INTERIOR DESIGN REFERENCE MANUAL

DAVID K. BALLAST, A.I.A.
NCIDQ Certified #9425

PROFESSIONAL PUBLICATIONS, INC.
BELMONT, CA

How to Get Online Updates for This Book

I wish I could claim that this book is 100% perfect, but 25 years of publishing have taught me that textbooks seldom are. Even if you only took one architectural course in college, you are familiar with the issue of mistakes in textbooks.

I am inviting you to log on to Professional Publications' web site at **www.ppi2pass.com** to obtain a current listing of known errata in this book. From the web site home page, click on the "Errata" button. Every significant known update to this book will be listed as fast as we can say "HTML." Suggestions from readers (such as yourself) will be added as they are received, so check in regularly.

PPI and I have gone to great lengths to ensure that we have brought you a high-quality book. Now, we want to provide you with high-quality after-publication support. Please visit us at **www.ppi2pass.com**.

Michael R. Lindeburg, PE
Publisher, Professional Publications, Inc.

Although this book has been written to help candidates prepare for the NCIDQ examination, and NCIDQ recommends that it be used along with other materials by candidates preparing for the examination, NCIDQ does not warrant or guarantee that reliance on this or any other publication will assure successful completion of the NCIDQ examination. The author, and not NCIDQ, is solely responsible for the contents of this book.

INTERIOR DESIGN REFERENCE MANUAL

Printed in the United States of America

Library of Congress Catalog Card Number: 92-60051

ISBN: 0-912045-41-8

Professional Publications, Inc.
1250 Fifth Avenue, Belmont, CA 94002
(650) 593-9119
www.ppi2pass.com

Current printing of this edition: 9

TABLE OF CONTENTS

PART III: CONTRACT DOCUMENTS

PART VI: COMMUNICATION METHODS

PART VII: CODES AND STANDARDS KNOWLEDGE

PART VIII: BUSINESS AND PROFESSIONAL PRACTICE

PART IX: PROJECT COORDINATION

PART X: HISTORY

LIST OF FIGURES

LIST OF TABLES

ACKNOWLEDGMENTS

I would like to thank several people who helped me in the development and publication of this book. My first thanks go to Loren Swick of the National Council for Interior Design Qualification for his suggestions and support of the initial effort. Michèle Guest did a thorough reading of the manuscript and offered many helpful suggestions. Nancy Barsotti's comments also helped steer the direction of portions of the book.

All of the people at Professional Publications were of immense help, especially my editor, Wendy Nelson, and production editor, Lisa Rominger. Thanks are also due to Karie Youngdahl for the always arduous task of copyediting, Jennifer Pasqual Thuillier for the illustrations, Shelley Arenson for typesetting, and Jessica R. Whitney-Holden and Russ Beebe for proofreading.

For assistance with later printings of this book I would like to thank Jessica R. Whitney-Holden, Kate Hayes, Chuck Oey, Yvonne Sartain, David Nielsen, and Cathy Schrott.

My thanks also to Todd Bostick for his assistance in later revisions to this book.

INTRODUCTION

The National Council for Interior Design Qualification (NCIDQ) examination is a test for measuring the minimum level of competence needed to practice in the profession of interior design. Successful completion of the exam is mandatory for certification in those American states and Canadian provinces that have licensing, registration, or certification statutes governing the profession of interior design. Passing the NCIDQ exam is also required for membership in most of the professional interior design organizations and for advanced professional certification as offered by the Governing Board for Contract Interior Design Standards. This book will help you prepare for the NCIDQ exam.

In early 2000, the NCIDQ announced major changes to the examination. The new format will be administered for the first time during the fall, 2000 exam. The fall, 2000 test will also be a transition period for those candidates who have already passed one or more parts of the previous test. By the spring, 2001 sitting, only the new format will be offered. However, those candidates who have passed all but one section of the old exam will have until spring, 2003 to take the appropriate section of the new exam to complete the exam process. Current information on the changes is available from the NCIDQ on their web site at www.ncidq.org.

Regardless of which version of the exam you take, this book helps you to review the subject areas tested by the NCIDQ exam. Later editions of this book will focus specifically on the new exam format. You can use this book to review and test your readiness for the entire exam, or you can use it as a resource for studying particular topics you may have limited experience with. As an overview, this book will also help you decide which topics you need to study in more detail. Refer to the References section at the back of the book for suggested readings. Combined with an appropriate educational background and practical professional experience, this book will provide you with the knowledge and confidence you need to pass the NCIDQ exam.

The following sections briefly describe both the old format and the revisions in the new format.

1 THE NCIDQ EXAMINATION

The NCIDQ examination is developed and administered by the NCIDQ. Formed in 1974, the Council's purpose is to identify to the public those interior designers who have met the minimum standards for professional practice by passing the NCIDQ examination. In addition, the Council defines, researches, and updates bodies of knowledge; conducts field surveys; analyzes candidate performance; evaluates subject areas and item validity; develops and pretests questions and problems; improves scoring; implements grading and jury procedures; reviews education and practice requirements; and identifies public health, safety, and welfare issues.

The Council is composed of representatives from professional design organizations and regulatory agencies from those states and provinces having statutory requirements. The professional organizations represented include the American Society of Interior Designers (ASID), the Interior Design Educators Council (IDEC), the Interior Designers of Canada (IDC), and the International Interior Design Association (IIDA). To apply for professional membership in these organizations, you must pass the NCIDQ exam.

NCIDQ certification is also required in some states if you want to use the various titles defined by the legislative acts of those states. These titles include interior designer, certified interior designer, and registered interior designer. In addition, Washington, D.C., currently requires NCIDQ certification to qualify to practice in the jurisdiction. Some states require that designers pass the Building and Barrier-Free Codes examination. Until further notice from the NCIDQ, this section from the old exam will continue to be offered for those jurisdictions that require it by law.

At the time of this writing, states that have some type of statute governing the profession include Alabama, Arkansas, California, Connecticut, Florida, Georgia, Illinois, Louisiana, Maine, Maryland, Minnesota, Nevada, New Mexico, New York, Tennessee, Texas, Virginia, and Wisconsin. Puerto Rico and Washington, D.C., also have statutes governing the profession. The Canadian provinces with statutes include Alberta, British Columbia, Manitoba, New Brunswick, Nova Scotia, Ontario, Quebec, and Saskatchewan. Legislation is pending in several other states, and it is likely that more states will require certification in the future.

The exam is designed to reflect the skills and knowledge currently required in the profession. The current revision of the test was made in 2000 based on the 1998 study, Analysis of the Interior Design Profession, commissioned by the NCIDQ and conducted by Hale Associates, Inc. Using the 1998 study, the NCIDQ worked with Columbia Assessment Services, Inc. (CAS), recognized testing experts, to revise the examination program with the goal of providing the most up-to-date and appropriate examination possible.

2 ELIGIBILITY REQUIREMENTS

You must have at least six years of combined educational and practical experience to sit for the examination. This requirement includes one of the following combinations:

- four or five years of interior design education plus two years of practical professional experience
- three years of interior design education plus three years of practical professional experience
- two years of interior design education plus four years of practical professional experience

The NCIDQ has specific semester and quarter credit-hour requirements for each of the yearly educational experiences. Refer to their web site at www.ncidq.org for current information. Time worked as an intern/co-op in the field of interior design prior to graduation is credited at one-half the time earned, up to a maximum of one year, if the candidate did not receive educational credit for the intern or co-op experience.

In addition, you must provide three letters of reference along with academic transcripts.

All first-time exam candidates apply directly to the NCIDQ for determination of eligibility. Deadlines for candidates to submit applications are January 1 of each year for the spring exam and July 1 of each year for the fall exam. The examination is given twice a year, in the spring and fall, on a Friday and Saturday, always in April and October. The exam is offered at sites throughout North America. When you are accepted to sit for the exam, you are notified of the test location nearest the address on your application. All aspects of exam administration, including processing exam registration, securing appropriate exam sites, issuing letters of admission, training exam proctors, and providing the shipping and receipt of all exam materials are the responsibility of CAS, Inc.

The previous examination consisted of six parts: Identification and Application, Problem Solving, Building and Barrier-Free Codes, Programming, Three-Dimensional Exercise, and Project Scenario. The new exam is composed of three sections: two multiple-choice sections (which will replace the previous three multiple-choice sections) and one practicum (design) section (which will replace the current three practicum sections). You may take the entire exam at one sitting or individual sections at different times. If you do not pass a section, you need only to retake that section. Time limits on passing all sections of the exam may be imposed on candidates at the discretion of the states, provinces, or professional membership organizations for regulatory or administrative purposes.

The exam is priced by section. As with the previous exam, the cost for candidates who take all three sections at once is $495.00. The multiple-choice sections are priced at $175.00 for Section I and $125.00 for Section II. Section III (practicum) costs $295.00.

(These prices are current at the time of this writing. For current costs and the latest information on the application process for both the old and new exam, refer to the NCIDQ Web site at www.ncidq.org.)

3 CONTENT OF THE NCIDQ EXAMINATION

The content of the exam is based on studies of the profession. Using the 1998 Analysis of the Interior Design Profession, the NCIDQ determined that six performance domains characterize the work of interior design. These include the following:

- project organization
- programming
- schematics
- design development
- contract documents
- contract administration

The weighting structure of the new examination is derived from each domain's relative importance, criticality, and frequency. Questions relating to these six performance domains are spread out in one or more parts of the exam.

In contrast, the previous test included the content areas of theory; programming, planning, and predesign; contract documents; furniture, fixtures, and equipment; building and interior systems; communication methods; codes and standards; business and professional practice; project coordination; and history.

The new exam places greater importance on health, safety, and welfare issues and less on a few topics like history and communication methods.

4 QUESTION TYPES

There are three question types used in the examination. The first is multiple choice, which requires that you select from three or four choices. Questions may be based on written information and graphic materials such as drawings, pictures, and symbols. These questions are used in Sections I and II of the new exam and are machine-graded.

The second type is a written scenario, which puts you in the position of the interior designer for a specific situation and also requires a multiple-choice answer. These are used in Sections I and II of the new exam.

The third type of question requires you to complete a graphic presentation. This type of question is used in the three-dimensional and scenario parts of the old test and is now used in Section III of the new exam. In the new exam you are given a program based on a multi-functional facility (a commercial and residential facility of approximately 3,500 square feet), and you must produce a design solution. Your solution must address the principles of universal design. This section will be jury-graded in the near future, but the NCIDQ is looking at ultimately having this section administered and graded by computer.

The examination uses three varieties of questions: recall, application, and developmental. The first type of question requires you to name, identify, or remember the correct term or concept from a list. It requires you to recall, recognize, or discriminate.

Example:
The units used for the measurement and description of the brightness of a direct glare source are

1. footcandles
2. footlamberts
3. candelas
4. lumens

The second type requires you to apply a principle, concept, or skill. Comparison and contrast can be tested with this type of question.

Example:
To detail a door frame for a conference room where acoustical privacy is critical, which of the following is LEAST likely to be required?

1. an automatic door bottom
2. a heavy-duty, silent door closer
3. neoprene gasketing
4. a solid-core door

The third type of question requires you to make a judgment, solve a problem, or apply a skill, principle, or concept to a difficult, complex situation. You may be required to integrate many principles or concepts to answer a question or problem in an acceptable way.

Example:
A doorway is installed by a contractor according to drawings. After viewing the job, a building inspector tells the contractor that the door is not wide enough. Who is responsible for paying for correcting it?

1. the framing subcontractor
2. the interior designer
3. the owner
4. the contractor

Sample questions of each of these types are included at the end of each chapter in this book, with the solutions given in Chapter 25. While most questions can be answered based on information given in this book, some require that you draw on your own knowledge of interior design. This is because no one book can possibly provide all the information for all the possible questions you may find on the actual exam. These questions are included to give you a feel for what to expect on the test.

5 EXAMINATION FORMAT

The new examination is divided into three sections given during two days, Friday and Saturday. Section I, Principles and Practices of Interior Design, addresses the domains of project organization, programming, schematics, and design development. Section I contains 150 multiple-choice questions. Section II, Contract Development and Administration, addresses the domains of contract documents and contract administration and contains 125 multiple-choice questions. Section III, Schematics and Design Development, is the practicum section. You receive a program based on a multi-functional facility and must produce a design solution. Your solution must address the program requirements as well as the principles of universal design.

During the transition period for the fall, 2000 exam, the new Sections I, II, and III will be given. Additionally the programming, three-dimensional, and scenario practicums will be offered for candidates who have credit for one or more of the current practicum sections. Any candidate who has credit for passing two or fewer sections of the current practicum exam sections will have to complete the current format or be required to take the new practicum section of the new exam format.

The exact schedule for the new format was being finalized at the time of this writing. For current information on both the old and new exam schedules, refer to the NCIDQ web site.

6 HOW TO TAKE THE TEST

There is a wide variation in peoples' responses to tests. Some people are comfortable taking examinations, while others are terrified by any test, no matter how simple it is or how well-prepared they are. Some people review very little, while others spend months studying every piece of material they can find and taking every review course offered. Only you can determine the best approach for your experience, needs, time availability, and personality. However, the following suggestions and tips may help lessen your anxiety so you can focus on studying the subject matter. The NCIDQ examination is fair and accurately evaluates minimum competency to practice as an interior designer. Ultimately, it is your knowledge of the subject matter and your professional experience that will give you the confidence to pass the test.

A. Time Management

One of the biggest problems many candidates have in taking the NCIDQ exam is simply completing it in the amount of time allowed. This is especially true of the practicum section. In general, though, if you know the material, you will find there is plenty of time to complete Sections I and II as well as Section III.

Section III, the design practicum, requires you to assimilate, analyze, and communicate a great deal of information in a short time. The key is to budget your time so you can complete all the mandatory drawings.

Also remember that highly refined, drafted drawings are not required. Drawings may be freehand and can be rather rough as long as they show the jurors that you have solved the problem and satisfied the program requirements. Ultimately, when Section III is computerized, drawing quality will be less of an issue.

For the design practicum, you must read the program quickly and develop a design concept that meets all of the design requirements. You should do this quickly so you have plenty of time to develop the concept and complete all the drawings. Do not try to do something that is complicated or unusual or that requires you to figure out complex construction. Avoid shapes and construction elements that require a lot of drawing time. Remember that the jurors are not looking for innovative, award-winning solutions; they just want proof that you can respond to a program and integrate design principles, accessible design, and health, safety, and welfare issues into a three-dimensional solution.

Detailed suggestions for completing the three-dimensional practicum and scenario problems of the old exam are given elsewhere in this book. Although the test is changing, most of the same principles still apply.

For the portions of the exam that consist of multiple-choice questions, you may want to proceed in one of two ways. With the first approach, proceed from the first question to the last, trying to answer each one regardless of its difficulty. Divide the time allotted by the number of questions on the exam to give yourself an average time per question. Of course, some will take less time than the average, some more. If you are not able to confidently answer a question in your allotted time, make a note of it and move on to the next one. Leave yourself some time at the end so you can go back to the most difficult questions and at least make a best guess.

With the second approach, go through the test two times. During the first pass, read each question and answer the ones you are sure of and that do not take any lengthy calculation or study of the information given. Because you will be jumping around, make sure you are marking the correct space on the answer sheet. If a question does not fit into the first category of "easy to answer," leave it for the second pass. During the second pass, answer the remaining questions. These should primarily be the ones that you can confidently respond to after some deductive reasoning or with a calculation with which you are familiar. Again, make sure you are marking the correct spaces on the answer sheet. Some questions will simply be beyond your knowledge, or the choice between two responses will be so close that you will have difficulty deciding.

Using the two-pass method allows you to get a feeling for the difficulty of the test during the first pass and helps you budget the remaining time for the unanswered questions. One of the tricks to making this method work is not to go back and reread or reanswer any completed questions. In most cases, your fist response (or guess) is the best response. Regardless of which approach you use, answer every question, even if it is a wild guess. You are not penalized for guessing, but you have absolutely no chance if you mark nothing.

B. Tips on Taking the Test

Even if you are completely familiar with the subject matter, taking the NCIDQ exam can be an arduous process simply because of its length and the concentration required to get through it. This is especially true if you are taking all sections for the first time. As with any activity requiring endurance, you should be rested when you start the exam. You should have stopped studying a day or two before the first test day to relax as much as possible. Get plenty of sleep the night before and between test days.

Allow yourself plenty of time to get to the exam site so you do not have to worry about getting lost or stuck in traffic jams or other transportation problems. An early arrival at the exam room also lets you select a seat with good lighting and as far away from distractions as possible. Once in the room, arrange your working materials and other supplies so you are ready to begin as soon as you are allowed. The proctor will review the test instructions as well as general rules about breaks, smoking, allowable materials, and other housekeeping matters. You can ask any questions about the rules at this time.

Once the test begins, you should quickly review the material given to you in the test booklet. Check the number of questions and set up a schedule for yourself as described in the previous section. If you plan on tackling the questions in sequence, you should have completed about half the questions when half of your allotted time is up. In your scheduling, leave some time at the end of the period to double-check some of the answers you are most unsure of and to see that you have not marked two responses for any question.

Here are some additional tips:

- Make a notation of the answers you are most unsure of. If you have time at the end of the test, go back and recheck these if you really think it may help. Remember, your first response is usually the best.
- Many times, one or two choices can be easily eliminated. This may still leave you with a guess, but at least your chances are better between two than among three or four choices.
- Some questions may appear too simple. While a few easy and obvious questions may be included, more often the simplicity should alert you to rethink all aspects to make sure you are not forgetting some exception to a rule or special circumstance that would make the obvious, easy response the incorrect one. Sometimes just one simple word in the question that you don't think about can change its meaning.
- Watch out for absolute words in a question, such as *always, never,* or *completely.* These often indicate some little exception that can turn what reads like a true statement into a false statement or a false statement into a true statement.
- Be on the alert for words like *seldom, usually, best,* or *most reasonable.* These indicate that some judgment will be involved in answering the question, so look for two or more options that may be very similar.
- Occasionally, there may be a defective question. This does not happen very often, but if you think you have found one, make the best choice you can. The error is usually discovered, and either it is not counted in the test or any one of the correct answers is credited.
- Finally, try to relax during your studying and during the examination. Worrying too much is counterproductive. If you have worked diligently in school, obtained a wide range of work experience, and have started your exam review early, you will be in the best position possible to pass the exam.

C. Study Guidelines

Your method of studying for the NCIDQ exam should be based both on the content and form of the test and your school and work experience. Because the exam covers such a broad range of subject matter, it cannot possibly include every of practice. Rather, it focuses on what is considered minimum competency to practice interior design.

Your recent work experience should also help you determine what to study the most. If you have been involved with construction documents for several years, you will probably require less work in that area than in others with which you have not had recent experience.

This review manual was prepared to help you focus on those topics that will most likely be included in the exam. As you go through the manual, you will probably find some subjects that are familiar or that come back to you quickly.

Others may seem like completely foreign subjects, and these are the ones to give particular attention to when using this manual. You may even want to study additional sources on certain subjects, take review seminars, or get special help from someone who knows the topic.

Although Canadian equivalents have been included in most instances, there may be some cases where only U.S. terms or measurements are used. If you are taking the exam in Canada, make sure you are comfortable with the specific terms and measurement system used in your area.

The following steps provide a useful structure for organizing your study for the examination.

Step 1: Start early. You cannot review for a test like this by starting two weeks before the date. This is especially true if you are taking all portions of the exam for the first time.

Step 2: Go through the review manual quickly to get a feeling for the scope of the subject matter. Although this manual has been prepared based on the content covered, you may want to review the detailed list of tasks and considerations given in the NCIDQ study guide.

Step 3: Based on this review and a realistic appraisal of your strong and weak areas, set priorities for your study. Determine what topics you need to spend more time on than others.

Step 4: Divide the subjects you will review into manageable units, and organize them into a sequence of study. Generally, you should start with those subjects least familiar to you. Based on the date of the examination and when you begin your studies, assign a time limit to each of the units you identify. Again, your knowledge of a subject should determine the time importance you give it. For example, you may want to devote an entire week to building and barrier-free codes if you are unfamiliar with them and only one day to space planning if you know that well. In setting up a schedule, be realistic about other commitments in your life as well as your ability to concentrate.

Step 5: Stop studying a day or two before the exam to relax. If you do not know the material by this time, no amount of cramming will help.

Here are some additional tips:

- Know concepts first, then learn the details. For example, it is much better to understand the basic ideas governing interior design contracts and agreements than it is to attempt to memorize every word of the standard contracts.

- Do not overstudy any one portion. You are generally better off to review the concepts of all the parts of the test than to become an overnight expert in one area.

- When taking the Scenario and Three-Dimensional tests, follow the instructions outlined in the criteria. Do not spend time on unnecessary details or minor issues.

- Try to talk with people who took the test before you. Although the exam questions are continually changing, it is a good idea to get a general feeling for the types of questions asked, the general emphasis, and areas that previous candidates found difficult.

D. What to Take to the Test

Although the rules for the test may change slightly from year to year, the following items are generally allowed. Reference materials are not allowed for any of the three sections. For Sections I and II you may only bring number two or HB lead pencils, an eraser, and a battery-operated calculator that is not programmable.

For the practicum section you may (and should) bring the items listed as follows.

- portable drafting board (no smaller than 24″ × 36″ (610 mm × 914 mm) with a parallel bar if drafting boards are not supplied at the exam center. Check before the test to see if drafting boards and parallel bars are provided. If you must supply your own drafting board, *do not* bring a T-square. It is too difficult to use when you are rushed.

- architect's scale (imperial or metric depending on what scale you are using and where you are taking the test)

- 30/60- and 45-degree triangles

- templates such as plumbing, furniture, and circle

- pencils and marking pens

- erasers

- battery-operated calculator that is *not* programmable (make sure the batteries are fresh)

- pencil pointer and/or sharpener

- tracing paper

Bring any other drawing tools that will make your work easier. Bring a variety of grades of lead and types and thicknesses of marking pens because the vellum that is supplied may be softer or harder than you are accustomed to and it may smear one type of marker and not another. Some candidates also bring a predrawn grid of two-foot squares to use as a tracing guide under their reflected ceiling plan in the old scenario section or the new Section III.

In addition, you should consider taking "survival" items like the following.

- watch
- tissue
- snacks and bottled water if allowed in the test center
- aspirin
- eye drops

For more information about the old and the new examination and the NCIDQ, visit their web site at www.ncidq.org.

1 ELEMENTS OF DESIGN

There are several elements of design that interior designers use according to some basic principles to create spaces that satisfy the functional and aesthetic goals of a problem. These design elements and principles are the same ones used by painters, graphic designers, sculptors, and other visual artists. You must be familiar with these concepts and be able to manipulate them to successfully complete the NCIDQ examination. Your knowledge of these concepts is tested with the three types of multiple-choice questions discussed in the Introduction. You are also required to apply these elements and principles in the three-dimensional exercise. This chapter discusses the individual elements of design, and the next chapter shows how these elements can be combined according to several fundamental principles.

1 FORM

Form is the basic shape and configuration of an object or space. It is often the way we first distinguish one thing as being different from another. For example, the form of a chair is different from the form of the wall behind it. There are an infinite number of possible forms, but people most often generalize and describe forms with words such as *cylindrical*, or *flat*, or *square*, or *linear*. Although objects and spaces can be viewed in isolation, their form is usually viewed in relation to other forms according to the principles discussed in Chapter 2. Form gives the interior designer a powerful tool to create order, establish mood, and coordinate the diverse components of a finished space.

However, the form of an object or space can be affected by other factors such as light, color, and the other basic elements discussed in this chapter as well as by the effects of human perception. A circle seen obliquely becomes an ellipse, for example. Optical illusions may also alter the perceived form of an object.

Form or shape is generated with lines, planes, volumes, and, to a lesser extent, points. Each has its own characteristics, strengths, and limitations for interior design. Even though geometric points, lines, and planes do not have a third dimension, people perceive them when the second or third dimension greatly exceeds the theoretically nonexistent dimension. For example, in Figure 1.1(a) the balusters of the railing read as linear elements because their length is much greater than their width and depth.

A. Line

A line is an object or form whose actual or visual length greatly exceeds any actual width or depth it may have. Lines are also formed and perceived where one plane meets another, where edges occur, and where there is a change in material, texture, or color. Lines have a very strong directional sense and can affect a person's feeling about a space. Horizontal lines are generally perceived as restful, stable, and related to the plane of the earth. Vertical lines usually connote strength, equilibrium, permanence, and a strong upward movement. Diagonal lines are dynamic and often represent movement, either upward or downward depending on the slope of the line. Curved lines relate more to the natural world and the human body. They are graceful and suggest gentle movement. Curved lines can be either geometric, like circles, arcs, and ellipses, or free form.

Lines can also affect the perception of the space in which they are used. Vertical lines tend to make a space appear higher than it is, while horizontal lines lower the apparent height. Diagonal lines, if not used carefully, can create an imbalance in a space.

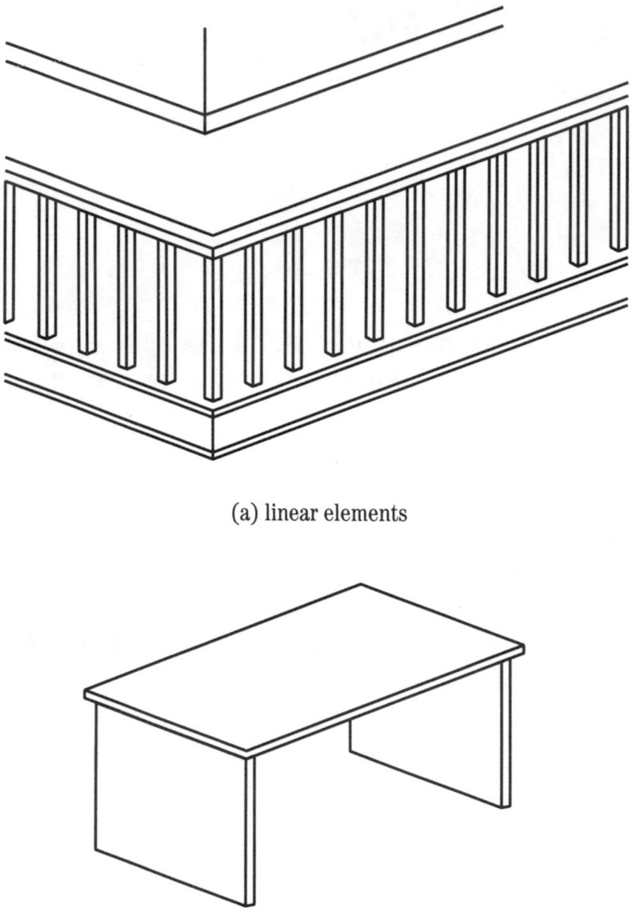

(a) linear elements

(b) planar elements

Figure 1.1 Linear and Planar Construction

Lines can be introduced into a space by using objects with strong linear forms, by structural elements, by applied decoration, with applied finish materials, and even with lighting. The designer can use line as a basic design element to create the desired effect in concert with other elements.

B. Plane

A plane is a form with two dominant dimensions, length and width. As with lines, all planes in the real world have some depth, but that dimension is not perceived as much as the dominant dimensions. For example, a three-foot square tabletop with a one-inch thickness appears planar, while the same three-foot top with a six-inch edge appears massive and three dimensional.

Planes are a significant component of interior design because space is typically defined by planar surfaces like walls, ceilings, and floors. Even furniture and other objects are usually constructed of planes. Unlike lines, planes help determine the form of a space with the additional characteristics of shape, texture, color, and pattern. Because of this, planes are a major factor in determining the character of a space.

A plane can be treated as a single surface with only one color and texture, or it can be subdivided like a painting, with different individual materials, textures, and colors. The planes used to define a space can be harmonized or contrasted with the planar forms of furniture, accessories, and other elements.

C. Volume

Volume is the true three-dimensional aspect of interior design because volume is clearly perceived as a spatial form having length, width, and depth. Volume can be either solid or void, sometimes referred to as positive or negative space. As shown in Figure 1.2, a solid is a form that has mass and appears to occupy space. A void is space itself defined by planes or other elements.

Volume has definite shape and is usually perceived and categorized as regular (such as cubic, cylindrical, or the like), as irregular (free-form shapes or very complex shapes), or by a dominant characteristic (such as tall, and narrow, curvilinear, or pie-shaped). As with other design elements, volume can be employed to enhance the overall desired effect of a spatial composition.

D. Shape

Shape is the unique characteristic of an object or space that defines it as distinct from adjacent objects or spaces. Shapes are clearly distinguished by planar or volumetric forms and can be geometric (like a square or circle or cylinder), irregular (like a free-form table), or natural (like a tree). It is also possible to combine these categories. A tree, for example, can have a globular, pyramidal, or ovoid geometrical shape.

Shape can have powerful symbolic or emotional qualities. The shapes of a cross or an outline of an

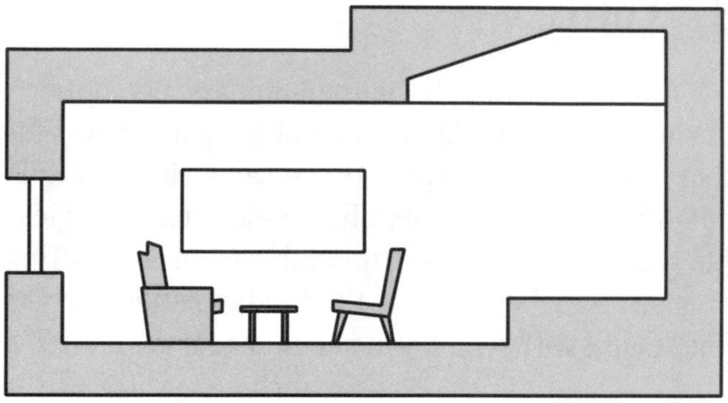

(a) solid—positive space

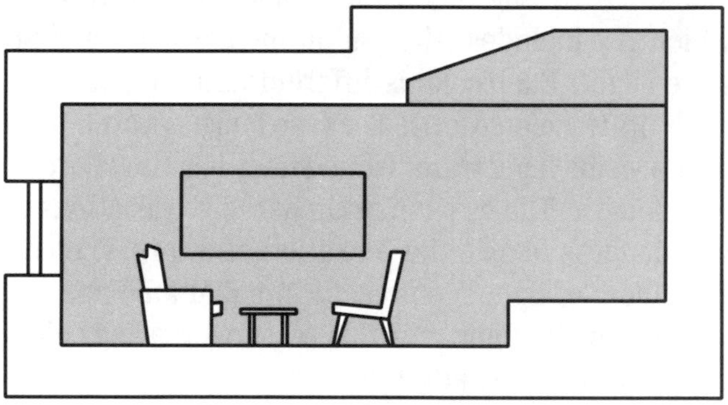

(b) void—negative space

Figure 1.2 Positive and Negative Space

apple, for example, are not just abstract forms but carry definite meanings for some people. That meaning can vary greatly depending on the culture, background, and experience of the person viewing the shape. On a more basic level, some shapes tend to have associative qualities that are similar for large groups of people. For example, a square generally suggests a rational, stable form with no directionality. A circle implies unity and completeness with a definite focus at its center. A triangle is a stable but dynamic shape. Structurally, it is a rigid shape because it cannot change shape unless the length of one of its sides is changed.

2 SCALE

Scale is the relative size of something as related to another element of known size. Proportion, discussed in Chapter 2, is simply the relationship between parts of a composition to each other and to the whole. Human scale is the most common scale, in which objects and spaces are judged relative to the size and form of the human body. This comparison can occur directly or indirectly. For example, the volume of a room can be compared with a person standing in the room, or the same space can be compared with something inanimate that has a direct relationship with a human, like a chair. In either case, the judgment of the room's scale is the same. See Figure 1.3.

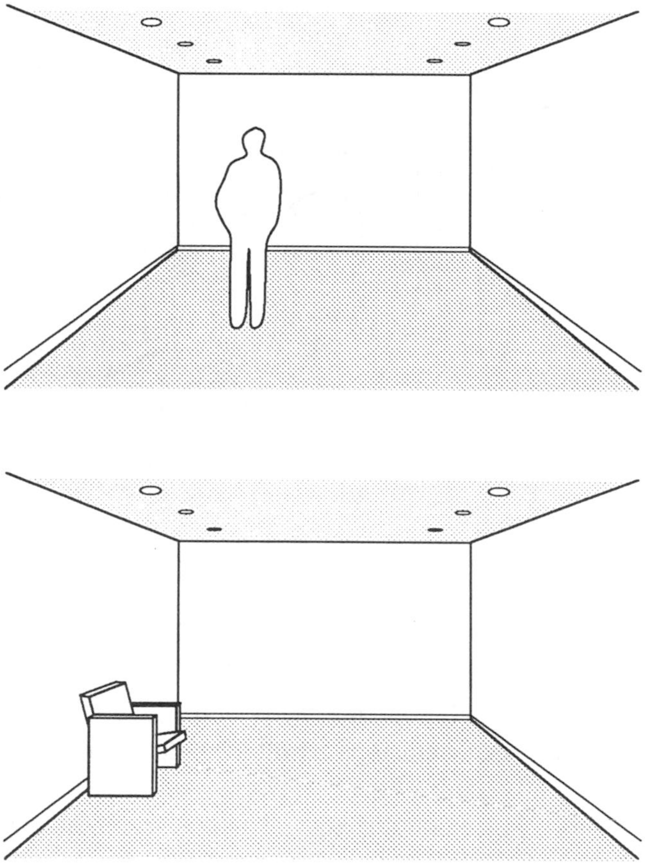

Figure 1.3 Scale Based on Known Objects

Other judgments of scale occur when one object or space is seen in relationship with the size of another object or space. For example, in Figure 1.4(a) the smaller openings make the major space onto which they open seem larger than the same space as it appears in (b). However, in neither case is there much of a clue as to the true size of the space because there is no relationship to a human or any other known size.

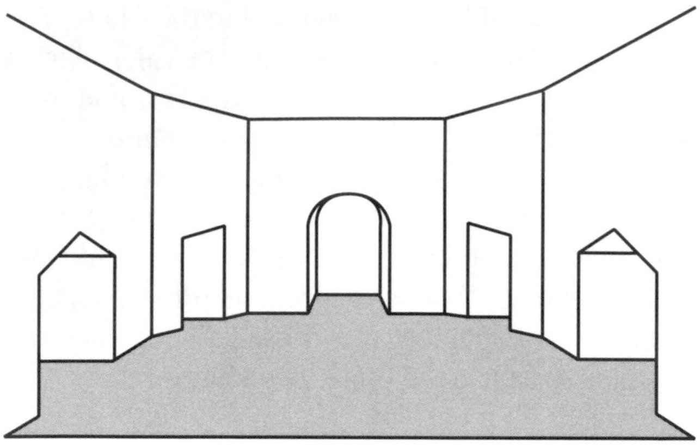

(a) small-scale space

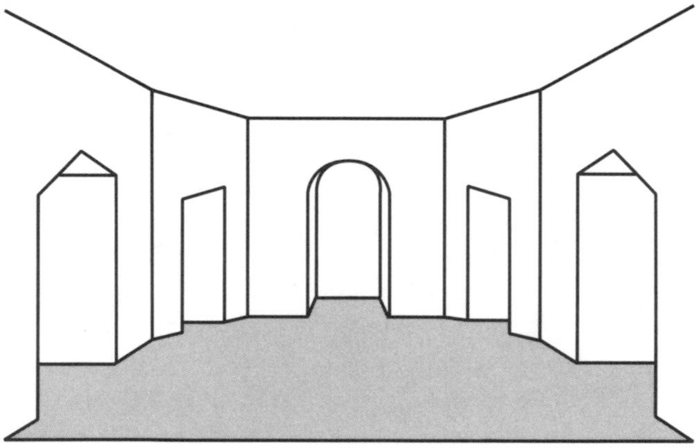

(b) large-scale space

Figure 1.4 Scale Relationships

Even though human scale is vitally important for interior design, decisions are often made based on the scale relationships between two or more nonhuman objects. For example, an eight-by-ten-inch framed photograph will look hopelessly out of scale on a wall twenty feet long with a ten-foot high ceiling regardless of how artfully it is positioned.

There are no definite rules for scale relationships. The judgment of scale is always complex because of the multitude of objects within a space, the form of the space itself, and the way the perception of objects and spaces is affected by color, value, texture, lighting, repetition, and other factors. The "correct" scale is also dependent on the design intent. Scale can be used to give spaces an intimate feeling or a monumental character. It can be used to provide emphasis and contrast or harmonize otherwise diverse forms.

3 COLOR

Color is one of the most dominant perceptions of the physical world and one of the most powerful tools for interior design. At the same time, color is one of the most complex physical and psychological phenomenon to understand and use correctly. This section describes some of the fundamentals of color and its use with which you should become familiar.

A. Color Basics

Color is a physical property of visible light that is one part of the larger electromagnetic spectrum, which also includes other radiation like X-rays and infrared light. Each color is differentiated from the others by its wavelength. Red has the longest wavelength of the visible spectrum, while violet has the shortest wavelength. The eye and brain perceive variations in wavelengths to give the sensation of color. When all the colors of light are present in equal amounts, we perceive white light. For this reason, creating colors with light is called additive.

The color of an object is perceived by the color of light it absorbs and the amount of light it reflects to the eye. For example, a blue object absorbs, or subtracts, most of the colors of light except blue, which is reflected to the eye. For this reason, creating colors with pigments is called subtractive. When all the colors of a pigment are present in equal amounts, we perceive no color, or black. When pigments are mixed in unequal amounts, they absorb various colors of light striking them.

The three primary colors of light are red, green, and blue. In various combinations and quantities, these three colors can create the other colors. They produce white light when combined equally. The three primary colors of pigments are yellow, red, and blue. Theoretically, all other colors can be produced by mixing various proportions of the primaries. This arrangement is typically shown on a circle known as the color wheel illustrated in Figure 1.5.

Color has three basic qualities: hue, value, and intensity (or chroma). The hue is the basic color, that attribute by which we distinguish blue from red, for example. The value describes the degree of lightness or darkness in relation to white and black. The intensity (or chroma) is defined by the degree of purity

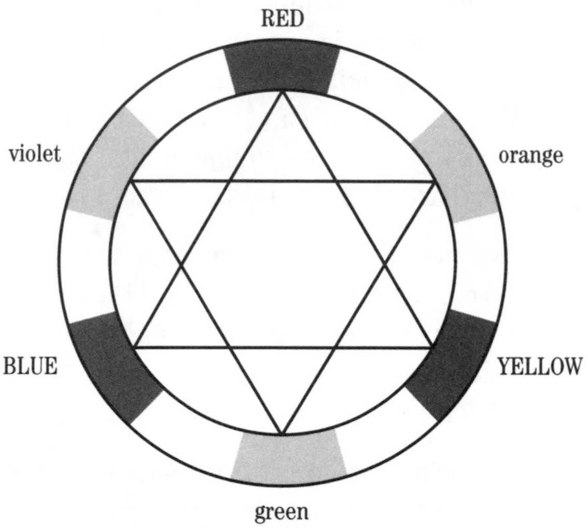

Figure 1.5 Brewster Color Wheel

of the hue when compared with a neutral gray of the same value. These basic qualities of color are represented diagrammatically in Figure 1.6. When white is added to a hue, its value is raised and a tint is created. When black is added, its value is lowered and a shade is created. Adding gray of the same value to a hue creates a tone. A tone can also be created by adding its complement, the hue of the color opposite it on the color wheel.

B. Color Systems

Many systems have been developed to describe and quantify color. Some deal with light and some focus on pigments, while others try to define color strictly in mathematical terms. For most interior design purposes you should be familiar with at least two of the commonly used systems: the Brewster system and the Munsell system.

The Brewster system, also known as the Prang system, is the familiar color wheel that organizes color pigments into the three primary colors of red, blue, and yellow. See Figure 1.5. In this case, "primary" means that these colors cannot be mixed from other pigments. When the primary colors are mixed in equal amounts, they produce the secondary colors of violet, orange, and green. In turn, when a primary color is mixed with an adjacent secondary color on the color wheel, a tertiary color is created.

The Munsell color system defines color more accurately than the color wheel and uses three scales

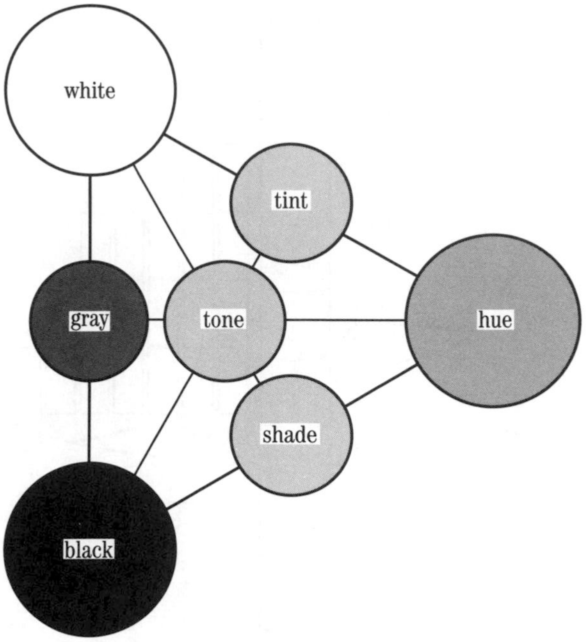

Figure 1.6 Modifying Values of a Hue

in three dimensions to specify the values of hue, value, and chroma (intensity). Figure 1.7 shows these scales. There are five principle hues (yellow, green, blue, purple, and red) designated by a single letter, and five intermediate hues, designated by two letters, all arranged in a circle. Each of these ten hues is subdivided into four parts and given the numbers 2.5, 5, 7.5, and 10. Each of the ten basic hues is given the number 5, indicating that they are midway between the adjacent hues and represent the most saturated color of that particular hue. When necessary, the colors can be further subdivided into 100 different hues.

Value (the degree of lightness or darkness) is represented by a scale at the hub of the circle and consists of nine neutral grays plus white and black. White is at the top of the scale and is given the number 10, and black is at the bottom with a value of 0.

Chroma is represented on a scale extending outward from the value axis. At the outside of the chroma scale the color is most saturated; as it moves toward the center it comes closer to a neutral gray of the same value. Because different hues have different maximum saturation strengths at different value levels, the number of chroma steps varies with the hue,

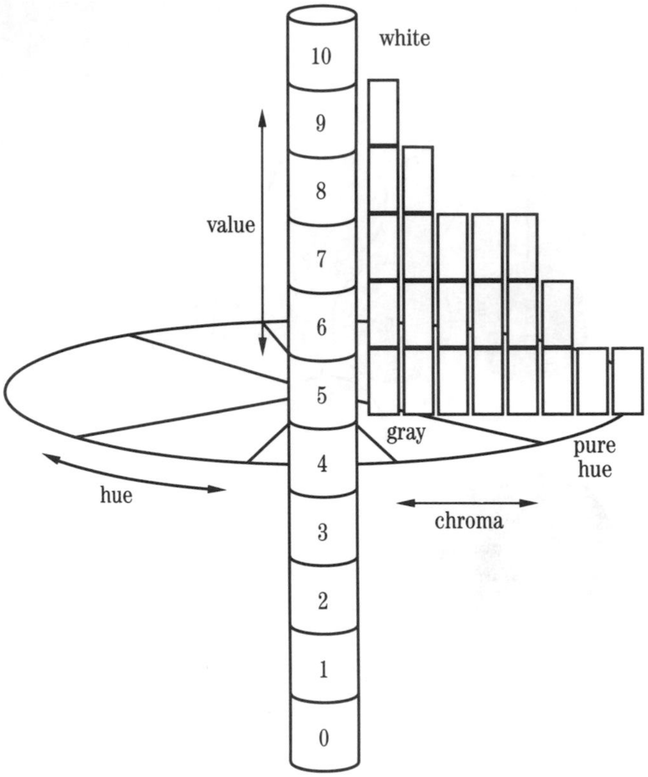

Figure 1.7 Munsell Color System

so the three-dimensional Munsell color solid is not a symmetrical form.

Any color in the Munsell system can be designated with a combination of letters and numbers. For example, G/6/3 is a principle hue of green with a value 6 and a chroma position of 3.

C. Effects of Adjacent Colors and Light

Like all other aspects of interior design, a single color does not exist in isolation. It affects and is affected by surrounding colors and by the color of the light striking it. There are many specific examples of how two colors affect each other when seen together. Some of the most common examples follow.

- Complementary colors (those opposite each other on the color wheel) reinforce each other. This phenomenon manifests itself in several ways. For example, when you stare at one color for some time and then look at a white surface, you see an afterimage of the color's complement. In addition, an object's color will induce its complement in the background. When two complementary colors are seen adjacent to each other, they each appear to heighten the other's saturation. When a small area of one color is placed on a back ground of a complementary color, the small area of color becomes more intense.

- Two noncomplementary colors placed together will each appear to tint the other with its own complement. This means that the two colors will seem farther apart on the color wheel than they are.

- Two primary colors seen together will tend to appear tinted with the third primary.

- A light color placed against a darker background will appear lighter than it is, while a dark color against a lighter background will appear darker than it actually is. Figure 1.8 shows an identical value placed against two contrasting backgrounds. This is known as simultaneous contrast.

- A background color will absorb the same color in a second, noncomplementary color placed over it. For example, an orange spot on a red background will appear more yellow because the red "absorbs" the red in the orange sample.

- A neutral gray will appear warm when placed on a blue background and cool when placed on a red background.

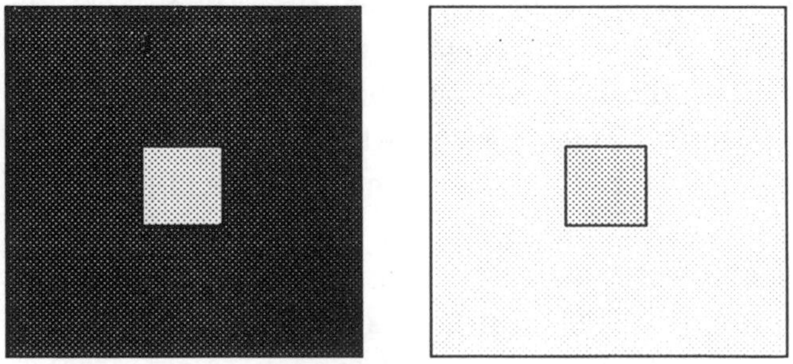

Figure 1.8 Simultaneous Contrast

One of the most important effects of interacting color that you must understand is how light affects the appearance of a color. Even though the human eye often perceives all light as white, each light source carries some colors more than others. For instance, incandescent light is very yellow while mid-day sunlight is predominantly blue. Cool white fluorescent lamps have a large blue and green component, and warm white fluorescent lamps have a higher yellow and orange spectral distribution.

In general, light that has a particularly strong hue component will intensify colors with similar hues and neutralize colors of complementary hues. For example, a red object seen under incandescent light will appear red and vibrant, while a blue object of the same value will appear washed out and muddy. The same blue object, however, would be rendered closer to its actual color if seen under mid-day light or under a cool white fluorescent light. Because of this fact, color selections should be made under the same type of lighting that is going to exist in the final interior installation.

The amount of light also affects color. Dim lighting reduces a color's value and diminishes its hue. High lighting levels can either intensify the hue or make the color appear washed out.

D. The Psychology of Color

In addition to its physical effects on the eye and brain, color carries with it many symbolic and associative meanings. For example, in many cultures red means danger or stop. Although there has been a large amount of research on the effects of color on humans, much of it is inconclusive or conflicting. This is partly due to the large number of variables that exist when talking about color, such as the physiology of color perception, the situation under which color is seen, cultural values, the value and chroma of the colors viewed, and the environment, to name just a few.

There are, however, some general statements that seem to hold true for most people. The first is that people distinguish between cool and warm colors. The cool colors are generally considered blue, green, and violet, while the warm colors are red, yellow, and orange. Cool colors are considered to be restful and quiet, warm colors active and stimulating. Reds are often seen as exciting and hot, yellows as cheerful. Greens are associated with nature and are sometimes used to connote cool, restful environments. Blues are also cool colors and can be calming and restful while implying dignity in some situations. Of course, much of the effect of color also depends on its value and intensity. A light value of a color will make a room appear larger, while the same hue in a dark value will make the room appear smaller.

E. Effect of Color on Spatial Perception

Hue, value, and chroma of color can be used in many ways to affect the appearance of a space and the objects in it. Bright, warm colors tend to make an object, such as a piece of furniture, appear larger. A dark color will make an object look smaller and heavier. Light, neutral colors extend the apparent space of a room while dark values close in. Warm colors tend to advance while cool colors recede.

These principles can be used to modify the spatial quality of a room. For example, a long, narrow room can be "widened" by painting the end walls with a bright, warm color and by painting the side walls a lighter, cooler color. A high ceiling can be "lowered" by painting it a darker color. Individual pieces of furniture can be made more prominent if they are much lighter than a background of dark floors and walls. Conversely, a large object can appear to be smaller by making its color light and similar to its background.

F. Color Schemes

There are five common methods of using color that are applicable regardless of the specific hues employed. These color schemes are monochromatic, analogous, complementary, triad, and tetrad.

A *monochromatic* color scheme employs one hue with variations only in intensity and value. Although monochromatic systems are fairly easy to develop and almost always work, they can become monotonous if used in an area that is occupied continuously. A monotone scheme is a variation of this type, but it consists of only a single hue of low intensity (near gray) in one or a very limited range of values. It is best used where a neutral background is needed for other activities, as in an art gallery where the space should not compete with the artwork.

Analogous color schemes use hues that are close to each other on the color wheel. This may include such combinations as one primary color, one secondary, and the tertiary between them, or one primary and one secondary with the colors on either side of them. Generally, the colors in an analogous scheme will not extend beyond one 90-degree segment of the color wheel. In most cases, analogous systems work best if one color is dominant and the others are subordinate.

When hues on opposite sides of the color wheel are used the scheme is called *complementary*. Because complementary hues can be harsh when viewed together, large areas of colors are generally of low chroma (grayer) and are a tint or shade of the color. Smaller areas or accents can have a higher chroma. One variation of this scheme is a split complementary in which a color on one side of the color wheel is used with two hues that lie on either side of the complementary color. A similar variation is the double complementary in which four hues are used: a pair on either side of two complements. In either case, one color should be dominant and used at low levels of chroma.

A *triad* color scheme uses colors equally spaced around the color wheel such as yellow-orange, blue-green, and red-violet. Because of the potential for producing a confusing, glaring appearance, triad schemes, like complementary schemes, employ low chroma tints or shades except for possibly one intense color that is used as an accent.

Finally, *tetrad* systems use four colors that are equally spaced around the wheel. Tetrad schemes are difficult to do well because a wide range of color is used. As with triad and complementary schemes, one or two colors should dominate and be of lower chroma.

4 TEXTURE

Texture is the surface quality of a material. It results from the inherent structure of the material or from the application of some type of coating over the material. Most people think of texture as the relative smoothness or roughness of a surface and associate certain textures with certain materials: metal is smooth while brick is rough.

Although every material has a specific texture, the perception of the texture is closely tied to its visual qualities, the relationship of the texture with surrounding textures, the viewing distance, and the lighting. Altering any one of these can affect the final, perceived appearance of the material.

Texture can be either actual or visual. Actual texture is the physical quality that can be sensed by touch: the smoothness of polished marble, the roughness of concrete, or the fuzziness of a wool fabric. Visual texture is what we imagine a surface to be simply by looking at it and based on our memory of similar textures. Viewed close up, we know concrete is a rough texture without touching it. Every actual texture has an associated visual texture, but visual textures do not necessarily have an actual texture. For example, artificial prints of wood grain or woven mat on a plastic laminate surface look textured but are actually quite smooth. Trompe l'oeil painting can produce a wide variety of apparent textures with very smooth, flat paint.

Texture is also affected by its relationship to nearby textures through scale relationships. Sand finish plaster may seem very rough next to a flat, smooth, shiny metal, but it will be perceived as relatively smooth next to an exposed aggregate concrete wall. It is important to remember this when combining a number of textures within the same space. See Figure 1.9.

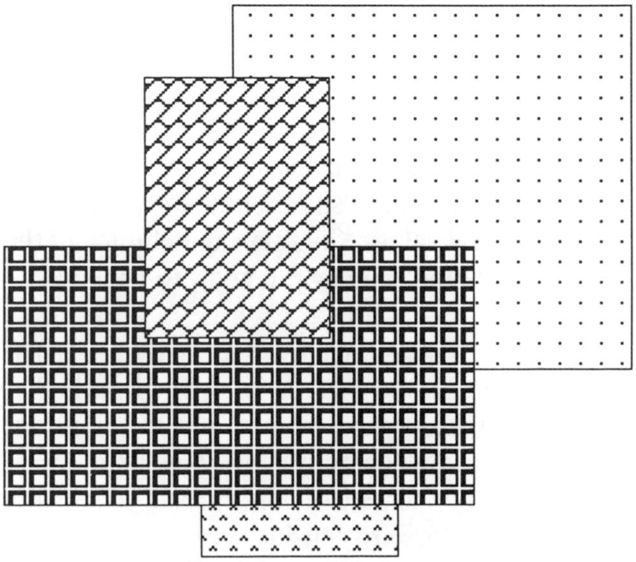

Figure 1.9 Perception of Textures

Similarly, texture changes based on viewing distance. Because of the limitations on the resolving powers of the human eye, any given surface appears smoother the farther away it gets. What may appear as a rough texture when selected in a showroom two feet away may become very smooth when applied to a wall that most people will see from twenty feet away.

Finally, the way a surface is lighted alters the apparent texture. Very diffuse lighting or strong, direct lighting tends to wash out texture, while strong side lighting will emphasize the actual texture. Conversely, texture affects our perception of light. Smooth, glossy surfaces reflect light sharply, often creating glare or showing the imperfections of the surface. Matte or rough textures tend to diffuse and absorb light, reducing the apparent brightness and color of a surface.

Texture can be a powerful design tool if used properly. Texture adds interest to a space, reinforces the design concept, helps differentiate objects and surfaces from each other, modulates light, and adds scale. For example, you can enhance a contemporary interior by using smooth or very finely textured materials. On the other hand, a "traditional" room may look best with heavier fabrics and dark wood textures. In another case, a large room can be made to seem smaller by using heavy textures, which tend to bring surfaces closer as diagrammed in Figure 1.10. Texture can also be used to provide emphasis or focus on one part of a space.

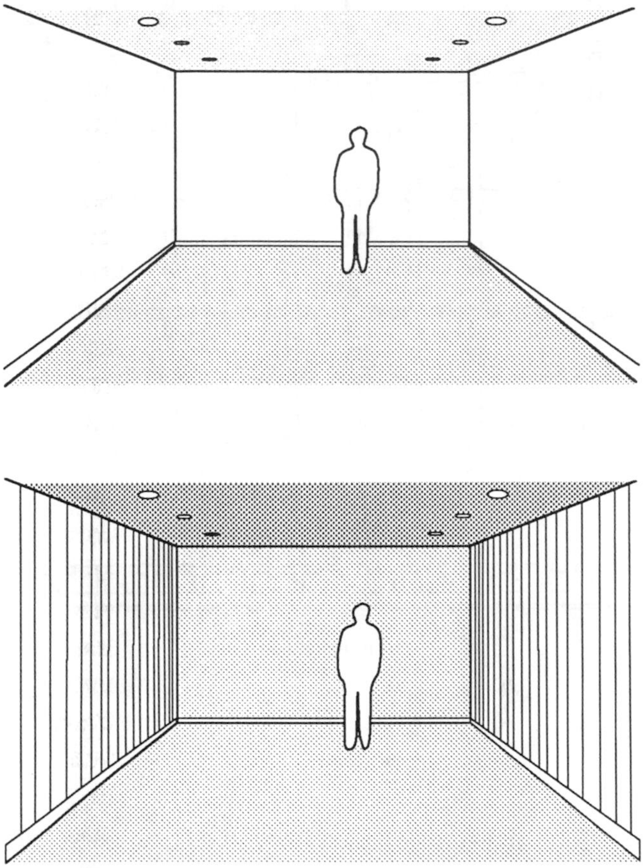

Figure 1.10 Modifying Space with Textures

5 PATTERN

Pattern is the repetition of a decorative motif on a surface. It is closely related to texture, but the individual elements of a pattern are usually discernible (at a reasonable viewing distance) as individual items whereas texture appears as an overall tone. See Figure 1.11. However, if a pattern becomes very small or is viewed from a distance, it can blend into a visual texture. Texture is also generally considered a two-dimensional quality of plane surfaces, while pattern can be a two-dimensional or linear composition.

Pattern can be built into a material, like ceramic tile or concrete block, or it can be applied with wallpaper or paint. However it is created, pattern, like texture, can add visual interest to a space, change the scale of a room, and reinforce the design concept. Like texture, though, it should be used carefully. Excessively bold patterns or the juxtaposition of too many patterns in the same space create a busy and overpowering space.

6 LIGHT

Light is basic to interior design. It is the means by which we see all the other aspects of the environment, and it strongly affects *how* we perceive space and objects. The same space can take on many different appearances simply by changing how it is illuminated. Because of this, lighting is a powerful design tool. This section briefly outlines some of the basic design elements of lighting. Chapter 13 describes in more detail the design and technical requirements of lighting.

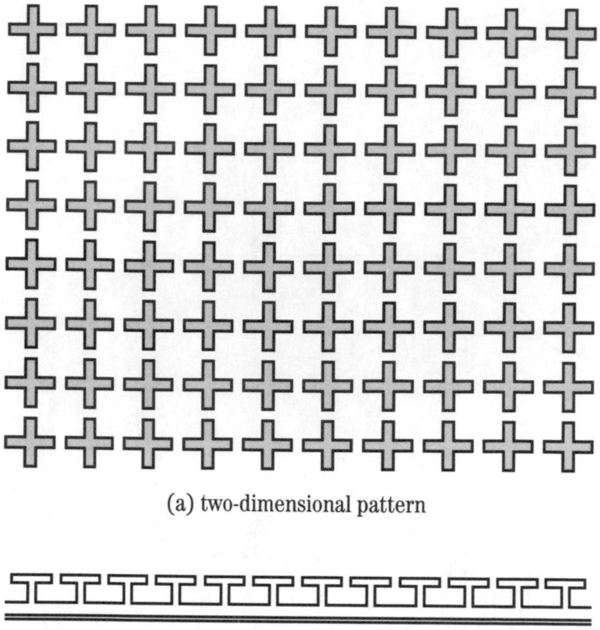

(a) two-dimensional pattern

(b) linear pattern

Figure 1.11 Pattern

Good lighting is an art as well as a science. Because it has both a physiological and emotional effect on people, it is not simply enough to provide a sufficient quantity of light. The quality of light must also be considered. For example, excessive contrast can cause the iris to open and close constantly as it tries to compensate for variations in illumination. This leads to physical fatigue, sore eyes, and other physical ailments. At the same time, absolute uniformity in lighting levels can be monotonous and dull.

You can consider both the light source and its effect as design elements. A light source can be a point, line, plane, or volume and can have the qualities of brightness and color. The illumination the light provides can, in turn, be seen as a point, line, or plane on objects and surfaces, each with its own brightness and color. With these effects, lighting can be used with other design elements to provide emphasis, rhythm, balance, and contrast.

Because lighting is both an art and science, a good lighting scheme requires a combination of technical and aesthetic sensibilities. The general lighting level must, of course, provide sufficient illumination for the activities taking place. You must also avoid detrimental situations like glare, excessive contrast, and inaccurate color rendition. Beyond this, however, a good lighting design can

- set or enhance the mood of the interior space
- add interest to the visual environment
- accent and emphasize objects and areas
- de-emphasize undesirable areas or architectural features
- highlight surfaces and textures
- enhance color
- affect spatial perception

The methods for achieving these effects and the lighting tools available are discussed in more detail in Chapter 13.

SAMPLE QUESTIONS

1. A client has asked a designer to create an intimate seating area for a hospital waiting room. Which of the following is likely to have the greatest impact on achieving the client's goal?

   1. pattern
   2. scale
   3. texture
   4. color

2. To give a sofa a heavy appearance, the designer should use which of the following color combinations for the sofa and the surrounding walls?

   1. a hue with a dark value for the sofa and a slightly lighter value for the walls
   2. a light colored sofa of any hue and a dark value wall color
   3. a sofa with a warm hue and dark value and a much lighter wall color
   4. a sofa with a light, cool color and a wall color of similar value and hue

3. A good selection for lighting to enhance the appearance of a rough, plastered wall would be

   1. fluorescent cove uplighting on all four sides of the room
   2. decorative chandeliers near the wall
   3. track lighting near the center of the room aimed at the wall
   4. recessed incandescents close to the wall

4. A Parsons table primarily uses which of the following types of design elements?

   1. plane and volume
   2. line and plane
   3. plane and point
   4. volume and line

5. To create the most vivid color-coding system in an elderly housing facility, the interior designer could create the most easily perceived system by using which of the following combinations?

   1. a bright color against a background of a non-complementary color
   2. complementary colors of high saturation
   3. either highly saturated warm or cool colors next to a neutral gray
   4. the primary colors and white

6. Which design elements could be used to lower the apparent height of a ceiling?

   1. a dark, highly textured ceiling
   2. strong horizontal lines on the walls
   3. fine-grained patterns on the ceiling and dark walls
   4. a light ceiling and textured walls

7. The Prang system organizes colors according to

   1. three scales of hue, value, and chroma in a three-dimensional form
   2. the hue and value in a matrix system
   3. their relationship to the primaries as organized in a circle
   4. five principle hues and their values on a wheel

8. Wallpaper is MOST useful to a designer in creating

   1. texture
   2. line
   3. scale
   4. pattern

9. When three colors near each other on the standard color wheel are used together, the scheme is called

   1. monochromatic
   2. triad
   3. complementary
   4. analogous

10. When black is added to a color, the result is called a

    1. tint
    2. shade
    3. tone
    4. value

2 PRINCIPLES OF DESIGN

1 BALANCE

Balance is the arrangement of elements in a composition to achieve visual equilibrium. Balance is important in interior design because every interior is composed of a wide variety of forms, shapes, colors, lines, patterns, textures, and light. Functional needs may determine much of the way an interior is designed, but the final composition must still be coordinated to establish a comfortable environment.

Balance depends on the idea of visual weight. To our eyes, some elements are "heavier" than others by the nature of their size, shape, complexity, color, texture, and location in space. These elements can be balanced by other objects in a variety of ways.

A good analogy is that of a balancing scale as diagrammed in Figure 2.1. Two identical objects are in balance if they weigh exactly the same and are placed an identical distance away from the fulcrum, or balance point. If one object is half as heavy as the other, things will still be balanced if the lighter object is placed twice as far from the fulcrum as the heavier one. Balance depends on both object (weight) and placement.

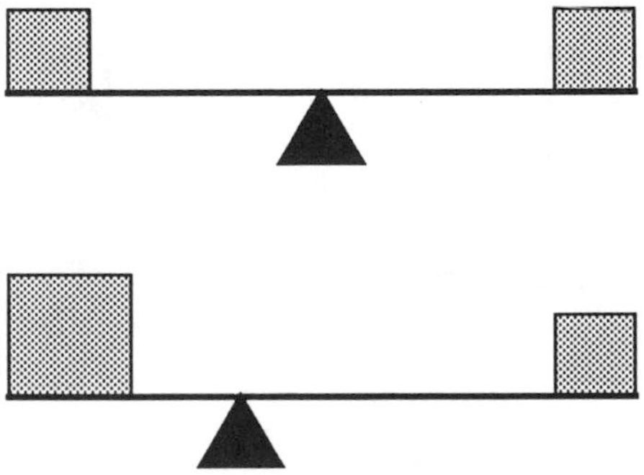

Figure 2.1 Balance of Visual Weight

For interior design (as well as architecture, graphics, and other visual arts) balance is not quite as exact or objective as weighing objects on a scale, but the principles still apply. Some of the ways objects or elements vary in visual weight include the following:

- large objects are heavier than smaller objects with the same form, shape, color, and texture
- highly textured or detailed elements are heavier than plain elements
- dark elements are heavier than lightly shaded elements
- bright colors carry more "weight" than neutral colors
- complex or unusual shapes weigh more than simple shapes
- several small objects closely grouped can balance a single object with the same area

Of course, each of these guidelines can be modified by combining them in different ways. A small form can become heavier than a much larger identical form by adding texture, or color, or other detail. See Figure 2.2.

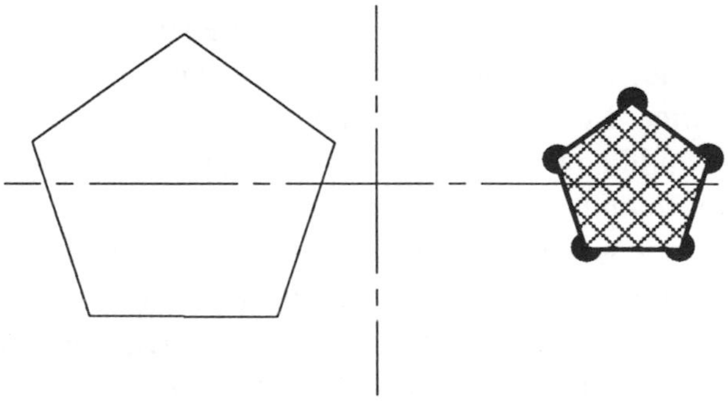

Figure 2.2 Variation in Visual Weight

As with the balancing scale analogy, position is important and all visual compositions have a balance point or axis or a field within which the balancing takes place. For example, in Figure 2.3(a) two adjacent shapes appear to be balanced about the imaginary vertical axis. If these objects are seen as pictures on the wall of a room (the field), they do not have the same balance if placed so that the physical distances from each of their edges to the ends of the room are identical. See Figure 2.3(b). Increasing the space between the end of the room and only one object places them even more out of balance. See Figures 2.3(c) and (d). However, when the center of the room coincides with the imaginary point of balance the composition appears balanced. See Figure 2.3(e). In many cases, the field of the objects, or negative space, also becomes an important part of the composition.

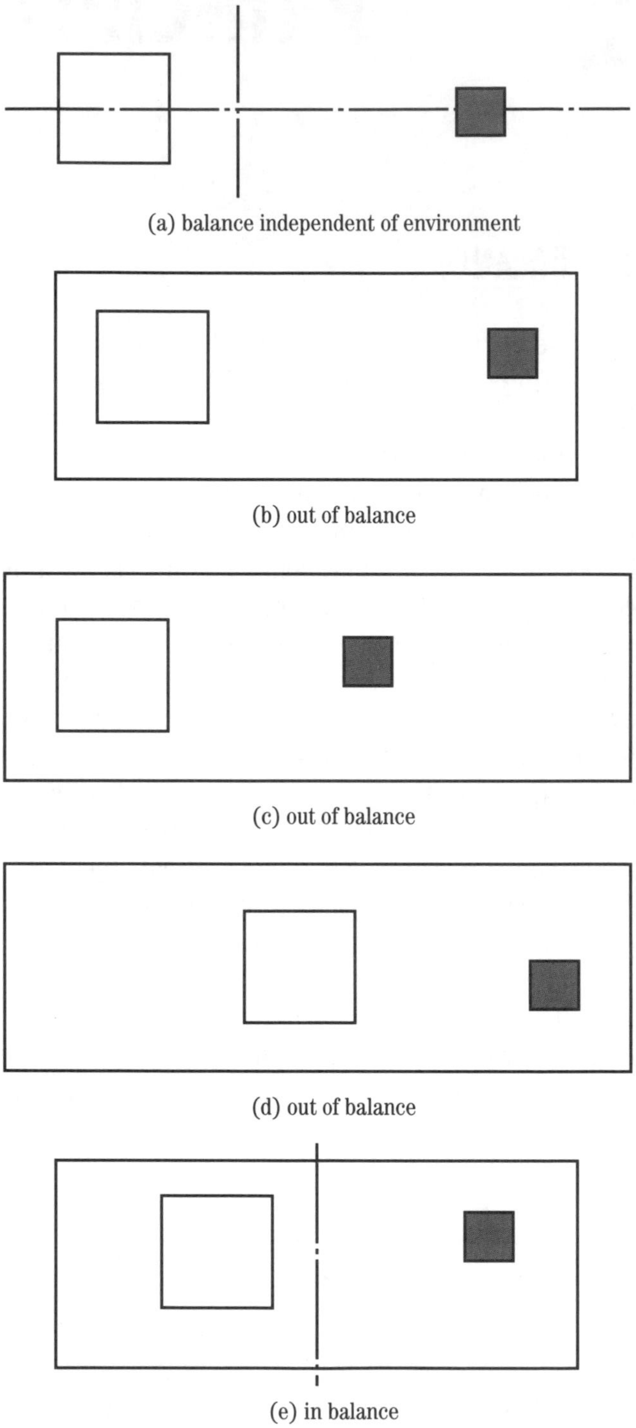

Figure 2.3 Balance of Different Elements

Establishing balance in interior design is a challenge because there are so many variables and because balance must be created in three dimensions, unlike a painting or graphic. What may appear balanced in a floor plan can be severely imbalanced when the space is viewed normally.

The three types of balance are described below. In most interior designs they are used together, but with one being dominant.

A. Symmetrical Balance

Symmetrical balance consists of identical elements arranged equally about a common axis as shown in Figure 2.4. This is also called bisymmetrical, bilateral, or axial symmetry. The common axis may be an actual object, like the peak of a cathedral ceiling, or an imaginary center line about which the elements are ordered. This type of balance is very stable and typically connotes formality. Many traditional interior designs are based on this kind of balance. Symmetry can emphasize either the area in the middle of the composition or a focal point at one or both ends of the axis.

In most cases, a purely symmetrical organization is not possible because of existing limitations of architectural space or required functional arrangements. Even if it is possible, absolute symmetry may not be desirable because it can be too static and formal. However, it can be used in combination with other organizational principles. For example, a perfectly symmetrical seating group may be placed asymmetrically within a room and balanced with another symmetrical arrangement of furniture.

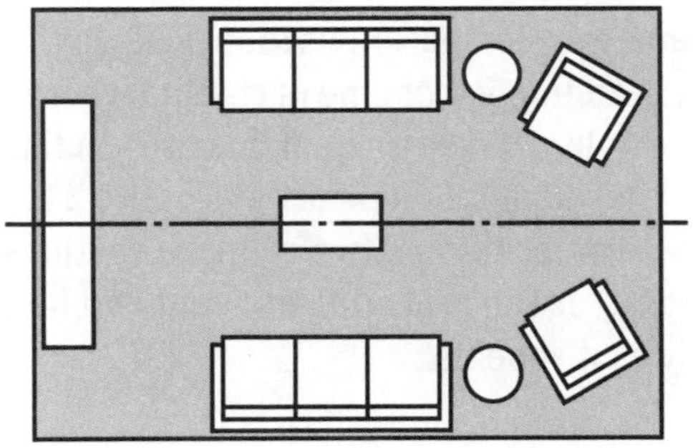

Figure 2.4 Symmetrical Balance

B. Asymmetrical Balance

Asymmetrical balance depends on equalizing the visual, or optical, weights of nonsimilar elements in a composition within a visual field or about a common axis. Figure 2.5 shows a symmetrically balanced seating group at one end of a room. This is balanced with the furniture and plants at the opposite end. Even though there is more furniture in the seating group, it is balanced by the visually more "complex" group of plants as well as the dining table. Some of the ways visual weights are established were outlined at the beginning of this chapter.

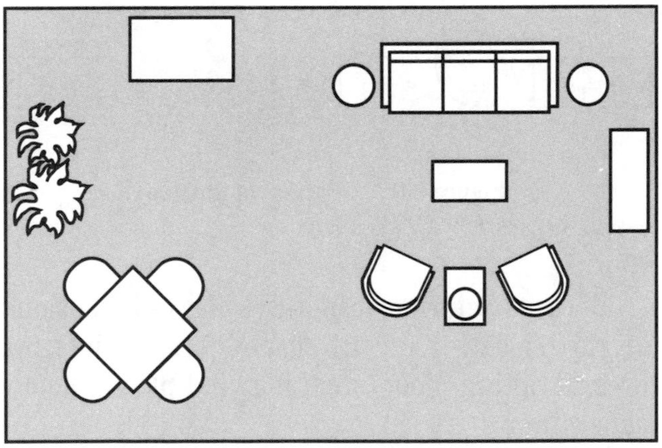

Figure 2.5 Asymmetrical Balance

Asymmetrical balance is generally considered informal and dynamic. It is capable of organizing a wide diversity of objects, forms, colors, and textures within either symmetrical or asymmetrical architectural spaces. Unlike symmetry, there are no fixed rules; each situation must be composed and arranged by the interior designer by "eye." For instance, a colorful, uniquely shaped chair near the corner of a room may balance the objects in other parts of the room, but placed in a room 50 percent larger the same chair may be hopelessly overpowered by other elements.

C. Radial Balance

Radial balance is a type of symmetrical balance in which elements are arranged uniformly about a central point as shown in Figure 2.6. By its very nature, radial balance usually focuses attention on the center of the grouping. However, individual elements can be oriented away from the center as well.

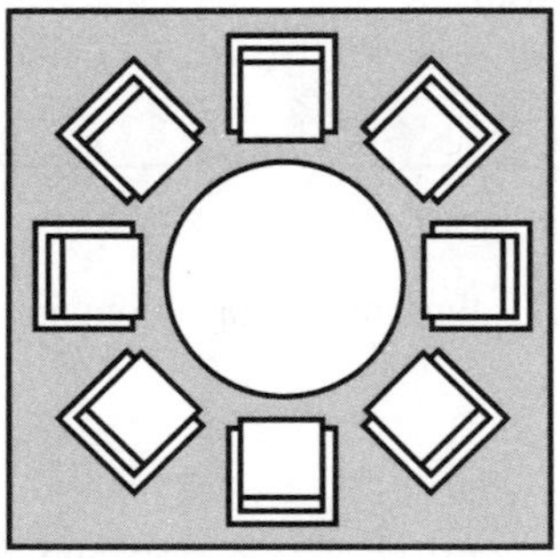

Figure 2.6 Radial Balance

2 HARMONY AND UNITY

Harmony in a composition is the agreement of the parts to each other and to the whole. It is often one of the most difficult design principles to apply because there are no fixed rules and because it includes the opposing concepts of unity/variety and rhythm/emphasis. Harmony results in a composition in which all the pieces seem to belong together and work to reinforce the overall design theme. Harmony is the way in which the wide variety of forms, shapes, colors, textures, and patterns found in any interior is balanced into a unified, satisfying composition.

Harmony is most often achieved by relating a number of different elements through a common characteristic. For example, a number of different furniture pieces may share the same basic scale and form. If the scale and form are different, they may harmonize by using the same colors. Harmony can also be achieved by grouping the elements close together, by relating them to a common architectural element, or by organizing them around a shared design feature. See Figure 2.7.

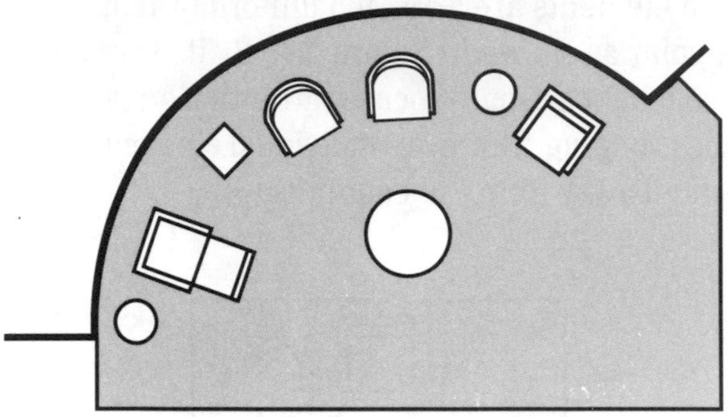

Figure 2.7 Harmony Using a Common Element

While harmony seeks to achieve a unity of appearance in which everything belongs, some variety is required to prevent the composition from becoming dull and monotonous.

3 RHYTHM

One of the most powerful design principles is rhythm, which is the repetition of elements in a regular pattern. Because rhythm sets up a sequence of multiple elements through space, it also has a factor of time as the eye or body moves past the individual pieces. In most situations, elements follow a common baseline to which they are related, either by physical connection or by an imaginary line that the eye and mind use to tie the elements together.

The simplest kind of rhythm is the uniform repetition of identical objects. More complex compositions include irregular spacing, emphasizing or changing elements and regular intervals, and uniformly increasing or decreasing the size of the elements, much the same way composers use musical rhythms. Gradation is an important type of rhythm where the size, color, or value of design elements are gradually modified as the elements repeat. See Figure 2.8. In more complex compositions, two or more rhythms can be juxtaposed or the repeating element can be changed slightly as it repeats.

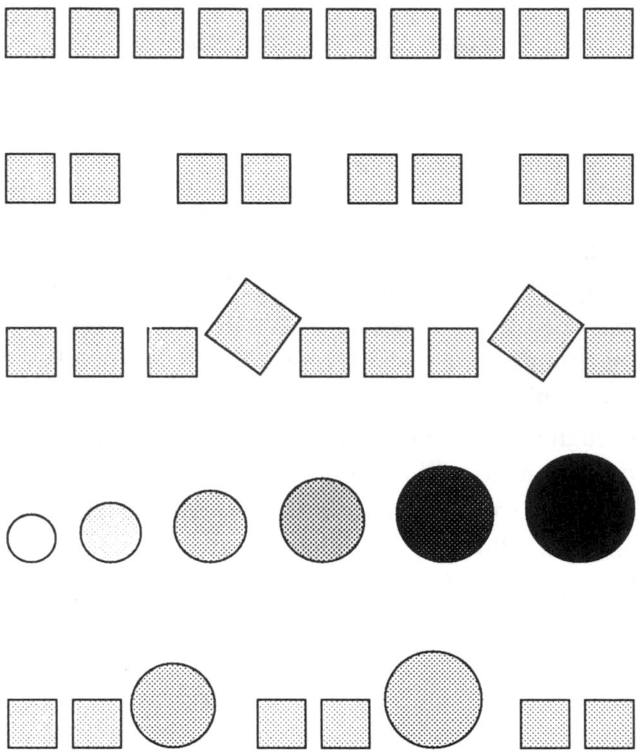

Figure 2.8 Variations of Rhythm

Because interior design is a three-dimensional art, rhythm can occur with shapes, forms, colors, textures, furniture, doors, lighting, and plants, among many others.

4 EMPHASIS AND FOCUS

Within any interior there are some elements that are more important than others. The important elements may be things like the table in a dining room, a spectacular view from a window, artwork in a museum, or a special merchandise display in a retail shop. The designer needs to understand the various dominant and subordinate parts of a space to create a design that enhances these hierarchies and provides a focus on the important features. A space in which everything is equally important tends to be bland and lifeless.

Emphasis can be created in a number of ways as shown in Figure 2.9. A part of the interior can be located in an important position. It can be centered, placed at the termination of an axis, or offset from a rhythmic grouping of other elements. An element can also be given emphasis by its size, color, shape, or texture, or in any way that creates a noticeable contrast between it and its surroundings.

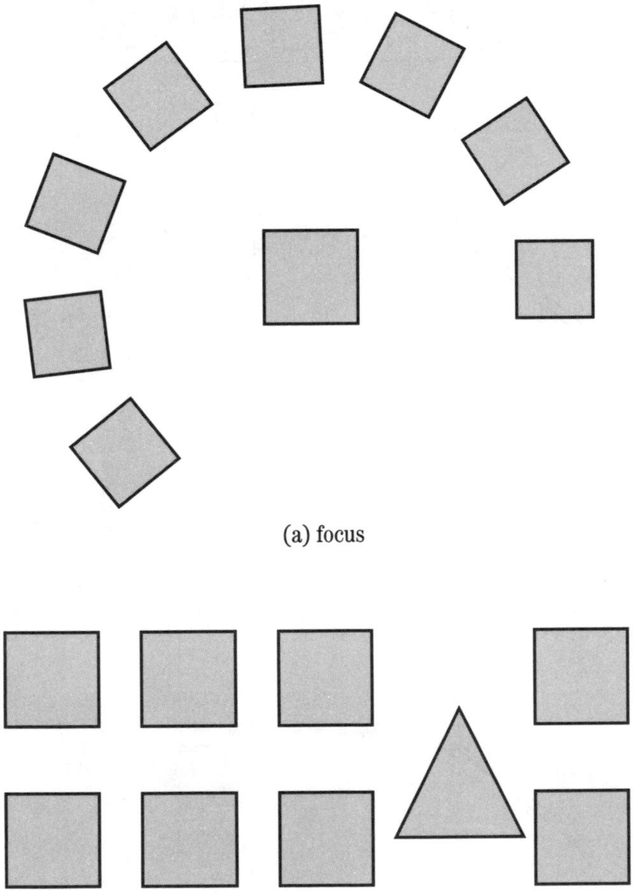

(a) focus

(b) offset and contrast

Figure 2.9 Methods of Emphasis

In most situations, there are several levels of emphasis and focus. For example, in a living room a seating group around the fireplace could be the main area of focus, while an art collection could be given secondary emphasis. All other furniture, finishes, and objects could be background elements. However, emphasis should be employed judiciously. If everything is emphasized, nothing is emphasized. There must be a clear differentiation between dominant and subordinate elements.

5 CONTRAST AND VARIETY

Contrast is a necessary condition of life. Black does not exist without white, left without right. Contrast is the way we perceive the difference between things, create importance, and add interest to our environment. Good interior design is a balance between harmony, or the unity of a space, and the liveliness and interest created by emphasis and contrast.

Contrast can be subtle, as between two minor shades of a color, or extreme, where two elements have completely different sizes, shapes, colors, textures, and proportions. The choice must be made by the designer based on the requirements of the space and the design objectives.

6 PROPORTION

Proportion is the relationship between one part of an object or composition to another part and to the whole, or between one element and another. It is similar to the element of scale discussed in Chapter 1, but it is not dependent on the relationship of one element to another of known size, such as the human body. For example, the parts of a table can be perceived as in or out of proportion to one another without knowing how large the table is. See Figure 2.10. In another situation, an object can appear out of proportion in one setting and perfectly correct in another. Figure 2.11 shows chairs crowded in one room while the same chairs seem proportionally correct in a room with a higher ceiling.

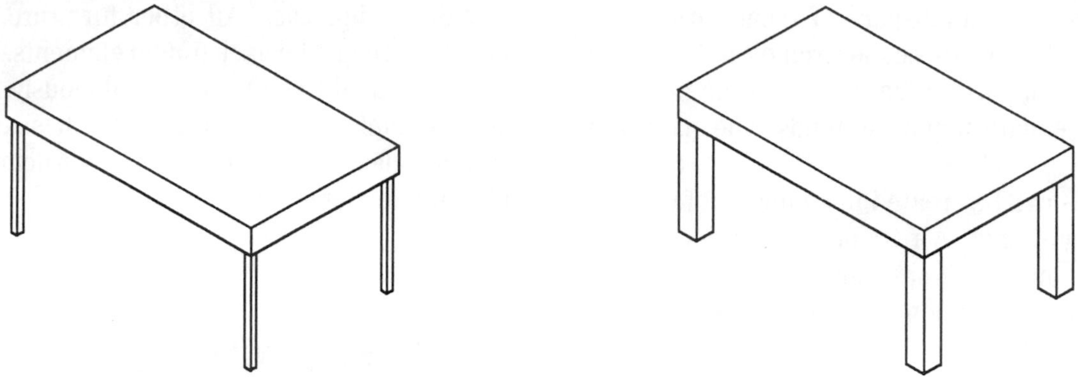

Figure 2.10 Proportions of Parts of an Object

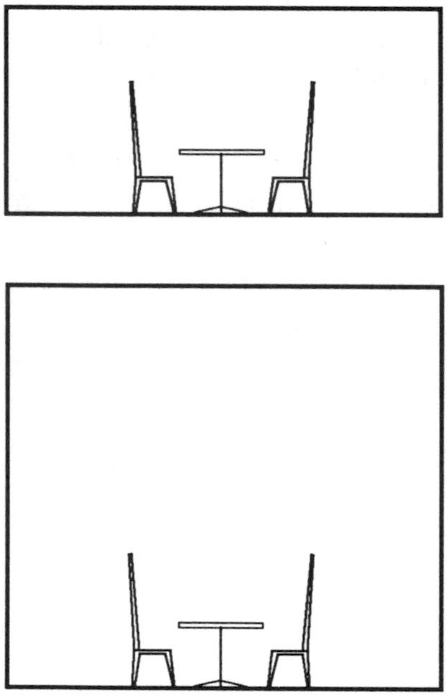

Figure 2.11 Correct Proportion Based on Situation

Proportion, by definition, is relative. It is also a matter of judgment and situation, and for interior designers it is dependent on the three-dimensional relationship of object and space. A tall, thin object may seem too skinny and top heavy if oriented vertically, but the same object might appear correct if laid on its side. See Figure 2.12. In some cases, something is deliberately made out of proportion to emphasize it or to create extreme contrast. Of course, the final judgment depends on the space in which the object is used, other furniture and accessories, color, lighting, and the other features of the immediate environment.

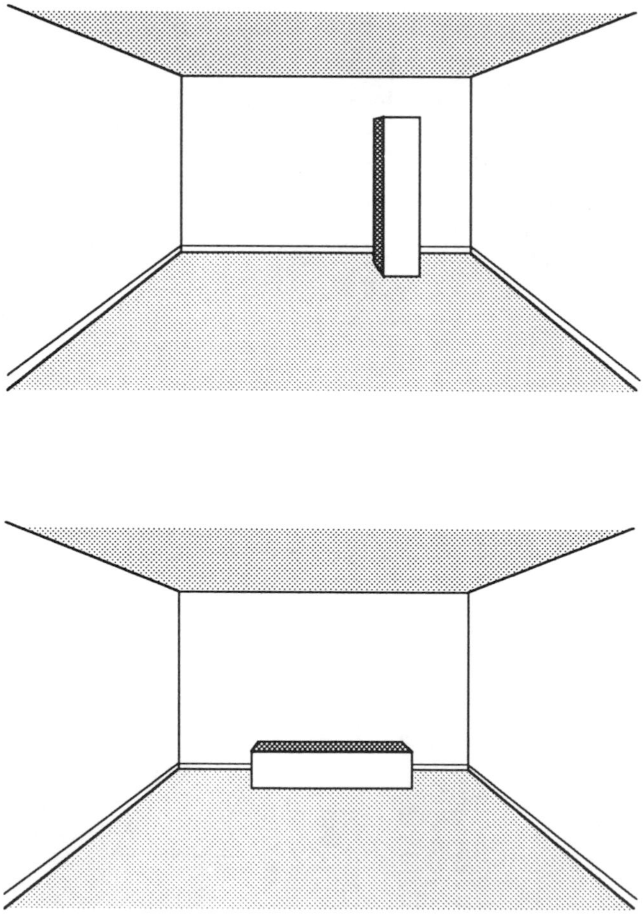

Figure 2.12 Proportion in Three-Dimensional Space

Because of these factors, most design decisions concerning proportion are made "by eye," adjusting size and shape until the visual relationships seem correct for the situation. However, throughout history, mathematicians, artists, and others have attempted to discover and quantify the ideal proportioning system. The most well known and studied of these systems is one in which a single line is divided into two unequal segments such that the ratio of the smaller part is to the larger part as the larger part is to the whole. This is the so-called *golden ratio,* and when translated to a rectangle it becomes the *golden section.* In fact, the golden ratio is developed by using a square to geometrically form the golden section. See Figure 2.13.

The ratio developed by dividing a line according to these proportions is an irrational number designated by the Greek letter phi, ϕ. It is approximately equal to 1.618. Since the time of the Greeks, the golden section has been believed to be the most pleasing proportion possible and has been found to occur repeatedly in nature as well as in human-formed structures, artwork, and musical harmony.

Another well-known proportioning system is the Modulor, developed by the architect Le Corbusier. It is loosely based on the golden section but uses the human body as a starting point. The system begins by dividing the height of a man (about 6 feet) at the waistline, or navel. Another proportion is developed by the distance from the top of the head to the fingertips when the arm is naturally raised above the head. From these three dimensions and proportions, all the others are developed. Le Corbusier believed that his system would facilitate prefabrication of building elements while avoiding the repetitive monotony of identical modular systems.

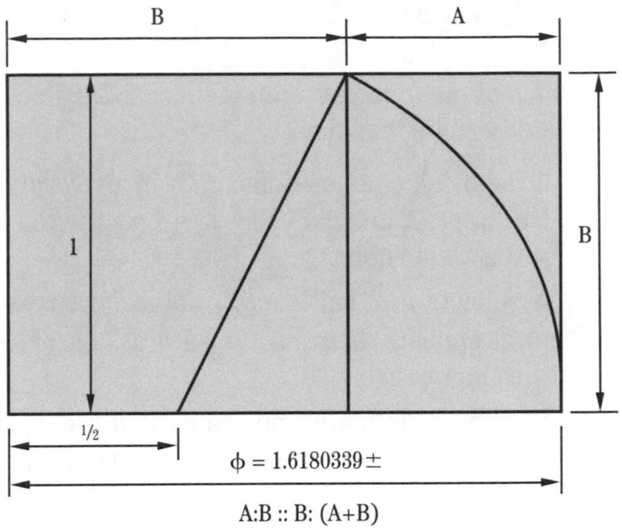

Figure 2.13 Golden Section

SAMPLE QUESTIONS

1. Which of the following statements is LEAST accurate in describing balance?

    1. A balanced composition drawn in an elevation can appear imbalanced when constructed in three dimensions.
    2. A collection of small elements of various textures appears "heavier" than a very large object with no texture.
    3. Placement is more important than the visual weight of an object when viewing an entire composition.
    4. Generally, neutral colors appear lighter than bright colors.

2. A designer uses the principle of harmony in order to

    1. develop a visual consistency and equilibrium to the individual elements
    2. establish an agreement of individual elements to each other and to the entire composition
    3. provide interest by developing one or two elements as more important than the other parts of a composition
    4. achieve a variation of the component parts without imbalance to the entire design

3. A series of workstations is arranged in a row. All are identical except that the acoustical panels surrounding each workstation are covered with a fabric that has a color of a lighter tint than the workstation in front of it. This best illustrates an example of which design principle?

    1. gradation
    2. unity
    3. repetition
    4. rhythm

4. A composition of furniture and architectural elements organized around three or more axes intersecting at a common point most likely represents what type of balance?

    1. bilateral
    2. asymmetrical
    3. symmetrical
    4. radial

5. If a designer wanted to emphasize one item in a retail client's store, which of the following design features would BEST achieve this goal?

    1. locating it on a main circulation axis and highlighting it
    2. arranging a grouping of several of the items among single pieces of the other items
    3. having an oversized model of the item made for display near the entrance
    4. putting it on a brightly colored pedestal in its usual place in the store

6. A casual restaurant uses dining tables with identical bases, but with table tops that are different shapes and colors. They are equally spaced and distributed evenly within a square space. This PRIMARILY illustrates which design principle?

    1. symmetrical balance
    2. variety
    3. harmony
    4. rhythm

7. Which of the following represents the golden proportion?

    1. $A : B :: B : (A + B)$
    2. $A : B :: A : (A + B)$
    3. $(A + B) : A :: 2B : A$
    4. $A : B :: B : 2A$

8. Which architect developed the Modulor system?

    1. Frank Lloyd Wright
    2. Mies van der Rohe
    3. Le Corbusier
    4. Walter Gropius

9. If a collection of 13 black and white photographs, all framed with different styles and colors of frames,

were grouped on a wall painted a light, cool gray, which design principle would the designer be using?

1. variety
2. rhythm
3. contrast
4. focus

10. The diagram below BEST represents which of the following principles?

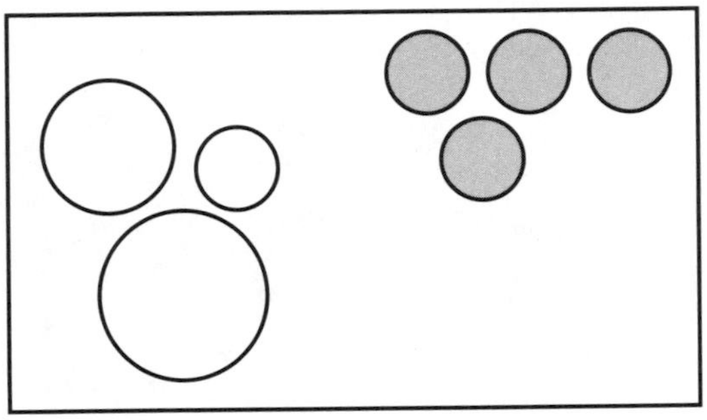

1. proportion
2. scale
3. rhythm
4. balance

3 HUMAN FACTORS

The field of human factors involves the correctness of fit between objects and spaces and the needs of the people using them. It encompasses a number of design disciplines that relate to the physical, psychological, and social needs of people. Because all interior design is based on the physical size of people and their physiological and psychological needs, you must have a good understanding of these topics of design theory.

1 ANTHROPOMETRICS

Anthropometrics is the measurement of the size and proportions of the human body. A large amount of research has been performed that establishes the range of human dimensions from foot length to shoulder width. These dimensions have been established for various population groups, ages, and by sex and include percentile distributions showing what percentage of the population falls within various measurement limits.

Based on anthropometric measurements, there is also a large body of knowledge about the minimum or optimum dimensions required for the average human to perform common activities. Room widths, heights of shelving, and clearances around furniture are examples of dimensions that are set by the interior designer and which must relate to the physical sizes, needs, and limitations of people.

Although there are hundreds of individual dimensions that have been found to be either minimum or optimum in a wide variety of situations, you should be generally familiar with some of the more basic ones. These are shown graphically in Figures 3.1 through 3.6. After you select the particular scenario problem you will solve before taking the exam (corporate, residential, retail, institutional, or hospitality), you may want to review some of the specific space needs of your chosen problem type.

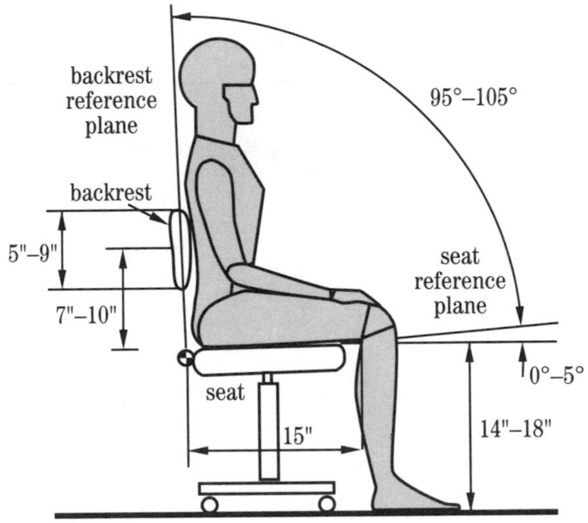

(a) work or secretarial chair

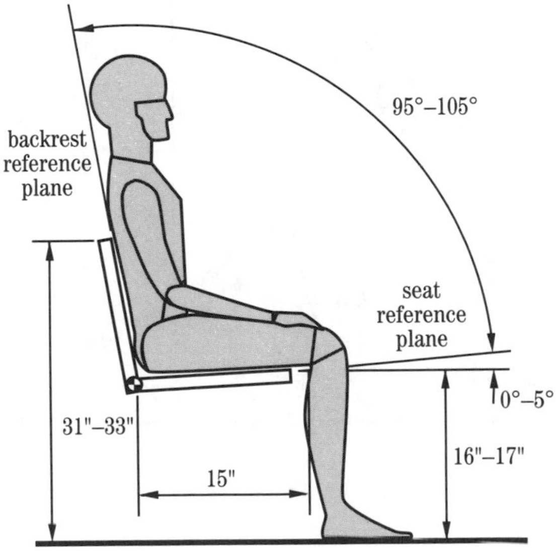

(b) general purpose chair

Figure 3.1 Seating Dimensions

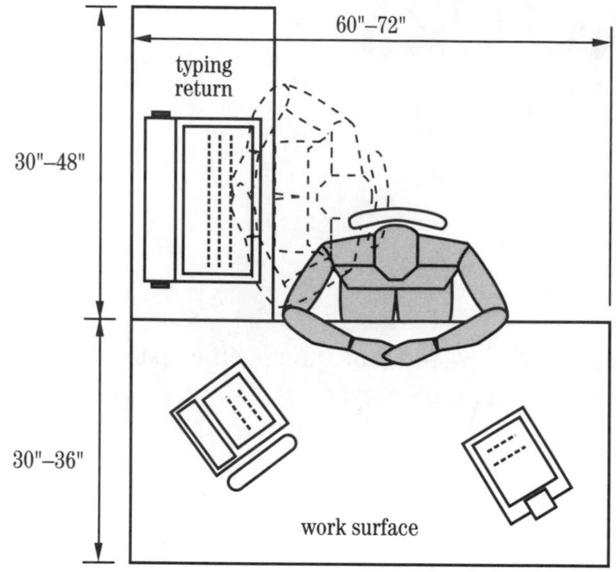

Figure 3.2 Office Workstation

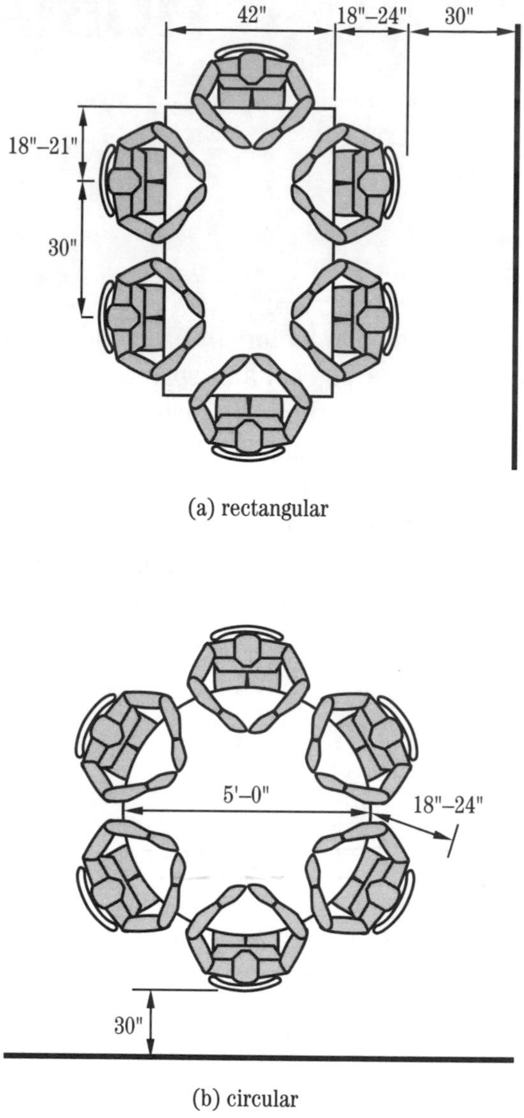

Figure 3.4 Conference Tables

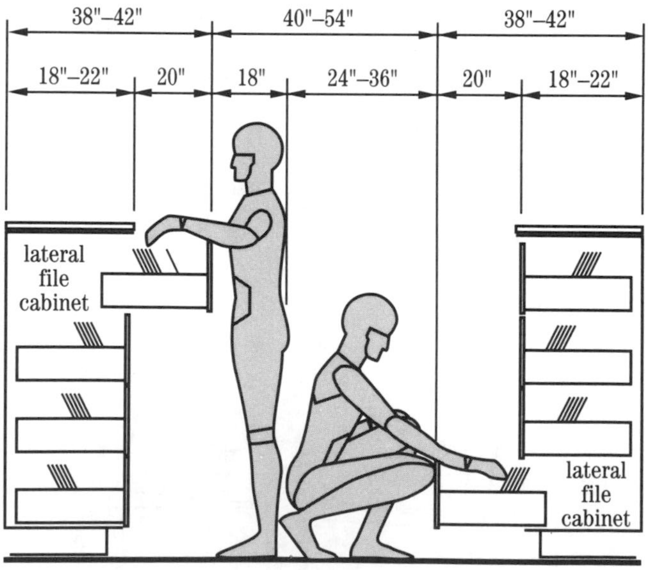

Figure 3.3 Lateral Filing Access Clearances

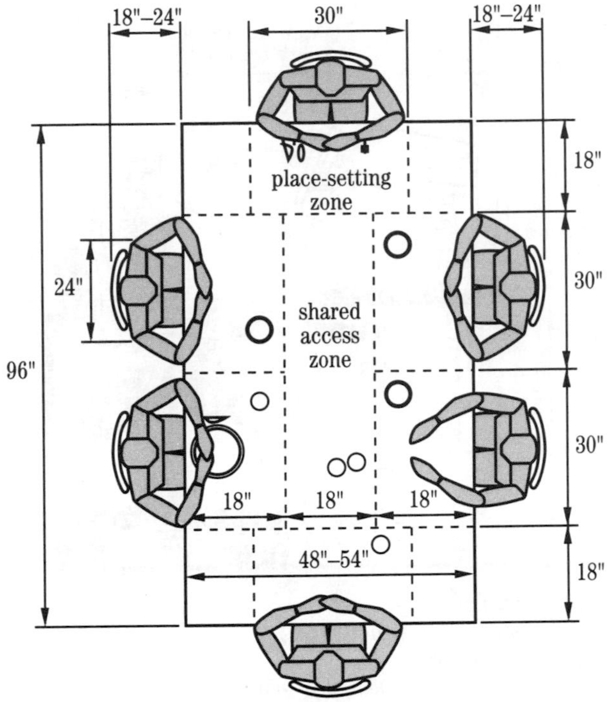

(a) rectangular table dimensions

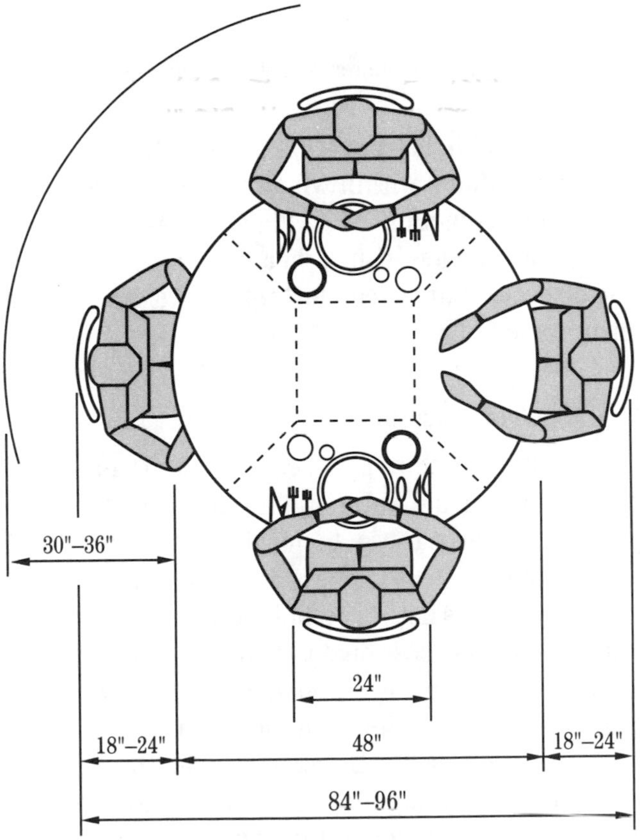

(b) round table dimensions

Figure 3.5 Dining Tables

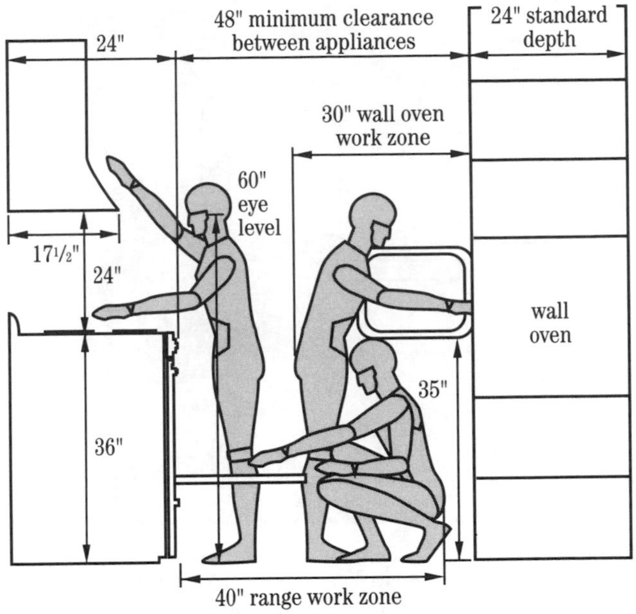

Figure 3.6 Kitchen Clearance Dimensions

2 ERGONOMICS

Ergonomics is the study of the relation between human physiology and the physical environment. Ergonomics uses the information developed by anthropometrics, but it goes further by studying exactly how humans interact with physical objects like chairs, control panels, desks, and the like.

Because of the increasing number of office workers, design guidelines for several workstation components have been developed based on extensive research. These include chairs, computer terminals, and work surfaces. Figure 3.7 shows some of the criteria for chair selection and design.

Figure 3.8 illustrates critical dimensions in computer workstation design. Note that one of the most important aspects of designing a computer station is keyboard height. The keyboard surface should be from 26 to $28^{1}/_{2}$ inches high and be adjustable. Reducing glare on the screen is also important but is usually accommodated in the design of the lighting or the layout and orientation of the workstation. When standup workstations are provided, they should have footrests.

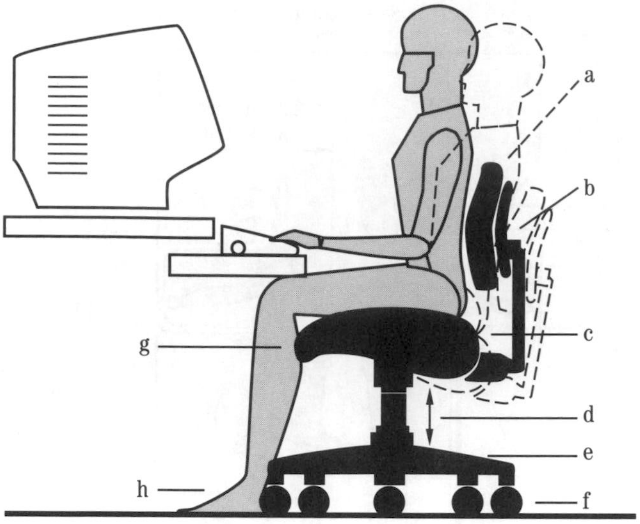

a. thoracic support, contoured backrest adjusts up and down, forward and backward; remains in constant contact with user's back regardless of tilt angle
b. lumbar (lower back) support: contoured seat sides support pelvic rotation, backward and forward regardless of tilt angle. Seat angle adjustment; pivot allows feet to remain on floor
c. foam construction not too soft; firm enough to cushion and support the body
d. pneumatic height adjustment
e. five-prong base for extra stability, balance
f. casters for smooth friction-free movement
g. waterfall front edge aids thigh circulation, reduces leg fatigue
h. feet comfortably flat on floor

Figure 3.7 Chair Design Criteria for Workstations

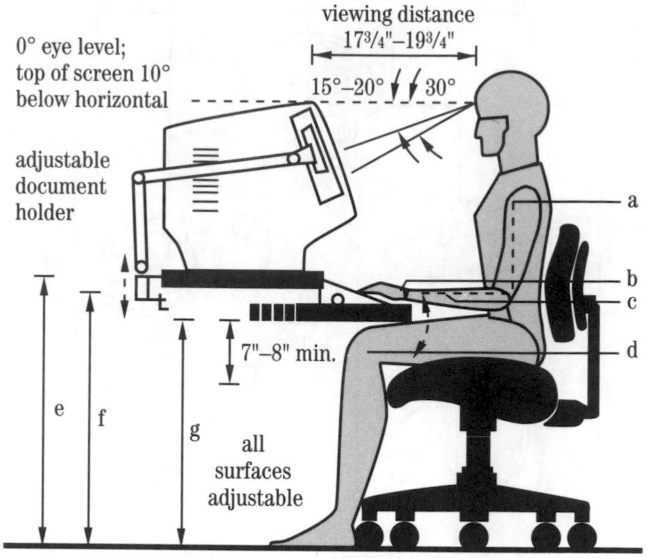

a. vertical upper arm
b. wrist incline no more than 10°
c. horizontal lower arm
d. adequate knee and leg clearance—no structural obstructions
e. work surface height to 30"
f. keyboard surface 26"–28½"; home row keys 28"–31"
g. leg clearance 27"

Figure 3.8 Computer Workstation Dimensions

One of the most important factors to include in the design of workstations and the selection of chairs is adjustability. Because there is no such thing as an average person, things like chair height, angle of a VDT (video display terminal), and keyboard position should be adjustable by the person using them. For chairs, the things that should be adjustable include the seat height, the angle of the back, the height of the lumbar support in the back, and the distance from the front of the chair to the back support. If armrests are provided, their height should also be adjustable, if possible.

3 HUMAN COMFORT

Human comfort is based on the quality of the following primary environmental factors: temperature, humidity, air movement, temperature radiation to and from surrounding surfaces, air quality, sound, vibration, and light. For each of these factors there are certain limits within which people are comfortable and can function most efficiently. Acoustics and lighting are reviewed in other chapters. This section discusses human comfort relative to the thermal environment.

A. Human Metabolism

The human body is a heat-producing machine. It takes in food and water and through the metabolic process converts these to mechanical energy and other bodily processes necessary to maintain life. Because the body is not very efficient in this conversion, it must give off excess heat to maintain a stable body temperature. The body loses heat in three ways: by convection, evaporation, and radiation.

Convection is the transfer of heat through the movement of a fluid, either a gas or liquid. This occurs when the air temperature surrounding a person is less than the body's skin temperature, around 85°F. Heat loss through evaporation occurs when moisture changes to vapor as a person perspires or breathes.

Radiation is the transfer of heat energy through electromagnetic waves from one surface to a colder surface. The body can lose heat to cooler surroundings or to a cooler surface.

The body loses heat (or is prevented from losing heat) through these three processes in various proportions depending on the environmental conditions. If the body cannot lose heat one way it must lose it another. For example, when the air temperature is above the body temperature of 98.6°F, there can be no convection transfer because heat always flows from a high level to a low level. The body must then lose heat by evaporation.

The sensation of thermal comfort depends on the interrelationship of air temperature, humidity, air movement, and radiation. Each of these is discussed below.

Air temperature: Temperature is the primary determinant of comfort. It is difficult to state precisely a normal range of comfortable temperature limits because the range depends on humidity levels, radiant temperatures, air movement, clothing, cultural factors, age, and sex, among other factors. However, a general comfortable range is between 69°F and 80°F, with a tolerable range from 60°F to 85°F. A value called the effective temperature (ET) has been developed that combines the effects of air temperature, humidity, and air movement.

Humidity: Relative humidity is the percentage of moisture in the air compared with the maximum amount of moisture the air can hold at a given temperature without condensing. Comfortable relative humidity ranges are between 30 and 65 percent with tolerable ranges between 20 and 70 percent. Relative humidity is particularly important in the summer because as the air temperature rises the body loses less heat through convection and must rely mostly on evaporation. However, as the humidity rises, it is more difficult for perspiration to evaporate, and therefore you feel much hotter than the air temperature might indicate.

Air movement: Air movement tends to increase evaporation and heat loss through convection. This is why you feel comfortable in high temperatures and humidities if there is a breeze. It also explains the wind-chill effect when a tolerably cold air temperature becomes unbearable in a wind. Wind speeds of from 50 feet per minute to about 200 feet per minute are generally acceptable for cooling without causing annoying drafts.

Radiation: Because the body can gain or lose heat through radiation, the temperature of the surrounding surface is an important factor in determining human comfort. If the surroundings are colder than the surface temperature of the skin, about 85°F, the body loses heat through radiation; if they are warmer the body gains heat.

The *mean radiant temperature* (MRT) is the value used to determine this aspect of comfort. The MRT is a weighted average of the various surface temperatures in a room, the angle of exposure of the occupant to these surfaces, and any sunlight present. The MRT is an important factor in comfort in cold rooms or in the winter because as the air temperature decreases the body loses more heat through radiation than by evaporation. Even a room with an adequate temperature will feel cool if the surfaces are cold. Warming these surfaces or covering them with wall hangings or drapes are ways to counteract this effect.

B. Ventilation

Ventilation is required to provide oxygen and remove carbon dioxide, to remove odors, and to carry away contaminants. The amount of ventilation required in a room depends on the activity in the room, the size of the room, and whether people smoke in the room. For example, a gymnasium needs a higher ventilation rate than a library. Building codes give the minimum requirements for ventilation, either by specifying minimum operable window areas, minimum mechanical ventilation rates, or both.

Building codes specify the minimum amount of fresh, outdoor air that must be circulated and the total circulated air in cubic feet per minute. Mechanical systems are designed to filter and recirculate much of the conditioned air, and they also introduce a certain percentage of outdoor air along with the recirculated air.

Where exhausting of air is required, such as in toilet rooms, kitchens, and spaces where noxious fumes are present, additional requirements are given.

Building codes either give minimum exhaust rates in cubic feet per minute per square foot of floor area or else they specify how often a complete air change within the room must be made. In these situations, the ventilation system must exhaust directly to the outside; none of the exhausted air can be recirculated. A toilet room exhaust fan, for example, will be connected to a duct that leads to the outside without connecting in any way with the building's ventilating system.

4 PSYCHOLOGICAL AND SOCIAL INFLUENCES

A well-designed interior should respond to the psychological and social needs of the people using it as well as to their physical needs. In many cases a general understanding of these human needs can be applied to any design situation. In other cases the particular needs must be identified during the programming process by determining the exact special needs of the users.

Although there has been much research in the field of environmental psychology, predicting human behavior and designing spaces that enhance people's lives is an inexact process. However, the interior designer must attempt to develop a realistic model of both the people who will be using the designed environment and the nature of their activities. This model can then serve as the foundation on which to base many design decisions. The following concepts are some of the more common psychological and social influences on interior design.

A. Behavior Settings

A behavior setting is a particular place with definable boundaries and objects in which a standing pattern of behavior occurs at a particular time. It is a useful concept for studying the effects of the environment on human activity. For example, a weekly board of directors meeting in a conference room can be considered a behavior setting. The activity of the meeting follows certain procedures, it occurs in the same place (the conference room), and the room is arranged to assist the activity (chairs are arranged around a table, audiovisual facilities are present, lighting is adequate, and so forth).

The behavior setting is useful for the interior designer because it connects the strictly behavioral aspects of human activity with the effects of the physical environment on people. Although a behavior setting is a complex system of activities, human goals, physical objects, and cultural needs, it provides the interior designer with a definable unit of design. By knowing the people involved and the activities taking place, programmatic concepts can be developed that support the setting.

B. Territoriality

Territoriality is a fundamental aspect of human behavior and refers to the need to lay claim to the spaces we occupy and the things we own. Although partially based on the biological imperative for protection, territoriality in humans is more related to the needs for self-identity and freedom of choice. When someone personalizes a desk at the office with family pictures, plants, individual coffee mugs, and the like, he or she is staking a claim to a personal territory, as small and temporary as it may be. In a more permanent living environment, such as a house or apartment, territorial boundaries are provided by walls, fences, and property lines. Often, boundaries are subtle. A row of file cabinets or a change in level may serve to define a person's or group's territory.

Territoriality applies to groups as well as to individuals. A study club or school class can claim a physical territory as their own, which helps give both the group and the individuals in the group an identity.

Closely related to territoriality is the concept of personal space that surrounds each individual. This idea, proposed by anthropologist Edward Hall, states that there are four basic distances that can be used to study human behavior and serve as a guide for designing environments. The actual dimensions of the four distances vary with the circumstances and with cultural and social differences, but they always exist. The interior designer should be aware of the fact of personal distance needs and design accordingly, as forcing people closer together than the situation warrants can adversely affect them.

The closest of Hall's distances is the intimate distance. See Figure 3.9. This ranges from physical contact to about 6 inches for the close phase to 18 inches for the far phase. People only allow other people to come within this distance under special conditions. If forced this close together (for example, on a crowded elevator) people have other defense mechanisms, such as avoiding eye contact, to minimize the effect of the physical contact.

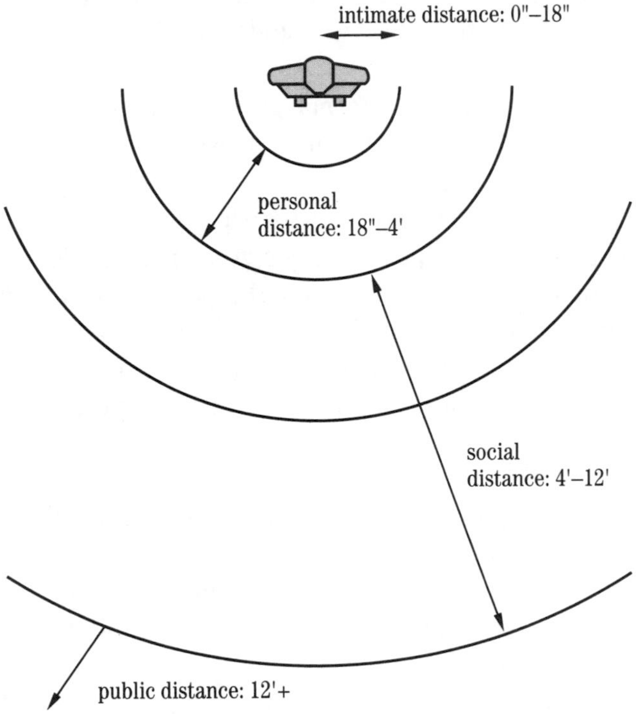

Figure 3.9 Personal Space

The next distance is the personal distance, from about 1½ feet to 2½ feet for the close phase and from 2½ feet to 4 feet for the far phase. If given the choice, people will maintain at least this distance between themselves and other people.

Social distance is the next invisible sphere, ranging from about 4 feet to 7 feet for the close phase and from 7 feet to 12 feet for the far phase. This is the distance at which most impersonal business, work, and other interaction takes place between strangers or in formal situations. In this area, speech and nonverbal communication are clearly understood but personal space is maintained. At about 10 feet it is not considered rude to ignore other people nearby, such as in a reception room or library.

Public distance is the farthest, ranging from about 12 feet outward. The greatest amount of formality can be achieved at this distance. In addition, this distance allows people to escape if they sense physical danger from another person.

Proxemics is how the theory of personal space is applied to the use of space. For example, proxemics suggests that where strangers will be sitting near each other, single chairs with their own definable space are preferable to sofas or benches. People will sit at the two ends of a sofa or bench, leaving the middle empty, rather than sit close to someone else or risk physical contact. In other cases, a knowledge of proxemics helps a designer decide the spacing between toilet fixtures or the density of public seating.

C. Personalization

One of the ways territoriality manifests itself is with the personalization of space. Whether it happens in one's home, at the office desk, or in a waiting lounge, people will often arrange the environment to reflect their presence and uniqueness. The most successful designs allow this to take place without major adverse effects to other people or to the interior as a whole. At home, people decorate their spaces the way they want. At the office, people bring in personal objects, family photographs, and pictures to make the space their own. In an airport lounge, people place coats and suitcases around them, not only to stake out a temporary territory, but also to make the waiting time more personal and a little more comfortable.

Another way people personalize space is to modify the environment. If a given space is not conducive to the needs of the people using it, they can either modify their behavior to adapt to the environment, change their relationship to the environment (leave), or try to change the surroundings. The simple act of moving a chair to make viewing a screen easier is an example of modifying and personalizing a space. If the chair is attached, the design is not as adaptable to the varying needs of the people using the interior space.

D. Group Interaction

To a certain extent, the environment can either facilitate or hinder human interaction. In most behavior settings, groups are predisposed to act in a particular way. If the setting is not conducive to the activities, the people will try to modify the environment or modify their behavior to make the activity work. In extreme cases, if the setting is totally at odds with the activity, stress, anger, and other adverse reactions can occur.

Seating arrangement is one of the most common ways of facilitating group interaction. Studies have shown that people will seat themselves at a table according to the nature of their relationship with others around them. For intimate conversation, two people will sit across the corner of a table or next to each other on a sofa. For more formal situations or when people are competing, they will sit across from one another. Where social contact is not desired, two people will take chairs at opposite corners of a table. See Figure 3.10.

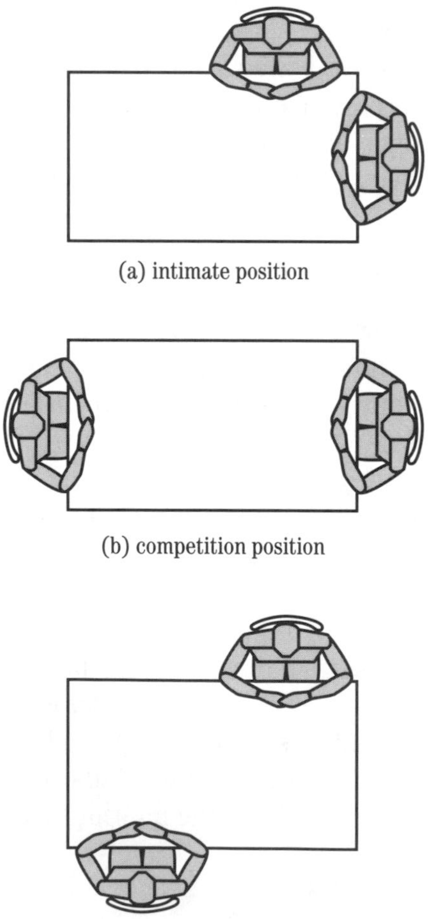

(a) intimate position

(b) competition position

(c) avoidance position

Figure 3.10 Table Seating

Round tables tend to foster more cooperation and equality among those seated around them. Rectangular tables tend to make cooperation more difficult and establish the person sitting at the end in a more superior position. Strangers do not like to share the same sofa or park bench. Knowing these basics of group interaction can assist the interior designer in making decisions. For example, individual study carrels in a library will be more efficient than large tables because the tables will seldom be fully occupied by strangers.

In places where informal group interaction takes place, studies have shown that over 97 percent of groups are comprised of two to four people. Designing to accommodate these sizes of groups makes more sense than anticipating larger groups of people, although a plan that allows for the possibility of very large groups while preferring small groups would be the best combination. In most cases, providing a variety of spaces for interaction is the best approach.

E. Status

The physical environment holds much symbolism for some human beings. Some people like houses with early American interiors because such designs symbolize to them the idea of "home." Some people expect banks to be of classical design with large lobbies because that is what they think a bank should look like.

In a similar way the environment can communicate status. In the United States, for example, someone with a corner office has more status than someone whose office has only one exterior wall. Office size is also equated with status in many cultures. Tables near the door of an exclusive restaurant are often considered the high-status position. Status can also operate at the scale of an entire interior project. The client may want the interior to symbolize some quality of the organization and give him or her a higher physical and psychological status in the community.

An interior design program should investigate the requirements or implications of status. Sometimes clients may clearly state what status-related goals they want to achieve. Other times, the interior designer must raise the issue, explore it with the client, and document the response as a programmatic concept.

SAMPLE QUESTIONS

1. Which of the following would be the MOST important consideration in the design of ergonomically correct chairs for air traffic controllers?

    1. adjustability
    2. firm cushions
    3. lumbar support
    4. tilt and swivel capability

2. If you were designing a computer workstation, which of the following would be the LEAST important?

    1. height of the keyboard
    2. angle of the VDT
    3. glare on the screen
    4. depth of the work surface

3. Symmetrically positioned identical furnishings in a college dormitory room shared by two people represent an attempt to satisfy which psychological need?

    1. personal space
    2. territoriality
    3. group interaction
    4. personalization

4. Proxemics might assist a designer in

    1. deciding on the size of a doctor's examination room
    2. determining where to locate the office of the president within an office suite
    3. planning the size and shape of a conference table
    4. making decisions about the type and spacing of seating in an audiovisual presentation room

5. Most people in the United States typically conduct business and relate to strangers at which distance?

    1. $1^1/_2$ feet to 4 feet
    2. 4 feet to 12 feet
    3. 7 feet to 12 feet
    4. 12 feet to 25 feet

6. A client complains that her office is too hot. The interior designer could MOST easily improve the situation by suggesting an accessory that affects

    1. convection
    2. ventilation
    3. evaporation
    4. conduction

7. The interior designer would most likely use anthropometric information to

    1. design countertops for a public rest room
    2. determine the percentage of children who would be comfortable on custom-designed benches in a puppet theater
    3. develop the best position for multiple VDT screens in a stock trader's workstation
    4. evaluate a new chair design that has just come on the market

8. Which type of information would be LEAST important for the interior designer to give to the mechanical engineer about a multipurpose room in an apartment building for the elderly?

    1. the ages of the residents in the apartment building
    2. the types of activities that commonly occur in the space
    3. an estimate of the number of people using the room
    4. a copy of the reflected ceiling plan

9. In addition to being decorative, tapestries in Gothic and Renaissance castles served which of the following functional purposes?

    1. They reduced the amount of sound reflection within a room.
    2. They minimized drafts.
    3. They increased the mean radiant temperature.
    4. They reduced heat loss by increasing the insulating value of the walls.

10. In which of the following situations would the interior designer most likely suggest to the mechanical engineer that additional ventilation or exhaust be provided?

1. private toilet rooms
2. a commercial kitchen
3. a corporation conference room
4. an exercise room in community recreation center

4 PROGRAMMING

Programming is a process during which information about a problem is collected, analyzed, and clearly stated to provide a basis for design. It defines a problem before a solution is attempted. Programming is problem analysis whereas design is problem synthesis.

Thorough programming includes a wide range of information. In addition to stating the goals and objectives of the client, a program may contain an analysis of the existing building, aesthetic considerations, space needs, adjacency requirements, organizing concepts, code restrictions, budget demands, and scheduling limitations.

1 THE PROGRAMMING PROCESS

There are several methods of programming. All of them can be used to establish the guidelines and information on which the design process can be based. For residential projects and small commercial jobs, a program may simply consist of a few sentences stating the goals of the project and a list of the required spaces and the furniture to be accommodated. On very large projects, like corporate office headquarters, the program may be a bound volume containing very detailed information about current and future needs of the organization. If a program has not already been completed, it is the responsibility of the interior designer to determine how much information is required before design can begin and to collect and analyze that information.

One popular programming method uses a five-step process in relationship to four major considerations of form, function, economy, and time. This method is described in *Problem Seeking* by William Peña (AIA Press, 1987).

A. The Five-Step Process

The five-step process involves establishing goals, collecting and analyzing facts, uncovering and testing concepts, determining needs, and stating the problem.

Establishing goals: Goals indicate what the client wants to achieve and why. They are important to identify because they establish the direction of programmatic concepts that ultimately suggest the physical means of achieving the goals. It is not enough simply to list the types of spaces and required square footages the client needs; you should know the objectives the client is trying to reach with those spaces and square footages. For example, a goal for a restaurant owner might be to increase revenues by increasing turnover, so the owner may want a design that discourages people from lingering over their meals.

Collecting facts: Facts describe the existing conditions and requirements of the problem such as the number of people to be accommodated, space adjacencies, user characteristics, the existing building within which the interiors will be constructed, equipment to be housed, expected growth rate, money available for construction and furnishings, and building code requirements. There are always many facts; part of your task is not only to collect them but also to organize them so they are useful. Information gathering is discussed at length later in this chapter.

Uncovering concepts: The programming process should develop abstract ideas that are functional solutions to the client's performance problems without defining the physical means that could be used to solve them. These are programmatic concepts and are the basis for later design concepts. It is important that you understand the difference between programmatic concepts and design concepts. A programmatic concept is a performance requirement about how a problem can be solved or a need satisfied. A design concept is a specific physical response about how a programmatic concept can be achieved.

For example, the following might be one of many programmatic concept statements developed for a retail store:

> Provide a medium level of security to protect against theft of merchandise without making the security methods obvious.

This statement identifies and responds to a particular problem (security), narrows its focus (security of property from theft as opposed to security of people or security from fire, for instance), and establishes a way of evaluating how well the goal was reached (is it obvious or not?). There could be many possible design concepts to satisfy the programmatic concept including the following:

1. Provide a central cash/wrap station at the entry/exit point to the store.
2. Tag all merchandise with concealed electronic identifiers and incorporate the detection device in the design of the entry.
3. Display only samples of merchandise as a basis for buying and have purchases delivered to the customer from a storage room.

An example involving the programming and design of a residential project might include the clients telling the designer that they entertain a lot and would like a place for parties, but the children are always in the way. From that need the following programmatic concept could be developed:

> Because the parents entertain frequently apart from the children's activities, the design should provide for functional separation of the children's spaces from the entertainment areas.

If this programmatic concept were approved by the client, the designer would later develop several design concepts for consideration and testing against other requirements of the problem. For example, Figure 4.1 shows five possible design concepts (diagrams that have actual physical implications) that respond to the programmatic concept. Diagram (a) shows splitting the parents' and children's areas into two wings of the house, each with its own entrance but connected with a corridor. Diagram (b) shows another physical response with both areas in the same building but separated with some type of buffer zone. Diagrams (c), (d), and (e) show other possibilities. Notice that because the various options are also concepts, there is still much detailed design work to do with whichever is selected.

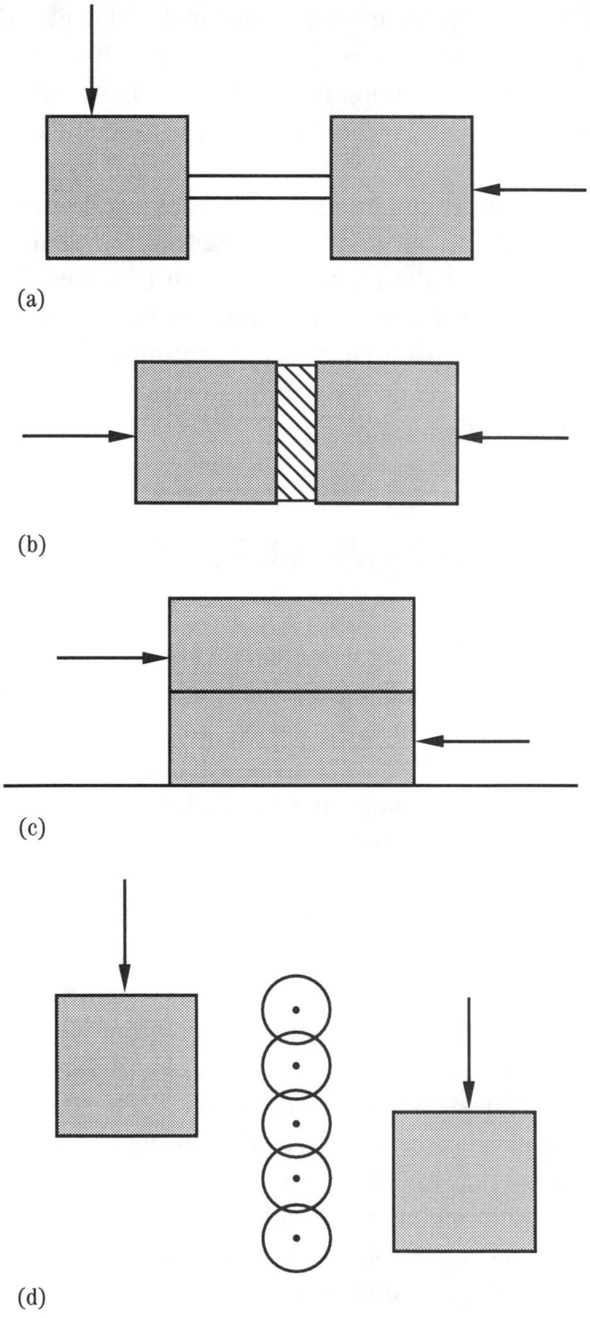

Figure 4.1 Design Concepts

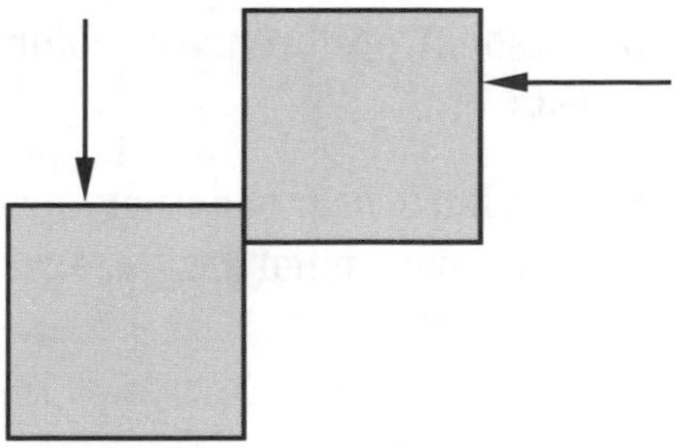

(e)

Figure 4.1 (cont'd)

Determining needs: This step of the programming process balances the desires of the client against the available budget or establishes a budget based on the defined goals and needs. It is during this step that "wants" have to be separated from "needs." Because most clients want more than they can afford, clear statements of true needs at this early stage can help avoid problems later. At this time, one or more of the four elements of cost (quantity, quality, budget, and time) may have to be adjusted to balance needs against available resources.

Stating the problem: The previous four steps are a prelude to succinctly stating the essence of the problem in just a few statements. The problem statements are the bridge between programming and the design process. They are statements, agreed upon by both the client and the programmer, that describe the most important aspects of the problem and serve as the basis for design and as the criteria by which the solution can be evaluated. There should be a minimum of four problem statements—one for each of the major considerations of form, function, economy, and time.

B. Four Major Considerations During Programming

The four major considerations of any design problem are form, function, economy, and time. Form relates to the existing conditions, the physical and psychological environment of the interior, and the quality of construction. Function relates to the people and activities to be performed in the spaces and their relationship. Economy concerns money: the initial cost of the interior, operating costs (if applicable), and life-cycle costs. Finally, time describes the ideas of past, present, and future as they affect the other three considerations. For example, the required schedule for construction is often a time consideration, as is the need for expansion.

C. Programming Format

Regardless of what programming method is used or how complex the project is, the programming process should produce some type of written document that records the information gathered and the conclusions drawn from analysis. This document should be reviewed and approved by the client before design begins, because any incorrect programming information will result in a design that may not meet the client's needs.

Although the exact format of the final programming document will vary depending on the size and complexity of the job, every program should include, as a minimum, the following information:

- a statement of goals and objectives. This may include result-oriented goals, such as "to increase sales by updating the image of the store," and functional goals, such as "to improve circulation and personal interaction among departments."

- a list of client requirements. This should include the number of people who will be using the space as well as information about the kinds of activities they engage in, the required adjacencies between people and activities, and the particular furniture and equipment each person requires. In addition, special needs for lighting, acoustic separation, flexibility in space use, and electricity should be noted.

- a list of spaces and their square footages. This information is basic and serves as a starting point for space planning. This kind of list should also include allowance for secondary spaces like corridors, closets, and other nonlisted spaces that are necessary to make the space functional.

In addition to these data, a program may also include a survey of existing conditions, budget requirements, scheduling constraints, and expansion requirements. The following sections describe in detail the kinds of information required, how it is collected, and how it is compiled and analyzed before beginning design.

2 INFORMATION GATHERING

There are four methods of collecting the information required to complete a program and prepare for design. Each has its own advantages and disadvantages. In most cases two or more methods are used together on any given project. Before these are discussed individually, the following lists provide a comprehensive itemization of the specific information you may need to gather for a project. Of course, not every item on the list is required for every project, but this should give you an overview of what information you should be looking for.

A. Checklist of Required Information

Goals and objectives:

- purpose for building a new or remodeled interior space
- functional goals (for example, larger space, more efficient operation, change in work flow)
- aesthetic goals

User requirements:

- individual users—by name, title, or position
- number and function of groups if not individual users
- whether the user is a specific, full-time user or public user
- number of people—at present, at move-in, and in future growth
- job description of the user
- user characteristics: age, sex, special needs (right- or left-handed, physical disabilities, etc.)
- personal preferences: colors, special interests, etc.
- location of user or activity space (for example, bedrooms on north side, executives in corner office, etc.)

Activity requirements:

- primary activity
- secondary activities
- nature of the activity: physical movement involved, work flow, etc.
- when the activity is performed (time of day or night)
- how often the activity is performed (number of times per day, week, etc.)
- part-time activities such as in conference rooms, reception areas, copy areas, etc.
- if the activity is done alone, in small groups, or in large groups
- visitors involved with the activity
- if the activity shares space with other activities
- special environmental requirements for the activity: lighting, acoustics, heating or cooling, ventilation
- special security requirements

Furnishings and equipment:

- kinds of furniture or equipment required
- whether existing furnishings will be used or new furnishings will be purchased
- sizes of reused and new equipment
- relationship of equipment or furnishings
- types and requirements of communication equipment: telephones, computers, facsimile machines, modems, etc.

- types and amount of storage: bookcases, shelves, drawers, file cabinets, etc.
- electrical requirements of equipment (voltage, special outlets, dedicated circuits, or special lighting)
- mechanical requirements of equipment (cooling, ventilation, etc.)
- private or shared furnishings and equipment
- accessories used: reference manuals, staplers, stamps, postage machines, etc.
- future needs
- required style, color, quality level, ergonomic needs, etc.
- display space required (tackboards, marker boards, etc.)
- audiovisual equipment requirements

Adjacencies:

- required person-to-person contacts
- required movement of objects, paper, or equipment
- degree of adjacency: mandatory, preferred, or not important
- required zoning of related activities, departments, or functional groups
- required adjacencies with the outside: visitors, service, views, shipping, etc.

Space requirements listed by area and square footage:

- space required by activity areas (people and equipment)
- space requirements determined primarily by equipment or activity alone rather than by full-time users in an activity area
- nonassigned space needs: corridors, closets, storage rooms, and other circulation space

Time and money requirements:

- total budget broken into construction budget, furnishing costs, equipment costs, taxes, contingencies, and others as required by project type
- life-cycle cost analysis
- move-in deadline or phasing requirements

B. The Client Interview

Interviewing users is one of the most valuable ways of collecting information. It combines observation (actually seeing what the user currently has), a structured process (following a pre-established set of questions), the ability to clarify ambiguous questions or responses (by elaborating or asking follow-up questions), and the opportunity for extemporaneous exploration of needs and ideas of the user not previously considered. If questionnaires have been used, interviews can verify their accuracy. In addition, a good interviewer can pick up on nonverbal clues about what the user may really be thinking or his or her attitudes toward certain aspects of the topics being discussed. The interview technique works with residential design as well as with large corporations.

However, interviewing takes time and requires that the person being interviewed be kept on the subject while still allowing for some open-ended questions and comments. The designer must also have the approval and direction of the management or of the supervisors of the interviewees. It is usually best to have the client send a memo or letter to all those being interviewed to explain why the process is being undertaken, what the answers will be used for, and that the interviews are approved and encouraged by management.

The number and types of people being questioned should be determined ahead of time and should represent a cross section of the organization. An individual worker may have a very different view of his or her needs than a department manager, but both opinions are valuable. The interviewer should prepare a list of specific questions for which answers are needed. This keeps the process on track and provides a common ground on which to compare interviews and compile results. However, there should be an opportunity for open-ended discussions or questions than can arise only when the interviewer actually sees and talks to an individual.

To conduct the interview, appointments should be made for a specific time and location (preferably the user's workplace or activity area) and limited to a predetermined length. Two interviewers should be present, one to ask the questions and observe and one to take notes and provide a second opinion on observation. It is usually impossible for one person to do everything well.

One part of the programming practicum portion of the NCIDQ exam simulates a client interview and requires that you read a descriptive situation. Then you may be asked either to write the eight most critical questions you would need to ask to gather the information required to proceed with the design or to select the eight questions from a longer list and write a brief explanation for why you selected each one. In either case, each question must focus on a separate programming concept or requirement and be intended to draw out different types of information. The questions on the test's checklist will most likely include the following requirements, from which you would select eight:

1. number of people involved
2. adjacencies
3. furniture requirements
4. equipment requirements
5. need for expansion (growth)
6. budget requirements
7. open versus closed space
8. reusing of furniture versus buying new furniture
9. circulation system
10. shared use of space
11. amount of time a space is used
12. spatial requirements of an activity

All of these requirements have physical implications for planning and design related to the number, size, location, quality, and furnishing of activity spaces. The most direct way to think of what questions you need to ask—on the NCIDQ exam or in a real design situation—is to imagine designing with the information you have. If you cannot make a design decision about something, then you need to ask.

C. Questionnaires

Questionnaires are written forms that people fill in with requested information. They are useful when a large number of people need to be surveyed and time or resources do not allow for individual interviews. However, to be effective, they must be well designed and their completion should be required by management.

No one likes to complete a form, even if it leads to improvements in the workplace. A questionnaire must be designed so that it is as short, unambiguous, and easy to fill in as possible. If an item is not clear, people will ignore it or provide questionable information. One of the best ways to develop an effective questionnaire is to design one and try it out on a select sample. Confusing or unnecessary questions can then be revised before the full sample is taken. A questionnaire should be accompanied with a cover letter from management explaining why the form is being distributed and encouraging or requiring that it be completed and returned. In some cases, information from questionnaires is verified by interviews.

A variation of the technique is to develop a questionnaire but have it administered by someone from the designer's office. This way unclear questions can be clarified and the questionnaire's completion is assured. Unlike an interview, only one person is required and the process usually requires less time.

D. Observation

Often, one of the most reliable ways to gather information is by observing what people do rather than by listening to what they say. The danger from observation, however, is jumping to conclusions without understanding why people are doing things a particular way. For example, a person may have numerous small appliances on a kitchen counter not because it is convenient but because there is nowhere else to store them. The client might prefer to have a storage location in a closet out of sight, while an observer might draw the conclusion that the client likes having appliances on the counter.

Observation is best used to verify information gathered by interviews or questionnaires or as a way of generating questions to determine the reason behind the observed behavior. Observation is also useful in situations where questionnaires or interviews are not possible—for example, to determine how people use a public space.

E. Field Surveys

Because interior design is accomplished within an architectural space, an important part of programming is to determine existing conditions. This is true whether the building already exists or is still in the planning stages. An existing building can be field measured and photographed and special on-site conditions can be noted. If a building is still being designed, the information must be determined from architectural drawings.

A field survey should determine the following things:

- the size and configuration of the building or space that will be used. This involves taking field measurements and drafting a plan to scale that can be used to lay out the final interior plan. The plan should include structural elements such as exterior walls, columns, and interior bearing walls. It should also include fixed architectural reference points from which interior dimensions can be made. These may include points like column center lines, faces of structural walls, or faces of permanent partitions.

- existing nonbearing partitions, cabinetry, and built-in items

- locations and sizes (width and height) of doors and windows

- types and heights of ceilings

- location of electrical and telephone outlets

- location and size of heating diffusers, radiators, and other exposed mechanical equipment

- location of plumbing fixtures and plumbing pipes

- location and type of existing artificial lighting

- condition and capacity of the electrical, plumbing, heating, and other mechanical systems in older buildings. This will need to be performed by engineering consultants.

- general condition of construction elements. This will help determine what can be reused and what will need to be repaired or replaced.

- location of true north and notes on the quality and amount of natural light in the space

- views from windows

- potential noise problems, either from within or outside the building

- special architectural features, moldings, or unusual elements

- potential environmental problems with asbestos, lead paint, and the like. The interior designer's survey can only suggest the possibility of these types of problems. Actual field testing and verification must be done by companies qualified to perform this type of work.

3 INFORMATION ANALYSIS

Once all the information about a problem has been gathered, you must organize and analyze it before beginning space planning and design. Of all programming data, area and adjacencies are two of the primary factors that determine the size and configuration of the interior space. In addition to the primary spaces, there are also support spaces that add to the overall space requirements. These include areas such as corridors and other circulation space, closets, toilet rooms, and nonspecified storage areas.

A. Determining Space and Volume Needs

Space needs are determined in a number of ways. Often, when programming begins the client will have a list of the required functional spaces and the corresponding square footages in addition to any special height requirements. These may be based on the client's experience or on corporate space standards, or they may simply be a list of what currently exists. For example, space standards of a corporation may dictate that a senior manager have a 225-square-foot office while a junior manager be allotted 150 square feet.

These types of requirements may provide a valid basis for developing space needs or they may be arbitrary and subject to review during programming. Where square footages are not defined by one of these methods, space for a particular use is determined in one of three ways: by the number of people that must be accommodated, by an object or piece of equipment, or by a specific activity that has its own clearly specified space needs.

The first way space can be determined is to multiply how much area one person needs by the total number of people in the same area. Through experience and detailed analysis, general guidelines for space requirements for one person engaged in various types of activities have been developed and are commonly used. For example, a student sitting in a standard classroom needs about 15 to 20 square feet. This includes space for sitting in a chair in addition to the space required for circulating within the classroom and space for the teacher's desk and shelving. To find the total square footage for the classroom, multiply the number of students by the standard 15 to 20 square feet requirement. An office worker needs from 100 to 250 square feet, depending on whether the employee is housed in a private office or is part of an open office plan. This space requirement also includes room to circulate around the desk and may include space for visitors' chairs, personal files, and the like. Multiply the number of office workers by the space required by one to find the space needs of the office.

Occasionally, space needs can be based on something other than the number of people that is directly related to the occupancy. For instance, preliminary planning of a restaurant kitchen may be based on a percentage of the size of the dining room, or library space can be estimated based on the number of books.

For the various parts of the NCIDQ exam you will not need to memorize the general guidelines for space requirements, but you will need to know how to apply given space and furnishing requirements to a problem. For example, in the practicum/scenario portion of the test, you may be given only the furniture and equipment requirements for a user and be asked to determine the total area required from that information. The program may tell you that a workstation must include 15 square feet of work surface, space for a computer terminal, 12 linear feet of filing, a chair, two visitors' chairs, and space for a calculator and telephone. You would then determine the space needed for this function.

The second way space needs are determined is by the size of an object or piece of equipment. The size of the printing press, for example, partially determines the area of a press room. Automobile size determines the space needs for an automobile showroom or a parking garage.

The third way space needs are defined is through a built-in set of rules or customs related to the activity itself. Space needs of sports facilities are determined with this method. A racquetball court must be a certain size regardless of the number of spectators present, although the seating capacity would add to the total space required. A courtroom is an example of a place where the procedures and customs of the trial process dictate an arrangement of human activity and spacing of individual areas that only partially depend on the number of people.

B. Determining Total Required Area

The areas determined with the methods described above result in the *net area* of a facility. As mentioned, these areas do not include general circulation space, closets, electrical and telephone equipment rooms, wall and structural thicknesses, and similar spaces. Sometimes the net area is referred to as the net assignable area and the secondary spaces are referred to as the unassigned areas.

The sum of the net area and these ancillary areas gives the *gross area*. The ratio of the two figures is called the net-to-gross ratio and is often referred to as the efficiency of the space. Efficiency depends on the type of occupancy and how well it is planned. A hospital with many small rooms and a great number of large corridors has a much lower efficiency ratio than a factory where the majority of space is devoted to production areas and very little to corridors and other secondary spaces.

Generally, net-to-gross ratios range from 60 to 80 percent, with some building types more or less efficient than this. Table 4.1 shows some common efficiency ratios.

Table 4.1

Net-to-Gross Ratios for Common Building Types

Building Type	Efficiency Ratio
office	0.75–0.80
retail	0.75
bank	0.70
restaurant, table service	0.66–0.70
bars, nightclubs	0.70–0.77
hotel	0.62–0.70
public library	0.77–0.80
museum	0.83
theater	0.60–0.77
school, classroom	0.60–0.66
apartment	0.66–0.80
hospital	0.54–0.66

In some cases it is important for the interior designer to understand an additional type of area measurement called the *rentable area*. This is the square footage that is used as the basis for leasing office and retail space. It is the total amount of usable space available but also includes structural columns, the thickness of some partitions, and often a portion of the exterior wall of the building.

When an office lease space only occupies a portion of a floor, the rentable area is measured from the inside glass surface of exterior walls (if the glass is more than 50 percent of the wall area) to the finished surface of the tenant side of the public corridor partition and from the centerlines of partitions separating adjacent tenant spaces. See Figure 4.2. The rentable area also includes a proportionate share of the corridor and rest rooms.

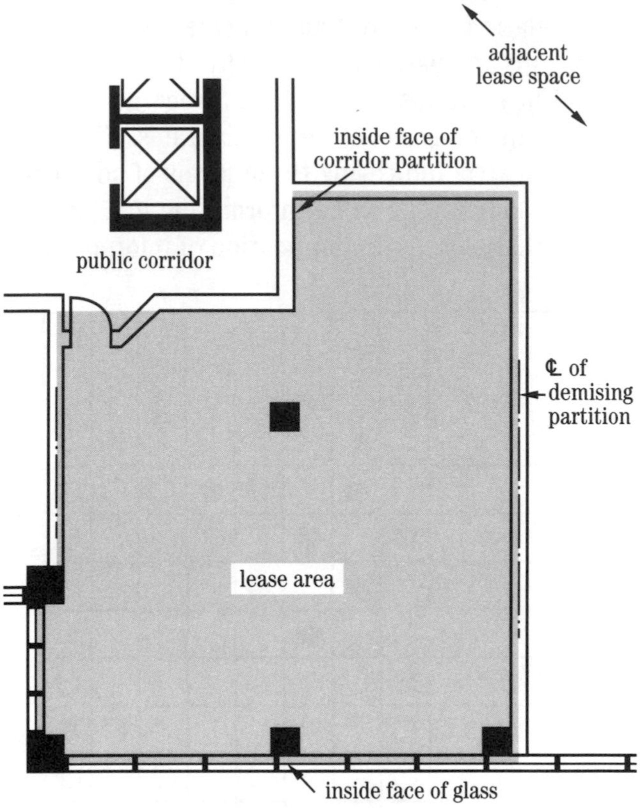

Figure 4.2 Method of Measuring Rentable Area

When a tenant occupies an entire floor, the rentable area includes all the space taken by the public corridors as well as the elevator lobby and the rest rooms on that floor. The partitions separating adjacent tenant spaces and separating a tenant space from public spaces are often called *demising walls*.

If your client gave you the rentable area to plan with, you would have to subtract the space required for corridors, closets, and the like to arrive at the net square footage for the spaces that are part of the program. Conversely, if you were developing a program with a list of spaces for a client, you would have to add in extra area to account for nonusable space. This total, plus an allowance for columns and demising walls, would then be the amount of rentable square footage your client would have to lease.

C. Determining Space Relationships

Spaces must not only be the correct size for the activity they support, but they also must be located near other spaces with which they share some functional relationship. Programming identifies these relationships and assigns a hierarchy of importance to them. The relationships are usually recorded in a matrix or graphically as adjacency diagrams. Figure 4.3 shows a matrix indicating three levels of adjacency. Figure 4.4 shows the same information in a "folded" version that eliminates duplication of information.

	entry	living room	dining room	kitchen	study	bedroom	bedroom	bath
entry		●		○	●	○	○	○
living room	●		●		○			○
dining room		●		●				
kitchen	○		●					
study	●	○						○
bedroom	○						○	●
bedroom	○					○		●
bath	○	○			○	●	●	

legend
mandatory adjacency ●
secondary adjacency ○
no adjacency required □

Figure 4.3 Adjacency Matrix

There are three basic types of adjacency needs: people, products, and information. Each type implies a different kind of design response. Two or more spaces may need to be physically adjacent or located very close to one another when people need face-to-face contact or when people move from one area to another as part of their activity. For example, the entry to a theater, the lobby, and the theater space have a particular functional reason for being arranged the way they are. In a house, the kitchen should be adjacent to the dining room but does not have to be adjacent to the bedrooms. With some relationships, two spaces may simply need to be accessible to one another, but this can be accomplished with a corridor or through another intervening space rather than with direct adjacency.

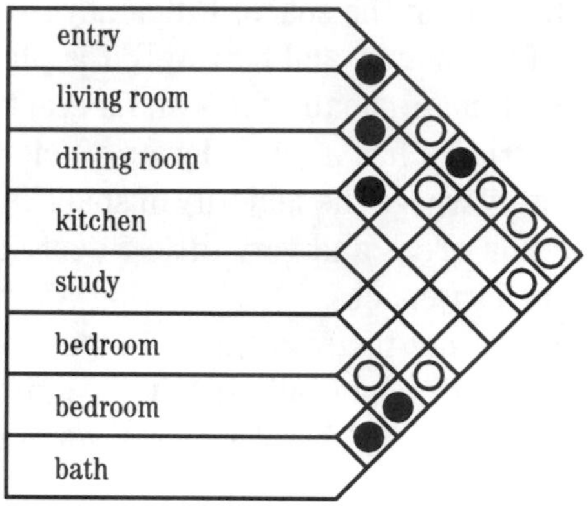

legend
mandatory adjacency ●
secondary adjacency ○

Figure 4.4 Folded Adjacency Matrix

Products, equipment, or other objects may need to be moved between spaces and require another type of adjacency. The spaces themselves may not have to be close to one another, but the movement of objects must be facilitated. Dumbwaiters, pneumatic tubes, assembly lines, and other types of conveying systems can connect spaces of this type without direct adjacency.

Finally, there may be a requirement only that people in different spaces exchange information. The adjacency may then be entirely electronic or with paper-moving systems. For example, a supervisor electronically monitoring telephone operators would not need to be physically adjacent (or even in the same building) even though there is a strong relationship between the two functions. Although quite frequently situations do not demand physical adjacency, informal human contact may be advantageous for other reasons.

The programmer analyzes various types of adjacency requirements and verifies them with the client. Because every desirable relationship can seldom be accommodated, the ones that are mandatory need to be identified separately from the ones that are highly desirable or simply useful. This is often indicated in adjacency diagrams (often called bubble diagrams) with varying weights of connecting lines or with varying numbers of lines: the more lines, the stronger the connection should be. Figure 4.5 shows the information given in the matrix of Figure 4.4 as a bubble diagram.

In one part of the practicum/programming section of the exam, you are required to draw a bubble diagram based on programming information and an adjacency matrix. The bubbles or area blocks must also show the approximate scale relationships between the spaces, and the diagram must have a legend showing what level of adjacency the connecting lines indicate. See Chapter 24 for more information on this part of the examination.

A special type of adjacency diagram is the stacking diagram. As illustrated in Figure 4.6, this is a drawing that shows the location of major spaces or departments when a project occupies more than one floor of a multistory building. A stacking diagram based on departments or major groupings of spaces is usually worked out before each floor area is planned in detail.

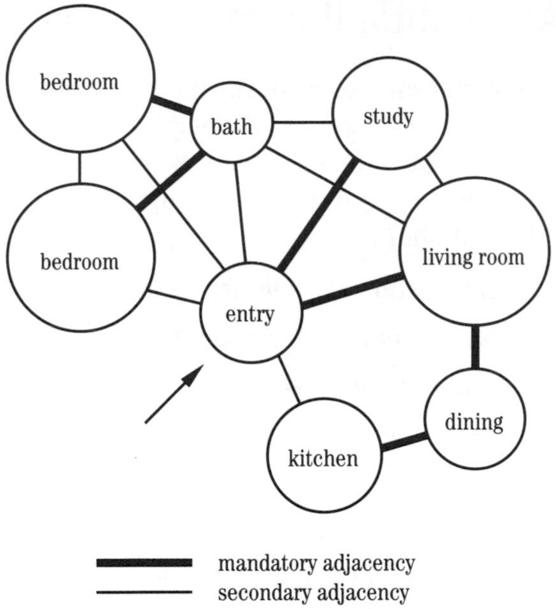

Figure 4.5 Bubble Diagram

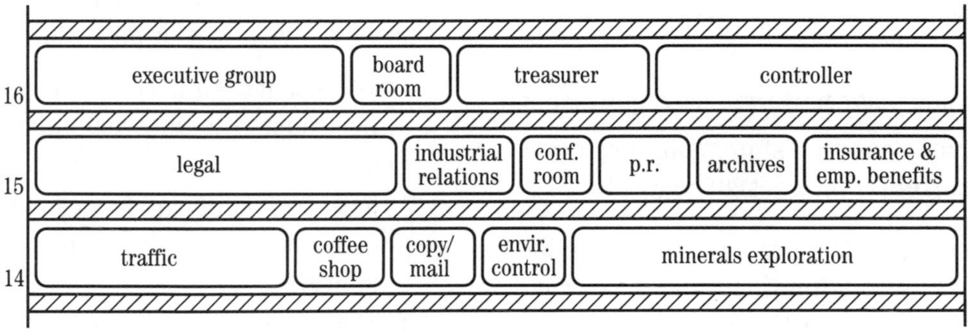

Figure 4.6 Stacking Diagram

SAMPLE QUESTIONS

1. What information would be the MOST important to obtain from a field survey if a complete set of drawings were also available for a building in which you were designing a library that was to occupy only one portion of the building?

    1. the location of structural elements
    2. existing natural light sources
    3. sources of noise within the building
    4. the location and capacity of electrical power

2. Of the following, what is true about the difference between a programmatic concept statement and a design concept statement?

    1. A design concept specifies a particular way to achieve the programmatic statement.
    2. There are as many programmatic concept statements for a problem as there are design concepts.
    3. A design concept is a performance requirement.
    4. Programmatic concept statements are developed concurrently with design concepts.

3. If you were conducting a programming interview with a client for a small clothing boutique, what would be the LEAST important question to ask?

    1. Which items are most frequently purchased on impulse?
    2. Will rest rooms be available to the customers?
    3. What amount of merchandise will be on display?
    4. What is the relationship between the cash/wrap counter and the dressing rooms?

4. What is generally NOT true about programming interviews?

    1. They can verify the accuracy of questionnaires.
    2. They minimize inaccurate results from ambiguous questions.
    3. They allow for information to be uncovered that the programmer may not have considered.
    4. They make efficient use of the interviewer's time.

5. The initial determination of area required for a client's program gives

    1. the net area
    2. the rentable area
    3. the gross area
    4. the efficiency ratio

6. Overall department relationships of a large company being planned to occupy a multistory building would most likely be shown in

    1. a block diagram
    2. an adjacency matrix
    3. a stacking diagram
    4. a bubble diagram

7. Preliminary space planning shows that it is impossible to satisfy all the programmed adjacencies shown on the adjacency matrix that has been approved by your client. What is your best course of action?

    1. Verify that the adjacencies require physical connection and then review the problem with the client.
    2. Satisfy as many adjacency connections as you can and present this to the client for review and approval.
    3. Ask the client to downgrade the importance of the adjacency that you are having difficulty achieving.
    4. Develop several alternatives that come as close as possible to the requirements and have the client select the one that best satisfies the program.

8. One commonly used programming technique considers which four elements when defining a problem?

    1. goals, facts, concepts, and needs
    2. form, function, facts, and the problem
    3. concepts, facts, form, and time
    4. time, function, form, and economy

9. During an initial interview with a client who has hired you to redesign a very large Victorian house into a bed and breakfast inn, the client says that he

wants to restore the interior to an original Victorian look as well as enlarge some of the bedrooms into larger suites so the inn will be the best in town. After hearing these comments, what should be your FIRST course of action?

1. Suggest that the client also retain an architect to determine the feasibility of enlarging rooms and removing walls.
2. Ask the client if he has a budget and suggest that you do a preliminary cost estimate to see if he can afford what he wants.
3. Tell the client that he needs to define what he means by "the best in town" so you have a more definite idea of how to design.
4. Recommend to the client that you do field measurements of the house and begin research on authentic Victorian furnishings and finishes.

10. In which case would the number of people occupying a space NOT be critical to the programming effort?

1. the dining room of a housing complex for the elderly
2. the workroom of a commercial laundry
3. a multipurpose meeting room in a neighborhood recreation center
4. a waiting area in a hospital

5 SPACE PLANNING

During programming, general concepts are developed as a response to the goals and needs of the client. These programmatic concepts are statements about functional solutions to the client's performance requirements. They differ from design concepts as discussed in this chapter because no attempt at an actual physical solution is made during programming. Programmatic concepts guide the later development of design concepts. For example, a programmatic concept might be that a corporate office facility should encourage interaction among all the employees by mixing circulation paths. The physical means to make that happen would be developed as a design concept. One possible design concept might be that the corridors cross near the center of the building at an informal lounge area.

This chapter summarizes the process used to translate programmatic needs into a physical plan of the space by organizing major rooms and areas, determining circulation systems, and laying out furniture. This process is often called *space planning* because it deals with the design of the arrangement of spaces and objects and not with the particulars of materials, finishes, colors, accessories, and the like.

1 CONCEPT DEVELOPMENT

The first step in designing is to develop an overall direction for subsequent work. This is known as concept development and is based on the project's programmatic needs generated earlier. A design concept is a statement of a specific physical response indicating how a programmatic concept can be satisfied. Refer to Chapter 4 for some examples of the difference between programmatic and design concepts.

Although design concepts specify particular physical responses, they are still a broad-brush approach that leaves some flexibility in deciding the details of the design. For example, a design concept for a restaurant located in a scenic area might be to design a neutral background of warm color finishes while maximizing the view to the outside. A statement like this would help determine such things as space planning of the rooms and tables (oriented to the view, possibly on stepped platforms like a theater, location of service spaces away from the primary view), selection of finishes (warm colors primarily), and the selection of materials (window coverings that do not obstruct the view, simple neutral forms and shapes, and so forth). The same statement precludes other decisions like a strong "theme" look or layout of tables and lounge areas focusing on the interior of the restaurant.

Although a concept statement may be simple or complex depending on the size and complexity of the project, it should be concise and define the essence of the design. Generally, a good concept statement can be made in one to four sentences. As with programmatic concepts, the concept statement can (and should) be reviewed with the client before more detailed space planning and material selection begins.

2 SPACE ALLOCATIONS

Regardless of the complexity of a program, there is a logical method to developing a space plan that satisfies the client's needs and the design concept. The steps involved in this process are outlined below. Additional design considerations are discussed in the following section.

A. Existing Conditions

Because the interior designer always develops a plan within the context of an existing architectural space (or one that is designed but not yet constructed), many preliminary space planning decisions are based on existing conditions. These are determined during the field survey and recorded on plans, elevations, and other sketches as necessary. You can also use photographs to document things like existing views, lighting, and the condition of materials and finishes that may be reused. If the building is still in the planning stages or existing drawings are available, you can get copies of the architectural plans. However, base building floor plans may not include certain information that you need for design, such as wall finishes, equipment added by the previous owner, or hardware types. If an existing floor plan is not available at the scale you will be using, a base plan should be drawn to use for subsequent planning and development of construction documents.

There are several aspects of existing conditions that can influence the space plan of an interior design project. These are briefly outlined below. Of course, depending on the nature of the project, not all will apply in every circumstance.

- *Relationship to surrounding areas:* The surrounding area includes exterior features such as entry doors to the building as well as interior points of connection like stairways and corridors. Obviously, you would want to locate the reception area of an office close to the main entrance or elevator lobby, or the primary furniture grouping of a living room near a focal point like a fireplace. In existing commercial buildings, the location of exits are always one of the primary determinants of how corridors and large spaces are planned.

- *Size of existing space:* The size of the existing space will also affect planning decisions. Some parts of the existing space may not accommodate some of the larger programmed spaces, so the location of these will be determined by the available large, unobstructed areas. If ceiling height is important, such as in athletic facilities and auditoriums, this too may influence how the project must be planned.

- *Views:* Views are important to residential and commercial interior design alike. Desirable views should be fully utilized, while undesirable views can be blocked or modified with window coverings. You can also plan space so that rooms where view is not important are located near windows with less desirable views. In commercial construction, you also have to decide what spaces are placed at the exterior wall. Guidelines for such decisions should be made during the programming phase. In many cases, offices with windows are a sign of status or hierarchy in an organization. In other cases, windows may be provided in common areas and open work areas for everyone to use.

- *Special features:* Both existing and new buildings often have unique characteristics that can be incorporated into the designer's planning. For instance, older structures may have ornate millwork or vaulted ceilings that can be featured in the primary interior spaces. The location of these spaces would, in turn, dictate the location of adjacent spaces. New buildings might have interior atriums or attractive public corridors that could suggest the positioning of certain rooms.

- *Structural considerations:* The location of columns and bearing walls is often one of the most troublesome existing factors for interior design. Columns cannot be moved and bearing walls may only be pierced or partially removed after review and design by a structural engineer and then only with significant expense. Existing structural elements may affect the spacing of rooms, the position of new partitions, or the location of large areas. New partitions can coincide with column locations so that columns do not awkwardly end up in the middle of a room. If a room is required to be of a size that exceeds the column spacing, it should be centered between the columns so that the columns are off to both sides as much as possible. In spaces used for open office planning or restaurant dining rooms, furniture placement can be planned around the columns or service spaces like closets and storage rooms, or space dividers can minimize the effect of the columns.

The existing bearing capacity of a building's floor system can also influence space planning. If heavy loading like library shelving, densely packed file cabinets, or heavy equipment is present, a structural engineer should be hired to review the situation. Some areas of a building may have a greater load-bearing capacity than others. In some instances, additional structural reinforcing may be required.

- *Plumbing:* Kitchens, bar sinks, toilet rooms, and other spaces that require water supply and drainage should be located close to existing building plumbing to minimize cost and simplify construction. For residential projects the plumbing lines can be easily located by the placement of existing bathrooms and kitchens or by inspecting the basement or crawl space. In commercial construction, the architectural plans may need to be reviewed because the location of plumbing lines is not always evident. In high-rise buildings, the plumbing is located in vertical stacks at the core of the building near the toilet rooms. Often, however, wet columns are provided. These are structural columns away from the core of the building next to which water supply pipes and drains are located to make it easier to tap into as required for tenant finish work.

B. Organization Concepts

After the pertinent existing conditions have been identified and noted, the next determinant of space planning is function. Required adjacencies and the relative sizes of various rooms and areas in conjunction with existing constraints dictate much of the organization of a plan. However, even with these objective requirements there are usually many ways the same program can be accommodated within any given architectural space. One of the designer's tasks is to develop organizing concepts that will satisfy the client's needs and then test them against criteria unique to the situation to find the best one to develop in more detail.

Given an open area (without constraining walls or other fixed elements), there are four basic organizing concepts (and their variations) that you can use to begin space planning. They are shown in Figure 5.1 and include linear, axial, grid, and central systems. You can apply these general concepts to large space planning problems as well as to individual rooms.

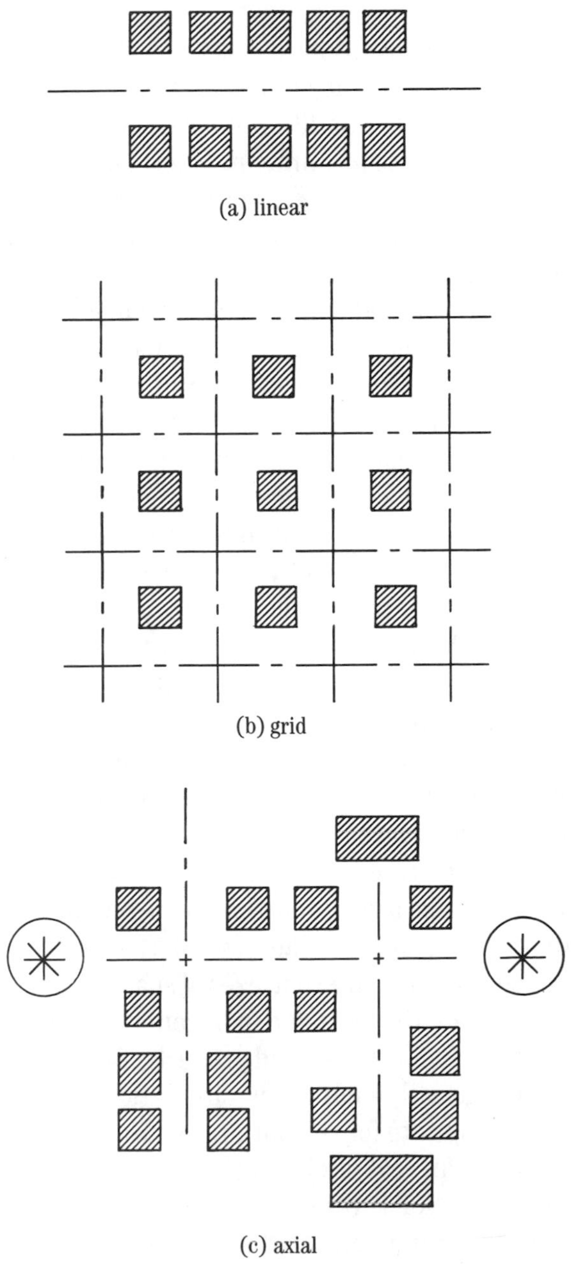

Figure 5.1 Organizing Concepts

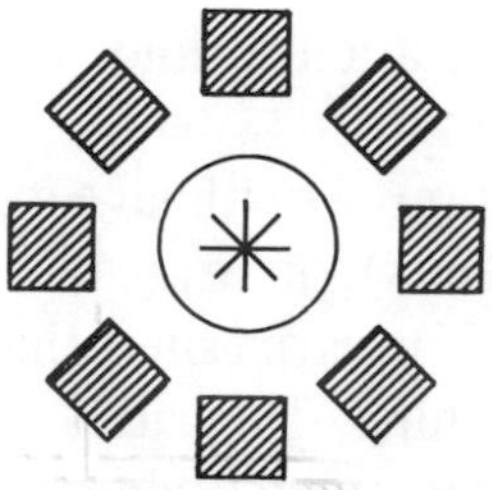

(d) central

Figure 5.1 (cont'd)

Linear organizations consist of a series of spaces or rooms that are placed in a single line. The spaces can be identical or of different sizes and shapes, but they always relate to a unifying line, usually a path of circulation. A linear organization is very adaptable; it can be straight, bent, or curved to work within an existing architectural space. It is easily expandable and can be planned in a modular configuration if desired. The typical layout of office space, with rooms positioned on either side of a corridor that encircles the building's core, is a variation of the linear concept.

Axial organizations have two or more major linear segments about which spaces or rooms are placed. There may be additional, secondary paths growing out of the primary axes, and the major linear segments may be at right angles to each other or at some other angle. Axial plans usually have a featured termination at one or more ends of the axis, or the axis is a major design element in itself.

Grid systems consist of two sets of spaced elements. The grid elements may be regularly spaced and perpendicular to each other or irregularly spaced and at angles to each other or to the architectural space. Within a grid, portions can be subtracted, added, or modified. The size of the grid can be changed to create different sizes of spaces or to define special areas. However, it can become very monotonous and confusing if not used properly. Because a grid system is usually defined by circulation paths, it is more appropriate for very large spaces or in buildings where a great deal of circulation is required. Open-plan workstations or restaurant tables are two examples where grid organizations are commonly used.

Central organizations are based on one space or point about which secondary elements are placed. It is usually a very formal method of organizing interiors and inherently places the primary emphasis on the central space. A hotel lobby is a common example of this type of concept.

When more than one linear organization extends from a centralized point, it becomes a radial organization. Radial plans have a central focus but also extend outward to connect with other spaces or rooms. Radial plans can be circular or assume other shapes as well.

C. Circulation Patterns

Developing a direct, efficient circulation plan is critical to successfully completing the scenario/practicum portion of the NCIDQ exam. You must demonstrate that you can allocate space efficiently, use circulation to maintain adjacencies, and provide the required arrangement and widths to satisfy barrier free and building code exiting requirements.

One of the common mistakes in space planning is to let adjacency requirements dictate the arranging of rooms and spaces in the preliminary planning and then to connect rooms with a circulation path as an afterthought. You are then left with a maze of awkward corridors and circulation routes that decrease efficiency and leave you with dead-end corridors or other exiting problems.

Circulation patterns are one of the primary ways of organizing a room, an open space, or an entire interior design project. They are vital to the efficient organization of space and provide people with their strongest orientation within an environment.

Circulation is directly related to the organizational pattern of a project, but it does not necessarily have to mimic it. For example, a major circulation path can cut diagonally across a grid pattern. See Figure 5.2. Normally, there is a hierarchy of paths. Major routes connect major rooms or spaces or are spaces themselves and have secondary paths branching from them. Different sizes and types of circulation are important for accommodating varying capacities and for providing an orientation device for people.

All circulation paths are linear by their very nature, but there are some common variations, many of which are similar to the organizational patterns described in the previous section. Because circulation

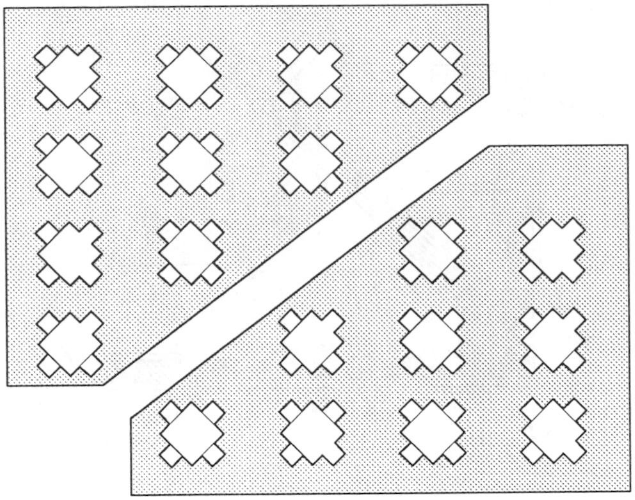

Figure 5.2 Juxtaposed Organizing and Circulation Concepts

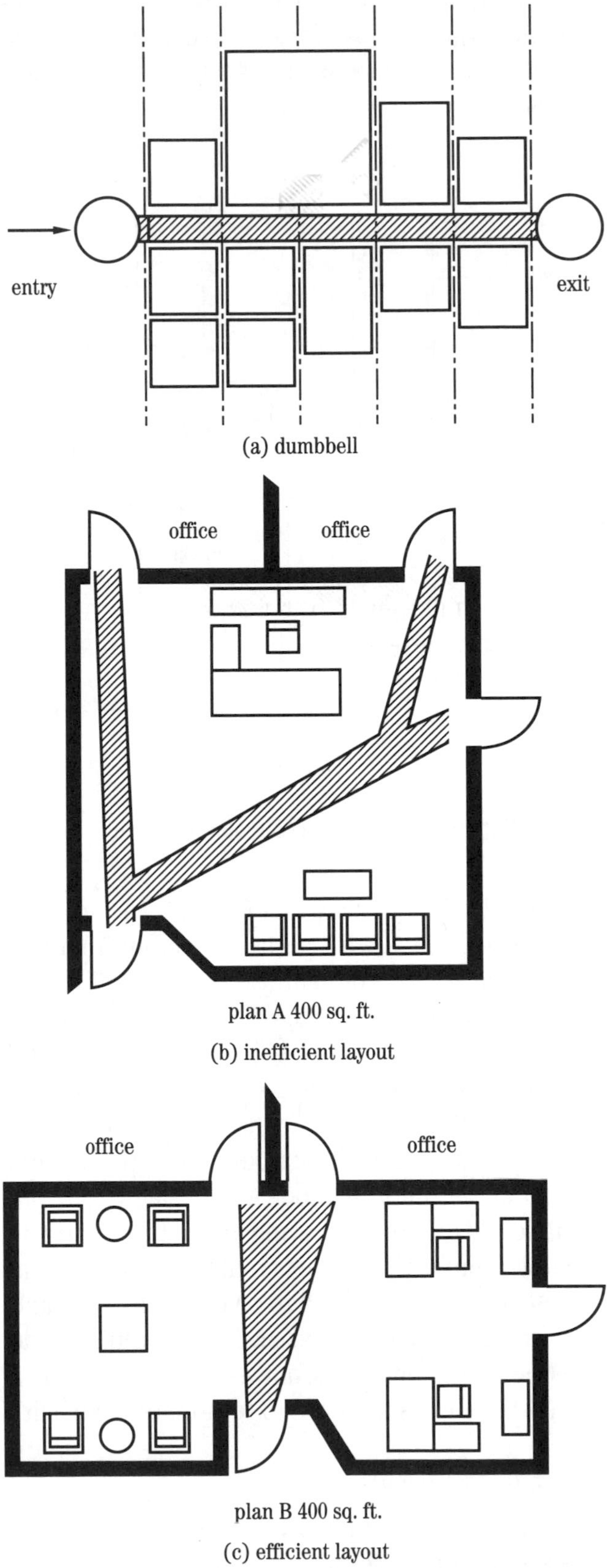

Figure 5.3 Circulation Layouts

is such an important part of space planning, you will find it helpful to have a mental picture of the various circulation concepts and the advantages and disadvantages of each before you take the test. There are three basic patterns as shown in Figures 5.3 through 5.5. You can apply these to an individual room when laying out furniture as well as to a group of rooms and spaces when planning a larger facility.

The linear, dumbbell layout diagrammed in Figure 5.3(a) is the simplest and one of the most flexible. Spaces are laid out along a straight path that connects two major elements at the ends. These are usually the entrance to the space or group of rooms at one end and an exit or other access point at the other, although the primary entrance can occur anywhere along the path. Spaces are laid out along the spine as required. The path can be straight, bent, or curved as required to accommodate the fixed architectural space. The typical double-loaded corridor arrangement (rooms on both sides of a common corridor) makes space planning very efficient. Figures 5.3(b) and 5.3(c) show the dumbbell layout applied to rooms of identical area in an efficient and inefficient way.

Making a complete loop results in a doughnut configuration as shown in Figure 5.4. This is also very efficient because it provides a double-loaded corridor and automatically makes a continuous exitway so two exits are always available if required by building codes. Entries, doorways, and exits can be located anywhere along the path. This pattern is only appropriate for larger groups of spaces because the ratio of circulation area to usable area should be kept as low as possible.

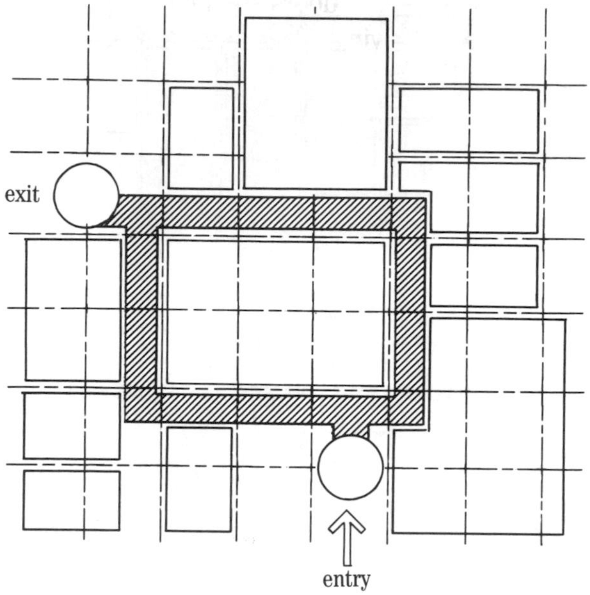

Figure 5.4 Doughnut Circulation Layout

The radial layout shown in Figure 5.5 is oriented on one major space with paths extending from this central area. This configuration is generally used when there is a major space that serves as the focal point for secondary spaces, such as with a hotel lobby. A well-planned house is another example of a radial layout with the entry hall being the central space from which the other circulation paths radiate. Because of the building code requirement in commercial construction for having at least two paths to an exit, the ends of the linear routes extending from the central space must lead to an exit or loop around to the central space. However, if the building code allows dead-end corridors not exceeding 20 feet, a short corridor does not have to terminate in an exit.

D. Furnishings Layout

Furniture layout is simply a space planning problem in miniature. Before you start work on a furnishings layout, however, you should determine the overall context of the room or space in which the

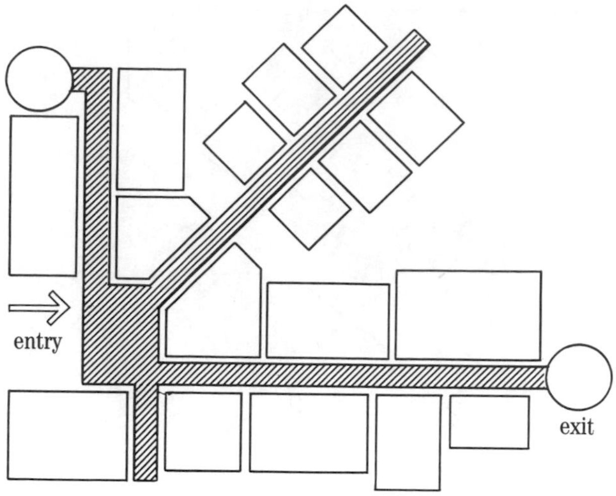

Figure 5.5 Radial Circulation Layout

furniture will be placed. This includes determining fixed items, such as window locations and structural elements, and planning those things you can control to give yourself as much flexibility as possible for furniture arrangement. For example, if you can locate a door anywhere in a new partition, it should be placed so it does not create an awkward circulation path through an area best used for a furniture grouping. The simplest way to avoid problems is to view furniture groupings as "rooms" and the spaces between them as circulation paths and follow the organizational and circulation concepts described in the previous two sections.

Nearly all furniture placement, whether in residential or commercial design, is designed as part of a furniture grouping. For example, a bedroom consists of a bed, nightstands, and storage cabinets, while an office workstation may consist of a desk, a desk return for placement of a computer terminal, a chair, and possibly a file cabinet or credenza. The grouping creates a planning module consisting of three elements: the individual pieces of furniture, the space around them, and the access points to get to the grouping (the "door" to the grouping). If you think of a furniture grouping in these terms it is easier to plan it efficiently.

The first step is to determine the types and number of individual pieces. Of course, the program defines the function of the grouping and often specifies the individual pieces of furniture. If the program simply specifies the function, like a "lounge seating group," you will need to make some assumptions about the exact number of people to be accommodated, the types of furniture (chairs versus sofas, for example), and other pieces like side tables, lamps, or coffee tables. If existing furniture is being reused, you can measure it to determine how much space is required. If new furniture is planned, you will have to assume an approximate size of the individual pieces.

Next, consider the space between the pieces and their orientation to each other. For example, the space between a desk and a credenza behind should be about 3$^1/_2$ to 5 feet. This allows for a chair and easy access to drawers. A well-planned seating group places chairs and sofas about 4 to 10 feet apart for comfortable conversation. Your knowledge of typical space planning dimensions and human factors discussed in Chapter 3 will help you determine spacing and orientation.

Finally, think about the general access to the grouping and its relationship to existing elements within the room. For example, a dining table in the middle of a room with three doors will require more space around the table for general circulation than a table at the end of a room, which would only need enough space between the table and walls to allow for seating and access to each chair.

E. Code Restrictions

Building code requirements concerning exiting, corridors, and doors affect initial space planning. Building code requirements are discussed in detail in Chapter 17, but the following guidelines summarize the requirements for preliminary planning. The problem statement of the practicum/scenario portion of the test will usually give you the major code requirements, but if not you can use the following checklist as a starting point.

- Verify that you have the required number of exits from individual rooms and from the entire space. Smaller rooms and nonassembly spaces usually require only one exit door. Spaces with large occupant loads like auditoriums and classrooms will require two exits.

- If two exits are required they must be separated by a distance at least one-half of the diagonal distance of the room or area they serve. See Chapter 17 for more information on this requirement.

- Make sure exit doors are a minimum of 3 feet wide and swing in the direction of travel.

- Use corridors of adequate exit width. Generally, the minimum is 36 inches for residential construction and 44 inches for commercial construction, but school and other occupancies may require wider corridors. In most cases, you will want to use 48-inch-wide to 60-inch-wide corridors anyway to provide adequate width for normal use.

- Although dead-end corridors of less than 20 feet are acceptable in some circumstances, try to develop the space plan to avoid these completely.

- Plan corridors for efficient layout so the total length is minimized. Refer to Chapter 17 for information on maximum travel distances.

- Verify that corridor widths, turns, and other clearances meet the requirements for accessibility for the physically disabled. This includes adequate clearance in front of and to the sides of door openings. See Chapter 19 for specific accessibility requirements.

3 DESIGN CONSIDERATIONS

The practicum/scenario portion of the exam requires that, in addition to fitting the programmed spaces on a given floor plan with efficient circulation, you must also maintain the required adjacencies, consider public versus private spaces, and include enclosed and open spaces as required by the program or based on a reasonable inference from the program.

A. Maintaining Adjacencies

One of the basic requirements of space planning is to maintain the programmed adjacencies. Bubble diagrams or matrices record these and indicate varying levels of connection such as mandatory, desired, or not important. Your plan should place rooms or areas with mandatory adjacencies next to each other. Spaces with less important adjacencies are often separated somewhat if they cannot be abutted. This is usually done with corridors.

During space planning, required adjacencies can be maintained by translating roughly scaled bubble diagrams to scaled, rectangular shapes representing individual rooms and spaces in such a way that as many lines of adjacency as possible are maintained. This diagram can then be laid over the base floor plan as a starting point for locating partitions and other area separations.

B. Public versus Private

Except for single rooms, almost all interior design projects have a hierarchy of privacy requirements. For example, a residential living room is considered more public than a bedroom or bathroom. The reception area of an office suite can be considered public, while a conference room is semiprivate, and individual offices are private.

A good space plan recognizes the need for different levels of privacy based on the type of occupancy and the function of the space. To achieve this you can use barriers (walls and doors), distance, sequencing, and other physical means to assure this need is met.

C. Enclosed versus Open

As with public and private spaces, different uses require or suggest varying levels of openness. These may be specified in the program or implied based on the type of space and its function. Generally, open spaces are used because they encourage communication, improve the appearance of the space, and reduce cost by making hard construction unnecessary. Open spaces can be created by using low partitions, systems furniture, or freestanding panels.

4 THE SPACE PLANNING PROCESS FOR THE NCIDQ EXAM

Your ability to complete a space plan is tested in the practicum/scenario portion of the NCIDQ exam. The space planning portion is worth 18 points and the lighting portion is worth 3 points. The project scenario type is selected by the candidate before the exam and can include one of the following project types: corporate, residential, retail, institutional, or hospitality. Refer to the Introduction for more information on the content of this part of the exam and to Chapter 24 for a sample scenario problem.

Although every designer has a slightly different method of space planning, each one follows an orderly process using a similar sequence of steps. If you have some experience with space planning, you may find that your particular approach will work for the NCIDQ exam. One of the most difficult challenges is completing the requirements of the problem within the allotted two and one-half hours. Strict time management is an absolute necessity to successfully completing the problem. The following guidelines are one possible method that you may want to consider when completing this portion of the test.

A. Read Program and Sketch Constraints

Your first step, of course, is to read thoroughly the problem statement. This will provide you with the basic rooms and areas that need to be laid out as well as suggest a direction for your overall design. However, for complex problems, you may find it helpful to translate the written word into graphic notations. One way of doing this is to lay a piece of tracing paper over the base plan and schematically mark the important requirements as given by the program. See Figure 5.6. These may include such items as entrance points and emergency exits, special features that you may want to use in your design, plumbing locations, views from windows or sources of daylight, mechanical system features such as air diffusers and vents, fixed partitions or removeable partitions, and similar fixed constraints of the problem. You may also want to diagrammatically indicate your design concept. Try to complete this step in 15 minutes.

B. Sketch Required Program Areas

The problem statement will give you the functional spaces. For some spaces, the area in square feet (or metric area if you elect to work in metric

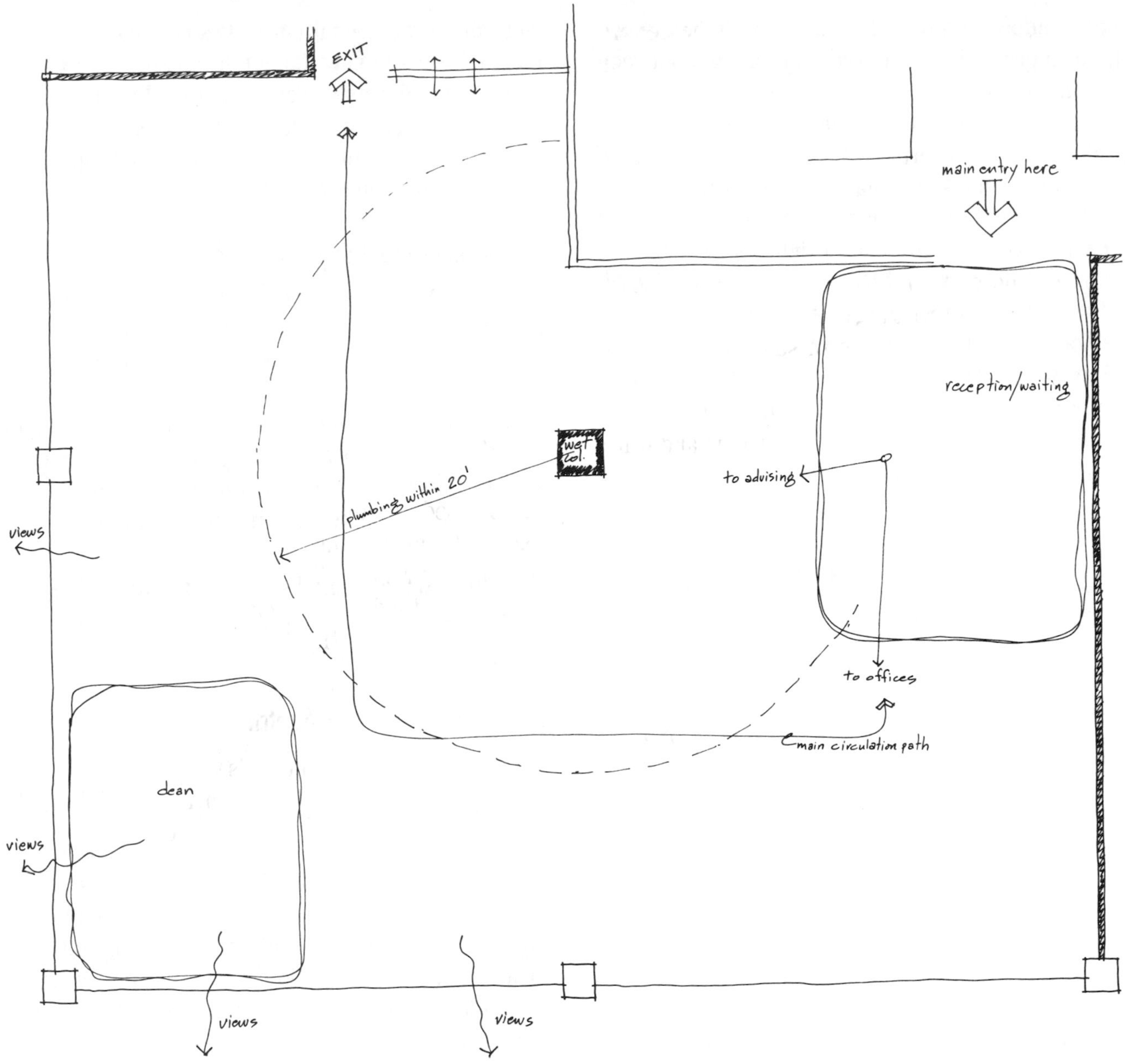

Figure 5.6 Programming Base Sheet

units) will simply be stated. For other areas requiring that you show a furniture layout, the detailed requirements for the furniture and accessories will be stated and you will have to arrange the furniture grouping to satisfy the program statements. For example, the program may state that a seating group must have six chairs, two end tables, space for magazine storage, and table lamps, but it is up to you to locate them and provide enough space to make the arrangement work.

However, the numbers given in the program are difficult to visualize. To give yourself a strong, graphic mental image of these numbers, translate the individual programmed spaces into graphic squares or rectangles at the same scale the final drawings must be. You can do this on a separate piece of tracing paper to help you visualize the spaces required as you begin the space planning. Use a consistent dimensional increment such as 2 feet for small projects or 5 or 10 feet for large projects or a module suggested by the window mullions. This will save you time and help you more easily see spatial relationships between functional groupings.

For areas where you will need to show furniture layout, sketch the area so you can develop a block of space that you know will accommodate the furniture and accessories. It is easier to work with this block of space during initial space planning than it is to redraw all the individual items of furniture. Sketch the furniture arrangement at the same scale of the base drawing sheet so you can trace it when you do the final drawing. Also, calculate the square footage of the block of space so you can add up all programmed areas to compare with the available space. Figure 5.7 shows examples of these areas and furniture sketches. Try to complete this step in 15 minutes.

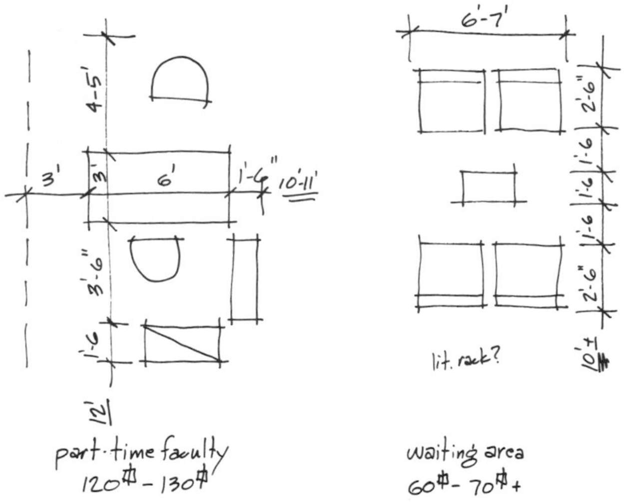

Figure 5.7 Individual Furniture Block Plans

You may also want to make graphic notes on program requirements unique to each space such as the number of exits or the room's relationship to some existing feature in the base floor plan. If two or more spaces must be adjacent or it seems logical to keep them together, you can develop a block area to show them as a group. Be sure to add some circulation if required.

When you are finished you should have every required space sketched roughly to scale on a piece of tracing paper. Remember that these diagrams are only notes to help you keep a mental image of the spaces. As you work on the floor plan base sheet, you will need to remain flexible so you can adjust the blocks to fit the specific conditions of the architectural plan. You may even need to split a functional grouping with a corridor, but such divisions need not compromise the adjacency requirements implied by the large functional grouping.

C. Develop and Analyze Adjacencies

If the problem statement does not give you an adjacency diagram, you will need to develop one from the matrix or other information given in the program. You may use a simple bubble diagram that is not to scale or use the scaled block diagrams you just developed to do this. Most of the adjacencies will be fairly straightforward and clearly stated in the program, so this step should take no more than 5 minutes.

D. Locate Required or Preferred Entrances and Exits

The number of required exits will probably be given as part of the problem statement. If not, you can make a reasonable inference from the requirements of the problem. These places will serve as the end points for your circulation scheme and are absolutely necessary to make sure you conform to building code exiting requirements. In most cases, they should be as far apart as possible. If the space you are planning is in a portion of a multistory building or located within a larger building, locate the main entry as close as possible to the elevator lobby or building entrance or where it seems most logical within the context of the building. Swing exit doors out and recess them if necessary so they do not swing into the corridor.

E. Sketch Preliminary Layouts

Before you start planning, quickly add the areas of all the programmed spaces, multiply by 1.25 or 1.33 to account for circulation, and compare the total square footage with the available area you have to work with. This comparison will tell you how generous the test makers have been and how careful you have to be with your space planning. If it appears that there is more than enough space, you will not have to waste as much time carefully squeezing in all the programmed areas.

You can now begin to lay out the spaces on the floor plan. Use tracing paper to do this rather than the final sheet you will turn in. You will find that the existing conditions of the architectural plan and the program requirements (that you have noted on your base sheet) will determine the location of many of the rooms and programmed spaces. For example, rooms requiring plumbing will need to be placed close to a wet column or plumbing lines, or a window with the best view and natural light should be used for one of the major spaces rather than for a secondary space like a storage room.

As you begin initial space planning, work from the general to the particular. That is, start laying out large blocks of space in their correct relationships before you start worrying about ancillary spaces or individual furniture groupings. This way you can quickly sketch several schematic alternatives to see which one works best for further refinement. At this time you should be thinking in terms of the organizational concepts and circulation schemes discussed earlier in this chapter. If you have a direct, simple circulation path and sensible organizational scheme, the spaces you allocate will probably accommodate the required furniture layouts.

At this early stage, a good circulation pattern is necessary because it will help organize the other spaces, satisfy required exiting, and provide for accessibility requirements. Try to complete the location of the entrances and exits and choose a preliminary layout of blocks of space and circulation in about 35 minutes. This is an incredibly short time even for a problem of limited size, but it must be done quickly if you are to have enough time for drawing the final floor plan and reflected ceiling plan.

F. Verify Space Allocations with Problem Requirements

After you have selected one plan that seems to work, take about 5 minutes to check it against the following performance criteria that the graders look for. Each one is worth one of the total of 18 points on the space planning portion of the scenario.

- Have you analyzed all the client requirements within the confines of the floor plan?
- Have you included all the programmed spaces in your plan?
- Do you have the required entries and exits based on the building code requirements?
- Have the corridors been sized to meet code requirements?
- Is there adequate space in corridors and activity areas to meet barrier-free codes?
- Does your plan meet all the adjacency requirements?
- Do you have an efficient, direct circulation system, both in the primary circulation system as well as any secondary circulation paths?
- Have you been sensitive to the needs for public and private spaces? At this preliminary sketch stage it may be too early to have all these requirements satisfied. This may be done in the next step.
- Does your preliminary layout suggest enclosed and open spaces as required by the program or inferred by the function of the spaces?
- Have you located spaces requiring plumbing within the specified distance to the existing wet columns or plumbing lines?

G. Draw the Final Plan

If you are satisfied that you have a good preliminary layout, you can now refine it and begin drawing the final floor plan on the base sheet provided. Make any necessary adjustments to your sketch plan until you can successfully answer the questions in the previous section. Allow yourself about 40 minutes to draw the final floor plan including the furniture and other items specified in the problem statement. You may either hard-line the drawing or use freehand sketching techniques. Use whichever one is easiest and fastest for you. Remember that no extra points are given for a perfectly drafted plan nor are points deducted for a very sketchy plan. The important thing is to communicate your design intent and show that you have met all the problem requirements. Your drawing only needs to be legible.

At this point, you can precisely locate partitions, doors, and other fixed elements like millwork, equipment, and space dividers. It is at this time that you should focus on relating your layout to the scale and position of existing architectural features. You should have been planning for this during the preliminary sketch stage, but now is the time to show the relationships in detail.

If you sketched furniture layouts for individual spaces as described earlier, you can slip your tracing paper under the final sheet and quickly trace them. Check your layout with the following additional grading criteria. These are worth one point each.

- Is your layout compatible with existing architectural features?
- Does your design show knowledge of the correct use of scale?
- Do you have all the required furniture to support the function of the space?
- Does furniture placement meet barrier-free codes?

Make sure that you clearly delineate the furniture (worth one point) and locate the placement of electrical and communications systems (worth one point) as well as any desk or table lamps.

H. Complete Lighting Layout

You will also need to complete a reflected ceiling plan showing your lighting design; this is discussed in Chapter 13. Be sure to leave yourself adequate time for this task. If you do not complete the reflected ceiling plan, your solution will not be graded and you will fail regardless of how perfect your floor plan is. You will need about 35 minutes to complete the reflected ceiling plan, which must also show switching and other elements called for in the problem statement.

SAMPLE QUESTIONS

1. Of the open plan workstations shown below, which is most efficient and most appropriate for frequent visitor conferences?

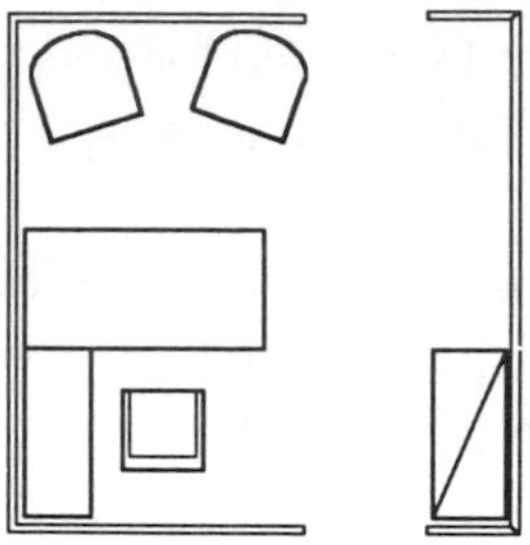

1.

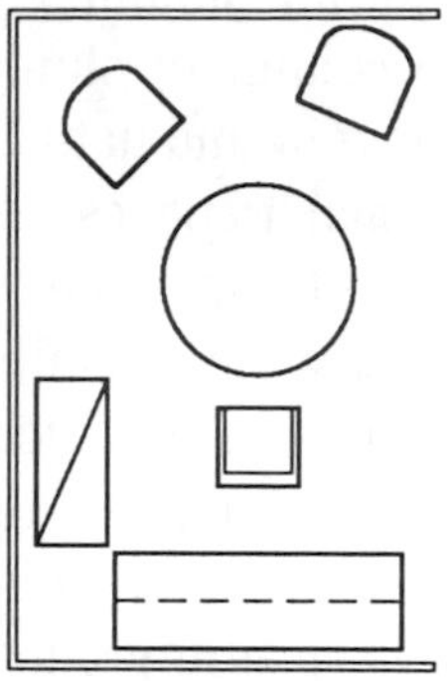

2.

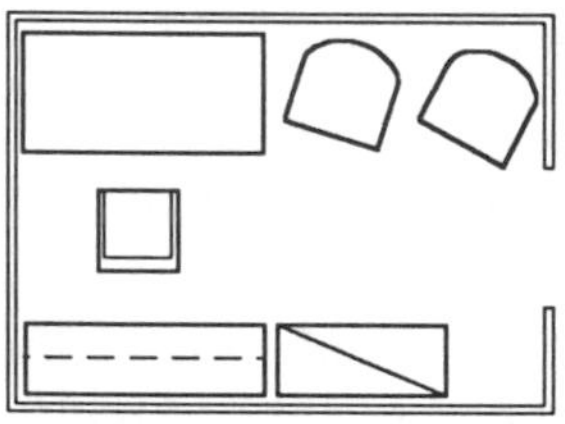

3.

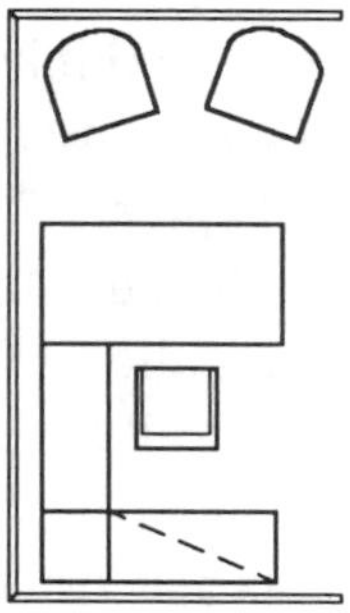

4.

2. In calculating lease area for tenant space occupying only a portion of a floor, to which of the following points are measurements taken?

   1. to the inside finish face of the tenant side of all demising walls
   2. to the centerline of the partitions separating tenants from each other and from the public corridor
   3. to the inside finish face of walls separating tenants and to the centerline of the public corridor wall
   4. to the centerline of walls separating tenants and to the inside finish face of the partition separating the tenant space from the public corridor

3. What would have the MOST influence over the planning of the dining area of a restaurant in an old building undergoing remodeling?

1. existing structural columns and walls
2. dimensions of the building
3. locations of existing plumbing
4. decorative millwork and existing ornate lighting fixtures

4. Planning an interior in a building with an atrium would suggest which of the following organizational concepts?

1. axial
2. grid
3. radial
4. central

5. What is MOST important in determining required space for a hospital nurses' station?

1. patient files and number of patient contacts
2. work surface and storage
3. movable carts and space for writing reports
4. electrical requirements and communication equipment

6. Which seating group shown below would be BEST for planning a waiting area to accommodate six people in a health clinic?

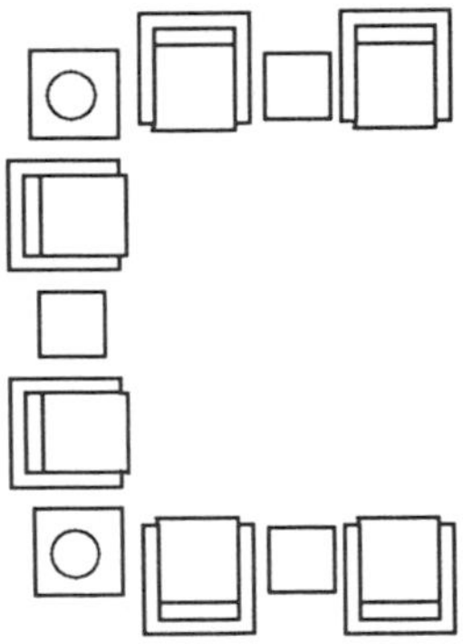

1.

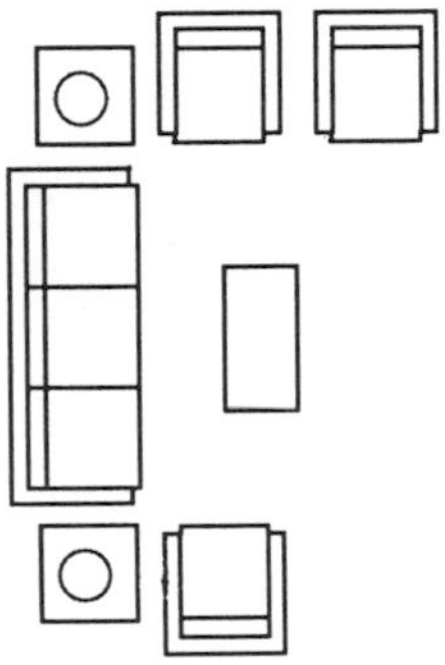

2.

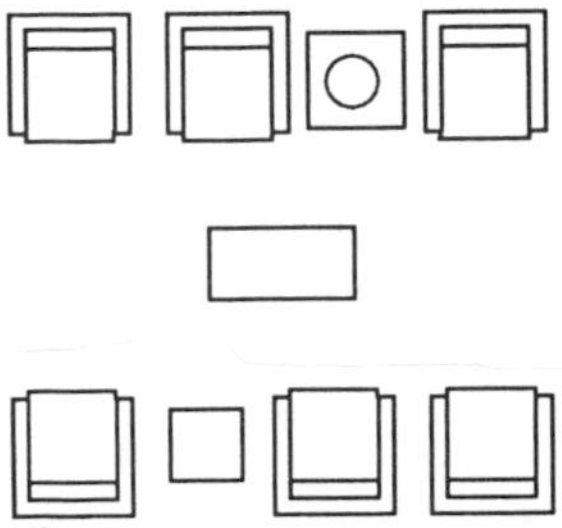

3.

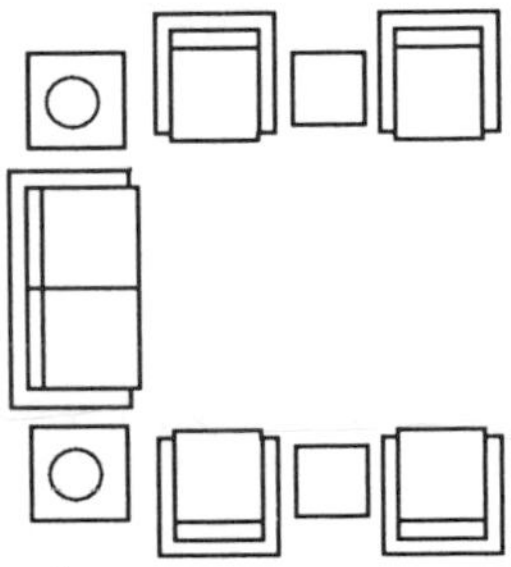

4.

7. The LEAST important consideration in planning exit corridors is

1. making sure dead ends do not exceed 20 feet
2. providing at least two exits from rooms where they are required
3. maintaining a minimum width as required by the occupancy type
4. having the corridors empty into approved exitways or stairways

8. The most efficient type of circulation system for the majority of planning problems is

1. a radial system
2. a single-loaded corridor
3. a double-loaded corridor
4. a grid system

9. A design concept statement for a public gathering area around a fireplace in a ski lodge would probably NOT include

1. the size of the fireplace
2. the number of individual seating groups
3. the type of finish materials
4. the method of lighting the space

10. In surveying existing conditions of an older building before beginning space planning, an interior designer would probably need to seek expert consulting assistance for determining which of the following items?

1. the number of supply air diffusers in the space
2. the existence of floor-mounted electrical outlets in an open space
3. the presence of adequate water pressure to add a sink in a washroom
4. the feasibility of opening a double-wide doorway in an existing wall

6 COST ESTIMATING

Establishing a budget early in the programming or design process is one of the most important aspects of design because it influences many design decisions and can help determine whether a project is even feasible. Once a budget is set, the interior designer must work within it and keep the client advised about any changes that might influence final costs.

Initial budgets can be set in several ways. In most cases, the client has already estimated the amount of money available and simply gives this figure to the interior designer. Corporate clients or organizations with on-going building programs usually have a good idea of what new or remodeled facilities cost, and their budgets are usually realistic. Residential clients or people who are contracting for interior design services and construction for the first time may have a very poor idea of the costs involved. Occasionally, budgets are set through public funding or legislation. The maximum project costs are set long before the design or construction begins and without the interior designer's involvement. The project, however, must be completed for that cost.

In other cases, the client will describe the extent of work he or she would like and ask the designer to develop an anticipated budget. From this preliminary figure, the client and designer can determine if there is enough money to do the job or whether the budget must be increased or the scope of work decreased.

There is always a relationship among quantity, quality, and money. Changing one affects the others. For example, if the client has a fixed budget and must build and furnish a specific amount of space, then the quality of materials or extent of work must reflect the budget and the space. If the client wants a particular level of quality and a given amount of space, then the required budget should reflect these two requirements.

1 COST INFLUENCES

There are many factors that affect the final project cost. The client must budget for more than construction costs and furnishings expenses. The following sections describe some of the possible expenses that can occur on an interior design project. Of course, not all of them apply on every job.

A. Construction Costs

Construction costs are the moneys required to build or remodel the interior, including such things as demolition, partitions, ceilings, millwork, finishes, and plumbing, electrical, and mechanical work—generally anything that is attached to and becomes part of the structure.

B. Furniture, Fixtures, and Equipment

This category can include many things. On most projects, furniture, fixtures, and equipment (FF&E) are separate budget items because the way they are specified, purchased, and installed is different from the way construction items are handled. Furnishings are either purchased directly by the interior designer, who arranges for delivery and installation, or specified by the interior designer for purchase and installation by one or more furniture dealers. They are also a separate budget item because of the various discounts the designer or client receives and the tax that must be paid. In most cases, clients also prefer to allocate money to these items separate from hard construction costs.

On some jobs, there may be a choice concerning whether to place an item in the FF&E budget or the construction budget. For example, a refrigerator and range may be specified by the designer and purchased and installed by the general contractor as part of the construction cost, or they may be purchased directly by the client or interior designer for installation after construction is complete. In the former case, the contractor will purchase the items at wholesale cost and charge the client a retail price in addition to adding fees for overhead and profit, while in the latter case the client may save on these charges by arranging for delivery and installation.

Some of the items that are normally part of the FF&E budget include the following:

- furniture
- appliances
- free-standing equipment such as vending machines and library bookshelves
- window coverings
- rugs and mats
- interior plants and planters
- lamps
- artwork
- accessories

C. Contractor's Overhead and Profit

This line item includes the general contractor's profit and cost of doing business. For construction projects, overhead can be divided into general overhead and project overhead. General overhead is the cost to run a contracting business and includes such things as office rent, secretarial help, utilities, and other recurring costs. Project overhead is the money it takes to complete a specific job, not including labor, materials, or equipment. Temporary offices, project telephones, trash removal, insurance, permits, and temporary utility hookups are examples of project overhead. The total overhead costs can range from about 10 percent to 20 percent of the total costs for the contractor's labor, materials, and equipment.

Profit is one of the most highly variable parts of a budget. It depends on the type of project, its size, the amount of risk involved, how much money the contractor wants to make (or thinks he or she can charge), the general market conditions, and, of course, whether or not the job is being bid or negotiated. For construction costs, profit is a percentage of the total of labor, materials, equipment, and overhead to do the job. During extremely difficult economic conditions, a contractor may cut the profit margin to almost nothing simply to get the job and keep his or her work force employed. If the contract is being negotiated with one contractor rather than with multiple contractors, the profit percentage is usually higher. In most cases, however, profit will range from 5 to 15 percent of the total cost of the job. Overall, overhead and profit can total about 15 to 25 percent of construction cost, with most jobs in a competitive market at the lower end of the scale.

D. Professional Fees

Professional fees include the charges for the interior designer's services as well as fees for other professionals such as architects, mechanical engineers, and electrical engineers. In addition, costs for special consultants, legal fees, and testing may be included here. If an interior designer is working on a retail basis where markups on purchased furniture account for the designer's fee, then this line item may not exist unless other professionals are involved.

E. Taxes

Taxes include sales tax paid on furniture, accessories, and other purchased items. If the interior designer buys these things, he or she is responsible for collecting tax from the client and paying it to the appropriate taxing jurisdictions. If the client has a total budget for purchased items, the tax must be deducted from the top so the designer knows how much money is actually available for buying the items. If you are working in a jurisdiction that collects taxes on professional services, such tax is usually included in the professional fees category, although it can be placed under taxes if it needs to appear as a separate line item. Taxes paid on materials used in construction are paid by the general contractor and subcontractors and are included in the total construction budget.

F. Moving Costs

Some clients prefer to include moving costs in their total building budget. It includes the money required to physically relocate and may also include things like the cost to reprint stationery and downtime caused by the move. For large companies, moving costs can be substantial.

G. Telephone and Data System Installation

Because telephone and data systems (computers, local area networks, and the like) are purchased separately and installed by specialty companies, the costs for these systems should be kept separate. In most cases, the client will coordinate these items separately without involving the interior designer. However, the designer may need to coordinate his or her work with the suppliers of these services to provide space for equipment, proper location of outlets and conduit, and other required mechanical and electrical support services.

H. Contingencies

A contingency should always be added to the budget to account for unforeseen changes by the client and other conditions that will add to the total cost of the job. For an early project budget, the percentage of the contingency should be higher than contingencies applied to later budgets, because there are more unknowns at the beginning of a project. Normally, from 5 to 10 percent of the total budget should be included. You may have one contingency to cover everything, or one for construction and one for furniture, fixtures, and equipment.

2 METHODS OF ESTIMATING

There are many methods of developing a budget and estimating the possible cost of a job. As previously stated, the client may already have a certain amount of money available and the interior designer must work backwards, subtracting money for fees, taxes, and similar costs to arrive at what is left over for the actual construction and furnishings. In other cases, the designer must determine the scope of the project with the client and assign costs to the various individual elements to arrive at the final figure.

Whichever method is used, the exact procedure for budgeting will vary depending on the time at which a budget is developed. Budgeting is an ongoing activity; it is revised at each phase of the project as more decisions are made. Very early in the project, little is known about the job except its overall size and general quality. Later, when construction documents are complete and furniture specifications finalized, a very detailed estimate can be calculated.

A. Square Footage

Budgets based on size are usually the first and most preliminary type of estimate done before much design work has started. The anticipated square footage of the project is multiplied by a cost per square foot to arrive at a number. The square footage costs may be based on the designer's or client's experience with similar projects, from knowledgeable contractors, or from commercially available cost books. Other costs, like contingencies, may in turn be generated by estimating them as a percentage of the basic construction cost. When you use a square foot cost, you must know if it includes additional costs such as contractor's overhead and profit, taxes, and the like.

Units other than square feet can also be used for certain facilities. For example, there are rules of thumb for costs per hotel room when budgeting for hotels, costs per hospital bed, and similar functional units. Whichever unit is used, it is usually best to develop three budgets based on a low, medium, and high cost per square foot or cost per functional unit. This way, the client can see the probable range of money that will be required.

B. Parameter

As design progresses and the interior designer and client have a better idea of the exact scope of the work, the budget can be refined. The procedure most often used at this time is the parameter method, which involves an expanded itemization of construction quantities and furnishings and assignment of unit costs to these quantities. See Figure 6.1.

For example, floor finishes can be broken down into carpeting, vinyl tile, wood-strip flooring, and so forth. The areas are multiplied by an estimated cost per square foot and the total budget for flooring is developed. If the design has not progressed to the point of selecting individual flooring types, an average cost of flooring can be estimated and assigned to the

Budget for Headquarters Remodel
Project #330

Section	Item	Quantity/Unit	Unit Price	Amount	Subtotal
100	Demolition				
100.01	partitions	3600 SF	2.00	7200	
100.02	ceilings	3700 SF	0.25	925	
100.03	carpet	3700 SF	0.25	925	
100.04	relocate entry	1 allowance	7200.00	7200	
					16250
200	Partitions				
200.01	full height	225 LF	27.00	6075	
200.02	partial height	24 LF	21.00	504	
200.03	partial glass	44 LF	100.00	4400	
200.04	operable partitions	50 LF	175.00	8750	
200.05	drywall facing	124 LF	20.00	2480	
					22209
300	Doors/Frames/Hardware				
300.01	entry	5 EA	600.00	3000	
300.02	interior—singles	3 EA	500.00	1500	
300.03	interior—pairs	2 EA	900.00	1800	
300.04	sliding	4 EA	800.00	3200	
300.05	closet-pairs	5 EA	1000.00	5000	
					14500
400	Finishes				
400.01	walls—paint	(included in partitions)		0	
400.02	walls—fabric tack panels	130 SF	6.00	780	
400.03	walls—wall covering	1 allowance	2000.00	2000	
400.04	floor—carpet	450 SY	22.00	9900	
400.05	floor—vinyl tile	140 SF	1.50	210	
400.06	floor—inset carpet	1 allowance	1000.00	1000	
400.07	ceiling	3740 SF	2.25	8415	
400.08	window coverings	342 SF	3.25	1112	
					23417
500	Millwork				
500.01	kitchen cabinets	28 LF	350.00	9800	
500.02	mail counter & boxes	14 LF	400.00	5600	
500.03	office alcoves counters	130 LF	100.00	1300	
500.04	wall storage	86 LF	150.00	12900	
500.05	president's office	9 LF	250.00	2250	
500.06	workroom	30 LF	200.00	6000	
500.07	display	21 LF	300.00	6300	
500.08	shelving	30 LF	50.00	1500	
500.09	admin. assistant	35 LF	300.00	10500	
					67850
600	Electrical				
600.01	fluorescent lighting	67 EA	175.00	11725	
600.02	incandescent downlights	7 EA	125.00	875	
600.03	wall outlets	36 EA	150.00	5400	
600.04	dedicated wall outlet	1 EA	250.00	250	
600.05	floor outlets	4 EA	300.00	1200	
600.06	telephone outlets	9 EA	100.00	900	
600.07	fire/security system	1 allowance	10000.00	10000	
600.08	upgrade power panel	1 allowance	3500.00	3500	
600.09	undercounter lights	47 EA	100.00	4700	
600.1	exit lights	6 EA	100.00	600	
					39150
700	Plumbing				
700.01	kitchen sink	1 EA	3000.00	3000	
					3000
800	Heating/Ventilating/A.C.				
800.01	additional roof unit	1 allowance	5000.00	5000	
800.02	secondary distribution	1 allowance	3000.00	3000	
800.03	controls	1 allowance	500.00	1000	
					9000
900	Equipment				
900.01	refrigerator	1 EA	600.00	1000	
900.02	microwave	1 EA	400.00	400	
900.03	garbage disposal	1 EA	300.00	300	
900.04	water heater (insta-hot)	1 EA	300.00	300	
900.05	dishwasher	1 EA	400.00	500	
900.06	projection screen/motor	1 EA	1600.00	1600	
					4100
				Subtotal $	199476
				10% for contingency	19948
				10% contractor's overhead and profit	21942
				TOTAL $	241366

Figure 6.1 Parameter Cost Estimate

total area of the project. Furniture can be estimated in a similar way. The final manufacturer and fabric of a seating group may not be decided, but costs for typical sofas, chairs, and coffee tables based on the designer's experience can be totaled to get a working budget number.

With this type of budgeting, it is possible to evaluate the cost implication of each building component and to make decisions concerning both quantity and quality to meet the original budget estimate. If floor finishes are over budget, the interior designer and the client can review the parameter estimate and decide, for example, that some wood flooring must be replaced with less expensive carpeting. Similar decisions can be made concerning any of the budget parameters.

Parameter line items are based on commonly used units that relate to the construction element or cost item under study. For instance, a gypsum wallboard partition would have an assigned cost per square foot or cost per linear foot (for a given height) of a complete partition of a particular construction type, rather than separate costs for studs, gypsum board, screws, and finishing. This way, it is an easy procedure to calculate the linear footage of partitions (even based on a preliminary space plan) and multiply by a unit cost. Secretarial chairs, however, would be budgeted on a "per each" basis because the number required is easily determined.

C. Detailed Quantity Takeoffs

The most precise kind of budget is developed by counting actual quantities of materials and furnishings and multiplying these quantities by firm, quoted costs. These detailed estimates cannot be done until late in the design and construction document phase of a project. At this point, the work of revising the budget to a fairly exact level generally is divided between the interior designer and general contractor.

For furnishing costs, the interior designer develops a list of all the individual pieces of furniture required along with other items like window coverings, accessories, artwork, and anything else that is being specified by the designer. The exact manufacturers and model numbers are known, along with color and fabric selections, applicable discounts, delivery costs, and required taxes. For some small projects, furniture may be supplied by the designer, but for large commercial projects, furniture is often purchased through dealers who develop the purchase orders and finalize exact costs to the client. In either case, the final cost to the client can be easily calculated.

If the project involves construction, detailed quantity takeoffs can be made several ways. For negotiated jobs, the selected contractor will take the construction documents and specifications and make a precise estimate, including overhead and profit. If the final quotation is too high, the client, interior designer, and contractor can work to change quantities or qualities of materials or the entire scope of the job to meet the budget. With several contractors bidding, the final quoted costs are not known until bids are in. Before hiring a contractor, the client may also hire an independent cost estimator to develop a reasonably accurate budget.

3 COST INFORMATION

One of the most difficult aspects of developing project budgets is obtaining current, reliable prices for the kinds of furnishings and construction units you are using. Furnishings costs are a little easier to develop than construction costs because items are priced on a unit basis and price quotes and discounts from dealers are available at any time. However, from the early phases of a project until the time when purchase orders are actually written, costs and taxes can increase or the client may change his or her mind and request a more or less expensive item.

For construction costs, there are several commercially produced cost books that are published annually. These books list costs in different ways; some are very detailed, giving the cost for labor and materials for individual construction components, while others list parameter costs and subsystem costs. There are even reference books oriented strictly toward interior design that give parameter costs for construction as well as furnishings.

You should remember, however, that commercially available cost information is the average of many past projects from around the country. Cost books may be of little use on your project, depending on local variations and particular conditions. A better source of information may be local contractors and other design professionals who have experience in the type of project you are budgeting.

SAMPLE QUESTIONS

1. What would be the primary reason for an interior designer to recommend that the client purchase appliances directly rather than through a general contractor?

   1. The client could avoid the contractor's markup.
   2. The client could not be overcharged for delivery and installation.
   3. The interior designer could provide the client a broader selection by acting as the client's agent.
   4. The client could get a better discount than the contractor.

2. Based on previous projects, you know that it costs about $45 per linear foot to construct a full-height partition. On the project you are now budgeting, there are about 350 feet of this type of partition. If you are estimating the contractor's overhead and profit to be 14 percent, what should you budget for this line item?

   1. $15,120
   2. $15,750
   3. $17,950
   4. $18,900

3. Bids have been submitted by four contractors on a midsize restaurant. The lowest bid is 10 percent over the client's budget and the next lowest bid is 12 percent over budget. As the interior designer, what is your best course of action?

   1. Suggest that the client obtain additional financing for the extra 10 percent and accept the lowest bid.
   2. Accept the lowest bid and tell the contractor that if he wants the job he should reduce his bid by 10 percent.
   3. Work with the client to redesign the project to reduce the cost.
   4. Remind the client that the designer is not responsible for construction costs, and tell the client that additional money must be found.

4. Which of the following is generally NOT considered FF&E?

1. a commissioned sculpture bolted to a wall
2. vending machines built into an opening
3. wall-to-wall carpeting
4. vertical blinds

5. If you were designing a project in an unfamiliar city, what would be your best source of cost data?

1. the most current cost data book with prices adjusted for geographical location and inflation
2. a local contractor who builds projects of the type you are working on
3. a computerized cost database targeted for the city you are working in
4. interior designers and architects who practice in the city and design projects similar to yours

6. In addition to construction, what are the major cost components of most interior design projects?

1. furnishings, taxes, signal systems, and moving
2. furnishings, professional fees, taxes, and telephone installation
3. fixtures, overhead and profit, moving, and telephone installation
4. furniture, fixtures, taxes, and moving

7. Which method provides the most accurate estimate of project cost?

1. square footage
2. functional unit
3. parameter
4. quantity takeoff

8. In preparing a budget, which of the following would you most likely ask the client to include in your budget?

1. legal fees and artwork consulting
2. taxes on furniture and computer system installation
3. contingencies and your fee
4. furnishings and furniture delivery

9. A line item included in a budget to account for unknown conditions is called a

1. unit price
2. parameter
3. contingency
4. budget adjustment

10. Furniture budgets can be accurately estimated by

1. the general contractor and the furniture manufacturer
2. the interior designer and furniture dealers
3. the furniture representative and the client
4. the furniture manufacturer and the interior designer

7 CONSTRUCTION DRAWINGS

One of the most important parts of the contract documents is the set of construction drawings (sometimes called working drawings) that describe, in detail, the extent of the work and the location, dimensions, and relationships of the various construction elements. The contractor and subcontractors use them, along with the construction specifications, to build the project. To pass the NCIDQ exam, you must be able to read and interpret construction drawings as well as have the knowledge to produce them for a project.

1 ORGANIZATION OF CONSTRUCTION DRAWINGS

Construction drawings are organized in a generally standardized sequence based on the normal sequence of construction and through many years of use. For interior design projects, the sequence may vary slightly depending on the size of the project and whether the interior drawings are part of a larger architectural set of drawings. For instance, a small residential project may include the floor plan, a finish schedule, and some interior elevations on the first sheet in a set of drawings, while these individual drawing elements may be shown on separate sheets as part of a set of drawings for a larger project.

For a set of construction drawings produced and coordinated by the interior designer, the drawings are usually organized in the following sequence:

- *Title and index sheet* (if used): On large projects, the first sheet often contains a large title and sometimes a graphic identifying the project. In addition, this sheet may contain an index to the set of drawings, a list of standard abbreviations and symbols used on the job, project data required by the building department (square footage, occupancy category, building type, and the like), and general notes that apply to the entire job. On small projects, this information, if included, is placed on the first sheet of the set, which is usually the floor plan.

- *Floor plans:* The number and types of plan drawings depend on the project. Small, residential designs may only have one floor plan that includes all the necessary information. Large projects may have several plans of the same area, each showing a particular type of information. Some of the types of plans commonly used on midsize to large projects include demolition plans, construction floor plans, finish plans, telephone and powerplans, and furniture plans. When the project is very complex, additional large-scale construction plans may also be required of certain portions of the small-scale floor plan.

- *Reflected ceiling plan(s)*

- *Elevations*

- *Details:* Details may include construction elements such as wall types, doors, glazing, ceilings, millwork, stairways, flooring, and any other special construction. The number of details depends on the size and complexity of the project and whether the job is being bid or negotiated. If the project is competitively bid, the details must be very complete and fully describe the extent of the work so the client will get a valid cost quote. On smaller, negotiated contract jobs where the majority of details are somewhat standard, there may be fewer details because some of the final decisions may be made during construction.

- *Mechanical drawings* (if required): If the project requires the services of a mechanical engineering consultant, the engineers prepare their own drawings with their professional seal. These drawings include (as necessary) information about the heating, ventilating and air-conditioning (HVAC) systems as well as any plumbing systems.

- *Electrical drawings* (if required): Electrical drawings are prepared by an electrical engineering consultant if the project includes new or revised power and lighting circuiting and specialty wiring such as fire alarms, communications systems, security systems, and the like. On most residential projects, light fixture and switch locations may be shown schematically by the interior designer. It is the electrical contractor's responsibility to show the correct gauge of wire and to circuit the system properly and according to local building codes.

- *Fire protection drawings* (if required): When a sprinkler system is required for commercial construction, fire protection plans are required to be completed by a mechanical engineer and are usually included with the complete set of construction drawings.

Occasionally, structural drawings are needed if work is being performed that requires the services of a structural engineer. If these are included, they are produced by the structural engineer and placed after the interior drawings and before the mechanical drawings. Drawing sets also include schedules (discussed in more detail in the following section). The locations of schedules may vary depending on the size and procedures of individual offices. However, they are generally located on the sheet where they most logically apply. For example, the room finish schedule and door schedule should be on the same sheet as the floor plan (assuming a separate finish plan is not used).

2 CONTENTS OF CONSTRUCTION DRAWINGS

Drawings should show the general configuration, size, shape, and location of the components of construction with general notes to explain materials, construction requirements, dimensions, and similar explanations of the graphic material. Detailed requirements for material quality, workmanship, and other items are contained in the technical specifications of the project manual discussed in Chapter 8. The following is a brief description of some of the more common items that should be included with the interior design drawings. This list is by no means inclusive.

A. Floor Plans

Construction plan: Construction plans, also called floor plans or partition plans, are the most common type of floor plan and are required for every project regardless of size or complexity. Construction plans are views seen as though a building were cut horizontally about four feet above the floor and the top section removed. The construction plan shows the building configuration with all walls shown, dimensions, existing construction to remain, references to elevations and details drawn elsewhere, room names (and numbers, if used), floor material indications, millwork, plumbing fixtures, built-in fixtures, stairs, special equipment, and notes as required to explain items on the plan. Construction plans are usually drawn at the scale of 1/8″= 1′-0″(1:100) or 1/4″= 1′-0″(1:50). If large-scale plans are required for very complex areas, they are typically drawn at 1/2″scale (1:25). If there are other plans in the set of drawings, they should be drawn at the same scale as the primary construction plan.

Demolition plans: If required by the complexity of the project, demolition plans show which existing construction is to remain and which is to be removed. A separate construction plan is then drawn to show new construction. If the extent of demolition work is minor, the portions of the building to be removed can be shown with dashed lines on the construction plan. A contractor needs some type of demolition plan before partitions on a remodeling project can be removed.

Power and telephone plan: For large or complex projects, the interior designer sometimes draws a separate plan showing the location of electrical outlets, telephone outlets, and other signal systems like the location of computer terminals and intercommunication systems. See Figure 7.1. A separate plan is usually required for large projects because there is not enough room on the construction plan to show the outlets and include dimension lines to precisely locate each one. The interior designer's plan only shows the location of the outlets. The electrical circuiting, conduit size, and other technical information are included on the plans prepared by the electrical engineer. If the interior designer does not produce a power plan, then the power plan drawn by the electrical engineer shows electrical outlets, telephone outlets, security systems, and fire alarm devices.

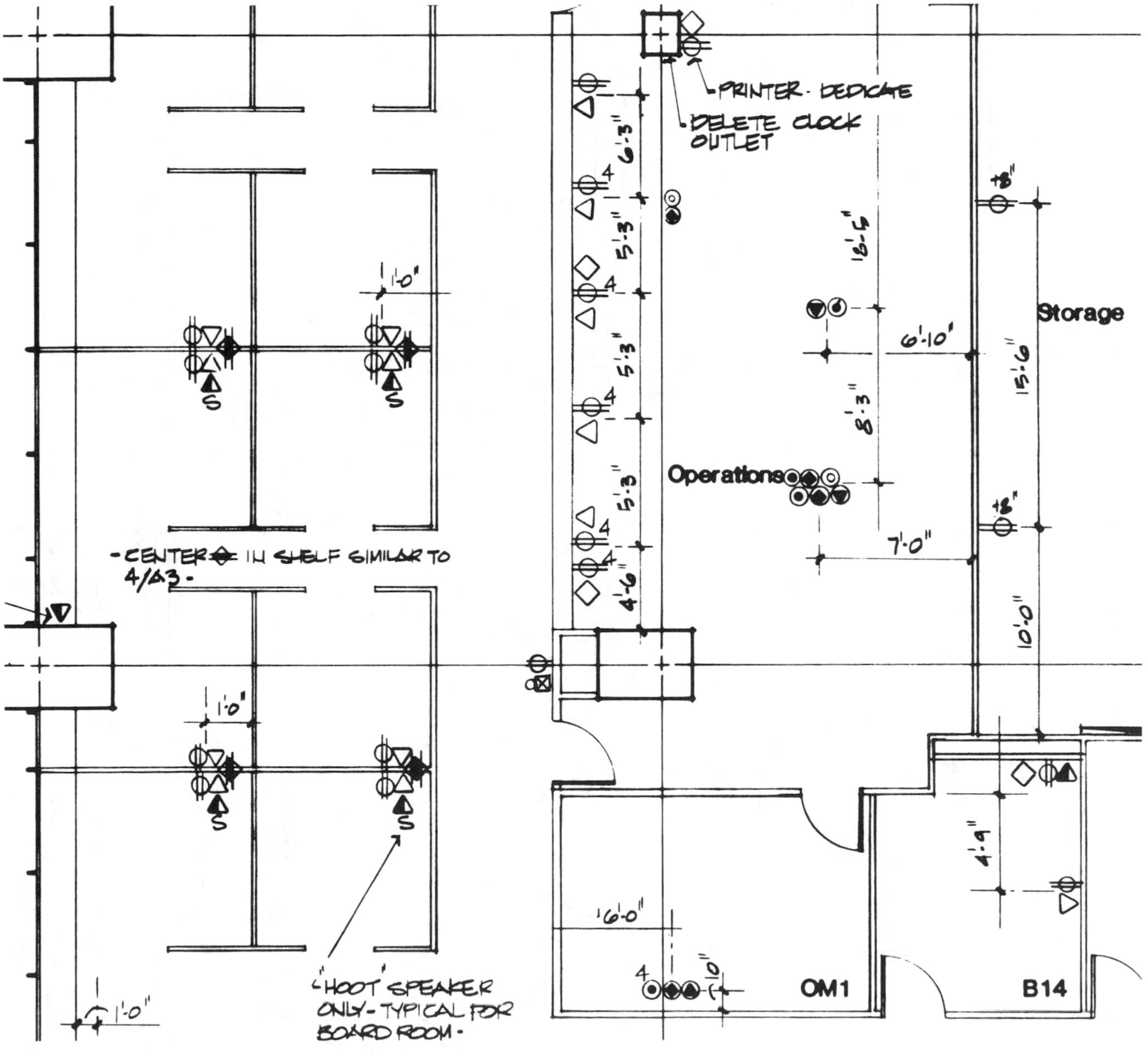

Figure 7.1 Interior Designer's Power Plan

Compare the power plan in Figure 7.2 with the designer's outlet plan in Figure 7.1.

Finish plan: There are a number of ways to communicate what finishes are required. Most commonly, a finish schedule is developed by the interior designer that lists, in tabular format, each room and the types and specifics of finishes for the floor, base, walls, and sometimes ceilings. Figure 7.3 shows a typical finish schedule. This method works well for fairly simple projects with only a single finish on each wall. However, when there are several finish types on each wall and other complex finish configurations, a separate finish plan can be used as shown in the partial plan of Figure 7.4. Here, each finish is given a code number that is listed in a legend specifying the exact manufacturer, catalog number, and color. For example, all wall fabric notations could be preceded with a WP and then given numerical designations such as WP1, WP2, and so on. However, specification items, such

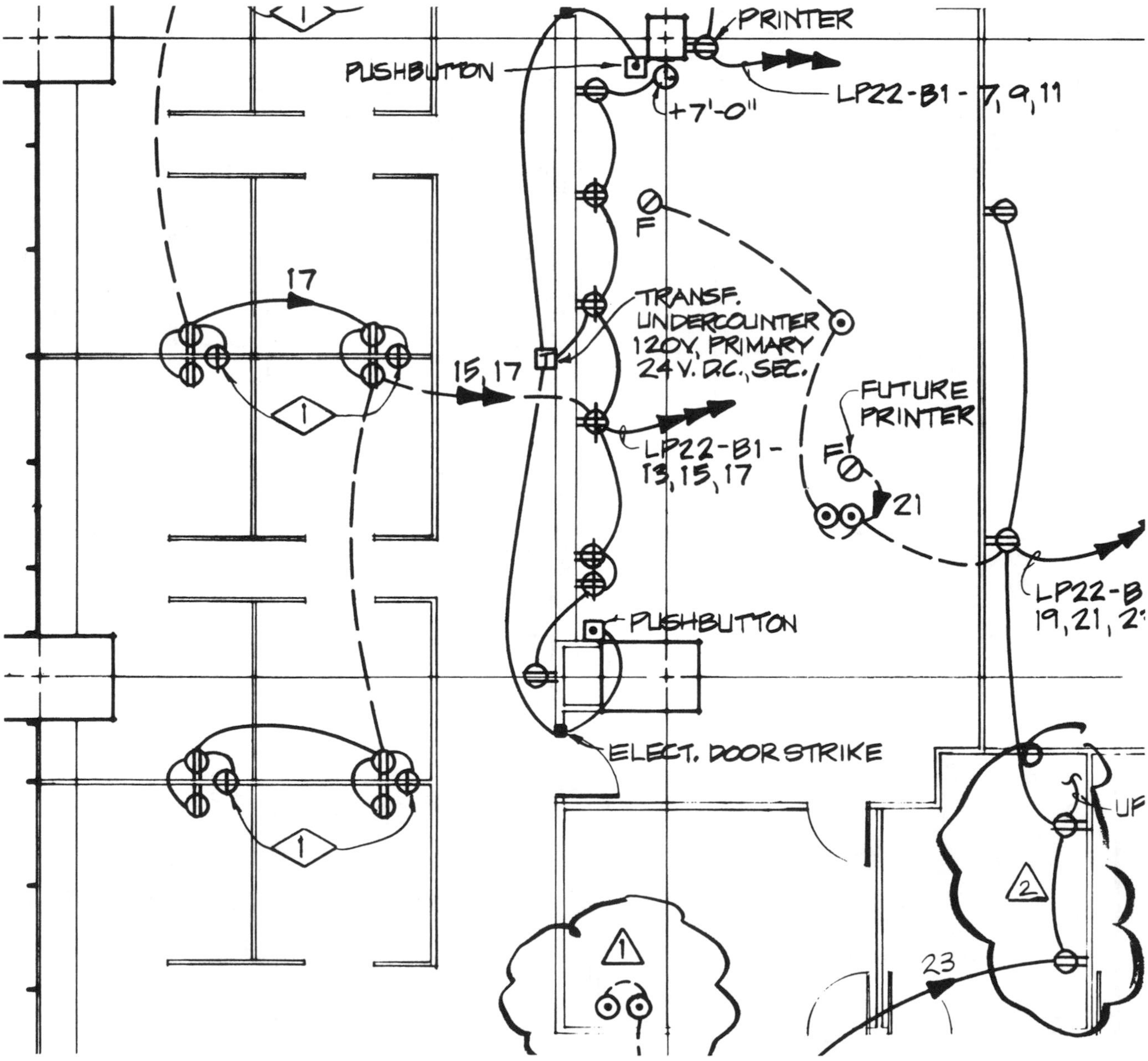

Figure 7.2 Electrical Engineer's Power Plan

FINISH SCHEDULE														
				East wall		North wall		West wall		South wall		Ceiling		
No.	Room	Floor	Base	Mat.	Color	Mat.	Color	Mat.	Color	Mat.	Color	Mat.	Mtl.	Remarks
201	Lobby	F1	B2	–		W2		–		W2		10'-0"	C1	
202	East Corridor	F1	B2	W2		W2		W2		W2		12'-0"	C2	W1 above trim
203	Vending	F1	B2	W2		W2		W2		W2		10'-0"	C3	Base surface applied
204	North Corridor	F1	B2	W2		W2		W2		W2		12'-0"	C2	W1 above trim
205	West Corridor	F1	B2	W2		W2		W2		W2		12'-0"	C2	W1 above trim
206	South Corr.	F1	B2	W2		W2		W2		W2		10'-0"	C1	
207	Service Corr.	Exist.	Exist.	W3		W3		W3		W3		Exist.	Exist.	
208	Corridor	F2	B3	W1		W3		W1&3		W1		Exist.	Exist.	
209	Not Used													
210	Closet	F1	B1	W1		W1		W1		W1		10'-0"	C2	
211	Conference	F1	B1	W1		W1		–		W1		12'-0"	C1	
212	Conference	F1	B1	W1		W1		W1		W1		10'-0"	C2	
213	Office	F1	B1	W1		W1		W1		W1		10'-0"	C2	
214	Lexis	F1	B1	W1		W1		W1		W1		10'-0"	C2	
215	Closet	F1	B1	W1		W1		W1		W1		10'-0"	C 2	
216	Law Library	F1	B1	W1		W1		*		W1		10'-0"	C1 &2	* Paint furred columns
217	Telephone	F1	B1	W1		W1		W1		W1		9'-0"	C2	
218	Telephone	F1	B1	W1		W1		W1		W1		9'-0"	C2	

Figure 7.3 Finish Schedule

as installation instructions, are included not on the plan but in the specifications.

Furniture plan: Because the exact location of furniture is important for an interior design project, separate furniture plans are often drawn. See Figure 7.5. These show the location of each piece of furniture on a floor plan with corresponding code numbers that identify each piece. The plans are used to itemize the furniture for pricing and ordering as well as to show the installers where to put each piece during move-in. The furniture plan is sometimes doubled up with a power and telephone plan because the exact location of many outlets is directly related to the location and orientation of furniture. For example, telephone and electrical outlets are best placed directly to the side of a desk.

Site plan: A site plan is a view of a building as seen from directly above, showing the roof of the building as well as the surrounding yards, walks, driveways, and other features within the property line. It also usually shows the streets and property immediately adjacent to the site. (The interior designer does not draw a site plan, but the NCIDQ exam may ask you to be able to identify its characteristics.)

B. Reflected Ceiling Plans

Reflected ceiling plans show a view of the ceiling as though it were reflected onto a mirror on the floor, or as though the ceiling were transparent and you could see right through it. This view of the ceiling is necessary to ensure that it has the same orientation as the floor plan. That is, if north is toward the top of the sheet on the floor plan, north will also be toward the top of the sheet on the reflected ceiling plan. Reflected ceiling plans should be drawn at the same scale as the construction floor plan.

Reflected ceiling plans show partitions that extend to the ceiling and those that extend through the ceiling (as on commercial projects where there is a suspended ceiling). They also show ceiling materials, building grid lines (if used), notes calling out ceiling heights, changes in ceiling heights, locations of all lights (including exit lights), sprinkler heads, air diffusers and vents, access panels, speakers, and

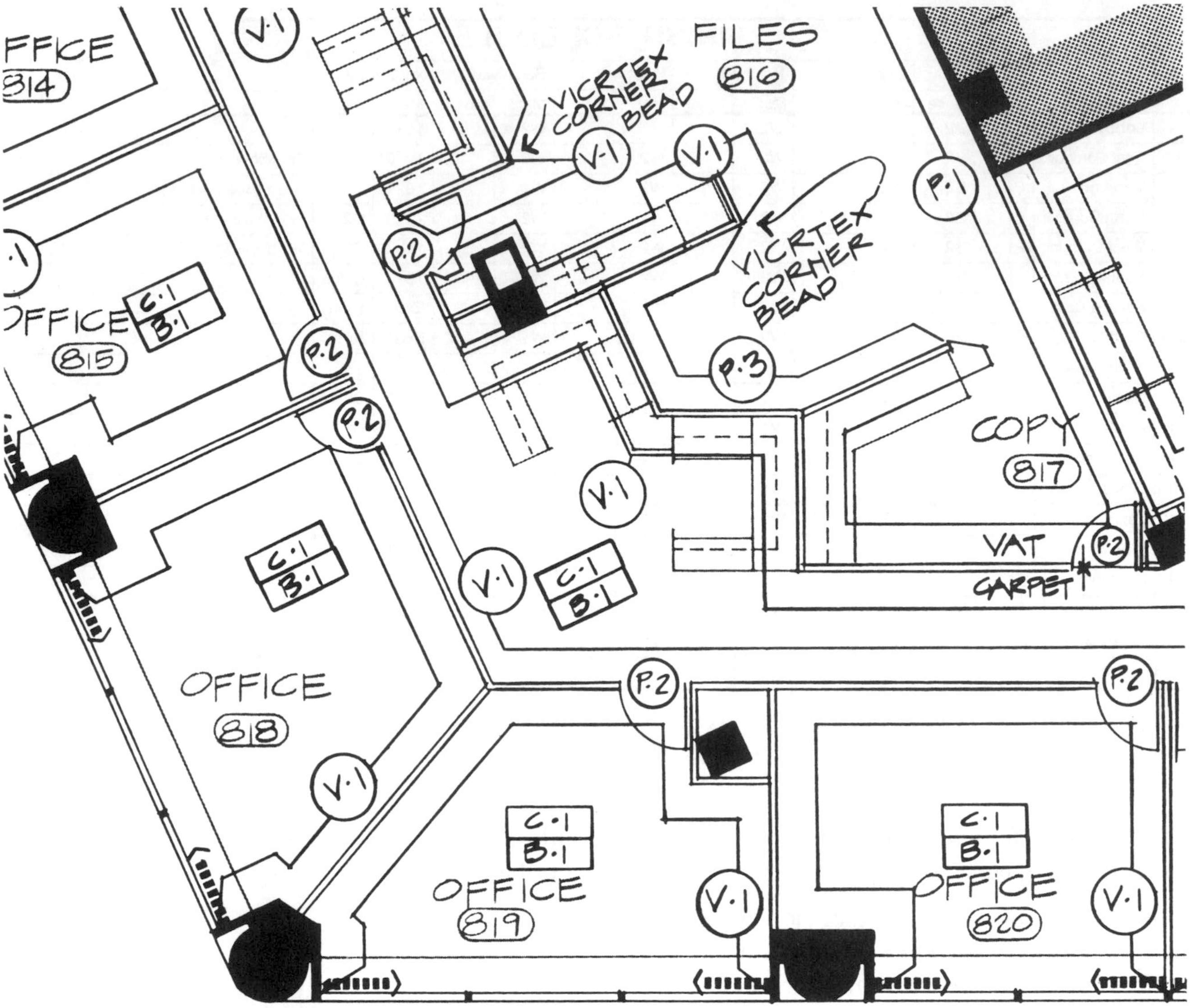

Figure 7.4 Finish Plan

any other item that is part of (or touches) the plane of the ceiling. In addition, dimensions are included where necessary to precisely locate elements that cannot be reasonably inferred by their relationship to something else. For example, recessed light troffers placed in a suspended ceiling can be located by the contractor by simply counting the number of tiles, but the position of a downlight in a gypsum wallboard ceiling must be dimensioned to its center point so the electrical contractor knows where to install it.

Although some items like lights and air diffusers will also be indicated on the engineering consultant's drawings, everything should be shown on the interior designer's reflected ceiling plan. This way, all items can be coordinated so the designer has a full understanding of what the final ceiling will look like.

The reflected ceiling plan will also have section cut reference marks and other notations referring to details drawn elsewhere in the set. One example is shown in Figure 7.6.

C. Elevations

An elevation is a drawing showing a vertical surface seen from a point of view perpendicular to the

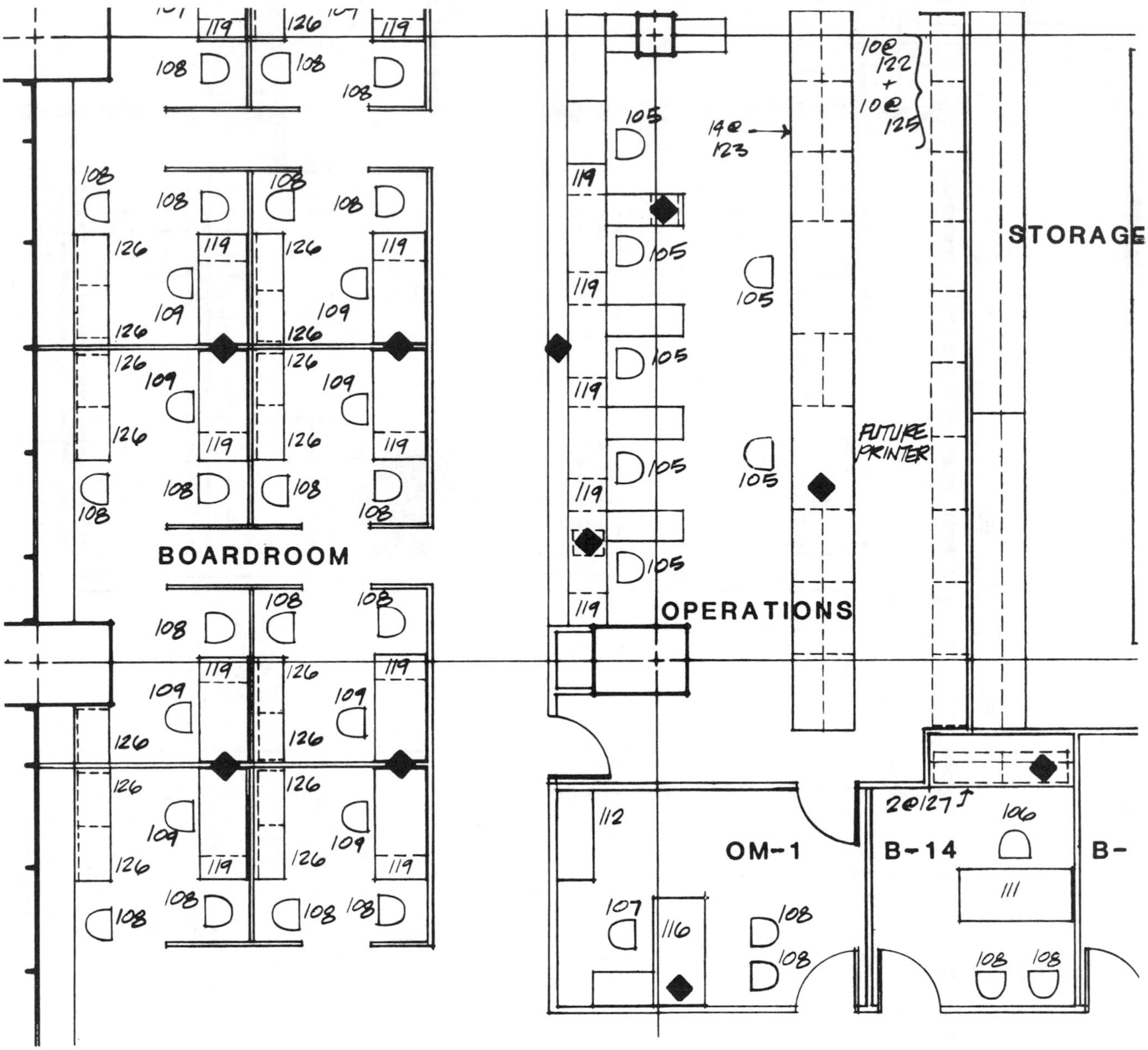

Figure 7.5 Furniture Plan

surface. Elevations are straight-on views, so there is no distortion as with perspective or isometric drawings. All portions of the drawing are done at the same scale, and if curves or angled surfaces are included, these are projected onto the flat plane of the elevation drawing. See Figure 7.7.

Elevations are drawn for interior design projects to indicate the configuration and finish of wall surfaces—something that is difficult, if not impossible, to do with a plan drawing. Elevations are also used to show the vertical dimensions and design of millwork and other freestanding construction.

Elevations are useful for showing the configuration of a surface, vertical dimensions, openings in walls, built-in items, materials and finishes on a wall, and the location of switches, thermostats, and other wall-mounted equipment. When there are numerous or complex horizontal dimensions, such as with

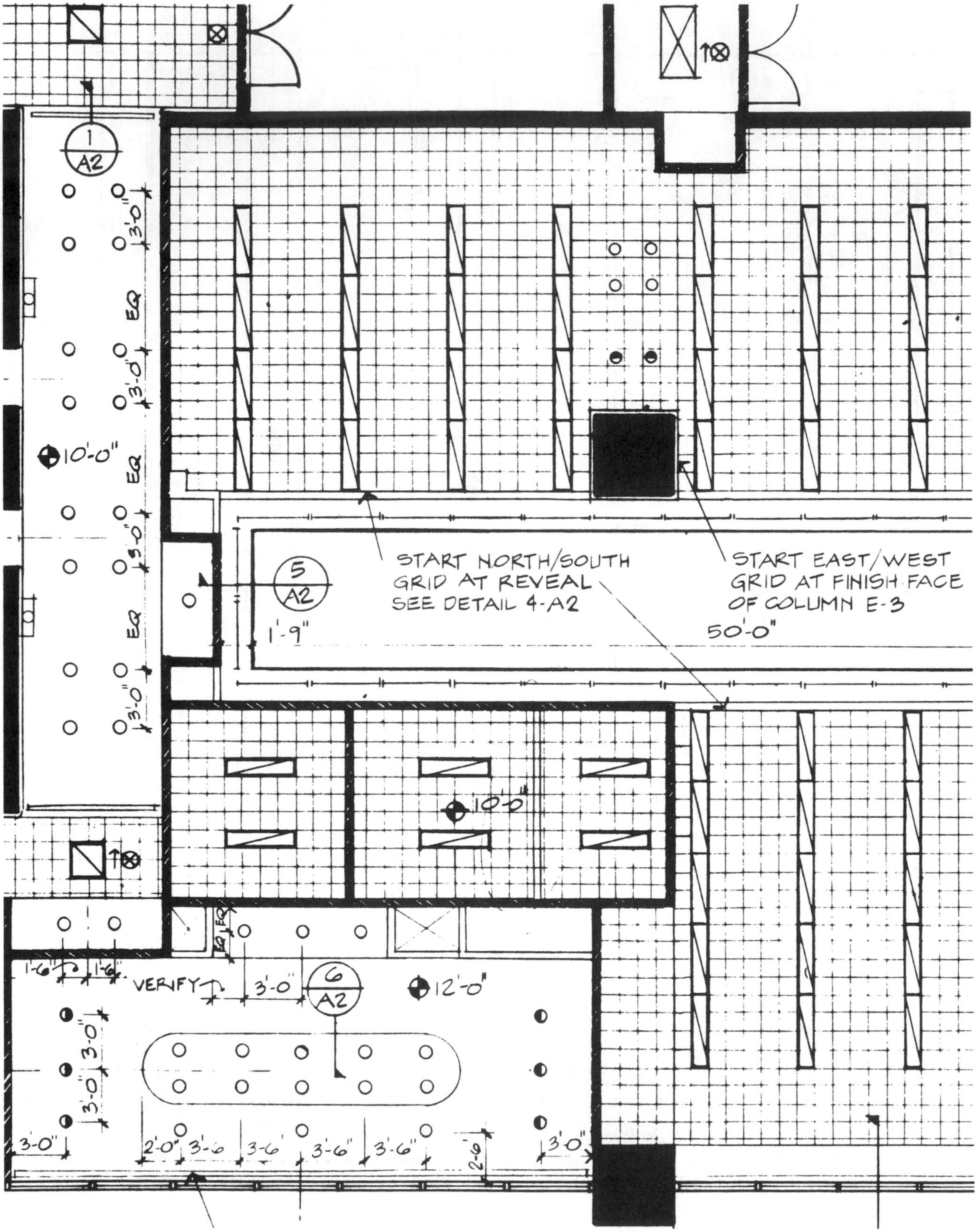

Figure 7.6 Reflected Ceiling Plan

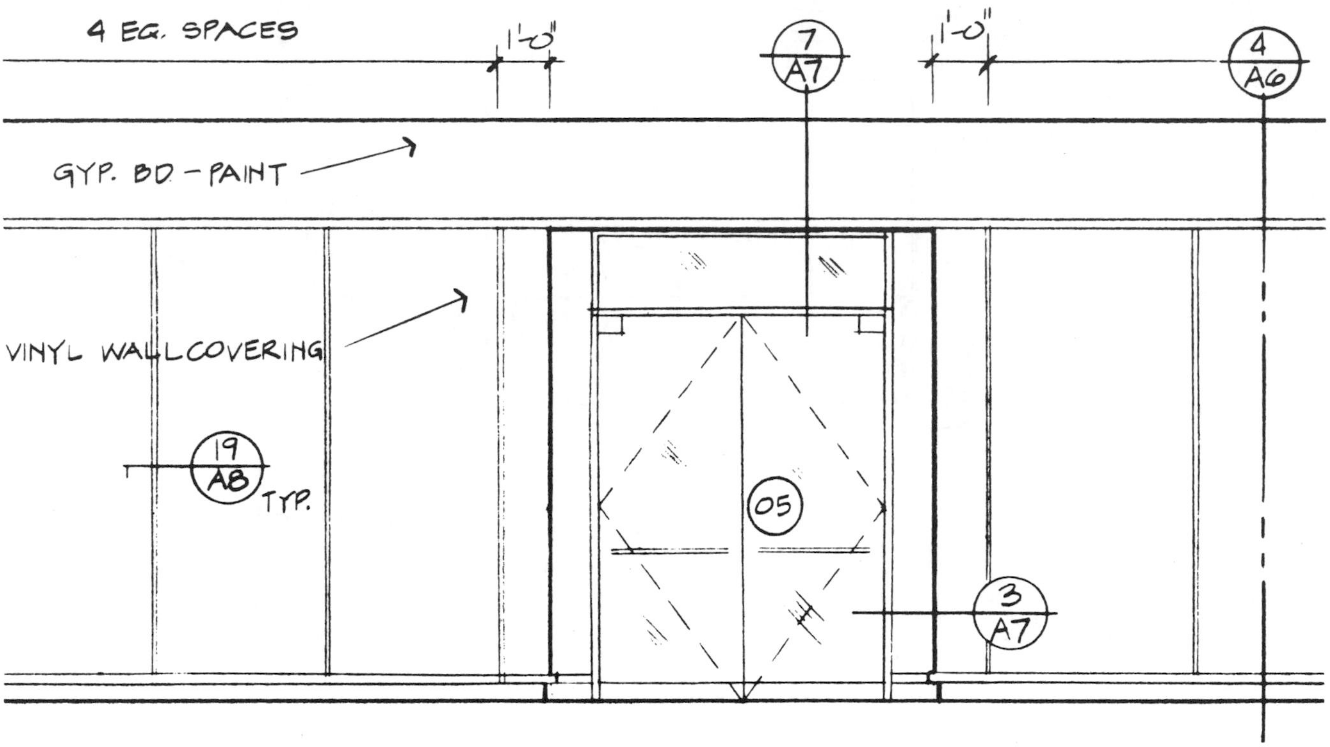

Figure 7.7 Interior Elevation

wall panels or cabinet units, elevations can include horizontal dimensioning that would not fit on a floor plan. They are also used to indicate references to other sections and details with the use of section cut lines. See Figure 7.7. The scale of elevations depends on the complexity of the surface to be shown, but common scales are 1/4″= 1′-0″(1:50) for simple wall planes to 3/8″(1:40) or 1/2″= 1′-0″(1:25) for more complex surfaces.

D. Sections

A section is a drawing showing what a part of the construction would look like if you cut straight through it. Because of this, it shows a view that does not really exist but one that is very useful for showing the relationships between materials. Figure 7.8 shows the section referenced in Figure 7.7. A section can be cut horizontally, as with a plan, or vertically, to show partition construction, for example. In either case, the section cut is perpendicular to the plane of construction that will be exposed in the detail.

Strictly speaking, an interior elevation is also a section cut because the outline of the elevation (the floor, side walls, and ceiling) is a portion of construction that is cut through to show the face of the wall. Generally, only the outline of the section is shown because the actual construction of the floor, walls, and ceiling is not the important element of an elevation drawing. See Figure 7.9. The details of these construction elements are shown elsewhere in the drawings, if needed.

There is sometimes confusion over the terms *section* and *detail* with interior construction drawings. This is because the majority of details are section cuts through small portions of construction, as described in the following text about details. In addition, the term section is used on architectural drawings to refer to sections through entire buildings. However, not all details are sections. A detail can also be a very large-scale plan view, an isometric view, or a large-scale partial elevation. Normally, a detail section is simply called a detail.

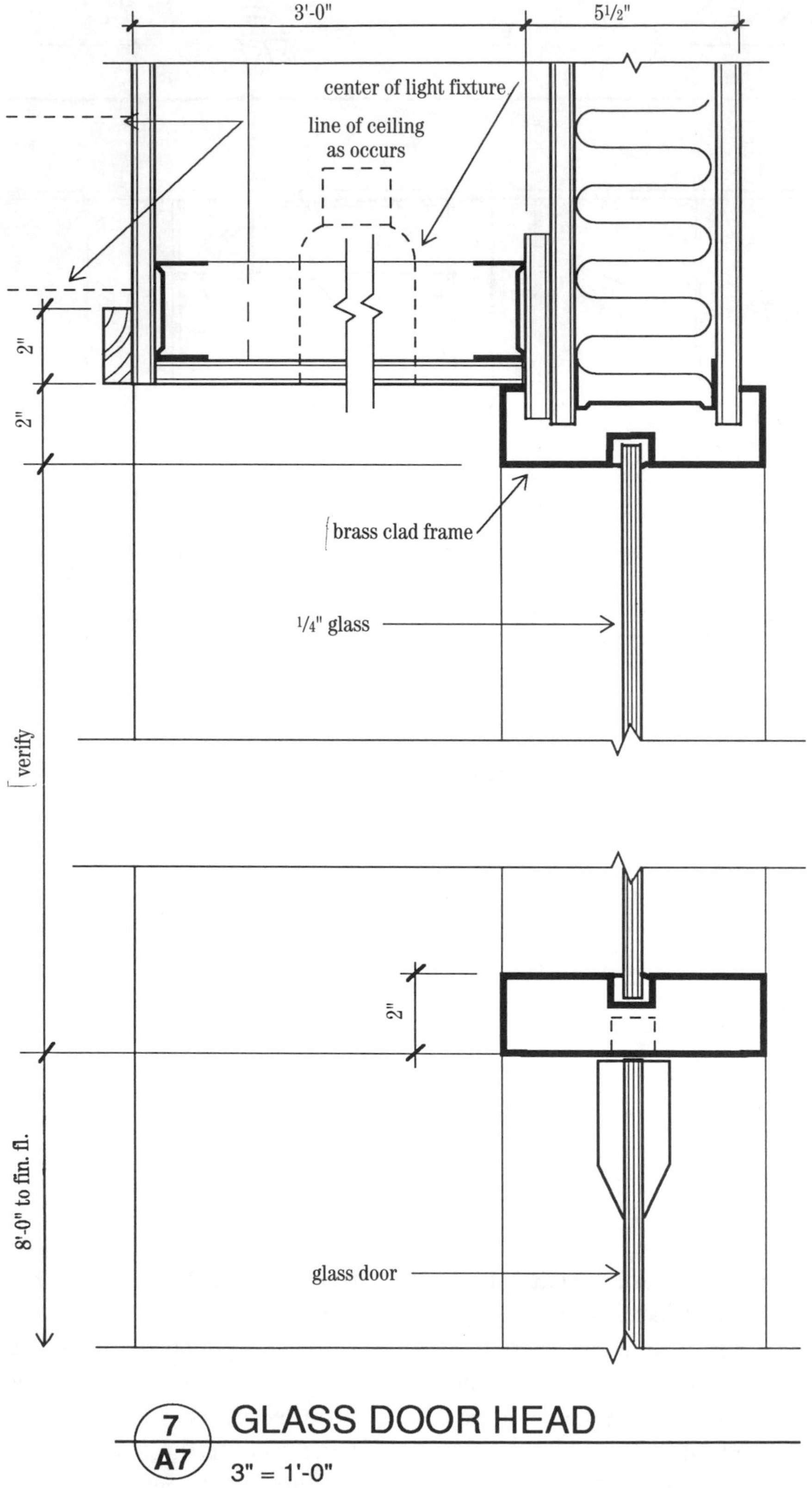

Figure 7.8 Section

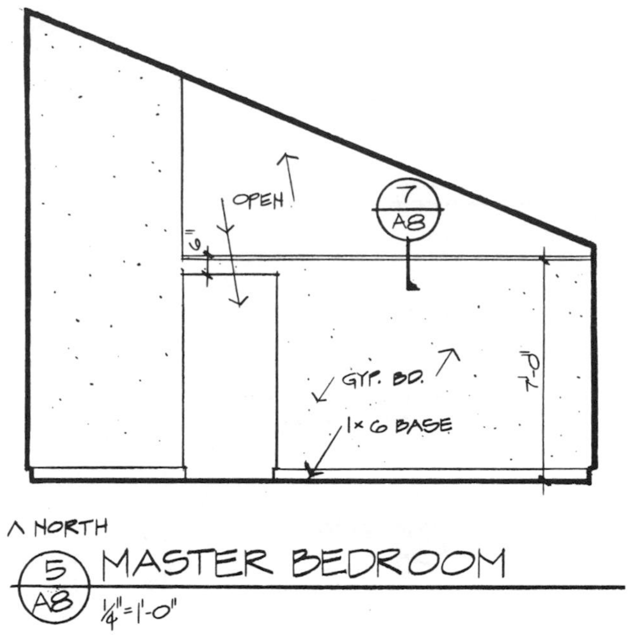

Figure 7.9 Elevation

E. Details

A building or interior design project is a complex collection of component parts, all of which are connected to other parts in various ways. The manner in which an assembly of several parts is organized and connected is commonly referred to as a detail. The construction drawing showing such a part is called a detail drawing or simply a detail, for short. A detail may be as simple as nailing wallboard to a stud or as complex as the intersection of the structural steel of a stairway and floor with the finish flooring, ceiling below, handrail, and concealed lighting, all of which might include dozens of different materials and connection techniques.

Because details show complex information, they are usually large-scale drawings of sections cut through a portion of construction as shown in Figure 7.10. However, it is also possible to have a detail plan or detail elevation if a large-scale view of something complex is required. In Figure 7.10, notice that in addition to showing the materials cut by the section, the detail also shows what is beyond the section cut. In effect, it is a small elevation of the portion of construction near the object through which you are drawing a section.

Details are commonly drawn at scales of 1″= 1′-0″(1:10), 1½″= 1′-0″(1:8), or 3″= 1′-0″(1:4). For very small and complex construction elements, half-size or even full-size drawings can be produced.

F. Schedules

Schedules show information in tabular format with rows and columns of data. They are used because they are a very efficient way to communicate a large amount of complex information in a small space. Common schedules for interior design construction drawings include room finish, door, kitchen equipment, millwork, and hardware schedules. Figure 7.11 shows a typical door schedule. Notice that there is a list of unique entities (in this case, door numbers), and each occupies one row of the table. Each entity has a number of attributes associated with it, such as type, size, material, and so on. These attributes are common for each of the rooms (entities) regardless of how many doors there are. This is typical of all construction schedules.

In addition to providing their own information, schedules may also refer to other parts of the drawings, if necessary. For example, the door schedule in Figure 7.11 has a column that lists the numbers and sheets on which details for the doors are drawn. Another column refers to the hardware groups listed in the specifications.

3 COORDINATION WITH THE CONSULTANT'S DRAWINGS

On nearly all projects, there are several consultants working with the interior designer. Small- to medium-size jobs may only require a mechanical and an electrical engineer. Larger projects may have additional consultants in architectural design, structural design, fire protection, food service, security systems, and acoustics, among others.

Each consulting firm develops its own drawings, so coordination among everyone on the team is critical. Someone must make sure that a recessed light fixture is not placed where it is in conflict with an air duct, for example. Although all consultants must be diligent in their efforts to work with others and

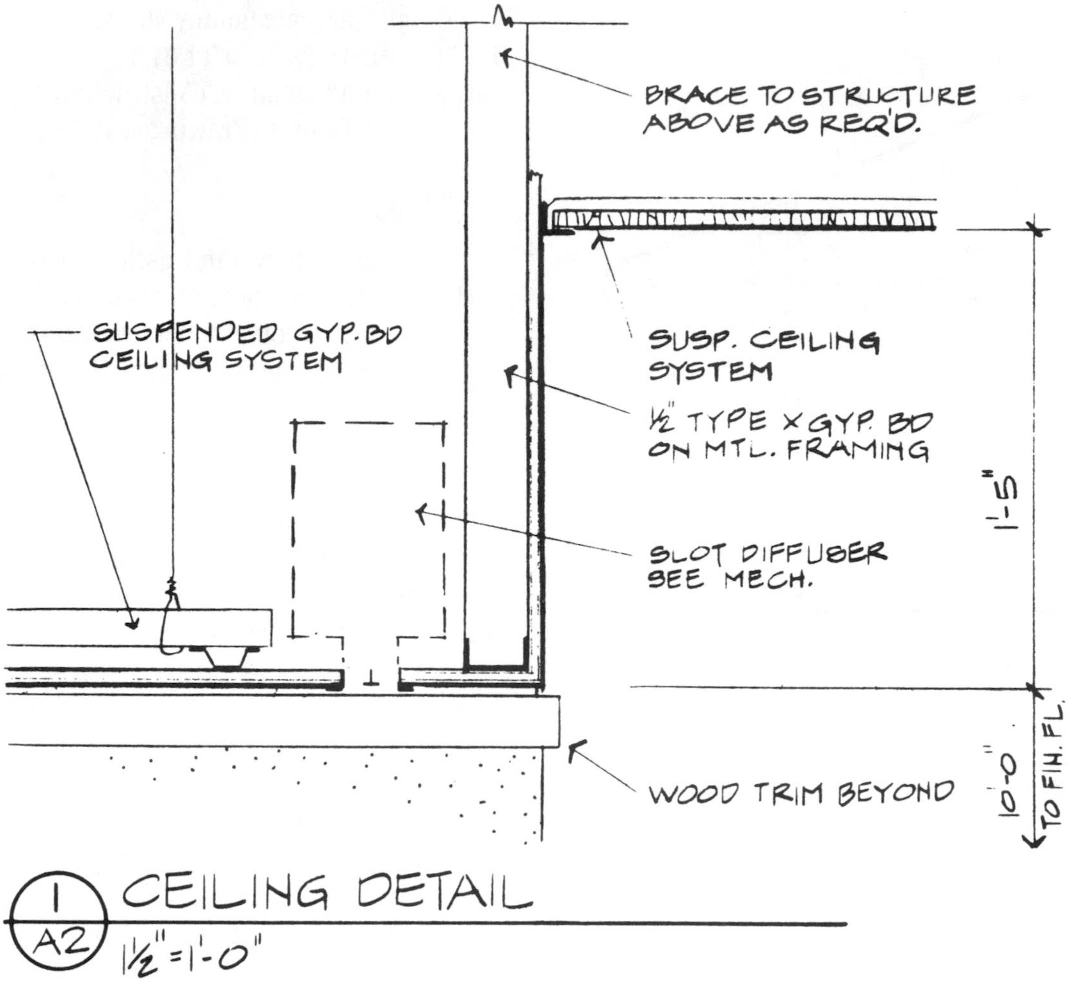

Figure 7.10 Detail

produce complete and correct documents, the primary responsibility for overall coordination should rest with one design professional. The specific terms of the client's contracts with the various professionals will ultimately determine who coordinates the team. On large projects, there may be an architect who coordinates the others, including the interior design consultant. On projects where the interior designer is the primary design consultant, he or she is responsible for coordination.

If the interior designer is responsible for retaining the services of other consultants, then the designer is usually responsible for directing and coordinating their work so the final set of construction documents (both drawings and specifications) represents a complete set of coordinated information. This does not mean that the interior designer is directly responsible for the work of any of the consultants; it means only that he or she is managing the efforts of the team. If the client hires the interior designer and other consultants separately, then someone other than the designer may be responsible for coordination.

A typical example of the coordination required between the consultants and, ultimately, the various subcontractors on the job is that of electrical design. The interior designer may develop the furniture plan and show the location of many of the electrical and telephone outlets and the basic lighting design. The electrical engineer is responsible for taking this information and developing the required electrical drawings, including circuiting and other

DOOR SCHEDULE														
	DOOR					FRAME								
No.	Type	Mat.	Width	Height	Thk.	Type	Mat.	Head	Jamb	Jamb	Sill	Fire rate.	Hwd Gp.	Remarks
01	A	HM	3'-0"	7'-0"	1 3/4	1	HM	1-A7	5-A7	5-A7		3/4	B	
02	B	HM	2-3'-0"	7'-0"	1 3/4	2	HM	1-A7	5-A7	5-A7		3/4	C	Relocate existing to new fm.
03	C	SC WD	3'-0"	7'-0"	1 3/4	1	HM	8-A7	11-A7	11-A7		1/3	D	
04	B	SC WD	2-3'-0"	7'-0"	1 3/4	*	Exist.	Exist.	Exist.	Exist.			E	Reuse existing frame
05	D	Glass	2-3'-0"	8'-0"	1/2	3	Brass	7-A7	3-A7	3-A7	10-A7		G	Glass transom above
06	Exist.						Exist.	10-A8	15-A8	16-A8			F	Existing door and frame
07	Exist.						Exist.	6-A8	1-A8	1-A8			F	Existing door and frame
08	C	SC WD	3'-0"	8'-0"	1 3/4	4	HM	2-A7	6-A7	6-A7		1/3	G	Use exist. bldg. std.
09	Exist.						Exist.	7-A8	3-A8	3-A8			F	Existing door and frame
10	D	Glass	2-3'-0"	8'-0"	1/2	3	Brass	7-A7	3-A7	3-A7	10-A7		G	Glass transom above
11	Not	used												
12	D	Glass	2-3'-0"	8'-0"	1/2	3	Brass	7-A7	3-A7	3-A7	10-A7		G	Glass transom above
13	Not	used												
14	C	SC WD	1'-10"	8'-0"	1 3/4	5	WD	9-A7	13-A7	13-A7			H	
15	C	SC WD	3'-0"	8'-0"	1 3/4	5	WD	9-A7	12-A7	13-A7			I	
16	C	SC WD	3'-0"	8'-0"	1 3/4	5	WD	9-A7	12-A7	13-A7			I	
17	C	SC WD	3'-0"	8'-0"	1 3/4	5	WD	9-A7	12-A7	13-A7			I	
18	C	SC WD	2-3'-0"	8'-0"	1 3/4	5	WD	9-A7	13-A7	13-A7			H	
19	F	SC WD	2'-6"	8'-0"	1 3/4	–	WD	12-A8	17-A8	17-A8			J	Glass panel in door
20	F	SC WD	2'-6"	8'-0"	1 3/4	–	WD	12-A8	17-A8	17-A8			J	Glass panel in door
21	E	SC WD	3'-0"	7'-0"	1 3/4	–	Exist.	6-A8 SIM	7-A6	7-A6			L	Dutch door, Match existing

Figure 7.11 Door Schedule

technical information. The designer's outlet plan must coordinate with the electrical power plan, and if one professional makes a change, everyone needs to know about it.

In most interior design offices (and other consultants' offices), the responsibility for coordination usually falls on the project manager, although in smaller firms or on small jobs the project designer may take on this task.

There are a number of ways to accomplish coordination during the design and production of contract documents. First, regularly scheduled meetings should be held to exchange information and alert everyone to the progress of the job. At these meetings, everyone should feel free to ask questions and raise issues that may affect the work of the others. Second, progress prints should be exchanged between the interior designer and the consultants for ongoing comparison of work being produced. Third, the project manager (or whoever is directing the job) must be responsible for notifying all consultants, in writing, of changes made as they occur. If overlay drafting or computer-aided drafting is being used, base sheets or electronic information can be exchanged according to the particular methods being employed. Finally, the interior designer must have a thorough method for checking and coordinating the entire drawing set before issue for bidding or negotiation of a construction contract.

4 REFERENCE SYSTEMS

A complete set of construction drawings is a carefully coordinated and interrelated grouping of individual graphic components. To refer someone looking at the drawings from one element (an elevation, for example) to another (a detail section of a portion of that section), standard graphic symbols are used.

To make any referencing system work, each drawing element, whether plan, elevation, or detail, must have a unique number. This is usually a combination of a sequential number starting with 1 on each separate sheet, and the number of the sheet on which the drawing element occurs. Drawing numbers are always combined with the title of the drawing. Some examples of these drawing titles are shown in Figure 7.12. For example, in the first example shown, the number 6 indicates that this is the sixth detail on drawing sheet A8.

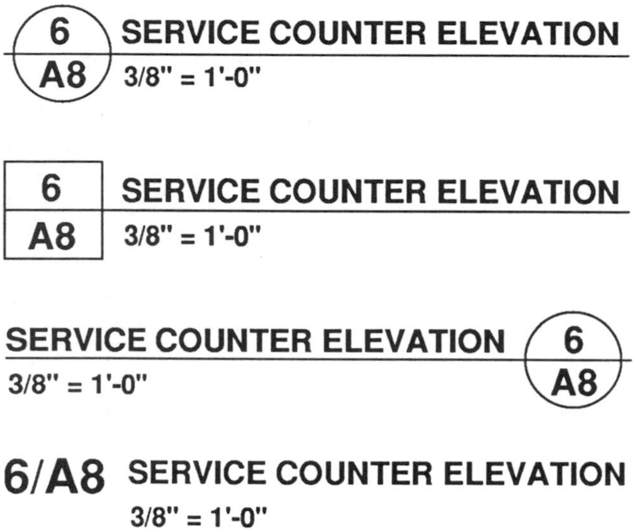

Figure 7.12 Drawing Titles

Various reference symbols are used with these unique drawing title numbers to direct someone to the correct, related drawing. Figures 7.13 through 7.15 show examples of the three commonly used reference symbols. These are also used in Figures 7.6 and 7.7.

Figure 7.13 shows several examples of elevation reference marks, often called elevation bubbles. Although these examples differ slightly, they all do the same job. An elevation reference mark is placed on a floor plan to indicate that an elevation of the wall (or walls) is drawn somewhere in the set. The number on top of the mark indicates the unique sequential number of the elevation drawing, and the number below the line indicates the sheet on which the drawing is placed. As shown in the examples, there can be a separate mark for each elevation drawn, or there can be only one symbol with arrows pointing to the elevations within a room that are drawn elsewhere in the set.

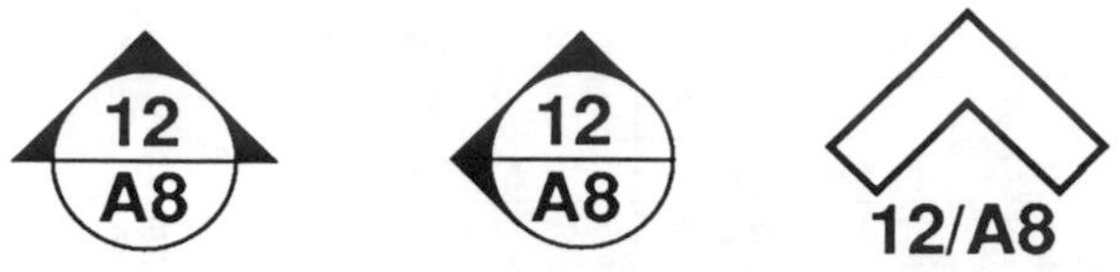

Figure 7.13 Elevation Reference Marks

Figure 7.14 shows two examples of detail section reference marks. A section reference mark is used to indicate where a section is cut through a portion of the construction. They can be used vertically or horizontally on plans, elevations, or even other sections to show that the drawing referred to shows a view that is 90 degrees to the plane in which the mark is made. For example, one of these marks oriented vertically on an elevation of a door indicates that there is a detailed drawing of a vertical section through the door. See Figures 7.7 and 7.8.

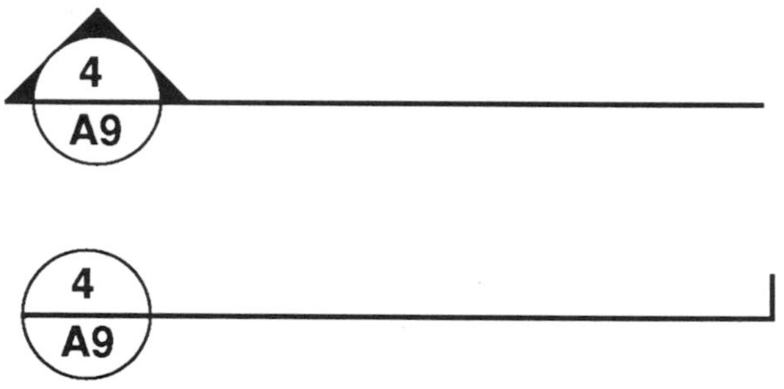

Figure 7.14 Section Reference Marks

Figure 7.15 shows two examples of a plan detail reference mark. This mark is used to show that a detail is drawn of the portion circled. Unlike the detail section reference mark, this symbol indicates that the detail is drawn in the same plane of the circled part of the plan, rather than being a view 90 degrees to the cut line. The detail differs from the plan only in that it is drawn at a larger scale. One way to remember the difference is that this symbol looks like a magnifying glass. As with the other marks, the top number is the detail identification while the bottom number is the sheet where the detail is drawn. If the circle around the detail is replaced with a larger rectangle with rounded corners, the meaning of the symbol does not change: it indicates an enlarged floor plan of the area highlighted.

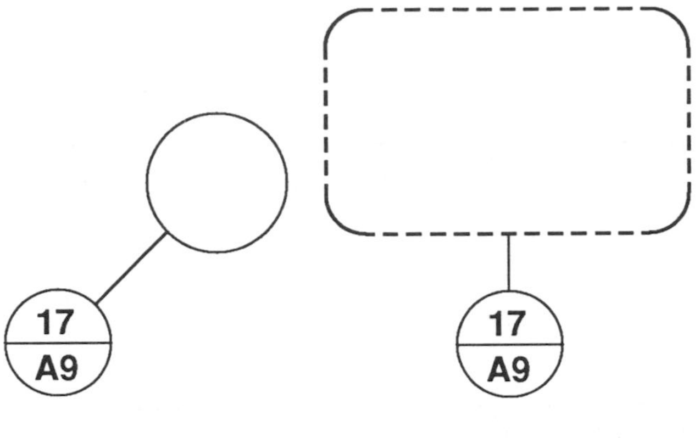

Figure 7.15 Plan Detail Reference Marks

5 DRAWING SYMBOLS

Standard drawing symbols are used to efficiently communicate various types of graphic information. In addition to the reference symbols discussed in the previous section, you must be familiar with some of the more common drafting conventions used to indicate materials, architectural features, electrical items, and miscellaneous drawing features. These are shown in Figures 7.16 through 7.19.

6 MILLWORK CONSTRUCTION DRAWINGS

Because cabinets, paneling, trim, and similar finish wood pieces are such common interior construction elements, the NCIDQ exam requires particular knowledge of millwork and the drawings required to describe its construction. This section describes common millwork details and graphic standards. Refer to Chapter 11 for information on basic millwork materials, finishes, and construction methods.

Millwork describes construction components that are primarily built of wood and that are manufactured in a mill shop. This includes common pieces like cabinets, bookshelves, paneling, and custom doors. A related type of wood construction is called finish carpentry and includes woodwork that is done on the job site. Wood base, door trim, wall moldings, and handrails are typical examples of finish carpentry items. Another related type of millwork is modular casework. These are prefabricated cabinets that are selected from a manufacturer's standard product line. Although similar in construction to custom millwork cabinets, the designer does not have to draw the details of modular casework because its construction is already set by the manufacturer.

A. Architectural Cabinets

Architectural cabinets include base cabinets, upper cabinets, open-front storage units, and similar components. Typical detail sections through a base cabinet and upper cabinet are shown in Figures 7.20 and 7.21. Because millwork is a custom-fabricated item, the exact dimensions, configuration, and finishes will vary depending on the design and the client's requirements. When appliances or other built-in equipment is planned, it is critical that the size and clearances required are noted on the millwork drawings. In the details shown in Figures 7.20 and 7.21, the finish of the exposed drawer and door fronts (as well as the countertop) may be plastic laminate, wood veneer, or other types of finishes such as paint, tile, or stone.

B. Paneling

There are two basic types of wood paneling: stile and rail, and flush. Stile and rail paneling is the traditional type composed of vertical pieces (stiles) and horizontal pieces (rails) enclosing a paneled area. See Figure 7.22. Flush paneling has a flat, smooth surface with the edges butted together or joined with a reveal or batten strip, as shown in Figure 7.23. In either case, the panels, which are fabricated in the shop, are installed with the use of cleats or metal Z-clips as shown in Figure 7.24. The cleats or Z-clips are attached to the wall and a corresponding cleat or clip is attached to the back of the paneling. The panel is then lifted into place.

C. Standing and Running Trim

Standing trim is an item of fixed length such as a door or window casing that can be installed with a single length of wood. *Running trim* is an item

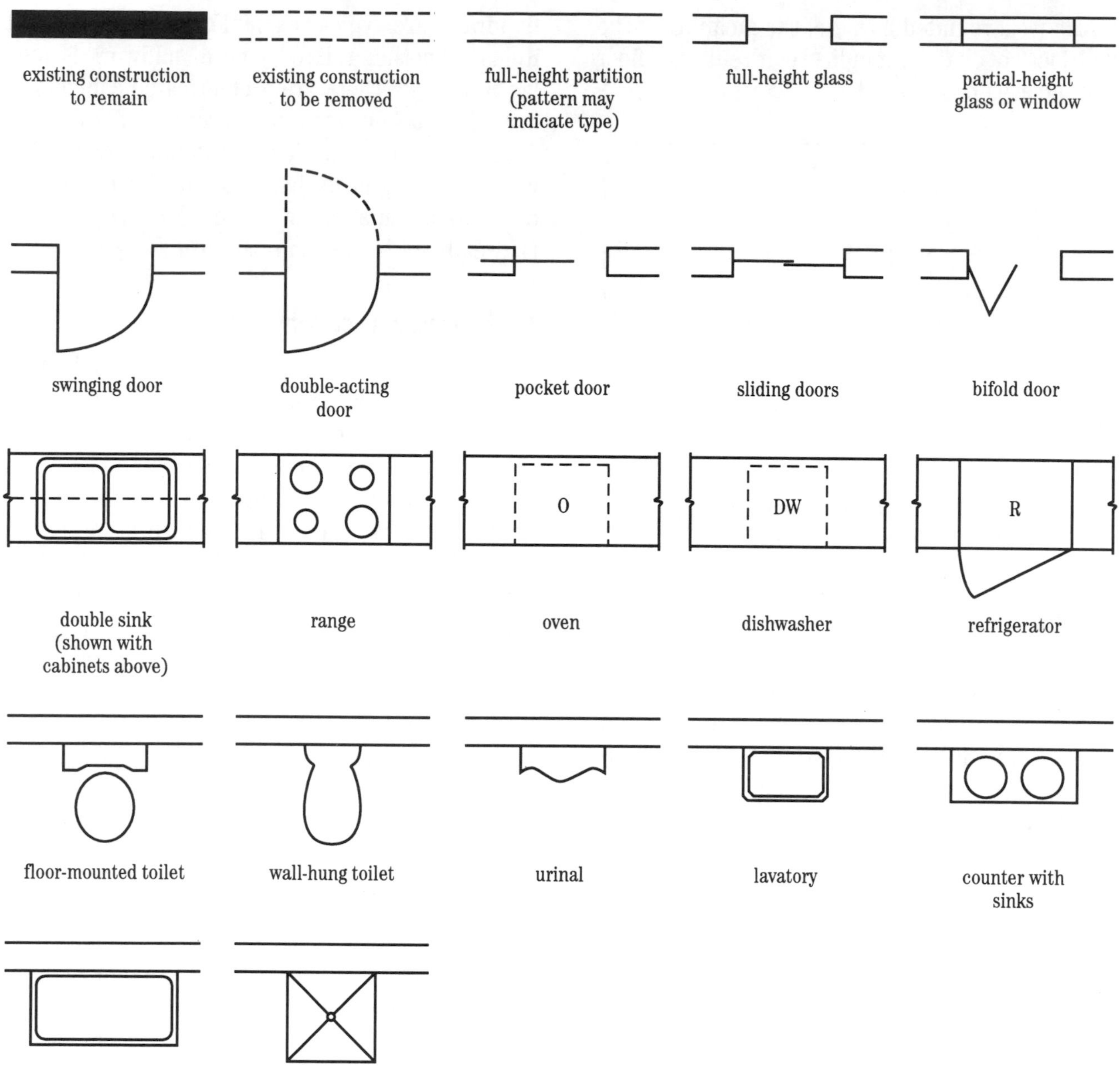

Figure 7.16 Architectural Plan Symbols

of continuing length such as a baseboard, chair-rail, or cornice. Standing and running trim is the term usually applied to wood pieces custom fabricated in a mill shop and then installed at the job site. *Wood molding* is a similar item but comes in standard profiles and sizes; it is ordered by number and installed as a finish carpentry item rather than a millwork item.

Standing and running trim can be custom fabricated in almost any profile and dimension the interior designer wants (subject to limitations in rough wood sizes and fabrication tools) and from any available wood species. If an unusual profile is needed, the mill shop custom-cuts a die that is then used to plane down wood stock to the desired size and profile. Wood molding, on the other hand, is available in only a few wood species (such as pine, oak, and walnut) and is limited to standard profiles. A few of these profiles are shown in Figure 7.25.

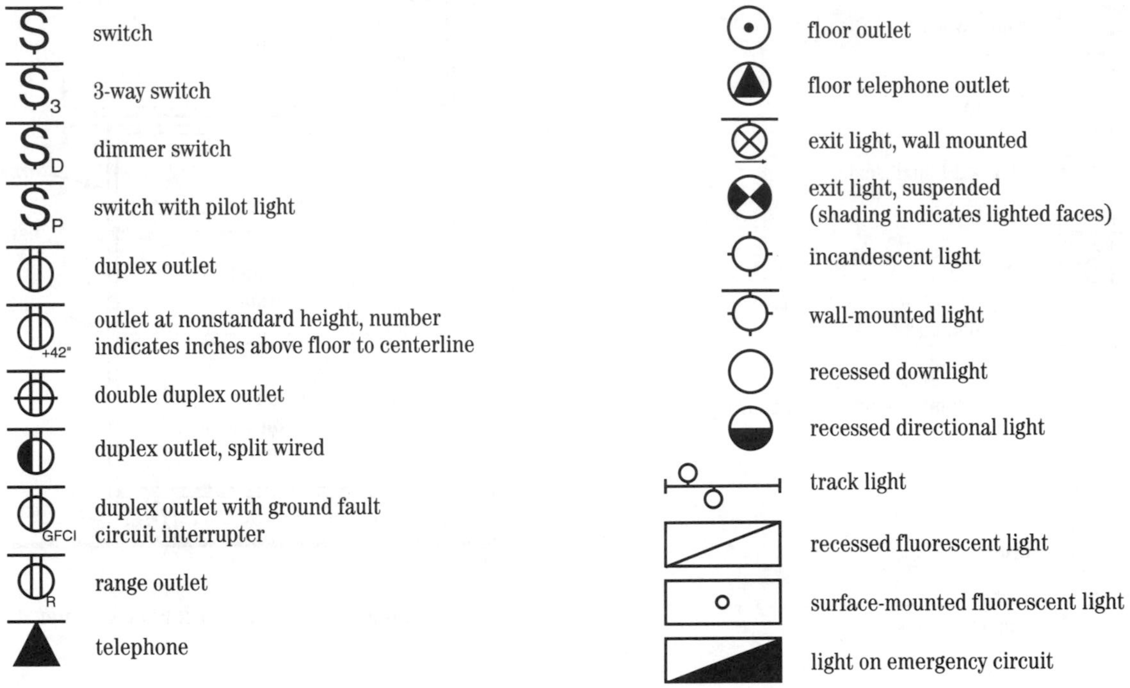

Figure 7.17 Electrical and Lighting Symbols

D. Specialty Millwork Construction

In addition to the usual types of millwork items, a wide variety of specialty items can be detailed and constructed. These include such things as conference tables, desks, fabric-wrapped panels, built-in shelving and furniture, bars, display cases, and counters. In addition to wood, the designer can incorporate other materials into the item (such as ornamental metal, tile, stone, glass, leather, and fabric).

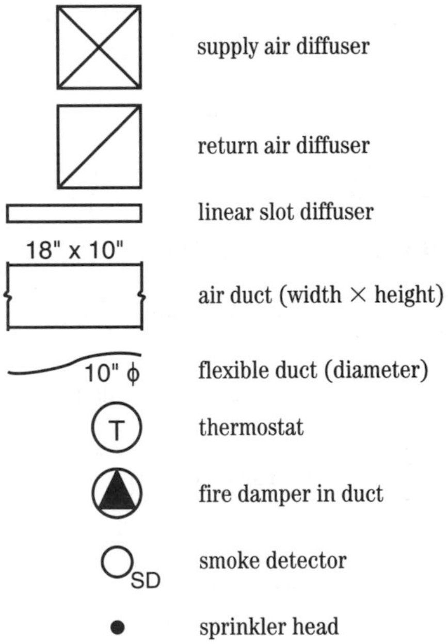

Figure 7.18 Mechanical Symbols

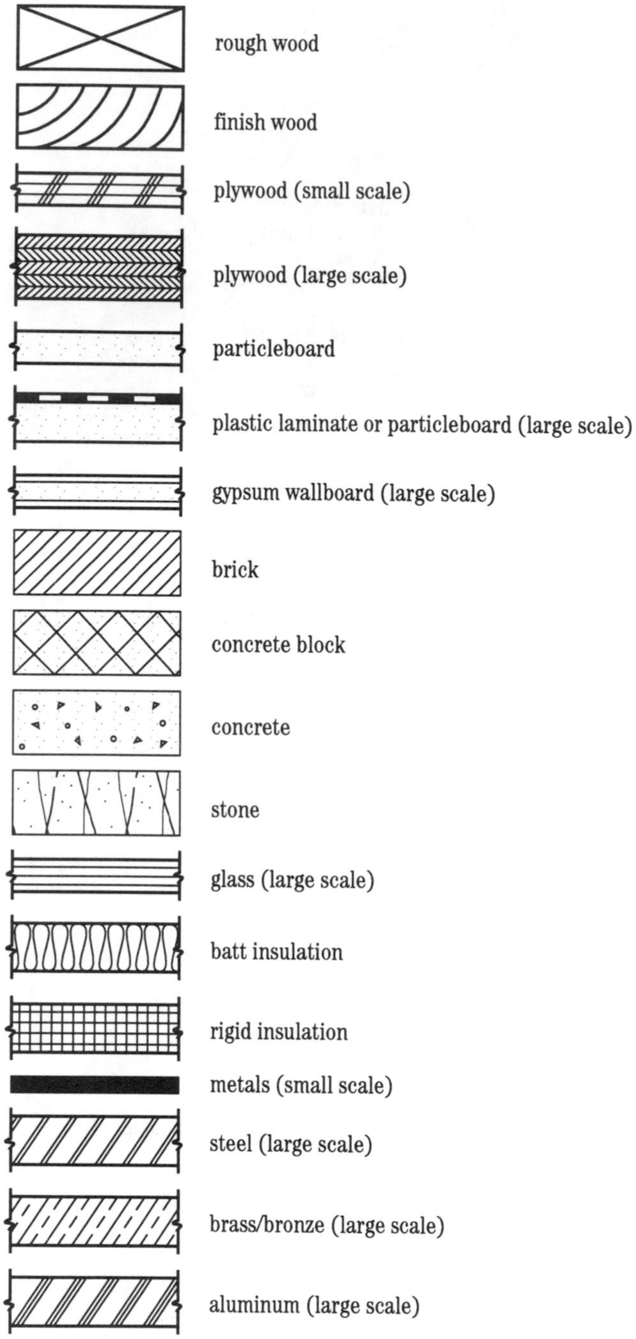

Figure 7.19 Material Indications in Section

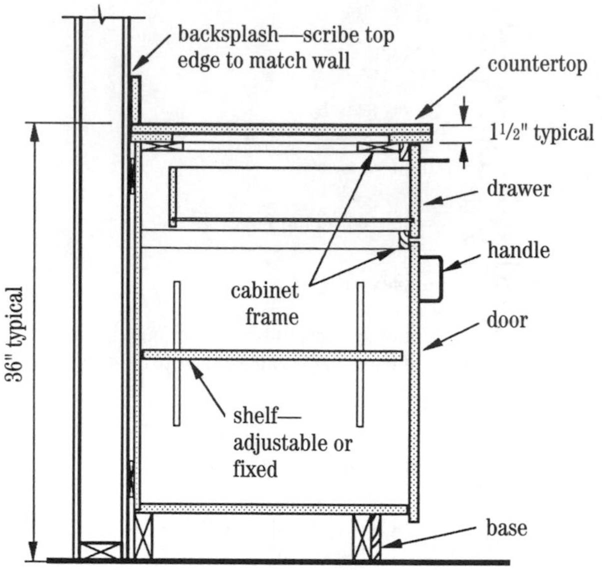

Figure 7.20 Millwork Base Cabinet

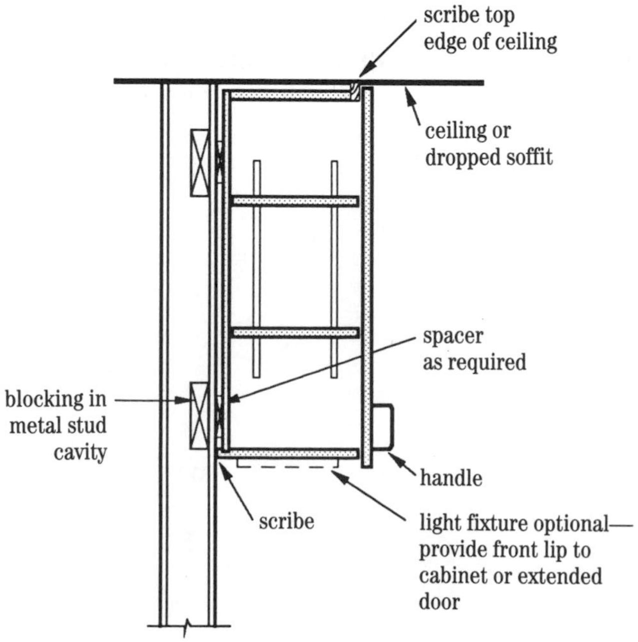

Figure 7.21 Millwork Upper Cabinet

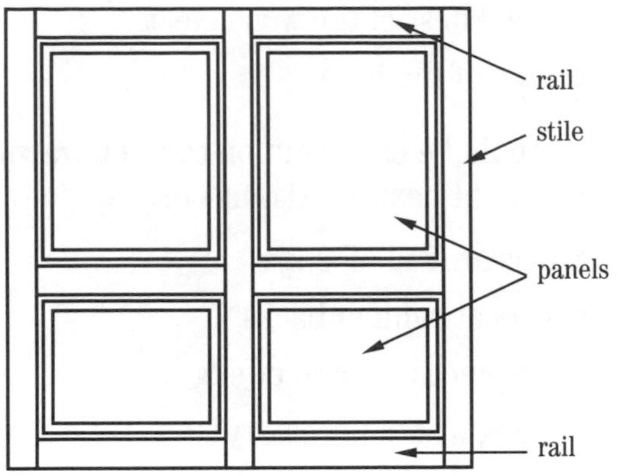

Figure 7.22 Stile and Rail Paneling

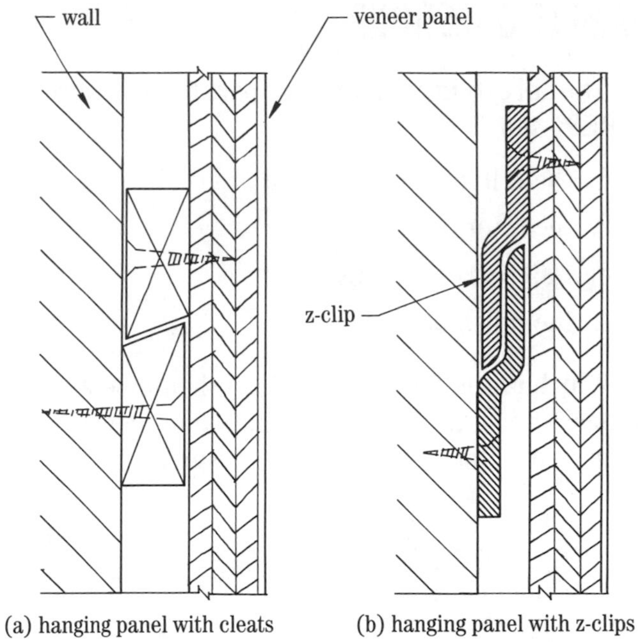

Figure 7.24 Methods of Hanging Panels

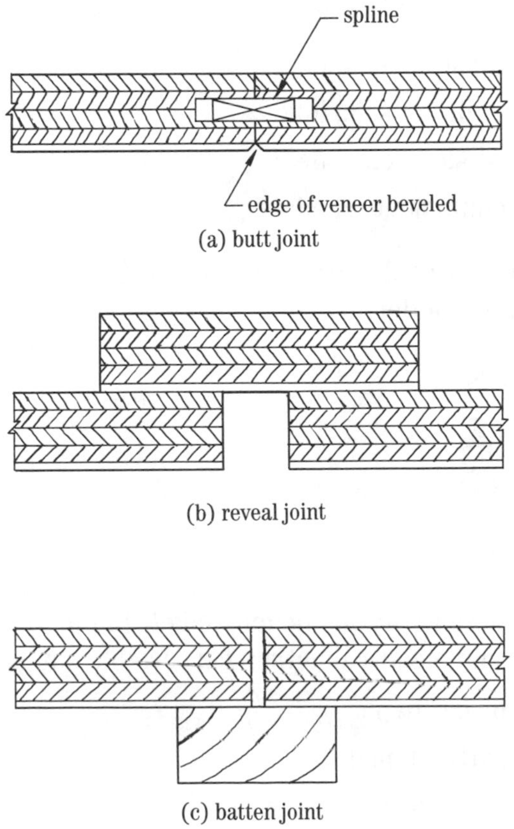

Figure 7.23 Flush Panel Joints

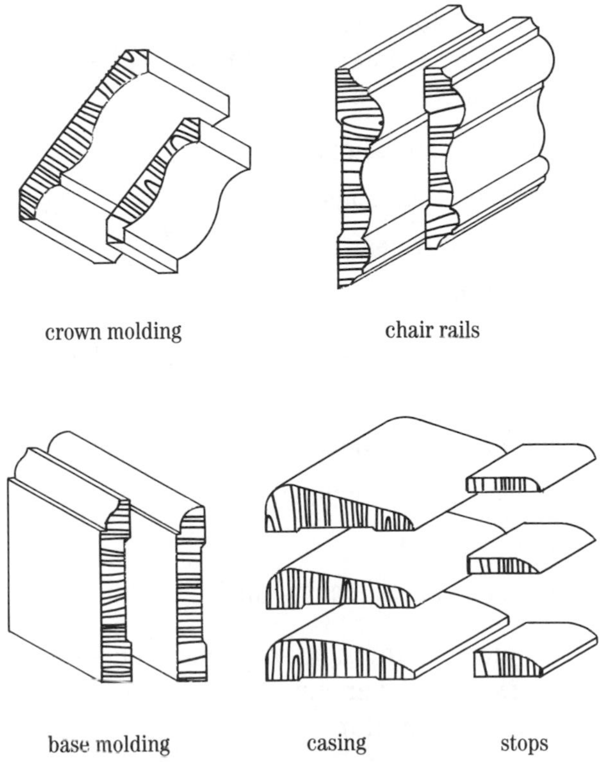

Figure 7.25 Wood Molding

SAMPLE QUESTIONS

1. The full extent of slab-to-slab partitions on a project is BEST shown on

    1. the reflected ceiling plan
    2. the interior elevations
    3. wall section details
    4. the finish plan

2. Which of the following symbols should be used to indicate that an interior glazing jamb shown on a floor plan is detailed on another drawing sheet?

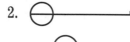

    1. 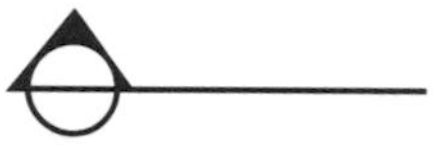
    2. 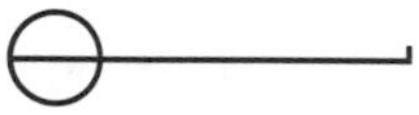
    3. 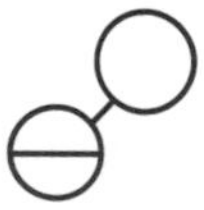
    4. 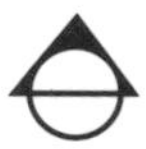

3. Who is responsible for verifying that recessed downlights do not interfere with ductwork shown on the mechanical plans?

    1. the mechanical engineer
    2. the electrical engineer
    3. the interior designer
    4. the architect

4. Who would be LEAST involved in the selection of an underfloor raceway system?

    1. the electrical consultant
    2. the structural engineer
    3. the architect
    4. the mechanical consultant

5. What piece of information is most important in doing drawings for paneling that will be suspended from a wall with cleats?

    1. the width of each panel along a wall
    2. the dimension between panel top and ceiling
    3. the thickness of the wood cleat
    4. the size of the base

6. What should be called out on cabinet drawings to assure a good fit next to existing construction?

    1. reveals around all edges
    2. spacers at cabinet backs
    3. scribe pieces at cabinet edges
    4. blocking where necessary

7. The symbol shown is used to indicate what type of control?

$$\overline{S}_3$$

    1. a light controlled from two locations
    2. a light controlled from three locations
    3. a light and a fan controlled from the same switch
    4. a three-position switch

8. What type of schedule would you LEAST expect to find on a set of interior design drawings?

    1. finish schedule
    2. millwork schedule
    3. window schedule
    4. equipment schedule

9. What symbol is used to indicate a floor-mounted telephone outlet?

    1. 
    2. 
    3. 
    4. 

10. Where would you be most likely to find information about electrical outlets for portable lamps?

    1. furniture plan
    2. partition plan
    3. power plan
    4. reflected ceiling plan

8 CONSTRUCTION SPECIFICATIONS

Any interior design project that involves construction requires written specifications as well as construction drawings. The drawings show the general configuration and layout of the interior space as well as the size, shape, and dimensions of the construction. The technical specifications describe the quality of materials and workmanship, along with general requirements for the execution of the work, standards, and other items that are more appropriately described in written, rather than graphic, form. Construction specifications differ from furniture specifications in their content, scope, and form. Furniture specifications are discussed in the last section of this chapter.

For small, simple projects, specifications may be typed on transparent adhesive material and placed on the drawings for convenience. On most projects, however, the specifications are included in a project manual and issued with the drawings and contract agreements as part of the complete package of contract documents.

1 ORGANIZATION OF THE PROJECT MANUAL

The project manual is a bound book containing all the contract and noncontract documents for a construction project except the drawings. The project manual contains the technical specifications, and it includes several other types of documents.

The manual is divided into four major parts: (1) bidding requirements (if needed); (2) parts of the contract itself, which may contain the agreement between owner and contractor, bond forms, and the like; (3) general and supplementary conditions of the contract; and (4) technical specifications.

A more detailed list of possible contents of the project manual includes the following:

- *Bidding requirements*
  invitation to bid
  prequalification forms
  instructions to bidders
  information available to bidders
  bid forms

- *Supplements to bid forms*
  bid security form
  subcontractor list
  substitution list

- *Contract forms*
  agreement (contract between owner and contractor)
  performance bond
  labor and materials payment bond
  certificates of insurance

- *General and supplementary conditions*
  general conditions of the contract (such as AIA Form 201 or similar preprinted forms)
  supplementary conditions (anything not covered in the general conditions)

- *Technical specifications*

Contracts, bidding documents, and general conditions of the contract are discussed in more detail in Chapter 9. This chapter focuses on the technical specifications.

2 TYPES OF SPECIFICATIONS

There are two broad categories of construction specifications: prescriptive and performance. Prescriptive specifications are sometimes called closed, while performance specifications are known as open.

Prescriptive specifications tell exactly what product or material you want the contractor to use by using brand names. Performance specifications tell what results you want the final construction assembly to achieve, but they give the contractor some choice in how they will be achieved. Most interior design specifications fall somewhere between these two extremes.

The type you select depends on several factors. Public projects usually require open specifications to encourage competitive bidding. Some private clients may require this as well. In other cases, you may want to use a closed specification to ensure that only one particular product is used. This is often the case with interior design projects because many finish materials and products are so unique that an equal substitute is not possible. Whether the job is bid or negotiated may also affect your choice. With bidding, you want to allow the contractor as much choice as possible so he or she can find the lowest price within the context of the specification requirements.

There are several types of prescriptive and performance specifications. Proprietary and base-bid are two common variations of prescriptive specifications while descriptive, reference standard, and pure performance are types of performance specifications.

A. Proprietary Specifications

Proprietary specifications are the most restrictive specifications in that they call out a specific manufacturer's product. These give the interior designer complete control over what is installed. They are easier to write than other types and are generally shorter. However, they do not allow for competitive bidding, and by limiting products, you may force the contractor to use materials or products that are difficult or expensive to procure or that require a long delivery time.

B. Base-Bid Specifications

A base-bid "or equal" specification is a type of specification that calls out a proprietary material or product but allows the substitution of other products that the contractor thinks are equal to the one stated. This is a risky method of specifying because the contractor may substitute a less expensive item that he or she thinks is equal, but which may not be equal.

Two variations of a base-bid specification give the interior designer more control over possible substitutions. The first lists several approved manufacturers of a product. The contractor is free to bid on any one listed. This type satisfies the requirements for public work where at least three different manufacturers must be listed, but it puts the burden on the interior designer to make sure that every one of the approved products or manufacturers listed is equal.

The second variation is a base-bid specification with "approved equal" language. This type of specification states that one product or an approved equal must be used. This means that the contractor may submit a substitution, but it is subject to review and approval by the designer before it can be incorporated into the bid. This gives the contractor some freedom in looking for lower-priced alternates, and it puts the burden of finding them on the contractor. However, the responsibility for fairly and accurately evaluating the proposed alternates is placed on the interior designer. During a hectic bidding period, this can be a large burden, so the specification should clearly state how much lead time the contractor must give the interior designer and how alternates will be evaluated.

C. Descriptive Specifications

A descriptive specification is a type of performance (open) specification that gives detailed written requirements for the material or product and the workmanship required for its fabrication and installation. It does not mention trade names. In its purest form, a descriptive specification is difficult to write because you must include all the pertinent requirements for the construction and installation of the product.

D. Reference Standard Specifications

A variation of the descriptive type is a reference standard specification. This describes a material, product, or process based on requirements (reference standards) set by an accepted authority or test method. For example, a product type can be required to meet the testing standards produced by such organizations as the American Society for Testing and Materials (ASTM), the American National Standards Institute (ANSI), or Underwriters Laboratories (UL). Reference can also be made to specific trade associations, such as the Architectural Woodwork Institute or the Gypsum Association.

For example, in specifying gypsum wallboard you can state that all gypsum wallboard products must meet the requirements of ASTM C36. This particular document describes in great detail the requirements for this product. You do not, then, have to repeat the requirements and can instead refer to the recognized industry standard.

Reference standard specifications are fairly easy to write and are generally short. Chances for errors are reduced and your liability minimized because you are using industry standards and generally recognized methods of building. However, you must know what is in the standard and how to refer to the appropriate part of the standard if it includes more provisions than you need for your job.

E. Performance Specifications

A pure performance specification is a statement setting criteria and results required of the item being specified. The results can be verified by measurement, tests, or other types of evaluation. The means of achieving the required results are not specified; this is left up to the contractor or vendor.

A true performance specification is often used for construction components when the specifier wants to encourage new ways of achieving a particular result. For example, a movable partition system could be specified by stating its required fire rating, acoustical properties, finish, maximum thickness, tolerances, size required, and all other required properties. It would then be up to the contractor and manufacturer to design and develop a system to meet the criteria.

Performance specifications are difficult to write because the specifier must know all the criteria, state the methods for testing compliance, and write an unambiguous document. Specifications of this type are rarely used for interior construction.

3 ORGANIZATION OF THE TECHNICAL SECTIONS

The organization of the technical sections has been standardized through the general adoption of the *Masterformat* system. This has been developed by the Construction Specifications Institute and Construction Specifications Canada to standardize the numbering and format of project-related information for use in specifying, cost estimating, and data filing. The organization is based on 16 broad divisions that represent major categories of work. Each division is subdivided into sections, each of which is assigned a five-digit number. The divisions and major sections are shown in Figure 8.1.

The sections in Figure 8.1 are considered broadscope sections, in that each may cover several types of materials, products, or systems. If more specific classification is required, then a so-called narrowscope section is used. For example, Section 09900, Painting, is a broadscope section than can include many different types of painting. A project manual can also be written using the narrowscope sections 09920, Interior Painting, and 09930, Transparent Finishes. Which level you use depends on the complexity of the job. For most interior projects, the broadscope divisions are usually adequate.

The *Masterformat* system also establishes a standard way of organizing any particular broadscope or narrowscope section. The first level of division within a section is the three-part format. This includes Part 1, General; Part 2, Products; and Part 3, Execution. All sections include three parts, while the specific articles within the parts vary with the type of material or product being specified.

Part 1 gives the general requirements for the section, such as the scope of the section, submittals required, quality assurance requirements, warranties, project conditions, and specifications for the delivery, storage, and handling of materials.

Part 2 details the specifications for the materials and products themselves, including acceptable manufacturer (if applicable), what standards and test methods the materials must conform to, how items are to be fabricated, and similar concerns.

Bidding requirements, Contract forms, and Conditions of the Contract

00010	Pre-bid information
00100	Instructions to bidders
00200	Information available to bidders
00300	Bid forms
00400	Supplements to bid forms
00500	Agreement forms
00600	Bonds and certificates
00700	General conditions
00800	Supplementary conditions
00900	Addenda

Division 1—General Requirements

01010	Summary of the work
01020	Allowances
01025	Measurement and payment
01030	Alternates/Alternatives
01035	Modification procedures
01040	Coordination
01050	Field engineering
01060	Regulatory requirements
01070	Identification systems
01090	References
01100	Special project procedures
01200	Project meetings
01300	Submittals
01400	Quality control
01500	Construction facilities and temporary controls
01600	Material and equipment
01650	Facility startup/Commissioning
01700	Contract closeout
01800	Maintenance

Division 2—Sitework

02010	Subsurface investigation
02050	Demolition
02100	Site preparation
02140	Dewatering
02150	Shoring and underpinning
02160	Excavation support systems
02170	Cofferdams
02200	Earthwork
02300	Tunneling
02350	Piles and caissons
02450	Railroad work
02480	Marine work
02500	Paving and surfacing
02600	Utility piping materials
02660	Water distribution
02680	Fuel and steam distribution
02700	Sewerage and drainage
02760	Restoration of underground pipe
02770	Ponds and reservoirs
02780	Power and communications
02800	Site improvements
02900	Landscaping

Division 3—Concrete

03100	Concrete formwork
03200	Concrete reinforcement
03250	Concrete accessories
03300	Cast-in-place concrete
03370	Concrete curing
03400	Precast concrete
03500	Cementitious decks and toppings
03600	Grout
03700	Concrete restoration and cleaning
03800	Mass concrete

Division 4—Masonry

04100	Mortar and masonry grout
04150	Masonry accessories
04200	Unit masonry
04400	Stone
04500	Masonry restoration and cleaning
04550	Refractories
04600	Corrosion resistant masonry
04700	Simulated masonry

Division 5—Metals

05010	Metal materials
05030	Metal coatings
05050	Metal fastening
05100	Structural metal framing
05200	Metal joists
05300	Metal decking
05400	Cold formed metal framing
05500	Metal fabrications
05580	Sheet metal fabrications
05700	Ornamental metal
05800	Expansion control
05900	Hydraulic structures

Division 6—Wood and Plastics

06050	Fasteners and adhesives
06100	Rough carpentry
06130	Heavy timber construction
06150	Wood and metal systems
06170	Prefabricated structural wood
06200	Finish carpentry
06300	Wood treatment
06400	Architectural woodwork
06500	Structural plastics
06600	Plastic fabrications
06650	Solid polymer fabrications

Division 7—Thermal and Moisture Protection

07100	Waterproofing
07150	Dampproofing
07180	Water repellents
07190	Vapor retarders
07195	Air barriers
07200	Insulation
07240	Exterior insulation and finish systems
07250	Fireproofing
07270	Firestopping
07300	Shingles and roofing tiles
07400	Manufactured roofing and siding
07480	Exterior wall assemblies
07500	Membrane roofing
07570	Traffic coatings
07600	Flashing and sheet metal
07700	Roof specialties and accessories
07800	Skylights
07900	Joint sealers

Division 8—Doors and Windows

08100	Metal doors and frames
08200	Wood and plastic doors
08250	Door opening assemblies
08300	Special doors
08400	Entrances and storefronts
08500	Metal windows
08600	Wood and plastic windows
08650	Special windows
08700	Hardware
08800	Glazing
08900	Glazed curtain walls

Division 9—Finishes

09100	Metal support systems
09200	Lath and plaster
09250	Gypsum board
09300	Tile
09400	Terrazzo
09450	Stone facing
09500	Acoustical treatment
09540	Special wall surfaces
09545	Special ceiling surfaces
09550	Wood flooring
09600	Stone flooring
09630	Unit masonry flooring
09650	Resilient flooring
09680	Carpet
09700	Special flooring
09780	Floor treatment
09800	Special coatings
09900	Painting
09950	Wall coverings

Figure 8.1 *Masterformat* System

Division 10—Specialties

10100 Visual display boards
10150 Compartments and cubicles
10200 Louvers and vents
10240 Grilles and screens
10250 Service wall systems
10260 Wall and corner guards
10270 Access flooring
10290 Pest control
10300 Fireplaces and stoves
10340 Manufactured exterior specialties
10350 Flagpoles
10400 Identifying devices
10450 Pedestrian control devices
10500 Lockers
10520 Fire protection specialties
10530 Protective covers
10550 Postal specialties
10600 Partitions
10650 Operable partitions
10670 Storage shelving
10700 Exterior protection devices for openings
10750 Telephone specialties
10800 Toilet and bath accessories
10880 Scales
10900 Wardrobe and closet specialties

Division 11—Equipment

11010 Maintenance equipment
11020 Security and vault equipment
11030 Teller and service equipment
11040 Ecclesiastical equipment
11050 Library equipment
11060 Theater and stage equipment
11070 Instrumental equipment
11080 Registration equipment
11090 Checkroom equipment
11100 Mercantile equipment
11110 Commercial laundry and dry cleaning equipment
11120 Vending equipment
11130 Audio-visual equipment
11140 Vehicle service equipment
11150 Parking control equipment
11160 Loading dock equipment
11170 Solid waste handling equipment
11190 Detention equipment
11200 Water supply and treatment equipment
11280 Hydraulic gates and valves
11300 Fluid waste treatment and disposal equipment
11400 Food service equipment
11450 Residential equipment
11460 Unit kitchens
11470 Darkroom equipment
11480 Athletic, recreational, and therapeutic equipment
11500 Industrial and process equipment
11600 Laboratory equipment
11650 Planetarium equipment
11660 Observatory equipment
11680 Office equipment
11700 Medical equipment
11780 Mortuary equipment
11850 Navigation equipment
11870 Agricultural equipment

Division 12—Furnishings

12050 Fabrics
12100 Artwork
12300 Manufactured casework
12500 Window treatment
12600 Furniture and accessories
12670 Rugs and mats
12700 Multiple seating
12800 Interior plants and planters

Division 13—Special Construction

13010 Air supported structures
13020 Integrated assemblies
13030 Special purpose rooms
13080 Sound, vibration, and seismic control
13090 Radiation protection
13100 Nuclear reactors
13120 Pre-engineered structures
13150 Aquatic facilities
13175 Ice rinks
13180 Site constructed incinerators
13185 Kennels and animal shelters
13200 Liquid and gas storage tanks
13220 Filter underdrains and media
13230 Digester covers and appurtenances
13240 Oxygenation systems
13260 Sludge conditioning systems
13300 Utility control systems
13400 Industrial and process control systems
13500 Recording instrumentation
13550 Transportation control instrumentation
13600 Solar energy systems
13700 Wind energy systems
13750 Cogeneration systems
13800 Building automation systems
13900 Fire suppression and supervisory systems
13950 Special security construction

Division 14—Conveying Systems

14100 Dumbwaiters
14200 Elevators
14300 Escalators and moving walks
14400 Lifts
14500 Material handling systems
14600 Hoists and cranes
14700 Turntables
14800 Scaffolding
14900 Transportation systems

Division 15—Mechanical

15050 Basic mechanical materials and methods
15250 Mechanical insulation
15300 Fire protection
15400 Plumbing
15500 Heating, ventilating, and air conditioning
15550 Heat generation
15650 Refrigeration
15750 Heat transfer
15850 Air handling
15880 Air distribution
15950 Controls
15990 Testing, adjusting, and balancing

Division 16—Electrical

16050 Basic electrical materials and methods
16200 Power generation—built-up systems
16300 Medium voltage distribution
16400 Service and distribution
16500 Lighting
16600 Special systems
16700 Communications
16850 Electric resistance heating
16900 Controls
16950 Testing

Figure 8.1 (cont'd)

Part 3 tells how the products and materials are to be installed, applied, or otherwise put into place. This part also describes the examination and preparation required before installation, how quality control should be maintained in the field, and the requirements for the adjusting, cleaning, and protection of the finished work.

Figure 8.2 shows the section format outline listing all the possible articles of each part. The specifier selects which ones are appropriate for the item being specified.

4 SPECIFICATION WRITING GUIDELINES

Because specifications are legal documents as well as a way of communicating technical information, they must be complete, accurate, and unambiguous. The language must be precise. Some of the important things to remember include the following:

- Know what the standards and test methods referred to include and what parts of them are applicable to your project. They must also be the most current editions.
- Do not specify together the results and the methods proposed to achieve those results, as the two may conflict. For instance, if you specify that a carpet must meet certain ASTM test criteria and then specify a particular carpet that does not meet the stated requirements, the specification will be impossible to comply with.
- Do not include standards that cannot be measured. For example, saying that the work should be done in "a first-class manner" is subject to wide interpretation.
- Avoid exculpatory clauses. These are phrases that try to shift responsibility to the contractor or someone else in a very broad, general way. An example is something like "contractor shall be totally responsible for all . . ." Unless the clause is generally accepted wording or makes sense in the context of the specification, current legal opinion disapproves of such clauses, especially when they favor the person who wrote them.
- Avoid words or phrases that are ambiguous. The combination *and/or,* for example, is unclear and should be replaced with one word or the other. The abbreviation *etc.* is also vague, implies that a list can go on forever, and may include something you do not want. The word *any* implies the contractor has a choice. This is acceptable if you want to allow a choice, but most often you do not.
- Keep specifications as short as possible. Specifications can be terse, and you may want to omit words like *all, the, an,* and *a.*
- Describe only one major idea in each paragraph. This makes reading easier and improves comprehension. It also makes changing the specifications easier.

5 COORDINATION WITH THE CONSTRUCTION DRAWINGS

The technical specifications and the drawings are complementary. They must be written and checked to avoid conflicting requirements, duplication, omissions, and errors. There are several areas of particular concern.

First, the specifications should contain requirements for all the materials and construction indicated on the drawings. A common checklist used by both the specifications writer and the project manager or senior designer is one way to accomplish this.

Second, the terminology used in both documents should be the same. If the term *gypsum board* is used in the specifications, the same term should be shown on the drawings.

Third, dimensions and thicknesses should be indicated only on one document. Generally, sizes are shown on the drawings, and the standards for the materials and components that those sizes refer to are stated in the specifications.

Fourth, in most cases, notes on the drawings should not describe methods of installation or material qualities; these belong in the specifications. However, if the project is a small one with a limited amount of construction and a separate project manual

SECTION FORMAT OUTLINE

PART 1 GENERAL

Summary
Section Includes
Products furnished but not installed under this section
Products installed but not furnished under this section
Related sections
Allowances
Unit prices
Alternates/alternatives*

References

Definitions

System Descriptions
Design requirements
Performance requirements

Submittals
Product data
Shop drawings
Samples
Quality control submittals
- Design data
- Test reports
- Certificates
- Manufacturer's instructions
- Manufacturer's field reports

Contract closeout submittals
- Project record documents
- Operation and maintenance data
- Warranty

Quality Assurance
Qualifications
Regulatory requirements
Certifications
Field samples
Mock-ups
Pre-installation conference

Delivery, Storage, and Handling
Packing and shipping
Acceptance at site
Storage and protection

Project/Site* Conditions
Environmental requirements
Existing conditions
Field Measurements

Sequencing and Scheduling

Warranty
Special warranty

Maintenance
Maintenance service
Extra materials

PART 2 PRODUCTS

Manufacturers

Materials

Manufactured Units

Equipment

Components

Accessories

Mixes

Fabrication
Shop assembly
Shop/factory finishing
Tolerances

Source Quality Control
Tests
Inspection
Verification of performance

PART 3 EXECUTION

Examination
Verification of conditions

Preparation
Protection
Surface preparation

Erection Installation Application
Special techniques
Interface with other products
Tolerances

Field Quality Control
Tests
Inspection
Manufacturer's field service

Adjusting

Cleaning

Demonstration

Protection

Schedules

Figure 8.2 *Masterformat* Section Format Outline

Reproduced with permission of the Construction Specification Institute, Inc. (CSI) and Construction Specifications Canada (CSC) is not produced, some designers describe materials and installation procedures in detail on the drawings.

Although the specifications and drawings are complementary, you must give careful attention to the written word. When there is a conflict between the drawings and specifications, the courts have held that the specifications are more binding and take precedence over the drawings.

6 FURNITURE SPECIFICATIONS

Although the *Masterformat* system provides a place to specify furnishings (Division 12), most interior design projects have separate specifications for construction and for furniture and accessories. This is because the procedure for specifying, contracting for, and building construction items is different from specifying, purchasing, delivering, and installing furniture.

The exact method of specifying and ordering furniture varies with the size of the project and the particular working methods of the interior design office. The responsibilities of the client, interior designer, furniture dealer, and others are described in the formal contract between the interior designer and the client. These contracts and responsibilities are discussed in more detail in Chapters 9 and 20.

For example, many interior designers select furniture for the client and assume the responsibility of writing purchase orders and coordinating delivery and installation. In this case, furniture specifications are not written. The selections that are approved by the client are directly listed on the purchase order that is sent to the furniture dealer. This is the procedure most commonly used for residential work.

For commercial work and some residential projects, the interior designer may select the furniture but turn the job of ordering, installing, and billing over to one or more furniture dealers who supply the specific brands of furniture needed. The dealer contracts directly with the client and assumes all responsibilities.

On larger commercial projects where a quoted price is requested from one or more dealers bidding on the same work, furniture specifications must be written to state clearly the client's requirements. These specifications not only list in detail all the individual items required but also state bidding requirements, responsibilities, installation procedures, and methods of invoicing. Figures 8.3 and 8.4 show one page of the general conditions of a furniture specification and one specified item.

d. If within one month after issuing a purchase order, the dealer has not received a written acknowledgment from the factory, he must contact the factory to obtain a written acknowledgment.

e. If requested by the interior designer one month prior to delivery and/or move-in, the dealer must contact all manufacturers confirming all scheduled shipping and delivery dates. Further, this checking with the factory is to continue on a no less than weekly basis until the installation of the goods. The intention of the above is to insure complete knowledge of the furniture status.

f. The dealer shall indicate time allotment that is required to install, assuming all merchandise is in his hands at one time to meet client occupancy schedule.

g. If it is necessary for the interior designer to carry out any undue installation procedures that are already a part of the contractor's agreement of work performance, this work will be computed at the hourly billing rate and the amount spent deducted from the final invoice submitted.

2.07 <u>DAMAGED FURNITURE</u>

a. In cases of merchandise damaged in shipment, bidder will be responsible for immediate repairs acceptable to the interior designer or, if necessary, replacement of such item with new merchandise from manufacturer on time for installation due date. If this is not possible because of delivery date from manufacturer, the interior designer must be informed immediately.

b. The successful bidder or bidders shall be responsible for all claims against the manufacturer for manufacturing defects and against the carrier for all freight and/or drayage damage.

2.08 <u>CLEAN UP</u>

No accumulation of packaging or crating materials permitted at the site. Remove debris daily. Upon completion of work within an area ready for inspection, remove temporary protection and leave area clean and ready for use by Owner.

Figure 8.3 Page from the General Conditions of a Furniture Specification

Code on plans	Item Description		Quantity	Unit Cost	Total Cost
	<u>B & B AMERICA</u>				
LO-1	Item:	Three Seat Sofa Coronado #05-103 OOY	2		
	Size:	83 ⅛" W × 36 ⅝" D × 30 ¾" H			
	Upholstery:	Jack Lenor Larsen Doria 1 I Henna Wool 54" W			
	Tag for:	Reception			
	Delivery Time:				

Figure 8.4 Page from a Furniture Specification

SAMPLE QUESTIONS

1. What would be the best way to assure that the finish on new millwork matches the finish on existing millwork on a remodeling project?

    1. Indicate on the drawings and in the specifications that the new work should match the existing work.
    2. Ask the client to find out what was used on the old job and include that in the specifications.
    3. Research the manufacturer and color of the existing finish and include that information in the specifications.
    4. Ask the painting contractor to investigate what finish was previously used and include that information on the finish schedule.

2. If a client wanted to obtain the most competitive bid price possible while still being assured that the product was acceptable, what type of specification should you write?

    1. open
    2. reference
    3. performance
    4. base-bid with approved equal

3. Which item in the following excerpt from a specification is a performance specification?

Part 2—Products

2.01 Metal Support Material

General: To the extent not otherwise indicated, comply with ASTM C754 for metal system supporting gypsum wallboard.

Ceiling suspension main runners: $1^1/_2$-inch steel channels, cold rolled.

Hanger wire: ASTM A641, soft, Class 1 galvanized, prestretched; sized in accordance with ASTM C754.

Hanger anchorage devices: size for 3 times calculated loads, except size direct-pull concrete inserts for 5 times calculated loads.

Studs: ASTM C645; 25 gage, $2^1/_2$ inches deep, except as otherwise indicated.

Runners: Match studs; type recommended by stud manufacturer for vertical abutment of drywall work at other work.

    1. ceiling suspension main runners
    2. hanger wire
    3. hanger anchorage devices
    4. runners

4. Where would you find application instructions for vinyl wall covering?

    1. in Part 1 of Section 09950, Wall Coverings
    2. in Part 2 of Section 09950, Wall Coverings
    3. in Part 3 of Section 09950, Wall Coverings
    4. in a finish schedule at the end of Section 09950, Wall Coverings

5. Which of the following is more legally binding?

    1. drawings
    2. specifications
    3. schedules
    4. all of the above

6. To minimize conflicts in the contract documents, what is the LEAST important action the interior designer can take?

    1. Show only dimensions on the drawings.
    2. Have someone check the drawings before they are issued.
    3. Write the specifications after the drawings are essentially complete.
    4. Make sure terminology in the specifications is the same as the drawings.

7. Specifications can be made most concise by following which of the following guidelines?

    1. Use reference standard specifications.
    2. Avoid the use of words like a, the, and all.
    3. Use phrases instead of complete sentences.
    4. Use descriptive specifications.

8. Which of the following would not be found in the project manual?

1. performance bond
2. testing requirements
3. cost estimate
4. instructions to bidders

9. What is the best way to get the exact product you and the client want?

1. Show the configuration of the product on the drawings and call it out specifically.
2. Write a closed, descriptive specification.
3. Require that the contractor submit samples of all items before purchasing.
4. List the information in a proprietary specification.

10. What does the phrase *or approved equal* mean in a specification?

1. The client must agree to the use of a product selected by the contractor.
2. The contractor may propose a substitution but it must be approved by the interior designer.
3. An alternate product may be bid on by the contractor if he or she is sure it provides the same quality of the product specified.
4. The interior designer and client can permit the substitution of an alternate product if they feel it is better than the one specified.

9 CONTRACT DOCUMENTS AND BIDDING PROCEDURES

Contract documents consist of the owner-contractor agreement; the general conditions of the contract; the supplementary conditions of the contract (if any); the drawings, specifications, and addenda issued before execution of the contract; any other documents specifically listed in the agreement; and modifications issued after execution of the contract. A modification is a change order, a written amendment to the contract signed by both parties, a written interpretation issued by the interior designer, or a written order for a minor change in the work.

Drawings and specifications have been discussed in previous chapters. Change orders are discussed in Chapter 22. This chapter outlines the major provisions of the other contract documents. In addition, bidding documents and bidding procedures are outlined. However, bidding documents are not part of the contract, although they are often bound into the project manual. Refer to Chapter 20 for information on owner-designer agreements.

Because the range of interior design services is wide, from selection of furnishings and accessories for a single residential living room to interior construction and furnishings installation for large corporate headquarters, the type and complexity of contract documents varies. This chapter describes the documents that define the contractual agreement between the owner and the contractor for mid- to large-scale projects.

1 METHODS OF COMPLETING INTERIOR DESIGN PROJECTS

The completion of an interior design project can occur in several ways. How it is accomplished, its size and complexity, and the specific responsibilities of the interior designer determine the types of contract documents that should be used.

In the simplest case, the owner hires the interior designer to perform a limited scope of work, such as selecting finishes and furniture. The designer works under a letter of agreement with the owner, completing the design work and preparing furniture and finish specifications, which are then given to various vendors and contractors. The owner contracts with these vendors directly to have the work completed. In some situations, the designer may purchase furniture directly for the client. This is the method commonly used for residential work.

For larger, more complex projects, the interior designer may be the owner's primary consultant, contracting with other consultants such as architects, structural engineers, electrical engineers, and mechanical engineers to develop the drawings and specifications for the job. Larger projects may consist of both interior construction and furniture, furnishings, and equipment (FF&E). The interior designer completes the design and preparation of drawings and specifications within the limits of state laws and local building code regulations and has other consultants do the design work in their particular area of expertise. This method is commonly used for commercial projects.

In other cases, the interior designer works as a consultant to the architect on the project or with an architect but under separate contract to the owner. In these instances, the architect is responsible for interior construction and the interior designer is responsible for only furniture, furnishings, and equipment. This approach is also common for commercial projects where the extent of the structural work and local laws require that certain drawings be prepared and stamped by a licensed architect.

Regardless of whether the interior designer is working alone or with an architect, interior design projects that involve both construction and furnishings are typically completed under two contracts, one for construction and one for furniture, fixtures, and equipment. The following sections describe commonly used FF&E contract documents.

2 OWNER-CONTRACTOR AGREEMENT

Although the owner enters into an agreement directly with the contractor (or contractors) for construction and FF&E, the interior designer must be familiar with the various provisions of this agreement. The owner-contractor agreement can be written by the designer's attorney or provided by the owner, or standard professional association forms may be used.

Two such forms are the Standard Form of Agreement Between Owner and Contractor for Furniture, Furnishings and Equipment and the Abbreviated Form of Agreement Between Owner and Contractor for Furniture, Furnishings and Equipment Where the Basis of Payment Is a Stipulated Sum. These documents, numbered A171 and A177, respectively, have been developed by the American Institute of Architects (AIA) and the American Society of Interior Designers (ASID). This section discusses the major provisions in these documents.

A. Identification of Contract Documents

The first article specifies that the contract documents include the agreement, the conditions of the contract (general, supplementary, and other conditions), the drawings, the schedules and specifications, all addenda, and all modifications issued after the execution of the agreement. It refers to a later article in which all the documents are listed in detail. The purpose of this article is to include all the other documents by reference.

B. Basic Provisions

Some provisions are common to all contracts. These include a description of the work, the time of commencement and substantial completion, and the contract sum. These are included in several articles in the AIA/ASID documents.

The work normally includes what is described in the contract documents, primarily the drawings and specifications. Any exclusions can be described in the owner-contractor agreement as well as in the other contract documents when they are identified as being the responsibility of other parties.

The date of commencement is an important time because it is from this date that construction completion time is measured. The date can be a specific calendar date specified in the agreement or can be the date when the contractor is given a notice-to-proceed letter by the owner.

The time of substantial completion is expressed with a specific calendar date or by a number of calendar days from the date of commencement. *Substantial completion* is defined as the stage in the progress of the work when the work or a designated portion thereof is sufficiently complete according to the contract documents so the owner can occupy or utilize the site though a few minor items may remain to be completed or corrected. Completion time may be extended as provided for in the general conditions when circumstances are beyond the control of the contractor. If a particular completion date is important to the owner, provisions for liquidated damages may be included. *Liquidated damages* are moneys paid by the contractor to the owner for every day the project is late. They represent actual anticipated losses the owner will incur if the project is not completed on time. For example, if an owner cannot move and must pay double rent, the liquidated damages may be the amount of the extra rent.

In many cases, a liquidated damage provision is accompanied by a bonus provision so the contractor receives a payment for early completion. This, too, is usually based on a realistic cost savings the owner will realize for early completion. If a penalty clause is included (which is different from liquidated damages), a bonus provision *must* also be included.

The contract sum states the compensation the contractor will receive for doing the work.

C. Progress Payments

Based on applications for payment submitted by the contractor, the owner makes periodic payments, usually monthly, to the contractor. The owner-contractor agreement defines how these payments are to be made.

In the standard AIA/ASID agreement forms, the amount due in any period is based on the percentage of completed work and any materials purchased and stored but not yet incorporated into the work, less any moneys already paid. A certain percentage of each payment, usually ten percent, is withheld until final completion of the work as a protection of the owner against incomplete or defective work on the part of the contractor. This percentage is called the *retainage* (or *holdback* in Canada).

To receive payment, the contractor must submit an application for payment to the interior designer listing the completed work and stored materials. The interior designer then reviews the application, verifies that it is correct, and recommends payment to the owner, who then makes payment. If there is work in dispute, the interior designer may choose not to certify payment of all or a portion of the amount until the problem is resolved.

3 GENERAL CONDITIONS OF THE CONTRACT

The General Conditions of the Contract for Furniture, Furnishings and Equipment (AIA/ASID Form A271) is one of the most important parts in the entire set of contract documents. It is incorporated by specific reference into the owner-interior designer agreement as well as the owner-contractor agreement. You should obtain a copy of the General Conditions and read the entire document before the NCIDQ exam. This section discusses the major articles in this document. Some of the topics included in the General Conditions but not discussed here include definitions and execution of the contract, subcontractors, insurance, termination of the contract, and miscellaneous provisions.

A shortened version of the General Conditions is given in the Abbreviated Form of Agreement Between Owner and Contractor for Furniture, Furnishings and Equipment Where the Basis of Payment Is a Stipulated Sum when the scope of the project does not require the separate version of the general conditions.

One area of particular interest to interior designers is the relationship of the Uniform Commercial Code (UCC) with the other contract provisions of a project. The Uniform Commercial Code is applicable in all states and governs all contracts dealing with the sale of goods costing more than $500. The provisions of the UCC may govern some aspects of an interior design project if specific written provisions are not included in the contract. The General Conditions of the Contract for Furniture, Furnishings and Equipment has been written to recognize the commercial standards of the UCC, especially in the areas of inspection, acceptance, and rejection of goods, but in some cases the UCC may take precedence over the contract. In other cases, state laws may override some provisions of the UCC. The interior designer must know the provisions of the UCC and his or her own state's laws if the designer is acting as a reseller of furniture and furnishings.

A. Duties and Responsibilities of the Interior Designer

Article 2 of the General Conditions states the interior designer's roles and responsibilities in contract administration. Some of these are discussed in more detail in Chapter 20, but the typical duties the interior designer performs are described here.

The interior designer acts as the owner's representative, advises and consults with the owner, and may act on behalf of the owner to the extent provided in the contract documents. The designer assists the owner in coordinating schedules for delivery and installation but is *not* responsible for the malfeasance of the contractor or any supplier to perform their duties.

The interior designer visits the project premises as necessary to become familiar with the progress of the work and to determine, in general, if the work is proceeding according to the contract documents. The designer keeps the owner informed of the progress and quality of the work but is not required to make exhaustive or continuous inspections. However, one paragraph reiterates that the interior designer does not have control over the means, methods, or procedures of construction, procurement, shipment, delivery, or installation. The designer is also not responsible for safety precautions or acts of omission of the contractor, subcontractors, or suppliers.

The interior designer can recommend to the owner to reject work that does not conform to the contract documents. The designer also has the authority to require special inspections or testing of the work. The interior designer does not have the authority to reject nonconforming work, to stop the work, or to terminate the contract on behalf of the owner. In any case, the actions or authority of the interior designer do not create any duty or responsibility to the contractor, subcontractors, or others.

The designer reviews shop drawings and other submittals for the limited purpose of checking for conformance with the design concept expressed in the contract documents.

The interior designer prepares change orders and may authorize minor changes in the work that do not involve adjusting either the contract sum or contract time and that are not inconsistent with the intent of the contract documents.

The interior designer interprets and decides on matters concerning the requirements of the contract documents and the performance of work if requested by either the owner or contractor. If the designer's interpretation is not acceptable, there are provisions in the General Conditions for arbitration. The designer's decisions concerning matters related to aesthetic effect are final if consistent with the intent shown in the documents.

The interior designer also conducts a final inspection to determine the dates of substantial completion and final completion and issues a final certificate for payment.

B. Duties, Rights, and Responsibilities of the Owner

Article 3 specifies the duties, rights, and responsibilities of the owner. Among these is the responsibility to furnish evidence, at the request of the contractor, that financial arrangements have been made to fulfill the owner's obligations under the contract—in other words, to pay the contractor.

The owner must furnish all drawings describing the physical characteristics of the job and must furnish, free of charge, three copies of the drawings and project manual required for the completion of the work. Additionally, the owner must provide (1) access to the area of work at reasonable times; (2) suitable space for the receipt and storage of materials, furniture, and equipment; and (3) temporary utilities on the job site and vertical transportation necessary for the execution of the work.

If the contractor fails to correct work not in conformance with the contract documents or persistently fails to carry out such work, the owner may order the contractor to stop the work until the cause for the order is eliminated.

The owner has the right to carry out the work if the contractor fails in his or her duties to correctly do so. The contractor has seven days from receiving written notice from the owner to commence corrections.

C. Duties and Responsibilities of the Contractor

The contractor is solely responsible for all fabrication, delivery, and installation means, methods, techniques, and procedures, and for coordinating all portions of the work. This includes visiting and inspecting the project premises before shipment and installation to confirm that everything is ready for the work. The contractor must report any problems to the owner. The contractor is also responsible to the owner for the acts and omissions of all subcontractors and other people performing work under a contract with the contractor.

It is not the contractor's responsibility to ascertain that the contract documents conform to building codes, ordinances, and other regulations. However, if the contractor notices some variance, he or she must notify the interior designer in writing. If the contractor does not give this notice and proceeds to perform work knowingly in variance with some regulation, the contractor assumes full responsibility for such work and must bear all costs to correct the situation.

The contractor is also obligated to provide a schedule for the owner's and designer's information, to keep it current, and to conform to it. The contractor must cooperate with the owner and designer in coordinating the schedule with the schedules of other contractors doing work.

The General Conditions includes a section on indemnification. To indemnify is to secure against loss or damage, and the indemnification clause is intended to protect the owner and designer against situations where a person is injured due to the negligence of the contractor or the contractor's agents. The clause also is intended to protect the owner and architect against claims from property damage other than to the work itself. Under the section on indemnification, it is stated that, to the extent provided by law, the contractor shall indemnify and hold harmless the owner, interior designer, and their agents and employees against claims, damages, and expenses arising out of performance of the work. However, this clause does not relieve the interior designer of his or her liability for errors in the drawings, specifications, or administration of the contract.

D. Work by Owner or Separate Contractors

The owner has the right to perform work related to the project with the owner's own forces and to award separate contracts for certain work. However, exercising this right does require the owner to provide for coordination of his or her own forces and to act with the same obligations and rights as any contractor would have. This clause is especially important for interior work because there are usually separate contracts for FF&E and construction.

E. Installation

Article 7 of AIA/ASID A271 specifies the procedures and responsibilities for installation of furniture, furnishings, and equipment. According to this article, the owner has the following responsibilities:

- To make adequate facilities available for the delivery, unloading, staging, and storage of furniture and equipment.

- To make sure that all delivery and staging areas and the route used to deliver furniture are free of obstacles or other trades that might impede the contractor.

- To provide the contractor with a firm schedule for the use of unloading facilities and elevators.

- To inspect the work upon delivery for the sole purpose of identifying materials, furniture, and equipment and to verify quantities. It is important to note that this inspection is not construed as final or as constituting acceptance of or taking charge or control over the items delivered even if they are partially paid for. If there is damage, the owner must notify the contractor, who should then have the opportunity to correct the problem. If any work or furniture is later found to be defective or not in accordance with the contract documents, the owner may revoke acceptance.

- To abide by the agreed critical dates in the progress schedule submitted by the contractor. If the owner fails to fulfill obligations according to these dates, then the owner is responsible for any costs or penalties incurred by the contractor.

- To provide security against loss or damage of furniture and equipment stored at the site between the dates of delivery and final acceptance by the owner.

The contractor, likewise, has certain responsibilities for installation. Among these are the following:

- To select the route to be used within the project premises for delivery, from point of delivery to final placement. The owner or designer, however, can make reasonable objection to a selected route.

- To tell the owner about any special equipment or services required for the proper delivery and installation of the work.

- To do all cutting, fitting, or patching required to complete the work and not to alter the work of others without first getting the written consent of the owner.

- To provide labor and means and methods of carrying out the work according to prevailing labor conditions at the job site.

F. Time

The contract time is the period from the starting date established in the agreement to the time of substantial completion, including any authorized adjustments. The contractor is expected to proceed expeditiously with adequate work forces and complete the work within the allotted time. The contract time may be extended by change order if delays occur beyond the contractor's control, such as acts or neglects of the owner or interior designer, labor disputes, fire, unavoidable casualties, or transportation delays.

G. Payments and Completion

Article 10 specifies the procedures for paying the contractor. The contractor makes monthly applications for payment based on the percentage of work completed. The interior designer reviews these applications and issues to the owner a certificate for payment or decides to withhold issuance if there is a valid reason. The General Conditions clearly states that the contractor warrants that title to all work, materials, furniture, and equipment covered by an application for payment will pass to the owner and that they are free of liens or other encumbrances. The exact procedures the designer must follow are described in more detail in Chapter 22.

H. Protection of Persons and Property

The contractor is exclusively responsible for onsite safety and precautions against damage to persons and property. This includes the contractor's employees, other people affected by the work, the work itself, furniture, furnishings, equipment, and adjacent property. If any damage to the work is sustained due to inadequate protection, the contractor must repair or correct it. However, this does not include damages caused by acts of the owner or interior designer.

I. Changes in the Work

The General Conditions allow for changes to be made in the work after execution of the contract. If changes are required, they are usually due to unforeseen conditions or changes desired by the owner. These changes are made by a *change order,* which is based on written agreement among the owner, contractor, and interior designer concerning the extent of the change and its cost and schedule implications. A change order is always required whenever there is a modification of contract cost or time, and it must be signed by the owner, the contractor, and the interior designer. The interior designer has the authority to make minor changes if they do not involve an adjustment in contract sum or the contract time. Change order procedures are discussed in more detail in Chapter 22, and a sample change order is shown in Figure 22.3.

J. Uncovering and Correction of Work

If the contract documents state that certain portions of the work are to be observed by the interior designer before being covered or enclosed and the contractor proceeds with covering them, then the contractor must uncover them at no additional charge on request by the designer. If there is no specific mention of an item to be observed before covering and if the work is in accordance with the contract documents, the interior designer may ask that it be uncovered, but the cost is borne by the owner through a change order. If it is found that there is nonconforming work, then the contractor is responsible for the additional cost.

The contractor must correct work recommended for rejection by the interior designer for failing to conform to the requirement of the contract documents. The contractor must bear the cost of such corrections, including testing, inspections, and compensation for the designer's services connected with the correction.

If the owner so chooses, he or she can accept nonconforming work. Because this entails a change in the contract, it must be done by written change order and, if appropriate, the contract sum may be reduced.

4 SUPPLEMENTARY CONDITIONS OF THE CONTRACT

Because of the unique nature of interior design construction and furnishings projects, not every condition can be covered in a standard document such as the General Conditions of the Contract for Furniture, Furnishings and Equipment. Each job must be customized to accommodate different clients, governmental regulations, and local laws. Information that is unique to each project can be included in one of four areas: in the bidding requirements if related to bidding, in the owner-contractor agreement if it relates to contractual matters, in the Supplementary Conditions if it modifies the General Conditions, or in Division 1 (General Requirements) of the specifications in the project manual. For example, limits of insurance and other bonding and insurance requirements are very specific to each client and project type. These are often placed in the Supplementary General Conditions.

The American Institute of Architects and the American Society of Interior Designers have jointly produced form A571, Guide for Interiors Supplementary Conditions, which suggests what types of modifications are typically required.

However, just as many clients may have their own standard forms for general conditions, they may also have their own requirements for modifications. You should use whichever form is most appropriate. In any case, modification to the general or supplementary conditions (as with any contract) should only be done with the advice of legal counsel.

5 BIDDING PROCEDURES

Price quotes and contracts between the owner and the contractor are established in one of two ways. With a *negotiated contract,* the owner (with the possible assistance of the interior designer) selects a contractor to do the work and then has the contractor look at the drawings and work up a price quote. The contractor may be selected based on a previous working relationship, on the recommendations of others, or both. With a *bid contract* (or *tendered contract* in Canada), the drawings and specifications are completed by the interior designer (and other consultants, if necessary) and then sent to several general contractors who bid on the work defined by the contract documents. The owner (again, with the assistance of the interior designer) can then select the contractor based on cost as well as experience, schedule, and other criteria.

Competitive bidding for construction and, when feasible, furniture and furnishings, is popular with many owners because it usually results in the lowest cost. For most public agencies, bidding is mandatory. However, it must be done within clearly defined guidelines to protect the owner from disreputable contractors and unethical bidding practices. Through many years of practice, bidding procedures have generally been standardized and codified in various industry association documents. Everyone involved with the process knows the rules and what is expected. This section describes the typical procedures and documents for bidding. These are described in more detail in AIA document A771, Instructions to Interiors Bidders.

A. Prequalification of Bidders

Bidding may be open to any contractor or restricted to a list of contractors who have been prequalified by the owner. The purpose of prequalification is to select only those contractors who meet certain standards of reliability, experience, financial stability, and performance. An owner contemplating the construction of a million-dollar corporate office headquarters would not be comfortable reviewing the bid of a small home contractor. Once these standards have been met, the owner is better able to review their bids based primarily on price, personnel, and completion time.

Prequalification is usually based on information submitted by contractors concerning their financial qualifications, personnel, experience, references, size, bonding capability, and any special qualities that make them particularly suited for the project under consideration. For public work, when prequalification is allowed, it is usually based on financial assets and the size of the firm.

B. Advertising for Bids

There are two ways to notify prospective bidders. The first is by advertising in newspapers and trade journals. This type of announcement simply states the project name and location and the fact that bids are being accepted. The advertisement gives a brief description of the project, the time and place for receiving bids, where bid documents can be obtained, the conditions for bidding, and other pertinent information. Advertising for bids is usually required for public work, although much private work is also advertised if it is open bidding.

For prequalified bidders, an invitation to bid is sent to the prospective bidders. The invitation contains the same information listed above for bid advertisements. Even with a prequalified list, there should be enough bidders to encourage price competition. If furniture and fixtures are being bid on private work, it is usually done on a prequalified basis because there are usually only a few dealers that can bid on the same furniture. These dealers are known ahead of time by the interior designer.

C. Availability of Bid Documents

Bid documents are generally made available through the interior designer's office. Each bidder receives the required documents including prints of the drawings, specifications, bidding documents, bid forms, and other required items. It is general practice to require that each bidder put down a deposit on each set of documents taken. The deposit may be returned when the documents are returned in usable condition after bidding. In some cases, the documents are loaned with no deposit required. Extra sets of documents over a certain number can be purchased by the contractor. In most large cities, documents are also put on file in a central plan room where subcontractors and material suppliers can review them.

D. Substitutions

During bidding, many contractors request that substitutions be considered for some of the materials specified. This most often happens when there are proprietary specifications or a very limited list of acceptable manufacturers. The conditions under which substitutions will be considered and the procedures for reviewing submissions should be clearly defined in the instructions to bidders.

Generally, bidders are required to submit requests for approval at least ten days before the bid opening. The requests must include the name of the material or equipment for which the substitution is submitted along with complete back-up information about the proposed substitution. The burden of proof of the merit of the substitution rests with the bidder. The interior designer then reviews the submission and may either reject it or approve it. If approved, the interior designer issues an addendum stating this fact and sends it to all the bidders.

E. Alternates

An *alternate* is a request included in the bidding documents asking the contractor to supply a price for some type of variation from the base bid. This may be a change in materials or level of quality of a material, a deletion of some component, or the addition of some construction element. For example, the base bid may include carpet as a floor covering in a room, while an alternate may be to substitute wood flooring for the carpet.

Alternates allow the owner some flexibility in modifying the cost of a project when the bids are submitted by varying the quantity or quality of portions of the job. They also allow the owner to select certain options based on firm prices rather than preliminary estimates.

Alternates are called *add-alternates* if they add to the base bid or *deduct-alternates* if they reduce the base amount. Because alternates require more time for both the interior designer and bidders to prepare, they should be used carefully and should not be a substitute for conscientious cost estimating and reasonable design for the base-bid amount.

When evaluating the bids, the selected alternates should be used to arrive at the lowest overall bid, but alternates should not be manipulated to favor one bidder over another.

F. Unit Prices

Unit prices are set costs for certain portions of the work based on individual quantities such as linear feet or square yards of installed material. When required, they are listed on the bid form and provide a basis for determining changes to the contract. For example, a cost per square foot for adding parquet flooring may be requested if the full extent of this type of flooring is unknown when bids are received. Even though the total cost may not be known, the unit costs of the bidders can be compared.

If unit prices are used when work is deleted from the contract, the amount of credit is usually less than the price for an additional quantity of the same item. Spaces should be provided in the bid form for both add and deduct amounts when applicable.

G. Addenda

An *addendum* is a written or graphic document issued by the interior designer before the execution of the contract that modifies or interprets the bidding documents by additions, deletions, clarifications, or corrections. During the bidding process, there are always questions that need answers, errors that are discovered, and changes that the owner or interior designer decides to make. Addenda are instruments to do this. They are issued during the bidding process before bids are submitted. An example of an addendum is shown in Figure 9.1. When an addendum is issued, it is sent to all bidders no later than four or five days before receipt of bids to give all the bidders ample opportunity to study the document and modify their proposals accordingly.

H. Prebid Conference

On some projects, it is advantageous to hold a prebid conference. This is a meeting with the interior designer, owner, architect (if one is involved), engineering consultants, and bidders during which the bidders can ask questions and the interior designer and owner can emphasize particularly important conditions of the project. On very large projects, there may be a separate conference for mechanical subcontract bidders, electrical bidders, and so on. During these conferences, the interior designer should have someone take complete notes concerning the items discussed. A copy of the notes should be sent to all bidders, whether or not they were in attendance.

I. Evaluation and Awarding of the Bid

The interior designer may assist the owner in evaluating the bids. This includes not only looking for the lowest proposed contract sum but also reviewing prices for alternates, substitutions, lists of proposed subcontractors, qualification statements, and other documentation required by the instruction to bidders. The owner has the right to reject any or all bids, to reject bids not accompanied by the required bid bond or other documentation, and to reject a bid that is in any way incomplete or irregular.

If all the bids exceed the project budget and the owner-designer agreement fixes a limit on construction costs, the owner has one of four options:

1. To rebid (or renegotiate if it is a negotiated contract).
2. To authorize an increase in the construction cost and proceed with the project.

ADDENDUM #2

Project: Global Transportation Headquarters
Project #: 9042
Date: July 27, 1990

Interiors by ABC, Inc.
2776 N. Ashley

To all general contract bidders of record on the project referenced above:

The contract documents are modified as follows:

1. Instructions to bidders, Page 1: Bid due date is changed to 4:00 pm, Tuesday, August 12, 1990.
2. Specification section 06400, Page 06400-3: Veneer cut is changed from quarter sliced oak to plain sliced oak.
3. Detail 5, Sheet A-6: Width of storage cabinet should be 1'-9", not 2'-0".

Figure 9.1 Addendum

3. To work with the interior designer in revising the scope of the project to reduce costs
4. To abandon the project.

Rebidding seldom results in any significant reduction in cost unless the bidding marketplace is changing rapidly. If the project is revised, the extra cost of having the interior designer modify the documents may be borne by the owner unless there are contract provisions specifying responsibility for changing the drawings or specifications if the project comes in over budget. One of the advantages of including alternates in the bid is having a flexible method of deleting or substituting materials or construction elements to reduce the project cost if the bid is too high.

6 BIDDING DOCUMENTS

Bidding documents are usually prepared by the interior designer using standard forms or forms provided by the owner. Many commercial clients who engage in much building have developed their own forms and procedures, but they are typically similar in content to standard forms. The bidding documents are usually bound into the project manual, but they are not a legal part of the contract documents.

The bidding documents usually include

- the advertisement or invitation to bid
- instruction to bidders
- bid forms
- bid security information
- requirements for a performance bond, if required
- requirements for a labor and material payment bond, if required

Other documents that are sometimes added include qualification forms, a subcontractor list form, requirements for certificates of insurance and compliance with applicable laws and regulations (such as equal employment opportunity laws), and information available to bidders, such as drawings of existing construction.

In addition to the bidding documents that are not part of the contract documents, the bidding package also includes the drawings, specifications, general and supplementary conditions of the contract, addenda issued before the receipt of bids, and the form of agreement between owner and contractor.

A. Advertisement to Bid

As previously mentioned, public bidding requires that bidding for the proposed project be advertised in one or more newspapers and trade publications. If a list of prequalified bidders is being used, an invitation to bid is sent to those contractors. On some projects, the interior designer may simply telephone the contractors on the prequalified list to ask if they would like to bid. The advertisement or invitation to bid is also printed and bound into the project manual with the other bidding documents.

B. Instructions to Bidders

The instructions to bidders outline the procedures and requirements that the bidders must follow in submitting bids, how the bids will be considered, and submittals required of the successful bidder. The AIA document A771, *Instructions to Interiors Bidders,* is often used. Other organizations also produce similar forms. Instructions to bidders normally include the following items:

- *Bidders' representation:* In making a bid, the bidder represents that he or she has read and understood the documents, reviewed the plans and specifications, and visited the site to become familiar with the conditions under which the work will take place.
- *Bidding documents:* This states where the documents may be obtained, provisions for bid security, and what the contractor and subcontractors should do if they discover an error or inconsistency. In such a case, they should make a written request to the interior designer for clarification at least seven days before bid opening. The interior designer then issues an addendum to all bidders answering the questions.
- *Substitutions:* The procedures required for submitting substitution proposals and having

them considered are outlined. No substitutions should be considered after the contract award unless there is a valid reason.

- *Bidding procedures:* This portion specifies how the bid form is to be filled in, what kind of bid security is to accompany the bid, how the bid should be physically submitted, and provisions for modification and withdrawal of bids. Bids are normally submitted in sealed envelopes with the name of the party receiving the bid on the outside, along with the project name and the name of the company submitting it.
- *Consideration of bids:* The procedure for opening bids and reviewing them is stated, including under what conditions bids may be rejected, how they will be evaluated, and conditions for award of the contract. Bids may be opened publicly or privately, although government projects require a public opening.
- *Bonds:* The required bonds and the time during which they must be delivered are outlined. The cost of bonds is included in the bidder's price.

C. Bid Forms

There should be a standard form on which all the bidders enter the required information to ensure that all bids will be identical in format, making it easier to compare and evaluate them. One such form is illustrated in Figure 9.2. The bid form should contain space for the amount of the base bid, the price for the alternates (if any), unit prices (if any), and the number of calendar or work days in which the bidder proposes to complete the work. Space should be provided for the bidder to acknowledge receipt of any addenda. The bid form must be signed by someone legally empowered to bind the contractor to the owner in a contract.

D. Bid Security

Bid security is used to ensure that the successful bidder will enter into a contract with the owner. The owner may not require it on small interior design contracts, and it is sometimes waived on larger projects. The final decision concerning the requirement for bid security is the owner's. The form of the bid security may be a certified check, cashier's check, or *bid bond.* If the successful bidder does not enter into an agreement, the bid security may be retained and compensates for the difference between the low bid and the next lowest bidder. The amount of the bid security is either set as a fixed price or as a percentage of the bid; it is usually about five percent of the estimated cost of the work or of the bid price.

E. Performance Bonds

A *performance bond* is a statement by a surety company that obligates the surety company to complete construction of the project should the contractor default on his or her obligations. If this happens, the surety company may complete construction by hiring another contractor, or it may simply supply additional money to the defaulting contractor to allow construction to proceed.

Performance bonds are usually mandatory on public work and advisable on private work. The cost of the performance bond is a percentage of the construction cost (around three percent) and is ultimately paid by the owner because it is included in the total amount of the contract price. The interior designer or owner should verify that the bond is written by a surety able to issue bonds in the particular state where the work will take place.

F. Labor and Material Payment Bonds

Although a performance bond ensures the completion of the contract, it does not guarantee payment for labor and materials by a defaulting contractor. The result of nonpayment could be liens against the property or litigation by subcontractors and material suppliers. Accordingly, a *labor and material payment bond* is usually required along with a performance bond to protect the owner against both types of problems.

BID FORM

We have received the documents titles

"____",

dated ____________________, as prepared by Interiors by ABC, Inc.

We have also received Addenda number ____________________________

and have included their provisions in this bid. We have examined both the documents and the site and hereby propose to furnish all labor, materials, equipment, and transportation in strict accordance with the documents for the full completion of the project for the sum of:

____ dollars,

($ __________________), which sum is hereby designated as BASE BID.

Overhead, profit, taxes, and freight costs are to included in the BASE BID sum.

ALTERNATES

ALTERNATE #1, add/deduct: $ __________________________.

ALTERNATE #2, add/deduct: $ __________________________.

ALTERNATE #3, add/deduct: $ __________________________.

ALTERNATE #4, add/deduct: $ __________________________.

Circle add or deduct as appropriate.

Alternates are itemized in Section 01005 of the Specifications.

Unit prices will be required at the time of bid and shall be attached to the bid form. Unit price is defined as the price per unit of measurement for materials and labor to provide the item, plus overhead and profit. Breakout labor and material for each case.

If the undersigned is notified of the acceptance of this bid, within thirty (30) days after the date set for opening thereof, or any time thereafter before this bid is withdrawn, he or she agrees to execute a Contract in the form of these documents and to furnish the necessary bonds together with certificate of Insurance as required by the Contract Documents and to provide the required work for compensation as computed from the bids sums included in this bid.

Time of completion: The undersigned agrees, if awarded the Contract, to commence work immediately after receiving official Notice to Proceed and to complete the Work not later than:

__________________.

Name of Firm: ____

Telephone: ________________________ Date: ________________________

Signed: __________________________

Printed: __________________________

Title: __________________________

Figure 9.2 Bid Form

SAMPLE QUESTIONS

1. Which of the following is NOT a part of the contract documents?

   1. addenda
   2. bid form
   3. specifications
   4. owner-contractor agreement

2. Two weeks before the bids are due on a large restaurant project, one of the contractors asks if he can price a type of ceiling tile that was not listed in the specifications. As the interior designer on the job, what action should you take?

   1. Advise the contractor that he should submit back-up proof with the bid that the proposed change is equal to what was specified.
   2. Refer the contractor to the owner, who will make the final determination and then notify the other bidders that this has been done.
   3. Tell the contractor to request approval in writing.
   4. Issue an addendum stating that one of the contractors has asked for permission to price an alternate and that all contractors may do this.

3. What method of selecting a contractor would be best for a client who wanted to get the lowest price for remodeling a complex data-processing facility?

   1. State the requirements of the project in an advertisement for bidders in local trade journals and newspapers.
   2. Select a qualified contractor and negotiate a fixed cost based on detailed drawings and specifications.
   3. Negotiate the lowest possible price with one contractor and then bid the project if the first cost is over the client's budget.
   4. Develop a list of contractors who have experience in the project type and then ask them to bid on the job.

4. If, during construction of a project, the contractor noticed that a handrail did not meet the local building codes, what action could the designer reasonably expect the contractor to take?

   1. The contractor should notify the designer in writing of the discrepancy.
   2. The contractor should correct the situation and submit a change order for the extra work.
   3. The contractor should build the handrail according to the contract documents because conformance to building codes is the designer's responsibility.
   4. The contractor should notify the designer of the problem and suggest a remedy.

5. Which of the following may the interior designer NOT do under terms of the General Conditions of the Contract for Furniture, Furnishings and Equipment?

   1. Prepare change orders and authorize minor changes in the work.
   2. Determine the date of substantial completion.
   3. Reject work that does not meet the requirements of the drawings.
   4. Demand that a special inspection be made to determine if the work conforms to the specifications.

6. What could the interior designer suggest that the owner require of the contractor to avoid liens against the project?

   1. bid bond
   2. bid security
   3. performance bond
   4. labor and material payment bond

7. As the designer for the interior furnishings of a large public hospital project financed with bond money, you have assisted the city government in preparing the bidding documents. When the bids are opened from five qualified contractors, they are all

over budget, ranging from four percent to ten percent of the approved costs. What should you do?

1. Recommend that the city accept the lowest bid and obtain the extra four percent from other sources.
2. Begin to study ways to reduce the scope of project so it meets the budget.
3. Suggest that the project be rebid because the lowest bid is so close to the budget.
4. Wait for the city to tell you how it wants to proceed.

8. Which standard form includes contract information about the owner's right to perform work separate from the main construction contract?

1. instructions to bidders
2. owner-contractor agreement
3. general conditions of the contract
4. supplementary conditions of the contract

9. Under what circumstances does the owner have to prove to the contractor evidence of the owner's financial resources to complete the project according the AIA/ASID General Conditions of the Contract?

1. whenever the contractor asks for such evidence
2. if the project is a public project
3. on request of the contractor if the job is being competitively bid
4. the owner does not have to offer any such proof

10. What type of agreement would a designer be advised NOT to work under when doing a residential project?

1. a letter of agreement
2. a series of purchase orders with terms printed on the back
3. a standard form of AIA/ASID agreement
4. a contract prepared by the designer's attorney

10 FURNITURE, FIXTURES, AND EQUIPMENT

Furniture, fixtures, and equipment (FF&E) describes freestanding interior components that are not physically attached to the construction and that are usually purchased under separate contract. Sometimes things like office equipment, storage shelving, bank teller equipment, and other built-in items that must be coordinated with construction are selected and specified by the interior designer while the construction itself may be the responsibility of the architect. FF&E is typically a separate line item on a client's budget and is purchased under a separate contract because the methods of specifying, ordering, and installing are different from a standard construction contract. The Uniform Commercial Code discussed in Chap. 9 governs contracts for FF&E.

1 SELECTION OF FURNITURE

There are three basic categories of furniture: ready-made, custom-designed, and built-in. Ready-made furniture is purchased from a selection of standard products of a particular manufacturer. The specifier usually has some choice of fabric types, fabric colors, and wood finishes, but the selection is limited to what is available on the market. Even with these limitations, there are thousands of possible variations of style, furniture type, cost range, and quality from which to choose. With ready-made furniture, the designer and client can look at the piece, touch it, sit in it, and have a good knowledge of its appropriateness before it is specified and purchased. Other advantages of selecting ready-made furniture include knowing its cost, having a guarantee, and being able to judge its quality based on a finished piece.

Custom-designed furniture allows the designer and client to get exactly what they want, but the burden of correctly designing the piece, having it manufactured, and being responsible for its ultimate quality is placed on the designer. In most cases, the time and cost of a custom-designed piece will be greater than a comparable ready made item. Some furniture pieces, like chairs, are so difficult to design well that they are seldom custom-designed for a single job. On the other hand, conference tables, storage units and the like can be developed and built as millwork.

Built-in furniture is custom designed but, as the name implies, it becomes part of the architectural construction of the project. This type of furniture usually makes more efficient use of space, is often less expensive than ready-made furniture for the same function, and its design is usually more consistent with the architectural appearance of the space. However, it is obviously less flexible and more difficult to change when styles change or the room's function changes.

A. Types of Furniture

Furniture can be grouped according to the function it serves. The following list describes some of the general considerations of each type.

- *Seating:* Seating must be appropriate for its use, comfortable, adaptable to a wide range of body types and sizes, strong, and have durable finishes. Because no one type of seating can serve all functions, there are thousands of styles of chairs, sofas, stools, and other designs for seating. A desk chair used eight hours a day must be quite different from a waiting-room lounge chair. In addition to comfort and function, furniture must be appropriate for the overall interior design concept of the space in which it is used.

  Regardless of the specific purpose of the chair or sofa, there are some criteria common to all seating that must be evaluated when purchasing or designing. These are described in Chapter 3. Of course, not all of the criteria are critical in all situations. A lumbar support on a chair, for example, may not be necessary if the seating is only for short-term use.

- *Tables:* Common table types include dining, conference, work-surface, and occasional tables. In addition to correct dimensions for their function, you should consider several other factors. These include a sturdy support structure, a durable surface, and a color and texture that will give the correct light reflectivity for the visual tasks performed. For dining and conference tables, plan enough space so that people are not crowded. Generally, this is from 24 inches to 30 inches per person along the edge.

- *Workstations:* Workstations are single pieces of furniture or groups of components providing a work surface and storage. When several components can be combined in a variety of ways to create one or more workstations in a modular fashion, it is called systems furniture.

  The most common type of workstation is the traditional pedestal desk with drawers in its base. Variations on this basic workstation include a desk with a typing or credenza return off to one side or a separate credenza behind the desk.

- *Storage:* Because storage is always required, its design must be given the same consideration as any other type of furniture. Basic parameters for designing storage include the types and sizes of items to be stored, the location of the storage, how often the stored items will need to be accessed, and the visibility desired.

- *Beds:* Most beds consist of a mattress or mattress set and some type of supporting framework, whether it is as simple as a platform base or an elaborate system of bedposts, a footboard, and headboard. Other types of sleeping furniture include simple floor pads, water beds, bunk beds, trundle beds, and sofa beds. The traditional type of Murphy bed that folds into a storage wall is also available for areas where space is at a premium. In addition to the actual sleeping surface, beds may be integrated with storage headboards, canopies, and built-in lighting, or simply used alone with side tables.

- *Systems furniture:* Systems furniture is a collection of modular components designed to fit together in various ways to make up office workstations. They most often consist of panels to divide workstations and define areas, work surfaces, storage units, and lighting and wire management facilities.

  Although there are hundreds of different systems from dozens of manufacturers, there are three basic varieties of systems furniture. The first uses freestanding panels with conventional freestanding furniture. The second type uses panels of various lengths and heights that link and provide support for work surfaces and storage units that are suspended from the panels. The third type consists of self-contained L-shaped or U-shaped workstations than include the work surface, storage, and other required components. The storage portion of this type of system is usually high enough to serve as a privacy barrier. Both the second and third types usually contain task lighting and sometimes ambient lighting.

  Systems furniture is used in open-office planning and where flexibility of layout is required. Systems furniture makes more efficient use of space than private-office layout, and a wide variety of individual needs can be satisfied by selecting the appropriate components from the manufacturer's catalog.

B. Selection Criteria

Furniture must satisfy a wide range of needs. It must first satisfy the functional needs of its intended use. Tables for a grade-school classroom, for example, will be quite different in size, appearance, and construction from a corporate boardroom table. Some of the functional considerations include the purpose of the piece of furniture, the type of people who will be using it, the need for adjustability, finish requirements, durability, and size.

Because people come in direct contact with furniture, comfort is another critical consideration. Chairs, especially, must be appropriately selected for their use and their effect on the human body. A chair used for long periods of time by many people must be adjustable. Even tables, storage cabinets, beds, and other pieces should be selected so they are sized correctly, are easy to use, and do not present safety hazards.

Furniture is also a major design element. Not only does each piece of furniture have its own aesthetic characteristics, but it also affects the appearance of its surroundings. It must be selected to be compatible with the size, shape, and visual characteristics of the space in which it is used. Qualities of scale, color, line, form, texture, and touch must all be considered.

Quality is a practical consideration. Balanced against cost, the level of quality selected depends on the furniture's use, the type of users, expected maintenance, and the length of time before replacement is expected.

Finish is a selection criterion that is closely related to several of the others. It affects the furniture's aesthetic impact, durability, maintenance, and flammability.

Finally, furniture selection is always governed by cost considerations. This must include the life-cycle cost as well as the initial cost. A higher-priced, well-built piece of furniture may have a high first cost, but it should last much longer and require less maintenance than a less expensive piece.

2 SELECTION OF FURNITURE FABRICS

The selection of fabric for upholstered furniture has a great influence on its appearance, durability, and safety. Because the same piece of furniture can be covered with a variety of fabrics, the interior designer must know what is available and the criteria for selecting fabrics and padding for specific uses. This is true whether the designer is selecting from fabric offered by the furniture manufacturer or specifying COM (customer's own material).

A. Types and Characteristics of Fabrics

Fibers used for furniture fabrics can be broadly classified into natural and synthetic. The natural fibers are further divided into cellulosic and protein. Cellulosic fibers, such as cotton and linen, come from plants, while protein fibers, such as wool, are manufactured from animal sources.

The most commonly used fibers are listed below.

- *Wool:* Obtained from the fleece of sheep, wool is one of the best natural fibers for all types of fabrics. It has excellent resilience and elasticity and wears well. Although wool will burn when exposed to flame, it is self-extinguishing when the flame is removed. It also accepts dyes well and can be cleaned easily.
- *Cotton:* Cotton is a cellulosic fiber that comes from the seed hairs of the cotton plant. It is relatively inexpensive and has moderately good abrasion resistance. However, cotton has poor resilience and recovery properties and degrades under prolonged sunlight exposure. It is also subject to mildew.
- *Linen:* Linen is made from the fibers of the flax plant. Linen is seldom used for upholstery because it lacks resilience, flexibility, and is susceptible to abrasion. In addition, it does not take printed dyes very well.
- *Silk:* Silk is obtained from fibers spun by silkworm larvae. It is very strong and has good resilience and flexibility. The finish and luster of silk are generally highly valued, but it is very expensive and degrades in sunlight.
- *Rayon:* Rayon is a regenerated cellulosic fiber that has very poor resistance to sunlight and poor resiliency. It is flammable and is seldom used for upholstery.
- *Acetate:* Acetate is a regenerated cellulosic fiber that is flammable and does not wear well. Like rayon, in its unmodified state it has poor sunlight resistance. Both light and flame resistance can be improved by treating the fiber.
- *Nylon:* Nylon is one of the most popular synthetic fibers. It is exceptionally strong with

high resiliency and elasticity. Nylon is resistant to many chemicals, water, and microorganisms. Some of the first nylons were not resistant to sunlight and had a shiny appearance, but these problems can now be compensated for by chemical formulations. Nylon is often combined with other synthetic or natural fibers to obtain the superior advantages of both.

- *Acrylic:* Acrylic is often used as a replacement for wool because of its appearance. It has moderately good strength and resilience and is very resistant to sunlight but can be flammable. Modacrylics have similar properties but have a much greater resistance to heat and flame.

- *Olefin:* Olefin is inexpensive and is highly resistant to chemicals, mildew, and microorganisms. It is highly resilient and nonabsorbent. Its desirable qualities make it useful for carpeting and carpet backing, but its low resistance to sunlight, heat, and flame makes it undesirable for most upholstery fabrics.

- *Polyester:* Polyester has many desirable qualities including good resilience and elasticity, high resistance to solvents and other chemicals, and good resistance to sunlight. Although is has undesirable burning properties, it can be treated to make it more flame-resistant. However, it tends to absorb and hold oily materials.

B. Selecting Fabrics

Selecting the correct fabric for a piece of furniture is a matter of balancing the functional and aesthetic requirements against cost and availability. The best fabric for a hospital waiting room must be quite different from that for a private office. Some of the important criteria for fabric selection are listed below.

- *Durability:* The durability of a fabric includes resistance to abrasion, fading, staining, and other mechanical abuses as well as its cleanability. Resistance to abrasion is the most important durability factor. The amount of abrasion-resistance a piece of upholstered furniture has depends on the type of fiber, how the yarn is made and applied to the piece, the fabric's backing, and the undercushion. In most cases, the most durable upholstery is achieved by using strong, smooth fibers like nylon or wool, having the yarn tightly twisted, specifying heavy or thick fabrics, using close-set weaves, and employing relatively soft undercushions to allow the fabric to flex under use.

  Some of the problems encountered with fabrics include snagging, fuzzing, and pilling. Snagging is catching and pulling a yarn out of the fabric surface. Fuzzing occurs when small fibers work out of the yarn onto the surface of the fabric. Pilling occurs when fuzzing fibers roll into small balls.

- *Flammability:* Flammability is one of the most important considerations for fabric selection, especially in public areas like waiting rooms, hospitals, or theaters. Some fabrics are inherently more flame-resistant than others, but nearly any fabric can be treated with various chemicals to enhance its resistance to ignition and smoldering. Many states and most federal agencies have flammability standards for furniture. These standards are discussed in more detail in the next section.

- *Dimensional stability:* This characteristic is a fabric's ability to retain its shape and fit over cushioning without sagging, wrinkling, stretching, or tearing. A fabric should be resilient enough to return to its original shape after being deformed by use. It is therefore critical that the fabric and cushion be matched. A cushion that allows for more deformation than a certain fabric can resist will cause problems.

  A fabric applied over a large area of cushioning may stretch or slip over the cushion if the fabric is not stable by itself. In many cases, fabric is attached to the cushion by buttoning, tufting, or channeling. Buttoning secures the fabric to the cushion with a lightly tensioned button and thread. Tufting is similar except that the button is pulled tightly against the cushion, resulting in a deeply folded surface. Channeling secures the fabric to the cushion in parallel rows.

- *Maintenance:* Because furniture fabric is subjected to much wear, it must be selected with the intended use in mind. (An ongoing program of regular maintenance must also be considered.)
- *Appearance:* An otherwise elegant, appropriately selected piece of furniture can be ruined by choosing a fabric that is the wrong color, texture, and pattern. You must consider both the other materials used in the furniture and the materials used in the space and adjacent furniture.
- *Scale:* Scale is the size of the fabric texture and pattern in relationship to the piece of furniture and to the space in which it is used. A large sofa in a large room, for instance, may be covered with large, bold patterns and heavy weaves without seeming out of scale.
- *Comfort:* People come in direct contact with furniture more than any other component of interior space, so comfort must be appropriate for the intended use and for ergonomic requirements. A waiting-room chair does not need to be as comfortable as an office worker's chair. Fabrics and cushioning can affect comfort by their porosity, resilience, surface texture and finish. A highly porous fabric can "breathe" and is more comfortable for long periods of sitting or where the temperature and humidity are high. Similarly, smooth fabrics are more comfortable than those with rough textures or finishes.
- *Touch:* Touch is how the fabric feels to a person's skin. In some cases, it is appropriate to use a smooth fabric, like satin, while in other instances a rough fabric is the correct choice. Sometimes the choice is purely a matter of preference, while other times it can be very practical. For example, a rough, heavily textured surface can make it difficult for people to slide in and out of restaurant banquette seating.

C. Cushioning and Seaming

Cushioning and seaming affect the comfort, wearability, and flammability of furniture. Some of the common cushioning materials include cotton batting, polyester batting, polyurethane foam, latex foam, rubberized fibers, and shredded fibers. These may be used alone or in cushions placed on coiled or sinuous spring support.

Because cushion material affects the flammability of upholstery as much as the surface fabric, it should be selected carefully. Untreated cellular plastic cushioning presents a particularly high fire hazard. These plastics include the following types of foams: polyurethane, polystyrene, polyethylene, polypropylene, PVC and ABS, cellulose acetate, epoxy, phenolic, urea, silicone, and foamed latex. Untreated cellulosic batting such as cotton batting is also dangerous when cigarette ignition resistance is required. When flammability resistance is a high priority, polyester batting is a better choice. The following list gives padding types from the most resistant to cigarette ignition and small flame to the least resistant:

- neoprene, and combustion modified polyurethane
- polyester batting
- smolder-resistant and flame-resistant polyurethane foam
- smolder-resistant and flame-resistant cellulosic batting
- mixed fiber batting
- untreated polyurethane foam
- cellulosic batting
- latex foam (rarely used)

One of the important considerations in upholstery fire safety is smoldering resistance or, as it is sometimes referred to, cigarette ignition resistance.

It is affected by the combination of fabric material, cushioning, and seating construction. Fire hazards are increased if you use tufting or any type of decorative treatment on the seats or arms of upholstery because dropped cigarettes may lodge in these areas. You should avoid welt cording and similar seaming on surfaces where cigarettes may be dropped. A welt is a fabric-covered cord sewn into the seam of upholstery for ornamental purposes or to improve the durability of the covering. Instead, seaming such as railroading can be used. Railroading is the application of fabric to furniture so that there are no intermediate seam details. Railroading is also used when vertical stripes on the fabric must run horizontally. In addition to specifying smooth seaming, you should specify that the back and seat of booths and other seating be separated by at least one inch so cigarettes cannot get lodged in this area.

Upholstery safety can be enhanced in two additional ways. Flammability can be minimized by treating the cushioning material with one of several chemicals. Cotton batting and polyurethane foam can both be treated to increase their resistance to smoldering and flame spread. Liners can also be used between the fabric and cushion to provide a barrier that slows or inhibits the spread of heat and flame from the fabric to the cushion.

In addition to safety, cushioning affects the comfort and wearability of furniture. Different types of cushion materials have different densities and resistance to compression. One method of measuring foam firmness is the indentation load deflection (ILD). To determine a cushion's ILD a metal plate eight inches in diameter is pushed against a sample of foam four inches thick. The number of pounds required to compress the foam down one inch is recorded and this number is the ILD rating. For example, an ILD rating of 35 percent means that 35 pounds were required to compress the foam sample to 25 percent of its height. Therefore, a higher ILD rating means a firmer foam.

The indentation load deflection rating can be used to specify cushioning material and determine the comfort factor or support ratio. The support ratio is the ratio of the ILD rating to the standard 25 percent ILD. By specifying a 50 percent ILD, for example, the support ratio is $(2)(50 \div 25)$. Generally, high support ratios (firm seating) from 2.25 to 4.0 should be used for medical, institutional, and assembly seating. Moderate firmness cushioning with support ratios from 2.0 to 2.5 should be used for light- to medium-use seating, while softer cushions are appropriate for the backs of chairs and booths.

Finally, cushioning affects wearability. While firm cushions give better support and are more appropriate in many situations, soft undercushioning permits fabric to give and resists the grinding action of normal use. Fabric is quickly abraded when it is pulled tightly over sharp corners or welts, so the correctly selected cushion can minimize these problems.

3 STANDARDS

A. Flammability Standards

Dozens of test methods for upholstery flammability have been developed and are used in flammability standards required by various states and many government agencies. These standards define limits on a material's flammability in terms of one or more of the following characteristics: resistance to ignition, resistance to flame spread, resistance to smoldering, prevention of smoke development, prevention of heat contribution to the growth of a fire, and prevention of toxic gas release.

One of the most common test methods classifies fabrics into four classes, A, B, C, and D, based on their resistance to charring. Class D is the least resistant to charring; when a lighted cigarette is placed on the fabric surface it chars more than 3 inches. Class C chars from 1.5 to 3 inches. Classes A and B char less than 1.5 inches, but a fabric receives a Class A rating if, when tested on cotton batting it chars less than 1.5 inches. All the fabrics that pass the test will not ignite. Similar tests that evaluate the smolder resistance of upholstered furniture also test for ignition and rate the material according to char size.

B. Wearability Standards

As with flammability, there are several tests that measure the wearability of a fabric. Abrasion resistance is tested with the Wyzenbeek or Taber tests. With the Wyzenbeek method, a sample of fabric is rubbed back and forth with a cloth-covered or wire-screen-covered roller several thousand times in both directions. A fabric is considered good if it withstands 15,000 double rubs. The Taber test involves mounting a sample of fabric on a platform and exposing it to the revolving action of two abrasive wheels. The number of revolutions the fabric withstands before breaking a yarn is the fabric's rating.

Fading is measured in a machine called a Fade-Ometer that exposes fabric to ultraviolet light at specific humidity levels. This tests the color loss at intervals of 20 hours. For most fabrics, 80 hours' exposure without color loss is considered a minimum rating. Another fading test rates fabrics on an international scale from one to eight, with four being adequate and five to six preferred.

4 DESIGN CLASSICS

The NCIDQ exam usually requires that you identify the designers of well-known chairs. Figure 10.1 shows some of the most common design classics.

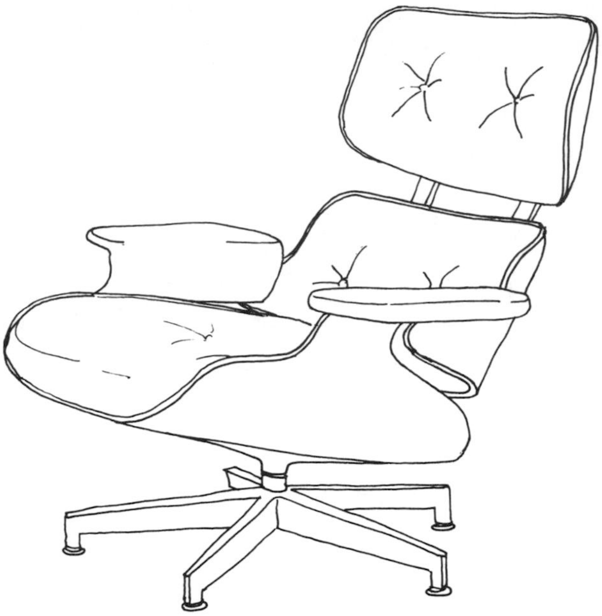

(b) Lounge chair
Charles Eames

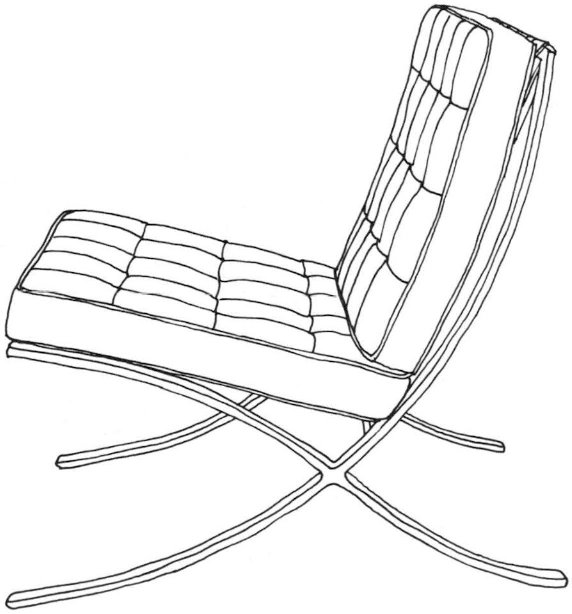

(a) Barcelona chair
Mies Van der Rohe

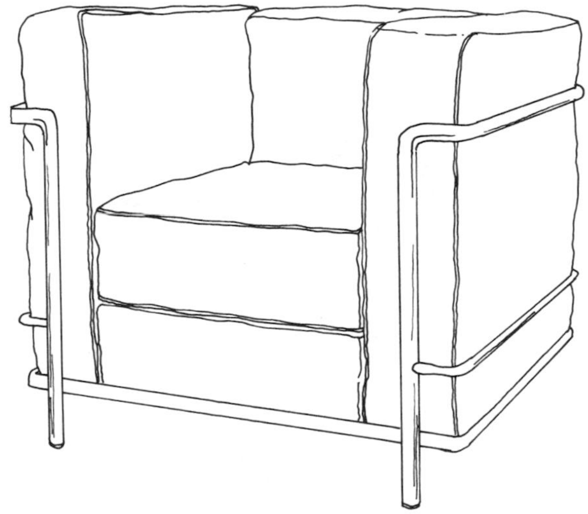

(c) Grand Confort
Le Corbusier

Figure 10.1 Classic Chairs

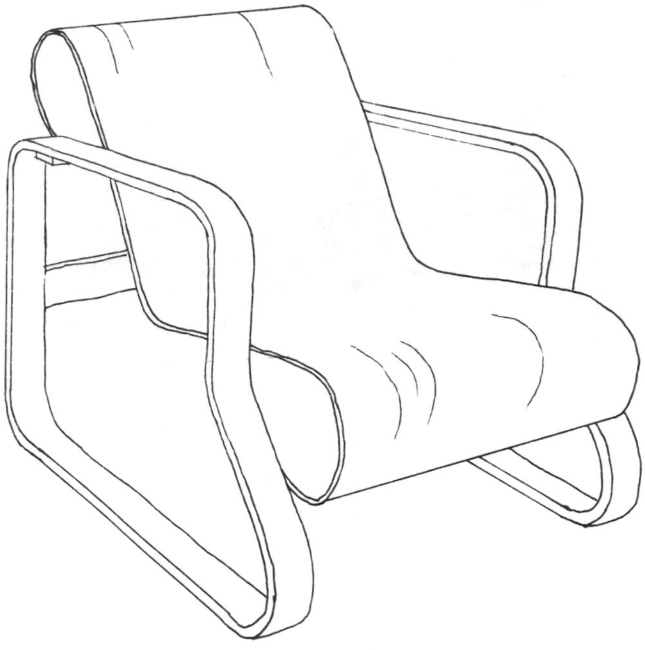

(d) Paimio chair
Alvar Aalto

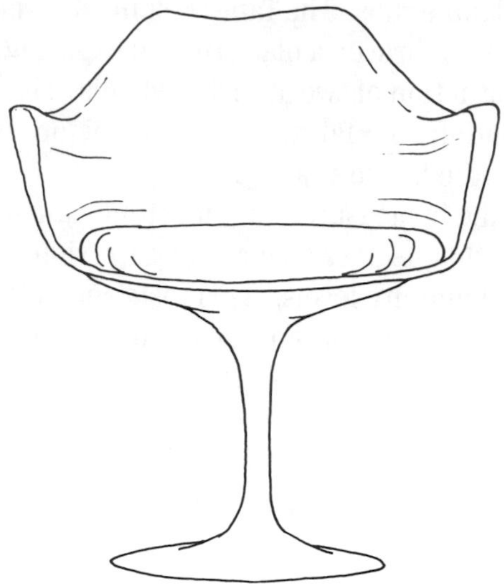

(f) Molded plastic chair
Eero Saarinen

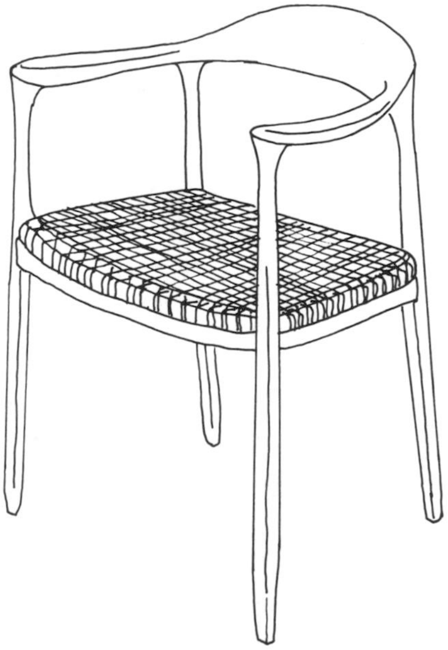

(e) "The Chair"
Hans Wegner

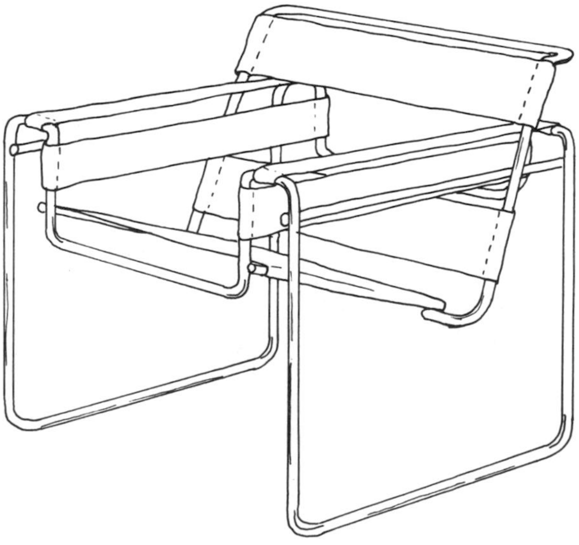

(g) Wassily chair
Marcel Breuer

Figure 10.1 (cont'd)

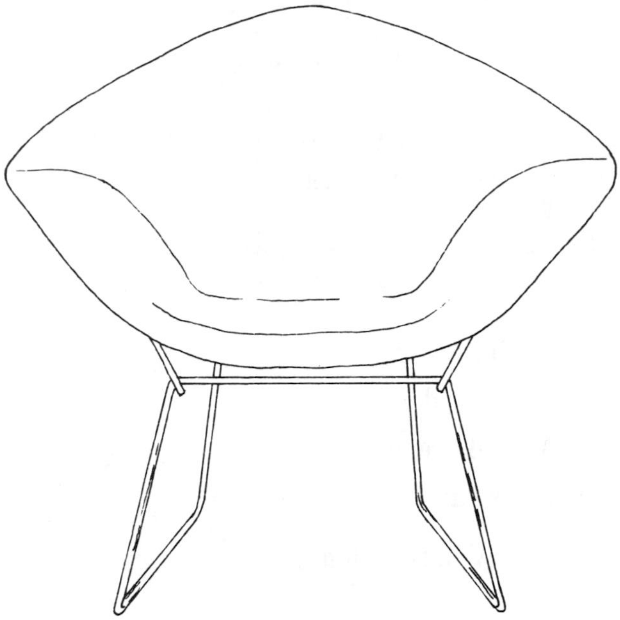

(h) wire frame chair
Harry Bertoia

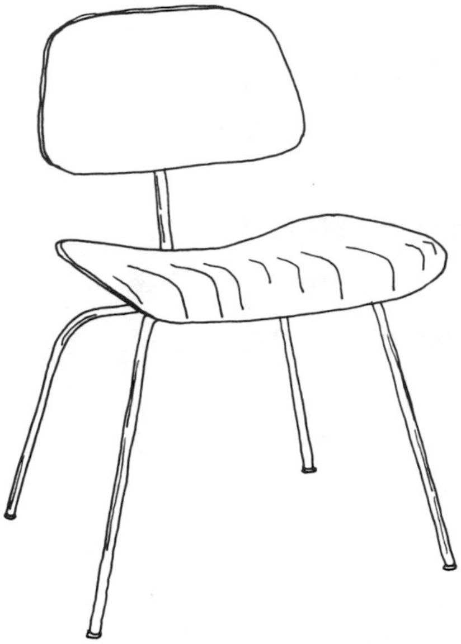

(i) dining chair
Charles Eames

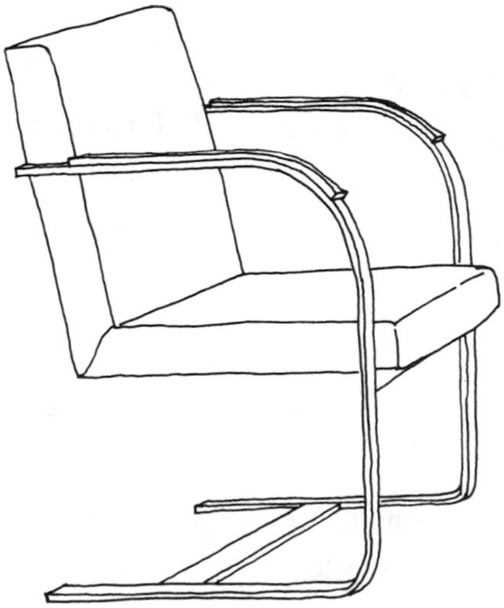

(j) Brno chair
Mies Van der Rohe

Figure 10.1 (cont'd)

SAMPLE QUESTIONS

1. What fabric would have the best appearance for the longest time when used in theater seating?

    1. vinyl
    2. wool/nylon blend
    3. acrylic/acetate blend
    4. cotton/rayon blend

2. What type of cushioning would be best for a hospital waiting room?

    1. high-density foam
    2. cotton batting
    3. combustion modified foam with a low ILD
    4. low-density polyurethane

3. In what order of importance should tables for a college library be selected?

    1. flammability, design, then comfort
    2. finish, flammability, then design
    3. durability, cost, then design
    4. quality, comfort, then finish

4. Which type of seaming would be LEAST appropriate for seating where cigarettes are likely to be dropped?

    1. channeling
    2. buttoning
    3. railroading
    4. welt cording

5. What performance tests should be specified for a custom-blended fabric to be used in a recreation center reception area?

    1. flammability and Fade-Ometer
    2. Wyzenbeek and fading
    3. Taber and Wyzenbeek
    4. indentation load deflection and Taber

6. Which architect designed the chair shown below?

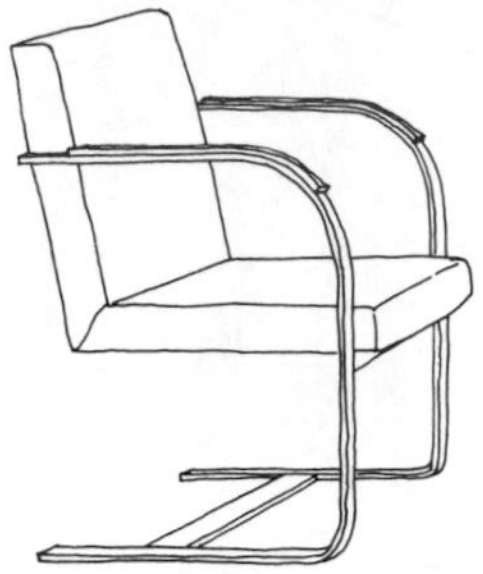

    1. Le Corbusier
    2. Mies van der Rohe
    3. Marcel Breuer
    4. Alvar Aalto

7. A Class A fabric will not

    1. char
    2. ignite
    3. smolder
    4. produce smoke

8. What most affects the flammability of upholstery?

    1. the type of chemical retardant used
    2. the cushioning and surface fabric
    3. the surface fabric and interliner
    4. the surface fabric

9. If you were specifying the fabric for sofas in a sunroom, which would be the LEAST desirable choice?

    1. polyester
    2. modacrylic
    3. rayon
    4. acrylic

10. What would be the best way to avoid fabric slippage over a cushion?

    1. Specify a heavy fabric pulled tightly over the cushion.
    2. Specify a high-density foam cushion with an interliner.
    3. Specify rounded corners with welts.
    4. Specify channeling.

11 INTERIOR CONSTRUCTION

1 PARTITIONS

Partitions are the most common construction element for both residential and commercial interior design. This section discusses three of the most frequently used materials for partitions: gypsum wallboard, lath and plaster, and masonry. Wallboard is the most common type of partition. Lath and plaster construction is seldom used for standard walls but is required for certain conditions. Masonry is least specified by interior designers, but it can be used in special situations.

A. Gypsum Wallboard

Gypsum wallboard consists of a gypsum core sandwiched between heavy paper or other materials. It is factory formed into standard-size sheets ready for dry application onto framing. Because of its many advantages, it is the most common material used for constructing partitions in both residential and commercial construction.

Advantages of gypsum wallboard include a low installed cost, quick and easy installation, fire resistance, sound control capability, easy availability, versatility (for a variety of uses), ease of finishing and decorating, and ease of installation of doors and other openings.

Gypsum wallboard is available in 4- and $4^1/_2$-foot wide sheets in lengths of 8, 10, and 12 feet. Thicknesses range from $^1/_4$ inch to $^5/_8$ inch, although a special, 1-inch core board is manufactured that is used for constructing elevator and stairway shafts when required. Wallboard is available with square edges, tapered edges, and (with 1-inch core board) tongue-and-groove edges. The tapered edge is the most commonly used because the slight taper allows joint compound and tape to be applied without showing a slight bulge in the finished surface.

Other available types include Type X for fire-rated partitions, foil-backed for vapor barriers, water-resistant for use behind tile and in other moderately moist conditions, backing board for two-layer applications, and predecorated with vinyl wallcovering already applied.

Gypsum wallboard is applied by nailing or screwing it to wood or metal framing, or with mastic when applying it to smooth, dry concrete or masonry walls or to a base layer of wallboard. The joints are finished by embedding paper or fiberglass tape in a special joint compound and allowing it to dry. Additional layers of joint compound are added and sanded after each application to give a smooth, finished wall surface. Various types of textured finishes can be applied, or the surface is left smooth for the application of wallpaper, vinyl wallcovering, or other finishes.

Either wood or metal studs are used to form wallboard partitions. Two-by-four-inch and two-by-six-inch studs are common framing members for residential construction, while metal framing is typically used for commercial construction because it is noncombustible and easier to install. Metal framing consists of light-gauge steel studs set in floor and ceiling runners (C-shaped channels). See Figure 11.1.

Steel studs come in standard depths of $1^5/_8$ inches, $2^1/_2$ inches, $3^5/_8$ inches, 4 inches, and 6 inches. Standard studs are very lightweight, but heavier gauges are available for high partitions or where other structural considerations are important. Hat-shaped furring channels are used for ceiling framing and to fur out from concrete or masonry walls if the walls are uneven or if additional depth is needed for electrical outlets or insulation. Wood furring strips of nominal 1″x 2″size can also be used in some situations. Resilient channels are used to improve the acoustical properties of a wall by isolating the wallboard from rigid attachment to the framing. Insulation is also

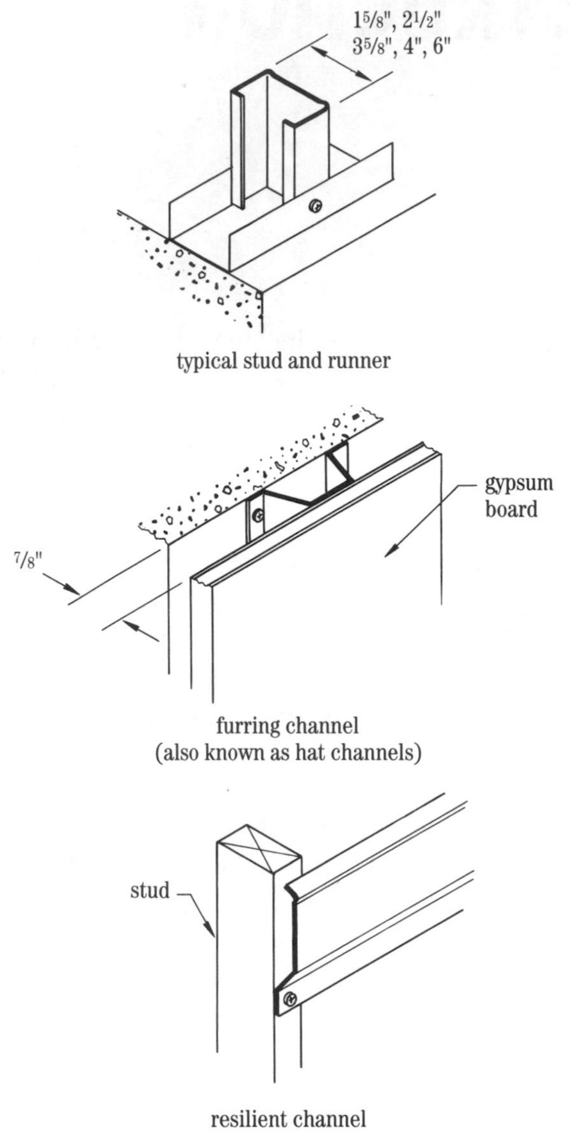

Figure 11.1 Gypsum Wallboard Framing

placed in the stud cavities to improve the acoustical quality of the partition.

The depth of the stud depends on the height of the partition, the gauge of the stud, the number of layers of wallboard, and the spacing of the studs. The most commonly used size is 2½ inches, which is sufficient for normal ceiling heights and slab-to-slab partitions and allows enough room for electrical boxes and small pipes. Metal studs are normally spaced 16 or 24 inches on center—the narrower spacing used for residential construction and the wider for commercial construction. Wallboard with ½-inch thickness is typically applied in residential construction and ⅝-inch thickness in commercial construction.

Because the edges of wallboard are rough, they must have fabricated edging whenever they are exposed. This includes a cornerbead, which is used for all exterior corners not otherwise protected and various types of edge trim. These trim pieces are shown in Figure 11.2 and include the following:

- LC *bead:* edge trim requiring finishing with joint compound.
- L *bead:* edge trim without a back flange; good for installation after the wallboard has been installed. It requires finishing with joint compound.
- LK *bead:* edge trim for use with various thicknesses of wallboard in a kerfed jamb (one with a small slot cut in). It requires finishing with joint compound.
- U *bead:* edge trim that does not require finishing with joint compound, but the edge of the metal is noticeable. It is sometimes called J metal by contractors.

Two of the most common types of commercial gypsum wallboard construction on metal framing are shown in Figure 11.3. Residential construction is similar except that wood studs are used and the partition stops at the ceiling joists. In commercial work, the standard partition is only built up to the suspended ceiling, while the slab-to-slab partition is used when a complete fire-rated barrier must be constructed or when sound control is needed. By adding additional layers of Type X wallboard, fire-resistive ratings of two, three, and four hours can be obtained. A slab-to-slab partition with a single layer of ⅝-inch Type X wallboard on each side provides a one-hour rated partition, while two layers on each side provide a two-hour rating. Gypsum wallboard is also used for ceilings and to provide fire protection for columns, stairways, and elevator shafts.

B. Lath and Plaster

Plaster is a finish material made from various types of cementing compounds, fine aggregate, and

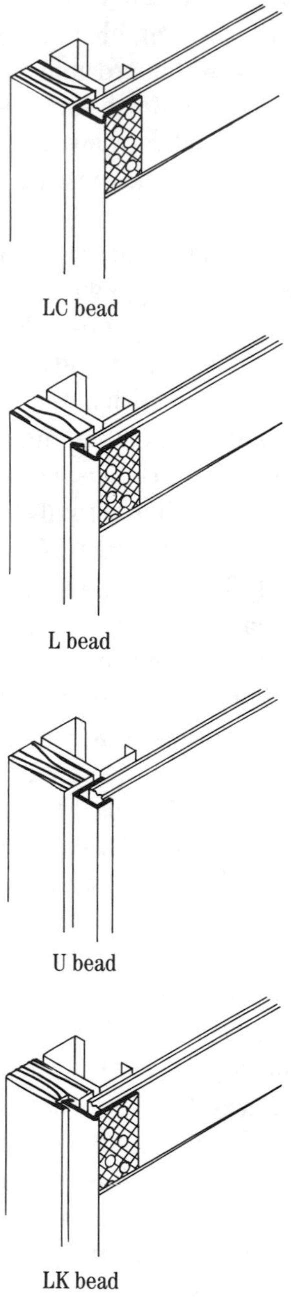

Figure 11.2 Gypsum Wallboard Trim

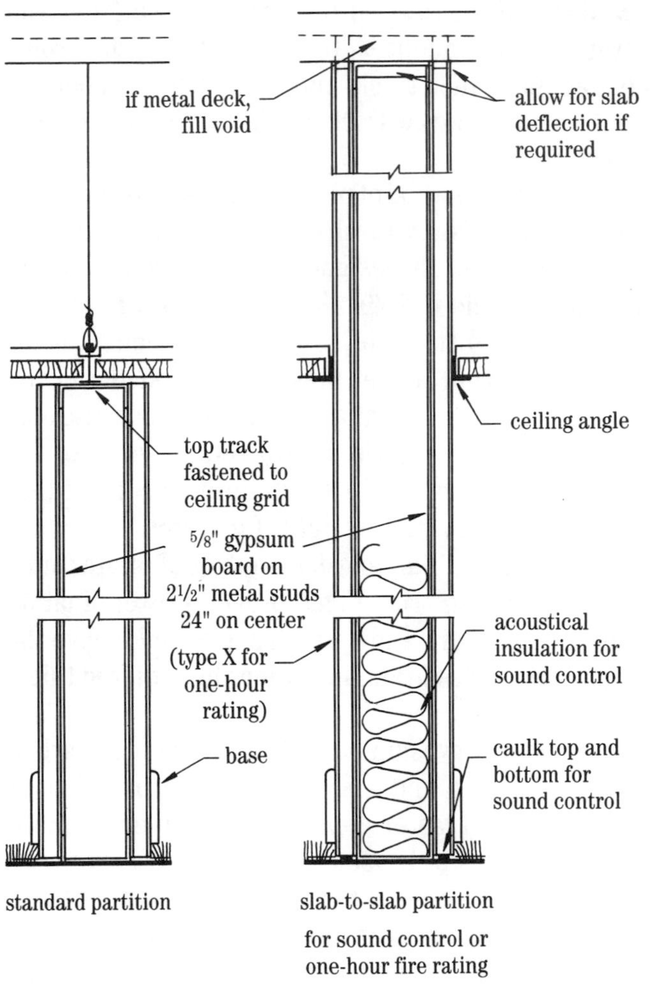

Figure 11.3 Gypsum Wallboard Partitions

water. It is applied over several kinds of base materials in one to three coats to form a smooth, level surface. Plaster describes various types of interior finish materials of this type, while stucco is an exterior type of plaster made with portland cement.

Plaster is made from gypsum, lime, water, and aggregates of sand, vermiculite, or perlite. Vermiculite and perlite are used when a lightweight, fire-resistant plaster is needed. For most interior construction, gypsum plaster can be used. However, in certain areas other types are required. Keene's cement, for example, is a plaster that has a high resistance to abrasion and water penetration. It is used in wet areas or on walls subject to scratching or other abuse. Portland cement plaster must be used as the base coat for Keene's cement or as a backing for tile walls.

There are two common types of plaster construction. The first is the traditional method using metal lath that is attached to wood or metal studs and serves as the base for the plaster. The first coat of plaster, called the scratch coat, is applied to the metal lath and runs between and partially around the lath, firmly keying the plaster to the lath. In standard plastering, the scratch coat is followed by the brown coat that is used to level the surface. The finish coat provides final leveling and the desired texture to the surface. The scratch coat is about $1/4$ to $1/2$ inch thick, the brown coat about $1/4$ inch thick, and the finish coat about $1/8$ inch thick. Two-coat work combines the scratch and brown coats.

The other method of plastering uses gypsum board lath instead of metal lath. This is a special gypsum product specifically designed for plastering. Gypsum lath is available in 16″x 48″ boards that are applied horizontally to studs, or as 48″x 96″ sheets. One or two coats of thin veneer plaster are applied over the boards. Veneer plastering reduces labor because only one coat is needed, but it still retains some of the advantages of plaster: a hard, durable surface that can be finished with a variety of textures.

Like gypsum wallboard, the edges of plaster must be finished with trim. This provides a termination point for the work and serves as a screed to give the plasterers guides for maintaining the required thickness.

In general, gypsum wallboard systems have largely supplanted lath and plaster work because of their lower cost and faster construction sequence. However, plaster is still used where curved shapes are required and where a hard, abrasion-resistant surface is needed. Plaster must also be used as a base for ceramic tile in areas subject to continual dampness like public showers, steam rooms, and the like. Ornamental plaster casting and plaster molding are also used in restoration work.

C. Masonry

Masonry is a general term that includes brick, concrete block, glass block, structural clay tile, terracotta, and gypsum block. In most cases, masonry materials are part of the architectural design of a building and are part of the architect's work. Occasionally, however, there are times when the interior designer may need to specify a non-loadbearing wall of masonry, most often concrete block or glass block. For example, in a renovation project, there may be a need to match an existing concrete block or brick wall.

Non-loadbearing concrete block partitions are usually specified for interior use to provide a strong, durable, fire-resistant partition. In institutional applications, such as schools or college dormitories, where heavy use is expected, concrete block may be a sensible choice. However, block is very heavy compared with gypsum wallboard and is generally not considered an attractive finish surface. If you are going to use it, you should verify with the architect or structural engineer that the existing floor structure can carry its weight.

Concrete block is manufactured with cement, water, and various types of aggregate, including gravel, expanded shale or slate, expanded slag or pumice, or limestone cinders. It is hollow and its size is based on a nominal 4-inch module with actual dimensions being $3/8$ inch less than the nominal dimension to allow for mortar joints. One of the most common sizes is an 8 x 8 x 16-inch unit, which is actually $7\,5/8$ inches wide and high and $15\,5/8$ inches long. Common nominal thicknesses are 4, 6, 8, and 12 inches. Various sizes and shapes are manufactured for particular uses.

Glass block is manufactured as a hollow unit with a clear, textured, or patterned face. It is a popular choice for interior use when a combination of light transmission, privacy, and security is required.

Glass block is manufactured in a nominal thickness of 4 inches and in face sizes of 6 x 6, 8 x 8, 12 x 12, and 4 x 8 inches. Glass block walls are laid in stack bond (with joints aligned rather than staggered) with mortar and horizontal and vertical reinforcement in the joints. Because of the coefficient of expansion of glass and the possibility of deflection of the floor structure, you must provide expansion joints around the perimeter of glass block walls.

Because glass block cannot be load bearing, individual panels are limited to 250 square feet or 25 feet in any dimension. Each panel must be supported with suitable structure both horizontally and vertically and with expansion joints provided at the structural support points.

2 DOORS AND INTERIOR GLASS

Doors and glass are two ways of selectively controlling openings between rooms. Doors are available in a variety of types and materials to meet various functional needs. Glass can be used to control passage and sound, but it admits light and vision.

There are three major components of a door system: the door itself, the frame, and the hardware.

Each must be coordinated with the other and be appropriate for the circumstances and design intent.

The common parts of a door opening are illustrated in Figure 11.4. To differentiate between the two jambs, the side where the hinge or pivot is installed is called the *hinge jamb* and the jamb where the door closes is called the *strike jamb* or *strike side* of the door.

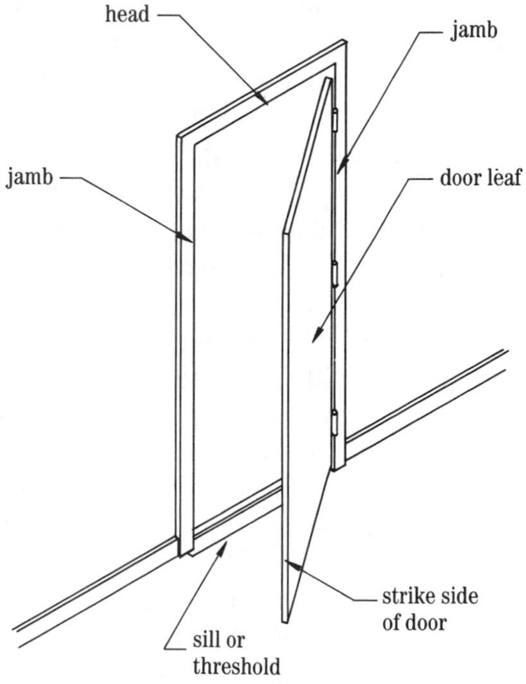

Figure 11.4 Parts of a Door

A. Wood Doors and Frames

Wood doors are the most common type for both residential and commercial construction. They are available in a variety of styles, methods of operation, sizes, and finishes.

The two styles of wood doors are shown in Figure 11.5. Which style you select depends on the functional needs of the opening as well as the aesthetic appearance required. For example, a panel door is not appropriate for an opening in a fire-rated partition because wood panel doors do not meet the required fire resistance.

Doors are also classified according to their method of operation, or how they open and close. The most common type, the swinging door, is attached to its frame with hinges or pivots. Swinging doors are easy to install and can accommodate high traffic volume. In addition, they are the only type acceptable as a required exit door. Pocket sliding doors are hung on a top track and can be used where space is limited. However, they are awkward to operate and should only be used where traffic is limited. Bypass sliding doors also are hung from a top track and are commonly used for closets only. Bi-folding doors are also used for closets. Unlike the bypass sliding door, which can only open half of a doorway, a bi-fold door allows full access. Accordion folding doors are often used to divide spaces or close very wide openings.

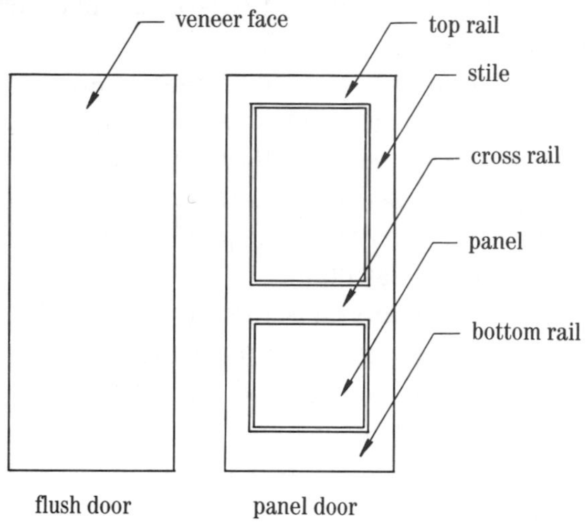

Figure 11.5 Types of Wood Doors

Flush wood doors are made of thin, flat veneers laminated to various types of cores. They are either hollow core or solid core. Hollow-core doors are made of one or three plies of veneer on each side of a cellular interior. The frame is made of solid wood with larger blocks of solid wood where the latching hardware is located. Hollow-core doors are used where only light use is expected and cost is a consideration. They have no fire-resistive capabilities.

Solid-core doors are made with a variety of core types depending on the functional requirements of the door. Cores may be particleboard, stave core (solid blocks of wood), or mineral core for fire-rated doors. Solid-core doors are used for their fire-resistive properties, as acoustical barriers, for security, and for their superior durability. Solid-core doors are available that have fire ratings of 20 minutes, 45 minutes, or 90 minutes.

The face veneers of wood doors are made from any available hardwood species using rotary-cut, plain-sliced, quarter-sliced, or rift-cut methods, as wood paneling (discussed later in this chapter) is made. Veneers of hardboard suitable for painting and plastic laminate are also available.

Panel doors are constructed of solid pieces of wood that frame various types of panels. Any number of panels can be constructed, and they can be the traditional raised panel style or simple flat panels.

Wood doors can be custom-made to any size, but the standard widths are 2′-0″, 2′-4″, 2′-6″, 2′-8″, and 3′-0″. Standard heights are 6′-8″and 7′-0″, although higher doors, often used in commercial construction, are available. Hollow-core doors are $1^3/_8$ inches thick and solid-core doors are $1^3/_4$ inches thick.

Frames for wood doors are made from wood, steel (hollow metal, discussed in the next section), and aluminum. A common wood-frame jamb is illustrated in Figure 11.6. This drawing shows a frame set in a commercial metal stud partition, but the construction is similar for a wood-frame wall. Although the stop and casing trim are shown as rectangular pieces, several different trim profiles are available and frequently used.

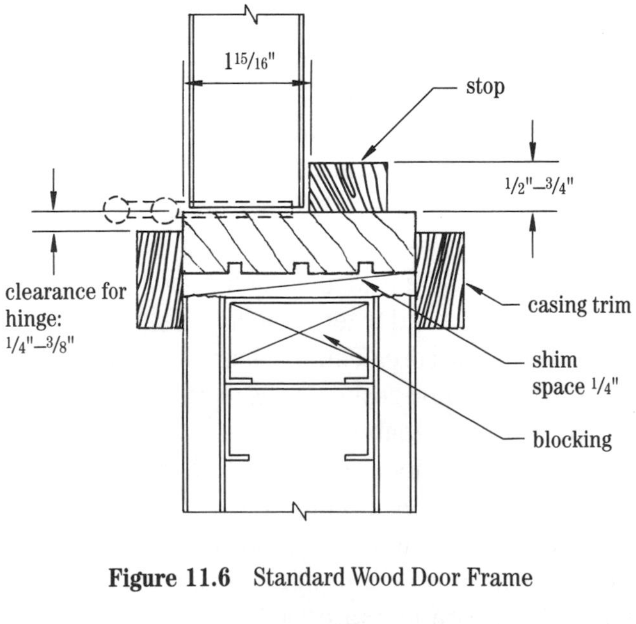

Figure 11.6 Standard Wood Door Frame

The decision concerning the type of frame to use for a wood door depends on the appearance desired, the type of partition the opening is being installed in, the fire-rating requirements, the security needed, and the durability desired. For example, wood frames are available for use in 20-, 30-, and 45-minute fire door assemblies, but a 1-hour door must be installed in a rated steel frame.

B. Metal Doors and Frames

Metal doors and frames (often referred to as hollow metal) are seldom used for residential construction. They are, however, frequently used in commercial construction because of their durability, security, and fire-resistive qualities.

The three most common types of metal doors are flush, sash, and louvered. Flush doors have a single, smooth surface on both sides, sash doors contain one or more glass lights, and louvered doors have an opening with metal slats to provide ventilation. Paneled steel doors, which resemble wood panel doors, are also available with insulated cores for residential use where energy conservation, durability, and a traditional appearance are required.

Metal doors are available in steel, stainless steel, aluminum, and bronze, but other door materials are available on special order. The most common material is steel with a painted finish. Steel doors are constructed with faces of cold-rolled sheet steel. 18-gauge steel is used for light-duty doors, but 16-gauge is most common. Heavier gauges are used for special needs. The steel face is attached to cores of honeycomb kraft paper, steel ribs, hardboard, or other materials. The edges are made of steel channels, with the locations for hardware reinforced with heavier gauge steel. Mineral wool or other materials are used to provide sound-deadening qualities, if required.

Although metal doors can be custom made in almost any practical size, standard widths are 2′-0″, 2′-4″, 2′-6″, 2′-8″, 3′-0″, 3′-4″, 3′-6″, 3′-8″, and 4′-0″. Standard heights are 6′-8″, 7′-0″, and 8′-0″. The standard thickness is $1^3/_4$ inches.

Steel door frames are used for either steel doors or wood doors and are made from sheet steel bent into the shape required for the door installation. Two of the most common frame profiles are shown in Figure 11.7 along with some standard dimensions and the terminology used to describe the parts. Different types of anchoring devices are used inside the frame to attach it to the partition. Where a fire rating over 20 minutes is required, steel frames are used almost exclusively.

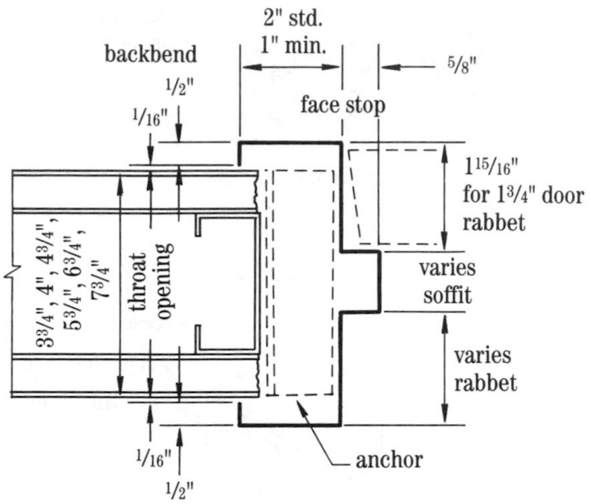

standard double rabbet

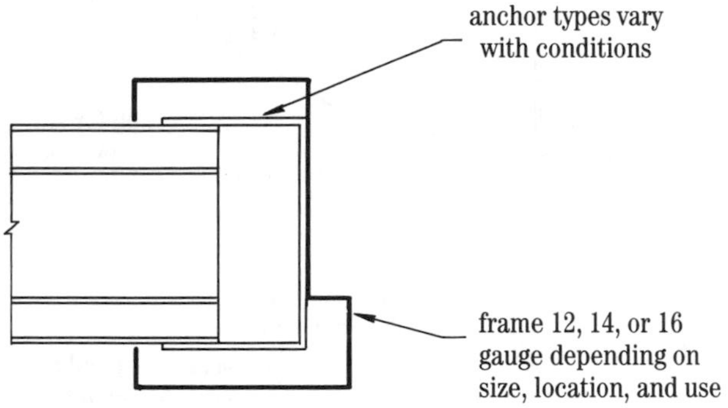

single rabbet

Figure 11.7 Standard Steel Door Frames

C. Hardware

- *Hinges:* Hinges are the most common method of attaching a door to its frame. Hinges consist of two leaves with an odd number of knuckles on one leaf and an even number of knuckles on the other. The knuckles are attached with a pin. The knuckles and pin form the barrel of the hinge, which is finished with a tip.

  The full mortise (also called a butt hinge) is the most common type and has both leaves fully mortised into the frame and the edge of the door so the hinge is flush with the surface of the frame and door. Other types are available that can be surface applied to the door, the frame, or both.

  There are also special types of hinges. Raised barrel hinges are used when there is not room for the barrel to extend past the door trim. The barrel is offset to allow one leaf to be mortised into the frame. Swing-clear hinges have a special shape that allows the door to swing 90 or 95 degrees so the full opening of the doorway is available. Without a swing-clear hinge, standard butt hinges decrease the opening width by the thickness of the door when it is open 90 degrees.

  Hinges are available with or without ball bearings and in three weights. The door weight and frequency of use determine which type to use. Low-frequency doors like residential doors use standard weight, plain-bearing hinges. Most commercial applications require standard weight, ball-bearing hinges. High-frequency applications such as office building entrances, theaters, and so forth require heavyweight ball-bearing hinges. In addition, ball-bearing hinges are required for fire-rated assemblies and on all doors with closers.

  The number of hinges is determined by the height of the door. Numbers of hinges are commonly referred to by pairs—one pair meaning two hinges. Doors up to 60 inches high require 2 hinges (1 pair). Doors from 60 inches to 90 inches require 3 hinges ($1^1/_2$ pair), and doors 90 inches to 120 inches require four hinges (2 pair).

- *Latchsets and locksets:* Latchsets and locksets are devices to operate a door, hold it in the closed position, and lock it. A latchset only holds the door in place with no provision for locking. It has a beveled latch extending from the face of the door edge and automatically engages the strike mounted in the frame when the door is closed. A lockset has a special mechanism that allows the door to be locked with a key or thumbturn. Various types and designs of knobs or lever handles are used with these devices to provide the actual gripping surface used to operate the door.

The most common types of locks and latchsets are the cylindrical lock (sometimes called a bored lock), the mortise lock, and the unit lock (sometimes called a preassembled lock). These are shown in Figure 11.8.

The *cylindrical lock* is simple to install in holes drilled in the door, and it is relatively inexpensive. It can be purchased in grades of light duty (least expensive), standard duty, and heavy duty. It is the most common type for residential construction, but it is also used for commercial projects.

A *mortise lock* is installed in a rectangular area cut out of the door. It is generally more secure than a cylindrical lock and offers a much wider variety of locking options.

A *preassembled lock* has its mechanism in a rectangular box that fits within a notch cut in the edge of the door. Because of this, it is easier to install than a mortise lock.

With all types of latches and locks, either a door knob or lever handle may be used to operate the latching device. In most cases, a lever handle is required to meet code requirements for accessibility.

- *Pivots:* Pivots provide an alternative way to hang doors where the appearance of hinges is objectionable or where a frameless door design may make it impossible to use hinges. Pivots may be center hung or offset and are mounted in the floor and head of the door. For large or heavy doors, an intermediate pivot is often required for offset-hung doors. Center-hung pivots allow the door to swing in either direction and can be completely concealed. Offset pivots allow the door to swing 180 degrees, if required.

- *Closers:* Closers are devices that automatically return a door to its closed position after it is opened. They also control the distance a door can be opened and thereby protect the door and surrounding construction from

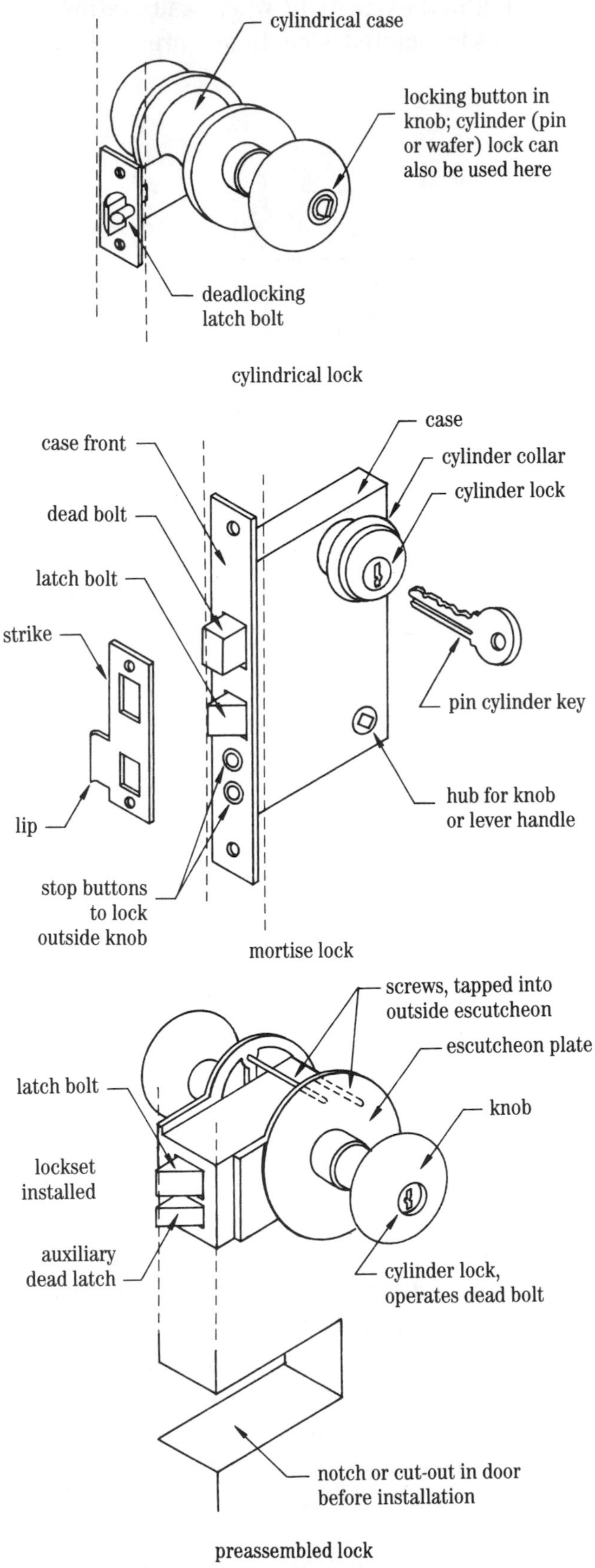

Figure 11.8 Types of Locksets

damage. Closers can be surface mounted on either side of the door, or in the head frame, or concealed in the frame or in the door. Closers can also be integral with pivots mounted in the floor or ceiling, either center hung or offset.

- *Panic hardware:* This type of operating hardware is used where required by the building code for safe egress by a large number of people. Push bars extending across the width of the door operate vertical rods that disengage latches at the top and bottom. The vertical rods can be surface mounted or concealed in the door.
- *Door stops and bumpers:* Some method of keeping a door from damaging adjacent construction is required. Closers will do this to some extent, but floor stops or wall bumpers provide more positive protection. These devices are small metal fabrications with rubber bumpers attached. Metal door frames also use silencers, which are small pads of rubber mounted on the door stop to cushion the door when it is closed.
- *Astragals:* Astragals are vertical members used between double doors to seal the opening, act as a door stop, or provide extra security when the doors are closed. An astragal may be attached to one door leaf or may be a separate unit against which both doors close. If the doors are required exit doors and an astragal is attached to one of them, they must have a door coordinator. This is a device that coordinates the closing sequence of the two doors so that they close completely, rather than having the leaf with the astragal close first and preventing the other leaf from closing.
- *Push plates and pull bars:* These are used to operate a door that does not require automatic latching. They are commonly used on doors to toilet rooms and commercial kitchens.
- *Automatic door bottoms:* These are devices that are mortised or surface applied to the bottom of the door to provide a sound or light seal. When the door is open the seal is up; as the door is closed a plunger strikes the jamb and forces the seal down against the floor.
- *Door seals:* Door seals are used along the edges of doors to provide a tight seal against smoke, light, and sound. Fire-rated seals are required on fire doors, and other types are often used for acoustical separation between two rooms. Different types of neoprene, felt, metal, and vinyl are used.
- *Thresholds:* Thresholds are used where floor materials change at a door line, where a hard surface is required for an automatic door bottom, or where minor changes in floor level occur.
- *Hardware finishes:* Hardware is available in a wide variety of finishes, and the choice of finish depends primarily on the desired appearance. The finish is either integral to the base metal from which the hardware is made or is a plated finish. There are five basic base metals: steel, stainless steel, bronze, brass, and aluminum. Fire-rated doors must have steel or stainless steel hinges.

D. Interior Glazing

Glazing is the process of installing glass in framing as well as installing the framing itself. There are a number of types of glass that are available for interior use. Among these are the following:

- *Float glass:* Float glass (annealed glass) is the standard type of glass used in common windows and other applications where additional strength or other properties are not required. For interior use, it is employed in small openings or where safety glazing is not required.
- *Tempered glass:* Tempered glass is produced by subjecting annealed glass to a special heat treatment. This glass is about four times stronger than annealed glass of the same thickness. In addition to its extra strength for

normal glazing, tempered glass is considered safety glass, so it can be used in hazardous locations (discussed in the next section). If it breaks, it falls into thousands of very small pieces instead of into dangerous shards. Tempered glass for interior use is commonly 1/4 inch thick.

- *Laminated glass:* Laminated glass consists of two or more layers of glass bonded together by an interlayer of polyvinyl butyral resin. When laminated glass is broken, the interlayer holds the pieces together even though the glass itself may be severely cracked. This type of glass is used where very strong glazing is required or where acoustical control is needed. It can be bullet resistant and provides high security against intentional or accidental breakage. Like tempered glass, it is considered safety glazing and can be used in hazardous locations.

- *Wire glass:* Wire glass has a mesh of wire embedded in the middle of the sheet. The surface can be either smooth or patterned. Wire glass is used primarily in fire-rated assemblies where it is required by most building codes. Wire glass cannot be tempered and does not qualify as safety glazing for hazardous locations.

- *Patterned glass:* This specialty glass is made by passing a sheet of molten glass through rollers on which the desired pattern is pressed, which may be on one or both sides. Vision through the panel is diffused but not totally obscured; the degree of diffusion depends on the type and depth of pattern.

- *Fire-rated glazing:* In addition to wire glass, there are three types of fire-rated glazing with ratings from 30 to 90 minutes. One is a visually clear ceramic, one is a special tempered glass (maximum 30-minute rating), and one is made with two or three panes of glass with a transparent gel between. When subjected to fire the gel foams and forms a heat shield. For each type there are limits on the hourly rating, maximum areas, and special requirements for detailing. Some types cannot be used in hazardous locations.

Interior glass can be set in wood or metal frames. Figures 11.9 and 11.10 show two common framing methods. When glass is framed conventionally, as in Figure 11.9, glazing beads are used to hold the glass in place. Glass can also be set in frames at the top and bottom and simply butt-joined on the sides as shown in Figure 11.11. The gap between adjacent pieces of glass may be left open or filled with silicone sealant.

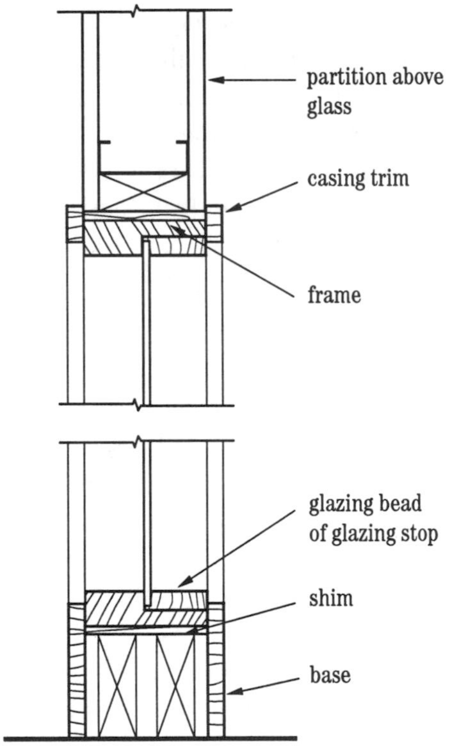

Figure 11.9 Standard Glass Framing

In addition to wood or metal doors with glass panels, solid glass doors are available. These are tempered glass, typically 1/2 or 3/4 inch thick with top and bottom metal rails and some type of door pull. There are no vertical framing members on either side of the door. The metal rails allow the door to be set on pivots in the floor and above the door and provide a place for a cylinder lock.

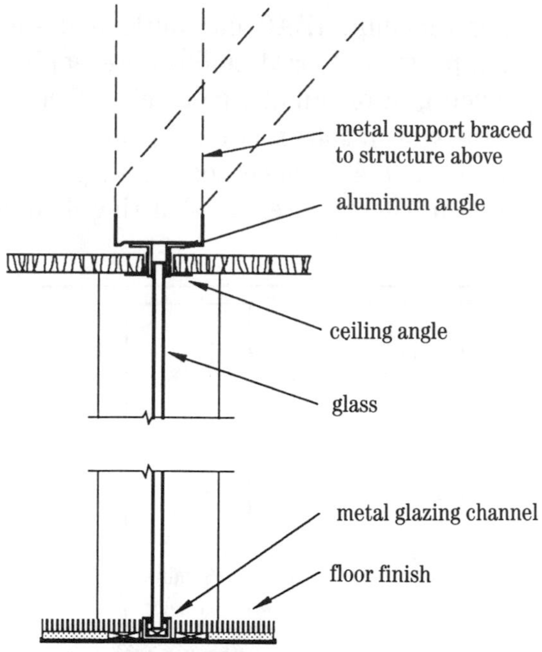

Figure 11.10 Frameless Glazing

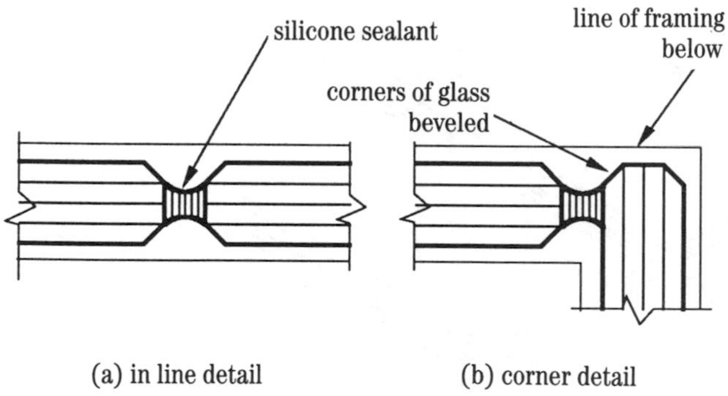

Figure 11.11 Butt Glazing

E. Building Code Requirements for Glazing

The two primary interior glazing situations that are regulated by building codes are limitations on glass in fire-rated assemblies and safety glazing subject to human impact in hazardous locations.

The Uniform Building Code (as well as the other model codes in the United States and Canada) places limits on the amount and type of glass in one-hour rated corridors. The UBC requires that the glazed openings must be protected by $^{1}/_{4}$-inch wire glass installed in steel frames. The maximum glazed area cannot exceed 25 percent of the area of the corridor wall of the room that it is separating from the corridor.

To prevent injuries, codes require safety glazing in hazardous locations. Hazardous locations are those subject to human impact such as glass in doors, shower and bath enclosures, and certain locations in walls. A composite drawing of where safety glazing is and is not required according to the UBC is shown in Figure 11.12. The exact requirements are given in two references, The American National Standards Institute ANSI Z97.1, Performance Specifications and Methods of Test for Safety Glazing Material Used in Buildings, and the Code of Federal Regulations, 16 CFR Part 1201, Safety Standard for Architectural Glazing Materials. Tempered or laminated glass is considered safety glazing. The National Building Code of Canada is a little less prescriptive. It requires tempered or laminated glass in doors, shower enclosures, and glass sidelights greater than 500 millimeters wide.

3 CEILINGS

There are many materials and construction techniques used for ceilings. Most residential ceilings are gypsum wallboard attached directly to the floor joists or ceiling joists. In most commercial construction, the ceiling is usually a system separate from the structure and is usually constructed with some type of suspended system, using acoustical tile, gypsum wallboard, or lath and plaster. This allows a flat ceiling surface for partition attachment, lights, and acoustical treatment while the space above the ceiling, called the plenum, can be used for mechanical systems, wiring, and other services.

A. Gypsum Wallboard

For residential construction, gypsum wallboard ceilings are constructed by screwing or nailing the wallboard directly to the ceiling joists. Any wiring or heating ducts are concealed between the joists. If additional space below the joists is required, it is boxed in with wood framing, and the wallboard is applied over the framing.

Because commercial construction typically requires clear space above the ceiling for piping, electrical conduit, HVAC ductwork, and sprinkler pipes, gypsum wallboard ceilings are applied to a suspended grid of framing members. Figure 11.13 shows the typical construction: $1^1/_2$-inch steel channels are located 4′-0″on center and suspended from the structural floor above. Metal furring channels are

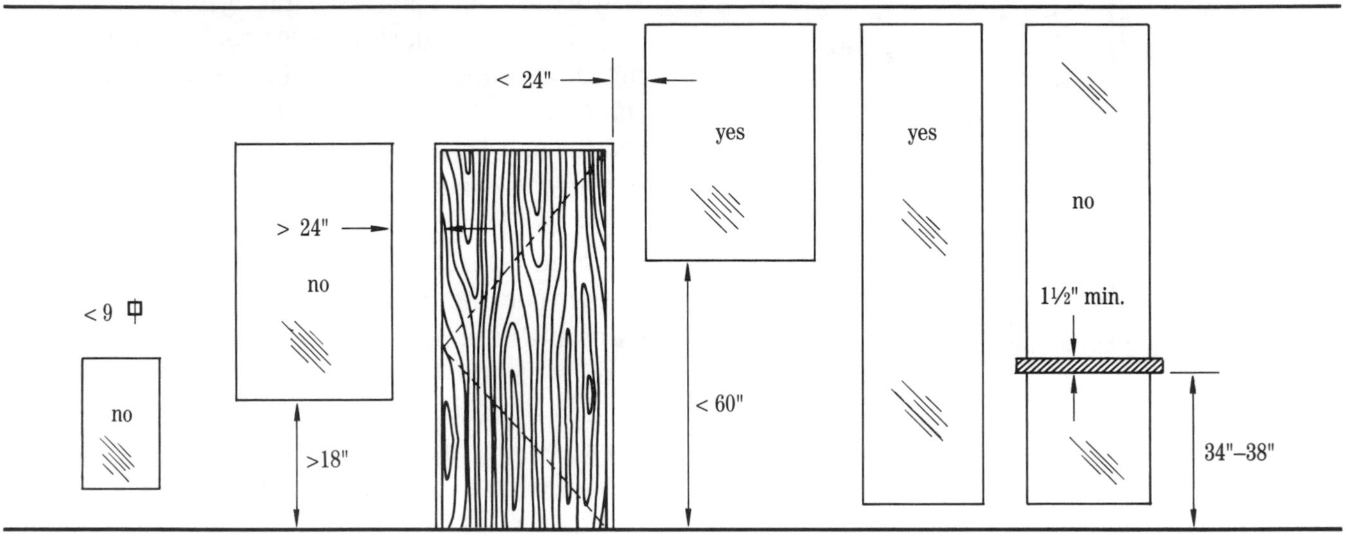

Figure 11.12 Safety Glazing Locations

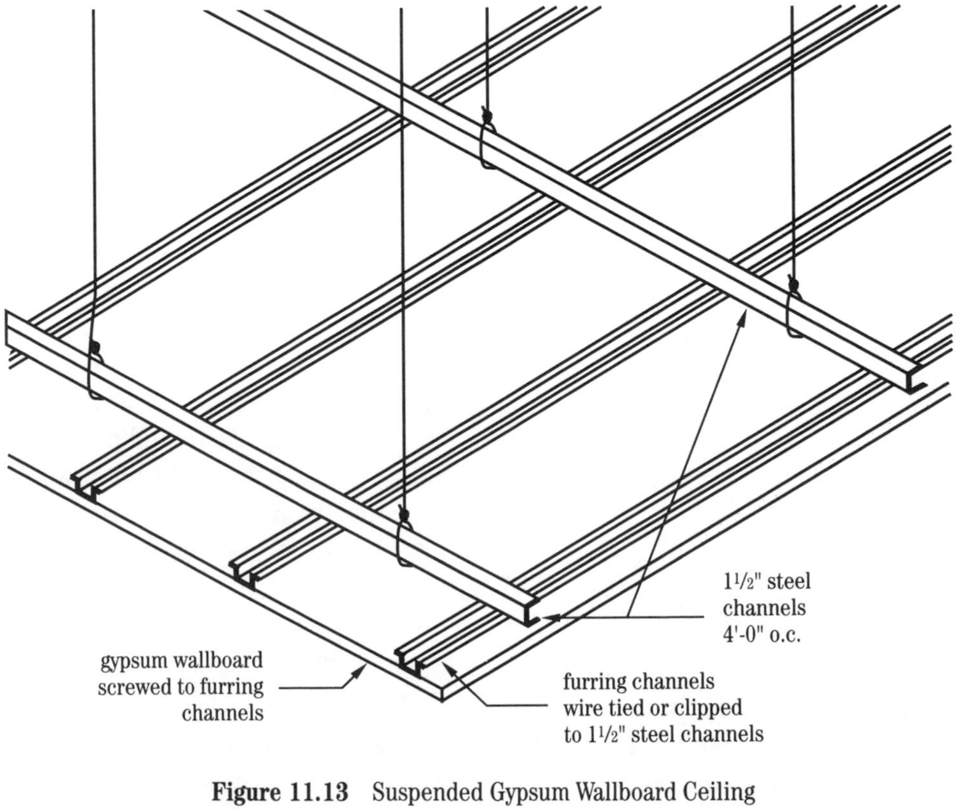

Figure 11.13 Suspended Gypsum Wallboard Ceiling

attached to the main runners either 16 or 24 inches on center with the wallboard screwed to them. Where access to valves, junction boxes, fire dampers, or other services is required, access panels must be installed in the ceiling.

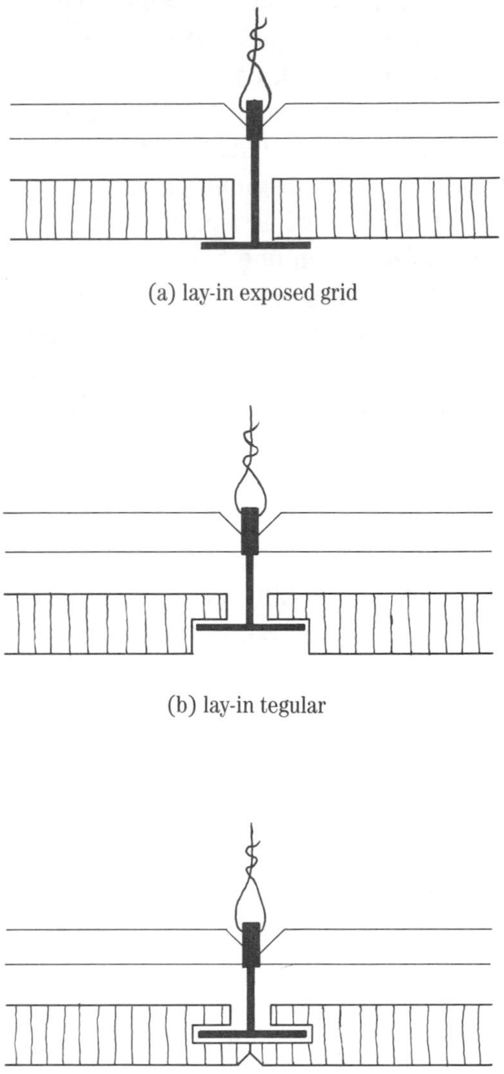

(a) lay-in exposed grid

(b) lay-in tegular

(c) concealed spline

Figure 11.14 Acoustical Ceiling Systems

B. Suspended Acoustical

Suspended acoustical ceilings consist of thin panels of wood fiber, mineral fiber, or glass fiber set in a support grid of metal framing that is suspended by wires from the structure above. The tiles are perforated or fissured in various ways to absorb sound. These ceilings, though, do not prevent sound transmission to any appreciable extent.

Acoustical ceiling tiles and the metal supporting grid are available in a variety of sizes and configurations. The most common type is the lay-in system in which panels are simply laid on top of an exposed T-shaped grid system. See Figure 11.14(a). A variation of this is the tegular system that uses panels with rabbeted edges, as shown in Figure 11.14(b). Systems are also available in which the grid is completely concealed. Concealed systems typically use 1′x 1′ tile sizes. See Figure 11.14(c). Whichever type is used, the tile at the perimeter walls is supported by a ceiling angle. This angle is also used to support light fixtures mounted next to the wall.

Lay-in acoustical ceiling systems are available in sizes of 2′x 2′, 1′x 2′, 2′x 4′(the most common), and 20″x 60″. The 20″x 60″system is used in buildings with a 5-foot working module. This allows partitions to be laid out on the 5-foot module lines without interfering with special 20″x 48″light fixtures located in the center of a module.

Other types of suspended systems that provide acoustical properties are available. These include metal strip ceilings, wood grids, and fabric-covered acoustical batts. They all serve the same purpose: to provide a finished ceiling with access and to absorb rather than reflect sound (like a gypsum wallboard ceiling does) to reduce the noise level within a space.

Because ceilings serve so many purposes in today's construction in addition to acoustical control, there are many elements that must be coordinated with the selection and detailing of ceiling systems. These elements include recessed lights; duct work; sprinkler piping, fire-alarm speakers, smoke detectors and similar items; and drapery pockets and other recessed fixtures.

In many cases in commercial construction, the space above a suspended ceiling is used as a return air plenum. Return air grilles are set in the grid and return air is simply allowed to pass through the grilles, through the ceiling space, and back to a central return air duct or shaft that connects to the HVAC system. If this is the case, building codes require that no combustible material be placed above the ceiling and that all plastic wiring be run in metal conduit. Some codes allow wiring used for telephone, computer, low-voltage lighting, and signal systems to be exposed if it is approved plenum-rated wiring.

Suspended ceilings may be rated or nonrated. If they are fire-rated, it means that they are part of a complete floor-ceiling or roof-ceiling assembly that is rated. Ceiling systems in themselves cannot prevent the spread of fire from one floor to the next. Rated acoustical ceiling systems consist of rated mineral tiles and rated grid systems, which include hold-down clips to keep the panels in place and expansion slots to allow the grid to expand when subjected to heat.

C. Lath and Plaster

Lath and plaster ceilings are constructed like lath and plaster walls. In a traditional plaster ceiling for residential construction, metal lath is attached to the ceiling joists and a three-coat plaster application is used. Like plaster walls, a ceiling can be finished in a variety of textures. In commercial construction, a framework is suspended from the structure like a gypsum wallboard ceiling, but instead of using wallboard, expanded metal lath is wired to the framework and the plaster is applied. Gypsum lath may also be used in place of metal lath and a thin veneer coat of plaster may be applied.

Like their partition counterparts, lath and plaster ceilings cost more than gypsum wallboard ceilings and are more difficult to construct. However, plaster ceilings can easily be curved in two directions for very complex shapes. Additionally, plaster castings of ornate molding can be applied to the ceiling.

D. Integrated Ceilings

Integrated ceilings are suspended ceiling systems specifically designed to accommodate acoustical ceiling tile, light fixtures, supply and return air grilles, sprinklers, and partition attachment in a consistent, unified way. There are many proprietary systems, each with its own characteristics, but all are intended to be used in commercial applications where the partitions, lights, and other elements connected with the ceiling change frequently.

4 MILLWORK

Millwork is custom, shop-fabricated components built of lumber and used for interior finish construction. It includes cabinetry, paneling, custom doors and frames, shelving, custom furniture, and special interior trim. Millwork makes it possible to produce superior wood items because most of the work is done under carefully controlled factory conditions with machinery and finishing techniques that cannot be duplicated on a job site.

Many of the aspects of the fabrication of cabinets and other millwork items have been standardized by the Architectural Woodwork Institute and are described in great detail in Architectural Woodwork Quality Standards, Guide Specifications and Quality Certification Program. Three grades of millwork are established: premium, custom, and economy.

A. Lumber and Veneers for Millwork

There are many wood species used for both solid stock and veneer. Material comes from domestic and foreign sources and varies widely in availability and cost. Because of the limited availability of many hardwood species, most millwork is made from veneer stock. A veneer is a thin slice of wood cut from a log (as described in the next section) and glued to a backing of particleboard or plywood, normally $^3/_4$ inch thick. Solid stock, by contrast, is a thicker piece of solid wood.

B. Types of Solid-Stock Lumber Cutting

The way lumber is cut from a log determines the final appearance of the grain pattern. There are three ways solid stock is cut from a log. The three methods used are plain sawing (also called flat sawing), quarter sawing, and rift sawing. These methods are illustrated in Figure 11.15.

Plain sawing makes the most efficient use of the log and is the least expensive of the three methods. Because the wood is cut with various orientations to the grain of the tree, plain sawing results in a finished surface with the characteristic cathedral pattern shown in Figure 11.15.

Quarter sawing is produced by cutting the log into quarters and then sawing perpendicular to a

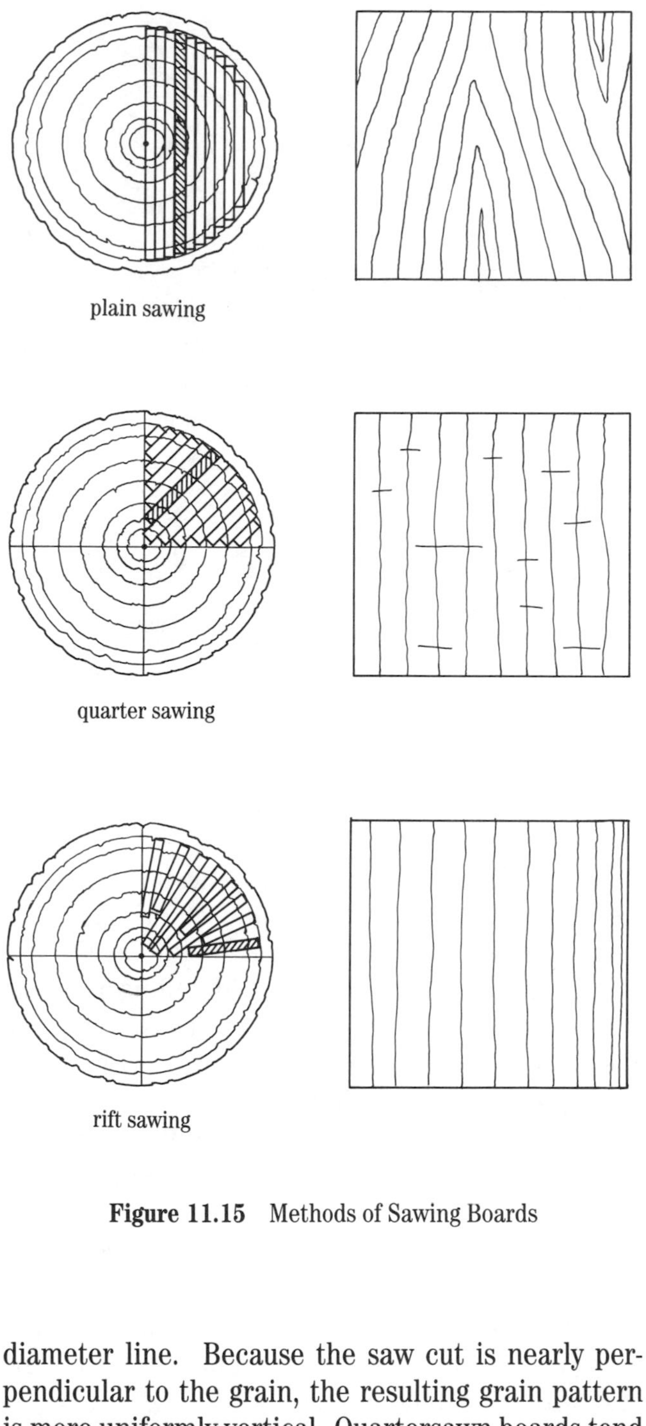

Figure 11.15 Methods of Sawing Boards

diameter line. Because the saw cut is nearly perpendicular to the grain, the resulting grain pattern is more uniformly vertical. Quartersawn boards tend to twist and cup less, shrink less in width, hold paint better, and have fewer defects than plainsawn boards.

Rift sawing provides an even more consistent vertical grain because the saw cuts are always madc radially to the center of the tree. Because the log must be shifted after each cut and because there is much waste, rift cutting is more expensive than quarter sawing and is seldom used.

Because of the limited availability of some species of wood and the expense of making certain cuts, not all types of lumber cutting are available in all species. The availability of cuts in the desired species should be verified before specifications are written.

C. Types of Veneer Cuts

Just as with solid stock, the way veneer is cut from a log affects its final appearance. There are five principal methods of cutting veneers, as shown in Figure 11.16. Plain slicing and quarter slicing are accomplished the same way as cutting solid stock, except the resulting pieces are much thinner. Quarter slicing produces a more straight-grained pattern than plain slicing because the cutting knife strikes the growth rings at approximately a 90-degree angle.

With *rotary slicing,* the log is mounted on a lathe and turned against a knife, which peels off a continuous layer of veneer. This produces a very pronounced grain pattern that is often undesirable in fine-quality wood finishes, although it does produce the most veneer with the least waste.

Half-round slicing is similar to rotary slicing, but the log is cut in half and the veneer cut slightly across the annular growth rings. This results in a pronounced grain pattern showing characteristics of both rotary-sliced and plain-sliced veneers.

Rift slicing is accomplished by quartering a log and cutting at a 15-degree angle to the growth rings. Like quarter slicing, it results in a straight-grain pattern and is commonly used with oak to eliminate the appearance of markings perpendicular to the direction of the grain. These markings in oak are caused by medullary rays, which are radial cells extending from the center of the tree to its circumference.

Because the width of a piece of veneer is limited by the diameter of the log or the portion of log from which it is cut, several veneers must be put together on a backing panel to make up the needed size of a finished piece. The individual veneers come from the same piece of log, which is called a *flitch.*

D. Joinery Details

Various types of joints are used for millwork construction to increase the strength of the joint and

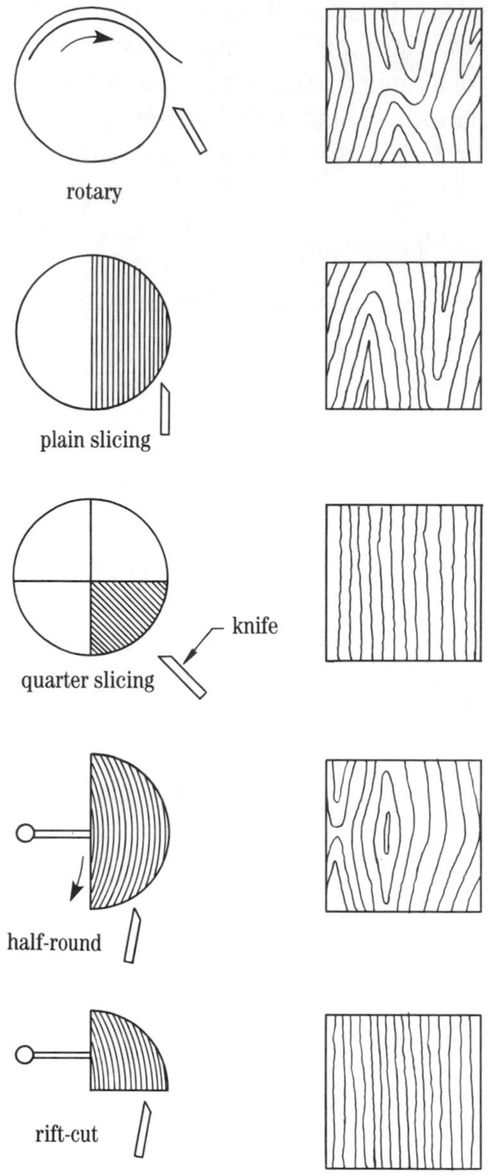

Figure 11.16 Veneer Cuts

improve the appearance by eliminating mechanical fasteners such as screws. With the availability of high-strength adhesives, screws and other visible mechanical fasteners are seldom needed for the majority of work produced in the shop. Field attachment, however, often requires the use of blind nailing or other concealed fastening to maintain the quality look of the work. Some of the common joints used in millwork are shown in Figure 11.17.

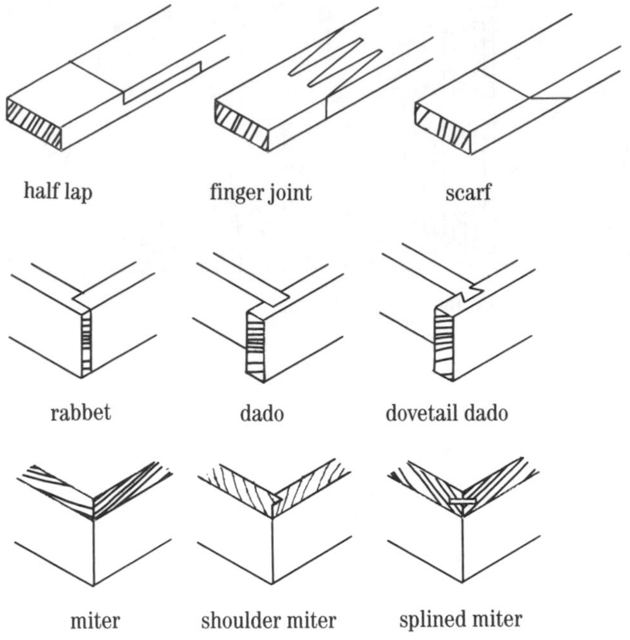

Figure 11.17 Wood Joints

E. Cabinetwork

Millwork cabinets are built in the shop as complete assemblies and are simply set in place and secured to the surrounding construction at the job site. There are several methods of detailing door and drawer fronts on cabinets, but the construction of most cabinet frames is fairly standard, as discussed in Chapter 7 and shown in Figures 7.20 and 7.21.

The two basic types of door and drawer front construction are overlay and face frame. With overlay construction, the fronts of the doors and drawers stop in front of the face frame of the cabinet. Edges of adjacent fronts may almost touch or be separated enough to show the face frame with a reveal. In face frame construction, the door and drawer fronts are flush with the cabinet frame.

F. Paneling

Millwork paneling includes the flush or raised panel construction used to cover vertical surfaces. Paneling is built up of thin wood veneers glued to backing panels of particleboard or plywood. Raised panel construction is the more traditional type, and its construction and components are illustrated in Figure 11.18. Flush paneling has a single, smooth surface. Its construction and installation are described in this section.

In addition to the way veneers are cut, there are several methods of matching adjacent pieces of veneer and veneer panels in a room that affect the final appearance of the job. The three considerations in increasing order of scale are matching between adjacent veneer leaves, matching veneers within a panel, and matching panels within a room.

Matching adjacent veneer leaves may be done in three ways, as shown in Figure 11.19. *Book matching* is the most common. As the veneers are sliced off the log, every other piece is turned over so that adjacent leaves form a symmetrical grain pattern. With *slip matching,* consecutive pieces are placed side by side with the same face sides being exposed. *Random matching* places veneers in random sequence, and veneers from different flitches may even be used.

Veneers must be glued to rigid panels (usually $^3/_4$-inch particleboard) for installation. The method of doing this is the next consideration in specifying paneling. If the veneers are bookmatched, there are three ways of matching veneers within a panel as shown in Figure 11.20. A running match simply alternates bookmatched veneer pieces regardless of their width or how many must be used to complete a panel. Any portion left over from the last leaf of one panel is used as the starting piece for the next. A balance match utilizes veneer pieces trimmed to equal widths in each panel. A center match has an even number of veneer leaves of uniform width so that there is a veneer joint in the center of the panel.

There are three ways panels can be assembled within a room to complete a project. Figure 11.21

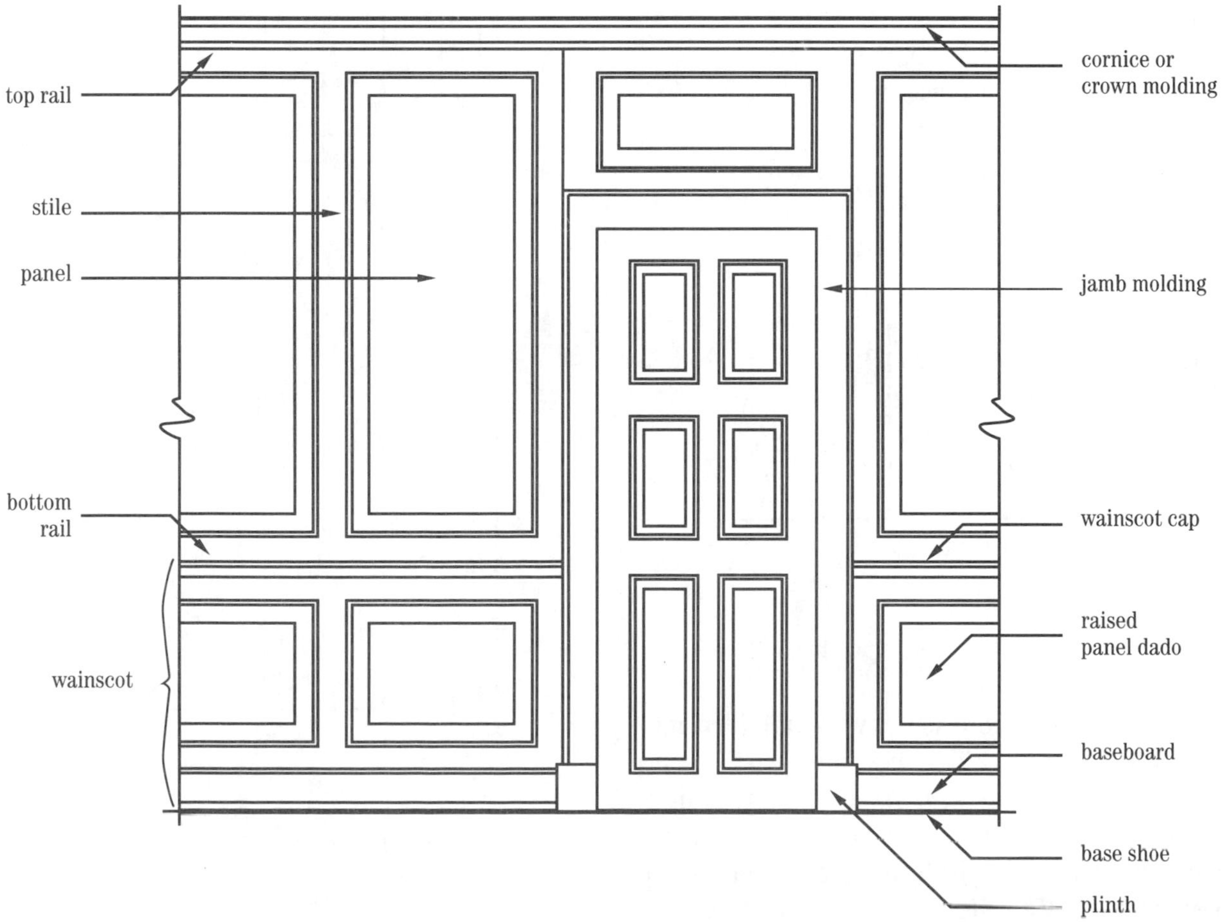

Figure 11.18 Raised Panel Construction

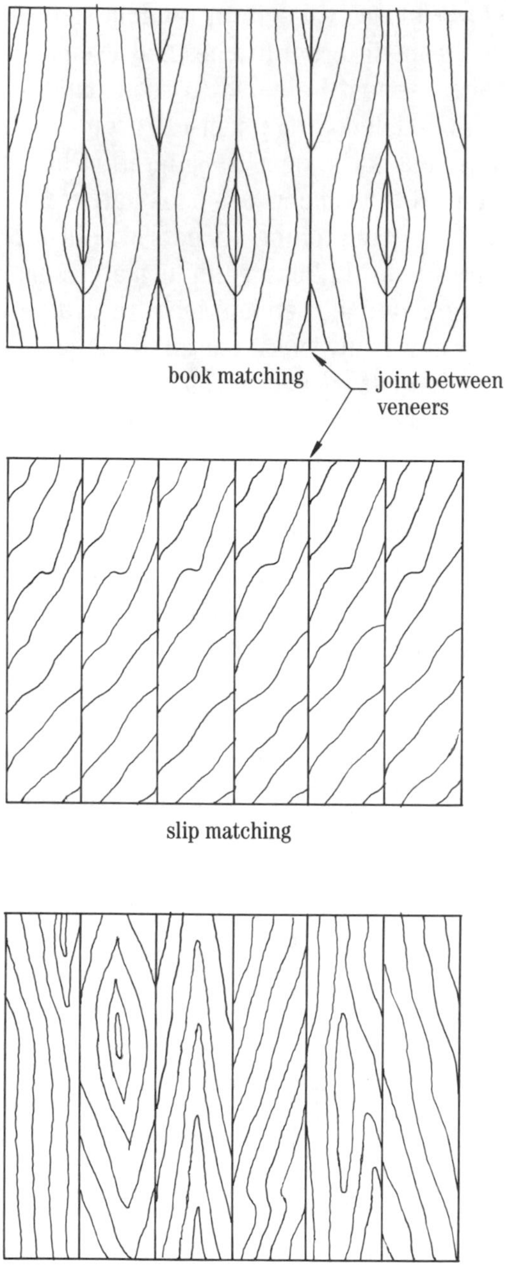

Figure 11.19 Veneer Matching

shows three sides of a room as if it were unfolded and the three walls laid flat. The first, and least expensive, is called *warehouse match.* Premanufactured panels, normally 4 feet wide by 8 or 10 feet long, are assembled from a single flitch that yields from six to twelve panels. They are field cut to fit around doors, windows, and other obstructions, resulting in some loss of grain continuity.

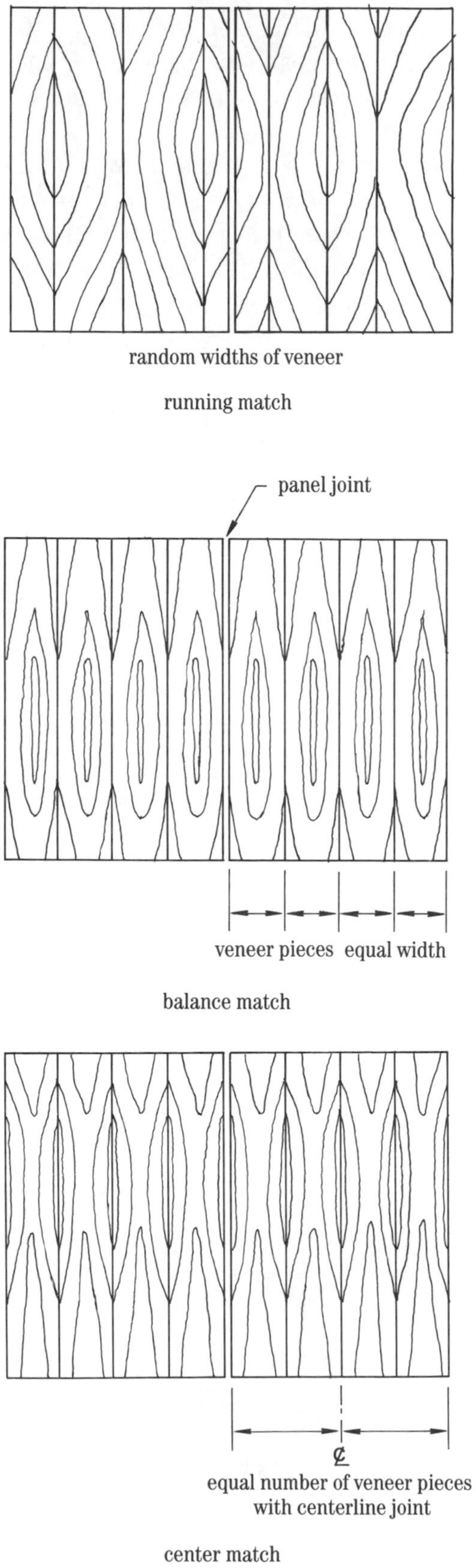

Figure 11.20 Panel Matching Veneers

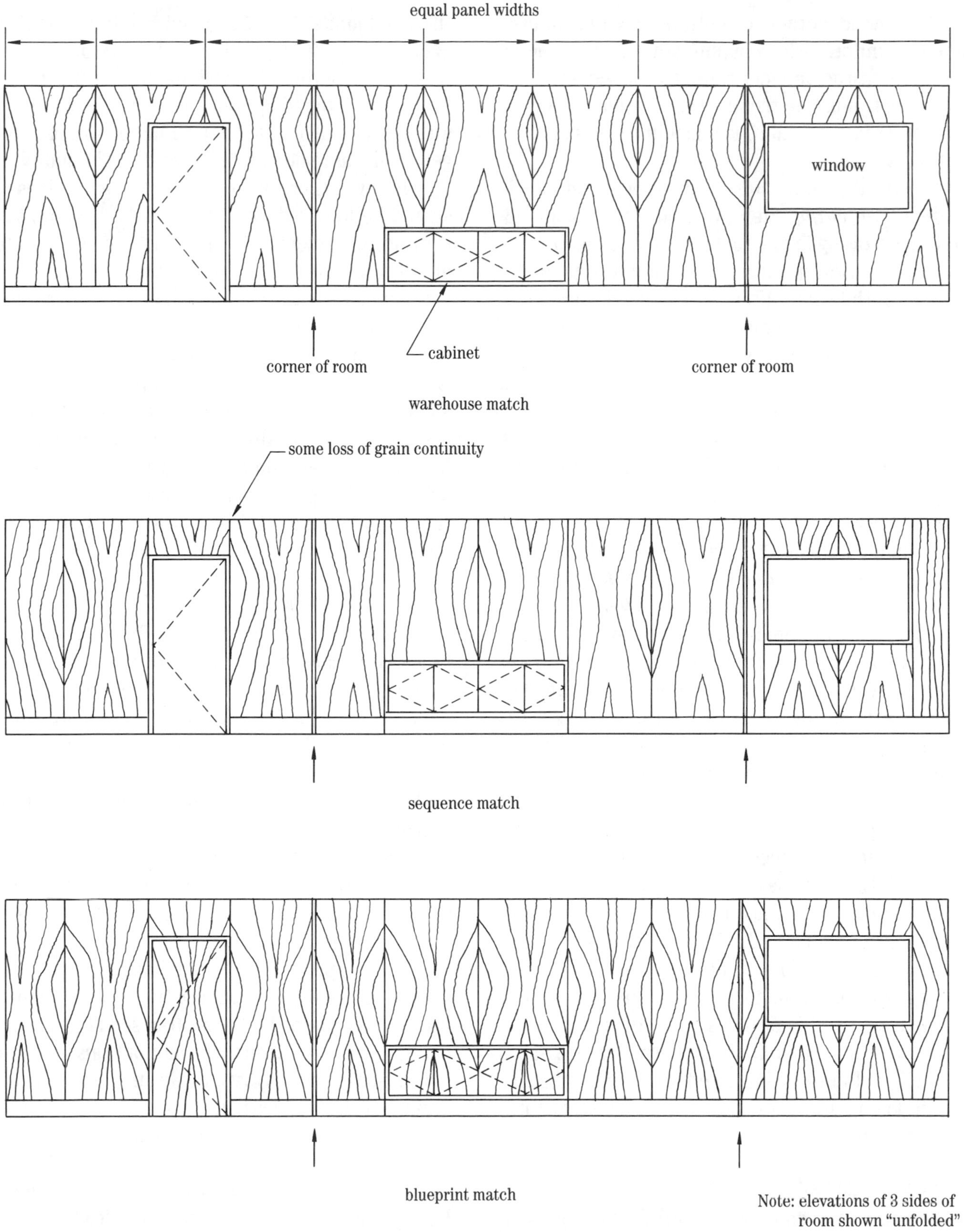

Figure 11.21 Matching Panels Within a Room

The second method, called *sequence match,* uses panels of uniform width manufactured for a specific job and with the veneers arranged in sequence. If some panels must be trimmed to fit around doors or other obstructions, there is a moderate loss of grain continuity.

The third, and most expensive, method is *blueprint matching.* Here, the panels are manufactured to precisely fit the room and line up with every obstruction so grain continuity is not interrupted. Veneers from the same flitch are matched over doors, cabinets, and other items covered with paneling.

Joints of paneling may be constructed in a number of ways depending on the finish appearance desired, as shown in Figure 7.23. Paneling is hung on a wall with either steel or aluminum Z-clips or wood cleats as discussed in Chapter 7 and shown in Figure 7.24.

G. Laminates

A common finishing material used with millwork is *high-pressure plastic laminate.* This is a thin sheet of material made by impregnating several layers of kraft paper with phenolic resins and overlaying the paper with a patterned or colored sheet and a layer of melamine resin. The entire assembly is placed in a hot press under high pressure where the various layers fuse. Plastic laminates are used for countertops, wall paneling, cabinets, shelving, and furniture.

Because laminates are very thin, they must be adhered to panel substrates such as plywood or particleboard. Smaller pieces can be glued to solid pieces of lumber. There are several types and thicknesses of plastic laminate, the most common being a general-purpose type, which is 0.050 inch thick. It is used for both vertical and horizontal applications. A post-forming type, 0.040 inch thick, is manufactured so it can be heated and bent to a small radius.

When plastic laminate is applied to large surfaces of paneling, it must be balanced with a backing sheet to inhibit moisture absorption and to attain structural balance so the panel does not warp.

H. Moisture Content and Shrinkage

Because all wood products shrink and swell with changes in moisture content in the air, all wood construction should be detailed to allow for this movement to take place without putting undue stress on the wood joints. Shrinkage and swelling in millwork is not as much of a problem as for site-built carpentry because of the improved manufacturing methods available in the shop and the fact that solid stock and veneer can be dried or acclimated to a particular geographical region and its prevailing humidity.

However, there are some general guidelines that should be followed. For most of the United States, Ontario, and Quebec, the optimum moisture content of millwork for interior applications is from 5 to 10 percent. The relative humidity necessary to maintain this optimum level is from 25 to 55 percent. In the more humid southern U.S. coastal areas, Newfoundland, and Canadian coastal provinces, the optimum moisture content is from 8 to 13 percent, while in the dry southwest, Alberta, Saskatchewan, and Manitoba, the corresponding values are from 4 to 9 percent. These values should be used when specifying the maximum allowable moisture content in architectural woodwork.

I. Millwork Finishes

Millwork can either be field-finished or factory-finished. Because more control can be achieved with a factory finish, it is the preferred method. Transparent finishes include penetrating oils, shellac, lacquer, and varnish. Oil finishes are easily applied and have a rich luster, but they have a short life and tend to darken with age. Shellac and lacquer become brittle and darken with age.

Other transparent finishes include the hard plastics such as polyurethane. They are very durable and will not darken with age, but they cost more. Gloss or matt sheens are available.

Before applying the final finish, wood may be stained to modify its color. The two types of stains are water-based stains and solvent-based stains. Water-based stains yield a uniform color but raise the grain. Solvent-based stains dry quickly and do not raise the grain, but they are less uniform.

On many open-grain woods such as oak, mahogany, and teak, a filler should be applied before finishing to give a more uniform appearance to the millwork. For shop-finished millwork, the American Woodwork Institute has developed 13 standard finishing systems that include specifications for both transparent and opaque finishes.

5 SECURITY

Security systems include methods for detecting intruders, for preventing entry, for controlling access to secure areas, and for notification in the event of unauthorized entry or other emergencies.

There are many types of intrusion detection devices. Motion detectors and heat detectors sense the presence of someone in a room or within the field of view. Microwave and infrared beams trip a circuit when the path of their beam is interrupted. Pressure sensors detect weight on a floor or other surface. Other types of systems can be installed on glass, in door openings, and in other parts of a building to set off an alarm when unauthorized entry is made through the opening.

In the event of an unauthorized entry or other emergency, alarm systems can include simple noise alarms, notification of the breach of security at a monitored central guard station, or automatic notification over phone lines to a central security service.

Access to secure areas can be controlled with a number of devices in addition to traditional mechanical locks. For example, locks can be connected to card readers. A plastic card containing a coded magnetic strip is used that unlocks the door when a valid card is passed through the reader. Numbered keyboards serve the same purpose by unlocking a door when the user enters the correct numerical code. At the same time the card or keyboard unlocks the door, the entry location and person entering is recorded at a central monitoring station. New devices are now being developed that can read individual biological features such as the retina of the eye or the palm of a hand, providing a counterfeit-proof method of identification.

SAMPLE QUESTIONS

1. Under what conditions would you use a $1^3/_4$-inch-thick hollow metal door?

1. when a fire-rating of over 90 minutes and high security and durability are required
2. when a fire-rating over 1 hour is required or a steel frame is necessary
3. when the door opening is expected to receive heavy use and a smoke-proof opening is required
4. when the door will receive minimal maintenance under heavy use

2. What type of locking device is MOST appropriate for an office building?

1. cylindrical lock
2. unit lock
3. card reader lock
4. mortise lock

3. Safety glazing is NOT required in which of the following locations?

1. in sidelites where the sill is greater than 18 inches above the floor
2. in glass sidelites next to a solid wood door
3. in shower doors
4. in full-height glass panels more than 12 inches from a door

4. What type of partition does the section shown below indicate?

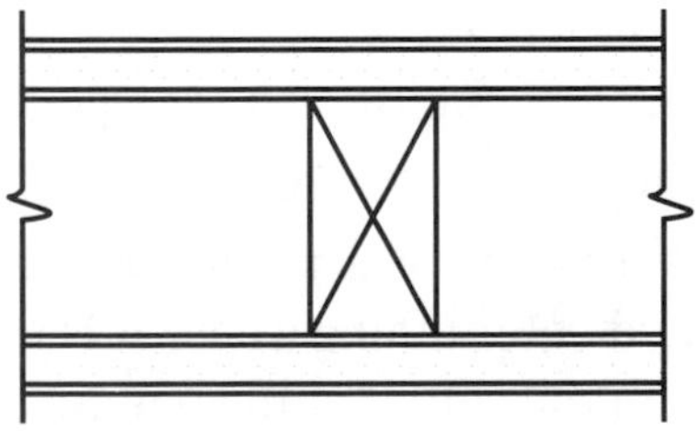

1. a $3^1/_2$-inch wood stud with gypsum wallboard
2. a $3^1/_2$-inch wood stud with wood paneling
3. a $2^1/_2$-inch metal stud with gypsum wallboard
4. a $2^1/_2$-inch metal stud with two layers of gypsum wallboard

5. What type of system would be MOST appropriate in a large commercial remodeling project where a decorative acoustical ceiling and plenum access are required?

1. integrated
2. linear metal strip
3. gypsum wallboard
4. concealed spline

6. What is the purpose of a glazing bead?

1. to seal the gap between edges of butt glazing
2. to cushion the glass against the frame
3. to hold the glass in place
4. to support the weight of the glass and separate its edge from the bottom frame

7. Which method of veneer cut would you specify if you wanted the straightest grain possible from most species of trees?

1. half-round slicing
2. quarter slicing
3. flat slicing
4. rotary slicing

8. If a client wanted to remove part of a partition you think might be a bearing wall, what is your best course of action?

1. Have a structural engineer or architect review the problem and make a recommendation.
2. Look in the attic to see if the wall supports any beams or joists.
3. Ask the client for the structural drawings of the building and review them.
4. Check for structural stability by tapping on the wall and determining where it is located in relation to the center of the building.

9. To detail a door frame for a conference room where privacy is critical, which of the following is LEAST likely to be required?

1. an automatic door bottom
2. a heavy-duty, silent door closer
3. neoprene gasketing
4. a solid-core door

10. In partition construction, what is the purpose of resilient channels?

1. to increase the thickness of a partition
2. to increase the acoustical properties of a partition
3. to increase the strength of a partition
4. to provide a suitable base for attaching wallboard over masonry

12 FINISHES

1 FLOORING

This section outlines some of the basic construction methods for flooring that is built with several components above structural floors as well as flooring that is simply applied as a single thin material such as resilient tile or carpet.

A. Wood Flooring

There are four basic types of wood flooring. *Strip flooring* is one of the most common and consists of thin strips from $^{3}/_{8}$ inch to $^{25}/_{32}$ inch thick of varying lengths with tongue-and-groove edges. Most strip flooring is $2^{1}/_{4}$ inches wide, but $1^{1}/_{2}$-inch wide strips are also available.

Plank flooring comes in the same thicknesses as strip but is from $3^{1}/_{4}$ to 8 inches wide. It is used where a larger scale is desired or to emulate wider, historic planking.

Block flooring is made of preassembled wood flooring in three basic configurations. *Unit block flooring* is standard strip flooring assembled into a unit held together with steel or wood splines. *Laminated block flooring* is flooring made from three to five plies of cross-laminated wood veneer. Both types of block flooring are from $^{3}/_{8}$ inch to $^{25}/_{32}$ inches thick. *Parquet flooring* is made of preassembled units of several small, thin slats of wood in a variety of patterns. It may be finished or unfinished. Parquet flooring is usually sold in 12-inch squares, $^{5}/_{16}$ inch thick, for mastic application. Parquet flooring is easier and less expensive to install than other types of flooring and can be installed in a wide range of designs.

The fourth type of wood floor is made from solid *end grain blocks.* These are solid pieces of wood from $2^{1}/_{4}$ inches to 4 inches thick laid on end. Solid block floors are very durable and resistant to oils, mild chemicals, and indentation. They are often used for industrial floors.

Wood flooring is graded differently from other wood products. Grading rules are set by the various trade associations such as the National Oak Flooring Manufacturers' Association and the Maple Flooring Manufacturers' Association. Unfinished oak flooring is graded as clear, select, no. 1 common, and no. 2 common. Clear is the best grade with the most uniform color. Plain sawn is standard, but quarter sawn is available on special order. Lengths of pieces are $1^{1}/_{4}$ feet and longer with the average length being $3^{3}/_{4}$ feet. Beech, birch, and maple are available in first, second, and third grades along with some combination grades.

Wood flooring must be installed over a suitable nailable base. Because wood swells if it gets damp, provisions must be made to prevent moisture from seeping up from below and to allow for expansion of the completed floor. Strip flooring is installed by blind nailing through the tongue. Figure 12.1 shows two methods of installing wood flooring over a concrete subfloor in commercial construction. In Figure 12.1(a), a sheet of $^{3}/_{4}$ inch plywood is attached to the concrete to provide the nailable base. A layer of polyethylene film is laid down first if moisture may be a problem.

In Figure 12.1(b), the wood flooring is laid on wood sleepers. This method of installation not only gives a more resilient floor that is more comfortable under foot, but it also provides an air space so any excess moisture can escape. In both instances, a gap of about $^{3}/_{8}$ inch to $^{3}/_{4}$ inch is left at the perimeter to allow for expansion and is concealed with the wood base.

Figure 12.2 shows the typical installation over wood framing with a plywood or particleboard subfloor, as is typical in most residential construction. A layer of 15-pound asphalt felt may be laid to prevent squeaking and act as a vapor barrier. There are

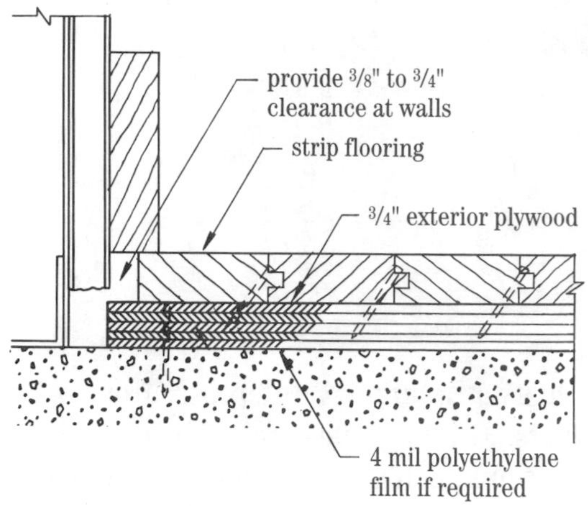

(a) strip flooring over plywood

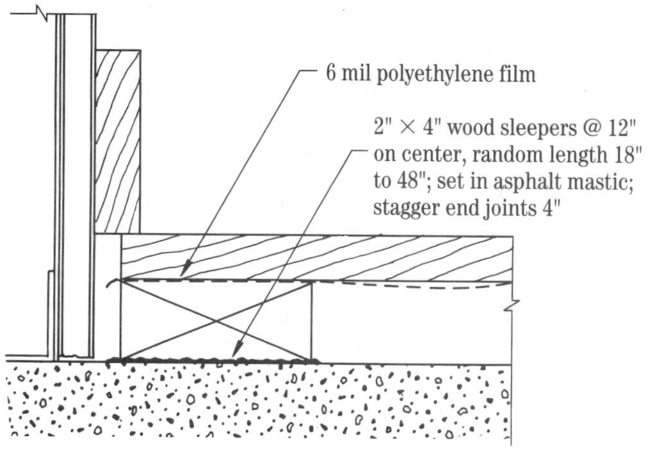

(b) strip flooring on sleepers

Figure 12.1 Wood Flooring Installation

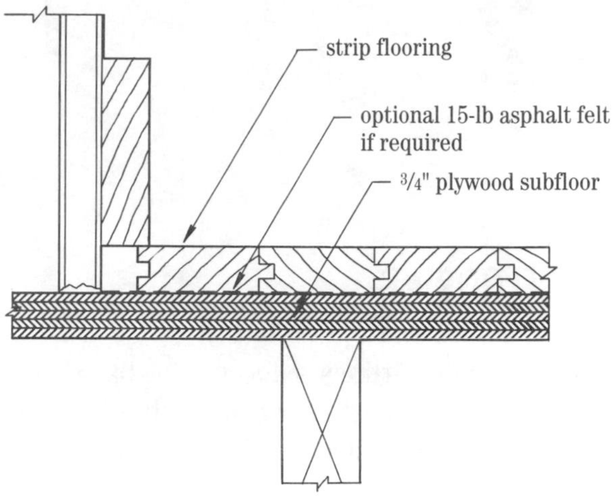

strip flooring over joists

Figure 12.2 Wood Flooring on Wood Framing

also resilient pads available that are used in place of sleepers for strip flooring installation. These provide an even more resilient floor and are often used for dance floors and gymnasium floors.

B. Stone Flooring

There are five types of stone commonly used in interior construction for flooring as well as for walls. These include granite, marble, limestone, slate, and sandstone.

- *Granite* is an igneous rock with visible grains. It is available in a wide variety of colors, including gray, beige, white, pink, red, blue, green, and black. For interior use, there are five common finishes. A polished finish has a mirror gloss with sharp reflection. A honed finish has a dull sheen, without reflections. Fine-rubbed finishes produce a smooth surface free from scratches, with no sheen. A rubbed finish has a surface with occasional slight "trails" or scratches. Finally, a thermal, or flame, finish has a coarse finish, the amount varying depending on the grain structure of the granite.

- *Marble* is a metamorphic rock formed by layers of shells, which, under heat and pressure, form into a composition of crystalline grains of calcite and/or dolomite. Like granite, marble is available in a range of colors and patterns from uniform, pure white to vivid greens and reds with wild streaked patterns. The smoothest finish for marble is a polished finish, which produces a glossy surface bringing out the full color and character of the marble. A honed finish has a satin-smooth surface, with little or no gloss. An abrasive finish has a flat, nonreflective surface suitable for stair treads and other nonslip surfaces. A wet-sand finish yields a smooth surface that is also suitable for nonslip floors.

- *Limestone* is most commonly used for exterior surfaces, but a type of limestone, called travertine, is frequently used for interior flooring. Because of the way it is formed, travertine has a network of holes in it. These must be filled with an epoxy resin (which can be colored to be compatible with the stone) to make a smooth surface. Travertine is a light, creamy color and is usually finished with a polished surface.

- *Slate* is a fine-grained metamorphic rock that is easily split into thin slabs, making it ideal for flooring as well as roofing. Slate is available in ranges of gray, black, green, brown, and deep red. A natural cleft finish shows the surface as it is cleaved from the rock, so it is rough and the surface level varies by about 1/8 inch. A sand-rubbed finish gives an even plane showing a slight grain. A honed finish is semipolished, without a sheen.

- *Sandstone* is a sedimentary rock made of sand and other substances. When cleaved from the original rock, it is called flagstone and has a naturally rough surface. It can be used with irregular edges as it comes from the rock, or it can be saw-cut into rectangular or square shapes.

Stone flooring can be installed in a number of ways; the two primary methods are a thin-set or a thick-set installation. With the first type, a uniform thickness of stone is set on the subfloor with a special thin-set mortar (about 1/8 inch or less in thickness) or with adhesive. A thick-set installation requires that a layer of mortar from 3/4 to 1 1/4 inches thick be applied to a suitably prepared, structurally sound subfloor. The stone is then set either in the semiwet mortar or the mortar is allowed to cure and the stone is set with another thin layer of dry-set mortar on top the first.

Thick-set applications are generally the best and must be used when the subfloor is uneven or when the stone varies in thickness, as with slate or sandstone. Thin-set applications are less expensive, add much less weight to the floor, and are faster to install. They are suitable for thin stone floors cut in uniform thicknesses in either residential or commercial construction.

The various types of stone flooring installation methods are shown in Figure 12.3. With thick-set methods, the mortar bed can be bonded to the subfloor or separated from it with a cleavage membrane.

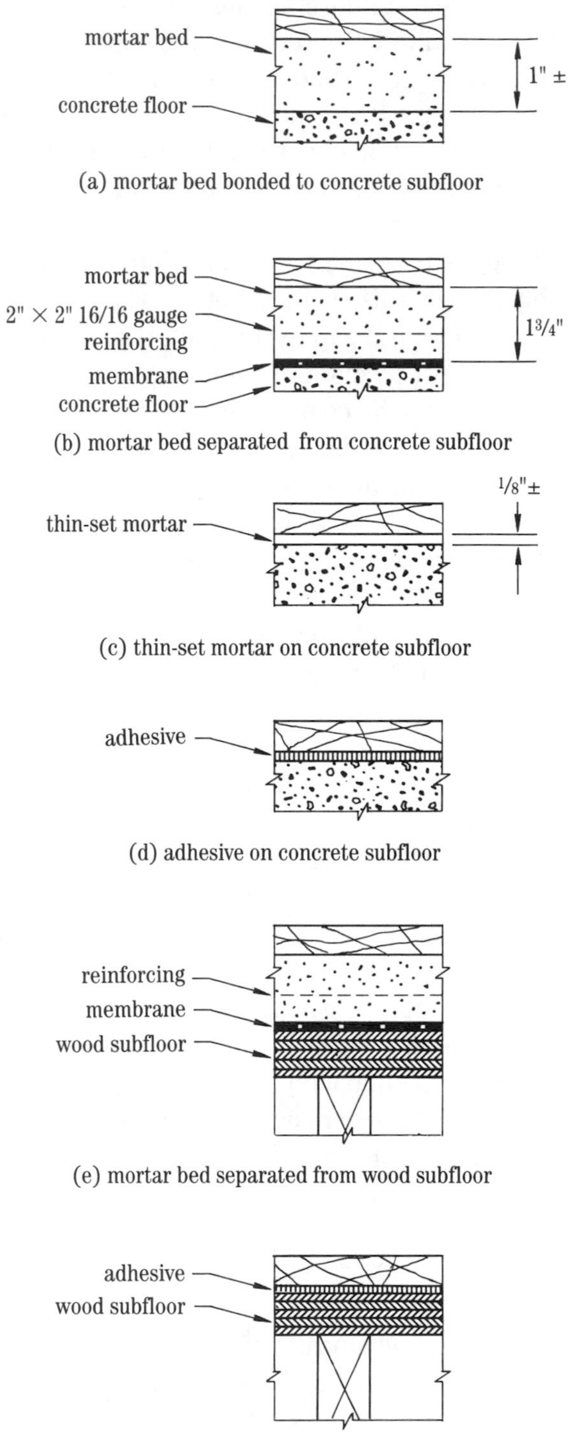

Figure 12.3 Stone Flooring Installation Methods

Used with steel reinforcing mesh in the mortar bed, this method allows the finish floor to be structurally separate from the subfloor. If the subfloor deflects or moves slightly, the stone flooring is protected from cracking because it is not bonded to the structural floor. Thin-set floors can be placed on either concrete or wood subfloors.

Stone floors can be set with the joints tightly butted together or with a space between the individual pieces. If there is a gap in the joint, it must be filled with grout or a portland cement/sand mixture that can be colored to be compatible with the color of the stone. Several special types of grout are available that are resistant to chemicals, fungus, and mildew. Another type of grout is latex grout, which provides some flexibility when slight movement in the floor is expected.

Whatever type of stone is used, you must consider the added weight the stone and mortar will add to the floor, the extra thickness required, and the finish that will be most appropriate. Most thin stones ($^1/_4$ to $^3/_8$ inch) that are applied with a thin-set mortar or adhesive do not add significant weight to the floor. Thick-set stone floors are very heavy and require an extra $1^1/_2$ to $2^1/_2$ inches above the subfloor. Structural capacities should be verified with a structural engineer.

Polished finishes should not be used in areas where the stone might get wet or on stairs because of the potential slippage problems. Flamed finishes with granite or an abrasive finish with marble are better choices in these applications and, in fact, are required by code in some applications.

C. Terrazzo

Terrazzo is a composite material poured in place or precast that is used for floors, walls, and stairs. It consists of marble, quartz, granite, or other suitable chips, in a matrix that is cementitious, chemical, or a combination of both. Terrazzo is poured, cured, ground, and polished to produce a smooth surface.

The advantages of terrazzo include durability, water resistance, ease of cleaning, fire resistance, and a wide choice of patterns and colors. An unlimited number of terrazzo finishes can be achieved by specifying various combinations of chips and matrix colors.

There are four basic types of terrazzo. Standard terrazzo is the most common type, using small chips no larger than $^3/_8$ inch. Venetian terrazzo uses chips larger than $^3/_8$ inch. Palladian terrazzo uses thin random-fractured slabs of marble with standard terrazzo between. Rustic terrazzo has the matrix depressed to expose the chips.

Terrazzo can be installed on walls as well as floors. Several common floor installations are shown in Figure 12.4. The sand cushion method (a) is the best way to avoid cracking of the terrazzo because the finish system is physically separated from the structural slab with a membrane much the same as one of the thick-set stone floor installation methods. Because the underbed is reinforced, the terrazzo system can move independently of the structure. If floor movement or deflection is not anticipated, the bonded method (b) can be used. Where the thickness of the installation is a problem, a monolithic (c) or thin-set (d) method can be used.

Terrazzo is generally finished to a smooth surface with an 80-grit stone grinder, but it can be ground with a rough, 24-grit to achieve a more textured surface. Rustic terrazzo exposes some of the stone when the matrix is washed before it has set, but this finish is usually not appropriate for interior flooring.

D. Resilient Flooring

Resilient flooring is a generic term describing several types of composition materials made from various resins, fibers, plasticizers, and fillers. It is formed under heat and pressure to produce a thin material, either sheets or tiles. Resilient flooring is applied with mastic to a subfloor of concrete, plywood, or other smooth underlayment. Some resilient floorings may be installed only on floors above grade, while others may be placed below, on, or above grade. The common types of resilient flooring used today include vinyl, rubber, and cork.

- *Vinyl flooring* includes pure vinyl, vinyl composition, vinyl tiles, and sheet vinyl. It is a good, durable resilient flooring resistant to indentation, abrasion, grease, water, alkalis, and some acids. Vinyl comes in a variety of colors and patterns and is inexpensive and easy to install. It can be used below

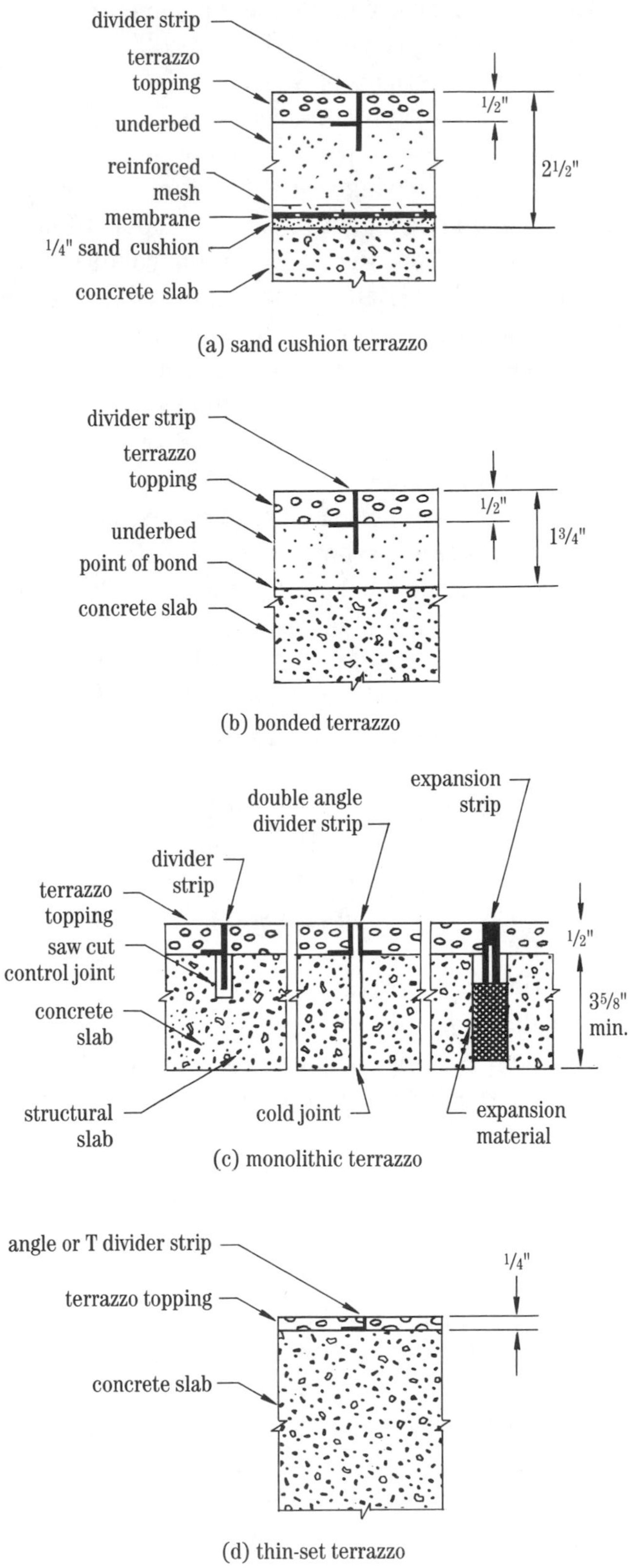

Figure 12.4 Methods of Terrazzo Installation

grade, on grade, or above grade. It must be installed over a clean, dry, smooth surface. Vinyl tiles are generally 12 inches square, although some are available in 9-inch squares. Either 1/16-inch or 1/8-inch thicknesses are available, but for commercial use and better residential floors, the 1/8-inch thickness is preferred. Sheet vinyl comes in 6, 9, or 12 foot wide rolls. Although slightly more difficult to install, it provides a floor with fewer seams.

- *Rubber flooring* is made from synthetic rubber and offers excellent resistance to deformation under loads, providing a very comfortable, quiet, resilient floor. Rubber, however, is not very resistant to oils or grease. This flooring is available with a smooth surface or with a patterned, raised surface, which allows water and dirt to lie below the wearing surface, helping to prevent slipping or excessive abrasion. Rubber flooring is available in tiles or sheet in several thicknesses.

- *Cork flooring* is available in tile form and is used where acoustical control or resilience is desired. However, some types are not resistant to staining, fading, moisture, heavy loads, or concentrated foot traffic. Cork is usually combined with resins to improve its durability and make it easier to maintain. Generally, cork should be used only on above-grade floors, although some types can be used below grade if installed according to the manufacturer's directions.

E. Carpet

Carpet is one of the most commonly specified flooring materials. If properly selected it is attractive, durable, quiet, easy to install, and requires less maintenance than many other types of flooring. There are three basic forms of carpet: rugs, sheet carpet, and carpet tiles. A rug is a soft floor covering laid on the floor but not fastened to it. It does not cover the entire floor.

Carpet tiles are individual pieces of carpet, typically 18 inches square, that are applied to the floor with pressure-sensitive adhesive. Because of their modular design, damaged or worn pieces can be replaced without removing the entire floor covering. They are generally specified for commercial installations where frequent change in room layout is expected, where maintenance may be a problem, or where flat undercarpet electrical and telephone cabling is used.

Fibers: Carpet is made from several fibers and combinations of fibers, including wool, nylon, acrylic, modacrylic, polyester, and olefin.

Wool is a natural material and overall one of the best for carpet. It is very durable and resilient, wears well, has a superior appearance, is flame resistant, and is relatively easy to clean and maintain. Unfortunately, it is also one of the most expensive fibers for initial cost.

Nylon is an economical carpet material that is very strong and wear resistant. It has a high stain resistance and excellent crush resistance, it can be dyed with a wide variety of colors, and it cleans easily. Some nylons have static problems and a glossy sheen, but these problems have generally been alleviated with improved fiber construction and by blending nylon with other fibers. Because of its many advantages, including cost, nylon is the most widely used fiber for residential and commercial carpet.

Acrylic has moderate abrasion resistance, but it has a more wool-like appearance than nylon. Like nylon, it can be dyed with a variety of colors, has good crush resistance, and is easy to maintain. Modacrylic is a modified version of acrylic.

Polyester carpet fiber is made from synthetic polymers and is highly abrasion resistant, has good crush resistance, cleans well, is mildew resistant, and is low in cost. It is sometimes blended with nylon.

Olefin (polypropylene) is used primarily for indoor-outdoor carpet and as an alternative to jute for carpet backing. It is very durable, stain resistant, and cleans easily. However, it is the least attractive of the artificial fibers and has a low melting point.

Manufacturing processes: Carpet is manufactured by weaving, tufting, needle punching, fusion bonding, and, less frequently, by knitting and custom tufting.

Weaving is the traditional method of making carpet by interlacing warp and weft yarns. It is a method that produces a very attractive, durable carpet, but it is the most expensive method of manufacturing carpet by machine. As shown in Figure 12.5, there are three primary methods of weaving.

Wilton carpet (a) is produced on a Jacquard loom that allows complex patterns to be woven into the carpet as well as allowing several types of surface textures, including level cut pile, level loop, cut/uncut, and multilevel loop. Because different colors of yarn run beneath the surface of the carpet and are pulled up only when they are needed for the pattern, Wiltons are generally heavier and more expensive than the other woven types for the same total weight.

Velvet carpet (b) is the simplest form of weaving and places all the pile yarn on the face of the carpet. Velvet carpets are generally solid colors, but multicolored yarns can also be used in a variety of surface textures including plushes, loop pile, cut-pile, multilevel loop, and cut-and-loop styles.

Axminster carpets (c) are made on a modified Jacquard loom that delivers different colors of yarn at different times according to the pattern desired. Because of the weaving process, Axminster carpets can be produced in a range of patterns and colors, from geometric to floral. Unlike the Wilton process, most of the pile yarn is placed on the surface. The carpet has an even, cut-pile surface with a heavily ribbed backing.

Tufting is a process in which the pile yarn is punched through the backing with rows of needles, much like a sewing machine. As the needle goes through the backing, the yarn is caught and held while the needle makes the next pass. The loop of yarn can be left as is for loop carpet or cut for cut-pile carpet. Because of the speed and relative low cost of tufting, this process accounts for the majority of the carpet manufactured.

Needle punching is similar to tufting except the fiber is pulled through a backing with barbed needles. It produces a carpet of limited variation in texture and accounts for a very small percentage of the total carpet market.

Fusion bonding embeds the pile yarn in a backing of liquid vinyl. When the vinyl hardens, the tufts are permanently locked in the backing. It is used primarily for carpet tiles.

The appearance and durability of a carpet are affected by the amount of yarn in a given area, how

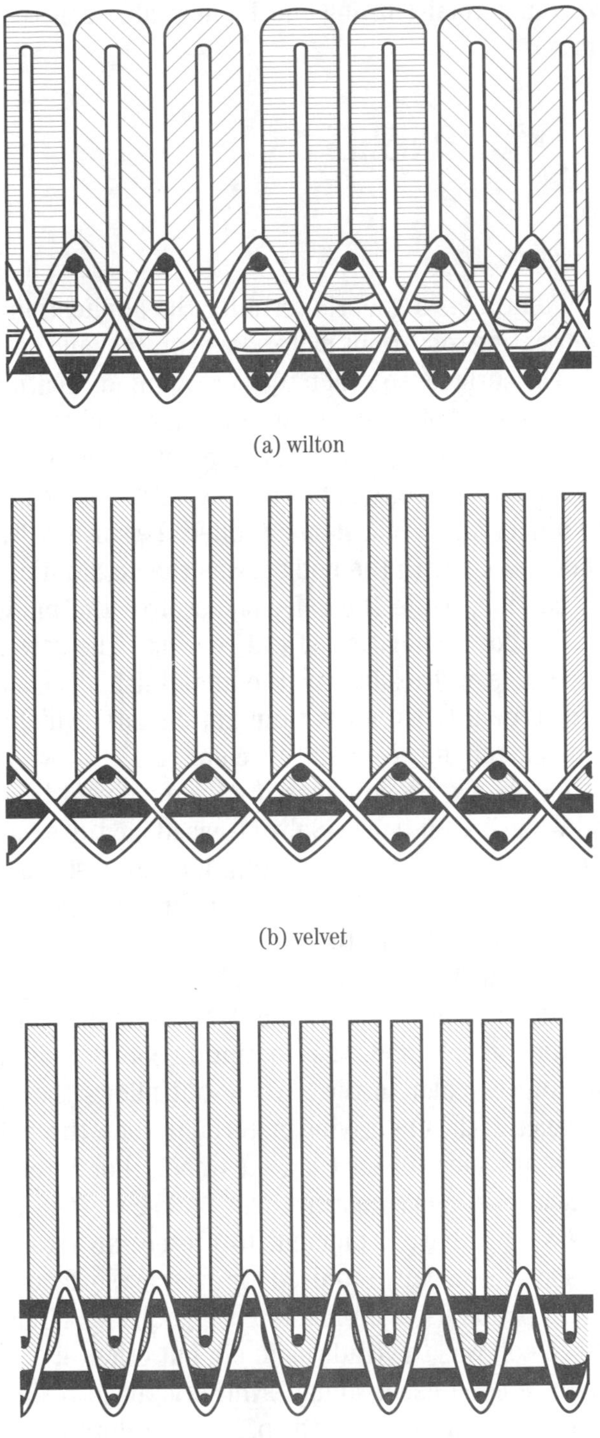

Figure 12.5 Woven Carpet Types

tightly that yarn is packed, and the height of the yarn. The pitch of a woven carpet is the number of ends of surface yarn in a 27-inch width. For tufted carpet, this measurement is called the *gauge*, which is the spacing in fractions of an inch between needles across the width of the carpet. Gauges of $^5/_{64}$ inch, $^1/_{10}$ inch, and $^1/_8$ inch are common for contract carpet. The *stitch* (or stitch rate) is the number of lengthwise tufts in one inch. The higher the pitch or gauge number and stitch numbers are, the denser the carpet is. The *pile height* is the height of the fiber from the surface of the backing to the top of the pile. Generally, shorter and more tightly packed fibers result in a more durable but more expensive carpet.

Carpet backing and cushion: Carpet backing provides support for the pile yarn and gives added strength and dimensional stability to the carpet. With woven and knitted carpet, the pile yarns and backing yarns are combined during the manufacturing process. Polypropylene backing yarn is the most common for woven carpet, but others include jute, cotton, and polyester. Tufted carpet is manufactured by punching the yarns through a primary backing of woven or nonwoven polypropylene or woven jute. A secondary backing, usually of latex, is then applied.

An important part of carpet installation is the carpet cushion, sometimes called padding. Cushion is not required for all carpet (such as with direct glue-down) but increases the life of the carpet, provides better resiliency and comfort, helps sound absorption, and lessens impact noise. Common cushion materials include felt, foam and sponge rubber, urethane, and polyester.

Installation: Carpet is installed in one of two ways: direct glue-down or stretched-in installation. With direct glue-down, the carpet is attached to the floor with adhesive. The carpet may have an attached cushion or be installed without a cushion. A stretched-in installation uses tackless strips attached around the perimeter of the room. These strips have embedded sharp points that face toward the walls. The carpet is stretched against these strips, which hold the carpet in place. Carpet cushion is either stapled to wood floors or glued to concrete floors after the tackless strips are in place.

F. Tile

Tiles are small, flat finishing units made of clay or clay mixtures. The two primary types are ceramic tile and quarry tile. The advantages of tile include durability; water resistance (if glazed); ease of installation and cleaning; a wide choice of colors, sizes, and patterns; fire resistance; fade resistance; and the ability to store heat for passive solar collection.

Ceramic tile is a surfacing unit, usually relatively thin in relation to facial area, made from clay or a mixture of clay and other ceramic materials, having either a glazed or unglazed face. It is fired above red heat during manufacture to a temperature high enough to produce specific physical properties and characteristics. *Quarry tile* is glazed or unglazed tile, usually with 6 square inches or more of facial area, and is made by the extrusion process from natural clay or shale.

Some of the common types of tile include glazed wall tile, unglazed tile, ceramic mosaic tile, paver tile, quarry tile (glazed or unglazed), abrasive tile, and antistatic tile.

Ceramic mosaic tile is formed by either the dust-pressed or extrusion method, $^1/_4$ inch to $^3/_8$ inch thick, and having a facial area of less than 6 square inches. Dust pressing uses large presses to shape the tile out of relatively dry clay, while the extrusion process uses machines to cut tiles from a wetter and more malleable clay extruded through a die.

The United States tile industry classifies tile based on size: under 6 square inches is mosaic tile, over 6 square inches is wall tile. Glazed and unglazed nonmosaic tile made by the extrusion method is quarry tile. Glazed and unglazed tile over 6 square inches made by the dust-pressed method is called paver tile.

Tile is also classified according to its resistance to water absorption. Nonvitreous tile has a water absorption rate of more than 7.0 percent. Impervious tile has a water absorption rate of 0.5 percent or less. Semivitreous tile and vitreous tile are classified between nonvitreous and impervious tile.

Imported tile is not classified like tile produced in the United States. European manufacturers classify tile according to its production method (either the dust-press or extrusion method), degree of water absorption, finish, and whether it is glazed or unglazed.

The classifications of abrasion resistance are Group I, light residential; Group II, moderate residential; Group III, maximum residential; and Group IV, commercial (having the highest abrasion resistance).

2 WALL FINISHES

A. Paint

Painting is a generic term for the application of thin coatings of various materials to protect and decorate the surfaces to which they are applied. Coatings are composed of a vehicle, which is the liquid part of the coating, and the body and pigments if the coating is opaque. The vehicle has a nonvolatile part called the binder and a volatile part called the solvent. The binder, along with the body, forms the actual film of the coating, while the solvent dissolves the binder to allow for application of the coating. The solvent evaporates or dries leaving the final finish. The body of most quality paints is titanium dioxide, which is white. Pigments give paint its color.

Paints are broadly classified into solvent-based and water-based types. Solvent-based coatings have binders dissolved in or containing organic solvents, while the water-based type has binders that are soluble or dispersed in water.

Clear, solvent-based coatings include varnishes, shellac, silicone, and urethane. When a small amount of pigment is added, the coating becomes a stain, which gives color to the surface but allows the appearance of the underlying material to show through. Stains are most often used on wood. For interior applications, clear coatings can be used. It is not necessary to have a pigment to protect an interior surface as is usually required for exterior surfaces.

Oil paints use a drying, or curing, oil as a binder. Linseed oil was the traditional oil, but other organic oils have been used. Today, synthetic alkyd resin is used as the drying oil. Oil paints are durable but have a strong odor when being applied and must be cleaned up with solvents such as mineral spirits. In addition, they cannot be painted on damp surfaces or on surfaces that may become damp from behind.

Latex paints are water based, with vinyl chloride or acrylic resins as binders. Acrylic latex is better than vinyl latex. Both can be used indoors as well as outdoors and can be thinned with water.

For more durable finishes, epoxy is used as a binder for resistance to corrosion and chemicals. Epoxies also resist abrasion and strongly adhere to concrete, metal, and wood.

Urethanes are used for superior resistance to abrasion, grease, alcohol, water, and fuels. They are often used for wood floors and for antigraffiti coatings.

Successful application of coatings depends not only on the correct selection for the intended use but also on the surface preparation of the substrate, the primer used, and the method of application. Surfaces should be clean, dry, and free from grease, oils, and other foreign material. Application can be done by brushing, rolling, or spraying. The amount of coating material to be applied is normally specified as either wet or dry film thickness in mils (thousandths of an inch) for each coat needed. The coating should be applied under dry conditions when the temperature is between 55°F and 85°F.

B. Wallpaper

Wallpaper is available in a range of colors, patterns, textures, and materials for direct application to plaster or gypsum wallboard partitions. Wallpaper is generally packaged in rolls $20^1/_2$ inches wide by 21 feet long and may be all paper or paper backed with cotton fabric or other material. Double and triple rolls are also available. Before application, a liquid sizing must be applied to the wall to seal the surface against alkali, to reduce the absorption of the paste or adhesive used, and to provide the proper surface for the wallpaper.

C. Vinyl Wallcovering

Vinyl wallcovering provides a durable, abrasion-resistant finish that is easy to clean and can satisfy most code requirements for flammability. It is available in a range of colors and patterns. Vinyl wallcovering typically comes in rolls 52 or 54 inches wide and 30 yards long.

There are three grades of vinyl wallcovering: Type I (light duty), Type II (medium duty), and Type III (heavy duty). Type I has a total weight of 7 to 13 ounces per square yard, Type II has a total weight of between 13 and 22 ounces per square yard, and Type III has a weight of over 22 ounces. Type I is used for residential applications while Type II is used for commercial and institutional applications. Type III is used where extra heavy use is expected such as in public corridors, food-service areas, and hospitals.

D. Fabric Wallcovering

Several types of fabrics can be used for wallcovering including wool, silk, and synthetics, subject to flame-spread restrictions. If the fabric is heavy enough it can be applied directly to the wall with adhesives. Sometimes the fabric is backed with paper or other material to prevent the adhesive from damaging the material and to give it additional dimensional stability. An alternate installation method is to stretch the fabric over a frame and tack it into place. This is called an upholstered wall. Various proprietary stretch fabric wall systems are also available. When the fabric is placed over thick fiberglass batting, the assembly becomes an acoustic panel as described below. However fabric wallcovering is applied, it must conform to the required fire rating for finishes either by being fire resistant itself or by being treated with fire retardant.

E. Acoustic Panels

Sound-absorbent panels can be purchased or constructed for use in spaces that require acoustical treatment in addition to acoustical ceilings and carpeting. These are made from a sound-absorbent material such as fiberglass and are covered with a permeable material such as a loose-weave fabric. The acoustical material should be at least 1 inch thick to be effective.

F. Stone

As with floors, stone can be used as a wall finish in thick slabs or in thin veneer sheets. With the traditional, standard-set method of applying stone, slabs about $^3/_4$ inch thick are attached to wall substrates (either masonry or gypsum wallboard) with stainless steel wires or ties. See Figure 12.6. These are anchored to the substrate and hold the stone by being set in holes or slots cut into the back or sides of the stone panel. Lumps of plaster of Paris, called spots, are placed between the substrate and the back of the stone panel at each anchor and hold the slab in place and allow for precise alignment before they harden.

For rooms with normal ceiling heights, the stone rests on the floor with the anchors simply serving to hold each panel in place. The joints can be filled with nonstaining portland cement mortar, sealant, or left open.

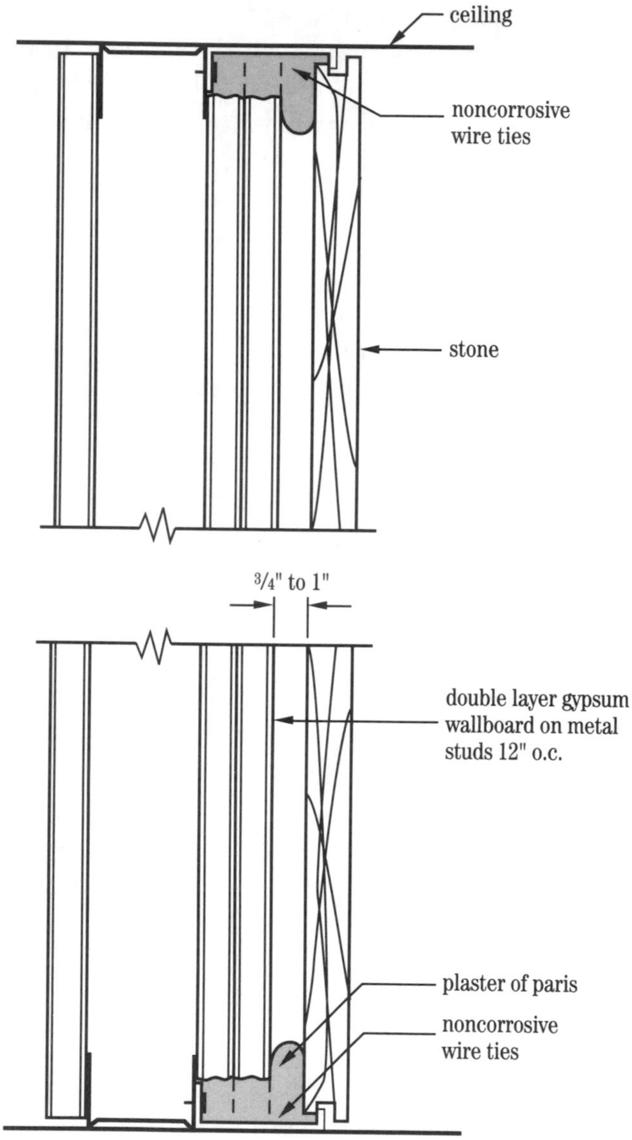

Figure 12.6 Thick-Set Stone Veneer

With new technology in cutting and laminating stone to various types of reinforcing backing, thin stone tiles are largely replacing the traditional thick slab construction. These tiles are about $^3/_8$ inch thick and come in sizes of 1′x 1′and 1′x 2′, although other sizes and thicknesses are available depending on the manufacturer. In many cases, the stone is simply mastic-applied to a suitable substrate. Some manufacturers provide special clips that hold the stone in place against the backup wall.

3 WINDOW TREATMENTS

Window treatments are used to enhance the appearance of windows, control light, provide privacy, reduce heat gain and heat loss, block off undesirable views, and reduce sound reflections within a space. They can also be used to unify or disguise an awkward or undesirable grouping of openings. Because they are such a dominate part of an interior space, they should be selected and designed to be suitable to the type of window they are covering as well as the overall design theme of the space.

Window coverings can be broadly classified into four categories: shades, blinds, soft coverings, and fixed. Within each of these categories are several variations, as shown in Figure 12.7.

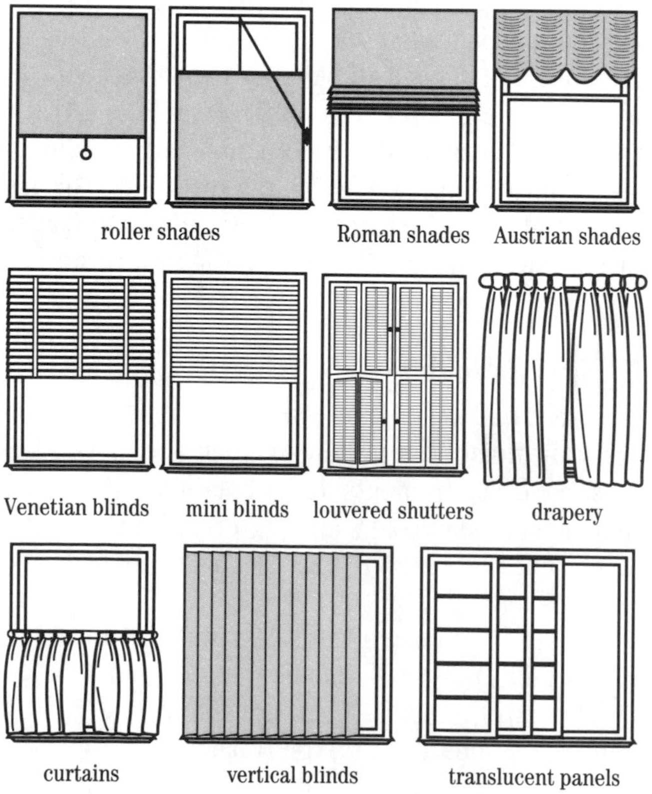

Figure 12.7 Window Coverings

- *Roller shades and inverted roller shades:* These coverings consist of a piece of cloth wound around a spring roller. They are normally pulled closed from the top but can also be mounted so a pulley-mounted cord unwinds them from the bottom up. They are inexpensive and can be covered with decorative fabric. These coverings, however, block off all the view when closed and can interfere with ventilation. They also block light unless made from a translucent material.

- *Roman shades:* Roman shades pull up with a cord into accordion folds.

- *Austrian shades:* These operate in a way similar to Roman shades but are made of several rows of fabric seamed in such a way that they fold into scallops when opened.

- *Venetian blinds:* Traditional venetian blinds consist of horizontal slats of wood, aluminum, or plastic whose angle can be adjusted with a control cord. The blinds can also be pulled up to varying levels with another cord.

- *Mini blinds:* Mini blinds are horizontal slats of aluminum like venetian blinds, but they are only $1/2$ inch to 1 inch wide. The angle of the slats is controlled with a plastic rod. They can be pulled up to expose the entire window area.

- *Vertical blinds:* Vertical blinds hang from a track and adjust only in the vertical direction. They can be pulled to the side to expose the window. They are available in several materials (primarily plastic), widths, and colors.

- *Louvered shutters:* Shutters are rigid panels, usually of wood, that are hinged so they can be opened or closed. Individual panels have thin, adjustable horizontal louvers to control view and light. Plantation shutters are similar in design but feature much wider louvers.

- *Drapery:* Drapery is one of most common types of window covering in residential and commercial interiors. Generally, drapery is any loosely hung fabric that covers the window. Most commonly, the fabric is attached to a traverse rod that allows the drapery to be drawn open and closed, but many styles of hanging are possible including fixed, tieback, and loose-hung swags. Drapery can be made from a variety of fabrics using several methods of pleating. Four common methods of pleating include pinch pleat, stack pleat, roll pleat, and accordion-type pleating.

  Drapery can be hung to cover just the window or can be sized to extend to the floor or so the drapery stacks clear of the window opening. When special light control is required, you can specify blackout drapery lining or linings for solar control. When selecting drapery for commercial, institutional, and public residential applications, one of the most important considerations is flammability. This takes precedence over other criteria such as durability, fading resistance, and style.

- *Curtains:* Curtains use fabric like draperies but are usually hung within the window frame and close to the glass. In most instances, curtains are not intended to be opened, but fixed across all or a portion of the window.

- *Translucent panels:* When a clear view is not required or desired, translucent panels can be used to admit diffused light. These can be constructed of various types of plastic, sheer fabric, frosted glass, or even paper using fixed or sliding Shoji screens.

- *Grilles:* Grilles can be used to modify strong light or minimize an undesirable view while still providing some visual connection between inside and outside. Grilles can be constructed of any durable material such as wood or metal and can be fixed or movable. Decorative metal grilles can also be used when security is required.

SAMPLE QUESTIONS

1. If a client wanted you to select a vinyl wallcovering for the family room in a single-family dwelling, which would you recommend?

   1. Type I
   2. Type II
   3. Type III
   4. Type IV

2. Which of the carpet types would allow you to design a complex, custom-patterned carpet with varying pile heights?

   1. tufted
   2. Axminster
   3. Wilton
   4. velvet

3. You are designing an entry lobby to a restaurant and have decided to use stone flooring. Which of the following types would be the MOST functional choice?

   1. granite with a flame finish
   2. marble with a honed finish
   3. travertine
   4. granite with a polished finish

4. Which type of wood flooring could be installed easily and LEAST expensively in a residential living room?

   1. block
   2. strip
   3. parquet
   4. plank

5. Which of the following would be the LEAST desirable choice for a carpet installation for hotel rooms that have concrete subfloors?

   1. nylon carpet stretched in over a foam cushion
   2. polyester carpet stretched in over a felt cushion
   3. acrylic carpet direct-glued
   4. wool carpet direct-glued

6. A window covering that is made from fabric and generally not intended to be opened is called

   1. a curtain
   2. an Austrian shade
   3. a vertical blind
   4. drapery

7. What is the purpose of construction element A in the following diagram of a wood floor?

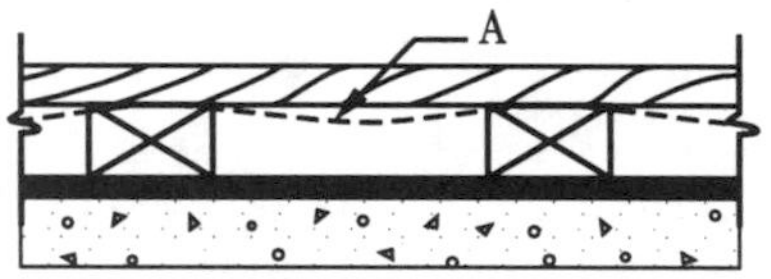

   1. to minimize squeaking
   2. to prevent chemicals from the subfloor from contaminating the wood
   3. to act as a vapor barrier
   4. to provide added resiliency

8. You have been retained as the interior designer for a building that is currently being planned by an architect with whom you are coordinating your design. If you were going to use slate flooring over a concrete subfloor on the second floor of the building, what type of installation should you ideally design for?

   1. a thick-set application using a cleavage membrane
   2. a bonded thick-set installation
   3. a $^1/_2$-inch layer of mortar with the stone dry-set on top
   4. a standard thin-set installation

9. What type of resilient flooring would be the best choice for a commercial kitchen?

   1. $^1/_8$-inch commercial grade vinyl tile
   2. sheet vinyl
   3. heavyduty cork flooring
   4. sheet rubber

10. If a sales person tells you a particular carpet has a 216 pitch what does this mean?

1. that its pile height is almost $^{1}/_{4}$ inch high
2. that it has 8 surface yarns per inch
3. that is has an equivalent gauge of $^{1}/_{6}$
4. that it has a commercial-grade stitch rate

13 LIGHTING

1 LIGHTING FUNDAMENTALS

Light is defined as visually evaluated radiant energy. Visible light is a form of electromagnetic radiation with wavelengths that range from about 400 nanometers (10^{-9} meters) for violet light to about 700 nanometers for red light. White light is produced when a source emits approximately equal quantities of energy over the entire visible spectrum.

A. Definitions

There is a relationship among several illumination definitions. Figure 13.1 shows these units of light.

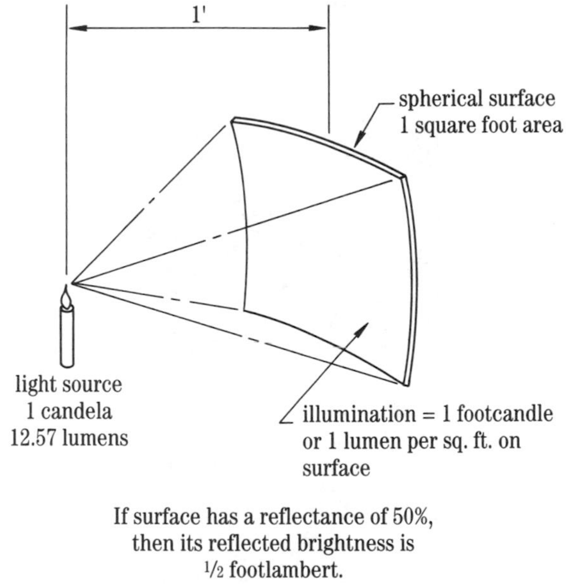

Figure 13.1 Relationship of Light Source and Illumination

Candlepower is the unit of luminous intensity approximately equal to the horizontal light output from an ordinary wax candle. In the SI (metric) system of measurement, this unit is the candela.

Lumen is the unit of luminous flux equal to the flux in a unit solid angle of one steradian from a uniform point source of one candlepower. On a unit sphere (1-foot radius), an area of 1 square foot will subtend an angle of one steradian. Because the area of a unit sphere is 4π, a source of one candlepower produces 12.57 lumens.

Illuminance is the density of luminous flux incident on a surface in lumens per unit area. One lumen uniformly incident on 1 square foot of area produces an illuminance of 1 footcandle. In SI units, the measurement is lux (lx), or lumens per square meter.

Luminance is the luminous flux per unit of projected (apparent) area and unit solid angle leaving a surface, either reflected or transmitted. The unit is the footlambert (fL), where one footlambert equals $1/\pi$ candelas per square foot. Luminance takes into account the reflectance and transmittance properties of materials and the direction in which they are viewed. Thus, 100 footcandles striking a surface with 50 percent reflectance results in a luminance of 50 footlamberts. Luminance is sometimes called brightness. A surface emitting, transmitting, or reflecting 1 lumen per square foot in the direction being viewed has a luminance of 1 footlambert.

B. Light Levels

Good lighting design involves providing both the proper quantity and quality of light to perform a task. This section discusses quantity; the next discusses quality. Different visual tasks under different conditions require varying levels of illumination. The variables involved include the nature of the task itself, the age of the person performing the task, the reflectances of the room, and the demand for speed and accuracy in performing the task.

The Illuminating Engineering Society (IES) has established a method for determining a range of illumination levels in footcandles appropriate to particular design conditions. Various areas and activities are assigned an illuminance category from A to I (A represents the lowest values for general lighting in noncritical areas, and I represents requirements for specialized and difficult visual tasks). These categories are used with other variables of age, surface reflectances, and importance of task to establish the recommended task and background illuminances.

To conserve energy, most codes require designers to develop a power budget for a project based on the building type and to design lighting systems within that budget. This most often requires that the recommended illumination level be provided for task areas only and that general background illumination (ambient light) be less, about one-third of the task level. Further, noncritical areas such as corridors are usually provided with less light than the background levels.

C. Light Quality

The quality of light is just as important as the quantity. Important considerations are glare, contrast, uniformity, and color.

There are two types of glare: direct and reflected. Direct glare results when a light source in the field of vision causes discomfort and interference with the visual task. Not all visible light sources cause direct glare problems. The extent of the problem depends on the brightness of the source, its position, the background illumination, and the adaptation of the eye to the environment.

To evaluate direct glare, the visual comfort probability (VCP) factor was developed. This factor is the percentage of people who, when viewing from a specified location and in a specified direction, will find the situation acceptable in terms of discomfort glare. Although the calculations are complex, some simplifications are made, and many manufacturers publish the VCP rating for their light fixtures when used under certain conditions.

For most situations, the critical zone for direct glare is in the area above a 45-degree angle from the light source. See Figure 13.2. This is because the field of vision when looking straight ahead includes an area approximately 45 degrees above the horizontal. Many direct glare problems can be solved by using a luminaire with a 45-degree cutoff angle or by moving the luminaire out of the offending field of view. One way to determine the amount of light being emitted by a luminaire at any given angle is to look at its footcandle distribution diagram. Figure 13.3 shows one such diagram that plots light output at various angles to the luminaire.

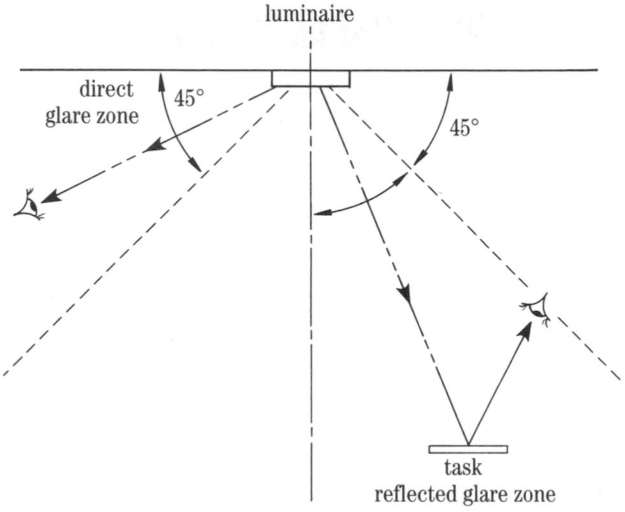

Figure 13.2 Glare Zones

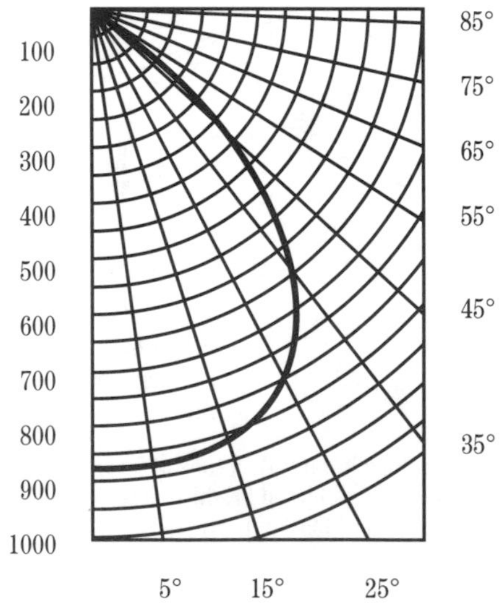

Figure 13.3 Candlepower Distribution Diagram

Reflected glare occurs when a light source is reflected from a viewed surface into the eye. If it interferes with the viewing task, it is also called *veiling reflection*. The effect of reflected glare is to decrease the contrast between the task and its background. For example, a strong light on paper with pencil writing can bounce off the relatively reflective graphite, making it almost as bright as the paper, and effectively obliterate the writing.

Veiling reflections are a complex interaction of light source and brightness, position of the task, reflectivity of the task, and the position of the eye. One of the simplest ways to correct veiling reflections is to move the position of the task or the light source. This is easy to calculate because, for light, the angle of incidence is equal to the angle of reflection. It is not always possible, however, because the exact use of the room and its furniture position is not always known. One way to avoid the problem is to provide general background illumination and specific task lighting that can be moved around by the user.

Contrast is the difference in illumination level between one point and nearby points. Because people see by contrast, it is vitally important to the quality of an environment. A printed word on a page is visible only because it contrasts with the brightness of the surrounding paper. However, too much contrast can be detrimental. It is difficult to see fine detail on a small, dark object when viewed against a bright background because the eye adapts to the brighter background and cannot admit enough light to see the darker object. The eye adapts by opening and closing the iris, but too much of this causes eyestrain and fatigue.

In most situations, brightness ratios should be limited to 3:1 between the task and immediate surroundings (for example, between a piece of paper and the desktop), to 5:1 between the task and nearby general surroundings, and to 10:1 between the task and more remote surroundings.

Uniformity of lighting affects a person's perception of a space as being comfortable and pleasant to be in. Complete uniformity is usually not desirable except for certain tasks like drafting or machine shop work. Some amount of shade and shadow provides highlight and interest to a space.

Color in lighting is an interaction between the color of the light source (lamp or daylighting) and the color of the objects that reflect the light. Color in lighting is a complex subject but it can affect people's comfort and their impression of an environment. Colors of light sources are discussed in the next section and the use of color in lighting design later in this chapter.

2 LIGHT SOURCES

In addition to daylight, there are three types of light sources: incandescent, fluorescent, and high-intensity discharge. Some of the considerations that influence the selection of a light source include its color rendition characteristics, initial cost, operating cost, efficacy, size, operating life, and ability to control its output from a luminaire. *Efficacy* is the ratio of luminous flux emitted to the total power input of the source and is measured in lumens per watt. It is an important measure of the energy efficiency of a light source. The amount of heat generated by a light source is also an important consideration because waste heat usually needs to be removed or compensated for with the air conditioning system, which can add to the total energy load of a building. A summary of some of the more common light sources is shown in Table 13.1. The color temperature and the CRI value shown in the table are explained in Section 4 of this chapter.

A. Incandescent

An incandescent lamp consists of a tungsten filament placed within a sealed bulb containing an inert gas. When electricity is passed through the lamp, the filament glows, producing light. Incandescent lamps are produced in a variety of shapes, sizes, and wattages for different applications. Some of the more common shapes are shown in Figure 13.4. Incandescent lamps are designated by their shape followed by a number that indicates the diameter in eighths of an inch at the widest point. Thus, an R-38 is a reflector lamp with a diameter of $4^3/_4$ inches ($^{38}/_8 = 4^3/_4$).

You should be familiar with the distribution characteristics of the various reflector lamps: types R, ER, PAR, and MR-16. The R lamp is the standard reflector lamp and has a wide beam spread. The ER, or elliptical reflector, provides a more efficient throw of light from a fixture by focusing the light beam at a point slightly in front of the lamp before it spreads out.

Table 13.1
Characteristics of Some Common Light Sources

Lamp Description	Watts	Initial Lumens	Color Temp. (°K)	CRI	Approx. Lamp Life (hours)
incandescent					
A-19	100	1750	2500	100	750
R30	75	850	2500	100	2000
PAR38	150	1730	2500	100	2000
fluorescent					
F40T12CW	40	3150	4300	62	20,000
F40T12WW	40	3170	3100	52	20,000
F40T12 triphosphor	40	4400	3000	80	20,000
tungsten-halogen					
T-H PAR	150	2900	3000	100	3000
T-H PAR	250	5000	3000	100	2000
high-intensity discharge					
mercury-vapor					
100 M-V	100	4400	5500	40	24,000
metal-halide					
70 M-H	70	4900	3000	75	6000
150 M-H	150	12,000	4300	85	6000
high-pressure sodium					
HPS 100	100	5200	2800	70+	10,000

Its spread is slightly smaller than the R lamp. The parabolic aluminized reflector, or PAR lamp, focuses the light in a tighter spread with the light rays more parallel because its reflector is a parabola with the filament at the focus of the parabola. PAR lamps, as well as R lamps, are available in both "flood" spreads and "spotlights." The MR-16 lamp is a low-voltage, miniaturized reflector. Several angles of beam spread are available, from a very narrow spot to a medium-wide spread. Generally, however, the MR-16 lamps have the narrowest beam spread of the four types of lamps, the next narrowest being a PAR.

Incandescent lamps are inexpensive, compact, easy to dim, can be repeatedly started without a decrease in lamp life, and have a warm color rendition. In addition, their light output can be easily controlled with reflectors and lenses. Their disadvantages include low efficacy, short lamp life, and high heat output. The combination of heat production and low efficacy makes incandescent lamps undesirable for large, energy-efficient installations. For example, a 150-watt lamp produces less than 20 lumens per watt, while a 40-watt cool-white fluorescent lamp has an efficacy of about 80 lumens per watt with much less heat output.

Tungsten halogen is one type of incandescent lamp. Light is produced by the incandescence of the filament, but there is a small amount of a halogen, such as iodine or bromine, in the bulb with the inert gas. Through a recurring cycle, part of the tungsten filament is burned off as the lamp operates, but it mixes with the halogen and is redeposited on the filament instead of on the wall of the bulb as in standard incandescent lamps. This results in longer lamp life, low lumen depreciation over the life of the lamp, and a more uniform light color. Because the filament burns under higher pressure and temperature, the bulb is made from quartz and is much smaller than standard incandescent lamps. Both standard voltage (120) and low-voltage tungsten halogen lamps are available.

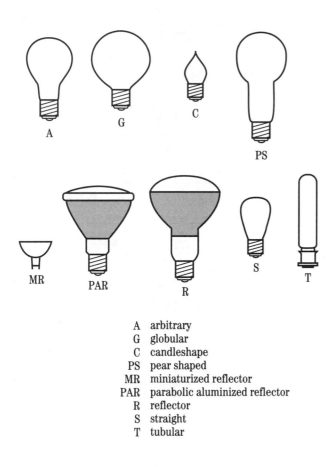

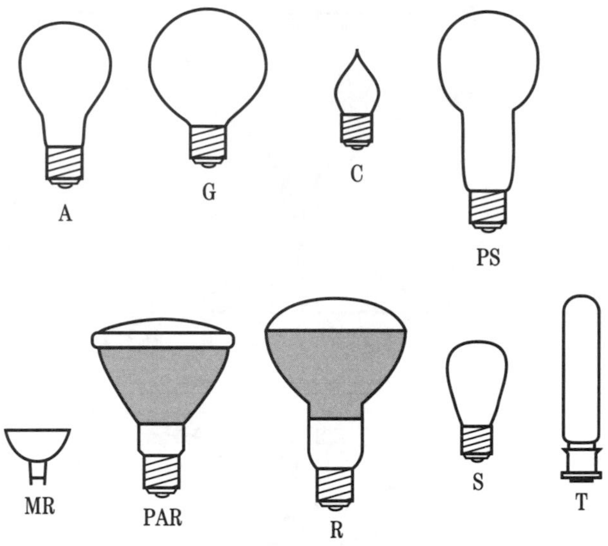

A arbitrary
G globular
C candleshape
PS pear shaped
MR miniaturized reflector
PAR parabolic aluminized reflector
R reflector
S straight
T tubular

Figure 13.4 Incandescent Lamp Shapes

B. Fluorescent

Fluorescent lamps contain a mixture of an inert gas and low-pressure mercury vapor. When the lamp is energized, a mercury arc is formed that creates ultraviolet light. This invisible light, in turn, strikes the phosphor-coated bulb, causing it to fluoresce and produce visible light. The three types of fluorescent lamps are preheat, rapid start, and instant start, according to their circuitry. Preheat lamps have been supplanted by rapid start types. All fluorescent lamps have a ballast, a device that supplies the proper starting and operating voltages to the lamp as well as limiting the current.

Lamps are produced in tubular shapes, normally straight, but U-shaped and circular lamps are also available. They are designated according to their type, wattage, diameter, color, and type of starting circuitry. Thus, an F40T12WW/RS describes a fluorescent lamp, 40 watts, tubular, $^{12}/_{8}$ of an inch in diameter ($1^{1}/_{2}$ inches), warm white color, with a rapid start circuit. Size is designated in eighths of an inch, so a T8 lamp is 1 inch in diameter. Fluorescent lamps come in a variety of lengths, 4 feet being the most common. Lengths of 2, 3, and 8 feet are also available, as well as special U-shaped sizes and compact shapes that are designed to be screwed into normal incandescent sockets.

In the past, one of the objections to fluorescent lighting was that it was too "cold." Actually, lamps are available in a wide range of color temperatures, ranging from a "cool" FL/D (daylight) lamp of 6500K color temperature to a WWD (warm-white deluxe) with a color temperature of 2800K, which has a large percentage of red in its spectral output. Color temperature designations are discussed in a later section.

Fluorescent lamps have a high efficacy (from 55 to 80 lumens per watt), relatively low initial cost and long life, and are available in a variety of color temperatures. They can also be dimmed, although fluorescent dimmers are more expensive than their incandescent counterparts. Because fluorescent lamps are larger than incandescent ones, it is more difficult to control them precisely, so they are usually more suitable for general illumination. However, in recent years, compact fluorescents have been developed that fit within a reflector housing similar to incandescent downlights and wallwashers.

C. High-Intensity Discharge

High-intensity discharge (HID) lamps include mercury vapor, metal halide, and high-pressure sodium. In the mercury vapor lamp, an electric arc is passed through high-pressure mercury vapor, which causes it to produce both ultraviolet light and visible light, primarily in the blue-green spectral band. For improved color rendition, various phosphors can be applied to the inside of the lamp to produce more light in the yellow and red bands. Mercury lamps have a moderately high efficacy, in the range of 30 to 60 lumens per watt, depending on voltage and the type of color correction included.

Metal halide lamps, which produce about 80 to 120 lumens per watt, are similar to mercury except that halides of metals are added to the arc tube. This increases the efficacy and improves color rendition but decreases lamp life.

High-pressure sodium (HPS) lamps produce light by passing an electric arc through hot sodium vapor. The arc tube must be made of a special ceramic material to resist attack by the hot sodium. High-pressure sodium lamps have efficacies from 80 to 140 lumens per watt, making them among the most efficient lamps available. Standard sodium lamps produce a very yellow light. However, with available color correction versions, color rendition is acceptable for some applications.

In addition to the three basic types of lamps, there are neon and cold-cathode lamps. Neon lamps can be formed into an unlimited number of shapes and are used for signs and specialty accent lighting. By varying the gases within the tube, a variety of colors can be produced. Cold-cathode lamps are similar to neon in that they can be produced in long runs of thin tubing bent to shape, but they have a higher efficacy, are slightly larger (about 1 inch in diameter), and can produce several shades of white as well as many colors.

3 LIGHTING TYPES

Lighting installations are broadly categorized by the overall system used to introduce light into the space and by how individual fixtures (luminaires) are mounted.

A. Lighting Systems

The types of systems can refer to individual luminaires or to an entire lighting installation and are described as direct, semidirect, direct-indirect, general diffuse, semi-indirect, and indirect. See Figure 13.5.

Direct lighting systems provide all light output on the task. A recessed fluorescent luminaire is an example of direct lighting. Semidirect systems put a majority of the light down and a small percentage toward the ceiling. Obviously, fixtures for this type of system must be surface mounted or suspended. Direct-indirect systems distribute light up and down about equally. Indirect systems direct all the light toward a reflective ceiling, where the light illuminates the room by reflection.

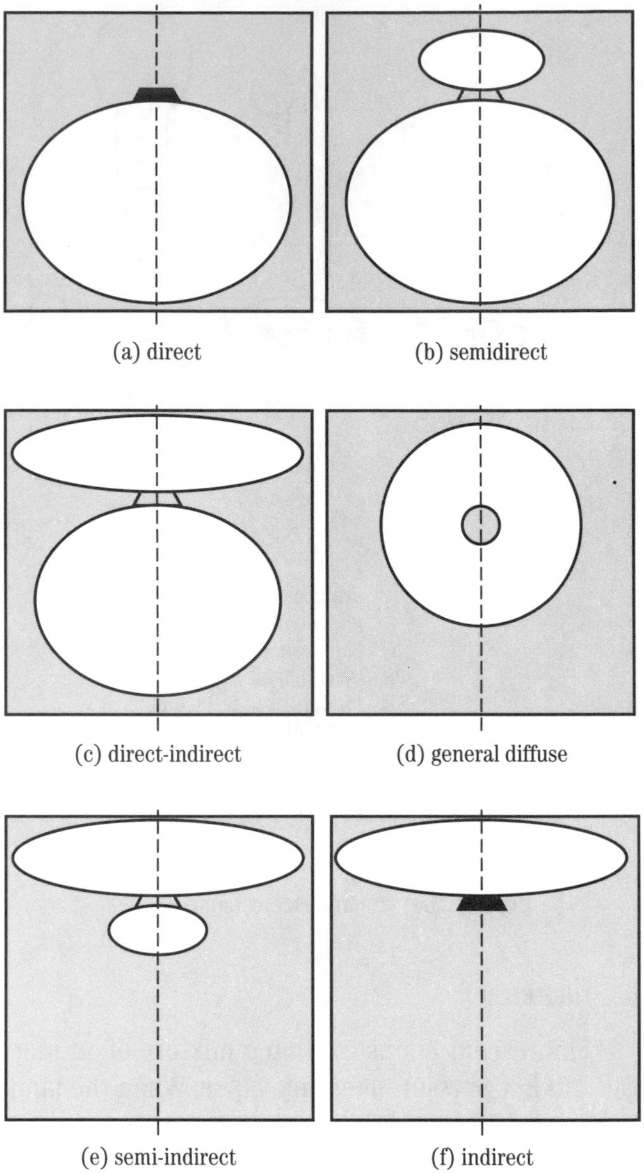

Figure 13.5 Lighting Systems

A task-ambient system is a common commercial lighting system. This system provides a general background illumination level with separate light fixtures used at individual workstations or wherever it is needed. This is done with desk lamps, directed spotlights, or by locating more fixtures near the tasks requiring more illumination. In addition to being energy efficient and responding to individual lighting needs, task-ambient systems create more pleasant work environments.

B. Surface-Mounted Fixtures

Surface-mounted fixtures are among the most commonly used types for residential and some commercial interior design. As the name implies, the luminaire is directly attached to the finished surface of the ceiling, directing all or a majority of the light into the space. These fixtures are used where there is not sufficient space above the ceiling to recess a fixture or where fixtures are added after the ceiling has been constructed. Surface-mounted fixtures include incandescent, fluorescent, or HID lights, as well as the various types of track lighting systems.

C. Recessed Fixtures

These fixtures are widely used in residential and commercial installations. Residential recessed lighting is usually limited to incandescent downlights because these can be located in the limited space between floor or ceiling joists. Commercial installations utilize both recessed incandescent lighting as well as recessed troffers that fit within suspended acoustical ceiling systems. When the entire ceiling is made up of lighting, a luminous ceiling is formed. Recessed incandescents can be general downlights for overall illumination or wallwashers, which direct light in one direction only. Continuous, narrow strips of fluorescent luminaires can also be recessed next to a wall to wash the wall uniformly with light.

D. Suspended Fixtures

Luminaires dropped below the level of the ceiling are called suspended fixtures. These can include direct incandescent or fluorescent fixtures, track lighting, indirect systems, chandeliers, and other types of specialty lights. Suspended mounting is required for indirect lighting systems. The fixture must be located far enough below the ceiling to allow for the proper spread of light to bounce off the surface. Suspended mounting is also used when the designer needs to get the source of light closer to the task area in a high-ceiling room. Sometimes, suspended specialty fixtures are used for strictly aesthetic reasons.

E. Wall-Mounted Fixtures

Wall-mounted fixtures can provide indirect, direct-indirect, or direct lighting. For general illumination, sconces direct most or all the light toward the ceiling. They are often used as decorative elements as well as light sources. Various types of adjustable and nonadjustable direct lighting fixtures are available that serve as task lighting, like bed lamps. Cove lighting can also be mounted on a wall near the ceiling and will indirectly light either the ceiling or the wall depending on how it is shielded.

F. Furniture-Mounted Fixtures

Furniture-mounted lighting is common with task-ambient systems. Individual lights are built into the furniture above the worksurface to provide sufficient task illumination, while uplighting is provided by lights either built into the upper portions of the furniture or as freestanding elements. Furniture-mounted lighting is also used on items like library bookshelves and study carrels.

G. Freestanding Fixtures

Floor lamps are the most common type of freestanding light fixture. These are available in thousands of different styles and sizes and can be custom designed and manufactured if needed. Freestanding lights that direct most of their output to the ceiling are called *torchères*. For task-ambient lighting systems, freestanding kiosks contain high-wattage lights for illuminating the ceiling for indirect lighting.

H. Accessory Lighting

Accessory lighting includes table lights, reading lamps, and fixtures that are intended for strictly decorative lighting rather than for task or ambient lighting. Like floor lamps, these are available from hundreds of manufacturers in an almost unlimited number of styles.

4 LIGHTING DESIGN

Lighting is both an art and a science. There must be a sufficient amount of light to perform a task without glare and other discomfort, but the lighting also enhances the interior design. Lighting must also be designed to minimize energy use and protect the health of the occupants.

A. Color of Light

In addition to the issues of glare and contrast discussed in a previous section, the color of light sources is an important factor in the overall quality of any lighting design. The color of any object we see is dependent on both the color of the object as well as the color of the light striking it. For example, incandescent light striking a blue object will tend to gray out the object, while the object will be enhanced if viewed under daylight.

Every lamp has a characteristic spectral energy distribution. This is a measure of the energy output at different wavelengths, or colors. One such energy distribution curve is shown in Figure 13.6. This energy distribution curve shows a discontinuous curve, typical of fluorescent and HID lights, with a continuous curve and with peaks at certain points. Daylight and incandescent light have continuous spectrum light without any sharp peaks.

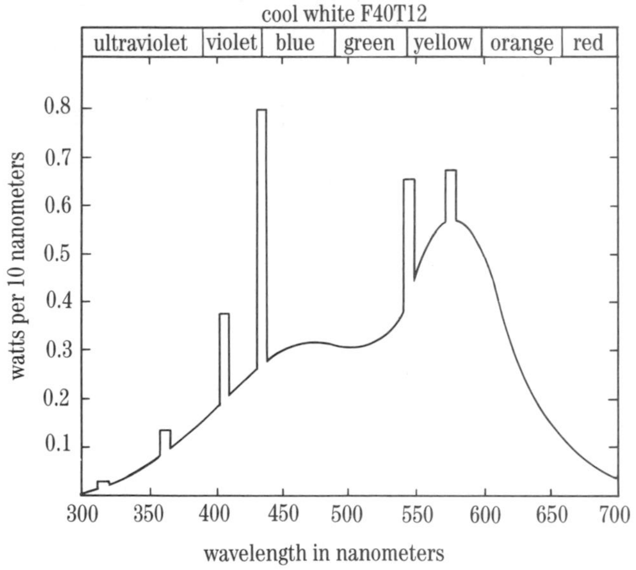

Figure 13.6 Spectral Energy Distribution Curve

Light sources are given a single number rating of their dominant color based on the temperature in degrees Kelvin to which a blackbody radiator would have to be heated to produce that color. Technically, only incandescent sources can have a color temperature designation, but an apparent color temperature is often used to describe the degree of whiteness of fluorescent lamps and other sources. However, even though a source with a discontinuous spectrum may have the same apparent color temperature as a continuous spectrum source, the two may render colors quite differently. Table 13.2 gives correlated color temperatures of some common light sources. Notice that the lower the color temperature, the "warmer" the light. As the temperature increases, the light becomes more blue and white.

Table 13.2

Correlated Color Temperature of Common Sources

Source	Color Temperature in Degrees Kelvin
hazy blue sky	9000
overcast sky	7500
60-watt incandescent	2790
150-watt incandescent	2800
tungsten-halogen	3000
cool-white fluorescent	4300
warm-white fluorescent	3100
cool-white deluxe fluorescent	4100
daylight fluorescent	6500
metal halide HID	3600–4200

Another method used to rate the color rendering of light sources is the color rendering index (CRI). This is a measure of how well one source renders the color of an object when compared with the same object lighted with a reference source of similar chromaticity whose CRI is 100. The index is a number between 1 and 100, and in many cases the reference source closely resembles a common incandescent lamp.

You must know the color characteristics of a light source when designing a lighting system because the light color affects the color of finishes, furniture, and other objects in the space. For example, using a lamp with a high complement of blue and violet will make finishes and furniture with the warmer colors of red appear dull, gray, and washed out. Where color appearance is important, finishes and materials should be selected under the same lighting used in the finished space.

B. Design Process

Although there is no one process for designing a lighting installation, this section summarizes the more important considerations and outlines a sequence of steps for completing a lighting design.

The first step is to determine the function of the space and the visual tasks to be performed. This includes determining the light levels needed (footcandle level), whether the space will be single or multiple use, and any special conditions that might dictate a particular kind of lighting solution. For example, a room with computer terminals will require particular care to avoid glare on the screens. An indirect lighting system with local, adjustable task lighting may be appropriate. Existing conditions that might affect the design should also be studied, such as daylighting contribution, ceiling height, ceiling construction, the size of the room, and other physical limitations.

Lighting should also enhance the character and function of the space. A lighting design for a library reading room will be quite different from a lighting design for a nightclub lounge. The character of a space includes not only the lighting level but also the types and styles of luminaires selected. Additional considerations include the degree of uniformity of lighting, light control, fixed lighting versus portable lamps, and the visibility of the light sources.

Next, lamp types are selected, whether they are incandescent, fluorescent, high-intensity discharge, or some combination. The decision is based on the color rendition required, overall economy (both initial cost and life cycle costs), and the type of control required. If spotlighting is required, for example, incandescent lamps will probably have to be used.

Concurrent with lamp selection is luminaire selection. This involves both technical knowledge and aesthetic sensibility. Of course, luminaires must be selected that control glare, are cost effective, provide adjustability if required, and fit into the structure of the room. They must also complement the design of the space and provide the quality of light required for the visual tasks. In most lighting designs, a variety of luminaires is required. For example, in a retail store direct or indirect fluorescent lights may be used for general illumination, incandescent wall-washers to highlight vertical surfaces, track lighting for adjustability and for highlighting special areas, and portable lamps for providing task illumination.

Finally, the number and location of the luminaires are determined. These decisions are primarily based on the light level required and the tasks to be performed. For residential design and some commercial design, the number of fixtures can be estimated based on experience or rules of thumb that relate the number of fixtures to a given amount of floor space.

For larger installations, the number and location should be calculated according to the zonal cavity method developed by the IES. In brief, this system determines the number of luminaires required to provide a given footcandle level by using the efficacy of the lamp (lumens per watt), the number of lamps in the luminaire, the coefficient of utilization of the luminaire, the gradual loss of light output of the lamps over time (called the lamp lumen depreciation factor), and the conditions under which the luminaire will be used, which affects the amount of dirt collected on the lamps over time (called the luminaire dirt depreciation factor). The coefficient of utilization (CU) is a number used in these calculations that represents how efficiently the luminaire distributes the light from the lamps under various degrees of finish reflectivity of the floor, walls, and ceiling. Manufacturers test each of their luminaires and publish individual CU tables for each fixture. All of these factors are used in formulas to calculate the number of luminaires, but it is unlikely that you will have to make such calculations on the NCIDQ exam. Nevertheless, you should know the factors that influence light level.

However, providing the number of fixtures to achieve a certain footcandle level on the task is not enough. Additional lighting may be required to minimize dark wall surfaces, to highlight certain areas, and to provide interest and contrast to the overall design. Fixtures must also be located to avoid direct and indirect glare and to provide the recommended contrast ratios discussed previously.

C. Reflected Ceiling Plans

The final lighting design is documented on a reflected ceiling plan. As defined earlier, this is a technical drawing located in the same orientation as the floor plan and drawn at the same scale. In addition to showing the construction of the ceiling and the location of air diffusers, smoke detectors, and other objects in the ceiling, it shows the location of all the built-in lighting. For residential construction and some commercial construction, the switching may also be indicated as shown in Figure 13.7. On larger commercial projects, the interior designer may develop a reflected ceiling plan showing only the luminaire locations, while the electrical engineering consultant develops a lighting plan that includes switching and circuiting. See Figure 7.6. Refer to Chapter 7, Section 2, for more information about reflected ceiling plans.

D. Circuiting

The interior designer should decide how the lights in a space will be switched. This decision is based on the function of the lighting, how much individual control is required, where the switches would be best located, energy conservation needs, and the maximum electrical load requirements on any one circuit.

The function of a space may simply require one on/off switch for all the lights in the space. In other cases, like a lecture room, it may be necessary to provide several circuits and switches so some lights can be turned off while some are on. Multiple switching also gives the users the flexibility of saving energy by not using all the lights when they are not required.

Switches generally should be located at the door into a space so they can easily be turned on and off as people enter or leave the room. If there are two doors or the space is very large, two-way or three-way switches can be used. These allow a light to be switched at two or three different locations, respectively.

The circuiting of lights is also dependent on the type of control required. Many lights connected to a dimmer switch must be on their own circuit. Both incandescent and fluorescent lights can be dimmed, but fluorescent dimmers are more expensive and special fixtures are required to minimize flicker as they are dimmed. Incandescent lights should generally be on a circuit separate from fluorescent lights. In commercial installations this is often mandatory because incandescent lights are on 120-volt circuits and fluorescent lights are connected to 277-volt circuits. Because they are more efficient, 277-volt circuits are often used in large commercial installations. Lights can also be switched by low voltage relay switching, by automatic time clocks, and by proximity devices that sense when people enter or leave a room.

Finally, the number of switches depends on electrical load limitations. This is determined by the electrical engineering consultant or, on small projects, by the electrical contractor. Electrical building codes limit the total wattage than can be connected to any one circuit, so a large space with a great deal of lighting will have several switches.

E. Daylighting

In many cases, daylighting is used to supplement or replace artificial lighting during certain times. Although the architectural design of a building determines the type of general success of daylighting, the interior designer must be sensitive to locating partitions, specifying office systems, and selecting colors and finishes that do not undermine the methods of the building's daylighting system. For example, in a space with clerestory lighting, partitions and office systems should be kept as low as possible to allow the light to flood the entire space. (A clerestory is a vertically glazed area placed between two different roof levels to admit light.)

F. Energy Conservation

In commercial buildings, lighting accounts for a large part of the total energy consumed. The interior designer can help minimize energy use with a variety of strategies: by using daylight as much as possible, selecting high-efficacy lamps, using efficient luminaires, minimizing unneeded ambient illumination, providing task lighting only where it is needed, and selecting high-reflectance ceiling, wall, and floor surfaces to reduce the total number of fixtures required to light a space. In addition, by working with a competent lighting designer or electrical engineer, other technical solutions can be used, such as automatic switching and return-air luminaires. Automatic switching shuts off lights in an unoccupied room after a certain amount of time, and return-air fixtures move exhaust air over the lamps, keeping them cooler and helping them to operate more efficiently.

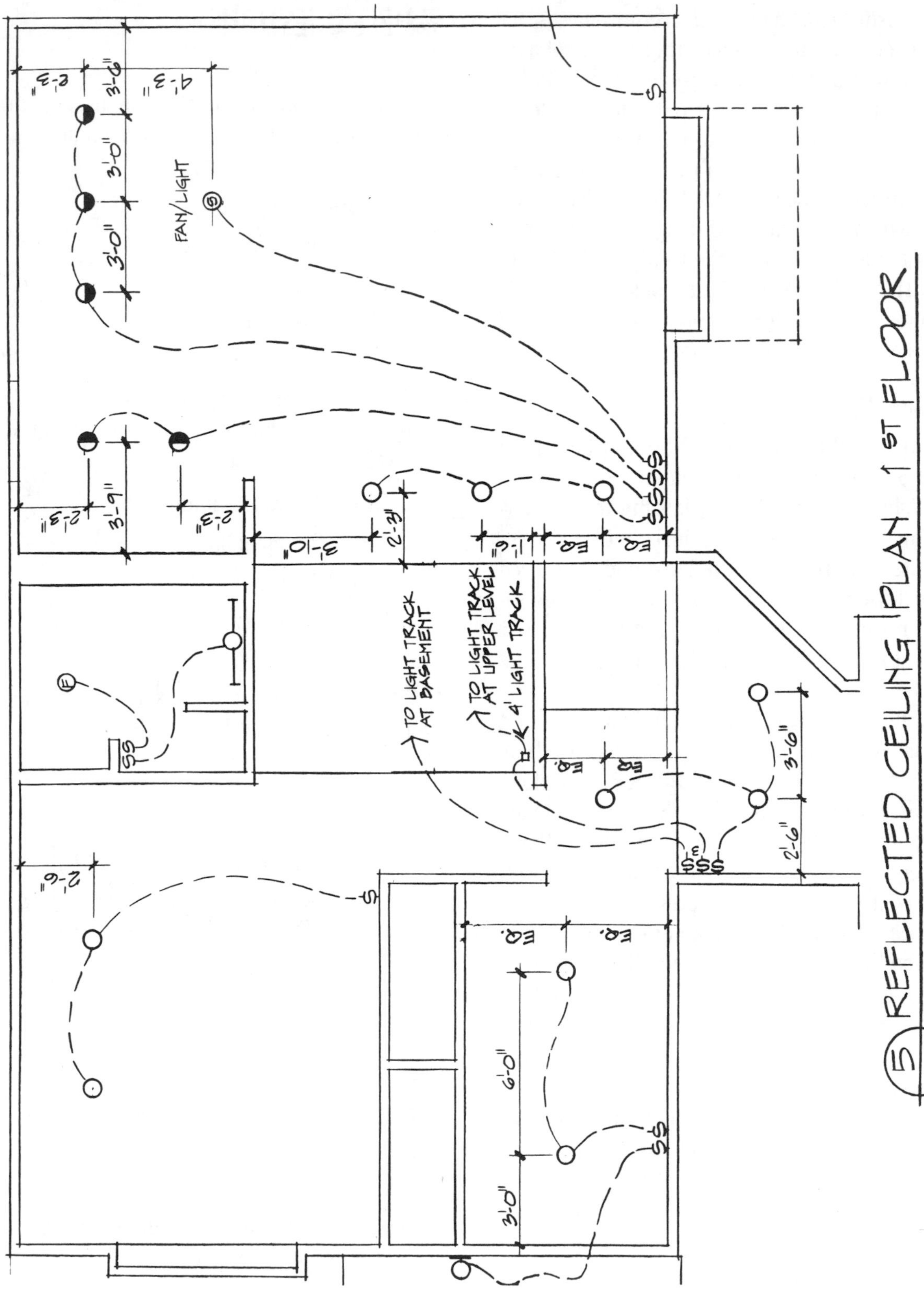

Figure 13.7 Switching on Reflected Ceiling Plan

Most jurisdictions have code requirements for commercial construction concerning the maximum amount of power that can be consumed in a building for lighting. This amount for a particular building type is determined according to certain procedures developed by the IES, and the designer must work within the guidelines so the total power budget is not exceeded. This allows for flexibility in design while conserving energy. Although the total power budget will vary with building type, a figure of approximately 2.3 watts per square foot for many types of commercial buildings is often considered a maximum.

G. Emergency Lighting

The Uniform Building Code, National Electrical Code, Life Safety Code, and Canadian codes all include provisions for emergency lighting in commercial buildings. Because each jurisdiction differs slightly in its requirements, the local codes in force must be reviewed. Generally, however, all codes require that in the event of a power failure, sufficient lighting must be available to safely evacuate building occupants.

Emergency lighting is required in exit stairs and corridors as well as in certain occupancies such as places of assembly, educational facilities, hazardous locations, and other places where occupancy loads exceed a given number. The usual minimum lighting level required is 1 footcandle at the floor level. Illuminated exit signs are also required in many situations. There must be an exit sign at each exit door, each door leading to an exitway, and directional exit signs at corridor intersections or where a corridor changes direction so that it is always evident to the occupants where the exits are. Emergency lighting circuits are usually a part of the architectural design of a building, but any extensive remodeling must include proper connection to the emergency circuits.

SAMPLE QUESTIONS

1. Who is responsible for the final design of the lighting and switching system in a commercial interior design project?

    1. interior designer
    2. architect
    3. electrical engineer
    4. electrical contractor

2. You are designing a jewelry store in an exclusive shopping mall. What type of lamps would be best to use in the display cases?

    1. 75 W PAR quartz lamps
    2. 150 W R quartz lamps
    3. 15 W T lamps
    4. 90 W MR-16 lamps

3. What is the commonly used designation for the lamp labeled X below?

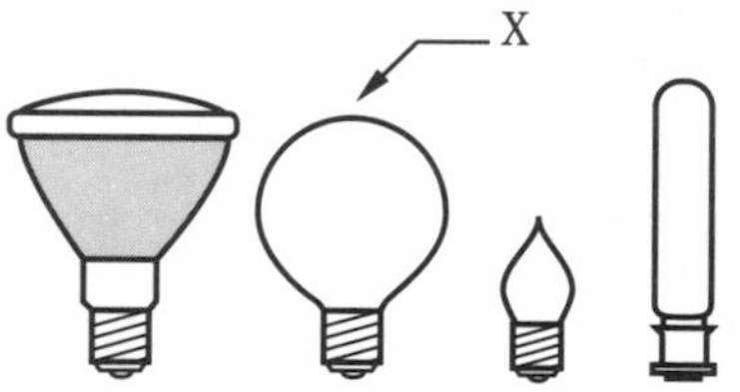

    1. C
    2. G
    3. A
    4. T

4. The units used for the measurement and description of the brightness of a direct glare source are

    1. footcandles
    2. footlamberts
    3. candelas
    4. lumens

5. One of the most frequent lighting problems in traditional drafting rooms is

1. veiling reflection
2. direct glare
3. visual comfort
4. excessive brightness ratio

6. After reviewing the plans for a large office suite that you have designed, the building department states that you have exceeded the lighting budget. If your design is composed of 80 percent fluorescent lighting and 20 percent incandescent lighting, what is your BEST course of action to begin redesign?

1. Reduce the number of luminaires by spacing them farther apart.
2. Substitute all incandescent lights with fluorescent lighting.
3. Change to a task-ambient lighting system.
4. Investigate whether lamps with higher efficacies will bring the design within the budget.

7. Which of the following sources would be MOST appropriate for the warehouse portion of a large furniture dealership?

1. high-pressure sodium
2. cool-white deluxe fluorescent
3. metal halide
4. mercury vapor

8. Surface-mounted luminaires are MOST often used for which of the following reasons?

1. Some side and uplighting is desired.
2. There is not enough space above the ceiling.
3. They are easier and less expensive to install.
4. They are used as a design feature.

9. What is the MOST important criterion for lighting a fabric showroom?

1. visual comfort probability
2. color rendering index
3. coefficient of utilization
4. apparent color temperature rating

10. In designing a room in which work will take place at both video display terminals and standard work surfaces, what approach to lighting design would be MOST appropriate?

1. Use indirect ambient lighting with individual task lights at each standard workstation.
2. Locate downlights over workstations and indirect lighting fixtures over the terminals.
3. Use low brightness troffers controlled by dimmers and task lighting on the work surfaces.
4. Specify a direct-indirect system locally controlled at each workstation.

14 MECHANICAL AND ELECTRICAL SYSTEMS

This chapter reviews some of the mechanical systems with which you should be familiar. For convenience, communication systems and stairway design are also included in this chapter. Although the interior designer is not responsible for designing or producing construction drawings for mechanical or electrical systems, he or she must often coordinate the location of plumbing fixtures, air diffusers, sprinklers, and other visible mechanical elements with the overall design.

In many cases, existing mechanical and electrical services are fixed and therefore dictate the location of interior design elements. In other cases, the interior designer may be able to relocate certain mechanical fixtures. For new construction, the interior designer often works with an architect or engineer to coordinate the desired location of mechanical and electrical equipment and devices.

1 HVAC

HVAC is the acronym for *heating, ventilating, and air conditioning* and includes all the systems used for these purposes. One system may combine all three, or there may be two or more systems to heat and cool a building.

A. Types of Systems

HVAC systems are often classified by the medium used to heat or cool the building. The two primary methods of heating and cooling use air or water. In some parts of the country, electricity is also used for heating. Some systems use a combination of media.

All-air systems cool or heat spaces by conditioned air alone. Heat is transported to the space with supply and return air ducts. A common example of an all-air system is a residential forced hot-air furnace. A boiler powered by oil or gas heats air that is distributed throughout the house in ductwork. Return air ducts in each room collect the cooled air and return it to the furnace for reheating. If necessary, an air conditioning unit is connected to the same ductwork to provide cooled and dehumidified air.

For commercial buildings, there are several variations of systems including variable air volume, high-velocity dual duct, constant volume with reheat, and multizone systems. All types require supply air ductwork, registers, and return air grilles in all spaces. Registers are connected to the supply air ductwork and can be adjusted to control the direction of air flow and the volume of air coming through them. In many instances, separate ductwork is not used for return air, but grilles are simply placed in the suspended ceiling to collect return air. The mechanical system draws the return air back to a central collecting point where it is then returned through ducts to the building's heating plant.

The space between the suspended ceiling and the structural floor above is called the *plenum*. If fire-rated partitions extend above the suspended ceiling, then supply air ducts and openings for return air must be provided. At the locations where the fire wall is penetrated, fire dampers are required that automatically close in the event of a fire.

Supply air registers are often connected to the main ductwork with flexible ducting. This allows some adjustability in the exact location of an air register if its location is in conflict with some other ceiling-mounted item. Because return air grilles are generally not connected to ducts in commercial construction, they may also be relocated if overall circulation is maintained. The mechanical engineer should be consulted to determine how much the registers can be moved.

All-water heating systems use some type of coil unit called a *convector* in each space through which hot water is circulated. The hot water heats the fins of the coil unit, and air is heated as it is drawn over the fins. The air may be circulated by convection, as with most baseboard residential fin-tube radiators, or by forced circulation created with a fan.

There are also combination systems that use ductwork for supplying fresh air but use water to heat or cool the air before it is introduced into the conditioned space. These are called terminal reheat systems. Other installations use an all-water system for heating and a separate duct system for ventilation and cooling. In geographical areas where electric heat is economical, radiant panels can be mounted in the walls or created by running cables in the ceiling. Sometimes electric panels are used where it is necessary to avoid drafts.

B. System Requirements

There are several things about HVAC systems the interior designer should keep in mind when designing a space. These considerations are discussed below.

Space for ducts and pipes: Small ducts and plumbing pipes are typically run within the walls and floor joists in residential construction. Occasionally, horizontal ducts in a house must be run below the floor joists and a dropped ceiling must be built to conceal them.

In commercial construction, horizontal ducts are normally run in the plenum and vertical ducts within their own chases. Large ducts may occupy most of the vertical distance between a suspended ceiling and the structure above, making it difficult, if not impossible, to recess light fixtures. You should verify the size and location of ductwork before locating light fixtures. Some commercial construction uses access flooring, which is a false floor of individual panels raised above the structural floor with pedestals. This provides space to run electrical and communication wiring as well as HVAC ductwork.

Small pipes can be run within walls in commercial construction, but larger pipes need to be placed in deeper walls or in chase walls that provide space between two widely spaced partitions.

Plenum requirements: In commercial construction when the plenum is used as a return air space, building codes prohibit the use of combustible materials such as wood or exposed wire within the space. However, some special types of telephone and communication wiring are plenum rated for use in such a location, and these may be used in place of running the wires in steel conduit.

Access: Building codes require that access be provided to certain components of mechanical and electrical systems. These include such things as valves, fire dampers, heating coils, mechanical equipment, and electrical junction boxes. If these components are located above a suspended acoustical ceiling, access is provided by simply removing a ceiling tile. In other locations such as gypsum wallboard ceilings and partitions, access doors are required for anything that might need to be adjusted or repaired.

Thermostats: The positions of thermostats are normally determined by the mechanical engineer so they are away from exterior walls, heat sources, or other areas that may adversely affect their operation. They are normally located 48 inches above the floor, but this should be coordinated with light switches and other nearby control devices.

Coordination with other ceiling items: The interior designer should coordinate the location of supply and return air diffusers with other ceiling items such as lights, sprinkler heads, smoke detectors, speakers, and the like, so the ceiling is as well planned as possible. However, the mechanical engineer must be consulted to verify that the desired locations do not adversely affect the operation of the HVAC system.

Window coverings: Window coverings can affect the heating and air conditioning load in a space and may interfere with supply air diffusers or other heating units near the window. Therefore, the interior designer should have the mechanical engineer or architect check their proposed type, size, and mounting to verify that they will not create a problem with the HVAC system.

Furniture placement: Most HVAC systems are designed to work independently of furniture placement. However, in some cases the interior designer may want to consider the location of floor registers, fin-tube baseboard radiators, and other equipment as it affects the placement of furniture and built-in woodwork.

C. Reading HVAC Plans

You should know the basics of reading HVAC plans so you can review drawings to verify existing conditions and coordinate the interior design work with the mechanical engineer's work. HVAC drawings are normally drawn with single lines representing piping and ductwork. Figure 14.1 shows a portion of a typical commercial mechanical plan. Note that ducts are indicated with a line and a number such as 18 x 12. The first number indicates the width of the duct in inches, and the second number indicates its height in inches.

Figure 7.18 shows some common mechanical drafting symbols with which you should also be familiar.

2 ELECTRICAL

A. Power System Requirements

Electrical systems include power for lighting (discussed in the previous chapter), convenience outlets, and fixed equipment. As with lighting, the electrical engineer or electrical contractor designs and specifies the exact type of circuiting, wire sizes, and

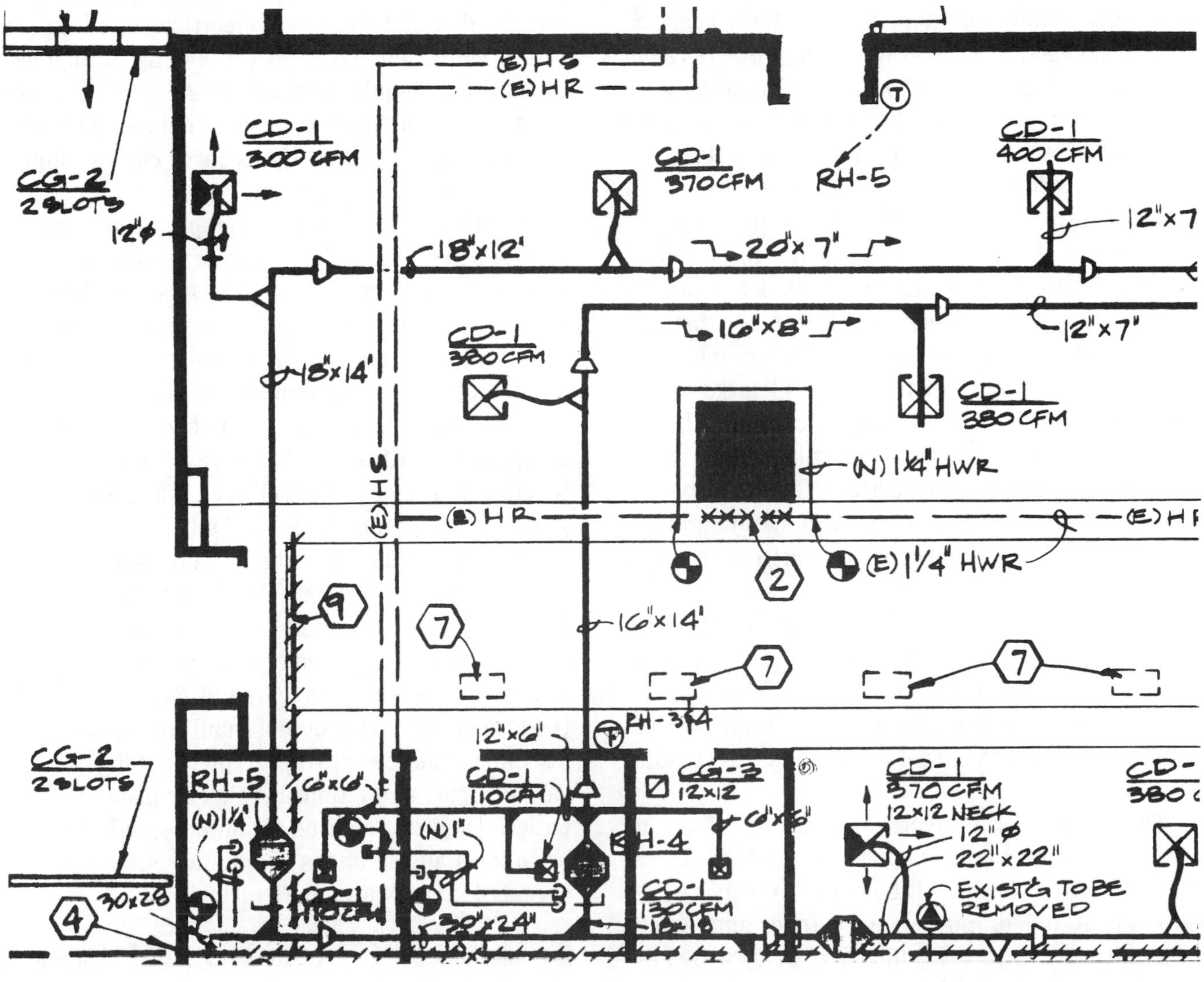

Figure 14.1 Partial HVAC Plan

other technical aspects of the electrical systems. The interior designer, however, is often responsible for schematically showing the desired location of outlets and switches, where power is required for special built-in equipment, and the appearance of cover plates and other visible electrical devices. The interior designer should also be familiar with the rudiments of power supply.

There are several types of conductors that supply power throughout a building. These extend from circuit breaker boxes to the individual switches, lights, and outlets. Nonmetallic sheathed cable, also known by the trade name *Romex*, consists of two or more plastic-insulated conductors and ground wire surrounded by a moisture-resistant plastic jacket. This type of cable can be used in wood stud residential buildings and buildings not exceeding three floors, as long as it is used with wood studs and protected from damage by being concealed behind walls and ceilings.

Flexible metal-clad cable, also known by the trade name *BX* (or the common term *flex*), consists of two or more plastic-insulated conductors encased in a continuous spiral-wound strip of steel tape. It is often used in remodeling work because it can be pulled through existing spaces within a building. It is also used to connect commercial light fixtures so they can be relocated in a suspended acoustical ceiling.

For commercial construction and large multifamily residential construction, individual plastic-insulated conductors must be placed in metal conduit or other approved carriers. Conduit supports and protects the wiring, serves as a system ground, and protects surrounding construction from fire if the wire overheats or shorts.

A relatively new type of cabling is under-carpet wiring. This is thin, flat, protected wire that can be laid under carpet without protruding. Cable for both 120-volt circuits and telephone lines is available, but it must be used with carpet tiles so that it is readily accessible.

Outlets and other types of connections to the power supply must be made in junction boxes. These are steel boxes to which the conduit or other cable system is attached. For single switches and duplex outlets, they measure about 2 inches by 4 inches. Larger boxes are 4 inches square, and several can be connected if there are more than two switches or two duplex outlets. Junction boxes are also required where light fixtures are connected to the electrical system.

Building codes specify requirements for all aspects of electrical systems, including the location of outlets. In residential construction, outlets must be spaced no farther than 12 feet apart, and there must be a duplex outlet on each wall surface where furniture might be placed so lamp cords and the like do not have to be stretched across door openings.

In many commercial projects, special power outlets must be placed on their own circuit. These are called *dedicated* circuits and prevent various types of electrical interference from disturbing sensitive electrical equipment (such as computers) connected to them. These circuits should be clearly differentiated on the plan and the exact electrical requirements of the equipment given to the electrical engineer. Circuits that require voltages greater than 120 volts must also be identified. These include outlets for electric ranges, clothes dryers, large copy machines, and other special equipment.

In addition to the protection provided by circuit breakers in the panel boxes that trip off if the circuit is overloaded, there are two other types of protection provided in electrical wiring. The first is grounding, which is a separate wire in addition to the two that provide power. The grounding of an electrical system prevents a dangerous shock if someone touches an appliance with a short circuit and simultaneously touches a ground path such as a water pipe. The ground provides a path for the fault.

A ground fault, however, can create other problems, because the current required to trip a circuit breaker is high and small leaks of current can continue unnoticed until someone receives a dangerous shock or a fire develops. Ground fault interrupters (GFI) are devices that detect small current leaks and disconnect the power to the circuit or appliance. GFIs can be a part of a circuit breaker or installed as an outlet. They are required for outdoor outlets and in bathrooms and kitchens as well as other locations specified in the National Electrical Code.

B. Telephone and Communication System Requirements

Telephone and communication systems are usually shown on the same plan as the power outlets.

The interior designer is responsible for showing the location of items like telephones, intercommunication systems, public address speakers, buzzers, computer terminals, and similar equipment. As with power outlets, the actual circuiting, wire sizes, and connections to central equipment are usually determined by the electrical engineer or the contractor responsible for installing the equipment.

Because telephone and communication systems are low-voltage systems, the requirements for conduit and other protection are not quite as stringent as for high-voltage power. In many cases, an outlet box is provided at the connection in the wall, and the wire is run within the walls and ceiling spaces without conduit. However, in some commercial construction all cable is required to be protected in conduit to avoid having it catch fire or release toxic fumes in case of a fire. Special plenum-rated cable is available that does not require conduit, but it is more expensive than standard cable.

C. Electrical System Plans

The interior designer can locate electrical, telephone, and communication outlets on one of several plans. For residential construction, they are often shown on the construction floor plan because the installation is fairly simple. On commercial projects where the floor plan may be crowded with other information, a separate power plan is often used. In addition to showing the outlets themselves, exact dimensions are given if their location is critical. Outlets can also be shown on the furniture plan because they most often directly relate to the placement of desks, seating groups, and other furniture. The power plans developed by the interior designer are then used by the electrical engineer to draw the electrical plan. This contains all the detailed information concerning circuiting, wire size, conduit size, panel boxes, and other data required by the electrical contractor. A typical power plan drawn by an interior designer is shown in Figure 7.1. As with mechanical plans, standard symbols are used to indicate common electrical items. Some of the more common ones are shown in Figure 7.17.

3 PLUMBING

Interior designers are often required to locate plumbing fixtures in both new construction and remodeling work. Because plumbing can be a significant cost item and imposes limitations on space planning, you should have a good understanding of plumbing basics and how to coordinate your work with existing building services.

A. Plumbing System Requirements

Plumbing systems consist of two major components: water supply and drainage. Water supply includes cold and hot water. In all plumbing installation, residential or commercial, water is supplied under pressure to individual plumbing fixtures. Because of this and because the pipes are generally small, it is relatively easy to locate pipes within wall cavities, ceiling structure, and other areas to supply a fixture, even if it is some distance from the main source of water. Figure 14.2 shows a schematic representation of a small water supply system.

Drainage systems present a more difficult problem because they work by gravity—drain pipes must be sloped downward to carry away wastes. In addition, vent pipes are required. Figure 14.3 shows a simplified diagram of a typical drainage and vent system. Beginning with the individual fixture, there are a number of components with which you should be familiar.

The first component attached to the fixture is the trap. With a few exceptions, traps are located at every fixture and are designed to catch and hold a quantity of water to provide a seal that prevents gases from the sewage system from entering the building. The locations where traps are not installed include fixtures that have traps as an integral part of their design, such as toilets, and where two or three adjacent fixtures are connected, such as a double kitchen sink.

Traps are connected to the actual drainage piping, but they must also be connected to vents. Vents are pipes connected to the drainage system at various locations, open to outside air, and designed to serve two purposes. First, they allow built-up sewage gases to escape instead of bubbling through the water in the traps. Second, they allow pressure in the system

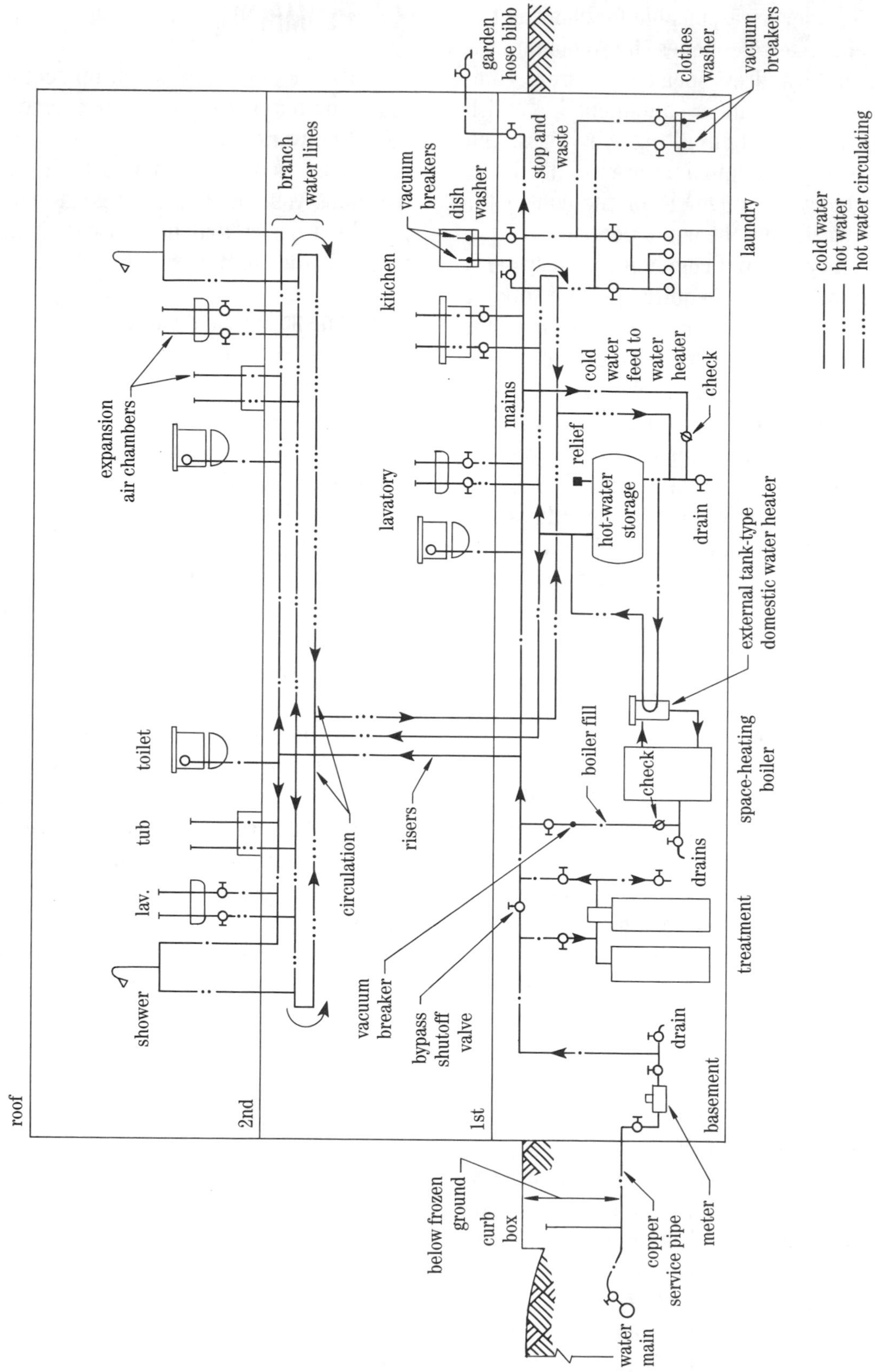

Figure 14.2 Water Supply System

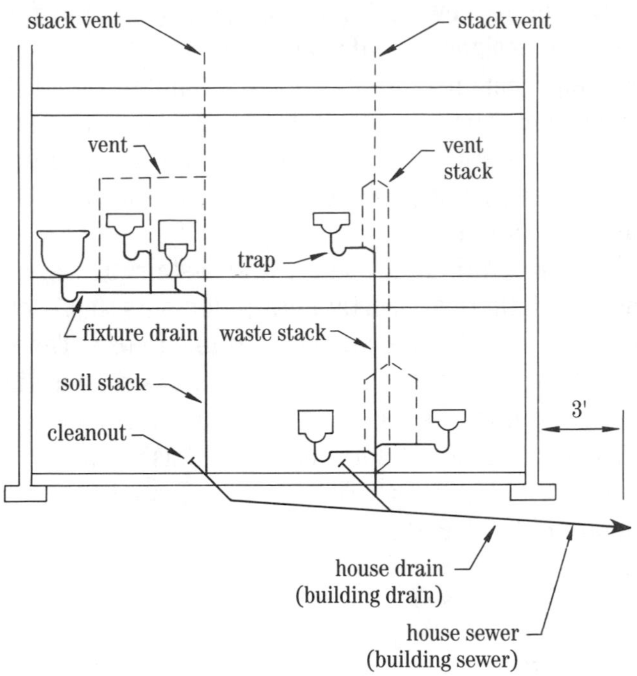

Figure 14.3 Drainage and Vent System

to equalize so discharging waste does not create a siphon that would drain the water out of the traps.

From the trap, sewage travels in fixture branch lines to a vertical stack. If the stack carries human waste from toilets, it is called a *soil stack*. If the stack carries wastes other than human waste, it is known as a *waste stack*.

Vents from individual fixtures are connected above the fixtures in two ways. If a vent connects to a soil or waste stack above the highest fixture in the system, the portion of the stack above this point is known as a *stack vent*. The stack vent extends through the roof. In multistory buildings, there is a separate pipe used for venting. This is called a *vent stack* and either extends through the roof or connects with the stack vent above the highest fixture as shown in Figure 14.3.

B. Locating Plumbing Fixtures

Because of the cost of plumbing and the necessity of sloping drainage pipes, plumbing fixtures should be located close to existing plumbing lines. These include horizontal lines or vertical risers that run continuously through a multistory building. Drains must be sloped a minimum of $^1/_4$ inch per foot (or $^1/_8$ inch per foot for pipes larger than 3 inches). If a pipe must be concealed within a floor space, then the slope and the size of the pipe itself will limit the distance from the fixture to a connection with a riser.

In commercial buildings, most plumbing is concentrated in one area near the core where it serves the toilet rooms, drinking fountains, and similar facilities. To provide service to sinks, private toilets, and the like, wet columns are sometimes included in the building. These are areas, usually at a structural column location, where hot and cold supply and drainage risers are located. Individual tenants can easily tap into these lines, if desired, without having to connect to more remote plumbing at the core of the building.

If extensive plumbing work is required, the necessary pipes may not fit within the space provided by standard partitions. Soil stacks from toilets, for example, require 4-inch diameter pipes that have an actual outside diameter somewhat larger than 4 inches. In this case, plumbing chases are required. These are constructed with two sets of studs with a space between large enough for the pipes.

C. Plumbing Plans

Like HVAC plans, plumbing plans are drafted by the mechanical engineer and represent piping and other components with single line diagrams and standard drafting symbols. Plumbing plan symbols you should be familiar with are shown in Figure 7.16.

4 FIRE PROTECTION

The most common type of fire protection is a sprinkler system. These are common in new construction and consist of a separate water system supplied by sprinkler mains that connect to sprinkler pipes on each floor that distribute the water to individual sprinkler heads.

In most construction, only the sprinkler heads are visible and a variety of styles are available, including recessed, upright, pendent, and sidewall. Recessed types have a smooth cover that is flush with the ceiling. When there is a fire, the cover falls away and the sprinkler head lowers and activates. Upright heads are used with exposed plumbing and high, unfinished ceilings. Pendent sprinklers are the traditional types for finished ceilings, but the head extends a few inches below the ceiling. Sidewall heads are used for corridors and small rooms when one row of sprinklers will provide adequate coverage for narrow spaces. Horizontal sidewall sprinklers also can be plumbed from the walls instead of from the ceiling, which makes them good for remodeling work.

Although the interior designer does not design sprinkler systems, you should recognize that the required location of sprinkler heads must be coordinated with other ceiling-mounted items. In addition, sprinkler pipes above the ceiling require additional space that may interfere with recessed lighting and other ceiling construction.

The design and installation of sprinkler systems are governed by each local building code, but most refer to the standard published by the National Fire Protection Association, NFPA-13. This standard classifies the relative fire hazard of buildings into three groups: light, ordinary, and extra hazard. The hazard classification and other requirements determine the required spacing of sprinklers.

For example, light hazard includes residences, offices, hospitals, schools, and restaurants. In these occupancies, there must be one sprinkler for each 200 square feet, or 225 square feet if the system is designed according to certain methods. For open wood joist ceilings, the area drops to 130 square feet. The maximum spacing between sprinkler heads is 15 feet for the 225-square-foot coverage requirement, with the maximum distance from a wall being one-half the required spacing. Within the limitations set by the building code, you can work with the fire protection engineer or fire protection contractor to coordinate placement of heads with other ceiling fixtures.

If water would damage the contents of a room, such as in a computer facility, a dry halon system can be used. This is a gas, released when the system is triggered, that smothers the fire while allowing people in the space to breathe.

5 VERTICAL TRANSPORTATION

Vertical transportation includes stairs, elevators, and escalators, but the NCIDQ exam only covers stairways. The design of stairs is usually the responsibility of the architect, but there are times when the interior designer must design them. Residential projects may require new or remodeled stairways, and the interior designer should be familiar with their basic requirements. If elevators are being installed or remodeled, the interior designer may be concerned with the interior finishes of the cab, the elevator entrances, and the signal system of call buttons and up/down lanterns.

Although there are many ways a stairway can be designed, there are certain basic elements that each must share to be safe and comfortable to use. These are shown in Figure 14.4. Building codes set certain restrictions on the rise and run of exit stairs (the vertical and horizontal portions) as well as on handrail design and landings. These are discussed in more detail in Chapter 18.

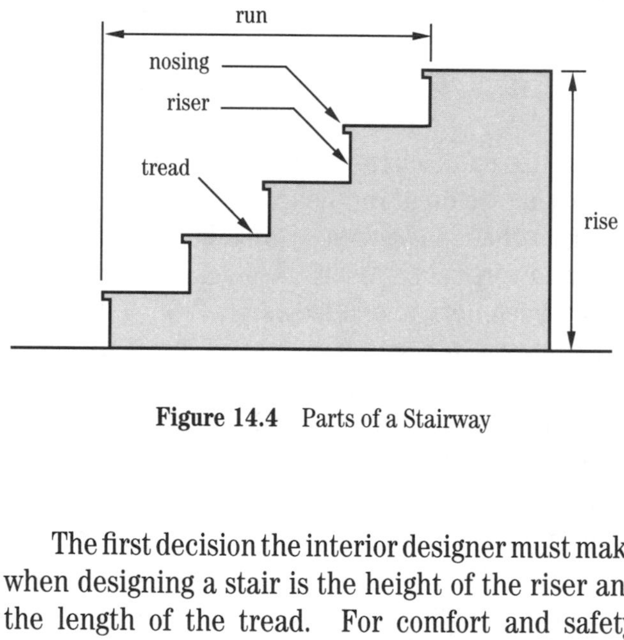

Figure 14.4 Parts of a Stairway

The first decision the interior designer must make when designing a stair is the height of the riser and the length of the tread. For comfort and safety, both of these dimensions are interrelated and are based on the normal adult stride. As the riser gets lower, the tread increases to maintain a certain relationship. Generally, the height of the riser must be determined first so each riser between the floors is identical within minimum and maximum code limitations. Then the appropriate tread dimension is calculated. There are several formulas for this but the most common is

$$2R + T = 25$$

R is the riser height in inches and T is the tread width in inches. For example, if the riser is $6^{1}/_{2}$ inches the tread should be

$$(2)(6.5) + T = 25$$
$$T = (25) - (2)(6.5)$$
$$T = (12) \text{ inches}$$

For most stairs a 7-inch riser and an 11-inch tread is a good combination and satisfies the Uniform Building Code, which limits risers to 7 inches in most stairways (8 inches in residential stairways). The minimum tread width by code is 11 inches (or 9 inches in residential stairways). If the riser height must be modified to equalize the stairs between a fixed floor height, a dimension between 6 and 7 inches should be used.

Additional considerations in stair design are the nosing, which normally extends about an inch from the back of the tread and the handrail as shown in Figure 14.4. To be accessible for the physically disabled, both the nosing and the handrail must be designed according to certain requirements as specified in Chapter 19.

SAMPLE QUESTIONS

1. The device that controls the volume of air and its distribution in an HVAC system is called a

1. convector
2. grille
3. register
4. duct

2. What type of system would be best for an open-office plan so the heating and cooling for each workstation could be individually controlled?

1. all-air
2. all-water
3. radiant panel
4. air-water

3. What is NOT allowed in a return air plenum?

1. fire dampers
2. electrical cable
3. water supply pipes
4. wood blocking

4. In working with an electrical engineer on a project, what information would you MOST likely put on the interior design power plan?

1. switch locations
2. dedicated outlets
3. conduit sizing
4. speaker locations

5. What type of sprinkler head should be used for a decorative, open-grid, wood slat ceiling suspended from the structural floor above?

1. upright
2. pendent
3. sidewall
4. recessed

6. In the diagram below, what is the portion of the stair called identified by A?

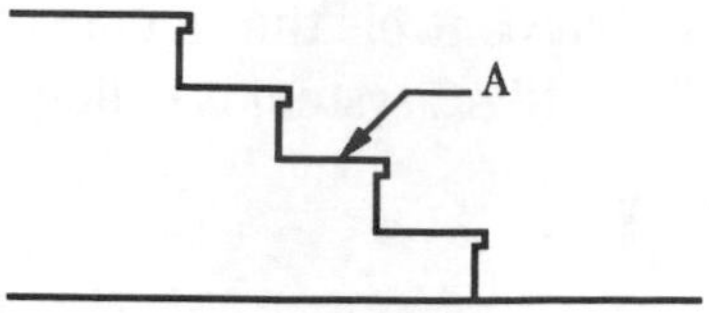

1. riser
2. tread
3. nosing
4. run

7. In specifying new window coverings and track to replace building standard window coverings, what coordination is LEAST important for the interior designer to undertake?

1. asking the electrical engineer if the new light reflectance is detrimental
2. verifying that the building owner does not care about the change in exterior appearance of the building
3. determining if the mechanical engineer objects to it
4. checking with the architect to see that the new coverings do not adversely affect the heating of the glass

8. What does the symbol shown below indicate?

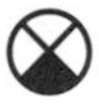

1. recessed directional light
2. suspended exit light
3. floor telephone outlet
4. fire alarm horn

9. What would be the BEST combination of dimensions for a stair serving a sleeping loft in a condominium where space was at a premium and the floor-to-floor dimension was 9 feet 4 inches?

1. 7-inch riser, 11-inch tread
2. 7-inch riser, 9-inch tread
3. 8-inch riser, 9-inch tread
4. 8-inch riser, 10-inch tread

10. What would NOT be allowed in an access floor with removable panels?

1. computer cable
2. plumbing
3. HVAC
4. electrical conduit

15 ACOUSTICS

Acoustics can greatly influence the overall quality of interior design. Spaces that are too noisy or reverberant are distracting at best and unusable at worst. Likewise, auditoriums or classrooms in which sounds are not audible are equally unsuitable. The interior designer can control the acoustic quality of a room with space planning, the design of walls and ceilings, and the selection of finishes. For many common situations, a basic knowledge of acoustics can help the interior designer make the best decisions. With more complex designs like concert halls or recording studios, the services of a qualified acoustical consultant should be used.

1 FUNDAMENTALS OF SOUND

A. Qualities of Sound

Sound has three basic qualities: velocity, frequency, and power. Velocity depends on the medium in which the sound is traveling and the temperature of the medium. Frequency is the number of cycles completed per second and is measured in Hertz (Hz). One Hz equals one cycle per second. The sounds that we call high notes or high-pitched sounds have higher frequencies; bass notes have lower frequencies. Power is the quality of acoustic energy as measured in watts. It is this power that people perceive as loudness.

B. Loudness

The human ear is sensitive to a vast range of sound power, from about 10^{-16} watts per square centimeter to 10^{-3} watts per square centimeter. Because of this and the fact that the sensation of hearing is proportional to the logarithm of the source intensity, the decibel (abbreviated dB) is used in acoustic descriptions and calculations. The decibel conveniently relates actual sound intensity to the way humans experience sound. By definition, zero decibel is the threshold of human hearing, and 130 decibels is the threshold of pain. Some common sound intensity levels and their subjective evaluations are shown in Table 15.1.

The change in loudness is subjective, but some common guidelines are shown in Table 15.2. These are useful for evaluating the effects of increased or decreased decibel levels in design situations. For example, spending money to modify a partition to increase its sound transmission class (defined later in this chapter) by three decibels probably would not be worth the expense because it would hardly be noticeable.

C. Human Sensitivity to Sound

Although human response to sound is subjective and varies with age, physical condition of the ear, background, and other factors, the following guidelines are useful to know.

- A healthy young person can hear sounds in the range of about 20 to 20,000 Hz and is most sensitive to frequencies in the 3000 to 4000 Hz range. Speech is composed of sounds primarily in the range of 125 to 8000 Hz, with most in the range of 200 to 5000 Hz.

- The human ear is less sensitive to low frequencies than to middle and high frequencies for sounds of equal energy.

- Most common sound sources contain energy over a wide range of frequencies. Because frequency is an important variable in how a sound is transmitted or absorbed, it must be taken into account in building acoustics. For

Table 15.1

Common Sound Intensity Levels

IL dB	Example	Subjective Evaluation	Intensity w/cm^2
140	jet plane takeoff		
130	gunfire	threshold of pain	10^{-3}
120	hard rock band, siren at 100 ft	deafening	10^{-4}
110	accelerating motorcycle	sound can be felt	10^{-5}
100	auto horn at 10 ft	conversation difficult to hear	10^{-6}
90	loud street noise, kitchen blender	very loud	10^{-7}
80	noisy office, average factory	difficult to use phone	10^{-8}
70	average street noise, quiet typewriter, average radio	loud	10^{-9}
60	average office, noisy home	usual background	10^{-10}
50	average conversation, quiet radio	moderate	10^{-11}
40	quiet home, private office	noticeably quiet	10^{-12}
30	quiet conversation	faint	10^{-13}
20	whisper		10^{-14}
10	rustling leaves, soundproof room	very faint	10^{-15}
0	threshold of hearing		10^{-16}

convenience, measurement and analysis is often divided into eight octave frequency bands identified by their center frequency.

Table 15.2

Subjective Change in Loudness Based on Decibel Level Change

Change In Intensity Level in dB	Change In Apparent Loudness
1	almost imperceptible
3	just perceptible
5	clearly noticeable
6	change when distance to source in a free field is doubled or halved
10	twice or half as loud
18	very much louder or quieter
20	four times or one-fourth as loud

2 SOUND TRANSMISSION

There are two basic problems in controlling noise (defined as any unwanted sound): preventing or minimizing the transmission of sound from one space to another and reducing the noise within a space. This section discusses sound transmission; the next section outlines the basics of sound absorption as the primary means of reducing noise in a space.

A. Transmission Loss and Noise Reduction

A common problem is unwanted sound transmission from one space to another. Transmission of sound is primarily retarded by the mass of the partition. The stiffness, or rigidity, of the partition is also important. Given two partitions of the same weight per square foot, the one with less stiffness will perform better than the other.

There are two important concepts in noise reduction: transmission loss and actual noise reduction between two spaces. Transmission loss takes into account only the loss through the partition. Noise reduction is dependent not only on the transmission loss but also on the area of the partition separating the two spaces and the absorption of the surfaces in the "quiet" room. Noise reduction can be increased by increasing the transmission loss of the partition, by increasing the absorption in the "quiet" room (the one not producing the noise), by decreasing the area of the common wall between the rooms, or by some combination of all three.

To simplify the selection of construction of walls and other building components, a single-number rating is often used to rate the transmission loss of construction. This is the *sound transmission class* (STC). The higher the STC rating, the better the barrier is (theoretically) in stopping sound. Table 15.3 shows some STC ratings and their effects on hearing.

Table 15.3

Effect of Barrier STC on Hearing

STC	Effect on Hearing
25	normal speech can clearly be heard through barrier
30	loud speech can be heard and understood fairly well; normal speech can be heard but barely understood
35	loud speech is not intelligible but can be heard
42–45	loud speech can only be faintly heard; normal speech cannot be heard
46–50	loud speech not audible; loud sounds other than speech can only be heard faintly, if at all

STC ratings represent the ideal loss through a barrier under laboratory conditions. Partitions, floors, and other construction components built in the field are seldom constructed as well as those in the laboratory. Also, breaks in the barrier such as cracks, electrical outlets, doors, and the like will significantly lessen overall noise reduction.

In critical situations, transmission loss and selection of barriers should be calculated using the values for various frequencies rather than the single STC average value. Some materials may allow an acoustic "hole," stopping most frequencies but allowing transmission of a certain range of frequencies. However, for preliminary design purposes the STC value is adequate.

B. Noise Criteria Curves

All normally occupied spaces have some amount of background noise. This is not undesirable because some noise is necessary to avoid the feeling of a "dead" space and to help mask other sounds. However, the acceptable amount of background noise varies with the type of space and the frequency of sound. For example, people are generally less tolerant of background noise in bedrooms than they are in public lobbies, and they are generally more tolerant of higher levels of low-frequency sound than of high-frequency sound.

These variables have been consolidated into a set of noise criteria curves relating frequency in eight octave bands to noise level. See Figure 15.1. Accompanying these curves are noise criteria ratings for various types of spaces and listening requirements. A representative sampling is shown in Table 15.4. Noise criteria curves can be used to specify the maximum amount of continuous background noise allowable in a space, to establish a minimum amount of noise desired to help mask sounds, and to evaluate an existing condition.

Table 15.4

Some Representative Noise Criteria

Type of Space	Preferred NC (dB)
concert halls, opera houses, recording studios	15–20
bedrooms, apartments, hospitals	20–30
private offices, small conference rooms	30–35
large offices, retail stores, restaurants	35–40
lobbies, drafting rooms, laboratory work spaces	40–45
kitchens, computer rooms, light maintenance shops	45–55

3 SOUND ABSORPTION

Controlling sound transmission is only part of good acoustic design. The proper amount of sound absorption must also be included to minimize noise

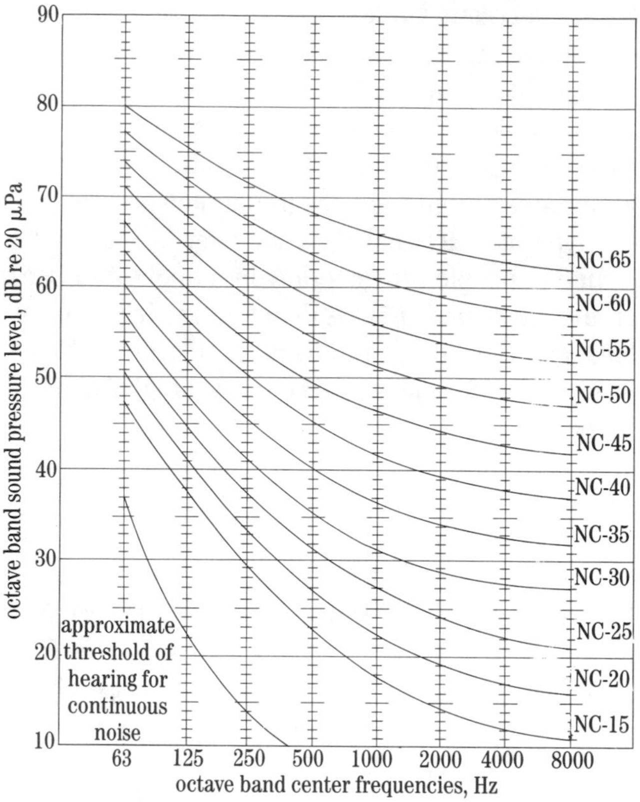

Figure 15.1 NC (Noise Criteria) Curves

within a space. Of course, the source of the noise may be reduced, but this is not always possible. Sound absorption, then, is used to control unwanted sound reflections (noise), to improve speech privacy, and to decrease or increase reverberation.

A. Fundamentals

The absorption of a material is defined by the coefficient of absorption, a, which is the ratio of the sound intensity absorbed by the material to the total intensity reaching the material. The maximum absorption possible, therefore, is 1, that of free space. Generally, a material with a coefficient below 0.2 is considered to be reflective, and one with a coefficient above 0.2 is considered sound absorbing. These coefficients are published in manufacturers' technical literature.

The coefficient of absorption varies with the frequency of the sound, and some materials are better at absorbing some frequencies than others. For critical applications, all frequencies should be checked, but for convenience the single- number *noise reduction coefficient* (NRC) is used. The NRC is the average of a material's absorption coefficients at the four frequencies of 250, 500, 1000, and 2000 Hz, rounded to the nearest multiple of 0.05. Some typical NRC ratings are shown in Table 15.5.

Table 15.5

Noise Reduction Coefficients

Material	NRC
vinyl tile on concrete	0.05
wood strip flooring	0.10
carpet, 1/2″ pile on concrete	0.50
gypsumboard walls	0.05
1″ fiberglass wall panel with fabric cover	0.80
plywood paneling	0.15
5/8″ suspended acoustic tile	0.60
1″ suspended acoustic tile	0.90

B. Noise Reduction Within a Space

The total absorption of a material is dependent on its coefficient of absorption and the area of the material. Because most rooms have several materials with different areas, the total absorption in a room is the sum of the various individual material absorptions. Although noise reduction can be calculated with complex formulas in critical situations, for most interior design the following rules of thumb may suffice:

- Avoid designing rooms with hard, reflective surfaces on the walls, floor, and ceiling. The space will be too "live" and noisy.
- The average absorption coefficient of a room should be at least 0.20. An average absorption above 0.50 is usually not desirable, nor is it economically justified. A lower value is suitable for large rooms, larger values for small or noisy rooms.
- Each doubling of the amount of absorption in a room results in a noise reduction of only 3 dB, hardly noticeable. To make any difference, you must increase the total absorption by at least three times to change the reduction by 5 dB, which is noticeable.

- Although absorptive materials can be placed anywhere, ceiling treatment for sound absorption is more effective in large rooms, while wall treatment is more effective in small rooms.

C. Reverberation

Reverberation is the prolongation of sound as it repeatedly bounces off hard surfaces. It is an important part of the acoustic environment of a space because it affects the intelligibility of speech and the quality of music. Technically, reverberation time is the time it takes the sound level to decrease 60 dB after the source has stopped producing the sound. It is a desirable quality if the reverberation time is appropriate for the use of the space. For example, the recommended time for speech in offices and small rooms is 0.3 to 0.6 seconds, while for auditoriums it is 1.5 to 1.8 seconds. Reverberation can be controlled by modifying the amount of absorptive or reflective finishes in a space.

4 SOUND CONTROL

This section reviews some of the specific strategies you can use to control sound and noise in various circumstances.

A. Control of Room Noise

There are three primary ways sound can be controlled within a space: by reducing the level of loudness of the sound source, by modifying the absorption in the space, and by introducing nonintrusive background sound to mask the unwanted sound.

Reducing the level of the sound source is not always possible if the sound is created by a fixed piece of machinery, people, or some similar situation. However, if the source is noise from the outside or an adjacent room, the transmission loss of the enclosing walls can be improved. If a machine is producing the noise, it can often be enclosed or modified to reduce its noise output.

Modifying the absorption of the space can achieve some noise reduction, but there are practical limits to adding absorptive materials. This approach is most useful when the problem room has a large percentage of hard, reflective surfaces.

In most cases, introducing nonintrusive background sound is desirable because it can mask unwanted noise. Some amount of background noise is always present.

This may come from the steady hum of HVAC systems, from business machines, from traffic, from conversation, or from other sources. For example, in an office, if the sound level on one side of a partition with an STC rating of 45 is 75 dB and the background noise on the other side of the partition is 35 dB, the noise coming through the partition will not be heard (theoretically) on the "quiet" side of the wall. See Figure 15.2. If the background noise level is decreased to 25 dB, then sounds will be heard.

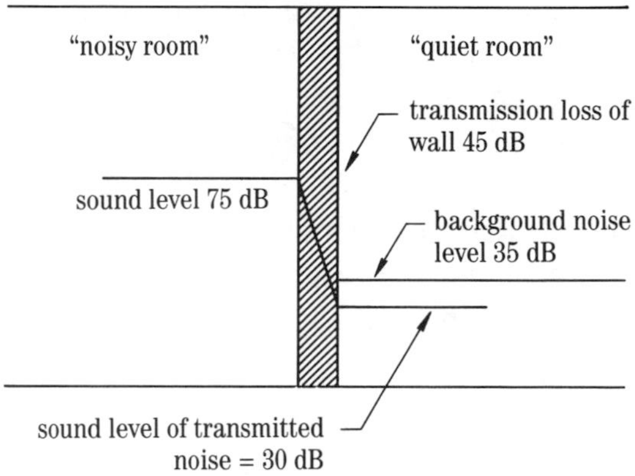

If transmitted sound level is below the background level, the sound is not perceptible.

Figure 15.2 Noise Reduction

This phenomenon is used to purposely introduce carefully controlled sound into a space rather than rely only on random background noise. Often called white sound, random noise, or acoustic perfume, speakers are placed in the ceiling of a space and connected to a sound generator, which produces a continuous, unnoticeable sound at particular levels across the frequency spectrum. The sound generator can be tuned to produce the frequencies and sound levels appropriate to mask the desired sounds. White sound is often used in open offices to provide speech privacy and to help mask office machine noise.

B. Control of Sound Transmission

The control of sound transmission through a barrier is primarily dependent on its mass and to a lesser extent on its stiffness. Walls and floors are generally rated with their STC value; the higher the STC rating, the better the barrier is at reducing transmitted sound. Manufacturers' literature, testing laboratories, and reference literature typically give the transmission loss at different frequencies.

There are several methods used to build a sound-resistant partition. These are shown diagrammatically in Figure 15.3. The first technique simply adds mass to the wall. This can be done by using a heavy material for the partition, such as masonry, or by using more than one layer of gypsum wallboard. Partitions with high STC ratings commonly have a double layer of wallboard on one or both sides of the stud. The second technique is to place insulation within the stud cavity. This absorbs sound (reduces its energy) that is transmitted through one layer of the wall before it reaches the other. Finally, resilient channels can be used as furring strips on one side of the partition. Because of their design, only one leg of the channel touches the stud so the wallboard "floats" and dampens sound striking it rather than transmitting it to the stud.

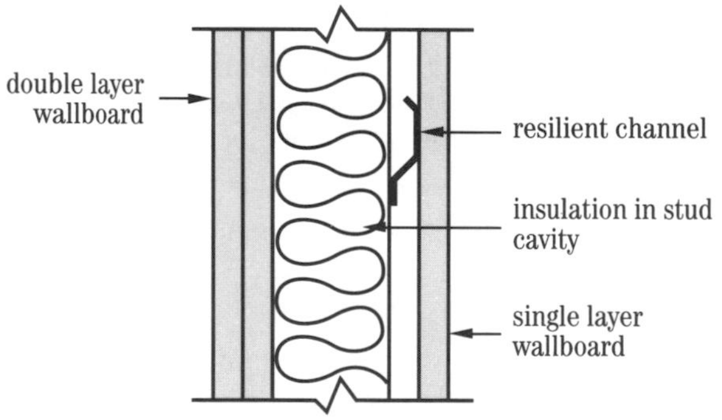

Figure 15.3 Sound-Resistant Partition

In addition to the construction of the barrier itself, other variables are critical to the control of sound transmission. Gaps in the barrier must be sealed. Edges at the floor, ceiling, and the intersecting walls must be caulked. Penetrations of the barrier should be avoided, but if absolutely necessary they should be sealed as well. For example, electrical outlets should not be placed back to back but staggered in separate stud spaces and caulked. Pipes, ducts, and similar penetrations provide a path for both airborne sound and mechanical vibration and should not be rigidly connected to the barrier. Any gaps between ducts, pipes, and a partition should be sealed and caulked.

Construction with a lower STC rating than the barrier itself should be avoided or given special treatment because it will decrease the overall rating of the barrier. Doors placed in an otherwise well-built sound wall are a common problem and can be dealt with in several ways. The perimeter should be completely sealed with weather stripping specifically designed for sound sealing at the jamb and head and with a threshold or automatic door bottom at the sill. An automatic door bottom is a piece of hardware that drops a seal from the door to the floor or threshold as the door closes. The door itself should be as heavy as possible, preferably a solid-core wood door. Often, two doors are used, separated by a small air gap.

Interior glass lights can be designed with laminated glass set in resilient framing. Laminated glass provides more mass, and the plastic interlayer improves the damping characteristics of the barrier. If additional transmission loss is required, two or more layers can be installed with an air gap between them.

Flanking paths for sound to travel should be eliminated or treated appropriately, including air conditioning ducts, plenum, and hallways.

C. Speech Privacy

In many spaces, the critical acoustic concern is not eliminating all noise or designing a room for music, but providing for a certain level of privacy while still allowing people to talk at a normal level. In many cases, speech privacy is regarded as a condition in which talking may be heard as a general background sound but not easily understood. This is most often required in open-plan offices.

Speech privacy in areas divided by full-height partitions is usually achieved by sound loss through the partitions and, to a lesser extent, by the proper use of sound-absorbing surfaces. In open areas, such as an open-plan office, speech privacy is more difficult to achieve. There are five important factors in designing for speech privacy in an open area. All of these must be present to achieve the optimum acoustic environment.

1. The ceiling must be highly absorptive. The ideal is to create a "clear sky" condition so that sounds are not reflected from their source to other parts of the space.

2. There must be space dividers that reduce the transmission of sound from one space to the adjacent spaces. The dividers should have a combination of absorptive surfaces to minimize sound reflections placed over a solid liner called a *septum*.

3. Other surfaces, such as the floor, furniture, windows, and light fixtures, must be designed or arranged to minimize sound reflections. A window, for example, can provide a clear path for reflected noise around a partial-height partition.

4. If possible, activities should be distanced to take advantage of the normal attenuation of sound with distance.

5. There should be a properly designed background masking system. If the right amount of sound-absorbing surfaces is provided, it absorbs all sounds in the space, not just the unwanted sounds. Background sound must then be reintroduced to maintain the right balance between speech sound and the background masking noise.

D. Control of Impact Noise

Impact noise, or sound resulting from direct contact of an object with a sound barrier, can occur on any surface, but it generally occurs on a floor and ceiling assembly. It is usually caused by footfalls, shuffled furniture, and dropped objects.

Impact noise is quantified by the *impact insulation class* (IIC) number, a single-number rating of a floor/ceiling's impact sound performance. The higher the IIC rating, the better the floor performs in reducing impact sounds in the test frequency range.

The IIC value of a floor can most easily be increased by adding carpet. It can also be improved by providing a resiliently suspended ceiling below, floating a finished floor on resilient pads over the structural floor, or by providing sound-absorbing material (insulation) in the air space between the floor and the finished ceiling below.

E. Room Geometry and Planning Concepts

There are many ways the acoustic performance of a group of spaces or an individual room can be affected by floor plan layout and the size and shape of the room itself. In addition to designing walls and floors to retard sound transmission and proper use of sound absorption, you can use the following ideas to help minimize acoustic problems in interior space planning.

- Plan similar use areas next to each other. For example, placing bedrooms next to each other is better than placing a bedroom next to a noisy space like the kitchen.

- Use buffer spaces such as closets and hallways to separate noise-producing spaces whenever possible. Using closets between bedrooms at a common wall is one example of this technique.

- Stagger doorways in halls and other areas to avoid providing a straight-line path for noise.

- If possible, try to locate furniture and other potential noise-producing objects away from the wall that is separating spaces.

- Minimize the area of the common wall between two rooms where a reduction in sound transmission is desired.

- Avoid room shapes that reflect or focus sound. Barrel-vaulted hallways and circular rooms, for example, produce undesirable focused sounds. Rooms that focus sound may also deprive some listeners of useful reflections.

SAMPLE QUESTIONS

1. What ratings are the MOST important in evaluating the acoustic quality of a floor and ceiling assembly?

    1. STC and NRC
    2. IIC and STC
    3. NC and IIC
    4. NRC and IIC

2. If a material supplier told you that adding his product to a wall assembly in a critical acoustical situation would increase the noise reduction (STC rating) between two rooms by slightly more than 3 dB, what should your reaction be?

    1. Determine what the additional cost would be and then decide whether or not to use the product.
    2. Thank him for stopping by but explain that you probably will not be using his product because that amount of noise reduction does not make it worth the effort or cost.
    3. Specify the product as long as it does not affect the construction cost by more than 5 percent.
    4. Inquire whether some modification can be made to the product to increase its rating to 6 dB, and say that then you might consider it.

3. During the design development phase of design, what method would NOT be used to reduce potential noise problems in a room whose exact size and shape had not yet been determined?

    1. Design the room to have the largest ceiling surface area possible.
    2. Plan for sound-absorbent material on the walls of the room.
    3. Study ways to increase the transmission loss of the room's partitions.
    4. Minimize the length of the wall separating the room from noisier areas.

4. The construction assembly shown would be BEST for controlling which of the following kinds of acoustic situations?

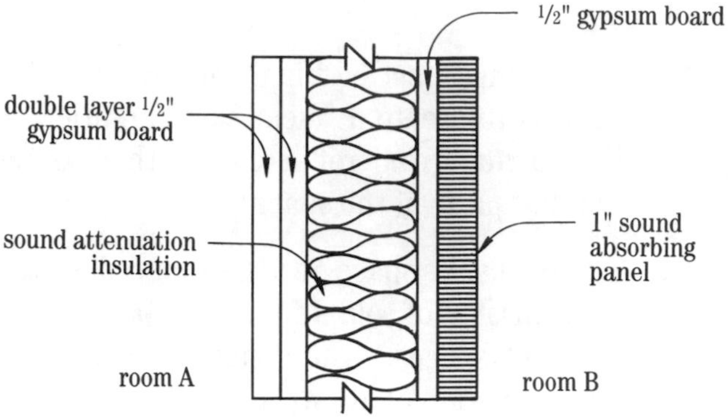

    1. impact noise
    2. transmission from room A to room B
    3. transmission from room B to room A
    4. mechanical vibration

5. Which is the MOST accurate statement about sound?

    1. A sound of 50 dB is twice as loud as a sound of 25 dB.
    2. A desirable goal of acoustic design is to eliminate all background noise.
    3. A reduction of 7 dB of the noise within a room would be clearly noticeable.
    4. A good acoustic material absorbs all frequencies equally.

6. To detail a door frame for a conference room where privacy is critical, which of the following is LEAST likely to be required?

    1. an automatic door bottom
    2. a heavyduty, silent door closer
    3. neoprene gasketing
    4. a solid-core door

7. What is the purpose of insulation in interior walls?

    1. to prevent heat transmission from one side to the other
    2. to improve the strength of the wall
    3. to improve the acoustic characteristics of the wall
    4. to increase the fire resistance of the wall

8. Changing a ceiling from gypsum wallboard to acoustic tile would MOST affect the room's

1. reverberation
2. sound transmission
3. decibel loss
4. impact insulation class

9. In a small lecture hall it would be best to avoid

1. a sound amplification system
2. a vaulted ceiling
3. carpet
4. parallel walls

10. Which of the following is NOT true about noise reduction between two rooms?

1. Noise reduction increases with an increase in the transmission loss of the wall separating the two rooms.
2. The stiffness of the wall can affect noise reduction.
3. To improve noise reduction, you should place absorptive materials on both sides of the wall.
4. An increase in wall area separating the two rooms is detrimental.

16 COMMUNICATION METHODS

The NCIDQ examination requires that you have a basic understanding of the common methods of graphic communication and that you can apply them to explaining your solution to a problem. Specifically, you must be able to draw a floor plan and reflected ceiling plan for the Practicum/Scenario section and use either an isometric drawing or elevations to complete the Practicum/Three-dimensional section. However, remember that your practicum drawings are not evaluated for your drafting technique but for your ability to communicate solutions.

This chapter briefly describes the four major types of drawings used by interior designers. Refer to Chapter 7 for a more detailed review of construction drawings and the standard graphic symbols used on drawings.

1 ORTHOGRAPHIC DRAWINGS

Floor plans, elevations, and sections are common types of orthographic drawings. These drawings use orthographic projection to enable a three-dimensional object to be seen in two dimensions. They are ideal for communication in the flat world of paper and computer screens because, by using multiple orthographic views, even the most complex object can be accurately and completely described.

Orthographic projection is a view of an object seen as though your line of sight were simultaneously perpendicular to every point on the face of the object. Another way to understand it is to imagine that each significant face of an object is projected onto a flat, transparent plane parallel to the face of the object, as shown in Figure 16.1.

In orthographic projection, all pieces are shown in their true relationship with other pieces, and the scale and proportion are the same for multiple views of the same object. There is no distortion for lines and planes parallel to the plane on which the view is projected. However, when a diagonal line or plane is shown it is foreshortened. For example, the top view of the building in Figure 16.1 shows a foreshortened view of the width of the roof while the length is shown true to scale. If you scale the length of the line from the eaves to the peak of the roof in the top view, the distance is shorter than the true length as scaled on the side view.

Orthographic drawings are most often drawn to scale; that is, one unit of measure is used to represent another, larger unit of measure. A floor plan, for instance, is often drawn so that one-fourth of an inch represents one actual foot. This is shown as $1/4''=$ $1'$-$0''$. Scale is used to accommodate large objects on paper and to regulate the amount of detail shown. Large scales have the effect of bringing the viewer closer to the object so more can be seen. A scale of $3''= 1'$-$0''$ is good for showing very complex construction details, while a small scale like $1/8''=1'$-$0''$ is sufficient for many floor plans.

The most common types of orthographic drawings are floor plans, reflected ceiling plans, elevations, and sections. Orthographic projection is also used as a basis for some types of three-dimensional drawings including axonometric drawings, elevation obliques, and one-point sectional perspectives.

A. Plans

A plan is an orthographic view of an object as seen directly from above. In architectural and interior design work, the floor plan is the most common type of plan, although strictly speaking a floor plan is really a section. The theory behind a floor plan is that a horizontal cut is made through a building (or portion of a building) about 5 feet above the floor. The top portion is removed. See Figure 16.2. What remains is drawn as the plan, including what shows on the floor. Cutting a section at this point makes it possible to show windows, doors, and other openings.

A view of a building seen from above without the section cut is a roof plan. If some of the ground on which the building sits, landscaping, walks, drives, and property lines are shown, the drawing is a site plan.

Of course, some compromises to the strictly theoretical approach are made with a floor plan. Even though a section would show all the construction materials within the walls, they are more commonly shown as just two parallel lines. In many cases, the walls are drawn with *poché,* which is a graphic pattern or solid black used to make the walls stand out or to indicate the wall construction type. Also, all

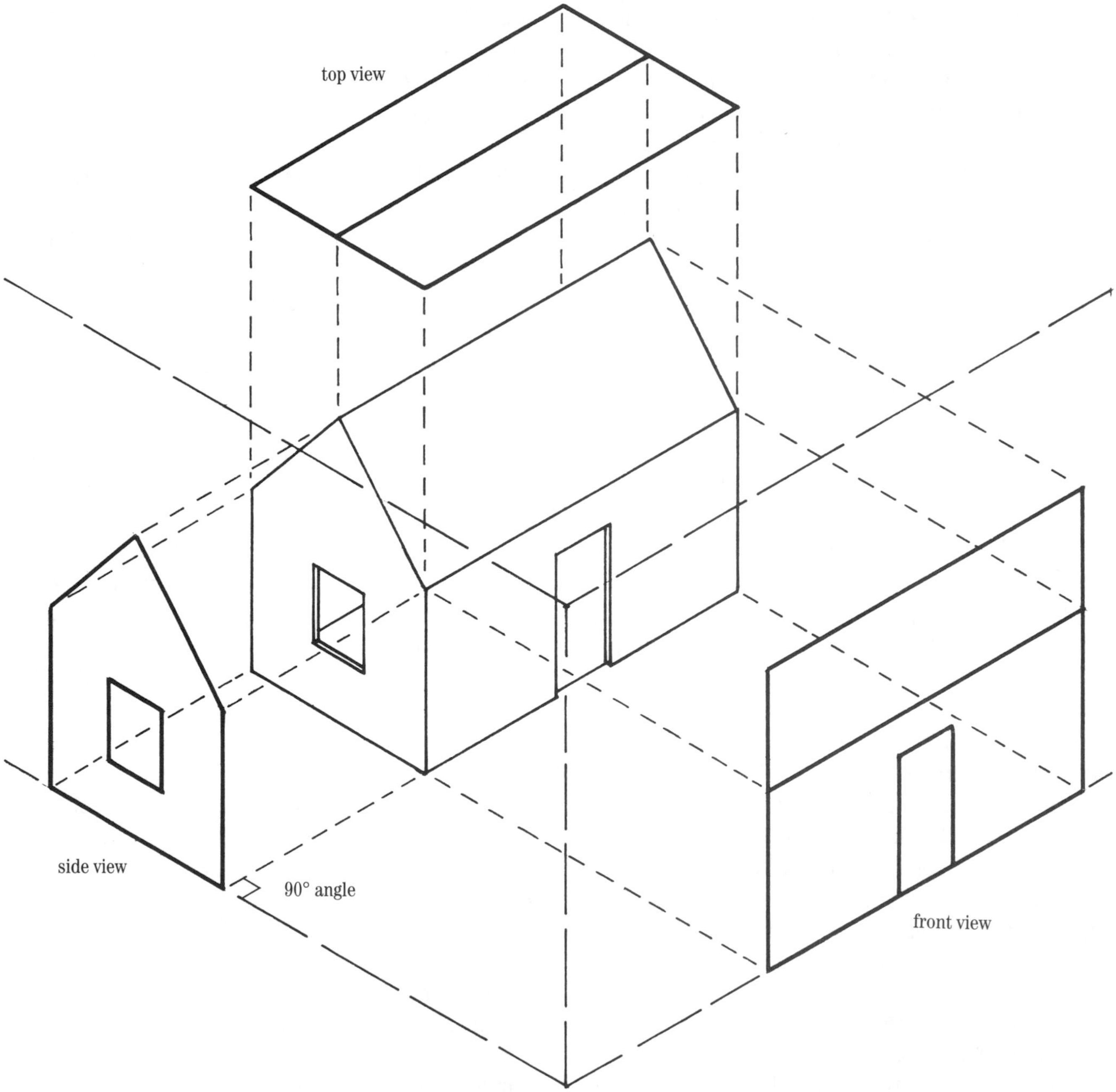

Figure 16.1 Orthographic Projection

openings are shown, even if their bottom edges are above the theoretical 5-foot-high section cut. Other construction elements that may also be above the 5-foot line are shown as well, such as kitchen cabinets, ceiling breaks, and shelving. Dashed lines are used for these items to indicate that they are above the normal section cut.

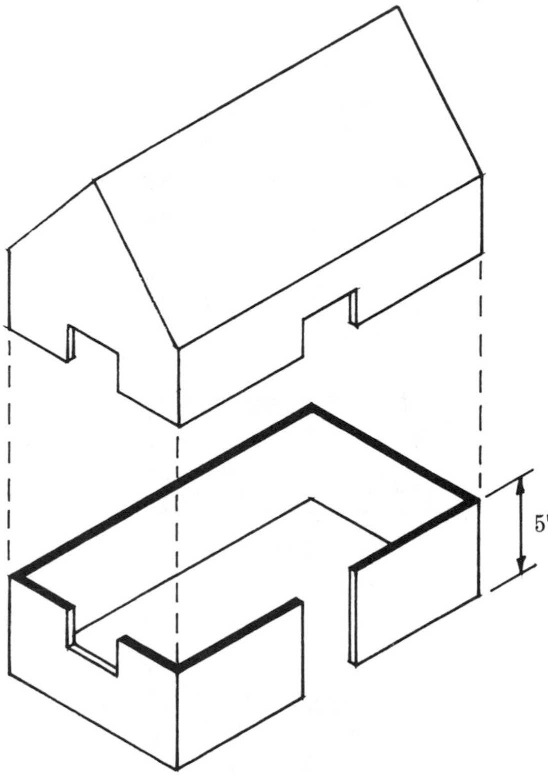

Figure 16.2 Floor Plan Generation

Variations of the floor plan are used to communicate different types of information. A floor plan rendered with color showing furniture, floor materials, and shading may be used for a client presentation. A construction drawing plan shows a very different set of data for the contractor's use. The various types of plan drawings are reviewed in more detail in Chapter 7.

B. Reflected Ceiling Plans

As shown in Figure 16.3, a reflected ceiling plan is an orthographic view of the ceiling of a room or building as though there were a mirror on the floor and you could see through the roof to see the ceiling's reflection. In other words, it is as though all the points on the ceiling could be projected through the roof onto a transparent plane above the building. Awkward as they may be, these views of the ceiling are important so that the orientation of the reflected ceiling plan is identical to the floor plan. That is, if the north side of the building is toward the top of the paper on the floor plan, north must also be toward the top on the reflected ceiling plan.

Reflected ceiling plans are another variation of a section, only the viewer is looking up rather than down. Theoretically, the reflected ceiling plan shows only those construction elements that touch the plane of the ceiling, as well as the ceiling itself and the objects in the ceiling. Therefore, walls that extend to or through the ceiling are drawn, but low walls are not. Likewise, the opening of a 7-foot-high door in a room with an 8-foot ceiling does not show. Instead,

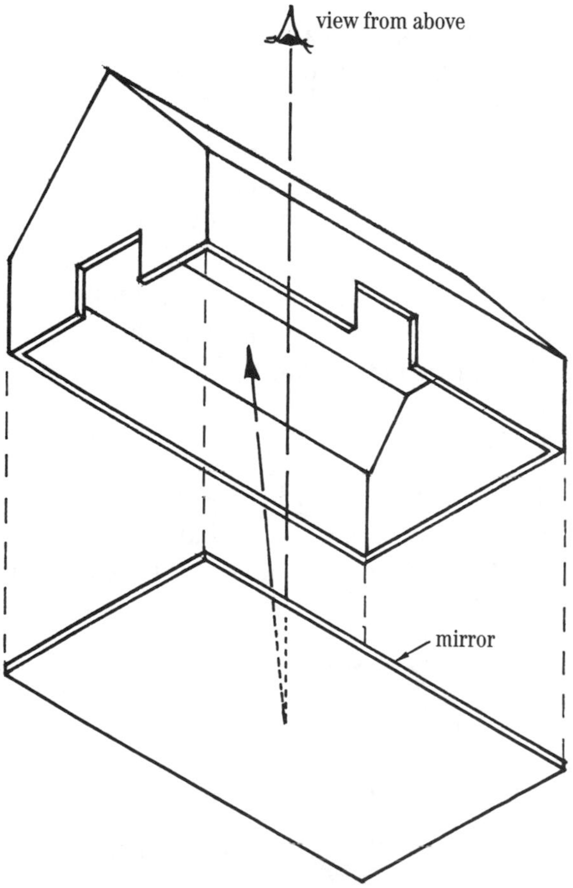

Figure 16.3 Reflected Ceiling Plan Theory

the wall above the door is drawn continuously, just as the wall touches the ceiling at that point.

In practice, however, liberties are taken with this strictly theoretical approach. Door openings may be shown to provide better orientation for the contractor. Elements that do not actually touch the ceiling, like cabinets, may be indicated to show their relationship to some part of the ceiling construction.

C. Elevations

Because plans can show only the dimensions of length and width, elevations are usually required. An elevation is an orthographic view of the side of an object. Interior elevations show the length and height of walls of a room. Two interior elevations of the building shown in Figure 16.1 are illustrated in Figure 16.4. Elevations can show not only vertical dimensions but also the types and extent of materials and finishes in a room that cannot be adequately described on other drawings.

Because elevations are often drawn at a slightly larger scale than the floor plans, some horizontal dimensions can also be described if there is not enough room on the plan or if the construction is complex. For these reasons, the spacing of wall panel joints or the width of cabinets is commonly shown on interior elevations rather than on plans. Notice that on the elevation of the length of the room, the diagonal plane of the ceiling is shown foreshortened because this is an orthographic projection.

D. Sections

Like a floor plan, a section is an orthographic view of an object after it has been cut and one portion removed. A section may be a view through an entire building as shown in Figure 16.5(a), or through a very small portion of construction like the front edge of a countertop as shown in Figure 16.5(b). Although sections are normally vertical slices through objects, they can be cut horizontally (as with plans) or at any angle that is convenient to show the internal construction of something.

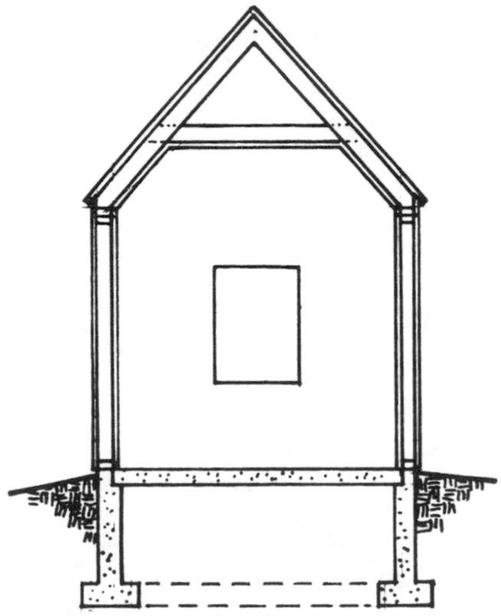

(a) small-scale section

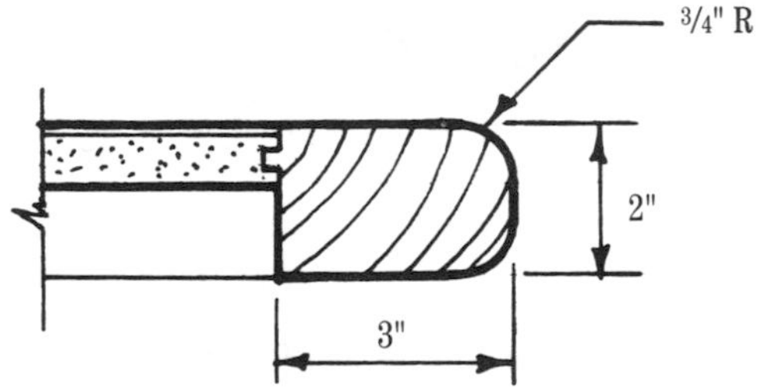

(b) large-scale section

Figure 16.5 Sections

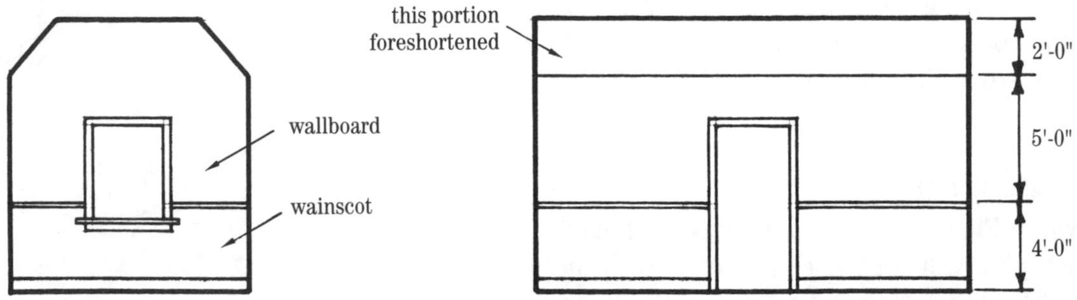

Figure 16.4 Elevations

Sections are invaluable drawings. Not only do they show the vertical dimension, but also they show hidden information about construction that cannot be described on plans or elevations. While architects frequently use building sections, as in Figure 16.5(a), to show the overall configuration of a structure, interior design sections typically illustrate larger scale views through walls, millwork, door frames, and other details. Because sections commonly show complex construction information at a relatively large scale, they are most often simply called details. Most details on a set of construction drawings are section views of one sort or another.

A section drawing shows a cut through both solids and voids. Because sections can be complex, certain graphic techniques are used to avoid confusion. Solid portions are often pochéd with standard material indications as shown in Figure 16.5(b). Voids are left blank and the lines separating solid from void are drawn very heavy. These are known as profile lines. To show the relationship between the material cut in section and adjacent construction, thin lines are used to show elements that occur beyond the section cut.

While any angle may be used to draw an isometric, the most common one is 30 degrees. Thirty degrees is a standard triangle angle and gives a fairly realistic view of an object. Smaller angles show more of the sides and less of the top, while larger angles show more of the top of the object. If a 45-degree angle is used, the drawing becomes an axonometric drawing as discussed in the next section.

Isometric drawings are quick and easy to draw and they can be measured at any convenient scale. However, because the horizontal plane is a parallelogram, floor plans and other planes must be redrawn at the selected angle. Then, the third dimension is shown by simply extending points vertically. Diagonal lines are drawn by projecting their endpoints from the basic three-dimensional grid and connecting them. See Figure 16.7.

Isometrics can be used to draw buildings, interior rooms (by omitting the top and two front sides), details, millwork, furniture, and any other object. Complex details can be shown by drawing a section in one plane and then extending the rest of the object with lines isometrically perpendicular to the section cut.

2 ISOMETRIC DRAWINGS

An isometric drawing is a three-dimensional view of an object in which the two sets of horizontal lines of the object are drawn at the same angle and all vertical lines are drawn vertically. All three axes have the same scale. These principles are illustrated with a simple cube in Figure 16.6.

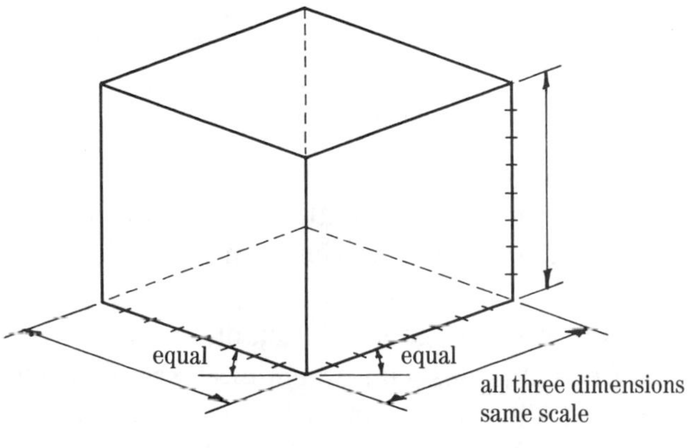

Figure 16.6 Principles of Isometric Drawing

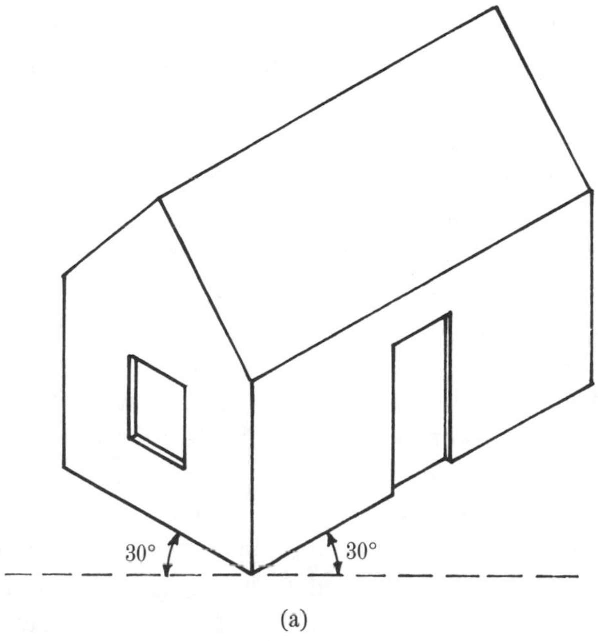

Figure 16.7 Isometric Drawing

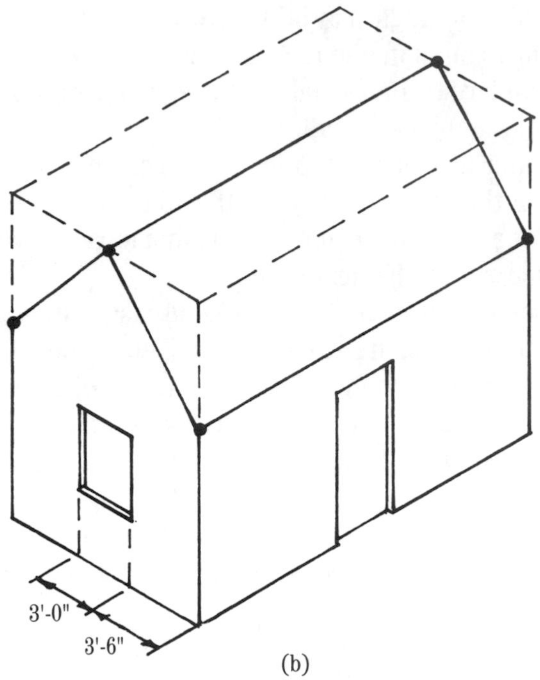

(b)

Figure 16.7 (cont'd)

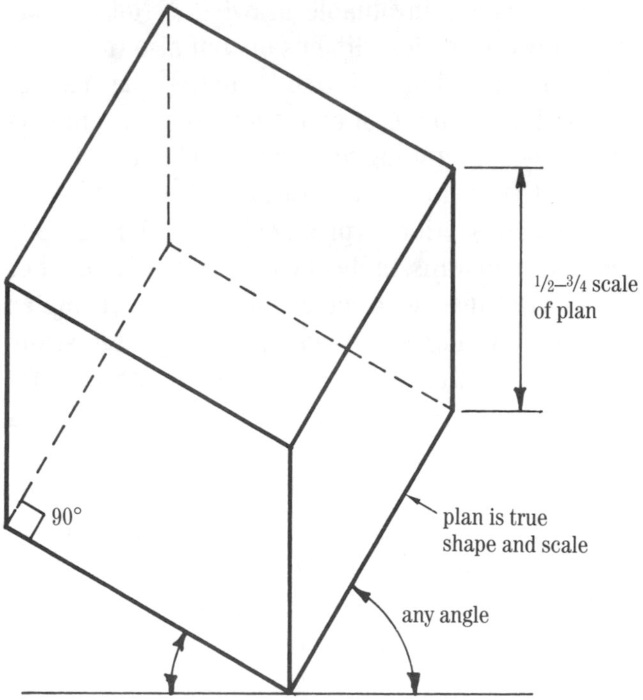

(a) plan oblique (axonometric)

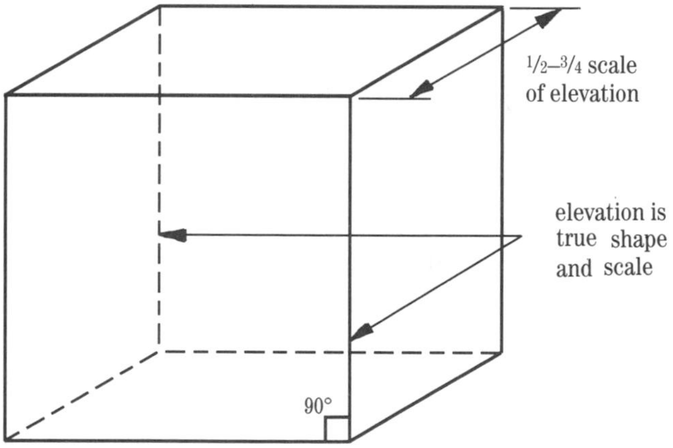

(b) elevation oblique

Figure 16.8 Principles of Axonometric Drawing

3 AXONOMETRIC DRAWINGS

An axonometric drawing is one type of oblique drawing. An oblique drawing shows one plane of an object (two dimensions) in true shape and scale with the third dimension drawn as lines at a fixed angle to the true plane. Figure 16.8 shows a plan oblique and an elevation oblique. An axonometric is a plan oblique drawing.

The advantage of an axonometric is that an existing orthographic floor plan can be used as the starting point without any redrawing. The plan is simply tilted at any desired angle. The third dimension is created by projecting vertical lines. However, if the third dimension is scaled the same as the true shape, the object often looks distorted, higher or wider than it really is. To compensate for this, the third dimension is usually drawn at one-half to three-fourths of the scale of the true plane. As with isometrics, diagonal lines in the nontrue plane dimension are drawn by determining the location of their endpoints through projection along one or more of the three main axes. See Figure 16.9. Interior views are created by omitting the top and two front sides of the room (or just the top) or by selectively cutting away portions of the enclosing planes to show what is inside.

The plan may be tilted at any angle as long as the walls are 90 degrees to each other, but, as with isometrics, it is most convenient to set the plan at 30, 60, or 45 degrees (the angle between a horizontal line and the wall). If 45 degrees is used, the drawing is both an axonometric and isometric.

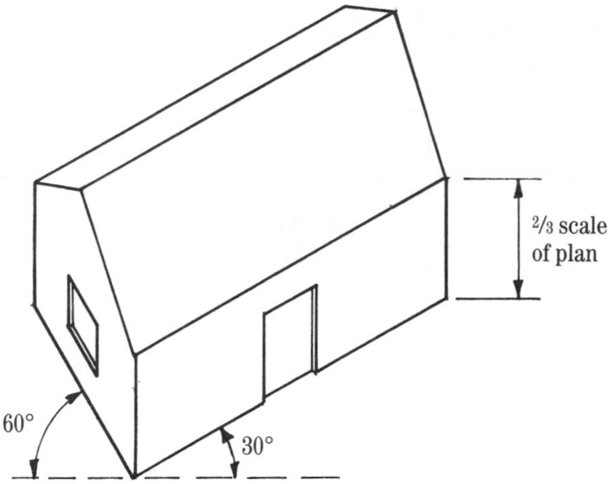

Figure 16.9 Axonometric Drawing

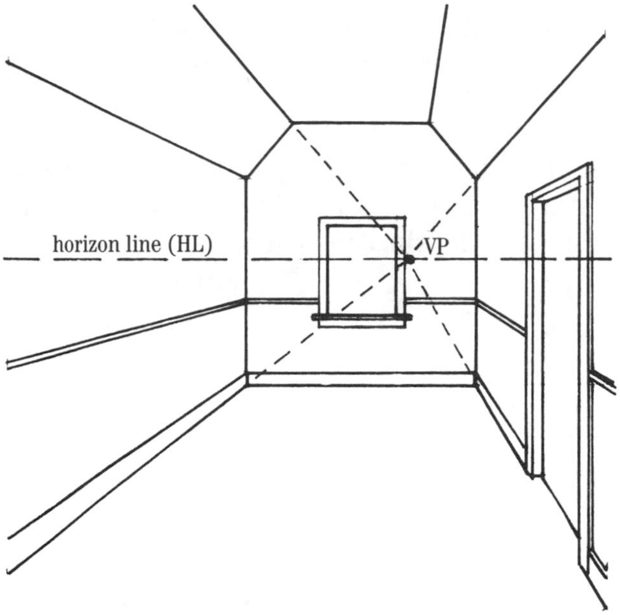

Figure 16.10 One-Point Perspective

4 PERSPECTIVE DRAWINGS

Of all the methods used to draw objects, perspectives give the most accurate two-dimensional representation of the three-dimensional world. This is because they use the principle of convergence, which is the apparent diminishing size of objects as they get farther from the eye. Convergence also explains how parallel lines seem to look nonparallel and point to, or converge on, the same imaginary spot in the distance.

When the point of view is perpendicular to one of the planes of the object, a one-point perspective is created. All vertical lines are drawn vertically, and all lines perpendicular to the line of sight are drawn horizontally. Lines parallel to the line of sight converge at the one vanishing point used to create the drawing. See Figure 16.10.

A two-point perspective is created when the point of view is at normal eye level and is not perpendicular to any plane of the object. Although the NCIDQ exam does not require that you draw a perspective for the test, you should be generally familiar with the theory behind perspectives, why they are used, and some of the common terminology. The following is a very brief description of perspective construction. If you are unfamiliar with perspective construction, you may want to review other books on the subject.

Figure 16.11 shows some of the basic elements of a two-point perspective construction. To construct a perspective, a plan is placed at a convenient angle on the drawing board. The angle selected determines how much of the two sides of the object you will see. A horizontal line is then drawn somewhere near the back edge of the plan. This is the picture plane (PP), the imaginary vertical plane on which all points of the object are projected to create the two-dimensional image. In plan view, of course, the picture plane appears just as a line.

In Figure 16.11, this line touches the back corner of the plan, but it can be placed slightly forward or back to decrease or increase the size of the perspective. For example, by moving this line farther away from the plan you change the projection of the sight lines from the station point (the point from which the object is being viewed), which widens the perspective when it is plotted.

Next, the station point (SP) is selected. Two lines are extended from the station point to the left and right parallel to the two major sets of parallel lines of the object. Because these lines are parallel to the object, they determine the vanishing points, or those imaginary points in the distance where the lines of the object appear to converge. Where these two lines intersect, the picture plane vertical lines are projected downward.

At some convenient point under the plan, a horizontal line is drawn across the paper. This is the horizon line (HL) and represents the place where the earth meets the sky, just as in the real three-dimensional world. The points where the horizon line intersects the two vertical lines projected from above become the vanishing points for the actual perspective drawing: the left vanishing point (VPL) and the right vanishing point (VPR). Sometimes these are simply noted as VP or v.p.

Where the picture plane touches the plan drawing, a vertical line is projected down to intersect the horizon line. This becomes the true height line, or simply the height line (HL) and is the only line on the perspective drawing where vertical dimensions can be directly scaled. All other vertical dimensions

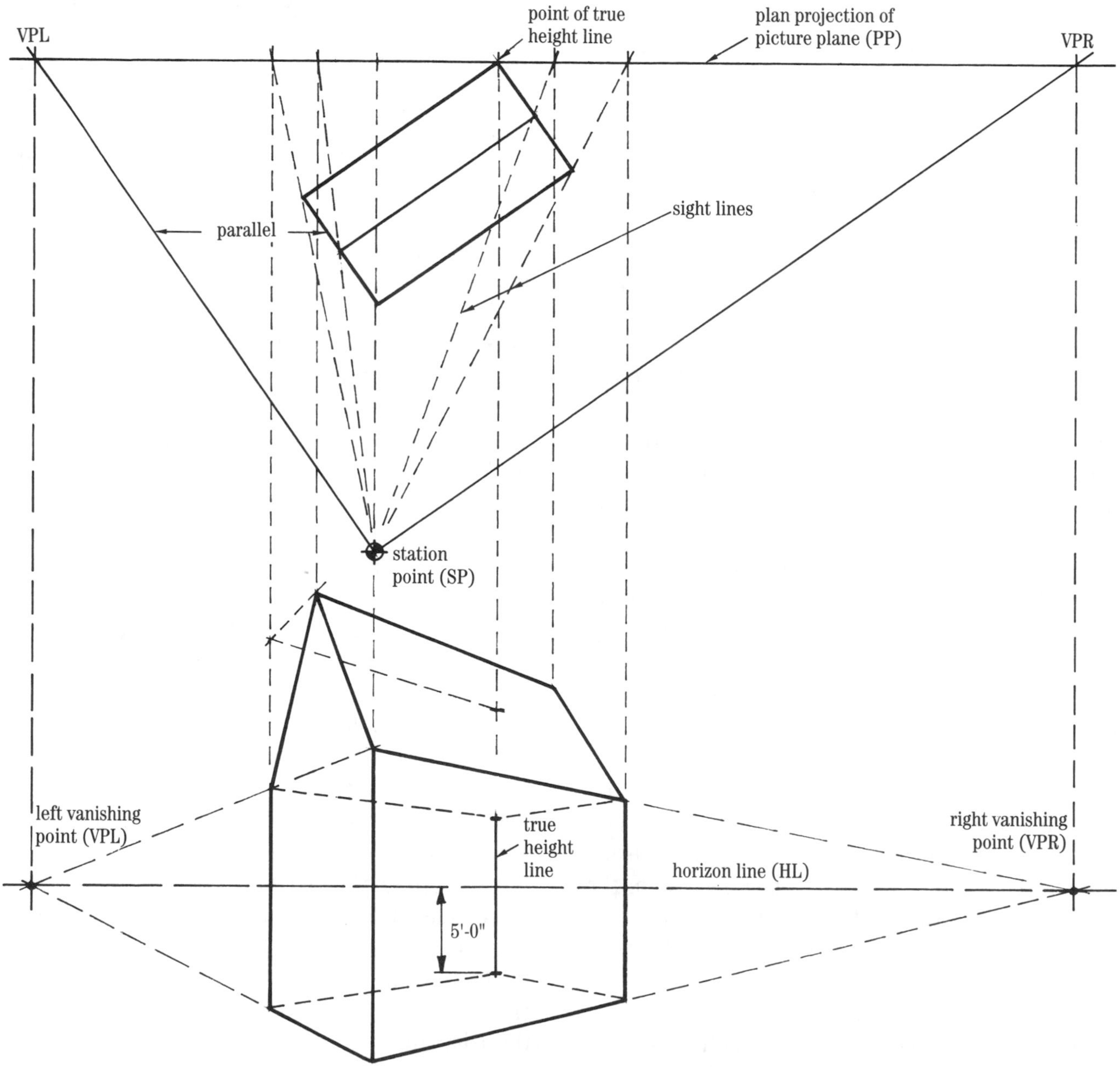

Figure 16.11 Two-Point Perspective Layout

must be developed by using dimensions from this line and one of the vanishing points as two points to project a line to other parts of the drawing to pinpoint the height of something.

At this point, the height of the corner of the building can be scaled on the height line where it crosses the horizon line. In most perspectives, the horizon line is assumed to be at eye level, or about 5′-0″ or 5′-6″ above the floor level. The bottom point of the height line (floor level of the building) is set by measuring 5 feet down from the horizon line. If the height of the wall is 9 feet, then the top point of the height line is set by measuring 4 feet above the horizon line.

Using the ends of the height line and the vanishing points, the two back edges of the building are drawn. The extent of how far they project is determined by drawing a guideline from the station point through the left and right edges of the building in the plan until they intersect the picture plan. Lines projected vertically downward from these points locate the corners of the building in perspective view. All other points in the horizontal planes are projected in a similar fashion. Vertical dimensions are scaled on the height line and projected from one of the two vanishing points along surfaces of the object until they intersect the appropriate vertical lines projected from the picture plane above.

SAMPLE QUESTIONS

1. What is a drawing that shows a top view of a building and its surroundings?

   1. floor plan
   2. site plan
   3. roof plan
   4. horizontal section

2. What does an axonometric drawing do?

   1. shows a two-dimensional floor plan and takes it into the third dimension
   2. equalizes the angle from the horizontal and the third-dimensional object
   3. describes all three faces of a room with the same scale
   4. requires that a floor plan be redrawn to the angle used for the 3-D drawing

3. Orthographic drawings are unreal views of objects primarily because

   1. more than one is required to describe an object
   2. the point of view is directly in front of every location on the object
   3. a transparent plane has to be imagined
   4. some planes may be foreshortened

4. What does SP in a perspective mean?

   1. standard perspective
   2. secondary point
   3. side plane
   4. station point

5. Why is a perspective the best drawing type to use when presenting to a client?

   1. It is the quickest method of rendering space.
   2. It most accurately shows vertical dimensions relative to the viewer.
   3. It is most like the way space and objects are perceived.
   4. It offers the widest choice of viewpoints.

17 BUILDING CODES

The NCIDQ exam places significant emphasis on knowledge of building and barrier-free codes. Although codes vary from one jurisdiction to another, there are basic concepts with which you must be familiar. You must also know how to apply a particular code requirement to a given situation. This chapter and Chapter 18 review general building code requirements. Chapter 19 summarizes the requirements for barrier-free design.

1 ADMINISTRATIVE PROVISIONS

A. Legal Basis of Codes

Building codes are adopted and enforced by local governments, either by a municipality or, in the case of sparsely populated areas, a county or district. Regulation in Canada is the responsibility of provincial and territorial governments. Codes are enacted as laws just as any other local regulation. Before construction, a building code is enforced through the permit process, which requires that builders submit plans and specifications for checking and approval before a building permit is issued. During construction, the department responsible for enforcement conducts inspections to verify that building is proceeding according to the approved plans. However, the design professional is ultimately responsible for making sure that the design meets all applicable codes.

B. Model Building Codes

Local jurisdictions may write their own building codes, but in most cases one of the model codes is adopted into law by reference. A model code is one that has been written by a group of experts knowledgeable in the field, without reference to any particular geographical area. Adopting a model code allows a city, county, district, or province to have a complete, workable building code without the difficulty and expense of writing its own. If certain provisions need to be added or changed to suit the particular requirements of a municipality, the model code is enacted with modifications. Even when a city writes its own code, it is usually based on one of the model codes.

Three model codes are used in the majority of the United States at the time of this writing:

1. the Uniform Building Code (UBC), which is used in the western and central portions of the United States
2. the BOCA National Building Code, which is used in the northeastern part of the country
3. the Standard Building Code (SBC), which is used in much of the southeastern United States

In 2000, the International Code Council (ICC) published the *International Building Code* (IBC), which will eventually replace the three model codes in the United States and possibly in some other countries. The ICC also publishes the *International Plumbing Code*, the *International Mechanical Code*, and the *International Private Sewage Disposal Code*.

The primary code for Canadian provinces is the National Building Code of Canada (NBC). Other Canadian codes regulate plumbing, housing, fire safety, and other specific areas of construction.

The Uniform Building Code (UBC) is used by the majority of the states and is the code on which the information in this and the next chapter is based. Because all three model codes, the International Building Code, and the NBC have very similar provisions, if you know the basic concepts of the UBC or IBC you can apply them to the NCIDQ examination. Of course, in practice, interior design work must conform to whatever code is used in the locale where the work is performed. If your area does not use the Uniform Building Code, make sure you know the specific local requirements for the topics discussed in this and the following two chapters.

C. Adjuncts to Building Codes

In addition to a building code, there are companion codes and standards that govern other aspects of construction. With the exception of the electrical code, these are published by the same groups that publish the model building codes. For example, the International Conference of Building Officials also publishes the Uniform Mechanical Code and the Uniform Plumbing Code. The electrical code used by all groups is the National Electrical Code published by the National Fire Protection Association (NFPA).

For interior designers, the most notable national regulation is American National Standard A117.1, American National Standard for Buildings and Facilities Providing Accessibility and Usability for Physically Handicapped People. This standard is typically referenced in most local building codes and is described in detail in Chapter 19. Another federal regulation separate from a local building code is the Americans with Disabilities Act, which regulates removal of barriers for the physically disabled.

Model codes also make extensive use of industry standards that are developed by trade associations, government agencies, and standards-writing agencies such as the American Society for Testing and Materials (ASTM), the American National Standards Institute (ANSI), and the NFPA. These are included in building codes by reference name and number and date of latest revision.

In addition to building codes and their adjuncts, local jurisdictions may also have required energy conservation codes, health and hospital codes, codes that regulate school buildings, fabric flammability regulations, and similar legal requirements for construction and finishes.

2 TESTING STANDARDS

All approved materials and construction assemblies referred to in building codes are required to be tested by approved agencies according to standardized testing procedures. There are hundreds of standardized tests for building materials and constructions. Some of the more common ones are listed in this section.

A. Testing Agencies

Any approved testing laboratory can perform tests on building materials as long as they follow standardized procedures. The American Society for Testing and Materials is one agency that publishes thousands of test procedures that prescribe in detail such things as how the test apparatus must be set up, how materials must be prepared for the test, the length of the test, and other requirements. If a product manufacturer has one of its materials successfully tested, it will indicate what tests the material has passed in its product literature.

One of the most well-known testing agencies is Underwriters Laboratories. They perform testing, approve building materials and assemblies, and publish the results in the UL Building Materials Directory.

B. Types of Tests

Materials fire testing for interior design components can be broadly classified into two groups: tests that rate the ability of a construction assembly to prevent the passage of fire and smoke from one space to another, and tests that rate the degree of flammability of a finish material. The following summaries include testing for building products and finishes. Flammability standards for fabric used in furniture construction are discussed in Chapter 10.

One of the most commonly used tests of the first type is ASTM E-119, standard methods of fire tests of building construction and materials. This test involves building a sample of the wall or floor/ceiling assembly in the laboratory and setting a standard fire on one side of it. Monitoring devices measure heat and other aspects of the test as it proceeds. In some cases, a standard fire hose stream is applied to the assembly to see how well it holds up to firefighting efforts. The test evaluates an assembly's ability to prevent the passage of fire, heat, and hot gases. A similar test for doors is NFPA 252, standard methods of fire tests of door assemblies.

Flammability tests for building and finish materials are more numerous. These tests determine (1) if a material is flammable and, if so, if it simply burns with applied heat or if it supports combustion (adds fuel to the fire), (2) the degree of flammability (how fast fire spreads across it), and (3) how much smoke and toxic gas it produces when ignited.

ASTM E-84, standard test method for surface burning characteristics of building materials, is one of the most common fire testing standards. It is also known as the *Steiner tunnel test* and rates the surface burning characteristics of interior finishes and other building materials by testing a sample piece in a tunnel test chamber that has a controlled flame at one end. The primary result is a material's flame-spread rating compared to cement-asbestos board (with a rating of zero) and red oak flooring (with an arbitrary rating of 100).

The Steiner tunnel test, useful for wall and ceiling materials, is not appropriate for carpeting because in the test the sample is placed on the ceiling of the test chamber—not a good replication of actual circumstances. The flooring radiant panel test, ASTM E-648, tests a sample of carpet in the normal horizontal position and measures the flame spread in a corridor or exitway that is under the influence of a fully developed fire in an adjacent space. The resulting test numbers are measured in watts per square centimeter; the higher the number, the more resistant the material is to flame propagation. For example, the National Institute of Standards and Technology recommends a minimum of 0.22 watts/cm^2 in corridors and exitways in commercial buildings.

Another test for carpet flammability is the methenamine pill test, which is required for all carpet produced in the United States. A test sample of the carpet is placed in a draft-protected cube and held in place with a metal plate with an 8-inch diameter hole. A timed methenamine pill is placed in the center and lighted. If the sample burns to within one inch of the metal plate, it fails the test.

The smoke density chamber test (NFPA 258) measures the smoke developed from both flaming and nonflaming (smoldering) solid materials. The result is a measure of optical density on a scale of 0 to 800. Many codes require a smoke-developed rating of 450 or less for finish materials. ASTM E-84 can also be used to generate a smoke-developed index.

C. Ratings

After a material is subjected to one of the standard tests, it is given a rating based on its performance during the test. With the ASTM E-84 test, materials are classified into one of three groups based on their tested flame-spread characteristics. These groups and their flame-spread indexes are listed below.

Class	Flame-Spread Index
I (A)	0–25
II (B)	26–75
III (C)	76–200

Class I is the most fire resistant. Product literature generally indicates the flame spread of the material, either by class (Roman numeral or letter) or by numerical value. Building codes specify the minimum flame-spread requirement for various occupancies in specific areas of the building. For example, Table 17.1 gives the maximum allowable flame-spread rating for three areas of a building based on occupancy as required by the UBC. In some cases, the building code will allow you to reduce the required class of the finish materials by one if an approved sprinkler system is provided. However, this may not apply to certain critical areas like enclosed vertical exitways or in certain occupancies.

Table 17.1

Maximum Flame-Spread Class

Occupancy Group	Enclosed Vertical Exitways	Other Exitways	Rooms or Areas
A	I	II	II
E	I	II	III
I	I	I	II
H	I	II	III
B, F, M, and S	I	II	III
R-1	I	II	III
R-3	III	III	III
U	No restrictions		

For construction assemblies tested according to ASTM E-119, the rating given is according to time, that is, the amount of time an assembly can resist a standard test fire without failing. The ratings are 1-hour, 2-hour, 3-hour, and 4-hour; 20-, 30-, and 45-minute ratings are also used for doors and other opening assemblies. The assemblies interior designers must be concerned with include permanent partitions, shaft enclosures (like stairways and elevators), and floor/ceiling constructions as well as doors and glass openings.

Thus, if a building code states that the partition separating an exit corridor from a tenant space must be a 1-hour rated assembly, then the interior designer must select and detail a design that meets the requirements for 1-hour construction. Building codes typically have tables showing what kinds of construction meet various hourly ratings. Other sources for acceptable construction assemblies include Underwriters Laboratories' Building Materials Directory, manufacturers' proprietary product literature, and other reference sources. Construction of fire-rated gypsum wallboard partitions is discussed in Chapter 11, but masonry and plaster partitions can also meet the requirements of rated walls.

Other tests have their own rating scales, but the idea is the same. A material is tested and given a rating, and the building code or other governmental agency states which minimum ratings are required in specific circumstances. Then, the interior designer must select and specify products that meet those minimum requirements.

3 REQUIREMENTS BASED ON OCCUPANCY

Occupancy refers to the type of use of the building or interior space, such as an office, a restaurant, a private residence, or a school.

A. Types of Occupancy

Every building or portion of a building is classified according to its use and is assigned an occupancy group. This is true of all the three model codes and specific city and state/province codes, although the lettering system may vary somewhat.

The philosophy behind occupancy classification is that some building uses are more hazardous than others. For example, a building where flammable liquids are used is more dangerous than a single-family residence. Similarly, a large auditorium holding hundreds of people is more dangerous than a meeting room that only holds a few dozen people. The Uniform Building Code classifies occupancies into seven major groups:

A	assembly
B	business
E	educational
F	factory and industrial
H	hazardous
I	institutional
M	mercantile
R	residential
S	storage
U	utility

Each of these classifications is divided into categories called *divisions* to distinguish subgroups that define the relative hazard of the occupancy. For example, in the residential group, an R-1 occupancy includes hotels and apartments while an R-3 occupancy includes dwellings.

Knowing the occupancy classification is important in determining other building code requirements (such as the maximum area, the number of floors allowed, and how the building is separated from other structures), many of which relate to the architectural design of a building. For the interior designer, occupancy classification affects the calculation of occupant load, ventilation and sanitation requirements, and other restrictions particular to any given classification. Occupant load is especially important to understand and is discussed in detail in Chapter 18.

B. Occupancy Separation

When a building contains two or more occupancies, it is considered mixed occupancy. This is quite common in architectural design as well as interior design. For instance, the design of a large office space can include office occupancy adjacent to an auditorium used for training, which would be an assembly occupancy. An interior designer might also be designing a new space of one occupancy that is next to an existing space of another occupancy. Each occupancy must be separated from other occupancies with a fire-resistive separation with an hourly rating defined by the particular code that applies.

The UBC shows required occupancy separations with a matrix table.

4 CLASSIFICATION BY CONSTRUCTION TYPE

Construction type refers to the fire resistance of certain building components. These include critical elements like exterior bearing walls, columns, stair and elevator enclosures, permanent partitions, and floors. Every building is classified into one of several types of construction. The UBC has five types, I through V, with several subgroups. Type I buildings are the most fire resistive and Type V are the least. For example, shaft enclosures like stairways must be protected with 2-hour rated walls in a Type I or II building, while only a 1-hour rating is required in Type III buildings.

The purpose of classifying buildings in this way is to protect the structural elements from fire and collapse. Also, by dividing a building into compartments, a fire in one area may be contained long enough to allow people to evacuate and to give firefighters time to arrive before the fire spreads. Like occupancy classification, construction type takes into account the relative hazard of buildings constructed with varying degrees of fire resistance. For example, a very large high-rise building in an urban area is potentially more dangerous than a house in the suburbs.

There are several interrelated variables concerning construction type, most of which are already determined by the architect when designing the building. For existing buildings, the construction type is already established. To determine the construction type of the project you are working on, you can ask the local building official for a determination or check with the building's architect.

Knowing the construction type is important for the interior designer, especially if major changes are being made. If the occupancy type of an existing building is being changed, the interior designer must know the type to verify that the maximum area is not exceeded. In addition, construction type can affect the required fire ratings of permanent partitions, new shaft enclosures, coverings of structural elements, ceilings, opening assemblies such as doors and glazing, and corridors in high-rise buildings.

5 FIRE-RESISTIVE STANDARDS OF MATERIALS AND FINISHES

There is no such thing as a fireproof building. There are only degrees of fire resistance. Building codes recognize this and specify requirements for two broad classifications of fire resistance: surface burning characteristics of finish materials and resistance of construction materials and assemblies.

In the first broad classification, single layers of finish materials are rated and their use is restricted to certain areas of buildings based on their rating. The most common test standard used to rate materials is ASTM E-84, the Steiner tunnel test, discussed earlier in this chapter. The purpose of this type of regulation is to control the rate of flame spread along the surface of a material and to limit the amount of combustible material in a building.

The materials tested and rated according to surface burning characteristics include finishes such as wainscoting, paneling, heavy wallcovering, or other finish applied structurally or for decoration, acoustical correction, surface insulation, or similar purposes. In most cases, the restrictions do not apply to trim, such as chair rails, base, and handrails, nor to doors, windows, or their frames, nor to materials that are less than $^1/_{28}$-inch thick cemented to the surface of the walls or ceilings.

In the second classification, the amount of fire resistance that a material or construction assembly must have is specified by the building code. For instance, exit corridors are often required to have at least a 1-hour rating, and the door assemblies in such a corridor may be required to have a 45-minute rating. The method of testing materials and rating them was discussed earlier in this chapter.

Remember that many materials by themselves do not create a fire-rated barrier. It is the construction assembly of which they are a part that is fire resistant. A 1-hour-rated suspended ceiling, for example, must use rated ceiling tile, but it is the assembly of tile, suspension system, and the structural floor above that carries the 1-hour rating. In a similar way, a 1-hour-rated partition may consist of a layer of $^5/_8$-inch Type X gypsumboard attached to both sides of a wood or metal stud according to certain conditions.

A single piece of gypsumboard cannot have a fire-resistance rating by itself.

6 FIRE DETECTION AND SUPPRESSION

Fire detection, alarm, and suppression systems have become important parts of a building's overall life safety and fire protection strategies. Almost all buildings are required to have some type of detection device, even if it is a single smoke detector in a residence. Other occupancies, such as high-rise buildings and hotels, must have elaborate detection and alarm systems, including communication devices on each floor to allow firefighters to talk with each other and occupants in the event of an emergency.

Sprinklers are the most common type of suppression system and are required in nearly all new high-rise buildings and hotels. They are also becoming commonplace in many other types of commercial buildings. The design and layout of a sprinkler system are the responsibility of the mechanical engineer or fire protection contractor, but the interior designer should be aware of sprinkler system requirements, most notably the spacing of sprinkler heads and the types of heads available.

The National Fire Protection Association has developed standards that are followed by most building departments for the design of sprinkler systems. Occupancies are classified as light-, medium-, or high-hazard. For light-hazard occupancies such as offices, stores, and restaurants, one sprinkler head is required for each 225 square feet of floor area (if the system is hydraulically designed), with a maximum spacing between heads of 15 feet. Every room, even closets, must have at least one head. No sprinkler head can be more than 7.5 feet from a wall.

There are several types of heads that can be used depending on the design objectives and type of ceiling. These are discussed in Chapter 14. For many interiors, the heads that are covered with a smooth, white coverplate and set flush with a ceiling are frequently used because they are less noticeable.

7 OTHER REQUIREMENTS

In addition to the provisions mentioned in the previous sections, all the model building codes regulate many other aspects of construction. These include things such as the use and structural design of individual materials, excavations, demolition, and elevators, among many others. In addition to the model codes, there are local, state/province, and federal codes that regulate projects. For example, some states/provinces have specific flammability codes that regulate the specification of furniture fabrics and other interior materials. Specific requirements for exiting and barrier-free design are discussed in the next two chapters. Other regulations you should be familiar with include the following items.

A. Glazing

The use of glass is regulated in hazardous locations such as doorways, shower doors, glass adjacent to doors, and any place where people are likely to accidentally fall through a piece of glass. In such locations, safety glazing, which is defined as tempered or laminated glass, must be used. Safety glazing is discussed in more detail in Chapter 11.

B. Plumbing Systems

Model codes specify in great detail how a plumbing system must be designed and specify the number of sanitary fixtures required based on the type of occupancy. In most cases, satisfying the requirements is the responsibility of the mechanical engineer and architect, but in some cases the interior designer may be involved with remodeling toilet rooms in commercial buildings. In this case, it is helpful to know how many fixtures are required while you are developing preliminary design layouts. The UBC gives the minimum number of toilets, lavatories, drinking fountains, and other fixtures required in a building based on the occupancy.

C. Sound Ratings

A building code may require that wall and floor-ceiling assemblies separating dwelling units or guest rooms in residential occupancies from each other and from public spaces be insulated for the control of sound transmission. If this is the case, the code specifies the minimum sound transmission class (STC) for walls or impact insulation class (IIC) for floors.

Construction details must then be selected that satisfy these requirements. Refer to Chapter 15 for more information on acoustics.

Recently, the questions in the Building and Barrier Free Codes section have been changed to include only three possible answer choices instead of four. The sample questions in this chapter and the next two chapters reflect this change.

SAMPLE QUESTIONS

1. The minimum number of toilet fixtures required for an interior design remodeling is determined by square footage and

    1. accessibility requirements
    2. building type
    3. occupancy group

2. Which test gives the most accurate evaluation of the safety of a partition system?

    1. ASTM E-84, standard test method for surface burning characteristics of building materials
    2. Steiner tunnel test
    3. ASTM E-119, standard methods of fire tests of building construction and materials

3. You are designing a library in which you want to use tall bookshelves. If the project is located in a city that has adopted the Uniform Building Code, where would you look to find requirements on the minimum allowable space between the top of the shelving and the sprinkler heads in the ceiling?

    1. Uniform Mechanical Code
    2. NFPA-13
    3. UPC

4. Where are flame-spread ratings in a building MOST restrictive?

    1. in exit enclosures
    2. on corridor floors
    3. in access ways to exits

5. Exit corridors must have a rating of

    1. 45-minutes
    2. 1-hour
    3. 2-hours

6. When selecting interior partition finishes to meet fire-resistive standards, the MOST important consideration is

1. whether or not the building has an automatic sprinkler system
2. the hourly rating of the partition on which the finish will be installed
3. the occupancy group and the location in the building where the finishes will be used

7. In starting a design project in a multi-use building, what information would you need to determine?

1. occupancy group, construction type, and accessibility requirements
2. occupancy separation, fire zone classification, and occupancy group
3. construction type, fire zone classification, and occupancy separation

8. In which building type are construction requirements likely to be LEAST restrictive?

1. Type III
2. Type IV
3. Type V

9. If you were selecting glass to meet the requirements for safety glazing in a hazardous location, you would select

1. tempered glass or laminated glass
2. heat-strengthened glass or wired glass
3. laminated glass or wired glass

10. Which test is MOST frequently used to evaluate carpet in the United States?

1. methenamine pill test
2. Steiner tunnel test
3. flooring radiant panel test

18 EXITING

Exiting is one of the most important requirements of any building code. You must be familiar with the basic concepts of exiting and know the commonly used dimensions for corridors, doors, and stairs. The NCIDQ exam tests your building code knowledge in both the Building and Barrier-Free Codes and Practicum/Scenario sections.

Because building codes vary across the country and in Canada, the exam does not cover specific provisions of any one model code but tests your understanding of common requirements and your ability to apply requirements to the scenario design problem. However, to provide an example, the information in this section is based on Chapter 10 of the 1997 Uniform Building Code. Its exiting provisions are very similar to the other model codes. You should be familiar with exiting provisions of the codes for your area.

1 OCCUPANT LOAD AND NUMBER OF EXITS

The occupant load is the number of people that a building code assumes will occupy a given building or portion of a building. It is based on the occupancy classification as discussed in Chapter 17, including assembly, business, educational, and the other categories. Occupant load assumes that certain types of use will be more densely packed with people than others and that exiting provisions should respond accordingly. For example, an auditorium needs more exits to allow safe evacuation than an office space of the same area.

Occupant load is determined by taking the area in square feet assigned to a particular use and dividing by an occupant load factor as given in the code. In the UBC the occupant load factor is given in Table 10-A, which also includes other requirements for providing two exits and barrier-free access. See Figure 18.1. These load factors range from a low of 3 square feet per person for waiting areas to a high of 500 square feet per person for warehouses. These numbers mean that, for the purposes of estimating exiting requirements, one person is occupying, on average, the number of square feet listed in the occupant load factor column of the table. In determining the occupant load, all portions of the building are presumed to be occupied at the same time. If there are mixed occupancies, each area is calculated with its respective occupant load factor and then all loads are added together.

Example 18.1

What is the occupant load for a restaurant dining room that is 2500 square feet in area?

In Figure 18.1, dining rooms are listed under the use of "Assembly areas, less-concentrated use," with an occupant load factor of 15 square feet. Dividing 15 into 2500 gives an occupant load of 167 persons (166.67 rounded up).

Example 18.2

What is the occupant load for an office with 3700 square feet that also has two training classrooms of 1200 square feet each?

An office has an occupant load factor of 100, so 3700 divided by 100 gives an occupant load of 37 persons. Classrooms have an occupant load factor of 20. Two classrooms of 1200 gives a total of 2400 square feet. 2400 divided by 20 gives an occupant load for the classrooms of 120. The total occupant load of all the spaces is therefore 37 plus 120, or 157 persons.

The number of exits from a space, group of spaces, or an entire building is determined based on the occupant load. All buildings or portions of a building

TABLE 10-A—MINIMUM EGRESS REQUIREMENTS[1]

USE[2]	MINIMUM OF TWO EXITS OTHER THAN ELEVATORS ARE REQUIRED WHERE NUMBER OF OCCUPANTS IS AT LEAST	OCCUPANT LOAD FACTOR[3] (square feet)
		$\times$ 0.0929 for m^2
1. Aircraft hangars (no repair)	10	500
2. Auction rooms	30	7
3. Assembly areas, concentrated use (without fixed seats) Auditoriums Churches and chapels Dance floors Lobby accessory to assembly occupancy Lodge rooms Reviewing stands Stadiums	50	7
Waiting area	50	3
4. Assembly areas, less-concentrated use Conference rooms Dining rooms Drinking establishments Exhibit rooms Gymnasiums Lounges Stages	50	15
5. Bowling alley (assume no occupant load for bowling lanes)	50	4
6. Children's homes and homes for the aged	6	80
7. Classrooms	50	20
8. Congregate residences	10	200
9. Courtrooms	50	40
10. Dormitories	10	50
11. Dwellings	10	300
12. Exercising rooms	50	50
13. Garage, parking	30	200
14. Hospitals and sanitariums— Health-care center	10	80
Nursing homes Sleeping rooms	6	80
Treatment rooms	10	80
15. Hotels and apartments	10	200
16. Kitchen—commercial	30	200
17. Library reading room	50	50
18. Locker rooms	30	50

(Continued)

TABLE 10-A—MINIMUM EGRESS REQUIREMENTS[1]—(Continued)

USE[2]	MINIMUM OF TWO EXITS OTHER THAN ELEVATORS ARE REQUIRED WHERE NUMBER OF OCCUPANTS IS AT LEAST	OCCUPANT LOAD FACTOR[3] (square feet)
		$\times$ 0.0929 for m^2
19. Malls (see Chapter 4)	—	—
20. Manufacturing areas	30	200
21. Mechanical equipment room	30	300
22. Nurseries for children (day care)	7	35
23. Offices	30	100
24. School shops and vocational rooms	50	50
25. Skating rinks	50	50 on the skating area; 15 on the deck
26. Storage and stock rooms	30	300
27. Stores—retail sales rooms Basements and ground floor Upper floors	50 50	30 60
28. Swimming pools	50	50 for the pool area; 15 on the deck
29. Warehouses	30	500
30. All others	50	100

[1]Access to, and egress from, buildings for persons with disabilities shall be provided as specified in Chapter 11.
[2]For additional provisions on number of exits from Groups H and I Occupancies and from rooms containing fuel-fired equipment or cellulose nitrate, see Sections 1018, 1019 and 1020, respectively.
[3]This table shall not be used to determine working space requirements per person.
[4]Occupant load based on five persons for each alley, including 15 feet (4572 mm) of runway.

Figure 18.1 UBC Egress Requirements

must, of course, have at least one exit. When the number of occupants of a use exceeds the number given in the building code (such as in the second column of Figure 18.1), then at least two exits must be provided. The idea is to have an alternate way out of a room, group of rooms, or building if one exit is blocked. Areas above the first floor must always have at least two exits if the occupant load is 10 or more, although there are some exceptions for residential occupancies. In addition, three exits are required when the occupant load is from 501 to 1000 persons, and four exits are required for occupant loads over 1001.

In Example 18.1, the restaurant dining room would require two exits because 167 persons exceeds the figure of 50 given in Figure 18.1 (Table 10-A of the UBC). In Example 18.2, the total area of the offices and classrooms would require two exits. In addition, note that each classroom would need two exits because the occupant load for each is 60 (1200 divided by 20 square feet per occupant). This is more than the 50 occupants given in the second column of the table, which is the trigger point for requiring a minimum of two exits.

2 ARRANGEMENT AND WIDTH OF EXITS

A. Arrangement of Exits

Once you know the number of exits required for each room, space, or group of rooms, you must then determine the arrangement and width of those exits. When two exits are required, they must be placed a distance apart equal to not less than one-half the length of the maximum overall diagonal dimension of the building or area to be served, as measured in a straight line between the exits. This rule is shown diagrammatically in Figure 18.2. The reason for this requirement is to position the exits far enough apart so that a fire or other emergency would not block both exits.

If three or more exits are required, two exits must be placed a distance apart equal to not less than one-half the length of the maximum overall diagonal dimension of the building or area to be served, measured in a straight line. Again, the additional exit or exits must be arranged a reasonable distance apart so that if one is blocked the others will be available.

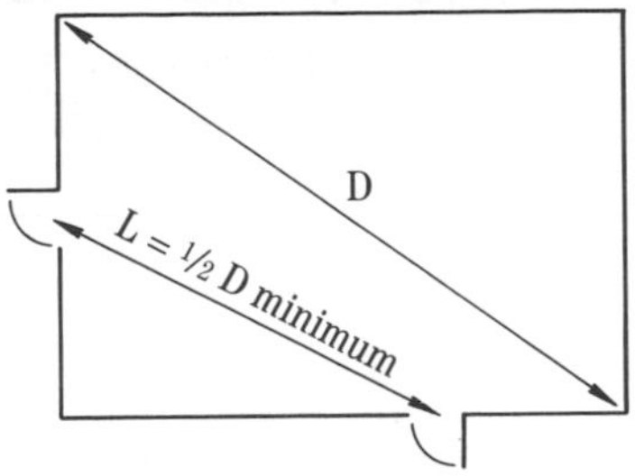

(a) exits from a room

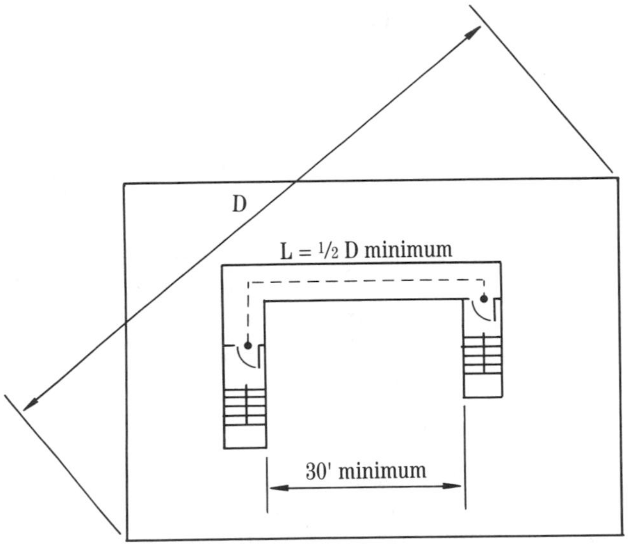

(b) exits from a building

Figure 18.2 Arrangement of Exits

B. Maximum Travel Distances

The maximum distances from any point to an exterior exit door, exit corridor, horizontal exit, or stairway are 200 feet in an unsprinklered building and 250 feet in a sprinklered building. See Figure 18.3. These distances may be increased a maximum of 100 feet when the increased travel distance is the last portion of the travel distance and is entirely within a one-hour-rated exit corridor. You will probably not have to worry about maximum travel distances in the practicum test because the problems are of much smaller scale, but your knowledge may be tested in the multiple-choice section.

C. Exits Through Adjoining Rooms

Most codes allow a room to have one exit through an adjoining or intervening room if it provides a direct, obvious, and unobstructed means of travel to an exit corridor or other exit as long as the total maximum travel distances, described in the previous section, are not exceeded. However, exiting is not permitted through kitchens, storerooms, rest rooms, closets, or spaces used for similar purposes. In the UBC, foyers, lobbies, and reception rooms constructed as required for corridors (with a one-hour-rated wall as described in the next section) are not considered intervening rooms, so you can exit through these spaces.

D. Widths of Exits

According to the UBC, for nearly all occupancies, the minimum total width of exits in inches is determined by taking the occupant load and multiplying it by 0.3 for stairways and 0.2 for other exits. (There are a few exceptions for hazardous and institutional occupancies.) This total width must be divided approximately equally among the separate exits. For instance, using Example 18.2 again, the occupant load of 157 multiplied by 0.2 gives 31.4 inches. A

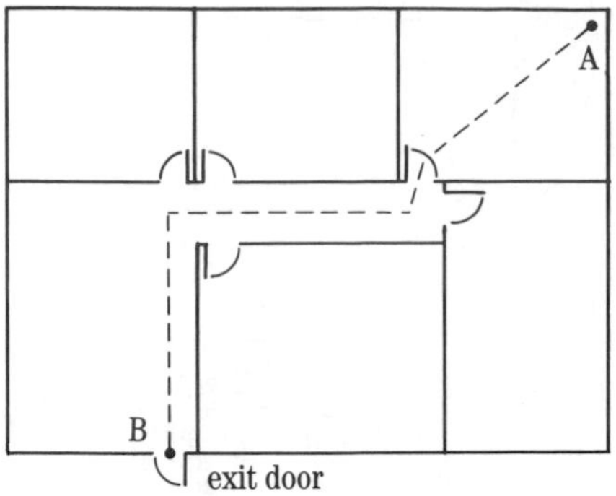

(a) exit from a room or space

A to B: maximum 150', unsprinklered bldg.
maximum 200', sprinklered bldg.

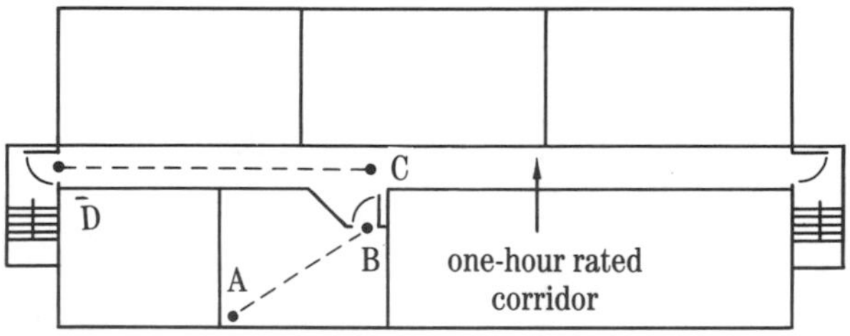

(b) exit from a building

A to B: maximum 150', unsprinklered bldg.
maximum 200', sprinklered bldg.
C to D: maximum 100'

Figure 18.3 Distances to Exits

corridor serving this occupancy would have to be at least this wide. However, as described in the next section, the minimum corridor width is 44 inches. For the doors, because at least two exits are required in this example, the total required exit width would be more than satisfied with two 3-foot-wide doors because they give a total exit width of 72 inches.

In most cases, for business, residential, and some educational occupancies of the square footages used on the NCIDQ exam, exit widths are usually satisfied by using the minimum 3-foot exit door width and having two exits. However, if you are dealing with an assembly occupancy (with a very low occupant load factor) or a very large space, you may want to verify the required exit width.

Another way to check that you have satisfied the code is to divide the total exit width (say 6 feet with two 3-foot doors) by 0.2 (or 0.3 for stairways), which gives a maximum occupant load of 360 served by these two exit doors. If your occupant load exceeds this figure, then you must provide another door. For corridors, get in the habit of using at least 5-foot wide corridors for commercial occupancies. This is a good, comfortable width for functional use and allows a maximum occupancy of 300 (60 inches divided by 0.2). If space is tight and there is not much traffic, you can consider using 4-foot wide corridors.

3 CORRIDORS

A corridor is an enclosed exit passageway connecting a room exit with a public way, enclosed exit stair, or horizontal exit. The purpose of a corridor is to provide a safe means of egress from a room or space to a building exit or to another approved exitway, such as a stairway. When two exits are required, corridors must be laid out so that it is possible to travel in two directions to an exit. If one path is blocked, then, occupants always have an alternate way out. Dead-end corridors (those with only one means of exit) are limited to a maximum length of 20 feet in the UBC. However, when completing the Practicum/Scenario portion of the exam, you should plan your spaces to avoid dead-end corridors altogether if possible.

The minimum width of a corridor in feet is determined (as discussed previously) by taking the occupant load it serves and multiplying by 0.2. However, the absolute minimum width for most occupancies is 44 inches if the corridor serves an occupant load of 50 or more. For occupant loads less than 50, the minimum width is 36 inches.

Certain occupancies, most notably educational and institutional in the UBC, require wider corridors. For instance, the UBC requires that corridors in schools must be 2 feet wider than the width as determined from UBC Chapter 10, but no less than 6 feet wide.

For most situations in the NCIDQ exam, you should plan on corridors 5 feet wide, if possible, for commercial design. This dimension satisfies most exiting requirements, provides enough space for barrier-free design, and is ample space for general circulation.

The width of a corridor must be unobstructed, but handrails and fully opened doors can protrude a maximum of 7 inches total. Other projections such as trim may extend into the width a maximum of $1^1/_2$ inches on each side.

With a few exceptions, corridors must be built of 1-hour fire-resistive construction when serving an occupant load of 10 or more in R-1 and I occupancies and when serving an occupant load of 30 or more in other occupancies. This must include the walls and ceilings. If the ceiling of the entire story is 1-hour rated, then the rated corridor walls may terminate at the ceiling. Otherwise, the 1-hour- rated corridors must extend through the ceiling to the rated floor or roof above.

Doors placed in 1-hour corridors must have a fire rating of at least 20 minutes and include approved smoke- and draft-control seals around the door. The door must also be maintained self-closing (with a door closer) or be automatic-closing by actuation of a smoke detector. Both the door and frame must bear the label of an approved testing agency, such as Underwriters Laboratories (UL).

Glass may be used in 1-hour-rated corridor walls only if it is listed and labeled as a $^3/_4$-hour fire-protection rating and the total area does not exceed 25 percent of the area of the corridor wall of the room that it is separating from the corridor.

When a duct penetrates a rated corridor, it must be provided with a fire damper, which is a device that automatically closes in the event of a fire.

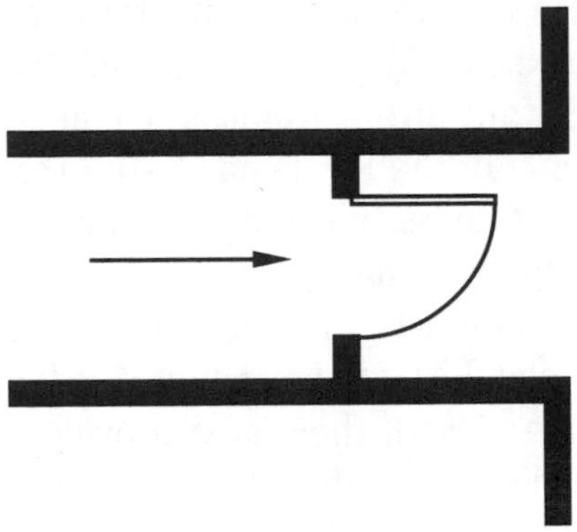

(a) doors must swing in the direction of travel

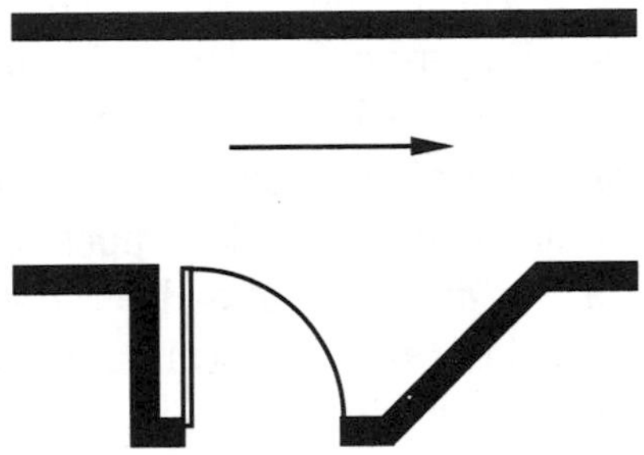

(b) doors must not swing into the required exit path

Figure 18.4 Exit Door Swing

4 DOORS

Building code provisions apply to exit doors serving an area with an occupant load of 10 or more. Exit doors must be pivoted or side-hinged and must swing in the direction of travel when serving any hazardous area or when serving an occupant load of 50 or more. This is to avoid a door being blocked when people are trying to get out in a panic. Make sure you show all required exit doors swinging in the correct direction, including doors to spaces with a high occupant load, stairway doors, and doors from corridors to other exitways. See Figure 18.4. Doors must also not swing into a required travel path, such as a corridor. In many instances, you may need to recess doors that swing into corridors as shown in Figure 18.4.

Exit doors must be a minimum of 3 feet wide and 6 feet 8 inches high. The maximum width is 4 feet. Exit doors must be operable from the inside without the use of any special knowledge or effort. For certain occupancies, such as educational and assembly, panic hardware is required. This is hardware that unlatches the door when pressure is applied against it rather than requiring a turning motion as with a door knob or lever handle. The door must swing to a full-open position when subjected to a maximum 30-pound force applied at the latch side.

Exit doors must have a fire rating compatible with the wall in which they are located. Doors are rated in hours the same way partitions are. A 2-hour partition, for example, must have a $1^1/_2$-hour-rated door assembly (also classed as a B-label door). This means that the door and frame have been tested by an approved laboratory and have a metal label certifying that they meet the requirements of their class. A 1-hour partition acting as a corridor wall needs a tight-fitting smoke- and draft-control assembly with a fire-protection rating of not less than 20 minutes. The types of doors commonly used in interior construction are summarized in Table 18.1, although the exact type required for any given circumstance depends on the requirements of the local code. Note that there are two B-labeled doors, one with a 1-hour rating and one with a $1^1/_2$-hour rating.

Exit doors must have automatic closers, and all hardware must be tested and approved for use on fire exits. When closed, they must provide a tight seal against smoke and drafts. Glass in exit doors must be wired glass, and its total area is limited depending on the door's fire rating.

In most cases, special doors such as revolving, sliding, and overhead doors are not considered required exits. Power-operated doors and revolving doors are sometimes allowed if they meet certain requirements. Revolving doors, for example, must have leaves that collapse under opposing pressure and must have a diameter of at least 6′-6″. There must also be at least one conforming exit door adjacent to each revolving door.

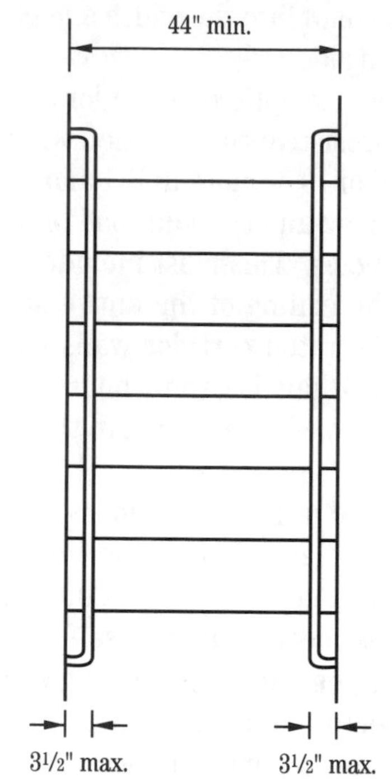

Figure 18.5 Stairway Width

5 STAIRWAYS

Stairways serving an occupant load of 50 or more must be at least 44 inches wide or as wide as determined by multiplying the occupant load by 0.3 as discussed previously. Those serving an occupant load of 49 or less must not be less than 36 inches wide. Handrails may project into the required width $3^1/_2$ inches on each side. See Figure 18.5.

The risers of the stair cannot be less than 4 inches or more than 7 inches, and the tread must be no less than 11 inches. Risers for barrier-free stairs cannot exceed 7 inches; treads must have an acceptable nosing design as discussed in the next chapter. For good design, you should determine either the required riser or tread and then use the stair formula discussed in Chapter 14 to calculate the other dimension. For residential occupancies and private stairways serving an

Table 18.1
Fire-Rated Door Classifications

Hour Rating	Class	Door Type	Frame Type	Use
20-minute	none	wood or hollow metal	wood or hollow metal	corridor doors in 1-hr partitions
$^3/_4$-hr	C	wood or hollow metal	hollow metal	1-hr corridor doors and exitway doors
1-hr	B	hollow metal	hollow metal	stairways in low-rise buildings and discharge corridors
$1^1/_2$-hr	B	hollow metal	hollow metal	2-hr vertical shafts for stairways
3-hr	A	hollow metal	hollow metal	3- or 4-hr walls

occupant load less than 10, the maximum riser may be 8 inches and the minimum tread may be 9 inches. See Figure 18.6.

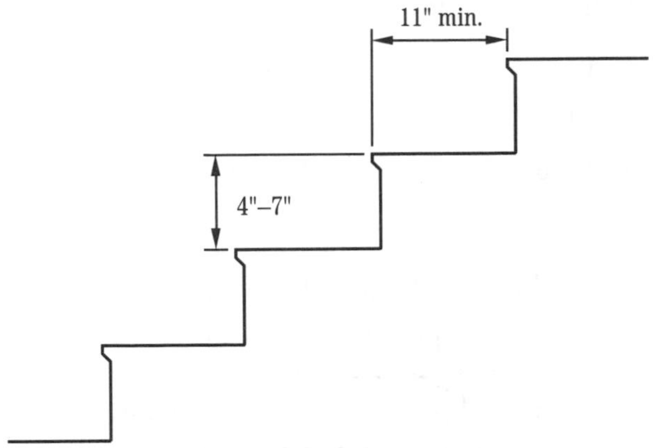

Figure 18.6 Stair Dimensions

Winding, circular, and spiral stairways may be used as exits in R-3 occupancies and in private stairways of R-1 occupancies only if they meet certain design conditions as specified in the code.

Landings must be provided at the top and bottom of every stairway. The minimum dimension in the direction of travel must not be less than the width of the stair but need not be more than 44 inches if the stair is a straight run.

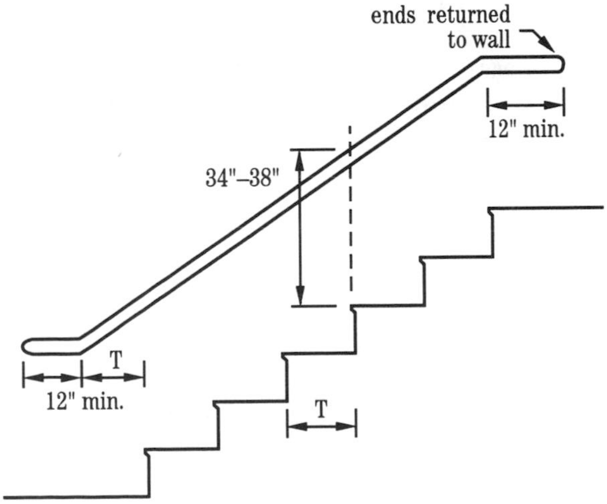

Figure 18.7 Handrail Design

Handrails must be provided on both sides of stairs as shown in Figure 18.7. Stairways less than 44 inches wide or stairways in residential occupancies only need one handrail. Stairways more than 88 inches wide need one intermediate handrail for each 88 inches of width. The top of the handrail must be between 34 inches and 38 inches above the nosing of the treads and must extend not less than 12 inches beyond the top and bottom risers. The ends must be returned or terminate in a newel post. The gripping portion cannot be less than $1^1/_2$ inches nor more than 2 inches in cross-sectional dimension. There must be a space at least $1^1/_2$ inches wide between the wall and the handrail.

6 RESIDENTIAL EXITING

Exiting requirements for individual dwelling units and single-family houses are not as stringent as those for commercial occupancies. Only one exit is required from the basement or second story of a house. However, basements and bedrooms must have an escape window with a minimum openable area of 5.7 square feet with the windowsill no more than 44 inches above the floor. The minimum clear opening height is 24 inches, and the minimum clear width is 20 inches.

Unlike most commercial construction, residential exits may pass through kitchens, storerooms, and similar spaces. Because the occupant load is less than 50, corridors may be a minimum of 36 inches wide (but this may be too narrow for accessibility in some instances). Also, because the occupant load is less than 10, doors may swing into rooms so there is not a problem with corridors being blocked.

Houses may have dead bolts or similar secondary locking devices provided that they are openable from the inside without a key or tool and are mounted no more than 48 inches above the floor. Houses may also have doorknobs instead of lever handles because they do not have to be accessible.

7 THE EGRESS SYSTEM

The UBC and other codes divide the means of egress into a system composed of three parts: the exit access, the exit, and the exit discharge. These must lead to a public way.

The exit access is that portion of the means of egress that leads to the entrance to an exit. Exit access areas may or may not be protected depending on the specific requirements of the code based on occupancy and construction type. They may include components such as rooms, spaces, aisles, intervening rooms, hallways, corridors, ramps, and doorways. In concept, exit access is the least protected of the entire egress system.

The exit is the portion of the egress system between the exit access and the exit discharge. Exits are fully enclosed and protected. Exits may be as simple as an exterior exit door or may include exit passageways, exit enclosures for stairs, and horizontal exits. Depending on building height, construction type, and passageway length, exits must have either a one- or a two-hour rating.

The exit discharge is the portion of the egress system between the exit and the public way. Exit discharge areas typically include portions outside the exterior walls such as exterior exit balconies, exterior exit stairways, and exit courts, but may also include, in some instances, building lobbies.

SAMPLE QUESTIONS

1. According the the UBC, dead-end corridors in sprinklered buildings are limited to a maximum of

   1. 10 feet
   2. 20 feet
   3. 50 feet

2. The abbreviated table below includes requirements for occupancy loads. A restaurant on the ground floor contains 3500 square feet of dining area, a 1000-square-foot kitchen, and a 1200-square-foot bar. What is the total occupant load?

Use	Occupant Load Factor
assembly areas, concentrated use (without fixed seats)	7
auditoriums	
dance floors	
lodge rooms	
assembly areas, less-concentrated use	15
conference rooms	
dining rooms	
drinking establishments	
exhibit rooms	
lounges	
stages	
hotels and apartments	200
kitchen—commercial	200
offices	100
stores, ground floor	30

   1. 202
   2. 318
   3. 380

3. What is included in the rise of a stairway?

   1. the vertical distance from one nosing to the next
   2. the average height of a step
   3. the distance from finish floor slab to finish floor slab

4. You have calculated that a total exit width of 8.5 feet is required from a store. What combination of door widths would meet most exiting requirements?

1. one 36-inch door remotely located from a pair of 34-inch doors
2. a pair of 32-inch doors remotely located from one 38-inch door
3. three 36-inch doors remotely located

5. In a 60,000-square-foot, single-story office building, what would be of greatest concern in space planning?

1. dead-end corridors
2. corridor widths
3. travel distances

6. A client has requested that you design and specify a new entry to her consulting business located in an old building that is being updated to conform to new building codes. Her current entrance consists of a pair of all-glass doors mounted on floor closers. What should you tell her to expect with the new entrance?

1. Smoke seals will have to be located around the edges of the glass doors.
2. The glass doors will have to be replaced with solid doors.
3. One of the doors will have to be removed.

7. Which of the following is an INCORRECT statement about fire-rated door assemblies?

1. Either hinges or rated pivots may be used.
2. Under some circumstances a closer is not needed.
3. Labeling is required for both the door and frame.

8. The MINIMUM width of a stair when handrails are required on either side is

1. 36 inches
2. 42 inches
3. 44 inches

9. Exits may NEVER pass through

1. foyers
2. kitchens
3. reception rooms

10. Which of the following is the MOST important in determining the number of exits that are required for a particular room or space?

1. the distance from the room exit to the building exit
2. the exit widths
3. the occupant load

19 BARRIER-FREE DESIGN

Barrier-free design is an important part of the NCIDQ examination section on building codes and is a topic with which all interior designers should be familiar. Although many federal and state agencies set requirements for accessibility, almost all of them follow the standards set forth in CABO/ANSI A117.1-1992, American National Standard for buildings and facilities providing accessibility and usability for physically handicapped people.

The Americans with Disabilities Act (ADA), which became law in 1992, requires that all commercial and public accommodations be accessible to people with disabilities. The specific regulations that accompany this legislation also follow CABO/ANSI A117.1 in most cases. The ADA does not cover single- or multi-family housing, but such housing is regulated by other federal and local codes, so these building types must also be accessible.

The standards discussed in this chapter include the basic requirements for accessibility related to interior design as defined in CABO/ANSI A117.1 and that are most likely to be tested in the NCIDQ examination. Remember that there are many other requirements for specific occupancies, parking, elevators, seating and work surfaces, and auditorium and assembly areas. You may want to review the CABO/ANSI standard or other reference sources for more detailed information.

1 ACCESSIBLE ROUTES

An *accessible route* is a continuous, unobstructed path connecting all accessible elements and spaces in a building or facility. It includes corridors, doorways, floors, ramps, elevators, lifts, and clear floor space at fixtures. The standards for accessible routes are designed primarily to accommodate a person using a wheelchair, but they can accommodate people with other disabilities.

Accessible routes and other clearances are based on some basic dimensional requirements of wheelchairs with which you should be familiar. The minimum clear width for an accessible route is 36 inches continuously and 32 inches at a passage point such as a doorway. The passage point cannot be more than 24 inches long. The minimum passage width for two wheelchairs is 60 inches. If an accessible route is less than 60 inches wide, then passing spaces at least 60 inches by 60 inches must be provided at intervals not to exceed 200 feet. These requirements are shown in Figure 19.1.

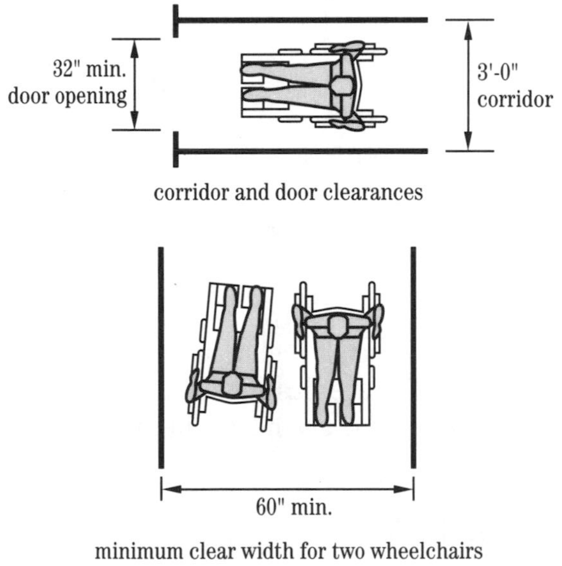

Figure 19.1 Wheelchair Clearances

The minimum clear floor space required to accommodate one stationary wheelchair is 30 inches by 48 inches. For maneuverability, a minimum 60-inch diameter circle is required for a wheelchair to make a 180-degree turn. In place of this, a T-shaped space may be provided as shown in Figure 19.2. When you are planning toilet rooms, make sure you have at least this 5-foot diameter clear space available. If turns in corridors or around obstructions must be made, the minimum dimensions are as shown in Figure 19.3.

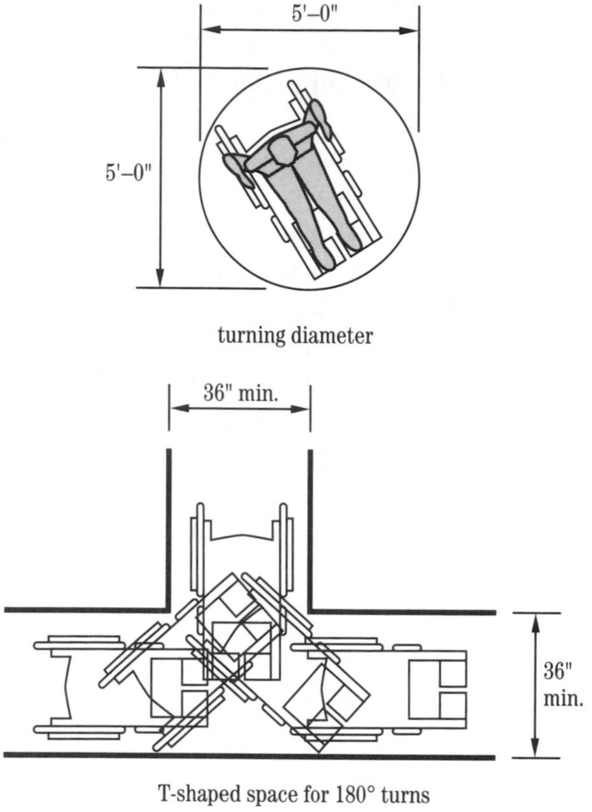

Figure 19.2 Maneuvering Clearances

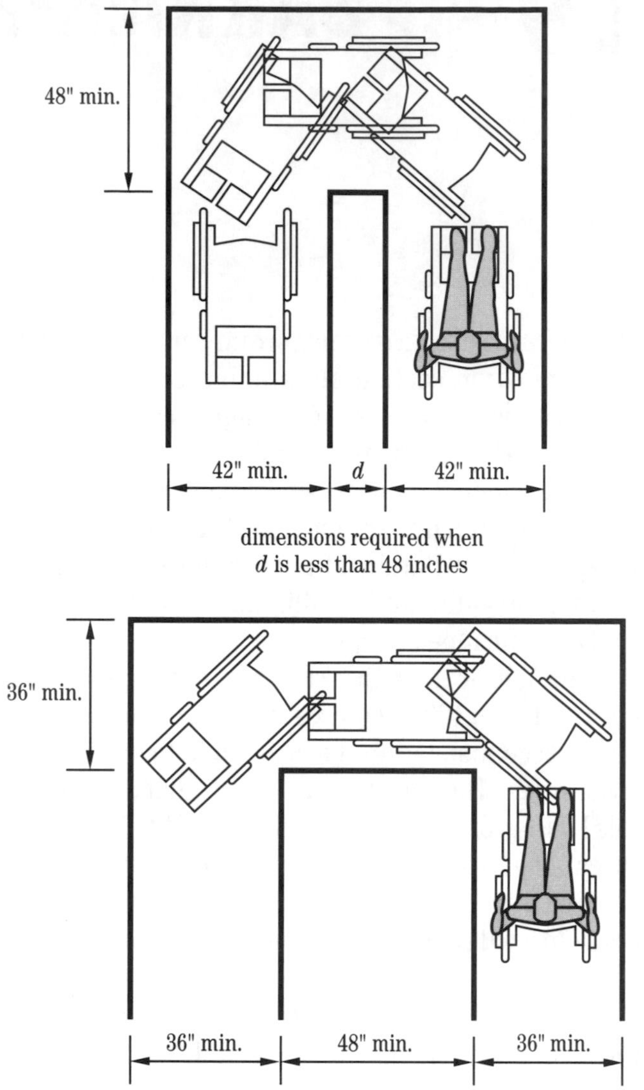

Figure 19.3 Turn in Corridors or Around Obstructions

An accessible route may have a slope up to 1:20 (1 inch in rise for every 20 inches in distance). Slopes any greater than this are classified as a ramp and must meet the requirements given later in this chapter.

2 DOORWAYS

Doors must have a minimum clear opening width of 32 inches when the door is opened at 90 degrees. The maximum depth of a doorway 32 inches wide is 24 inches. If the area is deeper than this, then the width must be increased to 36 inches. See Figure 19.4.

Maneuvering clearances are required at standard swinging doors to allow easy operation of the latch and provide for a clear swing. For single doors, the clearances are shown in Figure 19.5. The minimum space for two doors in a series is shown in Figure 19.6. Note the 48-inch space requirement. If sufficient clearance is not provided, then the doors must have power-assisted mechanisms or open automatically.

Barrier-free codes also require that door hardware meets certain specifications. Thresholds at doorways cannot exceed $1/2$ inch in height and must be beveled so no slope of the threshold is greater than 1:2. Operating devices must have a shape that is easy to grasp. This includes lever handles, push-type mechanisms, and U-shaped handles. Standard door knobs are not allowed. If door closers are provided,

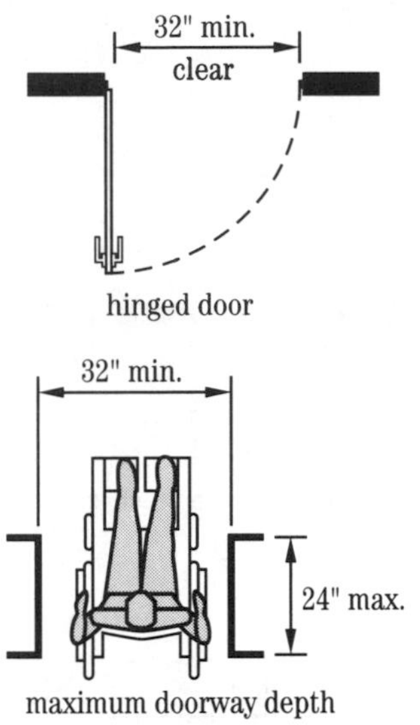

Figure 19.4 Doorway Clearances

they must be adjusted to slow the closing time. The opening force required to push or pull open an interior hinged door cannot be more than 5 pound-feet. Power-assisted doors may also be used.

3 PLUMBING FIXTURES AND TOILET ROOMS

CABO/ANSI A117.1 governs the design of the components of toilet rooms as well as individual elements such as drinking fountains, bathtubs, and showers. As mentioned in a previous section, toilet rooms must have a minimum clear turning space of a 5-foot diameter circle; however, the clear floor space at fixtures and controls and at the turning space may overlap.

A. Toilet Stalls

There are several acceptable layouts for toilet stalls. Minimum clearances for two standard stall layouts are shown in Figure 19.7. Alternate layouts are also acceptable as shown in Figure 19.8. The clearance depth in both cases varies depending on whether a wall-hung or floor-mounted water closet is used. In most cases, the door must provide a minimum clear opening of 32 inches and must swing out, away from the stall enclosure. Grab bars must also be provided as shown in the illustrations, mounted from 33 to 36 inches above the floor.

If toilet stalls are not used, the centerline of the toilet must still be 18 inches from a wall with grab bars at both the back and side of the water closet. A clear space in front of and beside open water closets should be provided as shown in Figure 19.9. Note that the dimension from the centerline of the toilet is 18 inches to both an adjacent wall and the closest edge of a lavatory. This may be important when you are laying out a toilet room in the Practicum/Scenario portion of the test.

B. Urinals

Urinals must be of the stall type or wall hung with an elongated rim at a maximum height of 17 inches above the floor. A clear floor space of 30 inches by 48 inches must be provided in front of the urinal, which may adjoin or overlap an accessible route.

C. Lavatories

Lavatories must allow someone in a wheelchair to move under the sink and easily use the basin and water controls. The required dimensions are shown in Figure 19.10. Notice that because of these clearances wall-hung lavatories are the best type to use when accessibility is a concern. If pipes are exposed below the lavatory, they must be insulated or otherwise protected and there must not be any sharp or abrasive surfaces under lavatories or sinks. Faucets must be operable with one hand and cannot require tight grasping, pinching, or twisting of the wrist. Lever-operated, push-type, and automatically controlled mechanisms are acceptable.

Mirrors must be mounted with the bottom edge of the reflecting surface no higher than 40 inches from the floor.

D. Drinking Fountains

Requirements for drinking fountains with a front approach are shown in Figure 19.11. If a drinking fountain is freestanding or built-in without clear space below, it must have a clear floor space in front of it at least 30 inches by 48 inches, which allows a person in a wheelchair to make a parallel approach.

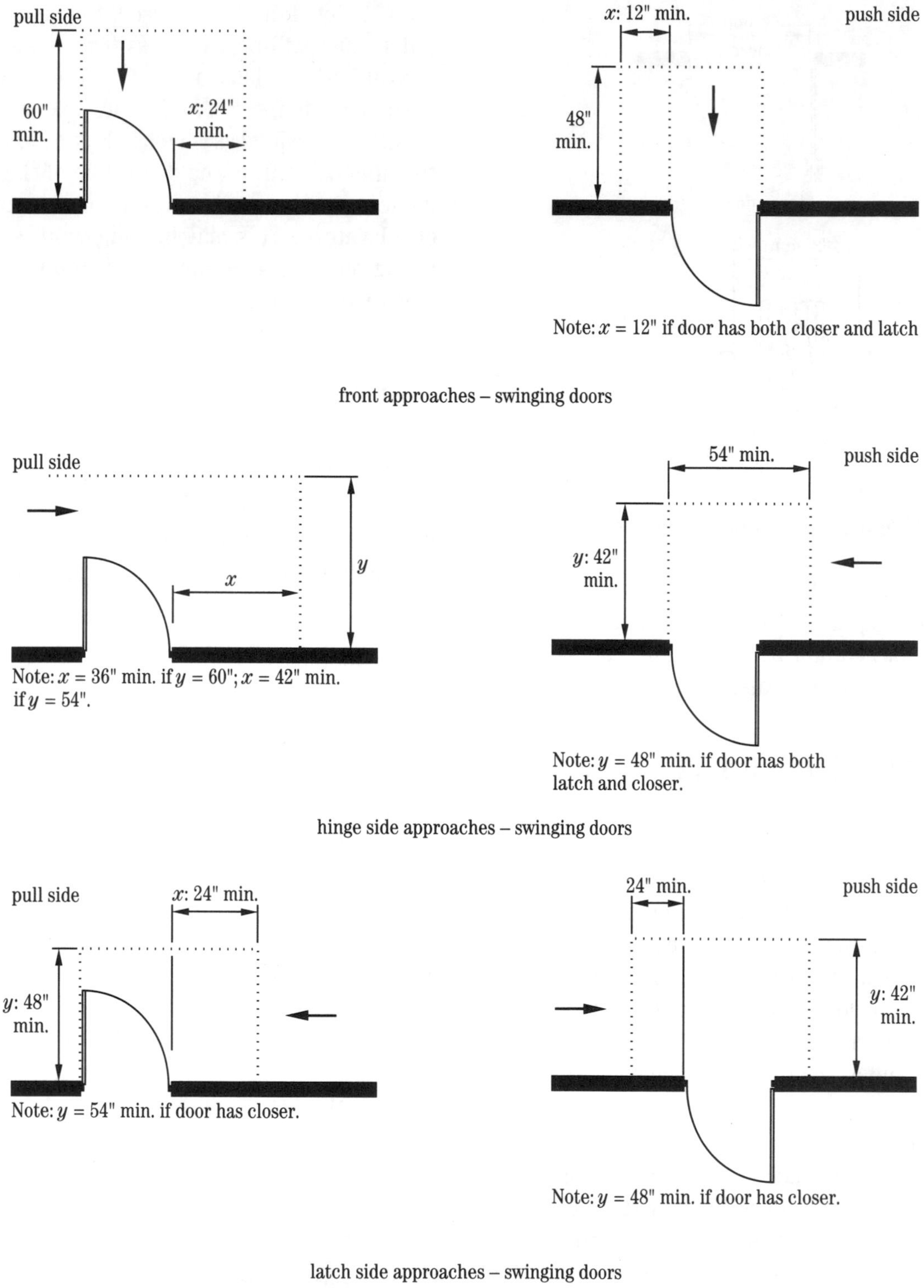
pull side
60" min.
x: 24" min.
x: 12" min.
push side
48" min.
Note: x = 12" if door has both closer and latch
front approaches – swinging doors
pull side
x
y
Note: x = 36" min. if y = 60"; x = 42" min. if y = 54".
54" min.
push side
y: 42" min.
Note: y = 48" min. if door has both latch and closer.
hinge side approaches – swinging doors
pull side
x: 24" min.
y: 48" min.
Note: y = 54" min. if door has closer.
24" min.
push side
y: 42" min.
Note: y = 48" min. if door has closer.
latch side approaches – swinging doors

Figure 19.5 Maneuvering Clearances at Doors

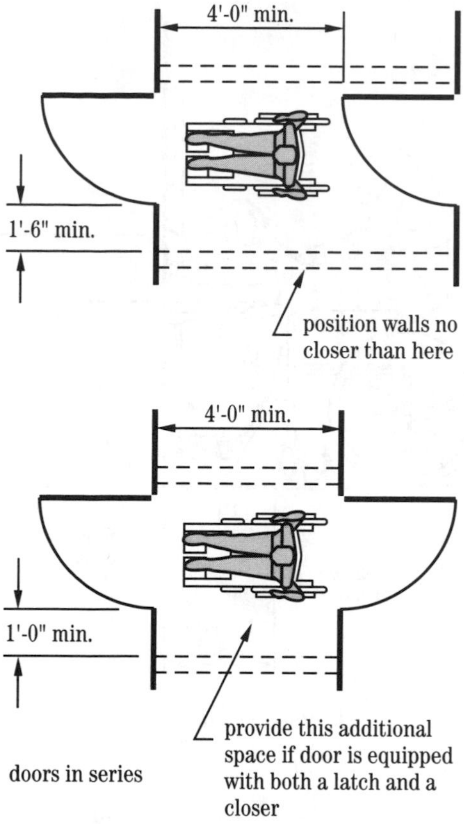

Figure 19.6 Double Door Clearances

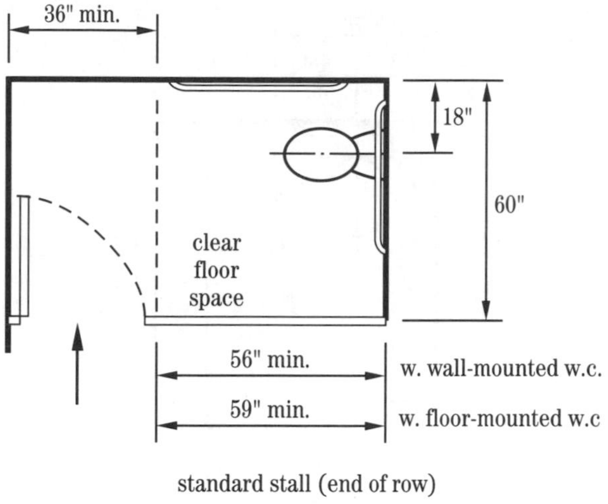

Figure 19.7 (cont'd)

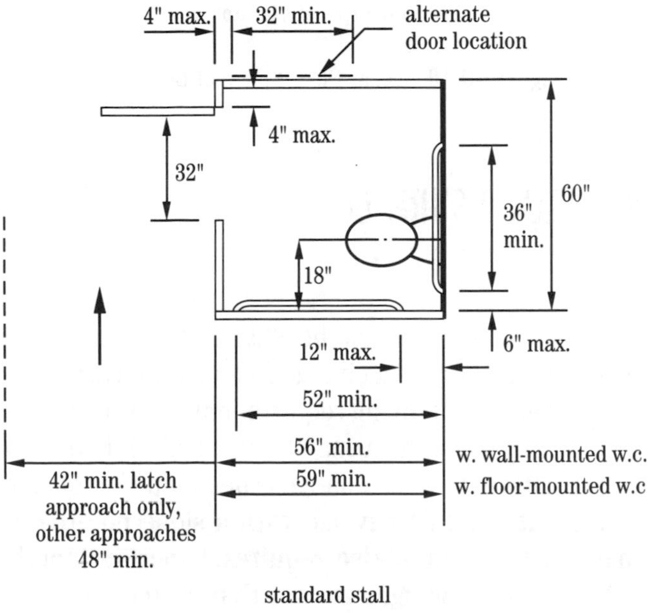

Figure 19.7 Toilet Stall Dimensions

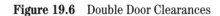

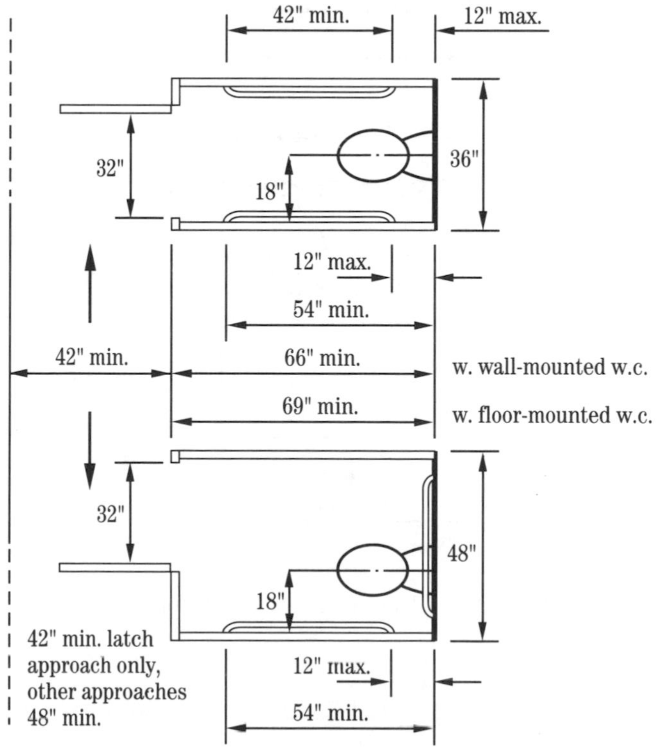

Figure 19.8 Alternate Toilet Stall Dimensions

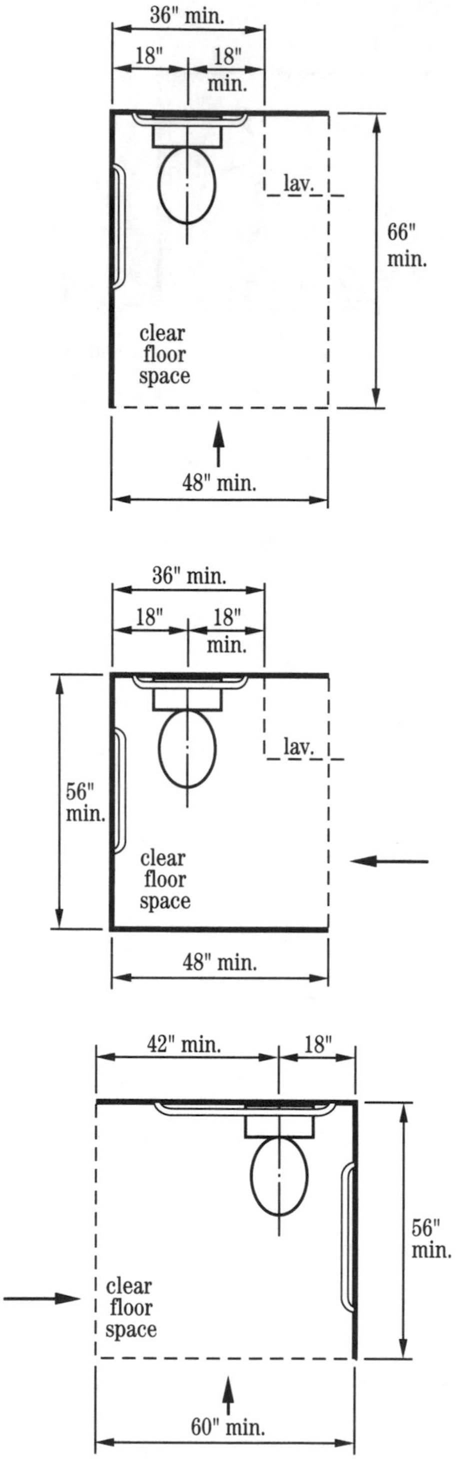

Figure 19.9 Clear Floor Space at Water Closets

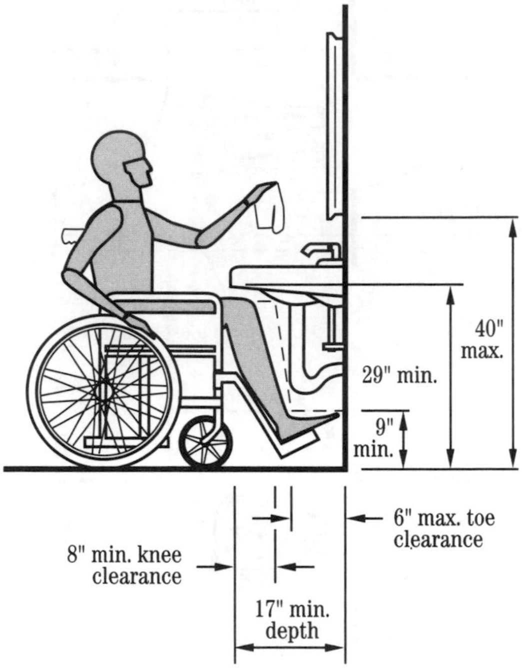

lavatory clearances

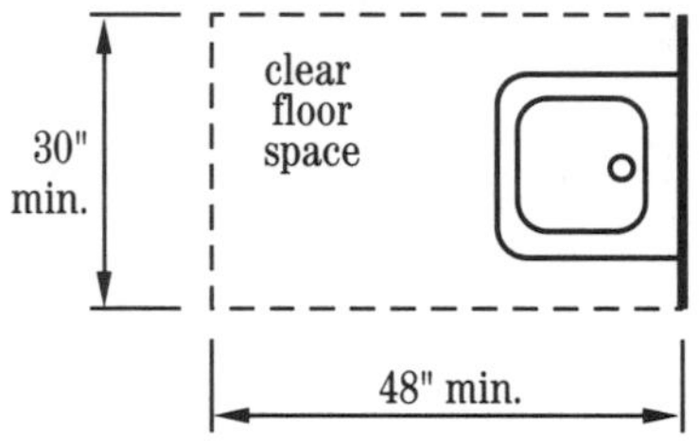

clear floor space at lavatories

Figure 19.10 Clear Floor Space at Lavatories

4 FLOOR SURFACES

Floor surfaces must be stable, firm, and slip-resistant. If there is a change in level, the transition must meet the following requirements. If the change is less than $^1/_4$ inch, it may be vertical and without edge treatment. If the change is between $^1/_4$ inch and $^1/_2$ inch, it must be beveled with a slope no greater than 1:2 ($^1/_2$ inch of rise requires 1 inch in length, for example). Changes greater than $^1/_2$ inch must be accomplished with a ramp meeting the requirements in the next section.

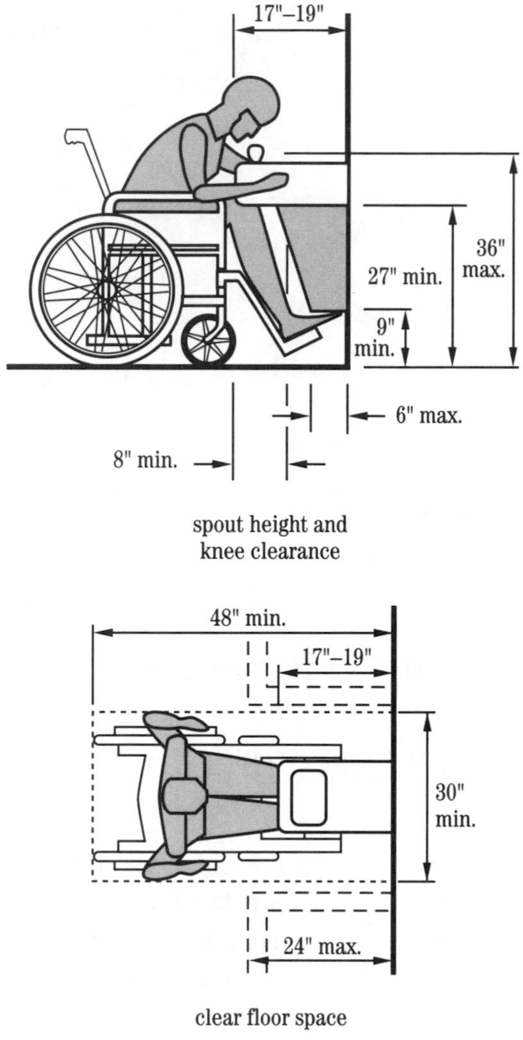

Figure 19.11 Water Fountain Access

Carpet must have a firm cushion or backing or no cushion and have a level loop, textured loop, level-cut pile, or level-cut/uncut pile texture with a maximum pile height of $^1/_2$ inch. It must be securely attached to the floor and have trim along all lengths of exposed edges.

5 RAMPS AND STAIRS

Ramps are required to provide a smooth transition between changes in elevation for both wheelchair-bound persons as well as those whose mobility is otherwise restricted. In general, you should use the least possible slope, but in no case can a ramp have a slope greater than 1:12 (1 inch in rise for every 12 inches in run). The maximum rise for any ramp is limited to 30 inches. Changes in elevation greater than this require a level landing before the next run of ramp is encountered. In some cases where exiting conditions prevent the 1:12 slope, a 1:10 slope is permitted if the maximum rise does not exceed 6 inches. A 1:8 slope is permitted if the maximum rise does not exceed 3 inches.

The minimum clear width of a ramp is 36 inches with landings at least as wide as the widest ramp leading to them. Landing lengths must be a minimum of 60 inches. If ramps change direction at a landing, then the landing must be at least 60 inches square.

Ramps with rises greater than 6 inches or lengths greater than 72 inches must have handrails on both sides with the top of the handrail from 34 to 38 inches above the ramp surface. They must extend at least 12 inches beyond the top and bottom of the ramp segment and have a diameter or width of gripping surface from $1^1/_4$ inches to $1^1/_2$ inches.

The ANSI code states that stairs that are required as a means of egress and stairs between floors not connected by an elevator must be designed according to certain standards specifying the configuration of treads, risers, nosings, and handrails. The maximum riser height is 7 inches and the treads must be a minimum of 11 inches as measured from riser to riser as shown in Figure 19.12. Open risers are not permitted. The undersides of the nosings must not be abrupt and must conform to one of the styles shown in Figure 19.13.

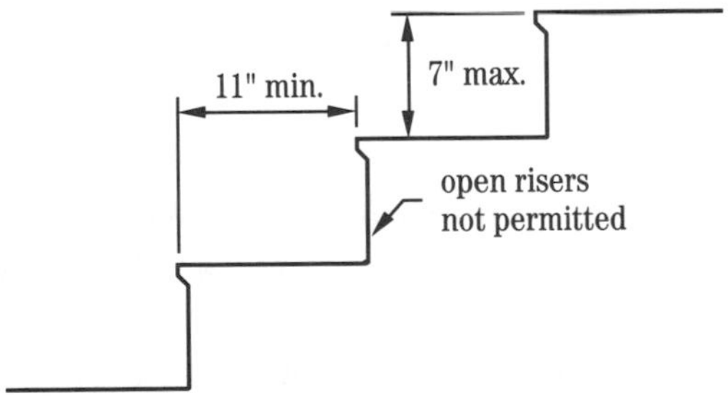

Figure 19.12 Stair Design Requirements

Stairway handrails must be continuous on both sides of the stairs. The inside handrail on switchback or dogleg stairs must always be continuous as

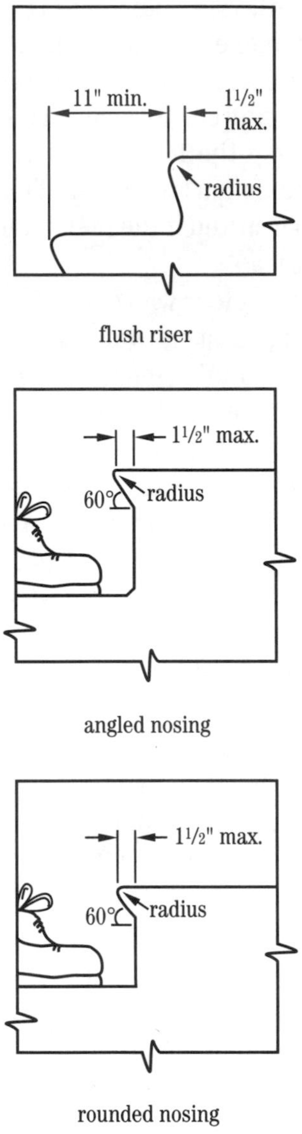

Figure 19.13 Stair Nosing Requirements

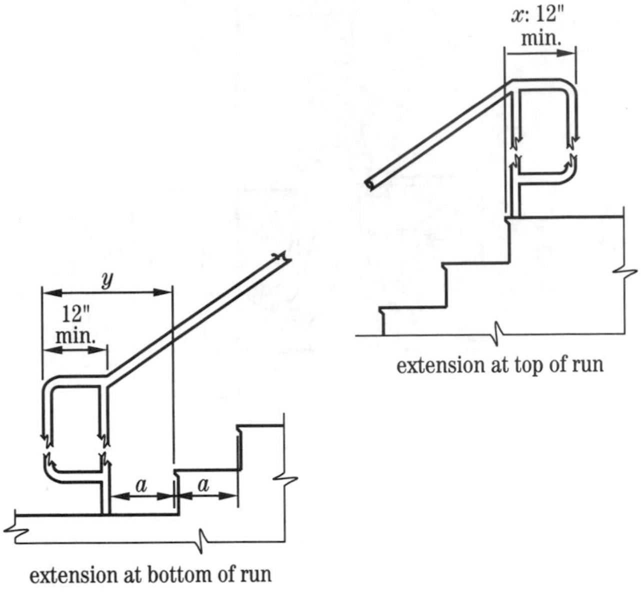

Figure 19.14 Handrail Design

it changes direction. Other handrails must extend beyond the top and bottom riser as shown in Figure 19.14. The top of the gripping surface must be between 34 and 38 inches above stair nosings. The handrail must have a diameter or width of gripping surface from $1\frac{1}{4}$ inches to $1\frac{1}{2}$ inches. There must be a clear space between the handrail and the wall of at least $1\frac{1}{2}$ inches. When an exit stairway is part of an accessible route in an unsprinklered building (not including houses), there must be a clear width of 48 inches between the handrails.

6 PROTRUDING OBJECTS

There are restrictions on objects and building elements that project into corridors and other walkways because they present a hazard for visually impaired people. These restrictions are shown in Figure 19.15 and are based on the needs of people with severe vision impairments walking with a cane. Protruding objects with their lower edge less than 27 inches above the floor can be detected by a person using a cane, so these objects may project any amount.

Regardless of the situation, protruding objects cannot reduce the clear width required for an accessible route or maneuvering space. In addition, if vertical clearance of an area adjacent to an accessible route is reduced to less than 80 inches, a guardrail or other barrier must be provided.

7 DETECTABLE WARNINGS

Detectable warning surfaces are required on walking surfaces in front of stairs, hazardous vehicular areas, and other places where a hazard may exist without a guardrail or other method of warning someone.

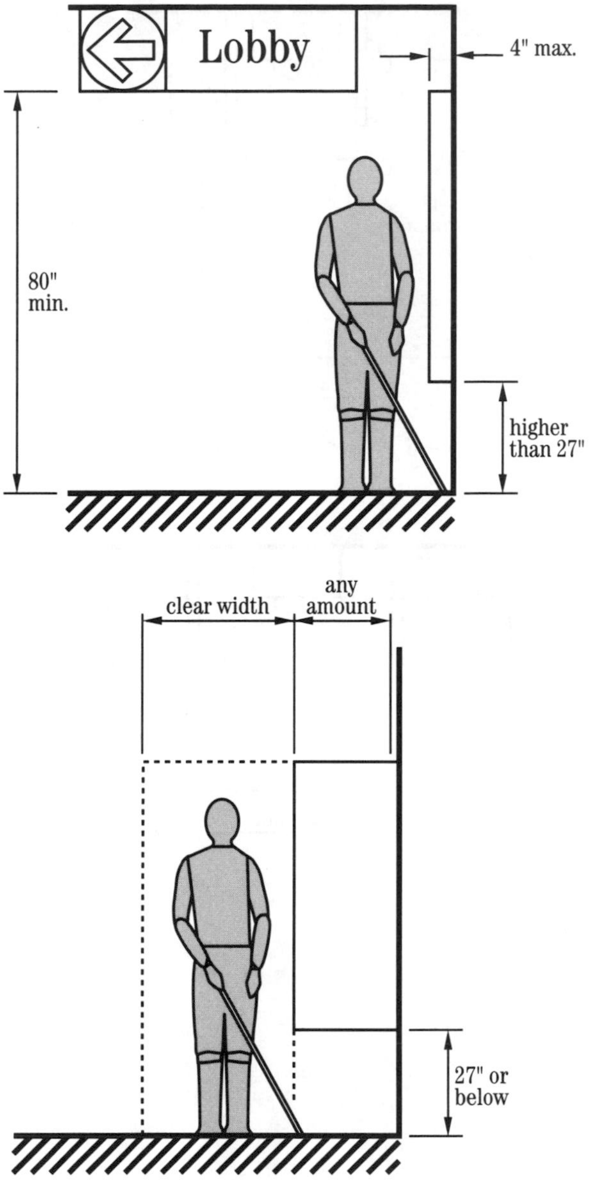

(a) walking parallel to a wall

Figure 19.15 Requirements for Protruding Objects

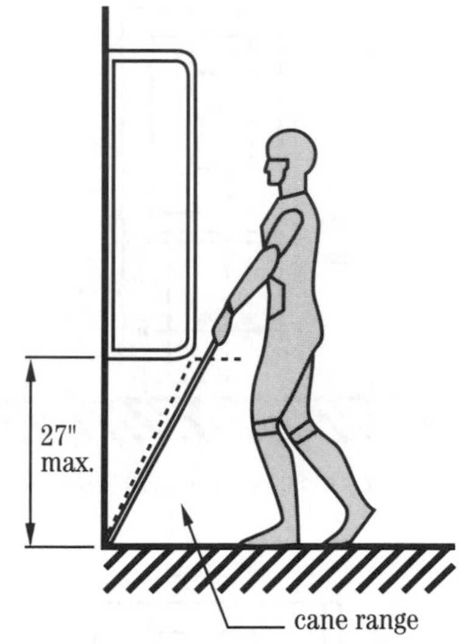

(b) walking perpendicular to a wall

Figure 19.15 (cont'd)

The surfaces must consist of exposed aggregate concrete, cushioned surfaces of rubber or plastic, raised strips, or grooves. Such textures must contrast with that of the surrounding surface.

Door handles are also required to have textured surfaces if they are part of a door that leads to an area that might prove dangerous to a blind person, such as doors to loading platforms, boiler rooms, and stages.

8 SIGNAGE AND ALARMS

Signage for visually impaired people should be provided that gives emergency information and general circulation directions. Signage is also required for elevators. The ANSI standards specify the width-to-height ratio of letters and how thick the individual letter strokes must be. They also require that characters, symbols, or pictographs on tactile signs be raised $1/32$ inch. If accessible facilities are identified, the international symbol of accessibility must be used.

Emergency warning systems are required that provide both a visual and audible alarm. Audible alarms must produce a sound that exceeds the prevailing sound level in the room or space by at least 15 decibels. Visual alarms must be flashing lights that have a flashing frequency of about one cycle per second.

9 TELEPHONES

Accessible telephones may be designed for either front or side access. The dimensions required for both of these types are shown in Figure 19.16. In either case a clear floor space of at least 30 inches by 48 inches must be provided. The telephones should have pushbutton controls and telephone directories within reach of a person in a wheelchair.

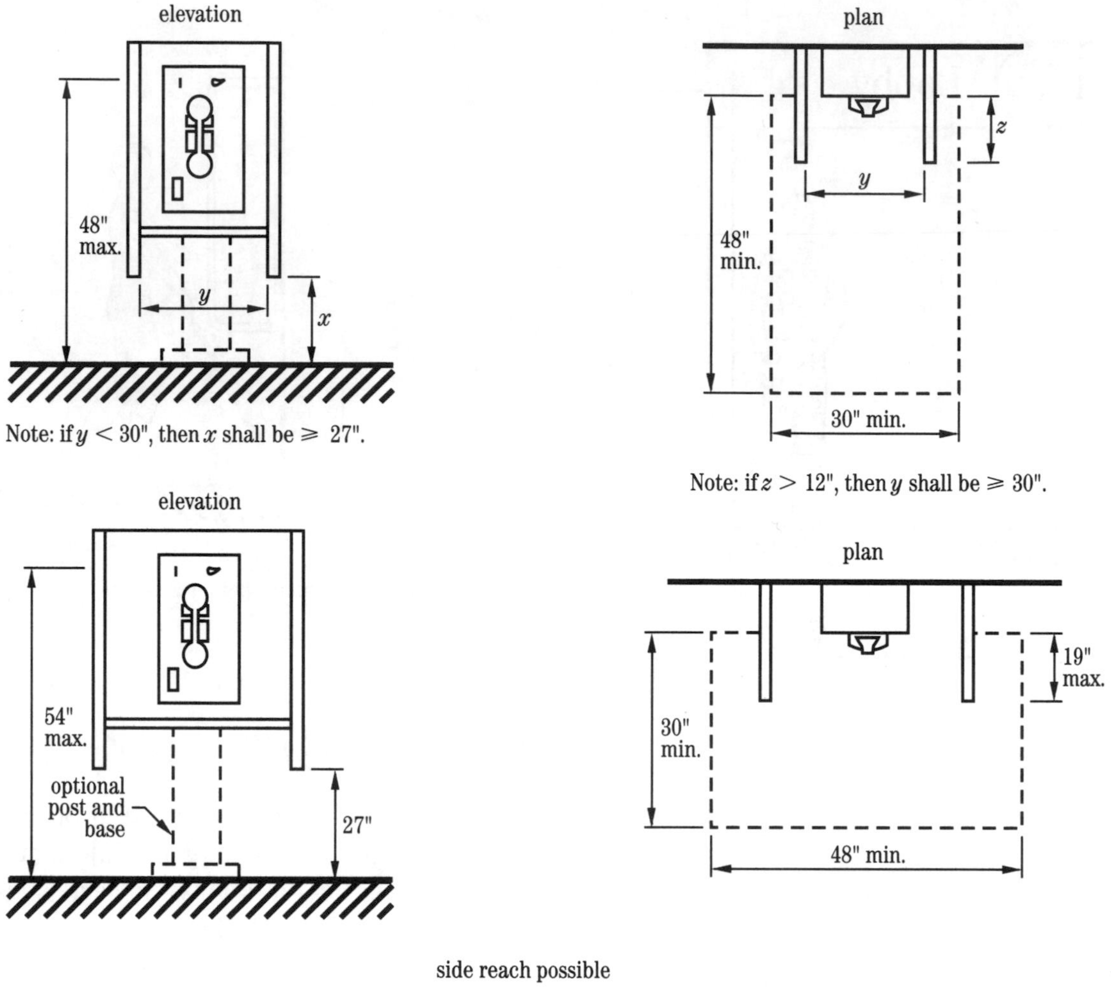

Figure 19.16 Telephone Access

SAMPLE QUESTIONS

1. The minimum clear width for a door must be

    1. 30 inches
    2. 32 inches
    3. 34 inches

2. When doing design work for remodeling toilet rooms to make them accessible you find that it is impossible to provide adequate clearance on one side of a door. What is your BEST course of action?

    1. Propose to the client that walls be demolished and replanned to provide the necessary clearances.
    2. Apply to the building department for a variance because of the remodeling problem.
    3. Specify a power-assisted door opener that meets accessibility standards and incorporate this into the design.

3. As measured from the nosing, how high must a handrail be for barrier-free design?

    1. 30 inches to 34 inches
    2. 32 inches to 36 inches
    3. 34 inches to 38 inches

4. In developing a signage system for a health care clinic you decide that the room identification signs should be horizontally mounted from the wall near the door to each room. What would be of LEAST concern in your design work?

    1. the color of the lettering and its background
    2. the amount Braille lettering is raised above the surface
    3. whether or not the width of the accessible route was reduced

5. What type of sink is BEST for barrier-free design?

    1. vanity
    2. pedestal
    3. wall hung

6. Standard accessible toilet stalls must have a clear width of at least

    1. 56 inches
    2. 60 inches
    3. 66 inches

7. What are the MOST important design elements to incorporate into a hotel to provide safe egress for physically disabled people?

    1. audible alarms and large emergency lettering
    2. visual and audible alarms
    3. tactile signage and visual alarms

8. An accessible route must serve

    1. all accessible spaces and parts of a building
    2. the corridors, stairs, elevators, and toilet rooms of a building
    3. entrances, parking, toilet rooms, corridors, and drinking fountains

9. What is the minimum distance between a pair of entry doors when one opens out and one opens in?

    1. 36 inches
    2. 48 inches
    3. 60 inches

10. In doing a minor remodeling project where only finishes were being changed, what would be of MOST concern?

    1. replacing existing thresholds
    2. providing lever handles on the doors
    3. the type of carpet and pad

20 OWNER-DESIGNER AGREEMENTS

For every job that an interior designer undertakes there is some form of mutual understanding about what the designer will do and what the client will give in return for services rendered. Such understandings are formalized in a contract, whether a simple one-page letter or a formal, multipage document. This chapter describes basic contract provisions and discusses some of the standard language in the agreement forms published by professional design organizations.

1 BASIC ELEMENTS OF A CONTRACT

A contract is a bargain between two or more parties who agree to exchange something each desires to obtain. For example, the client wants an interior space designed and the designer desires to be paid for his or her services. In a legal sense, there are two parts to this: an offer by one party and an acceptance by the other. Every contract, whether written or oral, must have both of these to be valid. If one person offers to do something and does it without acceptance and an agreement to receive something in return, a contract does not exist. There are other elements to a valid contract, such as a fair consideration (money) to be paid, but offer and acceptance are the most fundamental elements.

A contract between an interior designer and the client can take many forms. It may be a brief letter of agreement, a document developed by the designer's or client's attorney especially for a particular project, a standardized, preprinted form developed by a professional design organization like the American Institute of Architects (AIA) or the American Society of Interior Designers (ASID), or a standardized form that the client may use on all their design projects.

Wherever the contract originates, it should include the following provisions.

- *Parties to the contract and date:* The full legal name of both parties must be clearly stated along with their addresses and the date of the contract. You must be sure that the person signing the contract has the legal authority to do so. For residential work for a husband and wife, you may want to have both sign the contract so they are each separately responsible.

- *Scope of work and designer's responsibilities:* One of the most important parts of any agreement is the part that describes the exact amount of work the designer promises to do. This should include the actual area of the work (such as only the reception room and main conference room of an office suite) as well as a detailed description of services. The scope of work may be divided into common phases such as schematic design, design development, and construction and each phase subdivided in more detail. This is useful if you are billing for services after completion of each phase. Generally, fewer disputes will arise if you are very specific in itemizing services.

  It is also acceptable to itemize those services that you are specifically not going to provide, such as purchasing furniture or construction observation. This technique is useful to point out services that are normally included in a designer's contract and that the client may expect if they are not specifically excluded.

- *Purchasing agreements, if any:* If you are buying furniture and fixtures and reselling them to the client, you should specifically state your responsibilities as well as the client's for payment, acceptance, rejection of damaged goods, payment of delivery and installation costs, deposits, and methods of purchasing. Although the AIA Standard Form discourages the designer from procuring furniture except as agent for the client, many designers do act as resellers. If this is the case, you should be sure your contract is consistent with the Uniform Commercial Code and any specific laws of the state in which you are practicing.

- *Method of payment:* Any contract should state how much the client will be charged for services and how services will be paid for. There are several ways of charging for professional services including a fixed fee, multiple of direct personnel expense, percentage of project cost, and cost per unit area, along with several variations of these basic methods. These will be discussed in more detail in a later section. You should also clearly define when payment is to be made—whether it is monthly or paid at the completion of each phase, or some other method. You should also include payment due dates and any provision for late payments.

- *Reimbursable expenses:* Reimbursable expenses are costs that are not part of professional services but which are necessary to complete the project. These include things such as travel, long-distance telephone calls, reproduction costs, and postage. On large jobs these expenses can be significant, and it is important to itemize them so the client does not think they are part of your professional fee. Fees for consultants such as electrical and mechanical engineers may be included here or with methods of compensation. Many designers bill their clients the cost of consultants' fees plus ten percent to cover the cost of coordination and billing.

- *Extra services:* It is common for a client to request extra work from the designer once a project begins. This may include things like studying more design options, expanding the area of the job, specifying additional furniture, or requiring a longer time commitment due to delays. Many disputes can be avoided by clearly listing the types of extra services, charges for them, and how they will be billed to the client— the designer is then protected from providing extra work for free.

- *Responsibilities of the client:* Most projects require that the client perform certain actions or provide necessary information for the job to be completed. These may include things like buying and arranging for moving of client-supplied equipment, arranging for space to receive furniture delivered to the job site, or providing as-built drawings to the designer. If these responsibilities are not itemized in the General Conditions of the Contract as discussed in Chapter 9, they should be clearly stated in the contract. If timely completion of any action by the client is required to maintain the schedule, this should also be included.

- *Ownership of documents:* This provision states that the designer retains the rights of ownership to the documents and that they are only to be used to complete the specific project for which they were developed. The client may not reuse them to build other jobs without permission of and adequate compensation to the designer. This type of contractual provision is most often used with a copyright notice on the drawings themselves.

- *Provisions for arbitration:* Because disputes often arise, a contract should include procedures for arbitration. This is often more desirable than taking disagreements to court because it is generally faster and less costly, but both parties must agree to it in the contract.

- *Termination of the contract:* A termination clause gives both the designer and the client the right to quit the contract upon giving adequate written notice, usually at least seven days. If the contract is terminated by the client through no fault of the designer, the designer must be compensated for work performed up to the time of termination. Although a contract can be terminated without such a clause if both parties agree to it in writing, it is better to specify the conditions ahead of time.

- *Signatures:* To be legally valid, the contract need be signed only by the client, the person accepting the offer of the contract. However, it is better if both designer and client sign the agreement and date it.

In addition to these provisions, other articles may be added to cover such things as publication rights, time limits, responsibilities of third parties, and any special conditions of the project.

2 SCOPE OF BASIC INTERIOR DESIGN SERVICES

The amount and type of work that an interior designer does for a client vary widely and depend on the size and type of the project, what the client wants done, and what other professional consultants may be involved (such as architects, engineers, and specialized consultants). The following sections are based on the Standard Form of Agreement for Interior Design Services, B171, developed jointly by the American Institute of Architects and the American Society of Interior Designers. This agreement itemizes the most typical services that an interior designer performs. There is also a short form of agreement for small projects. You should be familiar with these provisions and the particular responsibilities the designer has during each phase of a project.

A. Programming

Although many contracts do not include programming as part of basic services, the AIA/ASID Standard Form of Agreement for Interior Design Services does. During this phase, the designer consults with the owner to develop the applicable requirements of the project and studies the feasibility of meeting the requirements within the constraints of the owner's budget and the building in which the project is to be located. This information and analysis are documented in a written program.

B. Schematic Design

Based on the approved written program, the designer prepares diagrams showing the general functional relationships required by the project and develops preliminary space allocation plans showing partitions, furnishings, and other pertinent planning ideas. The designer also prepares studies to establish the design concept of the project including types and qualities of materials, finishes, and furniture. This may include color and material sample boards and preliminary selection of furniture types as appropriate. The professional also prepares a preliminary statement of probable project cost based on the design concept and current costs for projects of similar scope and quality. As with all budgets, the designer is not responsible for final project cost.

C. Design Development

During the design development phase, the professional refines the approved schematic design work so that the size, scope, and character of the project are generally fixed. The drawings, color boards, samples, furniture selections, and other specifics of the job are presented to the client for approval or modification before work on the contract documents phase is commenced.

The design development documents usually include detailed plans showing partition and door locations, furniture and fixture layout, lighting design, sketches of special built-in cabinetry and furniture, and other elevation or three-dimensional drawings sufficient to describe the character of the design. In some cases, outline construction specifications may also be developed. At the end of this phase, the designer submits another statement of probable project cost for approval reflecting the changes and specific decisions made since the schematic design phase.

D. Contract Documents

Based on the approved design development submissions, the designer is responsible for preparing the detailed drawings, specifications, and other documents required to have the project constructed. The contract documents may include the work for both construction and furniture purchasing, or they may be developed separately so individual contracts can be let for construction and FF&E. The AIA/ASID Standard Form states that separate documents are to be prepared. This is usually the preferred method because interior construction is contracted for differently from furniture and equipment. The designer should advise the client of any adjustments or changes to the previous statements of probable project cost based on changes in the scope of work made during document preparation.

E. Bidding

The designer must assist the owner in the preparation of the bidding documents, the necessary procurement forms, the conditions of the contracts, and the forms of agreement between the owner and the contractor. The designer must also assist the owner in filing documents required for various governmental approvals. Notice that the designer's responsibility is to assist the owner, and not to perform all this work alone. After the necessary documentation is prepared, the designer assists the owner in obtaining bids (or negotiated proposals, if the project is not bid) and evaluating the bids (or proposals), and he or she assists in preparing contracts for interior construction and for FF&E. The designer is responsible for providing coordination of all these activities.

Note that in Canada and elsewhere the word *tender* or *tendering* are used to refer to bidding. Refer to Chapter 9 for more information on bidding procedures.

F. Contract Administration and the Designer's Responsibilities

In the AIA/ASID agreement, the scope of the designer's services during the contract administration phase is extensive. You should read the full text of these services in the agreement (B171), but the major provisions are outlined below.

The designer is a representative of the owner and advises and consults with the owner during the contract administration phase. Instructions to the contractors are forwarded through the designer, who has the authority to act on behalf of the owner, but only to the extent provided in the contract documents.

The designer assists the owner in coordinating the schedules for delivery and installation of the various portions of the work but is not responsible for neglect or malfeasance of any of the contractors or suppliers to meet their schedules or perform their contractual requirements.

To keep the owner informed and guard against defects and deficiencies in the work of the contractors, the designer must visit the project as necessary to become generally familiar with the progress and quality of the work and to determine, in general, if the work is proceeding according to the contract documents. The designer, however, is not required to make exhaustive or continual inspections.

One especially important provision is that the designer is not responsible for the means, methods, techniques, sequences, or procedures of construction. Nor is he or she responsible for fabrication, procurement, shipment, delivery, or installation of construction or furnishings. The designer is not responsible for job site safety or for the acts or omissions of the contractors, subcontractors, or suppliers.

During the construction and installation phase, the designer determines the amounts owed to the contractors and suppliers based on observations at the project site and on evaluation of the contractors' applications for payment. On this basis, the designer issues certificates for payment, usually monthly. In most cases, a single form is used as the application and certificate for payment.

The designer is considered the interpreter of the requirements of the contract documents and is expected to be an impartial judge of performance by both the owner and the contractors. His or her decisions should be consistent with the intent of the contract documents and reasonably inferable from them. The designer's decisions concerning aesthetic judgments are final if they are consistent with the intent of the contract documents.

As part of the day-to-day activities of contract administration, the designer reviews and takes appropriate action upon contractor submittals such as shop drawings and samples, prepares change orders when necessary, and may order minor changes in the work not involving an adjustment in the contract sum or an extension of the contract time. When the designer reviews shop drawings, it is only for conformance with the design concept expressed in the contract documents. The contractor is responsible for determining the accuracy and completeness of dimension, details, quantities, and other aspects of the shop drawings.

When the job is complete, the designer reviews the final state of construction and the final placement of all items and inspects for damage and function to determine if all the work has been supplied, delivered, and installed according to the contract documents.

The designer's responsibilities do not include the receipt, inspection, and acceptance on behalf of the owner of FF&E at the time of their delivery and installation. Nor is the designer authorized to stop the work, reject nonconforming work, or terminate the work on behalf of the owner. Instead, the designer can recommend to the owner that nonconforming work be rejected.

G. Purchase Orders

When the designer buys goods or services for the owner, either as a reseller or as an agent, a purchase order is used. This form gives the receiving party all the necessary information to supply the goods or services and authorizes the purchase of the listed items. Some of the information contained include the buyer's name and address; the vendor's name and address; a purchase order number; the quantity, description, and price of the items; and a shipping and billing address. In addition to providing written authorization, purchase orders are used as accounting devices to track the status of ordered goods and services and to serve as a basis for billing the client.

Once purchase orders are received by the vendor, they are usually followed up with an acknowledgment from the vendor. This lets the designer know the purchase order was received and allows the order to be double-checked to make sure all the information on the order is correct. The vendor creates a bill of lading when the goods are shipped, and later the vendor provides an invoice as a bill for the supplied items. Refer to Chapter 21 for more information on how purchase orders are part of the order processing procedure.

3 ADDITIONAL SERVICES

The specific services that the interior designer agrees to perform are itemized in the scope of work. The most common ones are described in the previous section based on the various phases of the work. The AIA/ASID Standard Form of Agreement lists many other services that are not commonly included in a standard contract. Including them in any type of contract helps avoid disputes because it makes clear what the client should not expect unless other arrangements are made. Some of additional services listed in the AIA/ASID form include:

- providing site evaluations or comparative studies of prospective sites
- providing services relative to future facilities and furniture and equipment that are not intended to be completed during the contract administration phase
- investigation of existing conditions or development of measured drawings
- providing services for planning tenant or rental spaces
- making revisions to drawings and specifications when those revisions are inconsistent with written approvals from the client or when they are required by revisions in codes or regulations after the preparation of the documents
- making inventories, surveys, or detailed appraisals of existing facilities or furniture
- providing services necessary by the default of any contractor or supplier or the failure of performance of either the owner or the contractor
- providing services relating to the work of any contractor after issuance to the owner of the final certificate for payment
- preparing to serve or serving as an expert witness

- providing services of consultants for structural, mechanical, and electrical engineering

- purchasing furniture, furnishings, or equipment with funds provided by the owner. Note that although this is an additional service according to the AIA/ASID agreement, many interior design contracts include this as a basic service

- providing services for the design or selection of graphics and signage

- providing services in connection with the procurement of art

4 OWNER'S RESPONSIBILITIES

The owner also has several responsibilities under the AIA/ASID agreement. He or she must furnish full information regarding requirements of the project, including a budget that provides for contingencies as well as for the basic cost items. The owner must furnish all legal, accounting, and insurance counseling services necessary for the project and must furnish any required laboratory tests, inspections, and reports as required by the contract documents. There must also be suitable space provided by the owner for the receipt, inspection, and storage of materials and equipment used on the job. The owner is also responsible for the removal or relocation of existing facilities, furniture, and equipment unless otherwise provided by the agreement.

The standard document also requires that the owner designate, when necessary, a representative who has the authority to act in the owner's behalf for the day-to-day decision-making required by the project. When the designer asks a question or submits documents for review, the representative must render decisions promptly to avoid delaying the job. If the designer is purchasing furniture and equipment for the project, the contract also requires that the owner maintain working funds that can be used for such purchases.

5 PROJECT COST

Project cost is defined as the total cost or estimated cost to the owner of all components of the project, including items designed or specified by the interior designer; labor; materials, furniture, and equipment furnished by the owner if it was designed or selected by the designer; and a reasonable allowance for the contractor's overhead and profit. It also includes the costs of managing or supervising construction and installation. Construction cost does not include professional fees of the designer, consultants, financing costs, or other costs that are the responsibility of the owner.

One of the most important provisions of contract language concerning project cost is that the interior designer does not warrant that bids or negotiated costs will not vary from the owner's budget or from any estimate prepared by the designer. The designer's estimated cost or statements of probable project costs represent only his or her best judgment as a design professional.

Language in the AIA/ASID agreement specifically states that no fixed limit of project cost shall be established as a condition of the agreement unless agreed to in writing by both parties. Only if the two parties thus agree to a fixed limit, and the lowest bid or negotiated price exceeds that limit, is the designer obligated to modify the drawings and specifications at no additional charge to reduce the project cost.

If the lowest bid or negotiated proposal exceeds the project budget or fixed limit of project cost, the owner has four options.

1. The owner can give written approval of an increase in the budget.

2. The owner can authorize rebidding or renegotiating of the project.

3. The owner can abandon the project.

4. If there is a fixed limit of project cost, the owner can have the designer modify the drawings and specifications without charge to reduce the project cost.

Of course, the owner may also work with the designer to reduce the scope of the project. If this occurs and there is no contractual fixed limit of project cost, the designer must be paid for his or her extra work in modifying the plans and specifications.

6 PROFESSIONAL FEES

There are many ways to charge for interior design work. Broadly speaking, these fall into two categories: those that are based only on professional services and those that are based on the retail method of reselling furniture and fixtures. For interior design firms, the most common method is to charge for services only, with furniture and fixtures being purchased by the client separately or through the design firm but without the design firm having any financial interest in the transaction. This method allows the interior designer to remain more objective about what type and quality of goods are specified because compensation is not tied to a particular manufacturer's discount or the total cost of the installation.

The AIA/ASID Standard Form of Agreement and other professional organizations only include methods of determining fees based on professional services. There are five basic ways this can be done, including some variations with each method.

- *Fixed fee:* This method states a fixed sum of money that the client will pay to the interior designer for a specific set of services. The money is usually paid out monthly according to the proportion of the basic phases of services described in the previous section, although other schedules can be arranged. With a fixed fee, the designer must accurately estimate all costs and allow for a profit. The fixed fee must include the salary costs of the people doing the job, customary benefits of employees, taxes, and office overhead. Reimbursable expenses are in addition to fees for the basic services.

  For a fixed fee to be profitable, the scope of services must be carefully itemized in the contract along with services that are not included. Methods and amounts of payment for additional services must be included in the contract so the client knows what to expect if extra work is requested. A fixed fee also requires the interior designer to carefully estimate the time for doing a project and to carefully monitor that time as the job progresses.

- *Hourly rate:* With an hourly rate, the client is charged for the actual amount of time that the professional spends on the project. The number of hours is multiplied by an hourly rate to arrive at the compensation charged to the client. The hourly rate must not only include the salary of the professional but also allowances for overhead and profit.

  The most common form of the hourly rate is the multiple of direct personnel expense. With this method, the direct hourly salary of employees is determined and multiplied by a factor to account for normal personnel expenses such as taxes, sick leave, health care, insurance, and other required and customary benefits. This hourly amount is then increased by a multiplier that includes provisions for overhead and profit. The exact amount of the multiplier depends on each office's overhead amount and profit margin, but it generally ranges from 2.75 to 3.00, although some offices use higher or lower multipliers. For example, if an employee was paid $20.00 per hour and personnel expenses (taxes, sick leave, etc.) accounted for 35 percent of the hourly rate, then the direct personnel expense would be calculated by multiplying 20.00 by 1.35 to get $27.00. This amount would then be increased by the multiplier. If the multiplier was 2.75, the final hourly rate charged to the client would be 27.00 times 2.75, or $74.25 per hour. Of course, there are different hourly rates for different employees based on their set salary or for different categories of work.

  The multiple of direct salary expense is a similar method except the multiplier is larger because it must provide for employee benefits as well as overhead and profit based on the direct hourly wage of the employee.

  The hourly method is favored by many interior designers, because for every actual hour spent on the project they are assured of covering expenses and making a profit. It also protects the designer when a client keeps changing his or her mind or otherwise delays the completion of the job. The designer is also compensated if unforeseen problems develop during design, construction, or installation of the project. Because some clients do not like the open-ended nature of the hourly rate system, a contract can be written for hourly rates that sets a maximum amount that the client will pay.

- *Percentage of project cost:* With this method, the professional fee is determined based on the total cost of the project. It is most appropriate for projects where the interior designer can accurately anticipate the amount of work required and has a good idea of the expected cost of the project. In many cases, this method may not be good because an economical or low-cost project may require just as much or more work as an expensive project. From the client's standpoint, the designer may be encouraged to increase the cost of the project to increase the fee or, may lose incentive to reduce construction and furnishings costs.

- *Area fee:* Professional fees on an area method are determined by multiplying the square footage of a project by some fixed rate. This is generally used only in commercial construction and then only with project types with which the interior designer has much experience. Tenant finish planning is often priced on a square-foot basis because a designer will know what it takes to do the job and because tenants, building owners, and leasing agents base most of their negotiations on a square-foot basis.

  As with a fixed fee, the scope of services with this method must be clearly defined so the designer is not forced to do more work than the fee will allow. In addition, you must specify how the area of the project will be calculated. For example, the area for lease spaces may be based on gross square footage, net square footage, or rentable square footage.

- *Retail method:* Using one of the variations of the retail method, the designer's compensation is produced by acting as a reseller of goods: buying furniture, fixtures, and other items at a trade discount and then selling to the client at retail price. The difference in price covers the designer's cost of doing business, delivery and installation charges, overhead, and profit. This method is used by stores offering design services, but it is also used by many residential and some commercial designers. Generally, the retail method is discouraged as a method of charging for professional services.

SAMPLE QUESTIONS

1. During the preparation of the contract for construction, the client asks the designer to be sure to check with an insurance agent so the correct amounts of coverage can be included in the Supplementary General Conditions of the Contract. How should the interior designer respond?

   1. Suggest to the client that his agent and your agent need to meet to make such a determination.
   2. Tell the client that insurance requirements should be placed in the General Conditions of the Contract.
   3. Call the client's insurance representative and discuss the project so the correct amounts can be determined.
   4. Remind the client that advice on insurance must come from the client.

2. Which of the following is a reimbursable expense?

   1. health insurance
   2. in-house costs for copying
   3. telephone calls made in connection with the project
   4. charges for having a model built for office design work

3. What should the designer first do if the client decides to make major revisions after the project has been tendered but before construction has started?

   1. Tell the contractor not to proceed until the issues have been resolved.
   2. Return any shop drawings that you have to the contractor and tell him that revisions will be forthcoming.
   3. Advise the client that making major revisions may delay the job and increase its cost and that you will require additional fees for design and drawing revision.
   4. Estimate the amount of time and extra fees you will need to make the revisions, and suggest that the client reconsider major changes.

4. Under the Standard Form of Agreement, what activities are included in an interior designer's services?

   1. programming, schematic design, contract administration, and post-occupancy evaluation
   2. design development, specification production, shop drawing review, and final punch list
   3. financial feasibility study, design development, working drawing production, and contract administration
   4. schematic design, assistance with bidding, contract administration, and furniture acceptance

5. If a partially completed low partition constructed according to the interior designer's drawings falls over during construction and injures a worker, who is responsible?

   1. the interior designer
   2. the contractor
   3. the subcontractor
   4. the worker

6. If you specified file cabinets that did not fit within a space that the contractor built according to the contract documents, who is responsible for paying for the correction?

   1. the contractor
   2. the interior designer
   3. the cabinet supplier
   4. the owner

7. Which type of fee is most often disadvantageous to the interior designer?

   1. hourly rate
   2. multiple of direct personnel expense
   3. fixed fee
   4. retail method

8. Which of the following is NOT an extra service?

   1. designing and detailing custom built-in furniture
   2. arranging and paying for an electrical engineering consultant

3. designing signage for a project
4. making a detailed survey of existing space prior to design

9. A project construction budget prepared by the interior designer should probably NOT include

1. the contractor's profit
2. the designer's fees and reimbursables
3. estimates for built-in equipment
4. fixtures to be supplied by the owner

10. What document is used to approve the release of funds for furnishing a project?

1. application for payment
2. certificate for payment
3. purchase order
4. bill of lading

21 PROFESSIONAL PRACTICE

Being an interior designer involves more than just designing and preparing drawings and specifications. Business skills are also needed. These include general business management, marketing, financial management, carrying insurance, and managing employees. This chapter discusses these topics as well as professional ethics.

1 PROFESSIONAL ETHICS

An interior designer must conform to all the federal, state, province, and local laws that any other business person must follow. Beyond this, however, a professional's conduct should be guided by a general sense of what is ethically correct and incorrect. For most professions, this is defined by historical practice as well as by codified standards developed by a profession's trade organization.

There are several trade organizations for interior designers, including the American Society of Interior Designers (ASID) and the International Interior Design Association (IIDA). The ASID has a code of ethics with which you should be familiar. It establishes minimum standards of conduct for its members and sanctions for violators.

The ASID code of ethics is divided into four areas including responsibility to the public, to the client, to other designers, and to the profession. The major ethical guidelines include the following:

- The interior designer must not engage in any form of false or misleading promotion or advertising.
- The designer is allowed to offer services to clients as a consultant, specifier, or supplier on the basis of a fee, percentage, or markup. However, the designer must fully disclose to the client the basis of all compensation. Additionally, unless the client knows and agrees, the designer cannot accept any form of compensation from a supplier of goods and services in cash or in kind.
- The designer must perform services in the best interests of the client as long as those interests do not violate laws, regulations, and codes, the designer's aesthetic judgment, or the health, safety, or welfare of the occupants.
- The designer is prohibited from divulging any privileged information about the client or the client's project without the express permission of the client.
- The designer cannot initiate any discussion or activity that might cause unjust injury to another professional. However, the designer can render a second opinion to a client or may serve as an expert witness in a judicial proceeding.
- The designer cannot interfere with the performance of another designer's contractual arrangement with a client. The designer can only begin work for a client if he or she is satisfied that the client has severed any contractual relationships with a previous designer.
- The designer can only take credit for work that has actually been created by the designer or under the designer's direction.
- As a member of ASID, the designer also agrees, whenever possible and within the scope of his or her interests and abilities, to encourage

and contribute to the sharing of ideas and information among designers, allied professionals, and others in the industry, and to encourage and offer support to interior design students.

Although stated differently, the IBD code of ethics covers many of the same areas and provides for discipline of a member who is found to have violated the code.

In addition to the professional organization's codes of ethics, there are some standards of conduct that derive from legal or contractual relationships or that have simply developed through industry standard practice.

One of the primary sources of problems during design and construction is lack of communication. The designer has a duty to keep both the owner and contractor informed of problems, changes, or other information that might affect their work or the performance of their contractual obligations. In most cases, any communication should be in writing to either party with a copy to the other party. This helps avoid misunderstandings and provides documentation of all actions on the job should disputes arise. Even telephone conversations should be documented with memos or notes.

2 INSURANCE

There are many types of insurance, both required and optional, that pertain to doing business and completing an interior design project. Each of the three primary parties to a project—the designer, owner, and contractor—must have certain kinds of insurance to protect against liability, property loss, and personal loss. Because the issue is so complex and the designer is not qualified to give insurance advice, it is best that the owner's insurance counselor gives insurance recommendations for specific projects. The interior designer and contractor should also have their respective insurance advisers recommend needed insurance for their businesses.

A. Interior Designer's Insurance

Professional liability insurance: This type of insurance protects the designer in case some action by the designer causes bodily injury or property damage. Sometimes called *malpractice* or *errors and omissions* insurance, this coverage responds to problems resulting from things such as incorrect specifications, mistakes on drawings, and incorrect installation of furniture or fixtures.

General liability insurance: This includes a range of insurance to protect against claims of property damage, liability, and personal injury caused by the designer or employees, consultants, or other people hired by the designer. It may also include product liability insurance, which provides protection in case a product or an installation completed by the designer or a subcontractor does some injury to the client after the designer or the subcontractor gives up possession of the product. Sometimes the designer will also buy insurance to cover the possibility that contractors or subcontractors do not have their own valid insurance as they should.

Property insurance: Property insurance protects the designer's building and its contents against things such as fire, theft, flood, and other disasters. Even if you rent space, property insurance protects the contents and any stock you may be holding for the client.

Personal injury protection: This protects the interior designer against charges of slander, libel, defamation of character, misrepresentation, and other torts. A tort is a civil wrong (as contrasted with a criminal act) that causes injury to another person.

Automobile insurance: Automobile insurance covers liability and property damage to vehicles owned and used by the business and can include protection against claims made by employees using their own cars while on company business.

Workers' compensation: This insurance is mandatory in all states and protects employees in the event of injuries caused by work-related activities.

Other types of insurance that the designer may carry include health and life insurance for employees, special flood insurance, valuable papers insurance, and business life insurance.

B. Owner's Insurance

As stated in A271, General Conditions of the Contract for Furniture, Furnishings and Equipment, the owner is required to carry his or her own liability insurance as well as property insurance for the full insurable value of the work. This insures against physical loss or damage caused by fire, theft, vandalism, and malicious mischief. The policy must be the "all risk" type rather than the "specified peril" type. All risk insurance is broader in coverage and includes all hazards except those that are specifically excluded by the policy.

C. Contractor's Insurance

The General Conditions of the Contract requires that the contractor carry insurance that will protect from the following types of claims:

- claims under workers' compensation
- claims for damages because of bodily injury, occupational sickness, or death of employees
- claims for damages of bodily injury or death to people other than employees
- claims for personal injury, which include slander, libel, false arrest, and similar actions
- claims for damages other than to the work because of destruction of tangible property. This includes loss of use resulting from such damages
- claims for damages related to use of motor vehicles

In addition, the contractor must carry insurance for any portions of the work that are stored off the job site or that are in transit to the site. Additional coverage may include "products and completed operations" insurance that protects against claims resulting from the contractor's actions when the injury occurs after the job is complete and the contractor has left the site.

3 BUSINESS MANAGEMENT

Two critical elements of professional practice include setting up a legal form for doing business and managing it as a successful, ongoing enterprise. This section discusses the more common forms of business structures and the business activities you should be familiar with for the exam.

A. Business Structures

There are several types of organizational structures that an interior designer can use. Each has its advantages and disadvantages and may be more or less appropriate depending on the number of people in the firm, the laws of the state where the firm is doing business, the type of practice, and the size of the business.

The simplest form is the *sole proprietorship.* In this case, the company is owned by an individual and operates either under the individual's name or a company name. To set up a sole proprietorship, it is only necessary to establish a name and location for business, open a company bank account, and have stationery printed. If you plan to resell furniture and other goods, a resale license is also required. If employees are hired, other state, province, and local requirements must be met.

The advantages to this form of business include the ease of setting it up, total management control by the owner, and possible tax advantages to the owner because business expenses and losses may be deducted from the gross income of the business. The primary disadvantage is that the owner is personally liable for all debts and losses of the company. For example, if a client sues the designer his or her personal income (and possibly co-owned property of a spouse), personal property, and other assets can be seized to pay any judgments. Another disadvantage is that it is more difficult to raise capital and establish credit as a sole proprietorship unless the owner's personal credit rating and assets are adequate.

Another common form of business organization is the *corporation.* A corporation is an association of individuals created by statutory requirements having an existence independent from its members. The formation and conduct of corporations are governed by the laws of individual states, and formal articles of incorporation must be drawn up by an attorney and filed with the appropriate state office to legally form a corporation.

Because a corporation is a separate legal entity, it is financially and legally independent from the stockholders. As such, the stockholders are financially liable only for the amount of money invested in the corporation. If the corporation is sued, the personal assets of the stockholders are not at risk. This is the greatest advantage of the corporate form.

Another advantage is that a corporation is generally taxed at a lower rate than individuals, and this can result in considerable savings. Additionally, corporations have a continuity independent of changes in stockholders, death of members of its board of directors, or changes in the principles. It is also relatively easy to raise capital by selling stock in the corporation.

The primary disadvantages of a corporation are the initial cost and the continuing paperwork and formal requirements necessary to maintain the business. These, however, are usually outweighed by the reduced liability and tax benefits.

Variations on the corporate form include the subchapter S corporation and the professional corporation. Subchapter S corporations have certain eligibility requirements and offer all the advantages of a standard corporation, but the profits or losses are paid or deducted from the stockholders' personal income taxes in proportion to the share of stock they hold. Sometimes this is an advantage when there are losses or the tax rates of the state shift the financial benefits when the individual is taxed rather than the corporation.

A professional corporation is allowed by many states for professionals such as architects, lawyers, doctors, accountants, and interior designers. This form of business is similar to other corporations except that liability for malpractice is generally limited to the person responsible. However, each state has its own laws regarding the burden of liability in a professional corporation.

Partnerships are the third type of business organization open to interior designers. With a partnership, two or more people share in the management, profits, and risks of the business. Income from the business is taxed as ordinary income on personal tax forms. If necessary, employees can be hired as with any form of business.

Partnerships are relatively easy to form (a partnership agreement is usually advisable) and provide a business with the skills and talents of several people rather than just one, as with a sole proprietorship. In most cases, partnerships are formed because each of the partners brings to the organization a particular talent such as business development, design, or technical knowledge.

The primary disadvantage is that all the partners are responsible and liable for the actions of the others. As with a sole proprietorship, the personal assets of any of the partners are vulnerable to lawsuits and other claims. Because income is taxed at individual rates, this is another disadvantage of the partnership form.

A variation of the general partnership described above is the *limited partnership.* This type of organization has one or more general partners and other limited partners. The general partners invest in the company, manage it, and are financially responsible, as with a general partnership. The limited partners are simply investors and receive a portion of the profits. They have no say in the management of the company and are liable only to the extent of their investment.

B. Scheduling

There are two major parts of a project schedule: design time, and construction and installation time. The interior designer is responsible for developing the schedule for the design of the job and the production of contract documents. The designer may also be responsible for scheduling the ordering, delivery, and installation of furniture if that is part of the designer's agreement with the client.

Construction scheduling, on the other hand, is the responsibility of the contractor. However, the design professional must be able to estimate the entire project schedule so the client has a general idea of the total time that may be required to complete the project. For example, if the client must move by a certain date and normal design and construction sequences make this impossible, the interior designer may recommend a fast-track schedule or some other approach to meet the deadline.

At the beginning of a project, the designer must estimate the time required to complete the design and construction drawing production and apportion this work among the people assigned to the project. The time is based on the scope of work jointly defined by the client and designer and is generally divided into phases of work as described in Chapter 20, including programming, schematic design, and so on. To assign estimated time (usually in hours or days) to individual work tasks, the designer uses time records and experience in completing similar jobs. Ideally, this estimating process is used to establish the fees so there is enough time to do the job properly and still make a profit. The various methods of charging for professional fees are discussed in Chapter 20.

The time required for the various design phases is highly variable and depends on the following factors:

- The size and complexity of the project. Obviously, an 80,000-square-foot office will take much longer to design than a 4,000-square-foot office.
- The number of people working on the project. While adding more people to the job can shorten the schedule, there is a point of diminishing returns. Having too many people simply creates a management and coordination problem, and for some phases only a few people are required, even for very large jobs.
- The abilities and design methodology of the project team. Younger, less experienced designers will usually require a little longer to do the same amount of work as senior staff.
- The type of client and the decision-making and approval processes of the client. Large corporations or public agencies are likely to have a multilayer decision-making and approval process. The time required for getting the necessary information or approval on one phase may take weeks or even months, whereas a small, single-authority client or residential client can make the same decision in a matter of days or hours.
- Fixed dates such as move-in, agency approval, or lease expiration over which the designer has no control.

The construction schedule is established by the contractor, but it must often be estimated by the interior designer during the programming phase so the client has some idea of total project time. When the designer does this, it should be made very clear to the client that it is only an estimate and that the interior designer cannot guarantee any time frame for the construction schedule.

There are several methods used to schedule both design and construction. The most common and easiest is the bar chart, sometimes called a Gantt chart. See Figure 21.1. The various activities of the schedule are listed along the vertical axis, and a timeline is extended along the horizontal axis. Each activity is given a starting and finishing date, and overlaps are indicated by overlapping bars for each activity. Bar charts are simple to make and understand and are suitable for small to midsize projects. However, they cannot show all the sequences and dependencies of one activity on another.

Another scheduling tool often used is the critical path method (CPM) and the CPM chart. A CPM chart graphically depicts all the tasks required to complete a project, the sequence in which they must occur, their duration, the earliest or latest possible starting time, and the earliest or latest possible finishing time. It also defines the sequence of tasks that are critical or that must be started and finished exactly on time if the total schedule is to be met. A CPM chart for a simple design project is shown in Figure 21.2.

Each arrow in the chart represents an activity with a beginning and end point (represented by the numbered circles). No activity can begin until all activities leading into the circle have been completed. The heavy line in the illustration shows the critical path, or the sequence of events that must happen as scheduled if the deadline is to be met. The numbers under the activities give the duration of the activity in days. The noncritical activities can begin or finish earlier or later (within limits) without affecting the final completion date. For very large, complex projects using CPM, computer programs are often used to develop and update the schedule.

Another technique sometimes used by contractors for large jobs is the Program Evaluation and Review Technique, or PERT chart. This is similar to the CPM technique but uses different charting methods.

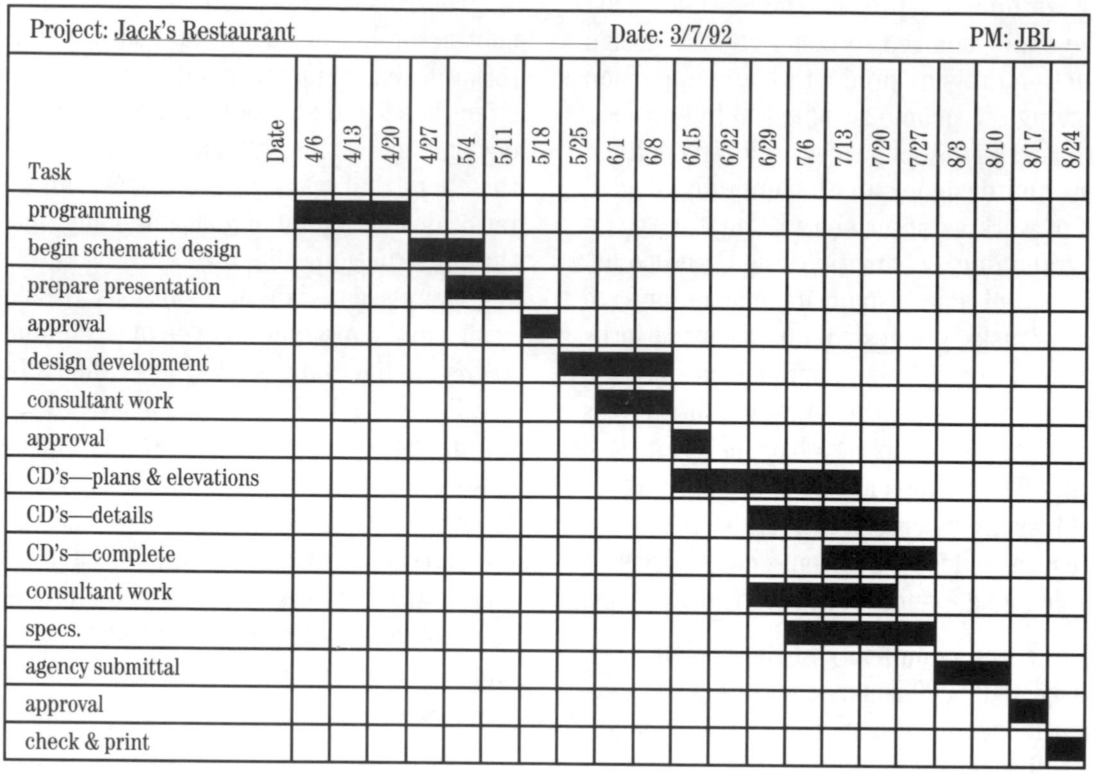

Figure 21.1 Gantt Chart

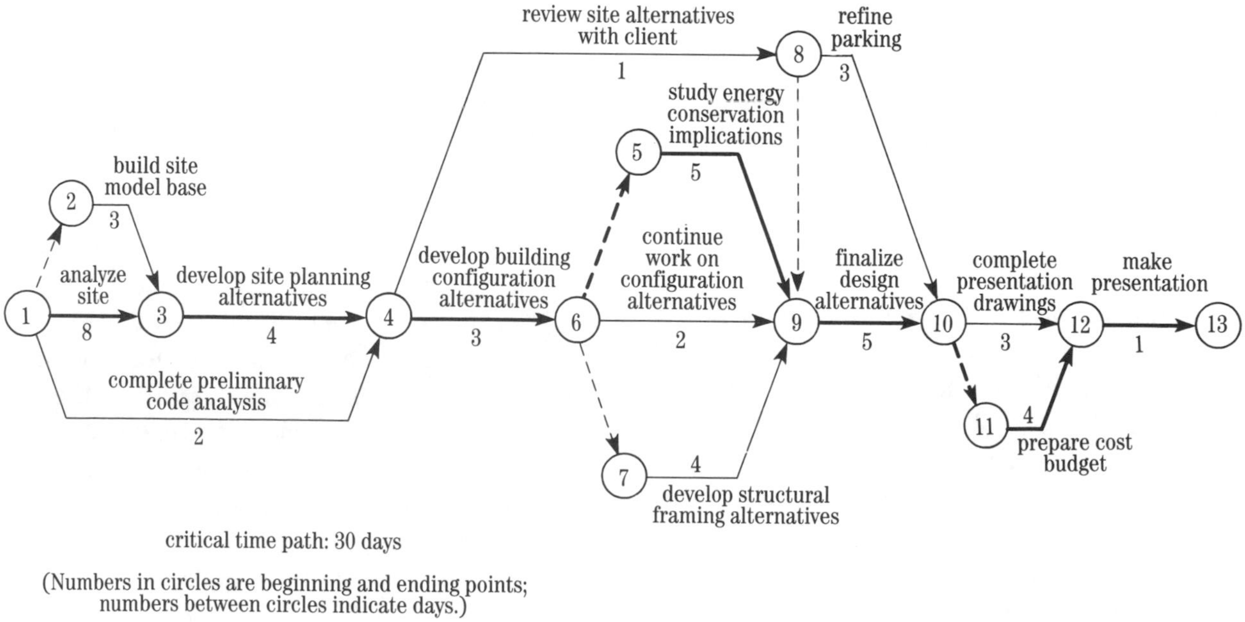

Figure 21.2 CPM Schedule

C. Order Processing and Purchase Orders

Depending on the agreement with the client and the type of design business, the interior designer can proceed in one of three ways after furniture and other purchased items have been selected and specified.

In the first case, the designer can simply give the furniture specifications to a dealer (or dealers) or furniture manufacturing representative who then assumes the responsibility for writing purchase orders, arranging delivery, troubleshooting problems, and billing the client directly.

In the second case, the interior designer acts as a purchasing agent of the client, writing purchase orders to send to dealers, manufacturers, and vendors and following up on the other paperwork in addition to coordinating delivery and installation, and then handling any problems that occur.

In the third situation, the designer acts as a reseller of goods. He or she writes purchase orders, accepts delivery, arranges for installation, and collects money from the client (including any applicable taxes) and pays the manufacturers or vendors.

In most situations, the interior designer is responsible for the following sequence of activities related to ordering furniture, fixtures, and accessories. These usually occur whether the designer is acting as a purchasing agent of the client or as a reseller.

The first step after the furniture and other goods have been selected is to receive a sales agreement or contract proposal signed by the client. This obligates the client to pay for the items listed in the agreement. Such forms typically list the name and address of the client, the items to be purchased, their price, and any labor, delivery, and taxes to be charged. If such an agreement is not signed by the client and the interior designer orders the goods, the designer is obligated to pay for them if the client does not.

Once the client has signed the agreement, a purchase order is written. This is a form sent to the manufacturer or vendor listing the items to be purchased, their exact catalog numbers, prices, shipping information, and other data. A separate purchase order is sent to each manufacturer or vendor if more than one is supplying goods to the project. In addition to providing the means to order goods, the purchase order serves as an internal record for the design firm that can be used to keep track of what orders are outstanding. It is also used as the basis for billing the client if payment is made by the client to the interior design firm rather than directly to the manufacturer.

After a manufacturer receives the purchase order, they send the designer an *acknowledgment* to confirm that they received it and to indicate how they interpreted it. The acknowledgment repeats the purchase order items, quantities, and costs, and indicates a scheduled shipping date and how the consignment will be shipped. It is the designer's responsibility to check the acknowledgment against the purchase order to make sure the order is correct.

When the manufacturer ships the merchandise, they normally also send an *invoice* to the designer (or whoever ordered the goods) at the same time. The designer (or whoever is responsible) pays from this invoice.

As the merchandise is shipped, there is a *bill of lading* that lists the contents of the shipment that the carrier (usually a trucker) carries with him or her. When the truck arrives at the final destination, the number of items should be checked against the bill of lading to make sure they match. There is also a *packing list*, which is sealed in an envelope attached to one of the items shipped. It is a detailed list of the number and description of items in the shipment and should also be checked against the items and the bill of lading.

When the merchandise is delivered to a warehouse before shipping to the job site, it should be inspected for any damage that may have occurred in transit. This should be done by the designer or the designer's representative. Any damage should be shown to the driver and notations made on the bill of lading. Some people also take photographs of the damaged merchandise to further back up their claims. Damage must be reported to the shipper as soon as possible.

When merchandise is delivered to the job site and the AIA/ASID General Conditions of the Contract is being used, the owner is responsible for inspecting delivered goods but only for the purposes of identifying the merchandise and verifying quantities. Such inspections are not considered final or as constituting acceptance of or taking control over the merchandise. If damage is found, the owner must notify the contractor who then has the opportunity to correct the situation.

4 BUSINESS DEVELOPMENT

In the competitive marketplace of professional services, it is no longer possible for an interior designer to sit in the office waiting for a phone call for a new job or for a referral from a previous client. Marketing and public relations have become integral parts of successful firms, and you should be familiar with the basic techniques.

A. Marketing

Marketing can be defined simply as a set of activities related to facilitating an honest exchange of something you have for something someone else needs. There are a number of marketing techniques used by interior design firms today. Which ones should be used by any particular office depends on the type of market the office is hoping to capture, the geographical area the office markets in, the type of work the office wants to perform, and the budget and personnel available for marketing, among others. The following marketing techniques are some of the more common methods used.

Corporate identification: Although a corporate identification is not a specific marketing technique in itself, it is a fundamental requirement for a professional firm and something that is applicable to other marketing aspects. A corporate identification is a distinct and consistently applied graphic image that connects the graphic with your firm in the minds of people who see it. It may include a specially designed logo, or mark, which is unique to your firm as well as a unique treatment of your firm name. All firms should have a well-designed corporate identification program that encompasses all the graphic and promotional items produced such as letterheads, envelopes, brochures, business cards, proposals, newsletters, forms, drawing paper, and similar items. A properly designed corporate identification program can visually communicate the philosophy of your firm, present a strong, visible identity to support your marketing efforts, organize your internal office procedures and project documentation, and give your firm a visual coherence and consistency.

Developing leads: A lead is a source of information about a particular client who may need the services of an interior designer now or in the future. A lead can also be a planned building project for which there is a need for design services. As more design firms target their marketing efforts to the types of clients they want or the kinds of projects in which they specialize, finding and developing leads are becoming increasingly important to a thriving business. For example, a design firm that specializes in law offices may develop a list of all the law firms in a given area so the marketing effort is directed only at those potential clients and not wasted on accounting firms.

Brochures: A brochure is a basic marketing tool for all design firms. It gives a brief description of the firm and its capabilities and service specialties, and includes representative photographs of past projects. Brochures are produced in a wide range of sizes and styles, from simple, pocket-size folders to hardbound books. In most cases, however, a brochure should be well designed, fairly brief, and laid out to give people an overall impression of the firm and its abilities. It should serve as a reminder of the firm and encourage a potential client to want more information from the designer.

Audiovisual presentations: Audiovisual presentations are often used to present more detailed information about a firm and its work or to focus on how a designer might approach a particular client's design problem. Slide shows are most commonly used because they are relatively easy to assemble and can be customized for each client. Videotape is being used increasingly by design professionals, but a professionally produced video is very expensive and does not allow questions or other interaction from the audience while it is being shown.

Newsletters: A newsletter is an effective way to keep a design firm's name and work in front of a large audience on a regular basis. Newsletters for promotional purposes are well-designed pieces that are sent to past, present, and potential clients, not the in-house type that are intended for the office staff. Newsletters are a relatively inexpensive marketing tool, but to be effective they must be produced on a regular basis, which takes a commitment of time and money.

Advertising: Advertising is any paid communication in some type of media, such as newspapers, magazines, or television. Although once considered professionally unethical, advertising is now being used to reach a wide market. Unlike press releases, articles, and other publicity tools, advertising has the advantage of being guaranteed to reach a given audience because you do not have to depend on the decision of an editor to place your promotion.

B. Public Relations

Public relations (or PR) differs from marketing in that it is not tied to a particular potential job or single potential client. Rather, it establishes and communicates the firm's presence to various groups of "publics" on many different levels. It attempts to create a positive image of your firm on the part of some group of people. Of course, the most important audience group a designer tries to communicate with are those people who may need the designer's services or are able to recommend you to others.

A public relations program should be a part of any office's marketing plan. To be effective, a public relations effort must identify who the "public" is and what their needs are, because the design firm is ultimately trying to communicate the overlap of services with the interests of a particular community of people. To get the message across most effectively, all the PR efforts must communicate on the public's terms and in the language they understand best.

There are several ways to promote an interior design firm through good public relations. One of the most common is through a press release. Such a release is simply a short statement concerning some newsworthy event related to the design firm that is sent to appropriate publications with the hope that the editors will use it. These may be local newspapers, trade newspapers, regional magazines, or national trade magazines.

Press releases are one of the most economical ways to publicize a design firm. Unfortunately, many releases never go to press because they are poorly written or incorrectly presented, do not conform to the requirements of the publication, or do not contain anything really newsworthy.

Another excellent form of publicity is an article about one of the design firm's projects in a magazine. It is better to be published in the magazines that clients receive than in a design trade magazine. (Remember, though, that it is flattering to be featured in a design trade magazine, and offprints of the article can be sent to existing and potential clients.) For instance, a bank interior featured in banking magazines will more likely impress other bankers looking for interior design services than if it was shown in an interior design trade journal. Technical articles written by an interior designer can also be used to promote an office name and its services.

Other methods of public relations include organizing seminars or workshops on a topic of interest to your "publics," volunteering for local service groups or projects, getting involved with local politics, winning design awards, and setting up open houses for the public.

5 TRADE SOURCES

A trade source is any dealer, manufacturer, representative, subcontractor, or tradesperson who supplies goods or services to an interior designer. In some cases, a trade source (most often a subcontractor) may not work for or with the designer directly but through a general contractor who is responsible for completing a project. For example, if a client has a contract directly with a general contractor to remodel a house, subcontractors such as carpenters, electricians, and plumbers will work for the general contractor and have no formal agreement with either the designer or the designer's client.

In most cases, trade sources are suppliers who provide information and products to the interior designer. One of the most common sources is the trade dealer. This is a local showroom that has the exclusive right to represent and display one or more manufacturers' lines of furnishings. These showrooms are typically open only to the trade—interior designers, architects, and others who work for end users.

A variation of the trade showroom is the retail furniture dealer, which is available to the general public as well as designers. These stores often carry a large stock and have interior designers on staff to assist retail clients. In most cases they sell merchandise at retail cost to the public but offer trade discounts to interior designers buying for their clients.

Representatives (or reps, as they are called) act as local agents for a particular manufacturer. Their primary services include giving out product information, acting as a contact with the manufacturer they represent, quoting prices, providing samples, giving out catalogs to designers, and generally assisting interior designers and architects with specific questions concerning the product line. They may have showrooms but many times do not. Some reps are independent, meaning that they work for themselves and may represent several product lines from several manufacturers. There are also factory reps who work for one manufacturer exclusively as an employee.

Specialty shops are similar to furniture dealers in that they are open to the public, but they specialize in one or a small number of goods. A lamp store or art gallery are examples of specialty shops. Like furniture dealers, they generally give interior designers and other professionals trade discounts below list price.

Finally, there are craftworkers who specialize in one type of construction or accessory such as furniture making, stained glass, or fiber art. Their working relationship on a project varies with the type of job and the preferred contracting methods of the designer or client. For instance, they may contract with the interior designer or work directly for the client while coordinating their efforts through the interior designer, or they may be hired by the general contractor as a subcontractor.

SAMPLE QUESTIONS

1. A week after furniture has been delivered to the job site, installed in its final position, and signed for by the owner, some damage is discovered before move-in. Who is responsible for correcting the damage?

   1. the owner
   2. the furniture dealer
   3. the trucking company
   4. the general contractor

2. On a small retail project, what type of schedule is the designer most likely to use?

   1. Gantt
   2. CPM
   3. PERT
   4. fast-track

3. The owner of a restaurant calls you and says she would like to hire you to complete a project because she is unhappy with the work the current designer is doing. What should be your FIRST response?

   1. Decline the offer and tell the restaurant owner the original designer must complete the project.
   2. Tell the owner that you could discuss a working agreement only if the other designer were no longer working on the job.
   3. Suggest that you and the other designer work together to complete the project to the owner's satisfaction.
   4. Tell the owner that you would begin work while you were waiting for a letter from the owner stating all contractual relationships had been severed with the original designer.

4. A shipment of furniture is vandalized in a storage area at the job site. Whose insurance will cover the loss?

   1. the interior designer's
   2. the owner's
   3. the contractor's
   4. the furniture dealer's

5. Which business organization allows the most control by its founders?

1. sole proprietorship
2. partnership
3. professional corporation
4. subchapter S corporation

6. After the final design presentation, your client authorizes you in writing to proceed with construction documents and furniture ordering. You write up the purchase orders and check the acknowledgments. Furniture is subsequently delivered, but the client refuses to pay for one sofa, claiming he does not like it and it isn't what he wanted. What should you do?

1. Tell the client that because written authorization to proceed was received he is obligated to pay for all the furniture.
2. Remind the client that the sofa was shown in the final presentation, which he approved.
3. Try to convince the client that the sofa is what he wanted, knowing that you may have to pay for it because you did not have him sign a sales agreement.
4. Pay for sofa because there was no contract proposal for furniture, order a new one, and write off the loss.

7. What would be the MOST appropriate type of marketing for a design firm just beginning business?

1. well-designed business stationery and a quarterly newsletter
2. a direct-mail campaign to targeted client types
3. advertising in local magazines where business is wanted
4. a corporate identification package and a capabilities brochure

8. Which of the following is NOT generally considered a trade source?

1. artisan
2. general contractor
3. manufacturer's representative
4. furniture showroom

9. What type of insurance is LEAST necessary for a practicing interior designer?

1. employee health
2. worker's compensation
3. general liability
4. automobile

10. What type of insurance is an owner NOT required to carry?

1. general liability
2. worker's compensation
3. property
4. errors and omissions

22 PROJECT COORDINATION

1 PROJECT MANAGEMENT

Project management is one of the most important activities of an interior designer. A project manager coordinates the entire process of a job, from its inception to final move-in and post-occupancy follow-up. Project management consists of planning, monitoring, coordinating and directing, documenting, and closing out the job.

A. Planning

The project manager should be involved from the first determination of the scope of work and estimating fees to the final follow-up. Planning involves setting requirements in three critical areas: time, fees, and quality. Time planning is scheduling the work required and making sure there are enough fees and staff to complete it. Methods of scheduling are discussed in Chapter 21.

A fee projection is one of the earliest and most important tasks that a project manager must complete. A fee projection takes the total fee the designer will receive for the project and allocates it to the schedule and staff members who will work on the project, after deducting amounts for profit, overhead, and other expenses that will not be used for professional time.

Ideally, fee projections should be developed from a careful projection of the scope of work, its associated costs (direct personnel expense, indirect expenses, and overhead), consultant fees, reimbursables, and profit desired. These should be determined as a basis for setting the final fee agreement with the client. If this is done correctly, there should be enough money to complete the project within the allotted time.

There are many methods for estimating and allocating fees, including computer programs available for microcomputers. Figure 22.1 shows one simple form that combines time scheduling with fee projections. In this example, the total working fee, that is, the fee available to pay people to do the job after subtracting for profit, consultants, and other expenses, is listed in the lower right corner of the chart. The various phases or work tasks needed to complete the job are listed in the lefthand column, and the time periods (most commonly in weeks) are listed across the top of the chart.

The project manager estimates the percentage of the total amount of work or fee that he or she thinks each phase will require. This estimate is based on experience and common rules of thumb the design office may use. The percentages are placed in the third column on the right and multiplied by the total working fee to get the allotted fee for each phase (the figure in the second column on the right). This allotted fee is then divided among the number of time periods in the schedule and placed in the individual columns under each time period.

If phases or tasks overlap (as they do in the example in Figure 22.1), you can total the fees in each period and place this figure at the bottom of the chart. This dollar amount can then be divided by an average billing rate for the people working on the project to determine an approximate budgeted number of hours that the office can afford to spend on the project each week and still make a profit. Of course, if the number of hours exceeds about 40, then more than one person will be needed to do the work.

By monitoring time sheets weekly, the project manager can compare the actual hours (or fees) expended against the budgeted time (or fees) and take corrective action if actual time exceeds budgeted time.

Quality planning involves determining with the client what the expectations are concerning design, cost, and other aspects of the project. Quality does not simply mean high-cost finishes but rather the requirements of the clients based on his or her needs.

These needs should be clearly defined in the programming phase of a project and written down and approved by the client before design work begins.

B. Monitoring

Monitoring is keeping track of the progress of the job to see if the planned aspects of time, fee, and quality are being accomplished. The original fee projections can be monitored by comparing weekly time sheets with the original estimate. One way of doing this is shown in Figure 22.2, which shows the same example project estimated in Figure 22.1.

In this chart, the budgeted weekly fees are placed in the table under the appropriate time period column and phase of work row. The actual amount of fees expended are written next to them. At the bottom of the chart, a simple graph is plotted that shows the actual money expended against the budgeted fees. The project manager can also plot his or her estimate of the percentage of work completed to compare with money expended. If either line begins to vary too much above the estimated, the project manager must find the problem and correct it.

Monitoring quality is sometimes more difficult. At regular times during a project, the project manager, designers, and office principles should review the progress of the job to determine if the original problems are being solved and if the job is being produced according to the client's and design firm's expectations. The work in progress can also be reviewed to see whether it is technically correct and if all the contractual obligations are being met.

C. Coordinating and Directing

During the job, the project manager (or whoever is responsible for managing the job) must constantly coordinate the various people involved: the design firm's staff, the consultants, the client, the building code officials, and the firm management. The individual efforts of the staff must also be directed on a

Project: Mini-mall | Project No.: 9274 | Date: 10/14/92
Completed by: JBL | Project Manager: JBL | Total Fee: $26,400

Period	1	2	3	4	5	6	7	8	9	% of total fee	fee allocation by phase or task	person-hrs. est.
Phase or Task / Date	11/16–22	11/23	11/30	12/7	12/14	12/21	12/28	1/4	1/11			
SD-design	1320	1320								10	2640	
SD presentation		1320								5	1320	
DD—arch. work			1980	1980						15	3960	
DD—consultant coord.			530	790						5	1320	
DD—approvals				1320						5	1320	
CD—plans/elevs.					1056	1056	1056	1056	1056	20	5280	
CD—details							2640	2640		20	5280	
CD—consultant coord.					440		440	440		5	1320	
CD specs.								1320	1320	10	2640	
CD—material sel.					660	660				5	1320	
budgeted fees /period	1320	2640	2510	4090	2156	1716	4136	5456	2376	100%	$26,400	
person–weeks or hours	53 / 1.3	106 / 2.6	100 / 2.5	164 / 4	108 / 2.7	86 / 2.2	207 / 5	273 / 6.8	119 / 3			
staff assigned	JLK	JLK AST JBC	JLK AST EMW-(1/2)	JLK AST JBC EMW	JLK AST EMW	JLK AST	JLK AST EMW →	JLK SBS BFD	JLK AST EMW			
actual fees expended												

Figure 22.1 Fee Projection Chart

weekly or even daily basis to make sure the schedule is being maintained and the necessary work is getting done.

D. Documenting

Everything that is done on a project must be documented in writing. This is to provide a record in case legal problems develop as well as to create a project history to use for future jobs. Documentation is also a vital part of communication. A written memo is more accurate, communicates more clearly, and is more difficult to forget than a simple phone call, for example.

Most design firms have standard forms for things such as transmittals, job observation reports, time sheets, and the like. These make it easy to record the necessary information. In addition, all meetings should be documented with meeting notes as well as phone calls, personal daily logs, and formal communications like letters and memos.

2 CONTRACT ADMINISTRATION

Contract administration consists of all the activities performed by the interior designer during the time the contract between the owner and the contractor is in force. The duties of the interior designer are itemized in the AIA/ASID General Conditions of the Contract for Furniture, Furnishings and Equipment (A271) if this document is used. The following sections outline some of the more important provisions of this document with which you should be familiar. Additional information on the duties of the designer is discussed in Chapter 20.

A. Submittals

After the contract is awarded, the contractor is responsible for providing submittals called for in the contract documents. These include shop drawings, samples, and product data. The submittals are sometimes prepared by the contractor, but most often they are prepared by the subcontractors, vendors, and material suppliers.

Project: Mini-mall			time												
Phase/People/Departments			1	2	3	4	5	6	7	8	9	10	11	12	total
schematic design	fee dollars	budgeted	1320	2640											
		actual	2000	2900											
design development		budgeted			2510	4090									
		actual			3200										
construction docs.		budgeted					2156	1716	4136	5456	2376				
		actual													
		budgeted													
		actual													
		budgeted													
		actual													
		budgeted													
		actual													
		budgeted													
		actual													
total (cumulative)		budgeted	1320	3960	6470	10,560	12,716	14,432	18,568	24,024	26,400				
		actual	2000	4900	8110										

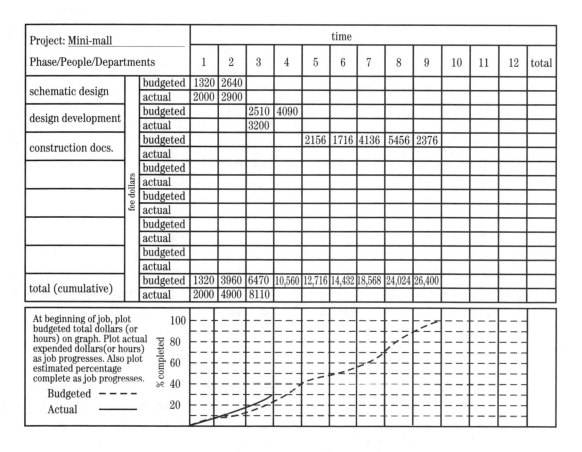

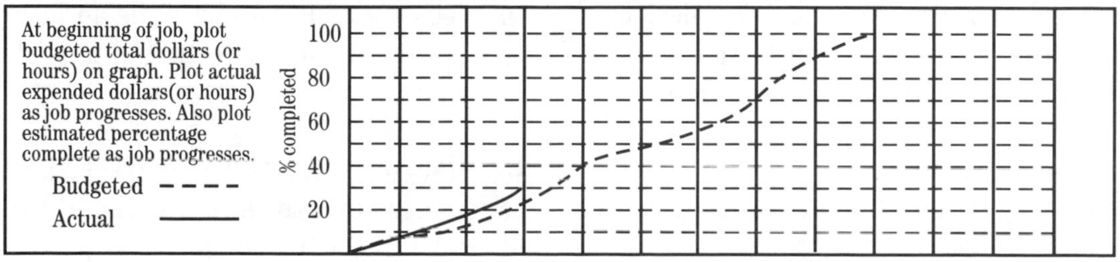
At beginning of job, plot budgeted total dollars (or hours) on graph. Plot actual expended dollars(or hours) as job progresses. Also plot estimated percentage complete as job progresses.
Budgeted
Actual
% completed
100
80
60
40
20

Figure 22.2 Project Monitoring Chart

Shop drawings are drawings, diagrams, schedules, and other data prepared to show how a subcontractor or supplier proposes to supply and install work to conform to the requirements of the contract documents. As such, they are usually very detailed drawings or product data that show how a portion of the work will be constructed. Samples are physical examples of a portion of the work intended to show exactly how a material, finish, or piece of equipment will look in the completed job. They become the standards of appearance and workmanship by which the final work will be judged. Product data include brochures, charts, performance data, catalog pages, and other information that illustrate some portion of the work. Although all submittals show in detail how much of the work is going to be built and installed, they are not contract documents.

When shop drawings and other submittals are prepared by the subcontractors and material suppliers, they are sent to the general contractor who is responsible for reviewing and approving them. By reviewing them, the contractor represents that field measurements have been verified, materials have been checked, and other construction criteria have been coordinated. Only after this review should the contractor send the submittals to the interior designer. If they are not checked and signed by the contractor, the interior designer should immediately return them without review.

The interior designer's review of submittals is only for the limited purpose of checking for conformance with information given and to see if they follow the design intent. The interior designer is not responsible for determining the accuracy of measurements, completeness of details, verifying quantities, or checking fabrication or installation procedures. The interior designer's review does not relieve the contractor of his or her responsibilities under the contract documents. This means, for example, that if the designer does not catch a mistake on the shop drawings the contractor is still responsible for building according to the contract documents and making sure the shop drawings conform to them.

If the submittals require the review of one of the interior designer's consultants, such as an electrical consultant, they are forwarded by the designer to the consultant who returns them to the interior designer after review. The designer then reviews them and returns them to the contractor who, in turn, returns them to the subcontractor or material supplier who prepared them. The interior designer may indicate on the drawings that no exceptions are taken, that marked corrections should be made, that they should be revised and resubmitted, or that they are rejected.

B. Field Administration

As part of basic services, the interior designer visits the project site at intervals appropriate to the stage of construction or as agreed in writing. The purpose is to become generally familiar with the progress and quality of the work and to determine, in general, if the work is progressing in such a way that, when completed, it will be in accordance with the contract documents.

The interior designer, however, is not required to make exhaustive or continuous inspections to check on the quality or quantity of the work. On the basis of his or her observations, the designer must keep the owner informed of the progress and quality of the work. Generally, after each visit, the designer should write a field report and send it to the client with copies to the contractor.

During construction and installation, the interior designer is not responsible for the means, methods, techniques, or procedures of construction, fabrication, shipment, or delivery and installation of the work. Nor is the designer responsible for safety precautions on the job or for acts or omissions of the contractor, subcontractors, or suppliers to carry out the work according to the contract documents.

While visiting the job, the interior designer may notice work that does not conform to the contract documents. In this case, the interior designer may recommend to the owner that the owner reject the work. The interior designer does not have the right to reject work but does have the authority to require special inspections or testing of part of the work to determine if it is in conformance.

Disputes inevitably arise during the work. The General Conditions of the Contract states that the interior designer is the interpreter of the requirements of the contract documents and the judge of the performance thereunder by both the owner and contractor. The designer must render interpretations necessary for the proper execution of the work. Any claims or disputes between the contractor and owner are first referred to the interior designer for a decision in writing. In these cases, the designer must be an impartial judge and render the decision consistent with the intent of the contract documents. If the decision is not accepted by either the owner or contractor, it is subject to arbitration upon written demand of either party according to the contract provisions.

Delays are another fact of life of design projects and one that can create many problems. If a delay is caused by any act or neglect of the owner or interior designer or by changes in the work, labor disputes, fire, and similar causes, the contractor is entitled to an extension of completion time. This extension must be made by a change order for such reasonable time as the interior designer determines. In most cases, the contractor will also ask for additional money to cover the cost of overhead and project supervision caused by the delay. Of course, if a delay is caused by the negligence of the contractor, then no additional time or money is due to the contractor.

C. Changes in the Work

During construction, changes in the work are nearly always required. They may be required by errors discovered in the drawings, by unforeseen site conditions, by design changes requested by the client, by rulings of building officials, and for many other reasons. During bidding and before contract award, changes are made by *addenda.* During construction, changes in the work are accomplished by a written order for a minor change or by formal change order.

When a change does not involve a modification of the contract sum or time and is consistent with the contract documents, the interior designer may issue a written order directing the contractor to make a change. For example, moving a door opening over six inches before it is framed is considered a minor change.

A *change order* is a document authorizing a variation from the original contract documents that involves a change in contract price, contract time, or both. See Figure 22.3. Technically, it is issued by the owner because the owner has the agreement with the contractor, but it is usually prepared by either the interior designer or, sometimes, by the contractor. It must be signed by the owner, interior designer, and contractor.

Any of the three parties may suggest a change order, but normally the interior designer submits a proposal request to the contractor. This is accompanied by supporting drawings or other documents as required to fully describe the proposed change. The contractor submits his or her quotation of price and time change. If these are acceptable to the client, the formal change order document is prepared and signed by all three parties.

D. Progress Payments

During the job the contractor requests periodic payments, usually monthly, against the total contract sum. Under the General Conditions of the Contract, the interior designer is responsible for making sure that the amounts requested are consistent with the amount of work done and the amount of materials stored.

To receive periodic payment, the contractor must submit to the interior designer a notarized application for payment at least ten days before the date established for each payment in the owner-contractor agreement. This application should include the value of work done to the date of the application in addition to the value of any materials purchased and in acceptable storage but not yet incorporated into the work.

Certification of the application for payment constitutes an acknowledgment by the interior designer that the work has progressed to the point indicated and that, to the best of the interior designer's knowledge, information, and belief, the quality of the work is according to the contract documents. Certification is not a representation that the interior designer has made exhaustive on-site inspections or that the designer has reviewed construction methods, techniques, or procedures. Further, certification is not a representation that the designer has reviewed copies of requisitions received from subcontractors and material suppliers or that the designer has determined how and for what purpose the contractor has used money previously paid.

If the application for payment is approved, the interior designer signs it and sends it to the owner for payment. An amount, called the *retainage,* is

Osprey Design Associates

Interior design and space planning

Date 8/16/92

Name Global Transportation Hqs.

To: PQF Constructors
1534 48th Street

Project No. 9231

Location 427 Zeneth Ave.

Change Order No. 1

You are directed to make the following changes in the Contract:

Hardware: Revisions per work authorization #1

Provide 2 ea. 3080, 4 hinge, LH, HM door frames	$ 117.00
Provide 2 ea. 3070, 1-hr. hollow metal doors	$ 482.92
Provide and install 1 ea. 3070 door to replace #12	$ 340.00
Subtotal	939.92
13% O & P	122.19
TOTAL	$1062.11

Original contract sum	$ 227,351.00
Net change by previous Change Orders	$
Contract Sum prior to this Change Order	$ 227,351.00
Contract Sum ☑ increased ☐ decreased by	$ 1,062.11
New Contract Sum including this Change Order	$ 228,413.11
Contract time ☑ increased ☐ decreased by	two (2) days
Revised completion date:	Jan. 15, 1993

Interior Designer	Contractor	Owner
Name	Name	Name
Address	Address	Address
Date	Date	Date
Signed	Signed	Signed

Figure 22.3 Change Order

withheld from each application until the end of the job. This retainage, which is usually ten percent of each application amount, gives the owner leverage in making sure the job is completed and can be used to provide money to satisfy any claims that may arise.

The interior designer may withhold all or a portion of the applications for payment to protect the owner if the designer cannot verify that the amount of work done or materials stored is in conformance with the application. The designer may also withhold payment for any of the following reasons:

- defective work
- third-party claims or evidence of probability of third-party claims
- failure of the contractor to make payments to subcontractors or suppliers
- reasonable evidence that the work cannot be completed for the unpaid balance of the contract sum
- damage to the owner or another contractor
- reasonable evidence that the work will not be completed on time
- persistent failure of the contractor to carry out the work in accordance with the contract documents

E. Installation

Installation is the final placement of furniture, fixtures, and equipment. If the project involves both construction and installation of furniture, one contractor may be responsible for both or there may be two or more contractors. In most commercial work, construction is carried out by one contractor, and the supply and installation of furniture is carried out by one or more furniture installation contractors.

In either case, the interior designer assists with the correct placement of furniture according to the contract documents and answers any questions that may arise. However, it is the owner's responsibility to provide for the following:

- adequate facilities for the delivery, unloading, staging, and storage of furniture, fixtures, and equipment
- the route to be used from the point of delivery to final placement
- that the route is free of unanticipated obstacles or other trades which might impede the installation contractor
- a firm schedule for the contractor for the use of unloading facilities and elevators
- any costs incurred by the contractor due to the owner's failure to conform to the schedule or other delays caused by the owner
- security against loss or damage to the furniture and fixtures stored at the site between the dates of delivery and final acceptance by the owner

The owner is also solely responsible for inspection when the items are delivered, final inspection of the installation, and rejection of any work that is damaged or that does not conform to the contract documents. The interior designer may assist and make recommendations, but the owner has the final authority and responsibility.

When the owner inspects delivery of furniture and fixtures, it is only for identifying them and verifying quantities to provide a basis for payment to the contractor or supplier. It is not final nor does it constitute acceptance of or taking charge or control over the furniture. If any defects are later found before final acceptance, previous acceptance may be revoked by the owner. This is an important distinction because the exchange of furniture may be governed by certain provisions of the Uniform Commercial Code or by state or province laws governing the sale of merchandise.

F. Project Closeout

Project closeout is an important part of the contract administration phase. It is during this time that the construction work is completed, the furniture and fixtures are finally installed, and all remaining documentation takes place.

The contractor initiates closeout by notifying the interior designer in writing and by submitting a comprehensive list of items to be completed or corrected. The contractor must proceed promptly to complete or correct these items. The designer then makes an inspection to determine if the work or a designated portion of it is substantially complete or if additional items need to be completed or corrected.

Substantial completion is defined as the stage of the work when it is sufficiently complete according to the contract documents so the owner can occupy or utilize the work for its intended purpose. The date of substantial completion is important because it has legal implications. For example, in many states, the statute of limitation of errors possibly caused by the interior designer begins with the date of substantial completion. The date is also the termination of the contractor's schedule for the project. If there are any bonuses or damages for late completion, they are based on this date.

The inspection and resulting list of items to be completed or corrected that is developed by the interior designer and owner is called the punch list (or deficiency list, in Canada). The contractor must correct or complete these items, after which another inspection is called for. If the final inspection shows the work is complete, the interior designer issues the certificate of substantial completion. The final application for payment is processed at this time.

In addition to the administrative chores, project closeout also includes other jobs that are important for the office and that create a good impression with the client and provide an opportunity to maintain contact with the client for future work. Some of these project closeout tasks include helping the client with problems during move-in and immediately after, making sure the client has any required operating manuals, and providing the cleaning procedures for finish materials. It is also helpful to both the client and design firm to make follow-up visits at six-month and one-year intervals to review maintenance problems, to look for defects that are covered by guarantees, and to see how materials and other design decisions are withstanding the test of time.

3 POST-OCCUPANCY EVALUATION

The interior designer will often return to the site after the client has occupied it for a time and evaluate how the design is performing. In most instances, this is an informal review undertaken at the interior designer's own time and expense. At other times, the client may hire the designer to do an extensive, formal post-occupancy evaluation. In either case, the exercise provides valuable information on design procedures, materials, construction details, and user satisfaction.

Post-occupancy evaluations try to provide answers to some or all of the following questions:

- Does the final space layout satisfy the original program requirements?
- Is the design image consistent with the stated goals of the client?
- Is adequate flexibility and expansibility provided consistent with the original needs of the client?
- Are rooms and spaces of adequate size for their intended function?
- Were all adjacencies provided for?
- Are finishes holding up to normal wear and tear?
- Are any materials and finishes providing maintenance problems?
- Are construction details adequate for their use?
- Do furniture and fixtures meet the design criteria established during programming?
- Is the furniture selected adequate for the functional requirements of the space and the type of use it receives?
- Are there any ergonomic problems with the furniture selected?
- Is the lighting adequate for the space?
- Are there any problems with the HVAC systems?
- Was adequate power and communication provided for?
- Are the acoustics adequate?
- How did the contractor, subcontractors, and other suppliers perform?

- Is the client satisfied with the project?
- Are the actual users satisfied with the performance and appearance of the finished space?
- What problems have arisen that may be covered by product or contractor warranties?

SAMPLE QUESTIONS

1. The last person to see the mechanical shop drawings before they are returned to the mechanical subcontractor should be the

    1. mechanical engineer
    2. architect
    3. interior designer
    4. general contractor

2. A project is being completed subject to the standard AIA/ASID General Conditions and contract agreement. If some millwork was installed with the incorrect finish, who is responsible if no sample was submitted to the designer?

    1. the millworker
    2. the interior designer
    3. the project manager
    4. the contractor

3. During a routine site visit, you notice a lack of barricades around a floor opening while interior construction is taking place. What should you do?

    1. Point out the situation to the contractor and write a letter to the client stating what you observed.
    2. Tell the contractor to correct the situation.
    3. Write a letter to the contractor with a copy to the owner stating your concern.
    4. Have the contractor stop the work until the problem is corrected.

4. What is the LEAST important part of a project manager's job?

    1. planning job tasks for the project staff on a weekly basis
    2. organizing the layout of the construction drawings
    3. keeping notes on daily decisions and meetings
    4. staying current with the client's opinion of the progress of the project

5. If it appears to the interior designer that the dollar amount requested on the contractor's application for payment exceeds the work completed and material stored, the designer should

1. certify only the amount that the designer believes represents the work completed and stored, and attach a letter explaining why the amount certified differs from the amount applied for
2. return the application to the contractor and request that it be revised to be more in line with actual work done and materials stored
3. reject the application with an explanatory letter attached
4. send the application to the client for his review and opinion about what amount should be certified

6. If an interior designer did not find an error in a dimension on the shop drawings for a custom steel door frame and it was subsequently fabricated, who is responsible for paying to have the mistake corrected?

1. the door frame supplier
2. the wall framing subcontractor
3. the general contractor
4. the interior designer

7. In order to allow the contractor extra time to complete a project because the owner asked for minor changes, the interior designer should issue

1. an addendum
2. a construction change authorization
3. a change order
4. a minor work order

8. A contractor would be within her rights if she asked the owner to provide which of the following?

1. extra insurance for the goods during transit from the warehouse to the site
2. final inspection and acceptance by the owner once the furniture was off the truck
3. extra space for storage and initial preparation of furniture after they were delivered to the site
4. additional workers to help with final installation

9. Which of the following is NOT a typical part of post-occupancy evaluation?

1. review of the HVAC system
2. interviews with representative users of the project
3. a check on maintenance problems
4. suggestions on how the client's next project can be improved

10. A doorway is installed by the contractor according to the drawings. After viewing the job, a building inspector tells the contractor that the door is not wide enough. Who is responsible for correcting it?

1. the framing subcontractor
2. the interior designer
3. the owner
4. the contractor

23 HISTORY

In the NCIDQ examination, questions about history account for three percent of the total content. They cover the identification of major periods and styles in architecture, art, and interior design furnishings. The questions are all in the identification and application section of the exam and consist of type A and B questions.

In addition to testing your knowledge of major periods in history, questions may ask you to associate a well-known building with its architect, identify a painter with an art style, or know who designed a particular chair. You may also be asked to identify the name of an architectural element based on a drawing. Although questions are drawn from all of history, the majority tend to ask about artists, architects, and interior design developments in the twentieth century.

Because the field of possible test questions is so vast and because history accounts for such a small portion of the exam, this chapter does not attempt to summarize over 2000 years of history. Instead, the major developments in art, interior design, and architecture are presented to help you review the overall sequence of eras and refresh your memory concerning important architects, artists, and interior design developments.

As you review the chapter, if any historical period seems unclear, you should study it in more detail by referring to the references listed in the bibliography. You should also concentrate on reviewing history in the 20th century. Finally, the sample questions at the end of the chapter will give you a sense of what to expect on the exam.

B.C. 3000

Periods and Art History

EGYPTIAN
c. 3000 B.C.–330 B.C.

Interiors and Furniture

Plaster and fresco were used to finish interior walls.

Chairs, stools, and tables were made of wood.

Loose cushions covered with cotton or leather were used on some furniture.

Architecture

Common buildings were built of sun-dried brick and wood. Temples and tombs were built of granite and finished with carved limestone.

Great pyramids at Giza, c. 2500 B.C.

Mortuary temple of Queen Hatshepsut, c. 1450 B.C.

Temple of Amen-Re, Karnak, c. 1280 B.C.

Temple of Ramses II, 1257 B.C.

Palace at Edfu, c. 237 B.C.

B.C. 600

GREECE
650 B.C.–30 B.C.

Depiction of the human figure became more representational in both painting and sculpture.

Caryatids, or female figures, were sometimes used in place of columns.

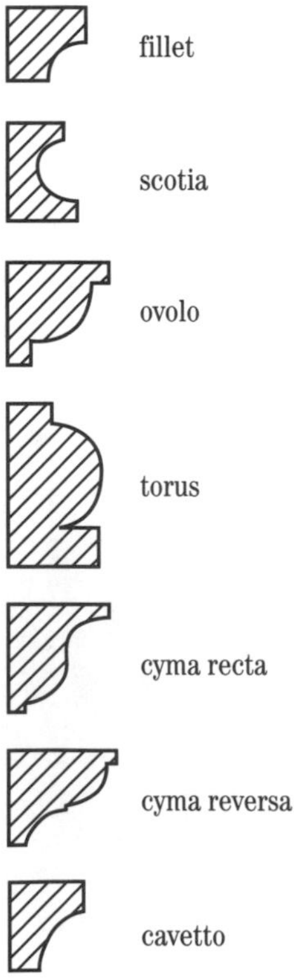

Figure 23.1 Molding Profiles

Moldings were used extensively in both Greek and Roman architecture for decorative effect and to divide a surface into smaller parts. Greek moldings used free-form curves while Roman moldings used geometric curves as shown in Figure 23.1.

Frescoes were used as wall murals and mosaics were used for flooring.

Greeks used proportion and geometry in planning their buildings.

Marble and limestone are used for most monumental buildings.

Three primary styles, or orders, are the Doric, Ionic, and Corinthian.

Major portions of the upper part of an order are shown in Figure 23.2.

Major buildings of the era:
- Temple of Apollo. c. 450 B.C.
- Parthenon, c. 440 B.C.
- Erechtheum, c. 410 B.C.

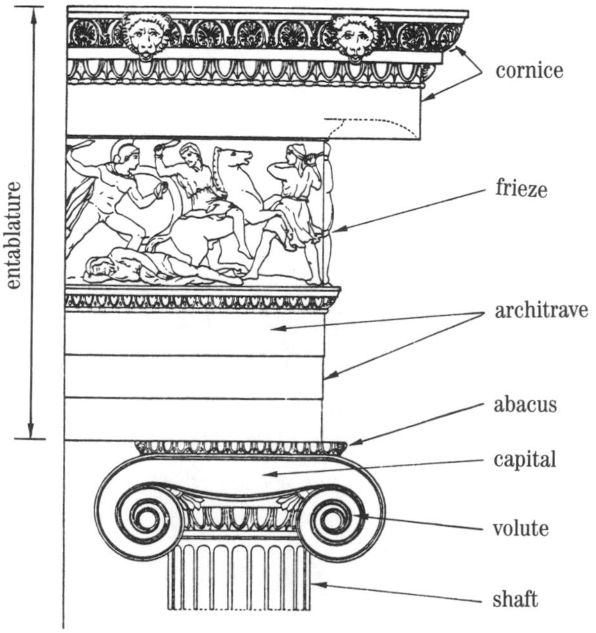

Figure 23.2 Ionic Order

Periods and Art History

ROME
500 B.C.–A.D. 365

Roman art represented space as surrounding the objects of the composition rather than just as something between them.

Mosaics were also used as art.

Alexander conquers Persia and Egypt, 332 B.C.

Destruction of Pompeii, 79 A.D.

Column of Trajan, 117 A.D. Carved with marble reliefs.

MIDDLE AGES—Includes the Early Christian, Byzantine, Romanesque, and Gothic.

EARLY CHRISTIAN
325–800
Constantine recognized Christianity, 325.

Art styles changed primarily in subject matter rather than in style of previous Roman periods.

BYZANTINE
330–1450

Symbolic interpretation of reality began to dominate Christian art.

Mosaics continued to be used in artistic expression.

Interiors and Furniture

Mosaics, stucco, and frescoes were used to finish interiors.

Interiors were elaborately painted with landscape scenes and figures, and buildings were depicted as framed views.

Architectural elements such as columns and arches were painted to frame a panel in which an architectural scene was painted.

Furniture, made of wood, consisted of chairs, stools, dining couches, beds, and cabinets.

Wool and linen were available as textiles.

Colored glass was used to decorate church windows.

Mosaics and tesserae of reflective glass were used extensively in the many churches built during the era.

Architecture

Principle building types included amphitheaters, circuses, baths, forums, and temples.

Romans developed the circular arch, barrel vault, and dome and were the first to model architectural space and interiors. Coffered ceilings and pilasters were used.

Concrete was used for walls and other compressive members were faced with stone.

Romans refined the Greek orders and added two more: the Tuscan and the Composite.

Pedestals were used as columns, which became the prototype for the dado of later periods.

Interior courtyards and atriums were used, which became the model for later cloisters and enclosed quadrangles.

Major buildings of the era:
 Pantheon, 120–124 A.D.
 Colosseum, 70–82 A.D.
 Baths of Caracalla, c. 215 A.D.
 Circus Maximus, from 46 B.C.

Churches dominated the architecture of the Christian era.

Old St. Peter's in Rome (333+) influenced subsequent church design with central nave, side aisles, narthex, and apse.

Santa Costanza in Rome, c. 350, used the central plan, a circular form surrounded by a barrel-vaulted corridor, or ambulatory.

Hagia Sophia, 532–537

Church construction used domes set on on a square base, making the transition with pendentives.

Timeline markers (left column): B.C. 500, B.C. 0 A.D., 200, 300, 400, 500

Periods and Art History

ROMANESQUE
800–1150

Stone relief carving was used extensively on the stone buildings of the era, including column capitals, tympanums, friezes, and other parts of the building.

Norman conquest of England, 1066

Universities were formed, 12th and 13th centuries.

GOTHIC
1140–1500

First accurately dated use of stained glass, 1144, at St. Denis. Stained glass was an integral part of cathedral architecture and replaced frescoes as a way to decorate walls.

Craft guilds protected artisans.

Women took on new importance in life, art, and religion. Cult of the Virgin Mary.

Black death, 1346–1348

Sculpture of human forms an integral part of church interiors and entries.

Timeline: 800, 900, 1000, 1100, 1200, 1300

Interiors and Furniture

Interiors were decorated with mural paintings of religious subjects.

Dominated by the vertical line. Exposed beams were common in castles and large houses. Floors were made of stone, brick, or tile.

Wood wainscot paneling was used in both church and domestic settings.

Furniture design was similar in form to architecture. Oak was used for woodwork and furniture.

Fireplace came into use in the 14th century.

Architecture

Romanesque architecture is characterized by geometric masses of easily definable rectangles, cubes, cylinders, and half-cylinders.

Exterior wall surfaces begin to reflect the interior organization of the structure.

Vaulted roofs of stone were used as in the church of St. Philibert at Tournus, c. 950–1020.
Speyer Cathedral, c. 1030–1060
Pisa Cathedral and campanile, 1053–1272

Church of St. Denis, 1140–1144, prototype of the Gothic style.

Skeletal construction and pointed ribbed vaults allowed light to flood interiors. Flying buttresses allowed the support of walls from the exterior. The ribbed vault made it possible for the crowns of arches to be at the same level.

Major buildings of the era:
 Chartres Cathedral, 1194–1220
 Notre Dame, 1163–1250
 Amiens Cathedral, 1220–1236
 Reims Cathedral, 1225–1290
 Cologne Cathedral, 1248–1322

Standard cathedral plan organization was developed. See Figure 23.3.

Westminster Abbey, 1245–1269
Florence Cathedral, 1296–1436
Doges Palace, Italy, 1345–1438

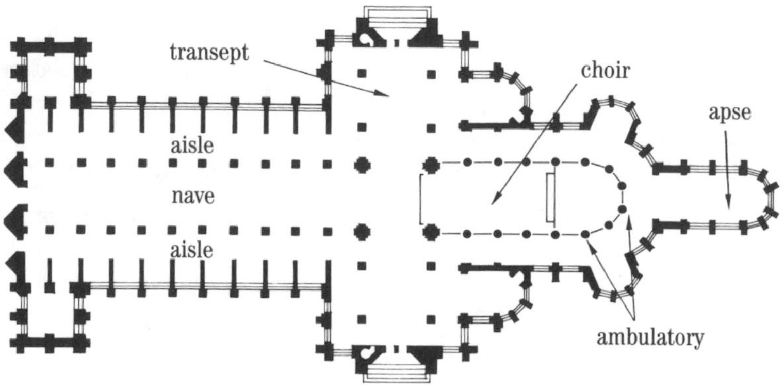

Figure 23.3 Parts of a Cathedral

	Periods and Art History	Interiors and Furniture	Architecture
1400	**RENAISSANCE** **1400–1600**	Renaissance interior space is bisymmetrical and horizontally oriented.	Classical elements were applied to contemporary buildings.
	Great importance was placed on the arts with leading families becoming patrons of artists.	Western tapestries were first used after 1400.	Dome of Florence Cathedral, 1420–1436, by Brunelleschi.
	Ghiberti's *Gates of Paradise* doors on the Baptistry of Florence Cathedral, 1425–1452.	Pedestals, pilasters, columns, pediments, and panels were used for both structural and ornamental purposes.	In Italy, pallazzos were divided into horizontal sections with different treatments, becoming visually lighter toward the top. Pallazzo Medici-Riccardi, 1444
1450	Gutenberg invented printing with movable type, 1450.	Windows and doors were trimmed with stone, plaster, and moldings.	
	Conquest of Constantinople by the Turks, 1453	Colored marble was used for walls and trim. Frescoes, tapestries, and velvets were used on walls.	Santa Maria Novella, c. 1458–1470, by Alberti.
	Linear perspective was invented by Brunelleschi and used in paintings and building design.	Paintings were used extensively on walls and ceilings of churches and palaces.	Proportion and mathematics were used by both Alberti and Brunelleschi to design facades.
1500	Copernicus published his planetary theory, 1512. The Protestant Reformation began, 1517.	Wood and plaster were used for ceilings, which were sometimes painted or gilded.	St. Peter's, Rome, 1506–1626 Andrea Palladio (1508–1580) Château de Chambord, 1519+
	Sculpture of the human form began to be separate from architecture. Paintings showed more depth and use of light to model space.	Floors were made of tile, marble, terrazzo, and parquetry.	Château Fountainebleau, 1528
		Furniture consisted of chests, cabinets, trestle tables, and chairs. Oak was used in France and walnut in Italy.	Louvre, Square Court, Paris, 1546
1550	Artists of the era: Jan van Eyck (1390?–1441) Leonardo da Vinci (1452–1519) Albrecht Dürer (1471–1528) Michelangelo (1475–1564) Raphael (Raffaello Santi) (1483–1520) Peter Paul Rubens (1577–1640)		16th-century English architecture followed classical forms with regular and symmetrical planning. St. Peter's completed, 1556–1612
1600	**BAROQUE** **1600–1720**	Palace walls were covered with brocades, velvets, and damasks. Mirrors also covered walls.	Surface enrichment was characteristic of the era with curved forms, elaborate trim, and detail. French Baroque remained more classical than Italian Baroque.
	American early colonial, 1608–1720 Art and architecture were more dynamic than in the Renaissance. Ceiling and landscape painting was used extensively. Galileo constructs the telescope, 1608.	Stucco ornamentation was used extensively.	
		More moveable furniture was used. Furniture was highly ornamented with irregular raised panels and stones, ivory, and other materials used for inlay.	Bernini's baldacchino for St. Peter's, 1624–1633 Sir Christopher Wren (1632–1723)
1650	Great fire of London, 1666 Baroque painters: Annibale Carracci (1560–1609) Nicolas Poussin (1594–1665) Claude Lorrain (1600–1682) Rembrandt (1606–1669) Jan Vermeer (1632–1675)		Palace of Versailles, 1662–1685
1700	Antoine Watteau (1684–1721)	Plate glass was developed in France, c. 1680.	East facade of the Louvre, 1667–1670 St. Paul's, London, 1675–1710

Year	Periods and Art History	Interiors and Furniture	Architecture
1720	**ROCOCO 1720–1760** Style began in France and was based on ornate natural forms like shells. Painting and sculpture is of elaborate, ornate, highly pictorial forms. American Georgian, 1720–1789. Rococo painters: William Hogarth (1697–1764)	Interiors and furniture had more sinuous curves and ornamentation with almost organic forms. Walls were covered with panels, wall painting, and wallpaper. Floors were of wood parquet, marble, and rugs. Furniture was scaled to human proportions and used curvilinear forms.	Classical orders of architecture were not used. Rooms were smaller than previous periods and had curved corners. Homes were divided into specific public and private uses. Pilgrimage church of Vierzehnheiligen, 1743–1772
1750	Jean Honoré Fragonard (1732–1806) Piranesi (1720–1778), *Views of Rome,* c. 1748		
1760	**NEOCLASSICISM 1760–1789** Thomas Gainsborough (1727–1788) Jacques Louis David (1748–1825)	Free forms of Rococo changed to regular curves and straight lines. Wall surfaces were composed symmetrically.	There was renewed interest in classic architectural orders and forms. Petit Trianon, Versailles, 1762–1768
1770	Steam engine was invented, 1769. Beginnings of the Industrial Revolution. American Revolutionary War, 1775 First cast iron bridge, 1779 French Revolution, 1789	Furniture was designed with straight lines and rectangular forms.	Robert Adam (1728–1792)
1780	American colonial painters: Gustavus Hesselius (1682–1755) Robert Fulton (1765–1815) Samuel F. B. Morse (1791–1872) Charles Peale (1741–1827)		State Capitol, Virginia, 1785–1789 by Thomas Jefferson (1743–1826)
1790	John Singleton Copley (1738–1815) Joseph Mallord William Turner (1775–1851) Thomas Sully (1783–1872) Benjamin West (1738–1820)		
1800	**19th CENTURY** Francisco Goya (1746–1828) Jean Auguste Dominique Ingres (1780–1867) Eugène Delacroix (1798–1863)	Openings between rooms became larger and the flow of space improved. Windows on houses were also larger. Jacquard loom was perfected, c. 1800.	Neoclassicism flourished in the first part of the century. Materials and techniques of the Industrial Revolution begin to change architecture. École des Beaux Arts influence, 1806+
1810	American Federal, 1789–1830 American Greek revival, 1815–1840	Design for the first complete bathroom, c. 1810 English Regency period, 1811–1830 Interiors became simpler.	
1820		Greek revival interiors were based on neoclassicism with simple interiors and plain paneling, moldings, and pilasters.	

	Periods and Art History	Interiors and Furniture	Architecture
1830	American Victorian, 1830–1901 Neo-gothic period in England and the United States, 1830–1870	Victorian interiors were a mixed collection of eclectic styles. Interior finishes were simpler, containing walls with unbroken areas and simple moldings and panels. Ceilings were plain.	
	Hudson River school: Asher B. Durand (1796–1886) Thomas Cole (1801–1848)		Houses of Parliament, London, 1836–1852
1840	George Inness (1825–1894) Frederick E. Church (1826–1900) Homer Martin (1836–1897) Alexander Wyant (1836–1892)	Furniture was influenced by the Empire period in France, the Regency period in England, and the Greek revival period in America.	
	Machine construction of carpets, c. 1850	Michael Thonet invented a process for making bentwood furniture.	
1850	James Bogardus erected the first cast iron frame building, 1851. Realism was the dominant art form in the latter half of the 19th century.	Industrial Revolution influenced hand-crafted furniture in the middle of the century.	Crystal Palace, London, 1850
	Bessemer process for manufacturing steel, 1856		First passenger elevator was installed, New York City, 1857.
1860	Arts and crafts movement began. American Civil War, 1861–1865	William Morris (1834–1896)	
	Mid-19th century American painters: James Abbott McNeill Whistler (1834–1903) Winslow Homer (1836–1910) Thomas Eakins (1844–1916)	American interiors of late 19th century used natural wood paneling.	Paris Opera house, 1861–1874
1870	Albert Ryder (1847–1917) John Singer Sargent (1856–1925)		
	Philadelphia Exposition, 1876		Richard Morris Hunt (1827–1895) Henry Hobson Richardson (1838–1886)
	Impressionist painters:		
1880	Camille Pissarro (1830–1903) Alfred Sisley (1839–1899) Claud Monet (1840–1926) Auguste Renoir (1841–1919)		
	The Barbizon school: Jean Baptiste Camille Carot (1796–1875) Honoré Daumier (1808–1879) Jean Francois Millet (1814–1875) Gustave Courbet (1819–1877) Édouard Manet (1832–1883) Edgar Degas (1834–1917)	Ernest Gimson, furniture designer, (1864-1919)	Marshall Field Warehouse, Chicago, 1885–1887 Home Life Insurance Building, Chicago, 1886, first "skyscraper." Galerie des Machines, use of cast iron on a large scale, 1889 Eiffel Tower, 1889

	Periods and Art History	Interiors and Furniture	Architecture
1890	Art nouveau, 1893–1905 Chicago Columbian Exposition, 1893 Post-impressionist painters: Gustave Moreau (1826–1898) Paul Cézanne (1839–1906) Henri Rousseau (1844–1910) Paul Gauguin (1848–1903) Vincent van Gogh (1853–1890) Georges Seurat (1859–1891) Toulouse-Lautrec (1864–1901) Vasily Kandinsky (1866–1944) Henri Matisse (1869–1954)	Elsie de Wolfe (1865–1950) was considered the first American woman professional decorator. Stanford White (1853–1906) was the leading interior designer with architectural firm of McKim, Mead, & White. Electric lights were first used in buildings.	Antonio Gaudî (1852–1926) Victor Horta (1861–1947) Hector Guimard (1867–1942) Burnham and Root's Reliance Building, 1894 Louis H. Sullivan, "form follows function," (1856–1924) Wainwright Building, 1890 Guaranty Building, 1894 Carson, Pirie, Scott Building, 1899–1904
1900		Furniture design at the beginning of the 20th century was similar to the previous era. Art nouveau designs began to be popularized. Arts and crafts movement was at its height in the U.S.	Early 20th-century architecture was largely determined by industrialization and by new materials and methods of construction. Josef Hoffmann (1870–1955) Casa Mila, Barcelona, Antonio Gaudî, 1907.
1910	Cubist artists: Pablo Picasso (1881–1973) Georges Braque (1882–1963) Marcel Duchamp (1887–1968) Juan Gris (1887–1927) Fernand Léger (1881–1955) Art deco, 1915–1940 De Stijl, 1917–1929 Piet Mondrian (1872–1944)	Furniture that was designed by architects for use in their own buildings became prevalent in the 20th century. Rietveld's geometric chair, 1917	Frank Lloyd Wright (1869–1959) Larkin Administration Building, 1904 Robie House, 1907 Taliesin, 1911 Falling Water, 1936–1939 Johnson Wax Administration Building, 1939 Morris Store, San Francisco, 1949 Guggenheim Museum, 1943–1959 The Bauhaus, 1919–1923
1920	**MODERNISM 1920+** International style, 1920–1975+ Surrealist painters: Paul Klee (1879–1940) Marc Chagall (1887–1985) Max Ernst (1891–1976) Joan Miró (1893–1983) René Magritte (1898–1967) Salvador Dali (1904–1989) Museum of Modern Art opened, 1929.	Marcel Breuer developed the continuous tubular steel frame chair, 1925. Danish furniture designers: Kaare Klint (1888–1954) founder of modern Danish furniture design Søren Hansen (1905–) Arne Jacobsen (1902–1971) Finn Juhl (1912–) Børge Mogensen (1914–) Hans Wegner (1914–) Barcelona chair, 1929	Mies van der Rohe (1886–1969) German Pavilion, Barcelona, 1929 Tugendhat House, 1930 Lakeshore Drive Apartments, 1949–1951 Farnsworth House, 1950 Seagram building (with Philip Johnson), 1956–1958 Walter Gropius (1883–1969) Fagus works, 1911 Shop Block, 1925–1926 Deutsche Werkbund exhibition, 1930

Periods and Art History

1930 Alexander Calder (1898–1976)
Henry Moore (1898–1986)

Plexiglas was invented, 1930.

Norman Bel Geddes' House of Tomorrow, 1931

Nylon was invented, 1937.

Fluorescent lighting was demonstrated, 1939.

1940 Abstract painters:
- Hans Hofmann (1880–1966)
- Josef Albers (1888–1976)
- Laszlo Moholy-Nagy (1895–1946)

Free-form shapes were common in painting, interiors, and furniture.

Abstract Expressionist painters:
- Mark Rothko (1903–1970)
- Willem de Kooning (1904–)
- Franz Kline (1910–1962)
- Jackson Pollock (1912–1956)
- Robert Motherwell (1915–1991)

1950

Post-war building boom began.

Interiors and Furniture

American Institute of Interior Designers was founded, 1931.

Swedish furniture designers:
- Josef Frank (1885–1967)
- Bruno Mathsson (1907–)

Alvar Aalto developed molded and bent birch plywood chair, 1934.

Finnish furniture designers:
- Eliel Saarinen (1873-1959)
- Alvar Aalto (1898–1976)

Knoll Furniture Company was founded, 1938.

Charles Eames' molded plywood dining chair, 1946.

Eames house, 1949

Suspended ceiling systems came into widespread use.

Harry Bertoia's wire chairs, 1952

Alexandar Girard's J. Irwin Miller house, with Eero Saarinen, 1952, first use of sunken conversation pit.

Eero Saarinen's unipedestal chair and table, 1957

Some interior design firms began to specialize in office planning.

Architecture

Le Corbusier (1887–1965)
- Villa Savoye, 1929–1931
- Unité d'Habitation, 1946–1952
- Notre Dame du Haut, Ronchamp, 1955

Eero Saarinen (1910–1961)
- TWA Terminal, 1956–1962
- General Motors Research Laboratories, 1955
- Hockey Rink, Yale University, 1959
- Dulles International Airport, 1960–1963

Alvar Aalto (1898–1976)
- Viipuri Library, 1927–1934
- Paimio Sanatorium, 1929–1933
- Dormitory at MIT, 1947–1949

Philip Johnson (1906–)
(influenced by Mies van der Rohe)
- Four Seasons restaurant in the Seagram Building, 1959
- Glass House, 1949
- New York State Theater, Lincoln Center, 1964
- Pennzoil Place, 1977
- AT&T Headquarters, 1978

Louis Kahn (1901–1974)
- Yale Art Gallery, 1951–1953
- Salk Research Center, 1965
- Richards Medical Research Building, 1957

I. M. Pei (1917–)
- East Wing of the National Gallery, 1978
- National Center for Atmospheric Research, 1967
- Louvre addition, Paris, 1989

Other notable architects:
- Kevin Roche
- Paul Rudolph
- Skidmore, Owings and Merrill
- Edward Durell Stone

1960

1970+

Periods and Art History

Pop art, 1960:
 Richard Hamilton (1922–)
 Jasper Johns (1930–)
 Robert Rauschenberg (1925–)
 Roy Lichtenstein (1923–)
 Claes Oldenburg (1929–)
 Andy Warhol (1927?–1987)

Optical art:
 Victor Vasareley
 Frank Stella
 Kenneth Noland
 Ellsworth Kelly

POST-MODERNISM 1974+

Interiors and Furniture

Systems furniture and office landscaping was popularized.

Interior Design Educators Council was founded, 1962.

Edgar Kaufmann, Jr., Conference Rooms, Alvar Aalto, 1964

Astroturf was invented, 1965.

Ergonomic seating developed.

Workstation design continued to be developed.

Interior designers of note:
 Davis Allen
 Benjamin Baldwin
 Ward Bennett
 Charles Pfister
 Warren Platner
 John Saladino
 Joseph D'Urso

Architecture

TWA terminal, 1962

Rebellion against International style began in 1960s.

Ford Foundation Building, Kevin Roche and John Dinkeloo, 1967

Minoru Yamasaki (1912–)
 McGregor Conference Center, Wayne State University, 1958
 Reynolds Metal Office Building, 1959
 World Trade Towers, 1975

Energy crisis affected building design.
Beaubourg museum, Paris, 1977, Richard Rogers and Renzo Piano.

Richard Meier (1934–)
Charles Gwathmey (1938–)
Robert Stern (1938–)
Michael Graves (1934–)
Robert Venturi (1925–)
Charles Moore (1925–)

SAMPLE QUESTIONS

1. Identify the component labeled A in the drawing below.

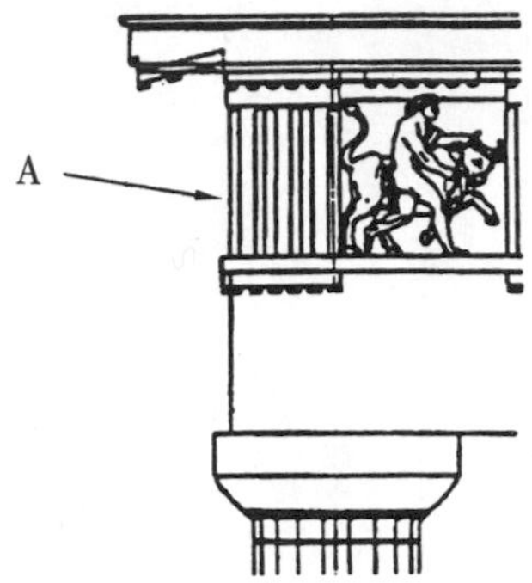

1. entablature
2. cornice
3. frieze
4. architrave

2. Tapestries were first used in the western world during which period?

1. Byzantine
2. Gothic
3. Renaissance
4. Baroque

3. What period attempted to unite art with technology?

1. De Stijl
2. Arts and crafts
3. Bauhaus
4. Art nouveau

4. Which building did I. M. Pei design?

1. Pennzoil Place
2. Dulles International Airport
3. World Trade Center
4. East Wing of the National Gallery

5. What development in furniture design did Alvar Aalto, Søren Hansen, and Charles Eames participate in?

1. the use of bent wood for structural support
2. widespread adoption of molded plastic
3. the Danish modern movement in the 1950s
4. the design of modular units

6. During which period was terrazzo first commonly used?

1. Gothic
2. Renaissance
3. Baroque
4. Modern

7. Who influenced Frank Lloyd Wright's early design work?

1. Henry Hobson Richardson
2. Louis Sullivan
3. Walter Gropius
4. Hector Guimard

8. Which architect is famous for designing a building and a particular chair to be used in it that has become a design classic?

1. Eero Saarinen
2. Frank Lloyd Wright
3. Le Corbusier
4. Mies van der Rohe

9. With what style is René Magritte associated?

1. cubist
2. surrealist
3. French baroque
4. impressionist

10. The portion of a church that is at right angles to the main axis is called the

1. transept
2. nave
3. apse
4. ambulatory

24 SAMPLE PRACTICUM PROBLEMS

The NCIDQ examination has three separate practicum sections. These portions test the candidate's ability to interpret information, devise a solution, and communicate the solution graphically. All the practicum questions are at the C level and are jury graded. They consist of programming (2 hours), a three-dimensional exercise ($1^1/_2$ hours), and a design scenario ($2^1/_2$ hours).

1 PROGRAMMING

The programming scenario is divided into two parts, each with equal grading value. The first part simulates a client interview. You are given a brief description of a common programming situation and must then identify the information that is missing or ambiguous. You do this by either writing the eight most critical questions to gather the information needed to proceed with the design or by selecting the eight most important questions from a longer list of possible questions. You then write a brief explanation of why you selected the questions you did. In either case, the written response should be very short, one or two sentences at the most. In addition, each response or question selection must relate to a separate programming concept or need. For example, there should only be one question asking for information about adjacencies or furniture requirements. The individual programming concepts or topics you should look for in the questions probably include eight of the following:

- number of people
- spaces required
- adjacencies
- circulation
- expansion
- furniture requirements
- equipment requirements
- reuse of furniture
- open versus closed
- time of use of a space
- cost
- phasing

The second part of the programming scenario requires that you interpret programming information and make a graphic representation of it. This usually involves reading a list or matrix of adjacencies and drawing a bubble diagram to show the major and minor relationships.

There is a total of six points for the programming scenario, three for the first part and three for the second. Selecting or writing four correct questions is worth one point, six questions earn two points, and eight questions earn you three points. You receive one point if you indicate the primary adjacencies in the bubble diagram. Showing the overall interrelationships gives you one point, and conveying the information in a generally acceptable graphic format is worth another point. To pass, you must receive a minimum of two points, one in the interview and one in the interpretation section.

A. Client Interview Sample Problem

A small general practitioner's office is planning to move to a new building due to growth in the practice. There are four doctors, a receptionist, two nurses, a lab assistant, and a part-time bookkeeper. Six examination rooms are needed in addition to a separate file room and two toilet rooms. The amount of space to be leased in the new building will be based on your programming study.

From the following list, select the eight MOST important questions that you would need to ask to collect more information to proceed with planning and designing their new space. After you have selected the eight questions, write a brief explanation in the space provided of why you selected each question.

1. What specialty does each doctor practice in?
2. What types of special lighting are required?
3. How much is the practice expected to grow in the next two years?
4. Do the doctors ever consult with each other?
5. How often does the bookkeeper work in the office?
6. Do the doctors require an office next to a private examination room?
7. How do the nurses work with the lab assistant and the doctors?
8. What is the age span of most of the patients?
9. How large are the examination tables?
10. What types of activities does the lab assistant engage in?
11. Are patients in wheelchairs frequently seen in the office?
12. What type of furniture do the doctors currently use and is it adequate?
13. Are most patient records computerized or in paper form?
14. What type of atmosphere do you want to create in the reception area?
15. How are patients commonly routed from the time they enter the reception area until they leave?
16. What ceiling height is required?
17. How much time does a typical patient spend in the office?
18. What kinds of durable finishes are required in the lab area?
19. How much time does each doctor spend outside the office on hospital rounds or other professional activities?
20. What types of major diagnostic testing are done in the office?
21. Do the nurses, bookkeeper, and lab assistant need separate work areas?
22. What is the budget for construction?
23. How many patients does each doctor see in an hour?
24. Is a conference room required?
25. How many patients are usually in the reception area waiting to see the doctors?
26. Does the receptionist sit in the waiting area or behind a counter?

Write your reasons for selecting the questions in the following spaces.

B. Program Interpretation Sample Problem

Based on the information shown below for a small branch bank, draw a bubble diagram using circles, blocks, lines, or other typical graphic elements to illustrate the major and secondary relationships. The graphic elements indicating spaces must show approximate scale relationships between the rooms. Include a legend with your diagram.

	receptionist area (250 sq. ft.)	customer service (500 sq. ft.)	loan officers (400 sq. ft.)	tellers (600 sq. ft.)	conference room (225 sq. ft.)	president (250 sq. ft.)	safe-deposit vault (600 sq. ft.)	main vault (200 sq. ft.)	break room (275 sq. ft.)	counting room (200 sq. ft.)	storage room (125 sq. ft.)	service entrance (50 sq. ft.)
receptionist area (250 sq. ft.)												
customer service (500 sq. ft.)	●											
loan officers (400 sq. ft.)	●	●										
tellers (600 sq. ft.)	●	●	○									
conference room (225 sq. ft.)	○	○	●									
president (250 sq. ft.)	○		●	○	●							
safe-deposit vault (600 sq. ft.)	○	●										
main vault (200 sq. ft.)				●			●					
break room (275 sq. ft.)				○	○	○						
counting room (200 sq. ft.)				●			○	●				
storage room (125 sq. ft.)				○						●		
service entrance (50 sq. ft.)				○		○	○	●		●	●	

primary relationships ●
secondary relationships ○

2 THREE-DIMENSIONAL EXERCISE

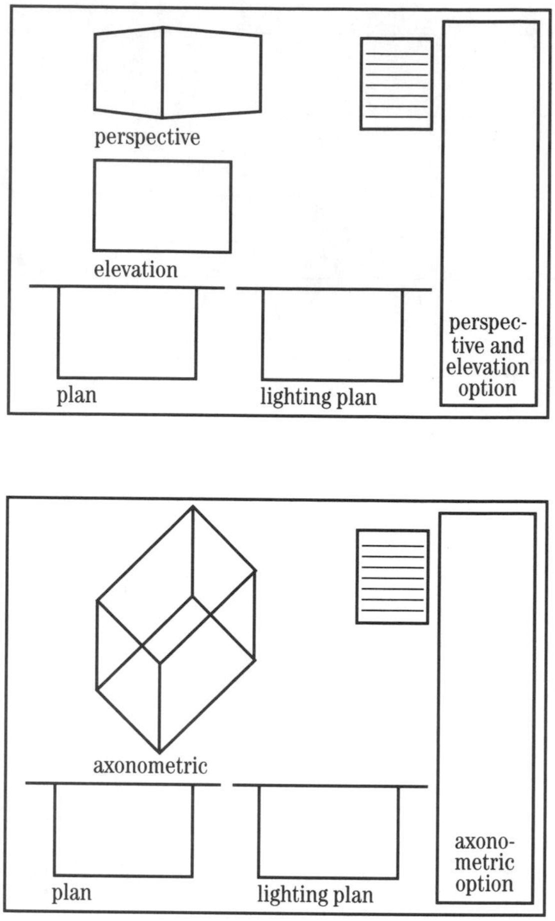

Figure 24.1 3-D Practicum Drawing Sheets

The Three-Dimensional Practicum tests your ability to apply the principles and elements of design with an integrated lighting solution into a three-dimensional volume of space within an existing building context. It also requires that you communicate your solution with some common drawing types.

You may select one of two sets of drawings to use. With the first option you must draw a plan, an elevation, a lighting plan, and a perspective. With the second option you must draw a plan, a lighting plan, and an axonometric. In both cases you must write a brief description about how your solution applies the principles and elements of design. You use one of two sheets of vellum provided, one for the perspective option or one for the axonometric option. There are areas for the plans and 3-D drawings outlined along with a little box in which you explain your design. Try to fit your explanation within the box. The vellum sheets you use are similar to the ones shown in Figure 24.1 and simply tell you where to place the various drawings. To test yourself on the following 3-D problem, use a sheet of 17″ × 22″ vellum for your work.

Although you must do a great deal of work in a short time ($1^1/_2$ hours), the physical extent of the problem is small. For example, the problem may state that your entire solution must fit within a box 14 feet on a side. However, you must include all the basic project requirements in your solution and complete all the required drawings. If you do not your solution will not be juried. All exams are prejuried to ensure that the minimum basic requirements are met. To achieve a passing score, it is necessary to meet the major program objectives as stated in the criteria (client requirements, building constraints, lighting, correct scale).

A brief program is given in the problem statement. You are told to include principles and elements of design along with a lighting scheme that complements the design concept and uses a combination of fixed, movable, and natural lighting (if applicable). You are told specifically which principles and elements to use. There is a total of 15 points in this section, six for principles of design, six for elements of design, and three for lighting. These include the following items:

- *Principles of design* (total of three principles worth two points each): balance, harmony, rhythm, emphasis/focus, proportion, and contrast
- *Elements of design* (total of three elements worth two points each): scale, form, line, color, texture, and pattern
- *Lighting*: overall lighting effect that complements the concept and a combination of fixed and movable lighting plus natural daylight (three points)

Sample 3-D Problem

A trade showroom located in a merchandise mart wants to construct a special area in which to display and feature new chair designs from the manufacturers of transitional and contemporary furniture they represent. The display pavilion must have some sense of enclosure and identify the space and chairs as special features. At the same time, it must be visible so customers in the showroom can see that something is being displayed and so sales staff can assist customers if they see someone looking at the display.

The display area must be contained within an area 10 feet wide, 15 feet long, and 10 feet high and will be placed against one wall of the existing showroom. It should be accessible from at least two of the other three sides. It must accommodate at least three spaces 36 inches square for chairs that can be viewed as well as sat on. In addition, there must be a way to display a small stock of promotional pamphlets for each of the three chairs.

The showroom is finished with warm-gray carpeted floors, fabric covered and painted gypsumboard walls, and natural-finish mahogany base and door trim, and has a suspended acoustical ceiling 12 feet above floor level. The wall against which the pavilion will be placed is an exposed concrete structural wall that has been painted a warm gray to match the other walls. You may leave this wall as it is or cover it within the length of the pavilion.

Design a display pavilion that satisfies the program requirements and that incorporates three principles of design and three elements of design. Use only one of the enclosed two sheets on which to draw your solution. In the box provided on the sheet, write a brief explanation of which principles and elements you are using and how you incorporated them into your solution. Use notes, dimensions, material indications, and other standard drafting conventions to fully describe your solution and use of materials, finishes, textures, and color. Your drawings must also indicate your use of general and specific lighting to enhance the design solution.

If you elect to draw an axonometric, show any ceiling partially removed to show the construction beneath if it would be otherwise obscured by your design.

In order for your solution to be juried, you *must* include all the basic project requirements and complete all the required drawings as well as the written explanation. You may use other tracing paper for design studies, but all final drawing must be done on one of the sheets provided. Only the supplied drawing sheet you use will be juried. Your drawing may be in drafted form or sketched freehand as long as it is legible and communicates your solution clearly.

3 SCENARIO

The Practicum/Scenario evaluates your ability to analyze and interpret a written program, create a space plan, lay out furniture, and develop an accompanying reflected ceiling plan, all within an existing context. You are given a program that includes a description of the existing building, a general outline of the project type, and a detailed listing of the spaces. In some cases, you are simply given the name of the space and a square footage allotment. For other areas, you must plan the space based on a detailed list of the furniture and equipment that must be accommodated. Special requirements for adjacencies, exiting, and barrier-free access are also given.

As with the 3-D Practicum, preprinted vellum drawing sheets are provided, one for the floor plan and one for the reflected ceiling plan. Although you can use sketch paper in your planning, all your final work must be on the sheets provided. The supplied sheets include legends for symbols.

When you register for the test, you may select one of five project types for your scenario exam: corporate, residential, retail, institutional, or hospitality. Although the knowledge tested is identical for any of the selected types, allowing you to choose lets you work in a familiar area. At the same time you select your project type, you have the option of choosing $^1/_8$″(1:100) or $^1/_4$″(1:50) scale. You cannot change your project type or scale once you have registered.

Grading is based on a total of 21 points in six categories as outlined below. You must score a minimum number of points in each of the six sections. The total minimum number of points to earn a passing score is 14.

Planning:

1. Solution includes all required spaces with correct minimum programmed areas.
2. Space is fully utilized with effective proportions of rooms.
3. Required adjacencies are maintained.
4. Relationships and location of the spaces are logical.
5. Circulation easily supports space function and is logical.
6. Visual requirements and acoustical separations are correct.

Candidate must achieve a minimum of 4 out of 6 points.

Code:

7. Access and egress locations comply.
8. Corridors comply.
9. Spaces (other than bathrooms/restrooms) are accessible.
10. Restrooms/bathrooms are accessible.

Candidate must achieve a minimum of 3 out of 4 points.

Lighting:

11. All required lighting is shown.
12. Lighting plan/layout is correct.
13. The type and amount of lighting supports the space.

Candidate must achieve a minimum of 1 out of 3 points.

Technical:

14. Solution respects the existing building shell.
15. Solution respects interior building systems and constraints.

Candidate must achieve a minimum of 2 out of 2 points.

Furniture, Fixtures & Equipment (FF & E):

16. Knowledge of correct use of scale is shown.

17 & 18. All FF&E and storage units requested in program are shown and labeled as necessary for clarity (worth 2 points).

Candidate must achieve a minimum of 2 out of 3 points.

Concept:

19. The concept answers the statement of the design problem for the type of space and its intended use.
20. The solution of the concept is clearly illustrated.
21. The candidate has demonstrated an understanding of the project requirements and has exhibited minimum competency in the solution.

Candidate must achieve a minimum of 2 out of 3 points.

Sample Scenario Problem

College Administrative Offices

A small college of an urban university is expanding its administrative offices as part of the school's campus building program. The college currently occupies a portion of the fifth floor of a midrise building and has exercised its option on adjacent space that recently became available. The college wants to use its existing space for faculty offices and use the new area for administrative functions.

In addition to the administrative area, the new space will be developed as the main entrance to the office suite and contain a small advising area for new and currently enrolled students. The main portion of traffic into the suite will be those who work in the office as well as students coming only for advising. The reception and advising areas should be planned so that student traffic conflicts with office traffic as little as possible. Some teachers may use the main entrance, but most will use a door closer to the existing faculty offices. The new space must be connected to the existing space for access to the faculty office as well as to serve as the second required exit from the space.

Because the administrative office suite is where most new students and visitors get their first impression of the college, the reception and advising area should be pleasant and as open and inviting as possible. Circulation should also be planned to accommodate the high traffic volume of administrators, students, and faculty that use the space every day.

General requirements:

1. The waiting area in the reception space serves both students waiting for advising as well as people waiting to visit administrators and faculty.
2. All areas except the fixtures and counter in the lunchroom must be accessible to the physically disabled.
3. The dean and assistant dean's office require acoustical privacy.
4. Because the new office space overlooks a small park and part of the city, views and natural light should be taken advantage of whenever possible, especially for people who work in the facility.
5. Because the conference room is also used for informal gatherings where refreshments are served, it should be conveniently located near the lunchroom.
6. The visiting faculty office and part-time faculty work areas should be located near the existing faculty offices.
7. The dean's secretary works for both the dean and assistant dean so this space should be adjacent to both offices.
8. Lighting should be planned to provide for an adequate office working environment while creating an inviting space and highlighting the college's collection of three original art works (about 40 inches wide and 30 inches high).

Program requirements:

A. Reception area: The reception area must accommodate entry to the office suite, a receptionist, and a waiting area.

1. The reception station must have a work surface of at least 15 s.f. with a 42″ high transaction counter in front. There should be returns for a computer terminal (18″w × 21″d × 18″h), a small typewriter (17″w × 14″d × 6″h), and a small printer (20″w × 17″d × 10″h). There should also be space for a facsimile machine (18″w × 15″d × 9″h). The telephone will be placed on the work surface.
2. Provide 6 l.f. of lateral files adjacent to the receptionist.
3. The waiting area should have seating for four people with side tables or a coffee table as appropriate. There must be space for a wall-hung literature rack (36″w × 48″h × 4″d) to hold information about the college and curriculum.
4. The reception area should be planned to divert traffic either to the advising area or to the offices.

B. Advising area:

1. There must be two identical advising stations. These should be in an open area but have some provisions for visual privacy.
2. Each station must have a work surface of at least 15 s.f. with a return for a computer terminal (18″w × 21″d × 18″h) and telephone. Provide 6 l.f. of lateral filing adjacent to the station and two visitors' chairs in addition to the adviser's chair.

C. Dean's office: Provide an enclosed office between 240 s.f. and 270 s.f.

D. Assistant dean's office: Provide an enclosed office between 190 s.f. and 220 s.f.

E. Dean's secretary:

1. The secretary will be reusing an existing 30″× 72″ desk with a 16″× 42″ return on the left side of the desk.

2. Provide one secretarial chair and two visitors' chairs.

3. Provide 24 l.f. of lateral files in the secretary's work area.

F. Conference room: Provide a room between 350 s.f. and 380 s.f. located convenient to the lunchroom.

G. Workroom:

1. The workroom must accommodate a copy machine that requires a space 6′-6″ wide and 42″ deep.

2. There must be at least 24 s.f. of work surface for collating, binding, and punching with enclosed storage below.

3. Provide 24 l.f. of lateral files.

4. There should be a minimum of 8 s.f. of lockable closet space.

5. Provide as much overhead shelving as possible.

H. Lunchroom:

1. Provide a minimum of 20 s.f. of counter space with storage above and below.

2. Fixtures and equipment to be accommodated: undercounter refrigerator, single-bowl stainless steel sink, microwave (on countertop), coffee maker (on countertop).

3. Two tables with four chairs at each table.

I. Toilets:

1. Men's: one toilet, one urinal, one lavatory.

2. Women's: one toilet, one lavatory.

3. Toilet rooms must be accessible to the physically disabled.

J. Visiting faculty office: Provide an enclosed office between 150 s.f. and 170 s.f.

K. Part-time faculty area:

1. Provide space for two faculty workstations in an open area. Each should have a work surface with a minimum of 15 s.f. with a task light. One office chair and one visitor's chair must be provided. Provide at least 4 l.f. of lateral files and 6 l.f. of bookshelf space.

2. Provide space for an additional secretary who provides assistance for part-time and visiting faculty as well as overflow work from the dean's secretary. The secretary will require a new 30″ × 72″ desk with a 16″ × 42″ return.

3. Provide one secretarial chair and one visitor's chair.

4. Provide 12 l.f. of lateral files in the secretary's work area.

Building description: The existing building is a typical steel frame midrise structure with the exterior finished in precast concrete column covers and aluminum curtain walls. The floors are poured concrete over steel decking. Interior columns and building core are covered with gypsum wallboard. The building is ten years old and well built but has no distinguishing features.

The new space is in the southwest corner of the building and is to be connected to existing faculty offices to the north as shown on the floor plan. An existing partition separating the new space from the existing space near the window line must remain, but beyond that the connection between the two areas may occur anywhere from the end of this partition to the corridor wall. The views south and west from the new space are equally desirable.

The window mullions are on a 4′-0″ spacing in both directions. Window sills are at 30″ AFF with window heads at 7′-6″. The ceiling must be 8′-6″ AFF and consist of acoustical lay-in tiles in a 2′-0″ × 2′-0″ exposed grid system. All plumbing must be located within 20 feet of the interior wet column.

Presentation requirements: Use the base floor plans provided on the following two pages to draw a floor plan and a reflected ceiling plan. (The base plans have been reduced to 1/8″ scale for publication purposes. You may work at this scale or have the drawings enlarged 200 percent to create base sheets at a 1/4″ scale.) The floor plan must reflect the required sizes and adjacencies of rooms and spaces and must show all partitions, millwork, toilet fixtures, doors, glazing, and other fixed construction. In addition, all furniture must be shown that is itemized in the program requirements, except that only one advising station and one part-time faculty workstation need to be drawn as long as there is sufficient room for both in their respective areas. For rooms defined only with square footage requirements, you need only to show the partitions and door swings. Include room names and other notes as required to fully explain your solution.

The reflected ceiling plan must show the ceiling grid, lights, switching, ceiling height and slab-to-slab partitions, and any other specialty ceiling construction.

In order for your solution to be juried, you must complete *both* the floor plan and reflected ceiling plan. Although you may do preliminary studies on your own paper, all final work must be shown on the two sheets provided. Any sketches, notes, or other studies must be turned in with your solution, but they will not be juried.

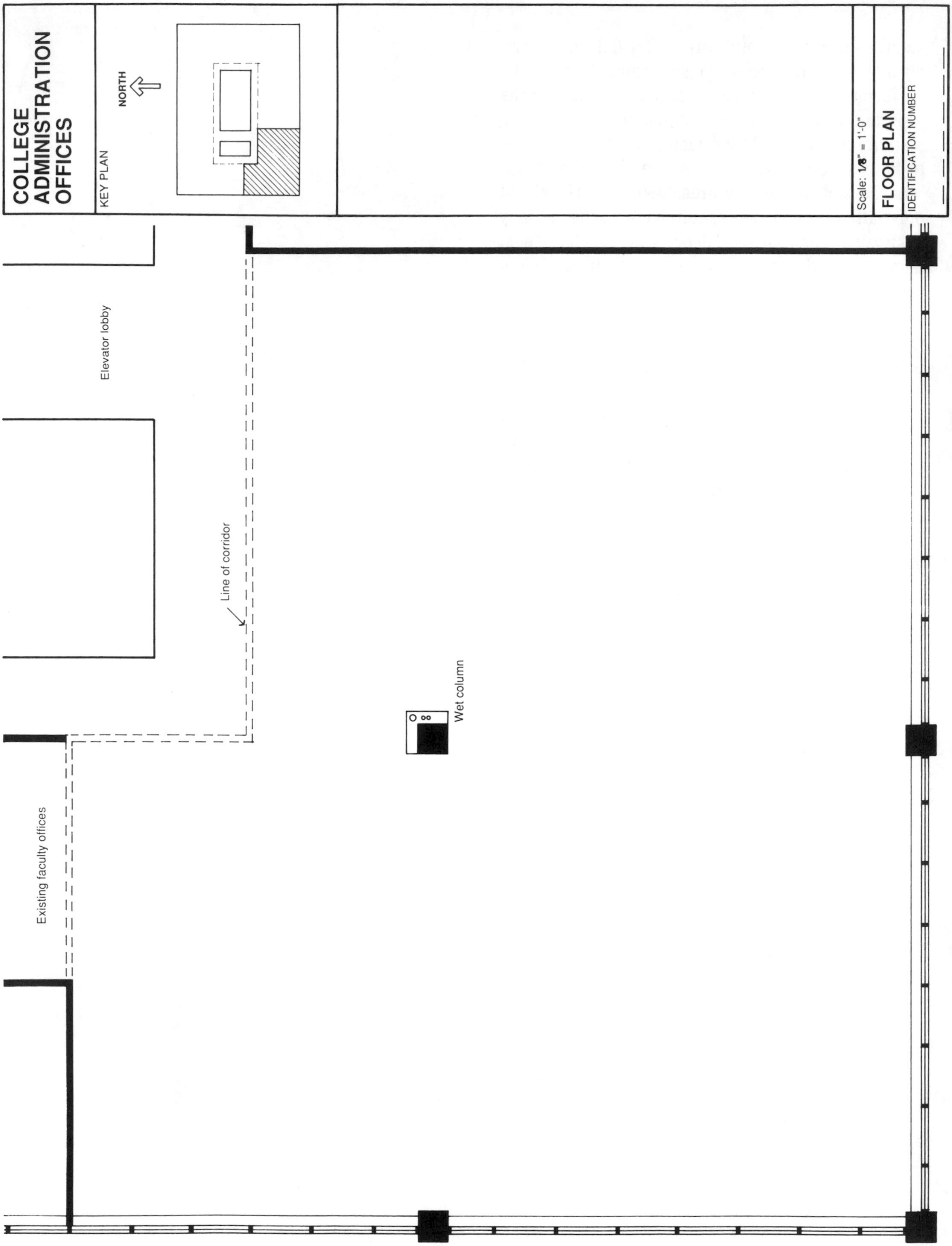
COLLEGE ADMINISTRATION OFFICES
KEY PLAN
NORTH
Scale: 1/8" = 1'-0"
FLOOR PLAN
IDENTIFICATION NUMBER
Elevator lobby
Line of corridor
Wet column
Existing faculty offices

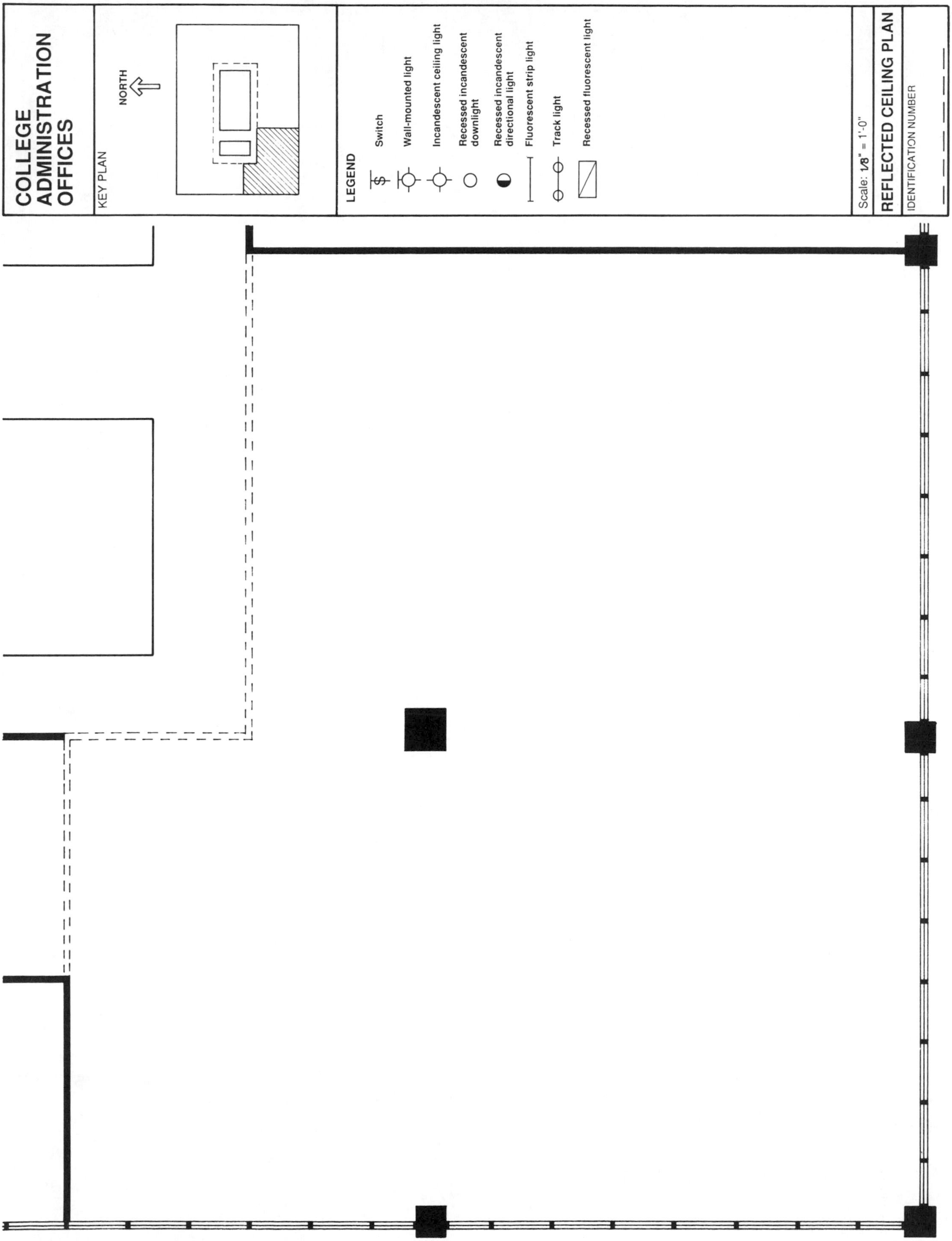
COLLEGE ADMINISTRATION OFFICES
KEY PLAN
NORTH
LEGEND
Switch
Wall-mounted light
Incandescent ceiling light
Recessed incandescent downlight
Recessed incandescent directional light
Fluorescent strip light
Track light
Recessed fluorescent light
Scale: 1/8" = 1'-0"
REFLECTED CEILING PLAN
IDENTIFICATION NUMBER

25 SOLUTIONS

1 ELEMENTS OF DESIGN

1. 2 is correct.

Manipulating scale through the physical placement of walls, ceilings, and other architectural elements would be most likely to create the feeling of intimacy. The use of pattern, texture, and color, while important elements in setting a mood, can be neutralized if the physical size of the space is too great.

2. 3 is correct.

Because warm colors tend to advance and darker values tend to make objects look heavier, answer 3 is the best choice, especially when the sofa is contrasted with a lighter background. Answer 2 is the next most correct response, but there is no indication whether the sofa is a warm or cool hue. A warm color, as in answer 3, would tend to make the sofa appear heavier.

3. 4 is correct.

To accentuate the rough wall, you would want grazing light. Among the choices listed, point sources close to the wall such as recessed incandescents would do the job best. The other types of lighting would tend to flatten the surface.

4. 1 is correct.

This question obviously requires that you know what a Parsons' table looks like. It has a square or rectangular thick top with thick legs set flush with the edges of the top. Such a table is very volumetric but also has a planar quality.

5. 2 is correct.

Because highly saturated, complementary colors reinforce each other, the second combination would create the highest contrast and be the easiest to see for people of all ages. Answer 4 would be the next closest answer, but the description does not explain how the colors and white would be used. For example, a sign with yellow lettering on a white background would be very difficult to see.

6. 1 is correct.

Dark values tend to make surfaces "close in" as do heavy textures. The two in combination would lower the apparent ceiling height.

7. 3 is correct.

The Prang system (also known as the Brewster system) is simply the familiar color wheel with the primary and secondary colors organized in a circle. Answer 4 is not correct because it states five principle hues (used in the Munsell system) rather than the three that the Prang system uses.

8. 4 is correct.

Although wallpaper can be used to show all the answer choices listed, it is most commonly used for pattern because of the repetitive nature of wallpaper printing.

9. 4 is correct.

Answers 2 and 3 are incorrect because they use colors that are widely separated around the color wheel. Answer 1 is incorrect because a monochromatic scheme uses only one hue with variations only in value and intensity.

10. 2 is correct.

As shown in Figure 1.6, as more black is added to a hue (color), it becomes a shade. A tone is created by adding gray.

2 PRINCIPLES OF DESIGN

1. 3 is correct.

All other things being equal, people tend to perceive the color, texture, shape, and other aspects of visual weight more than placement.

2. 2 is correct.

Answer 1 relates more to balance and repetition. Answer 3 describes the principle of emphasis. Answer 4 is incorrect because harmony seeks to unify a composition rather than provide variation even though variation is often part of a harmonious design.

3. 1 is correct.

Gradation is the gradual modification of some feature of a composition, which a series of color changes exemplifies. Answer 3 is incorrect because repetition is the multiple use of an element.

4. 4 is correct.

By definition, bilateral symmetry is organized around only one axis so answer 1 is incorrect. If the composition was asymmetrical the axes would probably not intersect in a common point, so answer 2 is incorrect. Because a radial balance is a type of symmetrical balance, answer 3 could be considered correct, but the question states that the three or more axes intersect in a common point, which makes it more likely that such a composition is radial.

5. 1 is correct.

Although all four answers could emphasize the object, answer 1 uses location, position, and lighting to focus attention on the item. Answer 3 is the next choice, but because the question does not specify what the item is, making an oversized model may distort its image.

6. 3 is correct.

Because the different table tops are related to each other by a common characteristic (the identical bases), this best represents harmony. The symmetrical balance of the equally spaced and distributed tables represents a secondary principle that would probably not be as visible as the difference in table tops. Variety is incorrect because the table tops are closely related to the bases.

7. 1 is correct.

The Golden Proportion is a line divided such that the ratio of the smaller length is to the larger length as the larger length is to the whole.

8. 3 is correct.

9. 1 is correct

Answer 2 is incorrect because the question does not give any information about how the photographs are grouped and whether they form a regular pattern. Answer 3 is incorrect because no single framed photograph would be different enough from the rest to create a significant contrast. Answer 4 is incorrect because if all the frames are different, no single one dominates.

10. 4 is correct.

From the diagram there is no apparent size relationship among the different forms and no relationship to an object of known size, so answers 1 and 2 are not good choices. Answer 3 is incorrect because there is no repetition of a regular pattern even though the forms are all circles.

3 HUMAN FACTORS

1. 1 is correct.

All the answers are important considerations for well-designed chairs, but because several people would be using the same chair for long periods of time, the chairs would have to be adjustable to accommodate variations in body size.

2. 3 is correct.

Answer 3 is least important because glare on the screen is a function of the lighting design more than the workstation design. All the other answers relate to items that you could control with the workstation design alone.

3. 2 is correct.

Identical furnishings organized around an imaginary (but perceived) line divides the room into two equal territories that each person could then personalize. Answer 1 is incorrect because personal space relates to actual distance, and the question gives no information about the size of the room or exactly how it is arranged.

4. 4 is correct.

Proxemics is the application of knowledge about personal space needs to actual space planning. Determining the design of seating where people will be close to each other is the most likely situation of the four choices where proxemics would be used.

5. 2 is correct.

Social distance, including both the close and far phase, ranges from about 4 to 12 feet. Answer 3 is incorrect because it includes only the far phase of social distance.

6. 3 is correct.

Because the question mentions an accessory and ease of use, a simple table fan would be the most logical suggestion to make. Creating air movement would increase evaporation from a person's skin, thereby cooling it.

7. 2 is correct.

Anthropometrics is primarily concerned with measuring the size of the human body and developing dimensional ranges within which certain percentages of a given population fall. Such raw data would be directly useful in comparing the height, depth, and other aspects of the benches with the percentages of children fitting those dimensions. The other answers relate more to ergonomics, or the interaction of the human with the environment.

8. 1 is correct.

Answers 2 and 3 directly relate to how much heat would be generated in the room and how much ventilation would be needed, both of which the mechanical engineer would have to design for. The reflected ceiling plan would tell the engineer what type of ceiling was planned and give an idea of the heat load generated by the lights. As long as the engineer knew the primary occupancy was elderly persons, the exact age is of little concern.

9. 3 is correct.

Tapestries served all four purposes listed, but the primary advantage was to decrease heat loss through radiation by covering the cold stone walls with an insulating material. This, in effect, raised the mean radiant temperature.

10. 3 is correct.

Of the four choices listed, only the interior designer would have the best knowledge of the use of the conference room, which might suggest increasing the ventilation or providing extra exhaust. In the other three situations, the ventilation and exhaust requirements would be evident to the engineer and in most cases governed by the building code.

4 PROGRAMMING

1. 3 is correct.

It is very likely that information concerning the other three questions would be available from a good, complete set of construction drawings. A field survey would be most necessary to determine what sources of noise exist and their magnitude.

2. 1 is correct.

Answer 2 is incorrect because there are usually more design concepts than there are programmatic concepts. Answer 3 is incorrect because a programmatic concept is a performance requirement, not the other way around. Answer 4 is incorrect because design concepts are based on and generated after programmatic concepts.

3. 2 is correct.

Answers 1, 3, and 4 relate directly to decisions about the location or size of elements in the store. If restrooms are provided at all (which they probably would be) they would be positioned away from the sales area whether or not they were available for customer use.

4. 4 is correct.

Because programming interviews consume so much time and often require two people to conduct and because interviewees tend to talk more than is necessary, interviews are a very *inefficient,* although valuable way to verify information.

5. 1 is correct.

Regardless of how the information is collected, area is based on the usable space (net area) that a client needs to perform a function. For example, the client knows that a 150-square-foot office is required but does not think of the corridor required to get to it or the thickness of walls to create it. Based on the net area and a knowledge of the project type, the programmer can estimate how much additional space is required, either the gross area or the rentable area.

6. 3 is correct.

By using the word *department* the question implies that the company is large and will occupy a multistory building and thus will occupy multiple floors. To show overall departmental relationships (rather than individual space relationships) a stacking diagram is used. Then individual block diagrams or bubble diagrams are developed for each floor.

7. 1 is correct.

The options given in answers 2 and 4 are possible but would require that you make guesses and do a lot of work before the client would review the problem with you. Answer 3 is risky because the adjacency that you are having difficulty achieving may turn out to be the most important one for the client, while the ones you have achieved may be unimportant to the client. Answer 1 lets the client clarify the programming adjacencies and, if necessary, modify them so you can proceed with good information. If the client does want to see some sketches to prove that the required adjacencies cannot be made to work, you already have these available.

8. 4 is correct.

The programming method to which the question refers was described in Problem Seeking and uses the four considerations of form, function, economy, and time.

9. 2 is correct.

Answers 3 and 4 are important but would be issues considered after the overall feasibility of the project has been determined. Answers 1 and 2 are very close to being the preferred response, but answer 1 would require additional costs to the client even before the feasibility was determined. In addition, in a case like this, a client is not likely to have a good grasp of the costs required for remodeling and may not have enough of a budget to do the job as he wants to.

10. 2 is correct.

The space in a laundry workroom would be determined more by the size, number, and configuration of equipment than by the limited number of people who would operate the equipment. The other choices all are highly dependent on the number of people that must be accommodated.

5 SPACE PLANNING

1. 4 is correct.

Layout 4 is the only one that satisfies both criteria. Layout 3 is also very efficient but not good for frequent visitor conferences because it is difficult for the worker to get to his or her desk and the arrangement of the visitor chairs makes talking awkward.

2. 4 is correct.

This is the standard BOMA (Building Owners and Managers Association) method of measuring lease space and one that is generally followed in the industry.

3. 2 is correct.

Although all the answers would have some influence, the actual dimensions (which would include the existing structural columns and walls) would determine if the proposed restaurant would even fit within the space available. This would be the most important thing to determine before worrying about plumbing or reuse of millwork or lighting fixtures.

4. 4 is correct.

An atrium could be incorporated into any of the concepts listed, but it is most often used in a central scheme where most of the functions focus on the atrium and its activities.

5. 2 is correct.

A nurses' workstation requires much record keeping and temporary and long-term storage of a variety of items. Answer 2 includes provisions for most of the elements that require a large amount of space, including patient files and movable carts. Answer 4 is incorrect because communication equipment and electrical outlets alone do not contribute significantly to the space required for the nurse's station.

6. 1 is correct.

Because a waiting area is generally filled with strangers who prefer not to share the same sofa, a layout that provides individual seating is best, which eliminates answers 2 and 4. Answer 1 is better than answer 3 because it makes it easier for people to circulate to and from the chairs and it minimizes the number of people facing each other if all chairs are occupied.

7. 2 is correct.

This is an obvious answer because the question relates to corridors, while answer 2 is the only one that describes exiting from a *room.*

8. 3 is correct.

Because a double-loaded corridor serves rooms on both sides of it in a straight line, this is the most efficient. A radial system and grid system generally have a much higher proportion of corridor to space served than a double-loaded system.

9. 1 is correct.

The fireplace size (although important in final planning) is the most detailed aspect of the choices and would probably affect the overall design and feeling of the space the least.

10. 4 is correct.

The information listed in answers 1, 2, and 3 could easily be determined by simple inspection. The adequacy of the air supply would have to be determined by a mechanical consultant, but the number of diffusers can easily be counted. Even water pressure for one additional sink could be verified by turning on a faucet. Answer 4 relates to structural considerations and the feasibility of cutting through a bearing wall, which may not be obvious to an interior designer.

6 COST ESTIMATING

1. 1 is correct.

Because general contractors add their overhead and profit charges (anywhere from about 10 percent to 20 percent) to all subcontracted work, the client would be paying that much extra for the appliances without the general contractor doing much work for the extra cost. Answer 4 is incorrect because the interior designer could get about the same discount for the client as the contractor could without the contractor's markup.

2. 3 is correct.

The base cost of the partition is \$45.00 times 350 feet or \$15,750. To that you must add an additional 14%:

$$0.14 \times \$15{,}750 = \$2{,}205$$

$$\$15{,}750 + \$2{,}205 = \$17{,}955$$

For preliminary budgeting, amounts are often rounded off to the nearest ten or one hundred dollars. \$17,950 is the closest to the figure so this is the correct answer.

3. 3 is correct.

Because the two lowest bids are so close, it is likely that they represent a true indication of the cost for the restaurant as designed rather than an overbid. Although the client has the option of trying to get more money, it is generally the designer's responsibility to be within ten percent of the expected bid. For this reason, the designer should offer to help the client redesign as necessary to reduce the cost.

4. 3 is correct.

Carpeting is a finish item (like paint or ceiling tile) that is attached to the construction and is typically part of the construction contract. Even though a sculpture is physically attached to the construction, it is commissioned directly with the artist and may be included in the FF&E budget. Vertical blinds are sometimes included in the construction contract but not as commonly as wall-to-wall carpeting is. Vending machines can also be part of a construction contract, but if there is both a construction and FF&E contract, they are usually part of FF&E. Although all four of the items mentioned may be part of either contract as the client wishes, the question asks which is *generally* not.

5. 2 is correct.

Answer 1 is incorrect because cost books are dated by the time they are published. Answer 3 is not the best choice because it does not account for current variations in prices or the unique nature of the job you are working on. Answer 4 is a possibility, but given the choice between designers and contractors, the contractors are most likely to be the best source of data.

6. 2 is correct.

Refer to the text for a complete explanation of cost items. Answer 1 is incorrect because it is missing professional fees. Answer 3 is incorrect because it does not include furnishings, an obvious, major component of an interior project. Answer 4 is incorrect because it is missing professional fees and telephone installation.

7. 4 is correct.

A quantity takeoff is the most detailed method, and therefore it is the most accurate.

8. 1 is correct.

Legal fees and specialty consulting like artwork advice are often separated from the construction and furnishing budget that the interior designer prepares. The items in the other three choices can be estimated by the interior designer (unlike legal fees) and are often placed in the designer's budget work.

9. 3 is correct.

10. 2 is correct.

Because the furniture dealer and interior designer are the two people closest to the specification and ordering of furniture, answer 2 is correct. Furniture manufacturers, general contractors, and clients are seldom, if ever, involved in budgeting furniture.

7 CONSTRUCTION DRAWINGS

1. 1 is correct.

The reflected ceiling plan should show slab-to-slab partitions as well as ceiling-high partitions. Although the information is usually indicated on wall-section details and sometimes on interior elevations, the reflected ceiling plan is the one place where they are all shown at once in an obvious manner.

2. 3 is correct.

Refer to Figure 7.15.

3. 3 is correct.

The interior designer is ultimately responsible for coordinating the drawings of the various consultants.

4. 4 is correct.

An underfloor raceway system uses metal enclosures buried in the concrete floor slab. The selection would obviously involve the electrical consultant and the architect because this is part of the architectural work. The structural engineer would also be involved because the size, spacing, and configuration of the system affects the thickness of the slab and its reinforcing.

5. 2 is correct.

Although all the information listed in the answer choices needs to be included, the most important is the clearance provided near the ceiling to allow the paneling to be installed. The installation of the panel is not really affected by the thickness of the wood cleat or the size of the base.

6. 3 is correct.

A scribe piece allows for field cutting so the edge of a cabinet or countertop can be trimmed to fit exactly the irregularities of the wall. A reveal can also be used to disguise the irregularities of the wall, but the question asks about a good fit, which implies direct contact between the cabinet and the existing construction. A reveal piece can also be a scribe piece, but the answer choices include a scribe.

7. 1 is correct.

This is a symbol for a three-way switch, which allows control from two locations. Refer to Figure 7.17. A four-way switch allows control from three locations.

8. 3 is correct.

Because windows are part of the architectural work in a building, a window schedule would not be found on interior drawings.

9. 3 is correct.

Refer to Figure 7.17.

10. 3 is correct.

Sometimes outlets are shown on the furniture plan and on the partition plan in small residential projects, but they would always be found on the power plan.

8 CONSTRUCTION SPECIFICATIONS

1. 1 is correct.

The first choice is the simplest and most reliable because it puts the entire burden on the contractor and painting subcontractor to match what you want. They are the people most likely to have the knowledge and experience to make the match. Also, by putting the notes on the drawings and specifications, the general contractor would be responsible for correcting the finish if it did not match.

2. 4 is correct.

A base bid with approved equal specifically lists one product and requires that the interior designer has final approval before any other product is substituted. The other choices leave the exact choice up to the contractor. Although a reference or performance specification could be written to make it very likely that the final product was acceptable, the base bid would assure it.

3. 3 is correct.

The ceiling suspension main runners are a descriptive specification. The hangar wires are a reference standard specification. The runners are also a reference standard specification because the wording refers to the reference standards of the studs.

4. 3 is correct.

Part 3, Execution, is the portion of any standard specification section that always contains installation or application requirements.

5. 2 is correct.

The courts have held in many past cases that information in the specifications takes precedence over the other documents in the case of conflicts. This provision is often written into contracts.

6. 3 is correct.

The specifications should be outlined and begun while the drawings are being done. The specifications writer and the job captain should be in constant contact while both documents are being completed to minimize conflicts.

7. 1 is correct.

The methods in answers 2 and 3 are useful in writing concise specifications but are not as good as using industry standards, which eliminate a great deal of text. Answer 4 is incorrect because a descriptive specification requires lengthy text to fully and accurately describe what the specifier wants.

8. 3 is correct.

Cost estimates are never placed in the project manual because the project manual is used for bidding. Including a cost estimate would defeat the purpose of bidding.

9. 4 is correct.

A proprietary specification calls out one single item by brand name, manufacturer, and model number. With a proprietary specification, you can also require that a sample be submitted to further verify that you will be getting what you want, but this method alone is not the best way.

10. 2 is correct.

Answer 1 is incorrect because both the interior designer and client must agree to the use of a contractor-selected product. Answer 3 is incorrect because the alternate product must be reviewed and approved by the interior designer, not just the contractor. Answer 4 is incorrect because the intent of the "or approved equal" language is to permit equal products, although sometimes the alternate does turn out to be better than the one specified.

9 CONTRACT DOCUMENTS AND BIDDING PROCEDURES

1. 2 is correct.

Although the bid form is often bound in the project manual along with the specifications, it is not part of the contract documents because it is only a proposal.

2. 3 is correct.

The contractor should always request approval in writing so the interior designer can review the information about the tile and make a determination whether the specification was an "or equal." If the request is approved, the interior designer would issue an addendum to all contractors telling them that the new product was approved.

3. 4 is correct.

The best way to get the lowest price is to open the project for bidding, so this eliminates answers 2 and 3. Because the project is a specialized building type, it would be best to use only prequalified bidders who have had experience with data processing facilities. This leaves answer 4 as the best choice.

4. 1 is correct.

Answer 1 describes the standard procedure that is written into most general conditions, including the AIA General Conditions for the Contract for Furniture, Furnishings, and Equipment. Answer 4 is close, but the response does not specify whether or not the contractor notifies the designer in writing. In addition, although the contractor often suggests how to solve a problem, that is the designer's responsibility.

5. 3 is correct.

The General Conditions states that the interior designer may only recommend to the owner that the owner reject work.

6. 4 is correct.

A labor and material payment bond is designed to pay subcontractors and vendors in case the general contractor defaults on his or her payments for labor and materials provided. When subcontractors or vendors are not paid for their work, they can file liens against the property. A performance bond provides money for completion of a project should the general contractor default but does not provide for payment of past due bills on the original construction.

7. 2 is correct.

Because bond money is a fixed amount, the budget must be met, so this eliminates answer 1. Rebidding takes additional time and does not guarantee that the new bids will be any better; in fact, they may be higher because prices will probably increase in the time it takes to rebid. This eliminates answer 3. You may want to wait for the city to tell you what to do, but the project must go forward. The amounts of the bids are so close to the budget that it is likely that costs could be reduced by four percent with some adjustment in the scope of the project.

8. 3 is correct.

9. 1 is correct.

The General Conditions clearly states the contractor may ask for such evidence.

10. 2 is correct.

All projects, no matter how small, should be completed under some form of written agreement, which answers 1, 3, and 4 indicate.

10 FURNITURE, FIXTURES, AND EQUIPMENT

1. 2 is correct.

Theater seating requires a fabric that is resilient, durable, and flame retardant. The only combination that meets these requirements is the wool/nylon blend.

2. 1 is correct.

A medical waiting area with a high usage would benefit from a firmer cushion. Cotton batting and low-density polyurethane do not meet this requirement. Also, any material with a low ILD (indentation load deflection) implies a soft cushion.

3. 3 is correct.

Because institutional furniture takes much abuse and must last a long time, its durability is important. This suggests answer 3 or 4 because quality can be considered a measure of durability. However, cost is usually an important factor in furniture selection for this type of client, so answer 3 is the best.

4. 4 is correct.

Answers 2 and 4 create the greatest hazard. However, welt cording provides the most likely condition where a cigarette could lodge and start a fire.

5. 2 is correct.

There are two ways you could select the best answer for this question. One of the most important tests for this application would be for wearability. This includes the Wyzenbeek and Taber tests, so answer 1 is eliminated. Because only one wearability test would probably be needed, this eliminates answer 3. An indentation load deflection test is for cushioning and the question asks about the fabric only so this eliminates answer 4.

Another way to view the question is to realize that wearability, flammability, and fading are three important standards for any custom-blended fabric in a public area. This leaves you with a choice between answers 1 and 2. Because they both include a fading test, you must choose whether wearability or flammability is more important. Any fabric can be flame-retardant treated, but only testing can determine if a custom fabric has sufficient wearability for a specific use, so answer 2 is the better choice.

6. 2 is correct.

This is the Brno chair designed by Mies van der Rohe.

7. 2 is correct.

Although Class A fabric chars the least of the four classifications, it still does char but will not ignite.

8. 2 is correct.

Although chemical retardants and interliners are important considerations in upholstery flammability resistance, the combination of surface fabric and cushioning affects it the most.

9. 3 is correct.

Rayon is one of the least desirable fabrics in general and specifically has very poor resistance to fading from sunlight.

10. 4 is correct.

Because channeling is a method of attaching fabric to a cushion and direct attachment is the best way to avoid slippage, answer 4 is the best choice.

11 INTERIOR CONSTRUCTION

1. 1 is correct.

Answer 2 is incorrect because you could use a solid-core wood door in a steel frame to meet the conditions. Answer 3 is incorrect because a smoke-proof opening can be achieved with a wood door as well as a hollow metal door. Answer 4 is a possible choice, but minimal maintenance under heavy use does not necessarily imply a metal door.

2. 4 is correct.

A mortise lock offers a variety of locking functions and is durable enough for the heavy use of an office building. The other types of lock could be used, but they are not the *most* appropriate.

3. 1 is correct.

Refer to Figure 11.12.

4. 1 is correct.

Refer to Figure 7.19 for material indications for rough wood and gypsum wallboard.

5. 4 is correct.

Plenum access precludes the use of gypsum wallboard for the ceiling. Both integrated ceilings and linear metal strip ceilings provide for some access, but their cost in a large commercial project would not be warranted. An integrated ceiling may be a good choice, but the question does not give enough information about the parameters of the problem to make this a reasonable choice.

6. 3 is correct.

Caulking or sealant seals the gap between butt glazing. Glazing tape or putty cushions the glass against the frame. Setting blocks support the weight of the glass and separate it from the bottom frame.

7. 2 is correct.

Refer to Figure 11.16.

8. 1 is correct.

In any situation that involves or might involve a structural question, an engineer or architect should be consulted.

9. 2 is correct.

The noise created by a door closer might be objectionable for the short time the door was closing, but it would have no effect on the privacy once the door was closed.

10. 2 is correct.

A resilient channel allows the gypsum wallboard attached to it to "bounce" when sound strikes it and minimizes the transmission of sound through the wall.

12 FINISHES

1. 1 is correct.

Type I vinyl wallcovering is the lightest weight of the three types and is appropriate for residential use. There is no Type IV wallcovering.

2. 3 is correct.

Both the Axminster and Wilton processes allow for complex patterns, but only the Wilton allows for varying pile heights.

3. 1 is correct.

The entry to a restaurant is a place that could be slippery due to spills or people tracking in snow, mud, or water, so a rough surface is best. A flamed finish granite would have the roughest surface of the four choices given.

4. 3 is correct.

Parquet flooring can be mastic-applied easily over most existing residential subfloors or finished floors or over a new subfloor. On a square-foot basis, the parquet would be least expensive considering both materials and installation.

5. 4 is correct.

Both nylon and polyester carpet over a cushion would be acceptable choices for this application. Of the two remaining choices, wool would be the least desirable because of its high cost, which could be substantial in a building with a large floor area, such as a hotel.

6. 1 is correct.

7. 3 is correct.

Although the sheet material indicated in the drawing may help minimize squeaking, the fact that a wood floor is shown over a concrete floor should indicate that it is a vapor barrier.

8. 1 is correct.

Because slate does not have a uniform thickness and a concrete subfloor above grade may deflect and cause cracking, the best installation is a thick-set method with cleavage membrane. The thick-set method allows the tile setter to adjust the bed according to the exact thickness of each stone, and a cleavage membrane (with reinforcement) allows the finish floor to float above any slight deflection of the concrete floor.

9. 2 is correct.

Sheet vinyl minimizes the number of joints and is resistant to grease, oils, and water.

10. 2 is correct.

Pitch is the number of ends of surface yarn in a 27-inch width. To convert this measurement to gauge (the spacing between stitches) divide 27 into 216. This gives 8 stitches per inch, or 8 surface yarns per inch. Its equivalent gauge is therefore $^1/_8$.

13 LIGHTING

1. 3 is correct.

Of the choices given, the electrical engineer is responsible for designing the circuiting, panel box layout, and other technical aspects of a lighting layout. The interior designer may choose the types of fixtures, lamps, and light and switch locations, but a detailed drawing stamped by a licensed electrical engineer is required for submission to the building department. The one exception to this is on small projects, such as residences, where the electrical contractor can handle technical issues such as wire sizes, circuits, and the like and have the job approved and inspected by the building department. However, because the answer choices included "electrical engineer," this is the better choice.

2. 4 is correct.

MR-16 lamps are the smallest of the choices given and could fit within the small area of a display case. They are also tungsten halogen lamps, which give good color rendition and sparkle to jewelry.

3. 2 is correct.

Refer to Figure 13.4.

4. 2 is correct.

Footlamberts describe brightness either reflected or transmitted from a source or surface and account for the projected area, that is, only the area that you see when looking at the source.

5. 1 is correct.

Any lights in the ceiling of a drafting room are reflected off plastic triangles, parallel bars, and similar instruments causing veiling reflections.

6. 4 is correct.

Answer 1 is not the best action because you can easily lower the illumination below an acceptable level. Answer 2 is a possibility and may ultimately be necessary, but other options should be explored first as the question asks what you should do to begin redesign. Answer 3 is also a possibility, but the original design was developed for a reason and your first action should be to try to make that work. Answer 4 allows you to leave everything the way it is, changing only lamps. If this investigation did not bring the design within the budget, then you could explore the other options consistent with your design.

7. 3 is correct.

Metal halide lamps are the best choice because they have a high efficacy (80 to 120 lumens per watt) and good color rendition. These two advantages would militate against using mercury vapor lamps, which have a longer life.

8. 2 is correct.

Although all the choices are possible reasons for using surface-mounted luminaires, they are most often employed when space is inadequate for recessing.

9. 2 is correct.

In a fabric showroom, accurate color rendition is an important concern. Therefore answers 2 and 4 are the most likely choices. Although the color temperature rating of a lamp gives a general indication of its "whiteness," the color rendering index (CRI) is a more accurate indication of how appropriate it is for a specific application.

10. 1 is correct.

Any design with provided direct lighting as in answers 2, 3, and 4 might result in reflections off the screens. Because the question does not state that the video display terminals are in known locations, an ambient/task light system is best.

14 MECHANICAL SYSTEMS

1. 3 is correct.

A convector transfers heat from a hot water system to the air. A grille may control the distribution of air but has no provisions for controlling the volume of air. A duct simply directs the transfer of air from one point to another.

2. 1 is correct.

An all-air system can be subdivided into as many individually controlled areas as needed. Radiant panels could be used, but it would be awkward to locate them in the ceiling and the cost would be much higher than that of an all-air system.

3. 4 is correct.

Most building codes do not allow any combustible material in a return-air plenum (the space above the suspended ceiling). Electrical cable is allowed if it is enclosed in steel conduit.

4. 2 is correct.

The interior designer would not determine conduit size or put speaker locations on the power plan. This eliminates answers 3 and 4. Switch locations would be placed on the reflected ceiling plan.

5. 1 is correct.

Upright sprinklers disperse the water upward so coverage is provided above and below the suspended wood slat ceiling.

6. 2 is correct.

Refer to Figure 14.4.

7. 1 is correct.

New window coverings can affect the exterior appearance of a building and the heat load, which affects the mechanical system. Also, they can put additional heat stress on the glass, causing cracking or breaking. Although light reflectance might be affected, it would be minor and probably not affect the overall light quality in the room.

8. 2 is correct.

Refer to Figure 7.17.

9. 3 is correct.

If space is at a premium and the floor-to-floor dimension is fixed, you must minimize the number of treads and the width of each one so the shortest possible total run is achieved. You can minimize the number of treads by using the 8″ riser, which is allowed by code in this type of use. (It requires 16 risers 7 inches high or 14 risers 8 inches high to equal 9′-4″. In turn, 16 risers require 15 treads while 14 risers require only 13 treads.) Because codes also allow a minimum 9-inch tread in residential uses like this, an 8-inch riser and 9-inch tread is the best combination (9″ times 13 treads requires a total run of only 9′-9″).

10. 2 is correct.

Computer cable and electrical conduit are commonly placed in access floors, such as below computer rooms. Duct work is also allowed. Plumbing is not allowed because pipe breaks can cause problems.

15 ACOUSTICS

1. 2 is correct.

Impact isolation class and sound transmission coefficient are both important ratings for evaluating transmission loss through a floor/ceiling assembly.

2. 2 is correct.

Because a change in intensity level of 3 decibels is considered just perceptible, you would probably be better off not using the material regardless of how low the added cost was. Trying to modify the material to 6 dB would also probably not be worth the trouble.

If you needed an STC rating of 6 dB or higher, you would be better off looking at another construction assembly instead of trying to make do with a modified material. Answer 4 could be correct if the material was such that simply doubling it would result in a 6 dB increase rather than modifying it, but the question does not include enough information to make this determination.

3. 1 is correct.

Answers 2, 3, and 4 are all important considerations in controlling noise both within a room and from being transmitted from outside the room. A large ceiling might be useful for applying sound-absorbent material, but the size of the ceiling is already determined by the time design development begins.

4. 2 is correct.

The assembly shown would not be the best for controlling impact noise (because it is a partition) or mechanical vibration, so these two answers are incorrect. Although the partition construction shown would be good for preventing sound transmission in both directions, it would be *better* from room A to room B. This is because noise transmission between two rooms is dependent on the transmission loss of the wall, the area of the wall, and the absorption of the surfaces in the *receiving* room.

5. 3 is correct.

Refer to Table 15.2, which shows that any change above 5 dB is clearly noticeable.

6. 2 is correct.

This is a repeat of question 9 in Chapter 11. If you take all parts of the exam at one sitting, you may find questions repeated on the test, but in different sections.

7. 3 is correct.

For interior partitions, insulation is only good to dampen sound within the cavity of the partition.

8. 1 is correct.

Changing from wallboard to acoustic tile affects the total absorption of a room and thereby changes the reverberation time.

9. 2 is correct.

A vaulted ceiling would focus sound reflections into one concentrated area and produce annoying echoes or quiet spots in the hall.

10. 3 is correct.

Although placing absorptive materials on both sides of the wall would not hurt and would decrease the noise level in the "noisier" room, the three most important variables are the transmission loss of the wall, its stiffness (damping qualities), and its area.

16 COMMUNICATION METHODS

1. 2 is correct.

If just the top of the building is shown, it is a roof plan. If the surroundings are shown, it is a site plan.

2. 1 is correct.

Answers 2 and 3 refer to an isometric drawing. Answer 4 refers to an isometric or elevation-oblique drawing and could refer to a perspective drawing.

3. 2 is correct.

Orthographic drawings assume the impossible situation that your eye is perpendicular to every point on an object at the same time when, in fact, we see something in perspective from only one point of view, even when standing directly in front of it.

4. 4 is correct.

Refer to Figure 16.11.

5. 3 is correct.

Even for laypersons, perspectives show the most realistic view of three-dimensional space on two-dimensional media.

17 BUILDING CODES

1. 3 is correct.

The Uniform Plumbing Code and similar model codes base toilet fixture requirements on the basic use of the building.

2. 3 is correct.

ASTM E-119 tests the entire assembly, not just the finish materials like ASTM E-84 (also known as the Steiner Tunnel Test). The ASTM E-119 test is best at evaluating any barrier, like a partition, that is intended to prevent the spread of fire.

3. 2 is correct.

The Uniform Building Code refers to NFPA-13 in detailing the requirements of sprinkler system design and installation. The other model codes refer to NFPA-13 as well.

4. 1 is correct.

Refer to Table 17.1, which indicates that the most restrictive requirements for finish materials are in enclosed vertical exitway enclosures.

5. 2 is correct.

6. 3 is correct.

Table 17.1 indicates that the two variables occupancy group and location are the primary determinants of minimum flame-spread class. The code allows a reduction of one class in most instances if the building is fully sprinklered, but occupancy and location are the most important considerations.

7. 1 is correct.

For an interior designer, occupancy group is one of the most important things to know because it affects exiting requirements, finishes, and other design questions. This eliminates answer 3. Fire zone classification is of concern only to the architect, so this eliminates answer 2.

8. 3 is correct.

Construction type ranges from Type I as the most restrictive to Type V, which is the least restrictive.

9. 1 is correct.

Only tempered and laminated glass are, by definition, considered safety glazing.

10. 1 is correct.

The methenamine pill test is required for all carpet produced in the United States, while the other tests may or may not be used by a manufacturer.

18 EXITING

1. 2 is correct.

The 1991 edition of the Uniform Building Code limits dead-end corridors to 20 feet.

2. 2 is correct.

From the table, assembly areas including restaurants and bars have an occupant load of 15. Commercial kitchens have an occupant load of 200. Therefore,

$$\begin{aligned} 3500 \div 15 &= 233 \\ 1000 \div 200 &= 5 \\ 1200 \div 15 &= 80 \\ \hline \text{Total} &\quad 318 \end{aligned}$$

3. 3 is correct.

Refer to Figure 14.4. Answer 1 describes a riser.

4. 3 is correct.

Answers 1 and 2 both include doors that are less than 36 inches in width, which prohibits their use as exit doors.

5. 3 is correct.

A 60,000-square-foot building would be approximately 250 feet square or about 200 feet wide and 300 feet long. The size combined with typical rectangular planning of corridors would create very long distances to exits. Refer to Figure 18.3.

6. 2 is correct.

Smoke seals will be required, but the most important thing is that glass doors will not be allowed. Because this will significantly change the appearance of the existing entry, this should be first thing to tell her to expect.

7. 2 is correct.

Closers are always required with fire-rated door assemblies (protected openings).

8. 3 is correct.

Any stair 44 inches or wider requires handrails on both sides.

9. 2 is correct.

10. 3 is correct.

The occupant load factor as given in Table 10-A of the UBC (and similar tables in other model codes) is used to determine the number of exits.

19 BARRIER-FREE DESIGN

1. 2 is correct.

Refer to Figure 19.4.

2. 3 is correct.

The solution that is least expensive and most sensitive to accessibility requirements is to provide a power-assisted door opener.

3. 3 is correct.

4. 1 is correct.

Barrier-free design requires that objects do not protrude into the accessible path in such a way as to present a hazard. See Figure 19.15. In addition, tactile signs must have a minimum $^1/_{32}$-inch raised surface, and accessible routes must not be reduced in width.

5. 3 is correct.

All the sink installations listed as possible answers can work if they meet the measurement requirements shown in Figure 19.10, but a wall-hung lavatory gives the most open access, usually exceeding the minimum requirements.

6. 2 is correct.

Although alternate designs for toilet stalls can be 36 or 48 inches wide as shown in Figure 19.8, a standard stall must be 60 inches wide as shown in Figure 19.7.

7. 2 is correct.

Emergency warning systems must provide both visual and audible alarms.

8. 1 is correct.

9. 2 is correct.

Refer to Figure 19.6.

10. 3 is correct.

If only finishes were being changed, you would not be required to change door hardware. Both carpet and threshold selection should be reviewed, but incorrect carpet and cushion selection would have the most impact on accessibility, so this should be your primary concern. If only minor work was being performed, it is unlikely that existing thresholds would be a problem.

20 OWNER-DESIGNER AGREEMENTS

1. 4 is correct.

The Standard Form of Agreement for Interior Design Services, B171, clearly states that the client is responsible for providing all legal, accounting, and insurance counseling services necessary for the project.

2. 2 is correct.

Answers 2 and 3 are the closest choices. However, only long-distance telephone calls directly related to a project are generally considered reimbursable. Models are also considered reimbursable if they are special presentation types and not just study models built for office design work.

3. 3 is correct.

This question requires that you know the word *tendered* as well as the procedures for handling these types of changes. *Tender* is a term used in England and often in Canada that means the same as *to bid.* Making changes after a project has been bid can be a major problem, and you should be sure the client understands the implications of time delays and cost changes.

4. 2 is correct.

Answer 1 is incorrect because post-occupancy evaluation is not considered a standard service. Answer 3 is incorrect because financial feasibility studies are also not a standard service. Answer 4 is incorrect because the owner is responsible for furniture acceptance under the Standard Form of Agreement even though the interior designer may view the furniture when it arrives and help direct the installation.

5. 2 is correct.

The contractor is responsible for all means and methods of construction and all safety concerns on the job site.

6. 2 is correct.

The interior designer is responsible for knowing the size of built-in items and for designing and detailing construction into which those items are placed.

7. 3 is correct.

A fixed fee requires that you perform the services listed in your contract for a set amount, regardless of any problems that may arise, either caused by the client or yourself.

8. 1 is correct.

The AIA/ASID standard owner-designer agreement clearly lists providing consultants, designing signage, and doing detailed surveys as extra services. Designing and detailing custom built-in furniture is considered part of the millwork that the designer is responsible for.

9. 2 is correct.

If it is a construction budget, fees are generally not included. The other answer choices all relate to the actual construction of the project.

10. 3 is correct.

Furnishings are bought through the purchase order process. Releasing funds for construction is done with an application and certificate for payment.

21 PROFESSIONAL PRACTICE

1. 2 is correct.

Even though the owner signed off on the delivery, such inspection does not constitute final acceptance or taking control of the merchandise. This does not occur until a final inspection of the job by the owner and designer, the sign-off of the punch list, and final payment. In this case, the furniture dealer is the "contractor" of the furniture contract and has the opportunity to correct the defects or supply new merchandise. The trucking company is responsible only if damage was noted at the time of delivery and it can be shown that the trucker damaged the merchandise.

2. 1 is correct.

A Gantt is a simple bar chart that is easy to construct. More complex CPM and PERT charts are not appropriate for a small project. Fast-track is not a chart type.

3. 2 is correct.

Standard professional practice and ethical guidelines require that before taking on a job you know that another designer does not have any contractual relationships with the client.

4. 2 is correct.

According to the General Conditions of the Contract for Furniture, Furnishings and Equipment, the owner must carry property insurance to cover vandalism, loss by fire or theft, and similar causes. The contractor's insurance covers damages to the work, and the dealer's insurance does not cover furniture once it is at the site.

5. 2 is correct.

Because the question asks about founders in plural, this eliminates answer number one. Professional corporations and subchapter S corporations are entities in themselves and are managed by a board of directors, which may include only the founders, but overall partnerships have the most complete, long-term control over a business founded by two or more people.

6. 3 is correct.

Technically, you must have a sales agreement signed by the client that obligates him or her to pay for the goods. This is processed before a purchase order is written.

7. 4 is correct.

A corporate identification package includes basic items such as stationery, business cards, and other items with your name and address on them. A capabilities brochure is a basic tool to give to prospective clients and others to briefly explain your firm and the type of jobs you do.

8. 2 is correct.

9. 1 is correct.

Although an interior designer may find it very difficult to find employees who would work without employer-provided health insurance, it is not mandatory for operating a business. Workers' compensation is mandatory in all states. Even though general liability and automobile insurance may not be required by statute in every state, any business person would be foolish to be without it.

10. 4 is correct.

Errors and omissions insurance is carried by the design professional.

22 PROJECT COORDINATION

1. 4 is correct.

After the mechanical engineer and interior designer have reviewed the shop drawings, they are returned to the general contractor who reviews them again to see what comments the engineer and designer have made before returning them to the subcontractor.

2. 4 is correct.

The contractor should make sure that the necessary samples, shop drawings, and other required submittals are forwarded to the interior designer for review. Because the general contractor is responsible for coordinating the various trades and suppliers, he or she would be responsible.

3. 1 is correct.

The contractor is solely responsible for job site safety, and if the interior designer told the contractor to correct it or what to do the designer could be opening himself or herself to liability. The designer's duty would be to advise the owner in writing of what was observed. In addition, it would be expedient to point it out to the contractor to see why there were no barricades.

4. 2 is correct.

Although on small projects the project manager may organize drawing layout, this is usually the task of the job captain or whoever is in charge of preparing the drawings. The other three choices are more commonly activities of the project manager.

5. 1 is correct.

Answer 1 is the most common method of processing applications for payment. The designer may certify an amount less than what is requested as long as a written explanation is attached. Applications for payment are sometimes returned to the contractor for revisions, but this usually delays the normal payment schedule and keeps money from the contractor that he or she is entitled to.

6. 3 is correct.

The interior designer's review of the shop drawings is only for conformance to the general design intent of the job. The general contractor is responsible for coordinating the job, checking dimensions, and, in general, building the job according to the contract documents.

7. 3 is correct.

Anything that requires a change in contract cost or time must be approved with a change order. A construction change authorization and minor work order are only for minor changes that do not require a change in contract cost or time.

8. 3 is correct.

Standard contract documents require that the owner provide adequate space for the receipt and staging of furniture, fixtures, and equipment. Answer 1 is incorrect because the goods should already be adequately insured. Answer 2 is incorrect because the owner inspects delivery of furniture only for identifying and verifying quantities and checking for damage and does not constitute final acceptance. Answer 4 is incorrect because the contractor should have adequately estimated the number of workers needed for installation.

9. 4 is correct.

Although the designer may use lessons learned from one job to the next, this is generally not placed in a verbal or written post-occupancy evaluation.

10. 2 is correct.

The interior designer is responsible for designing the job according to governing building codes. The contractor often points out problem areas ahead of time, but he or she is under no obligation to do so.

23 HISTORY

1. 3 is correct.

Refer to Figure 23.2.

2. 2 is correct.

Although there are literary references to tapestries as early as the Egyptian era and in early eastern Asia and Japan, European tapestry flourished from the early Gothic period in the 13th century. Tapestries in the western European tradition were first woven in Paris during the 14th century. Tapestry weaving continued into the Renaissance and later into the 20th century.

3. 3 is correct.

The primary force behind the Bauhaus was to apply industrial processes and emerging technology in the early 20th century to well-designed objects, graphics, and architecture.

4. 4 is correct.

Pennzoil Place was designed by Philip Johnson. Dulles International Airport was designed by Eero Saarinen. The World Trade Center was designed by Minoru Yamasaki.

5. 1 is correct.

Alvar Aalto experimented with and produced chairs and other furniture with laminated wood, steamed and bent into various shapes. Søren Hansen revived the Thonet steamed bent wood process. Charles Eames used molded plywood for several of his chairs.

6. 2 is correct.

7. 2 is correct.

Frank Lloyd Wright worked in Louis Sullivan's office early in his career.

8. 4 is correct.

The Barcelona chair was designed for the German Pavilion in Barcelona in 1929. Although Frank Lloyd Wright designed furniture specifically for most of his buildings, they have not become design classics the way the Barcelona chair has.

9. 2 is correct.

10. 1 is correct.

Refer to Figure 23.2.

24 PRACTICUM PROBLEMS

A. Programming

For the client interview sample problem, the following question choices and explanations would most likely be the ones that would provide you with the additional information you need. In some cases it may be possible to use others to get at the same kind of information. It is the strength of your rationale that determines how any one question choice is deemed appropriate.

3. This question would give information about expansion needs, both in providing extra space at move-in or how to lay out the space so expansion would be easier.

6. The required adjacencies (if any) between offices and examination rooms would be given by this question.

10. Information about the lab assistant is needed to determine the amount of space needed for this person.

12. This question gives data about furniture, either new or reused.

15. Circulation information and how the space should be planned can be developed from this question.

20. This question gives information on equipment types.

21. This question relates to open versus closed space related to three users.

25. The number of people to plan for is clarified with this question. The bubble diagram shown in Figure 25.1 offers one solution that would be given a passing score. The diagram shows both the primary relationships and overall relationships and is in an acceptable graphic format with the areas representing the rooms in approximate scale relationship. Equally acceptable would be diagrams that used block forms rather than circles and other types of graphic symbols to show the relationships.

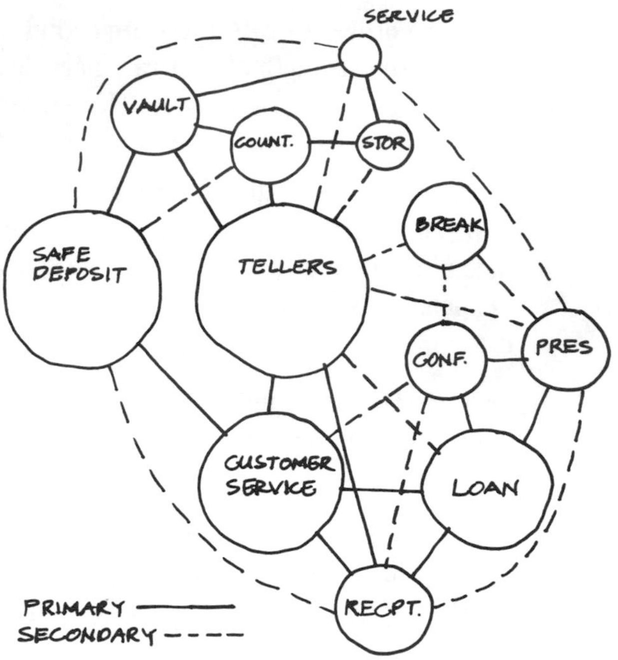

Figure 25.1 Solution to Programming Bubble Diagram

B. Three-Dimensional Exercise and Sample Problem

Figure 25.2 shows one well-developed solution to the problem. The design concept was quickly arrived at so there was plenty of time to spend doing the required drawings. The solution indicates that the candidate has an understanding of three-dimensional space and can apply the principles and elements of design as well as use lighting to support the design concept. All the basic requirements of the problem are satisfied and all the required drawings are complete enough to communicate the intent of the design.

A few of the principles are weakly applied, most notably the use of color and the neon tube for contrast, but overall the ideas are well applied for the short time allowed for the problem. Technically, it is not entirely clear about how the light boxes are suspended from the frame, but this is a minor point. Graphically, the axonometric does not show whether the concrete wall is exposed or covered, but this is also a minor point that does not detract from the explanation of the design.

This solution illustrates a wise choice of which drawing type to use. The solution would have been a little more difficult to show in perspective view. The short time allowed for the 3-D exercise does not allow for complicated drawings, so pick the easiest drawing types for your solution.

C. Scenario

Figures 25.3 and 25.4 illustrate one possible solution to the space planning problem. These show another well-developed scheme that was quickly planned so there was ample time for drawing, even though the reflected ceiling plan was a little rushed and there are a few items missing. As long as the problem requirements are satisfied, a graphically less-refined solution is acceptable.

In general, the solution would probably receive high marks. Although the overall concept is weak and there are some awkward spatial conditions, all the required spaces are included in correct size and proportion. The required adjacencies are also satisfied. The necessary furniture groups are shown with sufficient clearances.

Overall, the circulation is straightforward and efficient and provides for the required exiting as well as accessibility. The entry is well placed directly off the elevator lobby, although another entry location to the west would also be workable.

The circulation around the reception desk and into the two advising areas is a little tight and awkward because you have to pass one advising area to get to the second, but this is not enough to fail the solution.

Technically, all code restrictions are satisfied except that the entry into the advising area is too narrow for accessibility because the panels were drawn too long. However, this does not represent a major planning or structural problem. The rest rooms are shown larger than they need to be because of consideration given to sight lines, but this is not a detriment to the solution.

The reflected ceiling plan shows the required elements, and the location of the lighting generally supports the function of the spaces even though some areas could use refinement. A few lines representing switching are missing, but this is a minor problem. This drawing shows the full-height partition for acoustical control, which is acceptable, but it is better to show these partitions on both plans.

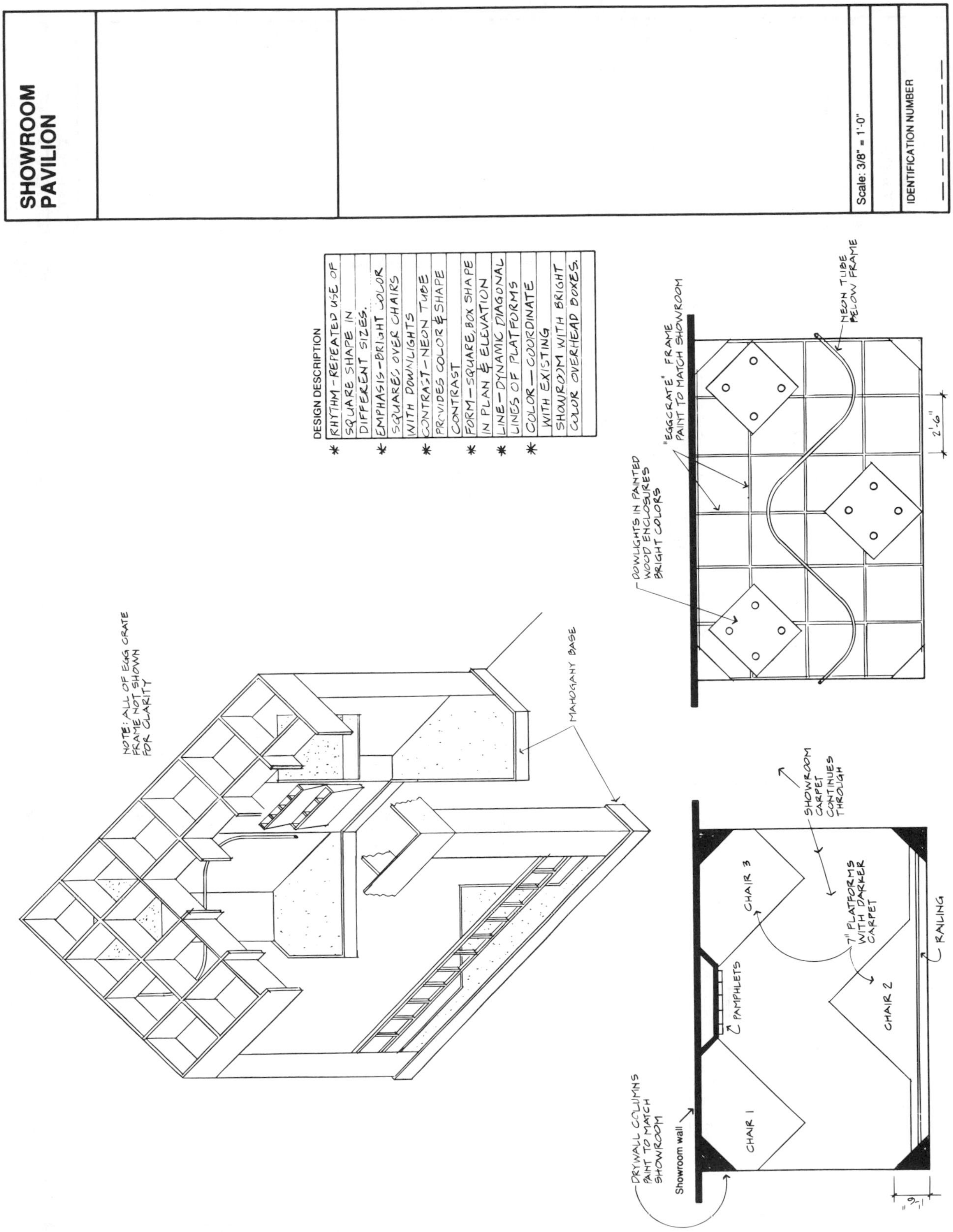

Figure 25.2 Solution to 3-D Practicum

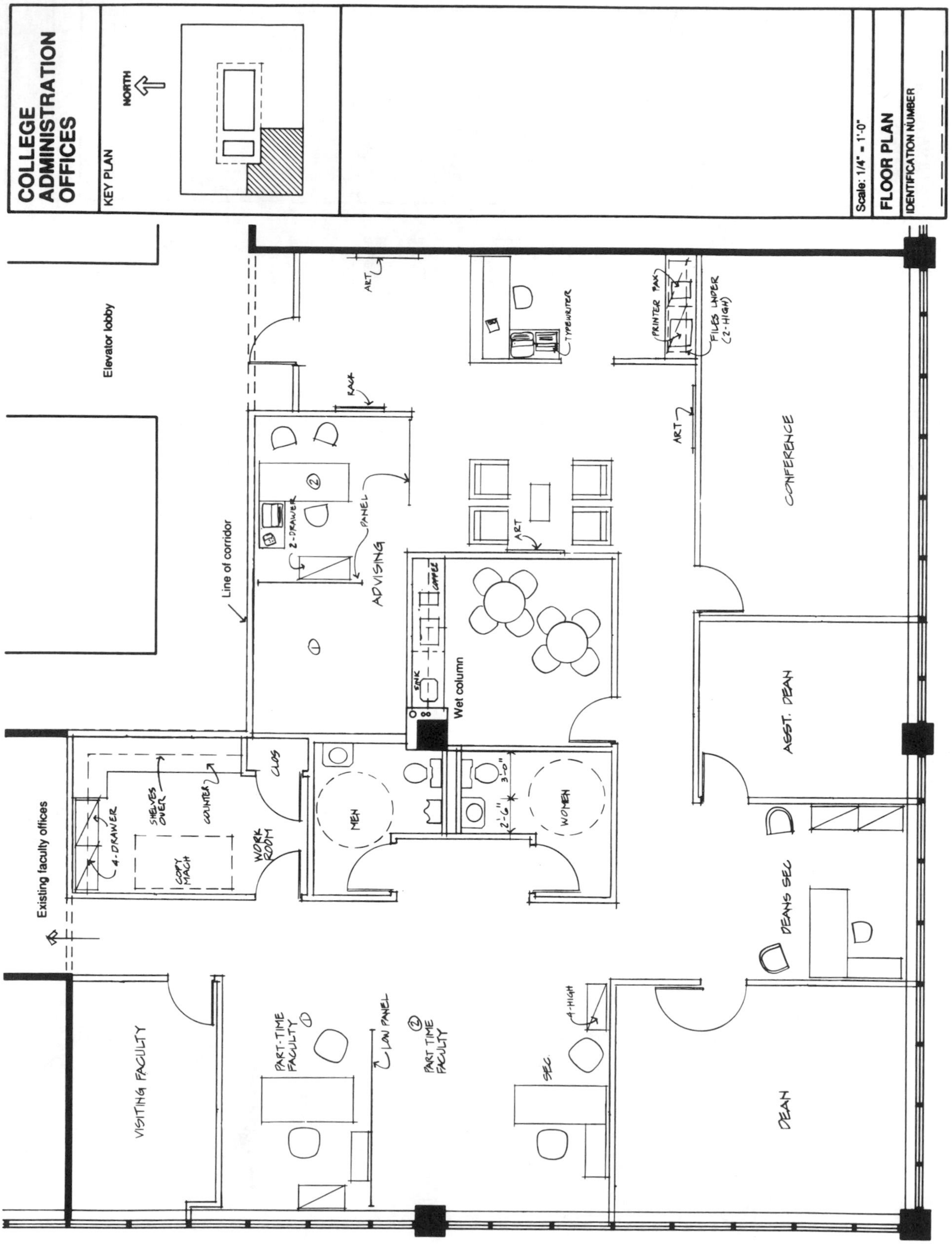

Figure 25.3 Floor Plan Solution to Practicum/Scenario

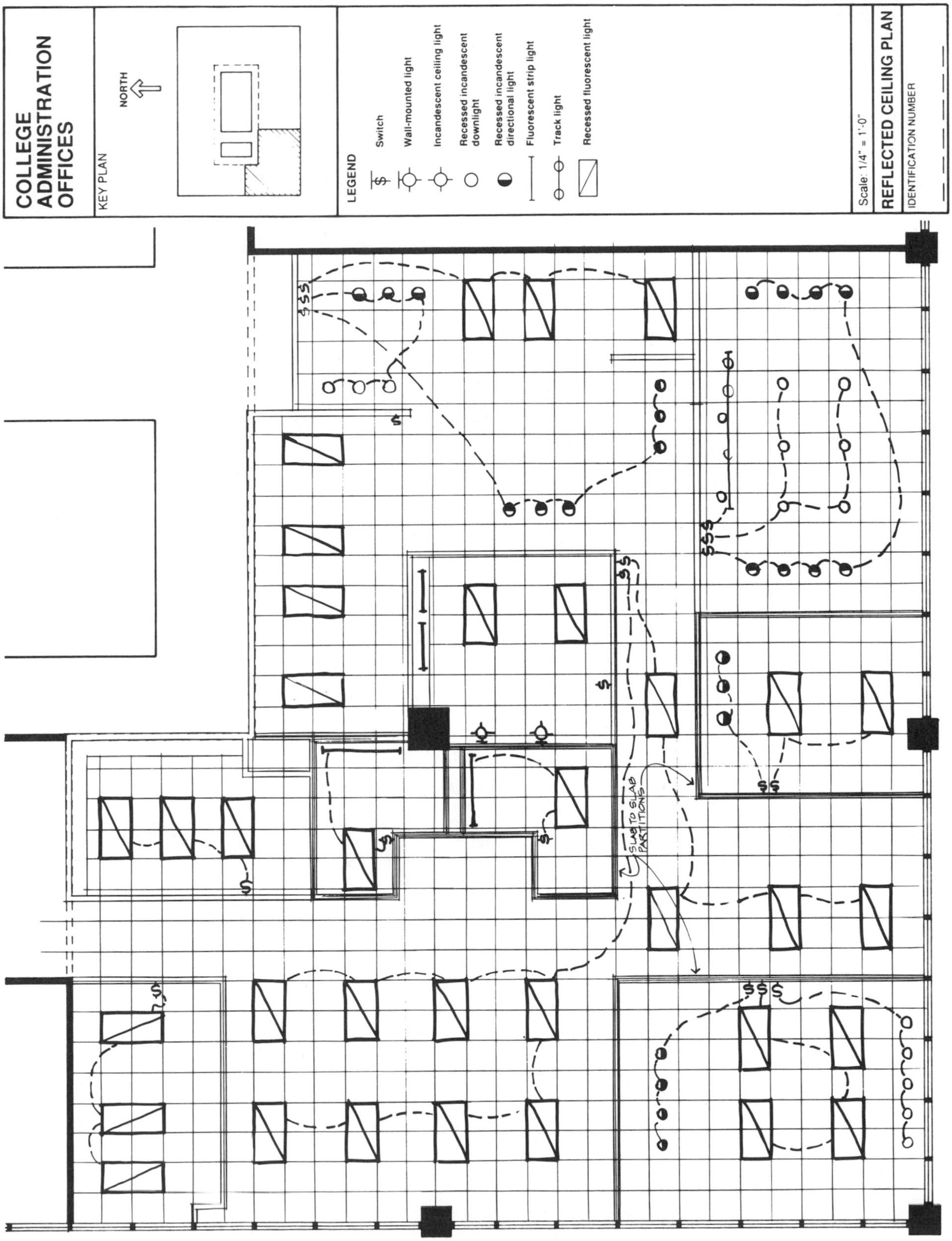

Figure 25.4 Reflected Ceiling Plan Solution to Practicum/Scenario

REFERENCES

The following books provide more detailed information on the topics covered in the NCIDQ examination. If you feel particularly weak in one or more areas, you may want to refer to additional sources. The matrix following this list will help you pinpoint the references related to various chapters in this book.

Ambrose, James. *Building Construction: Interior Systems.* New York: Van Nostrand Reinhold, 1991.

Ball, Victoria Kloss. *Architecture and Interior Design: A Basic History Through the Seventeenth Century.* New York: John Wiley & Sons, 1980.

—. *Architecture and Interior Design: Europe and America from the Colonial Era to Today.* New York: John Wiley & Sons, 1980.

Ballast, David Kent. *Interior Construction and Detailing for Designers and Architects.* Belmont, CA: Professional Publications, Inc., 2000.

Birren, Faber. *Color and Human Response.* New York: Van Nostrand Reinhold, 1984.

Ching, Francis D. K. *Architecture: Space, Form and Order.* New York: Van Nostrand Reinhold, 1980.

—. *Interior Design Illustrated.* New York: Van Nostrand Reinhold, 1987.

Deasy, C. M. *Designing Places for People: A Handbook on Human Behavior for Architects, Designers, and Facility Managers.* New York: Whitney Library of Design, 1990.

de la Croix, Horst, and Richard G. Tansey. *Gardner's Art Through the Ages,* 8th ed. New York: Harcourt Brace Jovanovich, 1986.

Diekman, Norman, and John Pile. *Drawing Interior Architecture.* New York: Whitney Library of Design, 1983.

Dizik, A. Allen. *Concise Encyclopedia of Interior Design.* New York: Van Nostrand Reinhold, 1990.

Egan, M. David. *Architectural Acoustics.* New York: McGraw-Hill, 1988.

Farren, Carole E. *Planning and Managing Interior Projects.* Kingston, Mass.: R. S. Means, 2000.

Friedmann, Arnold, John F. Pile, and Forrest Wilson. *Interior Design: An Introduction to Architectural Interiors,* 3rd ed. New York: Elsevier, 1982.

Gordon, Gary, and Nuckolls, James L. *Interior Lighting for Designers.* New York: John Wiley & Sons, 1995.

Hall, Edward T. *The Hidden Dimension.* Garden City, N.Y.: Doubleday, 1969.

—. *The Silent Language.* Garden City, N.Y.: Doubleday, 1959.

Harmon, Sharon Koomen. *The Codes Guidebook for Interiors.* New York: John Wiley & Sons, 1994.

Jackman, Dianne R., and Mary K. Dixon. *The Guide to Textiles for Interior Designers,* 2nd ed. Winnipeg: Peguis Publishers Limited, 1990.

Karlen, Mark. *Space Planning Basics.* New York: Van Nostrand Reinhold, 1997.

Larsen, Jack Lenor, and Jeanne Weeks. *Fabrics for Interiors.* New York: Van Nostrand Reinhold, 1975.

Loebelson, Andrew. *How to Profit in Contract Design.* New York: Van Nostrand Reinhold, 1983.

Mang, Karl. *History of Modern Furniture.* New York: Harry N. Abrams, 1978.

McGowan, Maryrose. *Specifying Interiors.* New York: John Wiley & Sons, 1996.

Miller, William E. *Basic Drafting for Interior Designers.* New York: Van Nostrand Reinhold, 1982.

Morgan, Jim. *Marketing for the Small Design Firm.* New York: Whitney Library of Design, 1984.

National Council for Interior Design Qualification. *Examination Guide.* New York: National Council for Interior Design Qualification, 1991.

Peña, William. *Problem Seeking.* Washington, D.C.: AIA Press, 1989.

Perritt, Henry H., Jr. *Americans with Disabilities Act Handbook.* New York: John Wiley & Sons, 1990.

Pile, John. *Interior Design.* New York: Harry N. Abrams, 1988.

Piotrowski, Christine. *Professional Practice for Interior Designers,* 2nd ed. New York: Van Nostrand Reinhold, 1997.

—. *Designing Commercial Interiors.* New York: John Wiley & Sons, 1998.

Porter, Tom, and Sue Goodman. *Manual of Graphic Techniques 4.* New York: Charles Scribner's Sons, 1985.

Reznikoff, S. C. *Interior Graphic and Design Standards.* New York: Whitney Library of Design, 1986.

—. *Specifications for Commercial Interiors.* New York: Whitney Library of Design, 1989.

Riggs, J. Rosemary. *Materials and Components of Interior Architecture,* 5th ed. Englewood Cliffs, N.J.: Prentice Hall, 1998.

Rupp, William, and Arnold Friedmann. *Construction Materials for Interior Design.* New York: Whitney Library of Design, 1989.

Sharpe, Deborah T. *The Psychology of Color and Design.* Chicago: Nelson-Hall, 1974.

Sommer, Robert. *Personal Space, The Behavioral Basis of Design.* Englewood Cliffs, N.J.: Prentice Hall, 1969.

Sorcar, Prafulla C. *Architectural Lighting for Commercial Interiors.* New York: John Wiley & Sons, 1987.

Stasiowski, Frank, and David Burstein. *Project Management for the Design Professional.* New York: Whitney Library of Design, 1982.

Stein, Ben M., Frederick H. Reynolds, and William McGinness. *Mechanical and Electrical Equipment for Buildings,* 8th ed. New York: John Wiley & Sons, 1991.

Tate, Allen, and C. Ray Smith. *Interior Design in the 20th Century.* New York: Harper & Row, 1986.

Wakita, Osamu A., and Richard M. Linde. *Professional Handbook of Architectural Working Drawings.* New York: John Wiley & Sons, 1984.

Whiton, Sherrill. *Interior Design and Decoration,* 4th ed. Philadelphia: J. B. Lippincott, 1974.

Wiggins, Glenn E. *A Manual of Construction Documentation.* New York: Whitney Library of Design, 1989.

● entire reference devoted to topic
○ one topic within reference

chapter topics

authors in reference list	elements and principles	human factors	programming	space planning	construction drawings	specifications	contract documents	furniture, fixtures	interior construction	finishes	lighting	mechanical systems	acoustics	communication methods	building codes	barrier-free design	professional practice	project coordination	history
Ambrose									○	○									
Ball																			●
Ball																			●
Ballast									●				○		○	○			
Birren	●																		
Ching	○			○															
Ching	○	○	○	○				○	○	○	○	○		○					
Deasy		●																	
de la Croix																			●
Diekman														●					
Dizik								○	○								○		○
Egan													●						
Farren			○		○	○	○											○	
Friedmann	○	○	○				○	○	○	○	○	○					○		○
Hall		●																	
Hall		●																	
Harmon															●				
Jackman								○		○									
Karlin				●															
Larsen								○		○									
Loebelson																	●		
Mang																			●
McGowan						○	○	○	○	○					○		○	○	
Miller					○									○					
Morgan																	●		
NCIDQ																			
Nuckolls											●								
Peña			●																
Perritt																●			
Pile	○	○						○		○	○						○		
Piotrowski							○										○	○	
Piotrowski	○		○	○		○	○	○		○	○	○			○		○	○	
Porter														●					
Reznikoff				○				○	○	○	○	○	○						
Reznikoff					○	○	○	○	○	○					○	○			
Riggs									○	○									
Rupp									○	○									
Sharpe	●																		
Sommer		●																	
Sorcar											●								
Stasiowski																	○	○	
Stein											○	○	○						
Tate	○													○					○
Wakita					●														
Whiton	○							○									○		○
Wiggins					●														

INDEX

Q

R

S

T

U

V

W